The Great Victory

الفوز العظيم

The Great Victory

© *Arnab Mubashir* 2021   *CC-BY-SA*

ISBN 978-0-578-86206-4

Free Islamic resources: arnabmubashir.com

The word of Allah   كلام الله

page 1

The Messenger of Allah (SAW)   رسول الله ﷺ

page 331

The way of Allah   دين الله

page 401

Scholars and sources

page 463

The word of Allah

Surah 1   Al-fatiha   [The Opener]

﴿ الحمد لله رب العالمين ﴾ الفاتحة ٢

{ **Praise to Allah, Lord of the worlds** } *Al-fatiha 2*

اختلف العلماء أيّما أفضل قوله العبد الحمد لله رب العالمين أو قول لا إله إلا الله فقالت طائفة قوله الحمد لله رب العالمين أفضل لأن في ضمنه التوحيد الذي هو لا إله إلا الله ففي قوله توحيد وحمد وفي قوله لا إله إلا الله توحيد فقط وقال طائفة لا إله إلا الله أفضل لأنها تدفع الكفر والإشراك وعليها يقاتَل الخلق قال رسول الله ﷺ أمرت أن أقاتل الناس حتى يقولوا لا إله إلا الله

تفسير القرطبي

Scholars differ on which of the two is better for a man to say: "Praise to Allah, Lord of the worlds" ["Al-hamdu Lillah Rabb al-'alamin"] or "There is no god but Allah" ["La ilaha illa Allah"]. One group says: It is better to say "Praise to Allah, Lord of the worlds", because this includes the assertion of one god [*tawheed*, unification] that is also found in "There is no god but Allah" – when he says this there is both *tawheed* and praise, whereas if he says "There is no god but Allah", there is only *tawheed*. But another group says: "There is no god but Allah" is better, since it averts disbelief [*kufr*] and associating others in worship to Allah [*ishrak*]. All of mankind is to be fought over this; the Messenger of Allah (SAW) said: I have been ordered to fight people until they say "There is no god but Allah."

Tafsir Al-Qurtubi

﴿ اهدنا الصراط المستقيم صراط الذين أنعمت عليهم غير المغضوب عليهم ولا الضالين ﴾

الفاتحة ٦-٧

{ Guide us in the straight path: the path of those upon whom you have bestowed favor, not those who are detested, nor those who are deluded } *Al-fatiha 6-7*

عن عدي بن حاتم عن النبي ﷺ قال اليهود مغضوب عليهم والنصارى ضُلال

جامع الترمذي كتاب تفسير القرآن

'Adi ibn Hatim related from the Prophet (SAW), who said: The Jews are detested, and the Christians are deluded.

Sunan Al-Tirmidhi, The book of tafsir

وقيل المغضوب عليهم هم اليهود لقوله عز وجل ﴿ من لعنه الله وغضب عليه ﴾ والضالين هم النصارى لقوله تعالى ﴿ قد ضلوا من قبل ﴾ فإن قلت ما معنى غضب الله هو إرادة الإنتقام من العصاة وإنزال العقوبة بهم وأن يفعل بهم ما يفعله الملك إذا غضب على من تحت يده نعوذ بالله من غضبه ونسأله رضاه ورحمته

تفسير الزمخشري

It is said that those who are detested are the Jews, based on the word of the Mighty and Sublime: { Those who Allah has cursed and become angry with } [Al-ma'ida 60]. And those who are deluded are the Christians based on the word of the Most High: { They have been deluded before } [Al-ma'ida 77]. If you should ask: What is the meaning of Allah's anger? It is a desire for vengeance against those who disobey, sending down punishment on them, and doing to them what a king does whenever he is angry at his subjects; we seek refuge in Allah from His anger and we ask of Him His good favor and His mercy.

Tafsir Al-Zamakhshari

عن عبدالله بن شقيق أن رجلاً أتى رسول الله ﷺ وهو محاصر وادي القرى فقال من هؤلاء الذين تحاصر يا رسول الله قال هؤلاء المغضوب عليهم اليهود ... عن عبدالله بن شقيق أن رجلاً أتى رسول الله ﷺ وهو محاصر وادي القرى قال قلت من هؤلاء قال هؤلاء الضالين النصارى ..... عن إبن عباس ﴿ ولا الضالين ﴾ قال وغير طريق النصارى الذين أضلهم الله بفريتهم عليه قال يقول فألهمنا دينك ألحق وهو لا إله إلا الله وحده لا شريك له حتى لا تغضب علينا كما غضبت على اليهود ولا تضلنا كما أضللت النصارى فتعذبنا بما تعذبهم به يقول امنعنا من ذلك برفقك ورحمتك وقدرتك

تفسير الطبري

Abdullah ibn Shaqiq related that a certain man came to the Messenger of Allah (SAW) while He was besieging Wadi Al-qura, and said: Who are these that you are besieging, oh Messenger of Allah? He said: These are the detested ones, the Jews. ... Abdullah ibn Shaqiq related that a certain man came to the Messenger of Allah (SAW) while He was besieging Wadi Al-qura, and said: Who are these? He said: These are the deluded ones, the Christians. ... From Ibn 'Abbas, regarding { Nor those who are deluded } ; he said: Nor the path of the Christians, those who Allah has deluded because of their slander of Him. Ibn 'Abbas said: Inspire us in your religion of truth, this being "There is no god but Allah alone, none is associated with Him", so that you will not be angry with us as you were angry with the Jews, and not delude us as you deluded the Christians, and not punish us by what you punished them with; moreover he said: Keep us from this by your kindness, your mercy, and your power.

Tafsir Al-Tabari

والضلال ضد الهدى وخصّ الله تعالى اليهود بالغضب لأنهم أشد عداوة

تفسير الماوردي

Delusion is contrary to guidance; and Allah Most High singled out the Jews to be detested, since they are the fiercest in enmity.

Tafsir Al-Mawardi

Surah 2   Al-baqara [The Cow]

﴿ مَن كَانَ عَدُوًّا لِّلَّهِ وَمَلَائِكَتِهِ وَرُسُلِهِ وَجِبْرِيلَ وَمِيكَالَ فَإِنَّ اللَّهَ عَدُوٌّ لِّلْكَافِرِينَ ﴾ البقرة ٩٨

{ Whoever is an enemy to Allah and His angels, and His messengers, and Jibril and Mikail; indeed Allah is an enemy of the Disbelievers } *Al-baqara 98*

من عادى أولياء الله فقد عادى الله ومن عادى الله فإن الله عدو له ومن كان الله عدوه فقد خسر الدنيا والآخرة كما تقدم الحديث من عادى لي وليًا فقد بارزني بالحرب
تفسير ابن كثير

Whoever shows enmity towards the associates of Allah has shown enmity towards Allah; and whoever shows enmity towards Allah, surely Allah is his enemy; and whoever has Allah as an enemy is lost in this world and the next. As was said before: "Whoever shows enmity towards an associate of mine has engaged me in war".

Tafsir Ibn Kathir

الله أنزل هذه الآية توبيخًا لليهود في كفرهم بمحمد ﷺ وإخبارًا منه لهم أن من كان عدوًا لمحمد فالله له عدو
تفسير الطبري

Allah sent down this verse to rebuke the Jews for their disbelief in Muhammad (SAW), and as a declaration from Him to them that anyone who is Muhammad's enemy, Allah is his enemy.

Tafsir Al-Tabari

﴿ عَدُوٌّ لِّلْكَافِرِينَ ﴾ أراد عدو لهم فجاء بالظاهر ليدل على أنّ الله إنما عاداهم لكفرهم وأن عداوة الملائكة كفر وإذا كانت عداوة الأنبياء كفرًا فما بال الملائكة وهم أشرف والمعنى من عاداهم عاداه الله وعاقبه أشدّ العقاب
تفسير الزمخشري

{ An enemy of the Disbelievers } : He intends to say an enemy to them, stating it clearly so as to establish that Allah is indeed at enmity with them due to their disbelief, and that enmity towards the angels is disbelief; and if enmity towards the prophets is disbelief, how then with the angels, who are even more honorable? The meaning therefore is that whoever is at enmity with them, Allah is at enmity with him, and will punish him with the severest of punishment.

Tafsir Al-Zamakhshari

﴿ ومن كان عدواً لله وملائكته ورسله وجبريل وميكال فإن الله عدو للكافرين ﴾ أراد بعداوة الله مخالفته عناداً أو معاداة المقربين من عباده

تفسير البيضاوي

{ Whoever is an enemy to Allah and His angels, and His messengers, and Jibril and Mikail; indeed Allah is an enemy of the Disbelievers } : By "enmity to Allah" He means stubborn opposition to Him or hostility towards His closest servants.

Tafsir Al-Baydawi

. . .

﴿ ما ننسخ من آية أو ننسها نأت بخير منها أو مثلها ألم تعلم أن الله على كل شيء قدير ﴾
البقرة ١٠٦

{ Any verse We abrogate, or cause to be forgotten, We bring something better than it or similar to it; do you all not know that Allah is able to do all things? } *Al-baqara 106*

قوله تعالى ﴿ ما ننسخ من آية أو ننسها نأت بخير منها ﴾ قال المفسرون إن المشركين قالوا أترون إلى محمد يأمر أصحابه بأمر ثم ينهاهم عنه ويأمرهم بخلافه ويقول اليوم قولاً ويرجع عنه غداً ما هذا القرآن إلا كلام محمد يقوله من تلقاء نفسه وهو كلام يناقض بعضه بعضاً فأنزل الله ﴿ وإذا بدلنا آية مكان آية ﴾ الآية وأنزل أيضاً ﴿ ما ننسخ من آية أو ننسها نأت بخير منها ﴾ الآية

أسباب النزول للواحدي

The word of the Most High: { Any verse We abrogate, or cause to be forgotten, We bring something better than it } . The expositors say that indeed the Idolaters [Mushrikun] would say: Do you all see Muhammad? He orders his Companions to do something, then He prohibits them to do it, and orders them to do the opposite. He says one thing today and takes it back tomorrow. What is this Qur'an but the words of Muhammad of his own accord, words which contradict each other. So Allah sent down: { And whenever We substitute one verse in place of another ... } and the rest of the verse [Al-nahl 101]; and He also sent down: { Any verse We abrogate, or cause to be forgotten, We bring something better ... } up to the rest of the verse.

Al-Wahidi, Asbab Al-nuzul

عن قتادة في قوله ﴿ ما ننسخ من آية أو ننسها ﴾ قال كان الله تعالى ينسي نبيه ما يشاء وينسخ ما يشاء ... عن الحسن أنه قال في قوله ﴿ أو ننسها ﴾ قال إن نبيكم ﷺ أقرئ قرآناً ثم نَسِيه ... عن إبن عباس ﴿ نأت بخير منها ﴾ يقول خير لكم في المنفعة وأرفق بكم ... وقال قتادة ﴿ نأت بخير منها أو مثلها ﴾ آية فيها تخفيف فيها رخصة فيها أمر فيها نهي

تفسير إبن كثير

From Qatada regarding His word { Any verse We abrogate, or cause to be forgotten } ; he said: Allah Most High would cause His Prophet to forget whatever He wished, and abrogate whatever He wished. ... From Al-Hasan, regarding His word: { Or cause to be forgotten } ; he said: Indeed your Prophet (SAW) would be made to recite a portion of the Qur'an, but then forgot it. ... Ibn 'Abbas, regarding { We bring something better than it } , said: More advantageous and milder for you all. ... And Qatada, regarding { We bring something better than it or similar to it ... } and up to the end of the verse, said: Something with relief in it, with permission in it, with an order in it, or with a prohibition in it.

Tafsir Ibn Kathir

* * *

﷽ وَلَا تَقُولُوا لِمَن يُقْتَلُ فِي سَبِيلِ اللَّهِ أَمْوَاتٌ بَلْ أَحْيَاءٌ وَلَٰكِن لَّا تَشْعُرُونَ ﴾ البقرة ١٥٤

{ Do not say of those who are killed in the cause of Allah that they are "dead", but rather "alive", just that you do not perceive it }

Al-baqara 154

يعني تعالى ذكره يا أيها الذين آمنوا استعينوا بالصبر على طاعتي في جهاد عدوكم وترك معاصيّ وأداء سائر فرائضي عليكم ولا تقولوا لمن يقتل في سبيل الله هو ميت فإن الميت من خلقي من سلبته حياته وأعدمتُ حواسَّه فلا يلتذّ لذّة ولا يدرك نعيماً فإن من قتل منكم ومن سائر خلقي في سبيلي أحياء عندي في حياة ونعيم وعيش هنيّ ورزق سنيّ فرحين بما آتيتهم من فضلي وحبوتهم به من كرامتي

تفسير الطبري

He (may His remembrance be exalted) means: Oh you who have believed! Appeal for steadfastness in obeying me in *jihad* against your enemy and abandoning rebellious deeds against me, and in fulfilling the rest of your obligations to me. And do not say of someone who is killed in the cause of Allah, "He is dead", for indeed someone of my creation who is dead, who I have stripped of his life and deprived of sensation, does not delight in any delight nor does he attain bliss. But whoever of you, and of the rest of my creation, is killed in my cause, is indeed alive with me in life and bliss, pleasurable living and splendid bounty, joyful in what I bring them of my abundance and of my honor which I have bestowed upon them.

Tafsir Al-Tabari

﴿ ولكن لا تشعرون ﴾ كيف حالهم في حياتهم وعن الحسن أنّ الشهداء أحياء عند الله تعرض أرزاقهم على أرواحهم فيصل اليهم الروح والفرح كما تعرض النار على أرواح آل فرعون غدوة وعشياً فيصل اليهم الوجع وعن مجاهد يرزقون ثمر الجنة ويجدون ريحها وليسوا فيها وقالوا يجوز أن يجمع الله من أجزاء الشهيد جملة فيحييها ويوصل إليها النعيم وإن كانت في حجم الذّرة وقيل نزلت في شهداء بدر وكانوا أربعة عشر

تفسير الزمخشري

{ Just that you do not perceive it } : what their condition in life is like. Al-Hasan related that martyrs are alive with Allah; their bounties are displayed before their spirits, and their spirits and their joy reach them, just like Hellfire is displayed before the spirits of the house of Pharaoh day and night, and torment comes to them. Mujahid related: They are bestowed with the bounty of the fruit of *Jannah*, and they perceive its aroma while they are yet not there. Some have said: It is permissible for Allah to bring together a group from among the martyrs, and give life to them, and bring them into bliss, even in the smallest amount. It is said that this verse came down regarding the martyrs at Badr, of which there were fourteen.

Tafsir Al-Zamakhshari

﴿ ولكن لا تشعرون ﴾ معنى لأن الخطاب للمؤمنين وقد كانوا لا يعلمون أنهم سيحيون يوم القيامة وأنهم ماتوا على هدى ونور فعلم أن الأمر على ما قلنا من أن الله تعالى أحياهم في قبورهم

تفسير الرازي

{ Just that you do not perceive it } : that is, since the message was for the Believers, as they did not know that they would live again on resurrection day, and that they died in guidance and light; and therefore they knew that the matter was as we have said – that Allah Most High will bring them to life in their graves.

Tafsir Al-Razi

وإذا كان الله تعالى يحييهم بعد الموت ليرزقهم على ما يأتي فيجوز أن يحيي الكفار ليعذبهم ويكون فيه دليل على عذاب القبر والشهداء أحياء كما قال الله تعالى وليس معناه أنهم سيحيون إذ لو كان كذلك لم يكن بين الشهداء وبين غيرهم فرق إذ كل أحد سيحيا ويدل على هذا قوله تعالى ﴿ ولكن لا تشعرون ﴾ والمؤمنون يشعرون أنهم سيحيون

تفسير القرطبي

If Allah Most High brings them to life after their death in order to bestow bounty on them, then it is conceivable for Him to bring the disbelievers [*Kuffar*] to life in order to punish them; and in this is evidence of the punishment of the grave. The martyrs are alive as Allah Most High says, but the meaning is not that they will be made alive; if it were so, there would be no difference between martyrs and others, as all will live. The word of the Most High makes this clear: { Just that you do not perceive } ; but the Believers do perceive that they will live.

Tafsir Al-Qurtubi

﴿ ولكن لا تشعرون ﴾ ما حالهم وهو تنبيه على أن حياتهم ليست بالجسد ولا من جنس ما يحس به من الحيوانات وإنما هي أمر لا يدرك بالعقل بل وبالوحي

تفسير البيضاوي

{ Just that you do not perceive it } : what their condition is. This is to advise that their life is not in the body, and not of a kind that animals can feel; indeed this is a matter which is not grasped by intellect, but rather by revelation.

Tafsir Al-Baydawi

﴿ أحياء ﴾ أرواحهم في حواصل طيور خُضْرٍ تسرح في الجنة حيث شاءت لحديث بذلك ﴿ ولكن لا تشعرون ﴾ تعلمون ما هم فيه

تفسير الجلالين

{ Alive } : their spirits are in the crops of green birds, who roam freely in *Jannah* wherever they wish, according to what is said of this: { Just that you do not perceive it } : you do not know what they are in.

Tafsir Al-Jalalain

﴿ وَقَاتِلُوا فِي سَبِيلِ اللَّهِ الَّذِينَ يُقَاتِلُونَكُمْ وَلَا تَعْتَدُوا إِنَّ اللَّهَ لَا يُحِبُّ الْمُعْتَدِينَ وَاقْتُلُوهُمْ حَيْثُ ثَقِفْتُمُوهُمْ وَأَخْرِجُوهُم مِّنْ حَيْثُ أَخْرَجُوكُمْ وَالْفِتْنَةُ أَشَدُّ مِنَ الْقَتْلِ وَلَا تُقَاتِلُوهُمْ عِندَ الْمَسْجِدِ الْحَرَامِ حَتَّىٰ يُقَاتِلُوكُمْ فِيهِ فَإِن قَاتَلُوكُمْ فَاقْتُلُوهُمْ كَذَٰلِكَ جَزَاءُ الْكَافِرِينَ فَإِنِ انتَهَوْا فَإِنَّ اللَّهَ غَفُورٌ رَّحِيمٌ وَقَاتِلُوهُمْ حَتَّىٰ لَا تَكُونَ فِتْنَةٌ وَيَكُونَ الدِّينُ لِلَّهِ فَإِنِ انتَهَوْا فَلَا عُدْوَانَ إِلَّا عَلَى الظَّالِمِينَ ﴾ البقرة ١٩٠-١٩٣

{ Fight in the cause of Allah those who fight you, and do not transgress; indeed Allah does not love those who transgress. And kill them wherever you get to them, and drive them away from where they drove you away; sedition is more severe than killing. But do not fight them at the Sacred Mosque until they fight you there, then if they fight you, kill them; such is the retribution of the Disbelievers. If they cease, indeed Allah is forgiving and merciful. And fight them until there is no more sedition and religion belongs to Allah; and if they cease, there is no hostility except against those who oppress } Al-baqara 190-193

ولما صدّ ﷺ عن البيت عام الحديبية وصالح الكفار على أن يعود العام القابل ويخلوا له مكة ثلاثة أيام وتجهز لعمرة القضاء وخافوا أن لا تفي قريش ويقاتلوهم وكره المسلمون قتالهم في الحرم والاحرام والشهر الحرام نزل ﴿ وقاتلوا في سبيل الله ﴾ أي لإعلاء دينه ﴿ الذين يقاتلونكم ﴾ الكفار ﴿ ولا تعتدوا ﴾ عليهم بالإبتداء بالقتال ﴿ إن الله لا يحب المعتدين ﴾ المتجاوزين ما حدّ لهم وهذا منسوخ بآية ﴿ براءة ﴾ وبقوله ﴿ واقتلوهم حيث ثقفتموهم ﴾ وجدتموهم ﴿ وأخرجوهم من حيث أخرجوكم ﴾ أي من مكة وقد فعل بهم ذلك عام الفتح
تفسير الجلالين

When He (SAW) was held back from the House [i.e. the Ka'ba] in the year of Hudaibiyya, He made a truce with the disbelievers that He would return the following year and that they would clear out Mecca for him for three days. And He made preparations for the pilgrimage of fulfillment ['umrah al-qadaa], but they feared that the Quraish would not keep the truce and would fight them, and the Muslims disliked fighting them in the sacred sanctuary and in a state of ritual purity [ihram], and during a forbidden month; { Fight in the cause of Allah } came down; that is, to exalt His religion; { Those who fight you } : the Disbelievers; { And do not transgress } : against them by initiating the fighting; { Indeed Allah does not love those who transgress } : those who go beyond what they have been restricted to. But this was abrogated by { Absolution ... } [Al-tawba 1] and by His word { And kill them wherever you get to them } : wherever you find them; { And drive them away from where they drove you away } : that is, from Mecca; and they in fact did this to them in the year of the conquest [fath] of Mecca.

Tafsir Al-Jalalain

قوله تعالى ﴿ واقتلوهم حيث ثقفتموهم ﴾ قيل نسخت الآية الاولى بهذه الآية وأصل الثقافة الحذق والبصر بالامور ومعناه واقتلوهم حيث بصرتم مقاتلتهم وتمكنتم من قتلهم ... ﴿ وقتلوهم حيث ثقفتموهم ﴾ أي حيث أدركتموهم في الحلّ والحرم وصارت هذه الآية منسوخة بقوله تعالى ﴿ ولا تقاتلوهم عند المسجد الحرام ﴾ ثم نسختها آية السيف في براءة فهي ناسخة منسوخة ... ﴿ وقاتلوهم ﴾ يعني المشركين ﴿ حتى لا تكون فتنة ﴾ أي شرك يعني قاتلوهم حتى يسلموا فلا يقبل من الوثني إلا الاسلام فإن أبى قُتل

تفسير البغوي

Regarding the word of the Most High { And kill them wherever you get to them } : It is said that the first verse was abrogated by this verse. The basis of getting to them is being astute and observant of affairs; the meaning is "And kill them wherever you see them fighting and you are able to kill them". ... { And kill them wherever you get to them } : that is, wherever you come across them in non-sacred or sacred occasions. This verse became abrogated by the word of the Most High: { But do not fight them at the Sacred Mosque } ; then the verse of the sword in the "Absolution" surah [Al-tawba] in turn abrogated it, making this verse both abrogating and abrogated. ... { And fight them } : that is, the idolaters; { until there is no more sedition } : that is, idolatry [shirk], meaning in effect: "Fight them until they enter into Islam"; for nothing else except Islam is to be accepted from the heathen [wathani, idol worshippers]; if they refuse, they are to be killed.

Tafsir Al-Baghawi

ثم أمر تعالى بقتال الكفار ﴿ حتى لا تكون فتنة ﴾ أي شرك قاله إبن عباس وأبو العالية ومجاهد والحسن وقتادة والربيع ومقاتل بن حيان والسدي وزيد بن أسلم ﴿ ويكون الدين لله ﴾ أي يكون دين الله هو الظاهر العالي على سائر الأديان ... ولما كان الجهاد فيه ازهاق النفوس وقتل الرجال نبه تعالى على أن ماهم مشتملون عليه من الكفر بالله والشرك به والصد عن سبيله أبلغ وأشد وأعظم وأطم من القتل ولهذا قال ﴿ والفتنة أشد من القتل ﴾ قال أبو مالك أي ما أنتم مقيمون عليه أكبر من القتل وقال أبو العالية ومجاهد وسعيد بن جبير وعكرمة والحسن وقتادة والضحاك والربيع بن أنس في قوله ﴿ والفتنة أشد من القتل ﴾ يقول الشرك أشد من القتل ... ثم أمر تعالى بقتال الكفار ﴿ حتى لا تكون فتنة ﴾ أي شرك قاله إبن عباس وأبو العالية ومجاهد والحسن وقتادة والربيع ومقاتل بن حيان والسدي وزيد بن أسلم

تفسير إبن كثير

Then the Most High ordered fighting the disbelievers { until there is no more sedition [*fitnah*] } : that is, idolatry [*shirk*]. Ibn 'Abbas, Abu Al-'Aliya, Mujahid, Al-Hasan, Qatada, Rabi', Muqatil ibn Hayyan, Al-Suddi, and Zaid ibn Aslam said this. { And religion belongs to Allah } : that is, the religion of Allah is the one high and manifest over all other religions. ... In that *jihad* involves demolishing lives and killing men, the Most High warned that the disbelief in Allah [*kufr*] that they embrace, the associating others with Him [*shirk*], and hindering His cause, are more drastic, severe, formidable, and engulfing than killing; for this reason He said { Sedition is more severe than killing }. Abu Malik said: That is, what you all are committing is more serious than killing. Abu Al-'Aliyah, Mujahid, Sa'id ibn Jubair, 'Ikrama, Al-Hasan, Qatada, Al-Dahhak, and Al-Rabi' ibn Anas, regarding His word { Sedition is more severe than killing } , said: He is saying that *shirk* is more severe than killing. ... So then the Most High ordered fighting the disbelievers { until there is no more sedition } that is, no more idolatry. Ibn 'Abbas, Abu Al-'Aliya, Mujahid, Al-Hasan, Qatada, Al-Rabi', Muqatil ibn Hayyan, Al-Suddi, and Zaid ibn Aslam said this.

Tafsir Ibn Kathir

قوله تعالى ﴿ وقاتلوهم حتى لا تكون فتنة ويكون الدين لله فإن انتهوا فلا عدوان إلا على الظالمين ﴾ فيه مسألتان الأولى ﴿ وقاتلوهم ﴾ أمر بالقتال لكل مشرك في كل موضع على من رآها ناسخة ومن رآها غير ناسخة قال المعنى قاتلوا هؤلاء الذين قال الله فيهم ﴿ فإن قاتلوكم ﴾ والأول أظهر وهو أمر بقتال مطلق لا بشرط أن يبدأ الكفار دليل ذلك قوله تعالى ﴿ ويكون الدين لله ﴾ وقال عليه السلام أمرت أن أقاتل الناس حتى يقولوا لا إله إلا الله فدلت الآية والحديث على أن سبب القتال هو الكفر لأنه قال ﴿ حتى لا تكون فتنة ﴾ أي كفر فجعل الغاية عدم الكفر وهذا ظاهر قال إبن عباس وقتادة والربيع والسدي وغيرهم الفتنة هناك الشرك وما تابعه من أذى المؤمنين ... الثانية قوله تعالى ﴿ فإن انتهوا ﴾ أي عن الكفر إما بالاسلام كما تقدم في الآية قبل أو بأداء الجزية في حق أهل الكتاب على ما يأتي بيانه في براءة

تفسير القرطبي

The word of the Most High: { And fight them until there is no more sedition and religion belongs to Allah; and if they cease, there is no hostility except against those who oppress } ; there are two points concerning this. The first: { And fight them } is an order to fight all idolaters everywhere, based on the view of those who take this to be abrogating. Those who take this to be non-abrogating say: The meaning is "Fight those about whom Allah has said: { If they fight you }". The first view is the clearest. This is an unrestrained command to fight, with no condition that the disbelievers initiate it; evidence for this is the word of the Most High: { And religion belongs to Allah } . He (peace be upon him) said: I have been commanded to fight people until they say: "There is no god but Allah" ["*La ilaha illa Allah*"]. Both the verse and the *hadith* make it clear that the reason for fighting is disbelief, since He said: { Until there is no more sedition } , that is, disbelief. He set the goal to be the absence of disbelief, and this is clear. Ibn 'Abbas, Qatada, Rabi', Al-Suddi, and others said: "Sedition" [*fitnah*] here is idolatry [*shirk*] and the harm to the Believers that this entails. ... The second point is the word of the Most High: { And if they cease } : that is, from disbelief, either by Islam as stated earlier in the verse, or by fulfilling the *jizya* according to the duty of the People of the Book based on what is given in the "Absolution" [surah *Al-tawba*].

Tafsir Al-Qurtubi

قال أبو جعفر إختلف أهل التأويل في تأويل هذه الآية فقال بعضهم هذه الآية هي أول آية نزلت في أمر المسلمين بقتال أهل الشرك وقالوا أمر فيها المسلمون بقتال من قاتلهم من المشركين والكفّ عمن كفّ عنهم ثم نُسخت ببراءة ... وقال آخرون بل ذلك أمر من الله تعالى ذكره للمسلمين بقتال الكفار لم ينسخ وإنما الإعتداء الذي نهاهم الله عنه هو نهيه عن قتل النساء والذراري قالوا والنهي عن قتلهم ثابت حكمه اليوم قالوا فلا شيء نُسخ من حكم هذه الآية ... فمعنى ﴿ واقتلوهم حيث ثقفتموهم ﴾ اقتلوهم في أي مكان تمكنتم من قتلهم وأبصرتم مَقاتلهم

... القول في تأويل قوله تعالى ﴿ فإن انتهوا فإن الله غفور رحيم ﴾ قال أبو جعفر يعني تعالى ذكره بذلك فإن انتهوا الكافرون الذين يقاتلونكم عن قتالكم وكفرهم بالله فتركوا ذلك وتابوا ﴿ فإن الله غفور ﴾ لذنوب من آمن منهم وتاب من شركه وأناب إلى الله من معاصيه التي سلفت منه وأيامه التي مضت ... عن قتادة ويكون الدين لله أن يقال لا إله إلا الله ذُكر لنا أن نبي الله ﷺ كان يقول إن الله أمرني أن أقاتل الناس حتى يقولوا لا إله إلا الله ... قال أبو جعفر يقول تعالى ذكره لنبيه محمد ﷺ وقاتلوا المشركين الذين يقاتلونكم حتى لا تكون فتنة يعني حتى لا يكون شرك بالله وحتى لا يُعبد دونه أحدُ

تفسير الطبري

Abu Ja'far said: The expositors differ regarding interpretation of this verse; some of them say this verse was the first verse to come down ordering the Muslims to fight those who commit *shirk* [idolatry; worshipping other than Allah alone]. They say: In this verse the Muslims order fighting against the idolaters [*Mushrikun*] who fight them, and desisting from those that desist from them; then it was abrogated by { There is absolution, from Allah and His Messenger, regarding the Idolaters with whom you made covenant ... } [*Al-tawba* 1] ... Others say that this is instead an order from Allah (may His remembrance be exalted) to the Muslims to fight the disbelievers [*Kuffar*], and has not been abrogated; rather the "transgression" that Allah prohibits is His prohibiting the killing of women and children. They say: The prohibition to kill them is firm, His command to this day; nothing of the command in this verse has been abrogated. ... The meaning of { And kill them wherever you get to them } : Kill them anywhere you are able to kill them and find a way to kill them. ... What is said regarding interpretation of the word of the Most High { If they cease, indeed Allah is forgiving and merciful } ; Abu Ja'far said: He (may His remembrance be exalted) means by this: If the disbelievers who are fighting you cease from fighting you, and from their disbelief in Allah, and abandon this, and repent, { Indeed Allah is forgiving } : of the sins of those of them who believe, and repent from their idolatry [*shirk*], and turn to Allah from their past misdeeds and past days. ... Qatada related that { And religion belongs to Allah } means that "There is no god but Allah" is to be said. It was mentioned to us that the Prophet of Allah (SAW) said: Indeed Allah has ordered me to fight people until they say "There is no god but Allah" ["*La ilaha illa Allah*"]. ... Abu Ja'far said: He (may His remembrance be exalted) is saying to His Prophet Muhammad (SAW): Fight the Idolaters, those who fight you, until there is no more sedition, that is, until there is no more *shirk* with Allah and until no one worships any but Him.

Tafsir Al-Tabari

﴿ والفتنة أشد من القتل ﴾ يعني الشرك أعظم عند الله عز وجل جرماً من القتل

تفسير مقاتل بن سليمان

{ Sedition is more severe than killing } : this means that in the sight of Allah Mighty and Sublime, *shirk* is a greater crime than killing.

Tafsir Muqatil ibn Sulaiman

قوله عز وجل ﴿ وقاتلوهم حتى لا تكون فتنة ﴾ أي قاتلوا المشركين حتى لا يكون شرك أي قاتلوهم حتى يسلموا فليس يقبل من الوثني جزية ولا يرضى منه إلا بالاسلام وليسوا كأهل الكتاب الذين يؤخذ منهم الجزية والحكمة في ذلك أنَّ مع أهل الكتاب كتباً منزَّلة فيها ألحق وإن كانوا قد أهملوها فأمهلهم الله بحُرمة تلك الكتب من القتل وأمر بإذلالهم بالجزية ولينظروا في كتبهم وليدبَّروها فيقفوا على ألحق منها فيتبعوه وأما أهل الأوثان فليس لهم كتب ترشدهم إلى ألحق وكان إمهالهم زائداً في شركهم فأبى الله أن يرضى منهم إلا بالاسلام أو القتل

التفسير الكبير للطبراني

The word of the Mighty and Sublime { And fight them until there is no more sedition } : that is, fight the idolaters until there is no more idolatry [*shirk*]; that is, fight them until they yield into Islam. No *jizya* is accepted from the heathens [*wathani*], and nothing but Islam is satisfactory from them. They are not like the People of the Book, from whom *jizya* is taken. The wisdom in this is that the People of the Book possess inspired books in which there is truth, and even if they have ignored it, Allah has granted them respite from killing, due to the sanctity of these books, and has commanded that they be abased by the *jizya*, and that they look into their books and be instructed by them, that they might comprehend the truth therein, and follow it. In contrast, the heathens do not have any books to guide them to the truth, and granting them respite only adds to their idolatry, and so Allah refuses to be pleased with them except either by Islam or killing.

Al-Tabarani, Al-tafsir Al-kabir

﴿ وقاتلوا في سبيل الله ﴾ دين الله وطاعته ﴿ الذين قاتلونكم ﴾ قال الربيع بن أنس وعبد الرحمن بن زيد بن أسلم هذه أول آية نزلت في القتال فلما نزلت كان رسول الله ﷺ يقاتل من يقاتله ويكف عمن كفّ عنه حتى نزلت ﴿ اقتلوا المشركين ﴾ فنسخت هذه الآية ﴿ ولا تعتدوا ﴾ أي لا تقتلوا النساء والصبيان والشيخ الكبير ولا من ألقى اليكم السلم وكف يده فإن فعلت ذلك فقد اعتديتم وهو قول إبن عباس ومجاهد ... ﴿ وقاتلوهم ﴾ يعني المشركين ﴿ حتى لا تكون فتنة ﴾ شرك يعني قاتلوهم حتى يسلموا ... ﴿ ويكون الدين الاسلام ﴿ لله ﴾ وحده فلا يعبد دونه شيء قال المقداد بن الأسود سمعت رسول الله ﷺ يقول لا يبقى على ظهر الأرض بيت مدر ولا وبر إلا أدخله الله عز وجل كلمة الاسلام إما بعز عزيز أو بذل ذليل إما أن يعزهم فيجعلهم الله من أهله فيعزوا به وإما أن يذلهم فيدينون لها

تفسير الثعلبي

{ Fight in the cause of Allah } : the religion of Allah and obedience to Him; { those who fight you } : Rabi' ibn Anas and 'Abd Al-Rahman ibn Zaid ibn Aslam said: This was the first verse to come down concerning fighting, and at the time it came down, the Messenger of Allah (SAW) would fight whoever fought him and desist from whoever desisted from him, until { Kill the idolaters } [Al-tawba 5] came down, and abrogated this verse. { And do not transgress } : that is, do not kill women, children, old men, or whoever extends peace to you and restrains his hand. If you do this, you have transgressed. This is what Ibn 'Abbas and Mujahid said. ... { And fight them } : that is, the idolaters; { until there is no more sedition } : idolatry [*shirk*]; that is, fight them until they yield into Islam. ... { and religion belongs } : Islam; { to Allah } : to Him alone, and none other than Him is worshipped. Al-Miqdad ibn Al-Aswad said: I heard the Messenger of Allah (SAW) say: Allah Mighty and Sublime will make the word of Islam penetrate into every Ma'add and Bedouin dwelling on earth, either by the might of the mighty or by the disgrace of the disgraced; either Allah will make them mighty, make them among His followers, and by this they will be mighty, or He will disgrace them, and they will be subject to the word of Islam.

Tafsir Al-Tha'labi

قوله تعالى ﴿ وقاتلوا في سبيل الله الذين يقاتلونكم ﴾ فيها قولان احدهما أنها أول أية نزلت في قتال المشركين أُمِر المسلمون فيها بقتال من قاتلهم من المشركين والكف عمن كف عنهم ثم نُسخت بسورة براءة وهذا قول الربيع وإبن زيد والثاني أنها ثابتة في الحكم أمر فيها بقتال المشركين كافة والإعتداء الذي نُهوا عنه قتل النساء والولدان وهذا قول إبن عباس وعمر بن عبد العزيز ومجاهد وفي قوله ﴿ ولا تعتدوا ﴾ ثلاث أقاويل احدها أن الاعتداء قتال من لم يقاتل والثاني أنه قتل النساء والولدان والثالث أنه القتال على غير الدين قوله تعالى ﴿ واقتلوهم حيث ثقفتموهم ﴾ يعني حيث ظفرتم بهم ﴿ وأخرجوهم من حيث أخرجوكم ﴾ يعني من مكة ﴿ والفتنة أشد من القتل ﴾ يعني بالفتنة الكفر في قول الجميع وإنما سمي الكفر فتنة لأنه يؤدي إلى الهلاك كالفتنة

تفسير الماوردي

The word of the Most High: { Fight in the cause of Allah those who fight you } ; there are two points of view concerning this. The first point is that this is the first verse to come down regarding fighting the idolaters; here the Muslims were ordered to fight the idolaters who fought them, and desist from those who desisted from them. Then it was abrogated by the "Absolution" surah [Al-tawba]; this is what Rabi' and Ibn Zaid say. The second point of view is that its ruling stands firm; here they are ordered to fight all the idolaters, and the transgression that they are prohibited from is the killing of women and children; this is what Ibn 'Abbas, 'Umar ibn 'Abd Al-'Aziz, and Mujahid say. Regarding His word { And do not transgress } there are three opinions: one is that "transgression" is killing people who do not fight, the second is that this means killing women and children, and the third is that this refers to killing for reasons other than religion [deen]. The word of the Most High { And kill them wherever you get to them } : this means wherever you get the upper hand over them; { and drive them away from where they drove you away } : this means from Mecca; { sedition is more severe than killing } : all say that by "sedition" [fitnah] He means disbelief [kufr] – indeed disbelief is called sedition because like sedition it leads to destruction.

Tafsir Al-Mawardi

وقوله تعالى ﴿ وقاتلوهم حتى لا تكون فتنة ﴾ أمر بالقتال لكل مشرك في كل موضع على قول من رآها ناسخة ومن رآها غير ناسخة قال المعنى قاتلوا هؤلاء الذين قال الله فيهم ﴿ فإن قاتلوكم ﴾ والأول أظهر وهو أمر بقتال مطلق لا بشرط أن يبدأ الكفار دليل ذلك قوله ﴿ ويكون الدين لله ﴾ والفتنة هنا الشرك وما تابعه من أذى المؤمنين قاله إبن عباس وقتادة والربيع والسدي و ﴿ الدين ﴾ هنا الطاعة والشرع

تفسير إبن عطية

The word of the Most High: { And fight them until there is no more sedition } ; this is a command to fight all idolaters everywhere, based on the view of those who take this to be abrogating. Those who take this to be non-abrogating say: The meaning is "Fight those about whom Allah has said: { if they fight you }" . The first view is the clearest. This is an unrestrained command to fight, with no condition that the disbelievers initiate it; evidence for this is His word: { and religion belongs to Allah }. "Sedition" here is idolatry and the harm to the believers that it entails; Ibn 'Abbas, Qatada, Rabi', and Al-Suddi said this. And { religion } here is obedience and the law of Islam.

Tafsir Ibn 'Atiyya

﴿ وقاتلوهم حتى لا تكون فتنة ﴾ شرك و ﴿ كان ﴾ تامة و ﴿ حتى ﴾ بمعنى كي أو إلى أن

مدارك التنزيل للنسفي

{ And fight them until there is no more sedition }: idolatry; and { is }: completely; and { until }: meaning "in order that" or "up to the point at which".

Al-Nasafi, Madarik Al-tanzil

قال أبو مسلم معنى الفتنة ههنا الجرم قال لأن الله تعالى أمر بقتالهم حتى لا يكون منهم القتال الذي إذا بدؤا به كان فتنة على المؤمنين لما يخافون عنده من أنواع المضار فإن قيل كيف يقال ﴿ وقاتلوهم حتى لا تكون فتنة ﴾ مع علمنا بأن قتالهم لا يزيل الكفر وليس من هذا أن يلزم أن لا يكون حقاً قلنا الجواب من وجهين الأول أن هذا محمول على الأغلب لأن الأغلب عند قتالهم زوال الكفر والشرك لأن من قتل فقد زال كفره ومن لا يقتل يخاف منه الثبات على الكفر فإذا كان هذا هو الأغلب جاز أن يقال ذلك الجواب الثاني أن المراد قاتلوهم قصداً منكم إلى زوال الكفر لأن الواجب على المقاتل للكفار أن يكون مراده هذا

تفسير الرازي

Abu Muslim said the meaning of "sedition" [*fitnah*] here is crime; he said: Since Allah Most High ordered them to be fought until there is no more fighting from them, that which, if they initiated it, would be an ordeal [*fitnah*] for the Believers when they fear any sort of harm in it. If someone asks: How can you say: { And fight them until there is no more sedition }, since we know that fighting them does not eliminate disbelief, and it is not possible that what Allah has stated is not true? We say: The answer is two parts. The first is that this is borne on what generally occurs, since generally when they are fought, disbelief and idolatry are eliminated, because whoever is killed – his disbelief ends, and whoever is not killed will be afraid to remain in disbelief. If this is generally the case, it is permissible to give this answer. The second part is that the goal in fighting them is the intent to eliminate disbelief from them, since anyone who fights the Disbelievers must have this as a goal.

Tafsir Al-Razi

وقيل الضمير لجميع الكفار أمروا بقتالهم وقتلهم في كل مكان فالآية عامة تتناول كل كافر من مشرك وغيره

البحر المحيط لأبي حيان

It is said: This refers to all disbelievers [Kuffar]; they have been ordered to fight them and kill them everywhere. The verse is general, encompassing all disbelievers, among the idolaters or otherwise.

Abu Hayyan, Al-bahr Al-muhit

﴿ حتى لا تكون فتنة ﴾ قيل أي شرك وكفر وعلى هذا فالآية محمولة على الأغلب فإن قتالهم لا يزيل الكفر رأساً وإنما الغالب الإزالة لأن من قتل منهم فقد زال كفره ومن لم يقتل كان خائفاً من الثبات على كفره ... وقيل فتنتهم أنهم كانوا يضربون أصحاب النبي ﷺ ويؤذونهم حتى ذهب بعضهم إلى الحبشة ثم إلى المدينة

تفسير النيسابوري

{ Until there is no more sedition } ; it is said: this means idolatry [shirk] and disbelief [kufr], and so the verse bears on what generally occurs. For if fighting them does not directly eliminate disbelief, it generally eliminates it, because whoever of them is killed – his disbelief ends, and whoever is not killed is afraid of remaining in his disbelief. ... It is said that their sedition was that they hurt the Companions of the Prophet (SAW), and harmed them, to the point that some of them went off to Ethiopia and then to Medina.

Tafsir Al-Nisaburi

﴿ ويكون الدين لله ﴾ قال حتى يقال لا إله إلا الله عليها قاتل رسول الله ﷺ وإليها دعا وذكر لنا أن النبي ﷺ كان يقول إن الله أمرني أن أقاتل الناس حتى يقولوا لا إله إلا الله ﴿ فإن انتهوا فلا عدوان إلا على الظالمين ﴾ قال وإن الظالم الذي أبى أن يقول لا إله إلا الله يقاتل حتى يقول لا إله إلا الله

الدر المنثور للسيوطي

{ And religion belongs to Allah } : He is saying: Until "There is no god but Allah" ["La ilaha illa Allah"] is declared. The Messenger of Allah (SAW) fought for this and called for this. It has been mentioned to us that the Prophet (SAW) said: Indeed Allah has ordered me to fight people until they say "La ilaha illa Allah". { And if they cease, there is no hostility except against those who oppress } : He is saying: Those who oppress are those who refuse to say "La ilaha illa Allah"; they are to be fought until they say "La ilaha illa Allah".

Al-Suyuti, Al-durr Al-manthur

﴿ وقد روي عن جماعة من المفسرين منهم قتادة أن قوله تعالى ﴿ فإن انتهوا فلا عدوان إلا على الظالمين ﴾ منسوخ بآية السيف

تفسير إبن الجوزي

It is related from a group of expositors, among them Qatada, that the word of the Most High { And if they cease, there is no hostility except against those who oppress } is abrogated by the verse of the sword [Al-tawba 5].

Tafsir Ibn Al-Jawzi

• • •

﴿ وأنفقوا في سبيل الله ولا تلقوا بأيديكم إلى التهلكة وأحسنوا إن الله يحب المحسنين ﴾
البقرة ١٩٥

{ Spend in the cause of Allah, and do not be thrown into ruin by your own hands, and do good; indeed Allah loves those who do good } *Al-baqara* 195

﴿ وأنفقوا في سبيل الله ﴾ وسبيل الله طريقه الذي أمر أن يسلك فيه إلى عدوه من المشركين لجهادهم وحربهم ... عن عبدالله بن عباس أنه قال في هذه الآية ﴿ ولا تُلقوا بأيديكم إلى التهلكة ﴾ قال تنفق في سبيل الله وإن لم يكن لك إلا مِشْقَصٌ أو سهم شعبة الذي يشك في ذلك ... عن إبن عباس ﴿ ولا تلقوا بأيديكم إلى التهلكة ﴾ قال ليس التهلكة أن يُقتل الرجل في سبيل الله ولكن الإمساك عن النفقة في سبيل الله ... وكذلك التارك غزو المشركين وجهادهم في حال وجوب ذلك عليه في حال حاجة المسلمين إليه مضيع فرضاً مُلقٍ بيده إلى التهلكة

تفسير الطبري

{ Spend in the cause of Allah } : the cause of Allah is His path, which He has ordered to be taken towards His enemy the idolaters [*mushrikeen*] in *jihad* and war against them. ... Abdullah ibn 'Abbas, regarding this verse { And do not be thrown into ruin by your own hands } , said: You are to spend in the cause of Allah, even if you only have an arrow or a dart that can be used to pierce for this. ... Ibn 'Abbas, regarding

{ And do not be thrown into ruin by your own hands } , said: "Ruin" is not someone getting killed in the cause of Allah, but rather holding back from spending in the cause of Allah. ... Anyone who neglects attacking the idolaters and waging *jihad* against them, when this is his duty, the Muslims being in need of this, has squandered an obligation, thrown by his own hand into ruin.

Tafsir Al-Tabari

فقال أبو أيوب نحن أعلم بهذه الآية اتما نزلت فينا صحبنا رسول الله ﷺ وشهدنا معه المشاهد ونصرناه فلما فشا الاسلام وظهر اجتمعنا معشر الأنصار نجياً فقلنا قد أكرمنا الله بصحبة نبيه ﷺ ونصره حتى فشا الاسلام وكثر أهله ... وقال الحسن البصري ﴿ ولا تلقوا بأيديكم إلى التهلكة ﴾ قال هو البخل ... قول الله ﴿ وأنفقوا في سبيل الله ولا تلقوا بأيديكم إلى التهلكة ﴾ وذلك أن رجالاً يخرجون في بعوث يبعثها رسول الله ﷺ بغير نفقة فإما أن يقطع بهم وإما كانوا عيالاً فأمرهم الله أن يستنفقوا مما رزقهم الله ولا يلقوا بأيديهم إلى التهلكة والتهلكة أن يهلك رجال من الجوع والعطش أو من المشي وقال لمن بيده فضل ﴿ وأحسنوا إن الله يحب المحسنين ﴾ ومضمون الآية الأمر بالإنفاق في سائر وجوه القربات ووجوه الطاعات وخاصة صرف الأموال في قتال الأعداء وبذلها فيما يقوى به المسلمون على عدوهم والإخبار عن ترك ذلك بأنه هلاك ودمار لمن لزمه واعتاده ثم عطف بالأمر بالإحسان وهو أعلى مقامات الطاعة فقال ﴿ وأحسنوا إن الله يحب المحسنين ﴾

تفسير ابن كثير

Abu Ayub said: We knew best about this verse, since it came down concerning us; the Messenger of Allah (SAW) went out with us, and we were there with him for the battles and stood by him; and when Islam spread and prevailed, we got together privately with some of the *Ansar* and said: Allah has honored us in being the Companions of His Prophet (SAW) and championing him until Islam spread and its people increased. ... Al-Hasan Al-Basri, regarding { And do not be thrown into ruin by your own hands } , said: This means being stingy. ... The word of Allah { Spend in the cause of Allah and do not be thrown into ruin by your own hands } : this was because some men went out on some missions that the Messenger of Allah (SAW) dispatched, without spending anything – either He affirmed them or they were dependents of others. And Allah ordered them to spend of the bounty Allah had given them, and to not be thrown into ruin by their own hands; "ruin" is when men are destroyed by hunger and thirst, or by travelling on foot. He is saying to those who have bounty: { And do good, indeed Allah loves those who do good } : the implication of the verse is a command to spend in the cause of Allah, as one of the ways to draw close and to carry out acts of obedience, especially in disbursing wealth for fighting enemies, and in freely giving it to what strengthens the Muslims over their enemy; the statement is against neglect in doing this, given that this will be destruction and perdition for whoever persists in this and becomes accustomed to it. Then He couples this with the command to do good [*ihsan*, excellence in faith and deed], this being the highest of the positions of obedience; He said: { And do good, indeed Allah loves those who do good } .

Tafsir Ibn Kathir

والإلقاء باليد إلى التهلكة أن نقيم في أموالنا ونصلحها وندع الجهاد فلم يزل أبو أيوب مجاهداً في سبيل الله حتى دُفن بالقسطنطينية فقبره هناك فأخبرنا أبو أيوب أن الإلقاء باليد إلى التهلكة هو ترك الجهاد في سبيل الله وأن الآية نزلت في ذلك

تفسير القرطبي

Being thrown into ruin by one's hand is when we secure our wealth, and put it in order, but disregard *jihad*. Abu Ayub was a *mujahid* in the cause of Allah until he was buried in Constantinople; his grave is there. Abu Ayub told us that being thrown into ruin by one's hand is neglecting *jihad* in the cause of Allah, and that this verse came down regarding this.

Tafsir Al-Qurtubi

﴿ وأنفقوا في سبيل الله ﴾ طاعته بالجهاد وغيره ﴿ ولا تلقوا بأيديكم ﴾ أي انفسكم وألباء زائدة ﴿ إلى التهلكة ﴾ الهلاك بالامساك عن النفقة في الجهاد أو تركه لأنه يقوي العدو عليكم

تفسير الجلالين

{ Spend in the cause of Allah } : in obedience to Him by *jihad* and otherwise; { and do not be thrown ... by your own hands } : that is, do not throw yourselves (the "by" is additional); { into ruin } : destruction, by holding back from spending for *jihad*, or abandoning it, since this would strengthen the enemy against you.

Tafsir Al-Jalalain

■ ■ ■

﴿ ومن الناس من يشري نفسه ابتغاء مرضات الله والله رؤوف بالعباد يا أيها الذين آمنوا ادخلوا في السلم كافة ولا تتبعوا خطوات الشيطان إنه لكم عدو مبين ﴾
البقرة ٢٠٧-٢٠٨

{ And among the people there are those who sell themselves seeking after the good pleasures of Allah; and Allah is compassionate to the servants. Oh you who have believed! Enter completely into peace and do not follow the steps of Satan; indeed he is a clear enemy to you all } Al-baqara 207-208

﴿ ومن الناس من يشري نفسه ﴾ يبيعها أي يبذلها في الجهاد أو يأمر بالمعروف وينهى عن المنكر حتى يُقتل ... ﴿ والله رؤوف بالعباد ﴾ حيث أرشدهم إلى مثل هذا الشراء وكلفهم بالجهاد فعرضهم لثواب الغزاة والشهداء ﴿ يا أيها الذين آمنوا ادخلوا في السلم كافة ﴾ ﴿ السلم ﴾ بالكسر والفتح الاستسلام والطاعة ولذلك يطلق في الصلح والاسلام

تفسير البيضاوي

{ And among the people there are those who sell themselves } : they sell themselves, that is, they sacrifice themselves in *jihad*, or they prescribe what is right and prohibit what is wrong until they are killed ... { And Allah is compassionate to the servants } : wherever He guides them towards such a transaction, charges them with *jihad*, and displays to them the reward of the fighters and martyrs. { Oh you who have believed! Enter completely into peace } : "peace" [*silm*] is surrender and obedience, and for this reason it applies to conciliation [*sulh*] and yielding [*islam*].

Tafsir Al-Baydawi

يعني جل ثناؤه ومن الناس من يبيع نفسه بما وعد الله المجاهدين في سبيله وابتاع به أنفسهم بقوله ﴿ إن الله إشترى من المؤمنين أنفسهم وأموالهم بأن لهم الجنة ﴾

تفسير الطبري

He (may His praise be exalted) means: Among the people there are those who sell themselves for what Allah has promised to the *mujahideen* in His cause, and for which He has bought them, according to His word: { Indeed Allah has bought, from the Believers, their lives and their wealth, so that *Jannah* may be theirs } [Al-tawba 111].

Tafsir Al-Tabari

ذكر المفسرون وجوهاً في تأويل هذه الآية احدها أن المراد بالآية المنافقون والتقدير يا أيها الذين آمنوا بألسنتهم ادخلوا بكُلّيتِكم في الاسلام

تفسير الرازي

The expositors have mentioned several points of view regarding the interpretation of this verse; one of them is that the verse is directed at hypocrites, and may be phrased as: Oh you who have believed by tongues [words] only! Enter fully into Islam.

Tafsir Al-Razi

لما بيّن الله سبحانه الناس إلى مؤمن وكافر ومنافق فقال كونوا على ملة واحدة واجتمعوا على الاسلام واثبتوا عليه فالسِّلم هنا بمعنى الاسلام قاله مجاهد ورواه أبو مالك عن إبن عباس

تفسير القرطبي

This was when Allah the Exalted made it clear to people – Believers, Disbelievers, and hypocrites; He said: Be of one religion, come together in Islam, and abide by it. "Peace" [*silm*] here means Islam; Mujahid said this and Abu Malik related it from Ibn 'Abbas.

Tafsir Al-Qurtubi

يقول الله تعالى آمراً عباده المؤمنين به المصدقين برسوله أن يأخذوا بجميع عُرى الاسلام وشرائعه والعمل بجميع أوامره وترك جميع زواجره ما استطاعوا من ذلك

تفسير ابن كثير

Allah Most High is saying as a command to His servants the Believers in Him, those who assert the truth of His Messenger, that they observe all the bonds of Islam and its laws, act according to all its commands, and abandon all its restrictions, as best they can.

Tafsir Ibn Kathir

﴿ يا أيها الذين آمنوا ادخلوا في السلم كافة ﴾ في شرائع دين محمد ﷺ جميعاً

تفسير للفيروز آبادي

{ Oh you who have believed! Enter completely into peace } : into all the laws of Muhammad's (SAW) religion [*deen*].

Tafsir Fairuz Abadi

إختلف أهل التأويل في معنى السلم في هذا الموضع فقال بعضهم معناه الاسلام ... وقال آخرون بل معنى ذلك ادخلوا في الطاعة ... والصواب من القول في ذلك عندي أن يقال إن الله جل ثناؤه أمر الذين آمنوا بالدخول في العمل بشرائع الاسلام كلها

تفسير الطبري

The expositors differ regarding the meaning of "peace" here; some of them say that it means Islam ... other say, rather, that the meaning is "Enter into obedience" ... The correct way to say it in my view is to say that Allah (may His praise be exalted) has commanded those who believe to take up observance of all the laws of Islam.

Tafsir Al-Tabari

• • •

﴿ كُتِبَ عَلَيْكُمُ الْقِتَالُ وَهُوَ كُرْهٌ لَكُمْ وَعَسَى أَنْ تَكْرَهُوا شَيْئًا وَهُوَ خَيْرٌ لَكُمْ وَعَسَى أَنْ تُحِبُّوا شَيْئًا وَهُوَ شَرٌّ لَكُمْ وَاللَّهُ يَعْلَمُ وَأَنْتُمْ لَا تَعْلَمُونَ ﴾ البقرة ٢١٦

{ Fighting is ordained for you, being something you dislike; but perhaps you dislike something that is good for you, and perhaps you like something that is bad for you; and Allah knows but you all do not know } *Al-baqara 216*

واستمر الاجماع على أن الجهاد على أمة محمد فرض كفاية فإذا قام به من قام من المسلمين سقط عن الباقين إلا أن ينزل العدو بساحة للإسلام فهو حينئذ فرض عين

تفسير إبن عطية

It rests unanimous that *jihad* is a collective obligation on the *ummah* of Muhammad, although whoever among the Muslims undertake it, the others are no longer obliged, except if the enemy descends into Islamic territory, it then becomes an individual obligation.

Tafsir Ibn 'Atiyya

قوله سبحانه ﴿ كتب عليكم القتال ﴾ يعني فرض عليكم كقوله ﴿ كتب عليكم الصيام ﴾ يعني فرض ﴿ وهو كرهٌ لكم ﴾ يعني مشقة لكم ﴿ وعسى أن تكرهوا شيئاً وهو خيرٌ لكم ﴾ فيجعل الله عاقبته فتحاً وغنيمة وشهادة ﴿ وعسى أن تحبوا شيئاً ﴾ يعني القعود عن الجهاد ﴿ وهو شرٌ لكم ﴾ فيجعل الله عاقبته شر فلا تصيبون ظفراً ولا غنيمة

تفسير مقاتل بن سليمان

His (may His praise be exalted) word: { Fighting is ordained for you } : that is, your obligation, just as He says: { Fasting is ordained for you } [Al-baqara 183], that is, an obligation. { Being something you dislike } : that is, harship for you; { but perhaps you dislike something that is good for you } : for Allah may give victory, spoils, and martyrdom as a result of it; { and perhaps you like something } : that is, sitting out from *jihad*; { that is bad for you } : for Allah may give a negative outcome in that you will attain neither victory nor spoils.

Tafsir Muqatil ibn Sulaiman

قال إبن عباس لما كتب الله الجهاد على المسلمين شُقَّ ذلك عليهم وكرهته نفوسهم وقبلته قلوبهم وأحب الله تعالى أن يطيّب نفوسهم بهذه الآية

التفسير الكبير للطبراني

Ibn 'Abbas said: When Allah ordained *jihad* for the Muslims, this troubled them; their souls were averse to it although their hearts consented to it, and so Allah Most High was pleased to ease their souls by this verse.

Al-Tabarani, Al-tafsir Al-kabir

قوله تعالى ﴿ كتب عليكم القتال ﴾ بمعنى فرض وفي فرضه ثلاثة أقاويل احدها أنه على أصحاب رسول الله ﷺ والثاني أنه خطاب لكل أحد من الناس كلهم أبداً حتى يقوم به من فيه كفاية وهذا قول الفقهاء والعلماء والثالث أنه فرض على كل مسلم في عينه أبداً وهذا قول سعيد بن المسيب

تفسير الماوردي

The word of the Most High: { Fighting is ordained for you } means an obligation; regarding its obligation there are three opinions. The first is that it was for the Messenger of Allah's (SAW) Companions. The second is that it addresses every individual among all people for all time, until enough have arisen to perform a collective duty; this is what jurists and scholars say. The third is that it is a personal obligation on every Muslim for all time; this is what Sa'id ibn Al-Musayyib said.

Tafsir Al-Mawardi

﴿ والله يعلم ﴾ أن الجهاد خير لكم ﴿ وانتم لا تعلمون ﴾ أن الجلوس شر لكم

تفسير للفيروز آبادي

{ And Allah knows } : that *jihad* is good for you; { but you do not know } : that sitting it out is bad for you.

Tafsir Fairuz Abadi

﴿ كتب ﴾ فرض ﴿ عليكم القتال ﴾ للكفار ﴿ وهو كره ﴾ مكروه ﴿ لكم ﴾ طبعاً لمشقته ﴿ وعسى أن تكرهوا شيئاً وهو خير لكم وعسى أن تحبوا شيئاً وهو شر لكم ﴾ لميل النفس إلى الشهوات الموجبة لهلاكها ونفورها عن التكليفات الموجبة لسعادتها فلعل لكم في القتال وإن كرهتموه خيراً لأن فيه إما الظفر والغنيمة أو الشهادة والأجر وفي تركه وإن أحببتموه شراً لأن فيه الذل والفقر وحرمات الأجر ﴿ والله يعلم ﴾ ما هو خير لكم ﴿ وأنتم لا تعلمون ﴾ ذلك فبادروا إلى ما يأمركم به

تفسير الجلالين

{ Ordained } : obligatory; { for you is fighting } : against the Disbelievers [*Kuffar*]; { being something you dislike } : undesirable; { to you } : because of its hardship by nature. { But perhaps you dislike something that is good for you, and perhaps you like something that is bad for you } : due to the soul's inclination towards desires that lead to its destruction, and its aversion towards the obligations that lead to its happiness; for perhaps in fighting – even if you dislike it – there is good for you, since in this there is either triumph over the enemy and spoils, or martyrdom and reward. But in abandoning it – even if you like this – there is harm, since in this there is humiliation and destitution, and deprivation from the reward. { And Allah knows } : what is good for you; { but you do not know } : this, so apply yourselves to what He has ordered you.

Tafsir Al-Jalalain

قوله تعالى ﴿ كتب ﴾ معناه فرض وقد تقدّم مثله وقرأ قوم ﴿ كتب عليكم القتل ﴾ هذا هو فرض الجهاد بين سبحانه أن هذا مما امتحنوا به وجعل وصلة إلى الجنة والمراد بالقتال قتال الأعداء من الكفار ... قوله ﴿ وعسى أن تكرهوا شيئاً ﴾ قيل عسى بمعنى قد قاله الأصم وقيل هي واجبة و عسى من الله واجبة في جميع القرآن إلا قوله تعالى ﴿ عسى ربه إن طلقكن أن يبدله ﴾ وقال أبو عبيدة عسى من الله إيجاب والمعنى عسى أن تكرهوا ما في الجهاد من المشقة وهو خير لكم في أنكم تغلبون وتظفرون وتغنمون وتؤجرون ومن مات مات شهيداً وعسى أن تحبوا الدعة وترك القتال وهو شر لكم في انكم تغلبون وتذلون ويذهب أمركم

تفسير القرطبي

The word of the Most High: { Ordained } : this means an obligation; similar has been presented. Some people recited this as { Killing is ordained for you } . This is the obligation of *jihad*; the Exalted has made known that this is part of what they were being put to the test for, and made a way to *Jannah*; the intended meaning of "fighting" is fighting the enemies from among the Disbelievers. ... The word of the Most High { But perhaps you dislike something } : "perhaps" is said with the meaning of possibility; Al-Asm said this. It is said that this is an obligation; "perhaps" from Allah means possibility throughout the Qur'an, with the exception of the word of the Most High: { Perhaps his Lord, if He divorces you all, will give him in exchange ... } [Al-tahrim 5]. Abu 'Ubaida said that "perhaps" from Allah means imposing an obligation, and the meaning is: Perhaps you dislike the hardship in *jihad*, although it is good for you, in that you prevail, and are victorious, and acquire spoils, and are rewarded; and whoever dies, dies a martyr. And perhaps you prefer to be gentle and refrain from fighting, although this is bad for you, in that you are prevailed over, and humiliated, and you end up as nothing.

Tafsir Al-Qurtubi

هذا إيجاب من الله تعالى للجهاد على المسلمين أن يكفوا شر الأعداء عن حوزة الاسلام وقال الزهري الجهاد واجب على كل أحد غزا أو قعد فالقاعد عليه إذا استعين أن يعين وإذا استغيث أن يغيث وإذا استنفر أن ينفر وإن لم يحتج إليه قعد ... ثم قال تعالى ﴿ وعسى أن تكرهوا شيئاً وهو خير لكم ﴾ أي لأن القتال يعقبه النصر والظفر على الأعداء والإستيلاء على بلادهم وأموالهم وذراريهم واولادهم ﴿ وعسى أن تحبوا شيئاً وهو شر لكم ﴾ وهذا عام في الأمور كلها قد يحب المرء شيئاً وليس له فيه خيرة ولا مصلحة ومن ذلك القعود عن القتال

تفسير ابن كثير

This is an obligation from Allah Most High on the Muslims for *jihad*, to restrain the evil of the enemies. Al-Zuhri said: *Jihad* is everyone's duty, whether he sets out to attack or sits it out. For the one who sits it out, it is obligatory for him, if he is asked to give support, to give support; if he is asked to assist, to assist; if he is called to mobilize, to mobilize; and if he is not needed, to sit it out. ... Then the Most High said: { Perhaps you dislike something that is good for you } ; that is, because victory and triumph over the enemies follows after fighting, as does taking possession of their land, their wealth, their women, and their children. { And perhaps you like something that is bad for you } : this refers in general to all affairs; a man might like something, although it has neither benefit nor gain for him, and this leads to sitting out from fighting.

Tafsir Ibn Kathir

قوله تعالى ﴿ كُتِبَ عَلَيْكُمُ الْقِتَالُ ﴾ أي فرض عليكم الجهاد واختلف العلماء في حكم هذه الآية فقال عطاء الجهاد تطوع والمراد من الآية أصحاب رسول الله ﷺ دون غيرهم وإليه ذهب الثوري واحتج من ذهب إلى هذا بقوله تعالى ﴿ فَضَّلَ اللَّهُ الْمُجَاهِدِينَ بِأَمْوَالِهِمْ وَأَنْفُسِهِمْ عَلَى الْقَاعِدِينَ دَرَجَةً وَكُلًّا وَعَدَ اللَّهُ الْحُسْنَى ﴾ ولو كان القاعد تاركاً فرضاً لم يكن يعده الحسنى وجرى بعضهم على ظاهر الآية وقال الجهاد فرض على كافة المسلمين إلى قيام الساعة

... قوله تعالى ﴿ وَهُوَ كُرْهٌ لَكُمْ ﴾ أي شاق عليكم قال بعض أهل المعاني هذا الكره من حيث نفور الطبع عنه لما فيه من مؤنة المال ومشقة النفس وخطر الروح لا أنهم كرهوا أمر الله تعالى وقال عكرمة نسخها قوله تعالى ﴿ سَمِعْنَا وَأَطَعْنَا ﴾ يعني أنهم كرهوه ثم أحبوه فقالوا ﴿ سَمِعْنَا وَأَطَعْنَا ﴾ قال الله تعالى ﴿ وَعَسَى أَنْ تَكْرَهُوا شَيْئًا وَهُوَ خَيْرٌ لَكُمْ ﴾ لأن في الغزو إحدى الحسنيين إما الظفر والغنيمة وإما الشهادة والجنة ﴿ وَعَسَى أَنْ تُحِبُّوا شَيْئًا ﴾ يعني القعود عن الغزو ﴿ وَهُوَ شَرٌّ لَكُمْ ﴾ لما فيه من فوات الغنيمة والأجر

تفسير البغوي

The word of the Most High: { Fighting is ordained for you } ; that is, *jihad* is your duty. Scholars have differed on what this verse stipulates. 'Ataa said: *Jihad* is voluntary, and the intended meaning of the verse is for the Messenger of Allah's (SAW) Companions, not anyone else. Al-Thawry took this view. But objection to those of this view was raised based on the word of the Most High: { Allah has preferred those who wage *jihad* with their wealth and with themselves by a degree over those who sit it out, but Allah has promised good things to both } [*Al-nisaa* 95]. If someone who sits it out is in fact abandoning a duty, a good thing would not be prepared for him. Some of the scholars took the verse at face value and said: *Jihad* is a duty on all Muslims until the final hour arrives.

... The word of the Most High: { Being something you dislike } ; that is, it is burdensome for you. Some of the interpreters said: This dislike is in regard to a natural aversion to it due to what it implies of supplying wealth, of personal hardship, and of menace to one's spirit, not because they dislike the command of Allah. 'Ikrama said: This was abrogated by the word of the Most High: { We have heard and obeyed } [*Al-baqara* 285] ; that is, because they disliked it, but then liked it, and so they said { We have heard and obeyed } . Allah Most High said: { But perhaps you dislike something that is good for you } since in going out on a raid there is one of two good things – either victory and spoils or martyrdom and *Jannah*. { And perhaps you like something } : that is, sitting out from raids; { that is bad for you } : due to forfeiture of spoils and reward.

Tafsir Al-Baghawi

إختلف علماء الناسخ والمنسوخ في هذه الآية على ثلاثة أقوال أحدها أنها من المحكم الناسخ للعفو عن المشركين والثاني أنها منسوخة لأنها أوجبت الجهاد على الكل فنسخ ذلك بقوله تعالى ﴿ وما كان المؤمنون لينفروا كافة ﴾ والثالث أنها ناسخة من وجه منسوخة من وجه وقالوا إن الحال في القتال كانت على ثلاث مراتب الأولى المنع من القتال ومنه قوله تعالى ﴿ ألم تر الذين قيل لهم كفوا أيديكم ﴾ والثانية أمر الكل بالقتال ومنه قوله تعالى ﴿ انفروا خفافاً وثقالاً ﴾ ومثلها هذه الآية والثالثة كون القتال فرضاً على الكفاية وهو قوله تعالى ﴿ وما كان المؤمنون لينفروا كافة ﴾ فيكون الناسخ منها إيجاب القتال بعد المنع منه والمنسوخ منه وجوب القتال على الكل

تفسير إبن الجوزي

The scholars of abrogating and abrogated texts differ regarding this verse, into three points of view. The first is that it is ruled as abrogating leniency towards the idolaters. The second is that it is abrogated, since it makes *jihad* incumbent on all, which was abrogated by the word of the Most High: { It is not for all of the believers to mobilize } [Al-tawba 122]. The third is that it abrogates in one sense and is abrogated in another sense. They say that the circumstances regarding fighting happened in three stages: the first was a prohibition on fighting, along the lines of the word of the Most High: { Have you not seen those to whom it was said: Restrain your hands } [Al-nisaa 77]. The second was a command for all to fight, including the word of the Most High: { Mobilize, light or heavy } [Al-tawba 41] , and this verse is similar. The third was fighting being a collective duty, this being the word of the Most High: { It is not for all of the believers to mobilize } . And so the abrogating portion of it is making fighting an obligation after prohibiting it, while the abrogated part of it is the necessity for all to fight.

Tafsir Ibn Al-Jawzi

أخرج إبن أبي حاتم عن سعيد بن جبير في الآية قال إن الله أمر النبي ﷺ والمؤمنين بمكة بالتوحيد وإقام الصلاة وإيتاء الزكاة وأن يكفوا أيديهم عن القتال فلما هاجر إلى المدينة نزلت سائر الفرائض وأذن لهم في القتال فنزلت ﴿ كتب عليكم القتال ﴾ يعني فرض عليكم وأذن لهم بعد ما كان نهاهم عنه

الدر المنثور للسيوطي

Ibn Abi Hatim reported from Sa'id ibn Jubair, who said regarding this verse: Indeed Allah ordered the Prophet (SAW) and the Believers in Mecca to assert one god [*tawheed*], to observe prayer, to present *zakat*, and to restrain their hands from fighting. But when He emigrated to Medina, the rest of the obligations came down, and they were given permission to fight. And { Fighting is ordained for you } came down, meaning that fighting is your obligation; and they were given permission after He had prohibited it to them.

Al-Suyuti, Al-durr Al-manthur

قوله تعالى ﴿ كتب عليكم القتال ﴾ كان النبي ﷺ غير مأذون له في القتال مدة إقامته بمكة فلما هاجر أذن في قتال من يقاتله من المشركين ثم أذن في قتال المشركين عامة ثم فرض الله تعالى الجهاد ... وأما منافع الجهاد فنها الظفر بالغنائم ومنها الفرح العظيم بالاستيلاء على العدو

تفسير النيسابوري

The word of the Most High: { Fighting is ordained for you } ; the Prophet (SAW) was not given permission to fight during his time in Mecca, but when He emigrated, He was given permission to fight those of the idolaters who fought against him. Then He was given permission to fight the idolaters in general, and finally Allah Most High made *jihad* an obligation. ... Regarding the benefits of *jihad*, these include attaining the spoils and the great joy in conquering the enemy.

Tafsir Al-Nisaburi

﴿ كتب ﴾ معناه فُرض واستقر الإجماع على أن الجهاد على أمة محمد ﷺ فرض كفاية وقوله تعالى ﴿ وعسى أن تكرهوا شيئاً ﴾ الآية قال قوم عسى من الله واجبة والمعنى عسى أن تكرهوا ما في الجهاد من المشقة وهو خير لكم في أنكم تغلبون وتظهرون وتغنمون وتؤجَرون ومن مات مات شهيداً وعسى أن تحبوا الدعة وترك القتال وهو شر لكم في انكم تُغلبون وتذلون ويذهب أمركم

تفسير الثعالبي

{ Ordained } : meaning it has been made obligatory; it rests unanimous that *jihad* is the collective duty of Muhammad's (SAW) people [*ummah*]. The word of the Most High: { And perhaps you dislike something ... } to the end of the verse; some people say: "Perhaps" is an obligation from Allah. The meaning is: Perhaps you dislike the hardship in *jihad*, although it is good for you, in that you prevail, and are victorious, and acquire spoils, and are rewarded; and whoever dies, dies a martyr. And perhaps you prefer to be gentle and refrain from fighting, although this is bad for you, in that you are prevailed over, and humiliated, and you end up as nothing.

Tafsir Al-Tha'alibi

. . .

﴿ يَسْأَلُونَكَ عَنِ الشَّهْرِ الْحَرَامِ قِتَالٍ فِيهِ قُلْ قِتَالٌ فِيهِ كَبِيرٌ وَصَدٌّ عَنْ سَبِيلِ اللَّهِ وَكُفْرٌ بِهِ وَالْمَسْجِدِ الْحَرَامِ وَإِخْرَاجُ أَهْلِهِ مِنْهُ أَكْبَرُ عِنْدَ اللَّهِ وَالْفِتْنَةُ أَكْبَرُ مِنَ الْقَتْلِ وَلَا يَزَالُونَ يُقَاتِلُونَكُمْ حَتَّىٰ يَرُدُّوكُمْ عَنْ دِينِكُمْ إِنِ اسْتَطَاعُوا وَمَنْ يَرْتَدِدْ مِنْكُمْ عَنْ دِينِهِ فَيَمُتْ وَهُوَ كَافِرٌ فَأُولَٰئِكَ حَبِطَتْ أَعْمَالُهُمْ فِي الدُّنْيَا وَالْآخِرَةِ وَأُولَٰئِكَ أَصْحَابُ النَّارِ هُمْ فِيهَا خَالِدُونَ ﴾ البقرة ٢١٧

{ They ask you about the sacred months – is there fighting during them? Say: Fighting during them is a great sin, although hindering from the cause of Allah, disbelief in Him and the Sacred Mosque, and driving its people out of it, are even greater in the sight of Allah; and sedition is worse than killing. They will not stop fighting you until they turn you away from your religion if they could; and whoever turns away from his religion and dies in disbelief - these are the ones whose deeds will come to nothing, neither in this world nor the next, and these are the inhabitants of Hellfire, abiding there forever } *Al-baqara 217*

عن الزهري قال أخبرني عروة بن الزبير أن رسول الله ﷺ بعث سرية من المسلمين وأمر عليهم عبدالله بن جحش الأسدي فانطلقوا حتى هبطوا نخلة ووجدوا بها عمرو بن الحضرمي في عير تجارة لقريش في يوم بقي في الشهر الحرام فاختصم المسلمون فقال قائل منهم لا نعلم هذا اليوم إلا من الشهر الحرام ولا نرى أن تستحلوا لطمع أشفيتم عليه فغلب على الأمر الذين يريدون عرض الدنيا فشدوا على إبن الحضرمي فقتلوه وغنموا عيره
أسباب النزول للواحدي

From Al-Zuhri, who said: 'Urwa ibn Al-Zubair told me that the Messenger of Allah (SAW) sent out a contingent of Muslims, and put Abdullah ibn Jahsh Al-Asadi in charge of them. They set out until they reached Nakhla, and found 'Amr ibn Al-Hadrami there with a trading caravan of Quraysh, on the last day of the sacred month. And the Muslims got into an argument; one of them said: The only thing we know is that today is still the sacred month, and we don't think you should make it lawful out of greed, which you are on the verge of doing. But those who desired the gains of this world got the best of the issue, and they assaulted Ibn Al-Hadrami, killed him, and took the booty from the caravan.

Al-Wahidi, Asbab Al-nuzul

كان أصحاب محمد ﷺ قتلوا إبن الحضرمي في الشهر الحرام فعير المشركون المسلمين بذلك فقال الله قتال في الشهر الحرام كبير وأكبر من ذلك صدٌ عن سبيل الله وكفر به ... قال مجاهد ﴿ قل قتال فيه كبير وصدٌ عن سبيل الله وكفر به والمسجد الحرام ﴾ قال يقول صد عن المسجد الحرام وإخراج أهله منه فكل هذا أكبر من قتل إبن الحضرمي ﴿ والفتنة أكبر من القتل ﴾ كفر بالله وعبادة الأوثان أكبر من هذا كله

تفسير الطبري

Muhammad's (SAW) Companions killed Ibn Al-Hadrami in a sacred month, and the idolaters disgraced the Muslims for this. So Allah said: Fighting in a sacred month is a great sin, but greater still is hindering from the cause of Allah and disbelief in Him. ... Mujahid, regarding { Say: Fighting during them is a great sin, although hindering from the cause of Allah, disbelief in Him and the Sacred Mosque } , said: Hindering people from the Sacred Mosque and driving away its people from it – all this is worse than killing Ibn Al-Hadrami. { And sedition is worse than killing } : disbelief in Allah and idol worship is worse than all of this.

Tafsir Al-Tabari

﴿ والفتنة أكبر من القتل ﴾ قال مجاهد وغيره الفتنة هنا الكفر أي كفركم أكبر من قتلنا أولئك وقال الجمهور معنى الفتنة هنا فتنتهم المسلمين عن دينهم حتى يهلكوا أي أن ذلك أشد إجتراماً من قتلكم في الشهر الحرام

تفسير القرطبي

{ And sedition is worse than killing } : Mujahid and others said: Sedition [*fitnah*] here is disbelief, that is, your disbelief is worse than our killing those people. The majority say that the meaning of sedition here is that they caused the Muslims to be drawn away from their religion to the point of destruction, and that this is a more severe crime than you all killing people during a sacred month.

Tafsir Al-Qurtubi

﴿ يسألونك عن الشهر الحرام قتال فيه ﴾ أي يسألونك عن قتال في الشهر الحرام ﴿ قل قتال فيه كبيرٌ ﴾ ولكن الصد عن سبيل الله وعن المسجد الحرام والكفر به أكبر من ذلك القتال ... قيل المفتون المجنون والجنون فتنة إذ هو محنة وعدول عن سبيل أهل السلامة في العقول فثبت بهذه الآيات أن الفتنة هي الإمتحان وإنما قلنا إن الفتنة أكبر من القتل لأن الفتنة عن الدين تفضي إلى القتل الكثير في الدنيا وإلى إستحقاق العذاب الدائم في الآخرة

تفسير الرازي

{ They ask you about the sacred months – is there fighting during them? } : that is, they ask you about fighting during the sacred months; { say: Fighting during them is a great sin } : but hindering from the cause of Allah and from the Sacred Mosque, and disbelief in Him, is even greater than such fighting. ... It is said: One who is enraptured is insane, and insanity is sedition, in that it is an ordeal and departure from the path of those of sound mind. It is affirmed from these verses that sedition [*fitnah*] refers to an ordeal; indeed we have said: Truly sedition is worse than killing, since the ordeal [*fitnah*] of being drawn away from the religion leads to much killing in this world, and to deserving eternal punishment in the next.

Tafsir Al-Razi

عن مجاهد قال النهي عن القتال في الشهر الحرام منسوخ نسخه قوله تعالى ﴿ فاقتلوا المشركين حيث وجدتموهم ﴾ الآية وقوله سبحانه وتعالى ﴿ يسألونك عن الشهر الحرام قتال فيه قل قتال فيه كبيرٌ ﴾ الآية وكذلك قال أبو حنيفة وقال أبو يوسف

كتاب السير الصغير للشيباني ٣١

Related from Mujahid, who said: The prohibition against fighting in a sacred month is abrogated; the word of the Most High abrogated it: { And kill the idolaters wherever you find them ... } and the rest of the verse [*Al-tawba* 5]. This is regarding the word of the Most High and Exalted: { They ask you about the sacred months – is there fighting during them? Say: Fighting during them is a great sin } and the rest of the verse. Abu Hanifa expressed this, and Abu Yusuf expressed it.

Al-Shaybani, Kitab Al-siyar Al-saghir, item 31

عن أبي إسحاق قال سألت سفيان عن قول الله ﴿ يسألونك عن الشهر الحرام قتال فيه قل قتال فيه كبيرٌ ﴾ قال هذا شيء منسوخ وقد مضى ولا بأس بالقتال في الشهر الحرام وغيره

السنن الكبرى للبيهقي كتاب السير باب ما جاء في نسخ العفو عن المشركين ونسخ النهي عن القتال حتى يقاتلوا والنهي عن القتال في الشهر الحرام

From Abu Ishaq, who said: I asked Sufyan about the word of Allah: { They ask you about the sacred months – is there fighting during them? Say: Fighting during them is a great sin } . He replied: This is something that has been abrogated, and is over; there is no issue with fighting in sacred months or any other month.

Al-Bayhaqi, Al-sunan Al-kubra, The book of campaigns, Section: what came regarding abrogation of pardoning the Idolaters, and abrogation of the prohibition to fight until being fought and the prohibition of fighting in a sacred month

﴿ إِنَّ الَّذِينَ آمَنُوا وَالَّذِينَ هَاجَرُوا وَجَاهَدُوا فِي سَبِيلِ اللَّهِ أُولَٰئِكَ يَرْجُونَ رَحْمَتَ اللَّهِ وَاللَّهُ غَفُورٌ رَحِيمٌ ﴾ البقرة ٢١٨

{ Indeed those who have believed and those who have emigrated and waged jihad in the cause of Allah – these hope in the mercy of Allah; and Allah is forgiving, merciful } *Al-baqara* 218

قوله تعالى ﴿ إن الذين آمنوا والذين هاجروا ﴾ في سبب نزولها قولان احدهما أنه لما نزل القرآن بالرخصة لأصحاب عبدالله بن جحش في قتل إبن الحضرمي قال بعض المسلمين ما لهم أجر فنزلت هذه الآية وقد ذكرنا هذا في سبب نزول قوله تعالى ﴿ يسألونك عن الشهر الحرام ﴾ عن جندب إبن عبدالله والثاني أنه لما نزلت لهم الرخصة قاموا فقالوا يا رسول الله أنطمع أن تكون لنا غزاة نعطى فيها أجر المجاهدين فنزلت هذه الآية قاله ابن عباس وقال ﴿ هاجروا ﴾ من مكة إلى المدينة ﴿ وجاهدوا ﴾ في طاعة الله إبن الحضرمي وأصحابه و ﴿ رحمة الله ﴾ مغفرته وجنته قال إبن الانباري الهجرة عند العرب من هجران الوطن والأهل والولد والمهاجرون معناهم المهاجرون الأولاد والأهل فعرف مكان المفعول فأسقط قال الشعبي أول لواء عقد في الاسلام لواء عبدالله إبن جحش وأول مغنم قسم في الاسلام مغنمه

تفسير إبن الجوزي

The word of the Most High { Indeed those who have believed and those who have emigrated } ; two things are said regarding its revelation. One of them is that when the portion of the Qur'an came down giving Abdullah ibn Jahsh license to kill Ibn Al-Hadrami, some of the Muslims said: There is no reward for them. And so this verse came down; we have already mentioned this in giving the reason for the revelation of the word of the Most High: { They ask you about the sacred months } [*Al-baqara* 217] from Jundab ibn Abdullah. The second thing that is said is that when license came down to them, they arose and said: Oh Messenger of Allah, are we being greedy that we should go on an attack for which we will be given the reward of the *mujahideen*? And so this verse came down; Ibn 'Abbas said this. And He said { who have emigrated } : from Mecca to Medina; { and waged *jihad* } : in obedience to Allah against Ibn Al-Hadrami and his companions; and { the mercy of Allah } : His forgiveness and His *Jannah*. Ibn Al-Anbari said: emigration [*hijra*] for the Arabs meant forsaking homeland, family, and children, and the idea of the emigrants [*muhajirun*] was that they were leaving family and children; they realized all that this implied and let it go. Al-Sha'bi said: The first banner that was solidified in Islam was the banner of Abdullah Ibn Jahsh, and the first spoils that were divided in Islam were his spoils.

Tafsir Ibn Al-Jawzi

ولما ظن السرية أنهم إن سلموا من الإثم فلا يحصل لهم أجر نزل ﴿ إن الذين آمنوا والذين هاجروا ﴾ فارقوا أوطانهم ﴿ وجاهدوا في سبيل الله ﴾ لإعلاء دينه ﴿ أولئك يرجون رحمة الله ﴾ ثوابه ﴿ والله غفور ﴾ للمؤمنين ﴿ رحيم ﴾ بهم

تفسير الجلالين

When the detachment assumed that, even if they were absolved of wrongdoing, they would still not be granted reward, this came down: { Indeed those who have believed and those who have emigrated }, breaking off from their homelands, { and waged *jihad* in the cause of Allah }, to elevate their religion, { these hope in the mercy of Allah } : his reward; { and Allah is forgiving } to the believers, { merciful } towards them.

Tafsir Al-Jalalain

* * *

﴿ ألم تر إلى الذين خرجوا من ديارهم وهم ألوف حذر الموت فقال لهم الله موتوا ثم أحياهم إن الله لذو فضل على الناس ولكن أكثر الناس لا يشكرون وقاتلوا في سبيل الله واعلموا أن الله سميع عليم ﴾ البقرة ٢٤٣-٢٤٤

{ Have you not seen those who left their homes by the thousands, wary of death, and Allah said to them: "Die!" but then brought them back to life? Indeed Allah is of bountiful favor towards people, but most people are not grateful. So fight in the cause of Allah, and know that Allah is hearing, knowing } Al-baqara 243-244

وقيل هو قوم من بني إسرائيل دعاهم ملكهم إلى الجهاد فهربوا حذراً من الموت فأماتهم الله ثمانية أيام ثم أحياهم

تفسير الزمخشري

It is said that these were some people from the children of Israel whose king called them to *jihad*, but they ran away out of fear of death. So Allah had them die for eight days, then He brought them back to life.

Tafsir Al-Zamakhshari

يعني تعالى ذكره بذلك وقاتلوا أيها المؤمنون في سبيل الله يعني في دينه الذي هداكم له لا في طاعة الشيطان أعداء دينكم الصادين عن سبيل ربكم ولا تجنبوا عن لقائهم ولا تقعدوا عن حربهم فإن بيدي حياتكم وموتكم

تفسير الطبري

He (may His remembrance be exalted) means: Fight, oh Believers, in the cause of Allah – that is, in His religion [*deen*] that He has guided you to, not in obedience to Satan – the enemies of your religion, those who obstruct the cause of your Lord; do not avoid facing them and do not refrain from war with them; for indeed your life and your death are in my hand.

Tafsir Al-Tabari

قوله عز وجل ﴿ وقاتلوا في سبيل الله واعلموا أن الله سميع عليم ﴾ قال أكثر المفسرين هذا خطاب لهذه الأمة معناه قاتلوا في طاعة الله تعالى ولا تهربوا من الموت كما هرب هؤلاء الذين سمعتم خبرهم فلا ينفعكم الهرب

التفسير الكبير للطبراني

The word of the Mighty and Sublime: { So fight in the cause of Allah, and know that Allah is hearing, knowing } . Most expositors say that this was addressed to this *ummah*; its meaning is: Fight in obedience to Allah Most High, and do not run away from death like how those you heard about ran away; running away is of no use to you.

Al-Tabarani, Al-tafsir Al-kabir

هذا خطاب لأمة محمد ﷺ بالقتال في سبيل الله في قول الجمهور وهو الذي ينوى به أن يكون كلمة الله هي العليا وسبل الله كثيرة فهي عامة في كل سبيل قال الله تعالى قل هذه سبيلي قال مالك سبل الله كثيرة وما من سبيل إلا يقاتَل عليها أو فيها أو لها وأعظمها دينُ الاسلام لا خلاف في هذا

تفسير القرطبي

This is an address to the *ummah* of Muhammad (SAW) to fight in the cause of Allah, in speaking to the gathering of people. This means anything by which the intent is that the word of Allah be the utmost. And the causes of Allah are many, and they prevail in every cause. Allah Most High has said: { Say: this is my cause } [*Yusuf* 108]. Malik said: The causes of Allah are many, and there is no cause that is not to be fought for, or in, or towards; and the religion of Islam makes them great. There is no disagreement about this.

Tafsir Al-Qurtubi

وقوله ﴿ وقاتلوا في سبيل الله واعلموا أن الله سميع عليم ﴾ أي كما أن الحذر لا يغني من القدر كذلك الفرار من الجهاد وتجنبه لا يقرّب أجلاً ولا يباعده بل الأجل المحتوم والرزق المقسوم مُقَدَّر مقنَّن لا يُزاد فيه ولا ينقص منه

تفسير إبن كثير

His word: { So fight in the cause of Allah, and know that Allah is hearing, knowing } ; that is, just as caution is of no avail against destiny, running away and avoiding *jihad* likewise neither hastens nor delays one's appointed time; rather, the preordained appointed time and the alloted bounty are decreed and legislated, neither added to nor taken away from.

Tafsir Ibn Kathir

﴿ وقاتلوا في سبيل الله ﴾ أي في طاعة الله أعداء الله ﴿ واعلموا أن الله سميع عليم ﴾ قال أكثر أهل التفسير هذا خطاب للذين أحيوا أمروا بالقتال في سبيل الله فخرجوا من ديارهم فراراً من الجهاد فأماتهم الله ثم أحياهم وأمرهم أن يجاهدوا وقيل الخطاب لهذه الامة أمرهم بالجهاد

تفسير البغوي

{ So fight in the cause of Allah } : that is, in obedience to Allah against the enemies of Allah; { and know that Allah is hearing, knowing } ; most of the scholars of *tafsir* have said that this is a direct address to those who were given life; they were ordered to fight in the cause of Allah, but they left their homes running away from *jihad*, and so Allah caused them to die, and then brought them back to life and ordered them to wage *jihad*. It is said that the address directed towards this *ummah* ordered them to wage *jihad*.

Tafsir Al-Baghawi

قال أبو جعفر يعني تعالى ذكره بذلك ﴿ وقاتلوا ﴾ أيها المؤمنون ﴿ في سبيل الله ﴾ يعني في دينه الذي هداكم له لا في طاعة الشيطان أعداء دينكم الصادين عن سبيل ربكم ولا تحتموا عن قتالهم عند لقائهم ولا تجبنوا عن حربهم فإن بيدي حياتكم وموتكم ولا يمنعنّ أحدكم من لقائهم وقتالهم حذر الموت وخوف المنية على نفسه بقتالهم

تفسير الطبري

Abu Ja'far said: He (may His remembrance be exalted) means: { So fight } oh Believers, { in the cause of Allah } , meaning for His religion that He has guided you to, not in obedience to Satan, the enemies of your religion, or those who hinder the cause of your Lord. And do not shelter yourselves from fighting them when you face them, and do not avoid war with them. For indeed I hold your life and your death in my hand, so let not anyone's caution against death, or fear of his own demise from fighting them, deter any of you from facing them.

Tafsir Al-Tabari

﴿ وقاتلوا في سبيل الله واعلموا أن الله سميع عليم ﴾ فيه قولان القول الأول أن هذا خطاب للذين أحيوا قال الضحاك أحياهم ثم أمرهم بأن يذهبوا إلى الجهاد لأنه تعالى إنما أماتهم بسبب أن كرهوا الجهاد ... وقيل لهم قاتلوا والقول الثاني وهو إختيار جمهور المحققين أن هذا إستئناف خطاب للحاضرين يتضمن الأمر بالجهاد إلا أنه سبحانه بلطفه ورحمته قدم على الأمر بالقتال ذكر الذين خرجوا من ديارهم لئلا ينكص عن أمر الله بحب الحياة بسبب خوف الموت وليعلم كل أحد أنه يترك القتال لا يثق بالسلامة من الموت كما قال في قوله ﴿ قل لن ينفعكم الفرار إن فررتم من الموت أو القتل وإذا لا تمتَّعون إلا قليلاً ﴾ فشجعهم على القتال الذي به وعد إحدى الحسنيين إما في العاجل الظهور على العدو أو في الآجل الفوز بالخلود في النعيم والوصول إلى ما تشتهي الأنفس وتلذ الأعين أما قوله ﴿ في سبيل الله ﴾ فالسبيل هو الطريق وسميت العبادات سبيلاً إلى الله تعالى من حيث أن الانسان يسلكها ويتوصل إلى الله تعالى بها ومعلوم أن الجهاد تقوية للدين فكان طاعة فلا جرم كان المجاهد مقاتلاً في سبيل الله ثم قال ﴿ واعلموا أن الله سميع عليم ﴾ أي هو يسمع كلامكم في ترغيب الغير في الجهاد وفي تنفير الغير عنه وعليم بما في صدوركم من البواعث والأغراض وأن ذلك الجهاد لغرض الدين أو لعاجل الدنيا

تفسير الرازي

{ So fight in the cause of Allah and know that Allah is hearing, knowing } : two things are said regarding this. The first is that this is a direct address to those who were given life. Al-Dahhak said: He gave them life and then ordered them to go out on *jihad*, since the Most High had indeed put them to death because they disliked *jihad*. ... And it was said to them: Fight! The second thing that was said, and this is preferred by the body of scholars, is that this is a continuation of an address to those present which included the call to *jihad*, except that the Exalted, in His kindness and mercy, brought the call to *jihad*, mentioning it to those who left their homes, lest they should shy away from Allah's order out of love for life owing to fear of death, so that everyone who abandons fighting may know that he can not trust in being safe from death, as said in His word: { Say: Running away will be of no use to you if you run away from death or killing, and even if so, you will be granted only brief enjoyment } [Al-ahzab 16]. And so He emboldened them to fight, for which one of the two good things is promised – either triumph over the enemy now; or in the future, the victory of eternity in bliss, and the attainment of the desire of souls and the delight of the eyes. Regarding His word: { In the cause of Allah } ; the cause means the path; acts of worship are called "path" to Allah Most High in that a man pursues it and thereby reaches Allah Most High. It is known that *jihad* fortifies religion, being obedience, and there is no blame of wrongdoing for a *mujahid* to be a fighter in the cause of Allah. Then He said: { And know that Allah is hearing, knowing } ; that is, He hears the things you say which rouse desire in others for *jihad* and which dissuade others from it, and He knows the motives and aims inside of you, and whether or not *jihad* is for the aim of the religion [*deen*] or for the immediate matters of this worldly life.

Tafsir Al-Razi

وإنما اللازم من الآية أن الله تعالى أخبر نبيه محمداً ﷺ إخباراً في عبارة التنبيه والتوقيف عن قوم من البشر خرجوا من ديارهم فراراً من الموت فأماتهم الله ثم أحياهم ليعلموا هم وكل من خلف بعدهم أن الإماتة إنما هي بإذن الله لا بيد غيره فلا معنى لخوف خائفٍ وجعل الله تعالى هذه الآية مقدِّمة بين يدَي أمره المؤمنين من أمة محمد ﷺ بالجهاد هذا قول الطبري وهو ظاهر رصف الآية

تفسير الثعالبي

Indeed what is central to this verse is that Allah Most High sends a message to His Prophet Muhammad (SAW), making known as a way of forewarning and restraint, regarding a group of men who had left their homes fleeing from death. Allah caused them to die, then brought them back to life, so that they and all who came after them would know that when death is caused it is indeed only by Allah's permission, not by the hand of any other. The fear of someone who is afraid is therefore meaningless. Allah Most High made this verse foremost in His command to the Believers of Muhammad's *ummah* to wage *jihad*; this is what Al-Tabari said, and is the clear way to affirm the verse.

Tafsir Al-Tha'alibi

﴿ وقاتلوا في سبيل الله ﴾ فحرض على الجهاد بعد الإعلام لأن الفرار من الموت لا يغني

مدارك التنزيل للنسفي

{ So fight in the cause of Allah } : So rouse people to *jihad* after giving notice, since running away from death is of no use.

Al-Nasafi, Madarik Al-tanzil

وفي القصة تشجيع للمسلمين على الجهاد والتعرض للشهادة وأن الموت إذا لم ينفع منه الفرار فأولى أن يكون في سبيل الله

تفسير النيسابوري

In this story there is encouragement for the Muslims to wage *jihad* and face martyrdom, and that death, whenever it is of no avail to flee from it, it is best for it to be in the cause of Allah.

Tafsir Al-Nisaburi

﴿ وقاتلوا في سبيل الله ﴾ أي لأعداء دينه ﴿ واعلموا أن الله سميع ﴾ لأقوالكم ﴿ عليم ﴾ بأحوالكم فيجازيكم

تفسير الجلالين

{ So fight in the cause of Allah } : that is, against the enemies of His religion; { and know that Allah is hearing } : what you say; { knowing } : of your situation, and He will reward you.

Tafsir Al-Jalalain

﴿ وقاتلوا في سبيل الله ﴾ في طاعة الله مع عدوكم ﴿ وعلموا أن الله سميع ﴾ لمقالتكم ﴿ عليم ﴾ بنياتكم وعقوبتكم إن لم تفعلوا ما أمرتم به

تفسير للفيروز آبادي

{ So fight in the cause of Allah } : in obedience to Allah against your enemy; { and know that Allah is hearing } : all that you say; { knowing } : your intentions and your punishment if you do not do what you are told.

Tafsir Fairuz Abadi

▪ ▪ ▪

﴿ لَا يُؤَاخِذُكُمُ اللَّهُ بِاللَّغْوِ فِي أَيْمَانِكُمْ وَلَٰكِن يُؤَاخِذُكُم بِمَا كَسَبَتْ قُلُوبُكُمْ وَاللَّهُ غَفُورٌ حَلِيمٌ ﴾
البقرة ٢٢٥

{ Allah does not hold you all to account for the slips in your oaths; Allah does however hold you to account for what your hearts have attained; and Allah is forgiving, forbearing }
Al-baqara 225

عن عطاء في اللغو في اليمين قال قالت عائشة إن رسول الله ﷺ قال هو كلام الرجل في بيته كلّا والله وبلى والله
سنن أبي داود كتاب الأيمان والنذور

'Ataa related regarding the slips [*laghw*] made in oaths; he said: 'Aishah said that the Messenger of Allah (SAW) said: This is what someone might say at home, like "By Allah, certainly not!" or "By Allah of course!"
Sunan Abu Dawud, The book of oaths and vows

﴿ لا يؤاخذكم الله باللغو في أيمانكم ﴾ أي لا يعاقبكم ولا يلزمكم بما صدر منكم من الأيمان اللاغية وهي التي لا يقصدها الحالف بل تجري على لسانه عادة من غير تعقيد ولا تأكيد ... عن عروة قال كانت عائشة تقول إنما اللغو في المزاحة والهزل ... عن إبن عباس قال لغو اليمين أن تحلف وأنت غضبان
تفسير إبن كثير

{ Allah does not hold you all to account for the slips [*laghw*] in your oaths } : that is, He will not punish you and He will not hold you accountable for the nonsensical oaths that come out from you all; these are things that the oath-taker does not intend to say, but roll off his tongue habitually without being considered and asserted. ... 'Urwa said: 'Aishah used to say: Indeed *laghw* is done in fun and jest. ... Ibn 'Abbas said: The *laghw* in oaths is what you swear to when you are angry.
Tafsir Ibn Kathir

عمرو بن شعيب عن أبيه عن جده أن النبي ﷺ قال من حلف على يمين فرأى غيرها خيراً منها فليتركها فإن تركها كفارتها أخرجه إبن ماجه
تفسير القرطبي

'Amr ibn Shu'aib related from his father, from his grandfather, that the Prophet (SAW) said: Whoever takes an oath, but then finds something else that is better, let him break the oath, and indeed breaking it is expiation for it. Ibn Majah reported this.
Tafsir Al-Qurtubi

إبن عباس في قوله ﴿ لا يؤاخذكم الله باللغو في إيمانكم ﴾ قال هذا في الرجل يحلف على أمرٍ اضرار أن يفعله أو لا يفعله فيرى الذي هو خير منه فأمر الله أن يكفر يمينه ويأتي الذي هو خير ... عن ابراهيم النخعي ﴿ لا يؤاخذكم الله باللغو في إيمانكم ﴾ قال هو الرجل يحلف على الشيء ثم ينسى فلا يؤاخذه الله به ولكن يكفّر ... عن سليمان بن يسار ﴿ لا يؤاخذكم الله باللغو في إيمانكم ﴾ قال الخطأ غير العمد ... عن ابراهيم ﴿ لا يؤاخذكم الله باللغو في إيمانكم ﴾ قال هو الرجل يحلف على شيء يرى أنه صادق وهو كاذب فذلك اللغو لا يؤاخذكم به

الدر المنثور للسيوطي

Ibn 'Abbas said regarding His word { Allah does not hold you all to account for the slips in your oaths } ; he said: This is regarding someone who swears to something that obliges him to do it or not do it, but then finds something better than it; Allah orders that he atone for his oath and take on what is better. ... From Ibrahim Al-Nakh'i, on { Allah does not hold you all to account for the slips in your oaths } ; he said: This is someone who swears to something but then forgets; Allah does not hold it against him, but he is to atone for it ... From Sulaiman ibn Yassar, on { Allah does not hold you all to account for the slips in your oaths } ; he said: This is someone who swears to something, thinking it is true, while in fact it is false; this is the *laghw* that you all will not be accountable for.

Al-Suyuti, Al-durr Al-manthur

﴿ لا يؤاخذكم الله باللغو في إيمانكم ﴾ وهو الرجل يحلف على أمرٍ يرى أنه فيه صادق وهو مخطئ فلا يؤاخذه الله بها ولا كفارة عليه فيها فذلك العفو

تفسير مقاتل بن سليمان

{ Allah does not hold you all to account for the slips in your oaths } : this is someone who swears to something, thinking that there is truth in it, while it is actually wrong; Allah does not hold him to account for it, and there is no atonement required of him for it – this is the forgiveness.

Tafsir Muqatil ibn Sulaiman

* * *

﷽ أَلَمْ تَرَ إِلَى الْمَلَإِ مِنْ بَنِي إِسْرَائِيلَ مِنْ بَعْدِ مُوسَى إِذْ قَالُوا لِنَبِيٍّ لَهُمْ ابْعَثْ لَنَا مَلِكًا نُقَاتِلْ فِي سَبِيلِ اللَّهِ قَالَ هَلْ عَسَيْتُمْ إِنْ كُتِبَ عَلَيْكُمُ الْقِتَالُ أَلَّا تُقَاتِلُوا قَالُوا وَمَا لَنَا أَلَّا نُقَاتِلَ فِي سَبِيلِ اللَّهِ وَقَدْ أُخْرِجْنَا مِنْ دِيَارِنَا وَأَبْنَائِنَا فَلَمَّا كُتِبَ عَلَيْهِمُ الْقِتَالُ تَوَلَّوْا إِلَّا قَلِيلًا مِنْهُمْ وَاللَّهُ عَلِيمٌ بِالظَّالِمِينَ ﷻ البقرة ٢٤٦

{ Have you not seen the assembly of the Children of Israel after Musa, when they said to a prophet of theirs: Raise up a king for us so we can fight in the cause of Allah. He said: Might it be, if fighting were ordained for you, that you would not fight? They said: And what have we got? Shall we not fight in the cause of Allah, when we have been driven from our homes and our sons? But when fighting was ordained for them, all but a small number of them turned away; and Allah knows who the wrongdoers are }

Al-baqara 246

وهذه الآية هي خبر عن قوم بني إسرائيل نالتهم ذِلّة وغَلَبَة عدو فطلبوا الإذن في الجهاد وأن يؤمروا به فلما أمروا كعّ أكثرهم وصبر الأقل فنصرهم الله

تفسير القرطبي

This verse tells about a group of the Children of Israel who were beset with the humiliation and subjugation of enemies, and so they sought permission for *jihad*, to be ordered to wage it. But when they were ordered, most of them grew weak and cowardly, while the few were steadfast, and Allah gave them victory.

Tafsir Al-Qurtubi

﴿ هل عسيتم ﴾ هل تعدون إن كتب يعني إن فرض عليكم القتال ألا تقاتلون يعني أن لا تفوا بما تعدون الله من أنفسكم من الجهاد في سبيله

تفسير الطبري

{ Might it be? } : Do you not promise, if fighting is ordained for you – that is, if it is made your duty – that you will fight, that is, make good on the *jihad* in His cause that you promised Allah of yourselves?

Tafsir Al-Tabari

﴿ والله عليم بالظالمين ﴾ وعيد لهم على ظلمهم في القعود عن القتال وترك الجهاد

تفسير الزمخشري

{ And Allah knows who the wrongdoers are } : a threat to them against their wrongdoing in sitting out from fighting and neglecting *jihad*.

Tafsir Al-Zamakhshari

﴿ والله عليم بالظالمين ﴾ أي هو عالم بمن ظلم نفسه حين خالف ربه ولم يف بما قيل من ربه وهذا هو الذي يدل على تعلق هذه الآية بقوله قبل ذلك ﴿ وقاتلوا في سبيل الله ﴾ فكأنه تعالى أكد وجوب ذلك بأن ذكر قصة بني إسرائيل في الجهاد وعقب ذلك بأن من تقدم على مثله فهو ظالم والله أعلم بما يستحقه الظالم وهذا بين في كونه زجراً عن مثل ذلك في المستقبل وفي كونه بعثاً على الجهاد وأن يستمر كل مسلم على القيام بذلك

تفسير الرازي

{ And Allah knows who the wrongdoers are } : that is, He knows who has wronged himself when he opposed his Lord and did not make good on what was spoken from his Lord. This is what provides evidence for the connection between this verse and His word prior to it: { Fight in the cause of Allah } , as if the Most High were affirming the obligation to do this by mentioning the story of the Children of Israel regarding *jihad*, and following this by stating that anyone who does something similar is a wrongdoer, and Allah knows best what the wrongdoers deserve. In its essence this makes the reproach clear against doing something similar in the future, and in its essence is a call to *jihad*, and that all Muslims are to continue fulfilling this.

Tafsir Al-Razi

* * *

﴿ لا إكراه في الدين قد تبين الرشد من الغي ﴾ البقرة ٢٥٦

{ There is no compulsion in religion; sensible conduct has been made clear from error } *Al-baqara 256*

قوله ﴿ لا إكراه في الدين ﴾ قال نزلت في رجل من الأنصار من بني سالم بن عوف يقال له الحصيني كان له ابنان نصرانيان وكان هو رجلاً مسلماً فقال للنبي ﷺ ألا أستكرههما فإنهما قد أبيا إلا النصرانية فأنزل الله فيه ذلك رواه ابن جريج وروى السدي نحو ذلك وزاد وكانا قد تنصرا على يدي تجار قدموا من الشام يحملون زيتاً فلما عزما على الذهاب معهم أراد أبوهما أن يستكرههما وطلب من رسول الله ﷺ أن يبعث في آثارهما فنزلت هذه الآية ... وقد ذهب طائفة كثيرة من العلماء أن هذه محمولة على أهل الكتاب ومن دخل في دينهم قبل النسخ والتبديل إذا بذلوا الجزية وقال آخرون بل هي منسوخة بآية القتال وإنه يجب أن يدعى جميع الأمم إلى الدخول في الدين الحنيف دين الاسلام فإن أبى أحد منهم الدخول فيه ولم ينقد له أو يبذل الجزية قوتل حتى يقتل وهذا معنى الاكراه قال الله تعالى ﴿ ستُدعون إلى قوم أولي بأس شديد تقاتلونهم أو يسلمون ﴾ وقال تعالى ﴿ يا أيها النبي جاهد الكفار والمنافقين وأغلظ عليهم ﴾ وقال تعالى ﴿ يا أيها الذين آمنوا قاتلوا الذين يلونكم من الكفار وليجدوا فيكم غلظة واعلموا أن الله مع المتقين ﴾ وفي الصحيح عجب ربك من قوم يقادون إلى الجنة في السلاسل يعني الأسارى الذين يقدم بهم بلاد الاسلام في الوثائق والأغلال والقيود والأجال ثم بعد ذلك يسلمون وتصلح أعمالهم وسرائرهم فيكونون من أهل الجنة

تفسير ابن كثير

His word: { There is no compulsion in religion } ; this came down concerning an *Ansar* man of the Banu Salim ibn 'Awf, known as Al-Husaini; he had two Christian sons but he was a Muslim man. He said to the Prophet (SAW): Shall I not compel them? For indeed they only accept Christianity. So Allah sent this down regarding him; Ibn Juraij related it and Al-Suddi related something similar, except he added: The two of them had become Christians because of some merchants who had come from Al-Sham carrying oil. And when the two of them made up their mind to go with them, their father wanted to compel them, and he asked the Messenger of Allah (SAW) to send people after them, but this verse came down. ... A large group of scholars hold the view that this verse pertains to the People of the Book, and those who entered their religion before the abrogation and modification, provided they fulfill the *jizya*. Others say, rather, that this verse is abrogated by the verse of fighting, and indeed all nations must be called to enter the true religion, the religion of Islam. If any of them refuses to enter it, not having criticized it, or fulfilled the *jizya*, he is to be fought until he is killed; this is the meaning of compulsion. Allah Most High said: { You will be called to a people of great might, to fight them or they yield } [*Al-fath 16*]; and the Most High said: { Oh Prophet! Wage jihad on the disbelievers and the hypocrites, and be harsh to them } [*Al-tahrim* 9]; and the Most High said: { Oh you who have believed! Fight the disbelievers who are near to you, and may they find harshness in you; and know that Allah is with the devout } [*Al-tawba* 123]; and in *sahih* hadiths: "Our Lord will marvel at people who are led to *Jannah* in chains", that is, prisoners brought by the people of Islam in a tight grip, shackles, chains, and handcuffs, then after this they yield into Islam and their deeds and their intentions are put in order, and they become among those who will be in *Jannah*.

Tafsir Ibn Kathir

وقيل هو إخبار في معنى النهي أي لا تكرهوا في الدين ثم قال بعضهم هو منسوخ بقوله ﴿ جاهد الكفار والمنافقين وأغلظ عليهم ﴾ وقيل هو في أهل الكتاب خاصة لأنهم حصنوا أنفسهم بأداء الجزية

تفسير الزمخشري

It is said: This is to inform regarding the meaning of the prohibition, that is, do not have an aversion regarding religion; then some said this is abrogated by His word: { Wage jihad on the disbelievers and hypocrites, and be harsh to them } [*Al-tawba* 73]. It is said that this is regarding the People of the Book in particular, since they have safeguarded themselves by giving *jizya*.

Tafsir Al-Zamakhshari

إختلف العلماء في معنى هذه الآية على ستة أقوال الأول قيل إنها منسوخة لأن النبي ﷺ قد أكره العرب على دين الاسلام وقاتلهم ولم يرض منهم إلا بالاسلام

تفسير القرطبي

Scholars differ on the meaning of this verse, into six points of view; the first is that it is said that indeed it is abrogated, because the Prophet (SAW) compelled the Arabs to the religion of Islam, and He fought them, and was not satisfied with anything but Islam from them.

Tafsir Al-Qurtubi

عن الضحاك في قوله ﴿ لا إكراه في الدين ﴾ قال أمر رسول الله ﷺ أن يقاتل جزيرة العرب من أهل الأوثان فلم يقبل منهم إلا لا إله إلا الله أو السيف ثم أمر فيمن سواهم بأن يقبل منهم الجزية فقال ﴿ لا إكراه في الدين قد تبين الرشد من الغي ﴾ ... عن قتادة في قوله ﴿ لا إكراه في الدين ﴾ قال كانت العرب ليس لها دين فأكرهوا على الدين بالسيف قال ولا يكره اليهود ولا النصارى والمجوس إذا أعطوا الجزية ... عن

إبن ابي نجيح قال سمعت مجاهداً يقول لغلام له نصراني يا جرير أسلم ... عن إبن عباس ﴿ لا إكراه في الدين قد تبيّن الرشد من الغيّ ﴾ قال وذلك لما دخل الناس في الاسلام وأعطى أهل الكتاب الجزية وقال آخرون هذه الآية منسوخة وانما نزلت قبل أن يفرض القتال

تفسير الطبري

Al-Dahhak, regarding His word { There is no compulsion in religion } , said: The Messenger of Allah (SAW) was ordered to fight the idol worshippers in the Arabian peninsula, and He did not accept anything from them except "There is no god but Allah" ["La ilaha illa Allah"], or else the sword. Then He was ordered regarding those like them to accept *jizya* from them; He said: { There is no compulsion in religion; sensible conduct has been made clear from error } ... Qatada, regarding His word: { There is no compulsion in religion } , said: The Arabs had no religion, and they were compelled to religion by the sword; he said: Neither the Jews, the Christians, nor the Magians were compelled if they gave *jizya*. ... Ibn Abi Nujaih said: I heard Mujahid say to a Christian servant boy of his: Oh Jarir! Yield into Islam! ... Ibn 'Abbas, regarding { There is no compulsion in religion; sensible conduct has been made clear from error } , said: This was when people entered into Islam and the People of the Book gave *jizya*. Still others have said: This verse is abrogated, since indeed it came down before fighting was imposed as an obligation.

Tafsir Al-Tabari

وقالوا قال الله تعالى ﴿ لا إكراه في الدين ﴾ فقلنا أول من يقول إن العرب الوثنيين يكرهون على الاسلام وإن المرتد يكره على الاسلام وقد صح أن النبي ﷺ أكره مشركي العرب على الاسلام فصح أن هذه الآية ليست على ظاهرها وانما هي فيمن نهانا الله تعالى أن نكرهه وهم أهل الكتاب خاصة وقولنا هذا هو قول الشافعي وابي سليمان وبالله تعالى التوفيق

المحلى لإبن حزم كتاب الجهاد

People say: Allah Most High said: { There is no compulsion in religion } . And we would answer: You all are the first to say that the idol-worshipping Arabs were compelled to Islam, and that apostates are compelled to Islam. It is true that the Prophet (SAW) compelled the Arab Idolaters to Islam, and it is also true that this verse is not in the strict sense; indeed it concerns those who Allah Most High has forbidden us to compel, these being the People of the Book in particular. Our view here is what Al-Shafi'i and Abu Sulaiman say; and prosperity is from Allah Most High.

Ibn Hazm, Al-muhalla, The book of jihad

Surah 3 Al 'Imran [The House of 'Imran]

﴿ قَدْ كَانَ لَكُمْ آيَةٌ فِى فِئَتَيْنِ الْتَقَتَا فِئَةٌ تُقَاتِلُ فِى سَبِيلِ اللَّهِ وَأُخْرَىٰ كَافِرَةٌ يَرَوْنَهُم مِّثْلَيْهِمْ رَأْىَ الْعَيْنِ وَاللَّهُ يُؤَيِّدُ بِنَصْرِهِ مَن يَشَاءُ إِنَّ فِى ذَٰلِكَ لَعِبْرَةً لِّأُولِى الْأَبْصَارِ ﴾ آل عمران ١٣

{ There has already been a sign for you in two squads that faced each other, one squad fighting in the cause of Allah and another that was disbelieving; they saw them as twice the like of them as the eye sees; but Allah upholds who He wills with His victory; indeed in this there is a lesson to be heeded by those who see }
Al 'Imran 13

﴿ فِى فِئَتَيْنِ ﴾ يعني في فرقتين وحزبين و الفئة الجماعة من الناس ﴿ الْتَقَتَا ﴾ للحرب وإحدى الفئتين رسول الله ﷺ ومن كان معه ممن شهد وقعة بدر والاخرى مشركو قريش
تفسير الطبري

{ In two squads } : meaning in two bands, parties; a squad is a group of people; { that faced each other } : for combat. One of the two squads was the Messenger of Allah (SAW) and those with him who had been present at the battle of Badr, and the other squad was the idolaters of Quraish.

Tafsir Al-Tabari

﴿ قَدْ كَانَ لَكُمْ آيَةٌ ﴾ عبرة وذكر الفعل للفصل ﴿ فِى فِئَتَيْنِ ﴾ فرقتين ﴿ الْتَقَتَا ﴾ يوم بدر للقتال ﴿ فِئَةٌ تُقَاتِلُ فِى سَبِيلِ اللَّهِ ﴾ أي طاعته وهو النبي وأصحابه وكانوا ثلاثمائة وثلاثة عشر رجلاً معهم فرسان وست أدرع وثمانية سيوف وأكثرهم رجالة ﴿ وَأُخْرَىٰ كَافِرَةٌ يَرَوْنَهُم ﴾ أي الكفار ﴿ مِّثْلَيْهِمْ ﴾ أي المسلمين أي أكثر منهم وكانوا نحو ألف ﴿ رَأْىَ الْعَيْنِ ﴾ أي رؤية ظاهرة معاينة وقد نصرهم الله مع قلتهم ﴿ وَاللَّهُ يُؤَيِّدُ ﴾ يقوي ﴿ بِنَصْرِهِ مَن يَشَاءُ ﴾ نصره ﴿ إِنَّ فِى ذَٰلِكَ ﴾ المذكور ﴿ لَعِبْرَةً لِّأُولِى الْأَبْصَارِ ﴾ لذوي البصائر أفلا تعتبرون بذلك فتؤمنون
تفسير الجلالين

{ There has already been a sign for you } : a lesson, the event being mentioned as a transition to { in two squads } : two bands; { that faced each other } : to fight on the day of Badr; { one squad fighting in the cause of Allah } : that is, in obedience to Him, and this was the Prophet and his Companions - three hundred thirteen men, plus two horses, six breastplates, and eight swords; most of them were on foot; { and another that was disbelieving; they saw them } : that is, the disbelievers [*Kuffar*] saw; { as twice the like of them } : that is, the Muslims, as more than them; and there were around a thousand of them; { as the eye sees } : that is, a vision in clear view, and Allah made them victorious despite their small number; { and Allah upholds } : strengthens; { who He wills with his victory } : He grants them victory; { indeed in this } : in what has been mentioned; { is a lesson to be heeded by those who see } : people who understand; so will you not take this as a warning and believe?

Tafsir Al-Jalalain

فعندما عاين كل الفريقين الآخر رأى المسلمون المشركين مثليهم أي أكثر منهم بالضعف ليتوكلوا ويتوجهوا ويطلبوا الإعانة من ربهم عز وجل ورأى المشركون المؤمنين كذلك ليحصل لهم الرعب والخوف والجزع والهلع ثم لما حصل التصاف والتقى الفريقان قلل الله هؤلاء في أعين هؤلاء وهؤلاء في أعين هؤلاء ليُقدم كل منهما على الآخر ﴿ ليقضي الله أمراً كان مفعولاً ﴾ أي ليفرق بين الحق والباطل فيظهر كلمة الإيمان على الكفر ويعزِّ المؤمنين ويُذل الكافرين كما قال تعالى ﴿ ولقد نصركم الله ببدر وانتم أذلة ﴾ وقال هاهنا ﴿ والله يؤيد بنصره من يشاء إن في ذلك لعبرة لأولي الابصار ﴾ أي إن في ذلك لمعتبراً لمن له بصيرة وفهم يهتدي به إلى حكم الله وأفعاله

تفسير إبن كثير

And when each of the two bands caught sight of the other, the Muslims perceived the idolaters [*mushrikeen*] as twice what they were, that is, twice as many as they were, so that they would rely on and turn to and seek aid from their Lord Mighty and Sublime. And the idolaters saw the believers in the same way, so that they would be struck with terror, fear, anxiety, and dread. Then at the time of lining up when the two groups faced each other, Allah diminished the one in the eyes of the other, and the other in the eyes of the one, so that each one of them would advance against the other, { So that Allah might fulfill a matter already accomplished } [Al-anfal 44] , that is, that He might discern between truth and falsehood, and in so doing manifest the word of belief over disbelief, strengthen the Believers, and disgrace the disbelievers, as the Most High said: { And Allah made you victorious at Badr, when you were feeble } [Al-'Imran 123]. And He says here: { But Allah upholds who He wills with his victory; indeed in this there is a lesson to be heeded by those who see } ; that is, indeed in this there is something to consider for those who have awareness and understanding, so that they might be guided by it to the judgment and decrees of Allah.

Tafsir Ibn Kathir

﴿ إِنَّ الدِّينَ عِندَ اللَّهِ الإِسْلَامُ وَمَا اخْتَلَفَ الَّذِينَ أُوتُوا الْكِتَابَ إِلَّا مِن بَعْدِ مَا جَاءَهُمُ الْعِلْمُ بَغْيًا بَيْنَهُمْ وَمَن يَكْفُرْ بِآيَاتِ اللَّهِ فَإِنَّ اللَّهَ سَرِيعُ الْحِسَابِ ﴾ آل عمران ١٩

{ Indeed religion in the sight of Allah is Islam, and those who have been given the book have not differed, except after knowledge came to them, out of agression among themselves. And whoever disbelieves in the signs of Allah, indeed Allah is quick to reckon } *Al 'Imran 19*

والاسلام هو الدخول في السلم وهو الانقياد والطاعة يقال أسلم أي دخل في السلم وإستسلم

تفسير البغوي

Islam means entering into a state of peace, which is compliance and obedience; it is said: "One has yielded into Islam"/"One has become a Muslim" ["*aslama*"], that is, he has entered into a state of peace and has surrendered.

Tafsir Al-Baghawi

قال أبو سليمان الدمشقي لما ادّعت اليهود أنه لا دين أفضل من اليهودية وادعت النصارى أنه لا دين أفضل من النصرانية نزلت هذه الآية قال الزجاج الدين إسم لجميع ما تعبد الله به خلقه وأمرهم بالاقامة عليه وأن يكون عادتهم وبه يجزيهم وقال شيخنا علي بن عبيد الله الدين ما التزمه العبد لله عز وجل قال إبن قتيبة والاسلام الدخول في السلم أي في الإنقياد والمتابعة ومثله الإستسلام يقال سلّم فلان لأمرك وإستسلم وأسلم كما تقول أشتى الرجل أي دخل في الشتاء وأربع دخل في الربيع

تفسير إبن الجوزي

Abu Sulaiman Al-Dimashqi said: When the Jews asserted that there is no religion better than Judaism, and the Christians asserted that there was no religion better than Christianity, this verse came down. Al-Zajjaj said: Religion [*deen*] is a name for everything that Allah's creation worships Him for, that He orders them to observe, that becomes their customary practice, and for which He rewards them. Our *shiekh* 'Ali ibn 'Ubaid Allah said: Religion is what a servant fulfills to Allah Mighty and Sublime. Ibn Qutaiba said: Islam is entering into a state of peace, that is, into compliance and consent, similar to surrender; it can be said: So-and-so submitted [*sallama*] to your orders, or surrendered [*istaslama*], or resigned himself [*aslama*], just as you might say a man "wintered", that is, he entered into winter, or he "sprang" – passed into springtime.

Tafsir Ibn Al-Jawzi

وقوله تعالى ﴿ إن الدين عند الله الإسلام ﴾ إخبار منه تعالى بأنه لا دين عنده يقبله من أحد سوى الإسلام وهو إتباع الرسل فيما بعثهم الله به في كل حين حتى ختموا بمحمد ﷺ الذي سد جميع الطرق إليه إلا من جهة محمد ﷺ فمن لقي الله بعد بعثة محمد ﷺ بدين على غير شريعته فليس بمتقبل كما قال تعالى ﴿ ومن يبتغ غير الإسلام ديناً فلن يقبل منه ﴾ ... ثم قال تعالى ﴿ ومن يكفر بآيات الله ﴾ أي من جحد ما أنزل الله في كتابه ﴿ فإن الله سريع الحساب ﴾ أي فإن الله سيجازيه على ذلك ويحاسبه على تكذيبه ويعاقبه على مخالفته كتابه

تفسير ابن كثير

The word of the Most High: { Indeed religion in the sight of Allah is Islam } ; a declaration from the Most High that there is no religion in His sight that He accepts other than Islam; this is adherence to the messengers in what Allah sent them forth with throughout the ages, until they were sealed by Muhammad (SAW), who closed off every path to Him except from the direction of Muhammad (SAW). Whoever faces Allah after the mission of Muhammad (SAW) with a religion founded on anything other than His law [shari'ah] – he is not accepted, as the Most High says: { Whoever aspires to a religion other than Islam, it will not be accepted of him } [Al 'Imran 85]. ... Then the Most High says: { And whoever disbelieves in the signs of Allah } ; that is, whoever controverts what Allah has sent down in His book, { Indeed Allah is quick to reckon } : that is, indeed Allah will discipline him for this, hold him accountable for his repudiation, and punish him for opposing His book.

Tafsir Ibn Kathir

﴿ ومن يكفر بآيات الله فإن الله سريع الحساب ﴾ وعيد لمن كفر منهم

تفسير البيضاوي

{ And whoever disbelieves in the signs of Allah, indeed Allah is quick to reckon } : a threat to those of them who disbelieved.

Tafsir Al-Baydawi

* * *

﴿ لَا يَتَّخِذِ الْمُؤْمِنُونَ الْكَافِرِينَ أَوْلِيَاءَ مِن دُونِ الْمُؤْمِنِينَ وَمَن يَفْعَلْ ذَٰلِكَ فَلَيْسَ مِنَ اللَّهِ فِي شَيْءٍ إِلَّا أَن تَتَّقُوا مِنْهُمْ تُقَاةً وَيُحَذِّرُكُمُ اللَّهُ نَفْسَهُ وَإِلَى اللَّهِ الْمَصِيرُ ﴾ آل عمران ٢٨

{ Let not the Believers take Disbelievers as associates in place of Believers, for whoever does this has nothing to do with Allah, except out of prudence if you fear from them; Allah warns you of Himself, and destiny is to Allah } *Al 'Imran 28*

نهى الله تبارك وتعالى عباده المؤمنين أن يوالوا الكافرين وأن يتخذوهم أولياء يُسِرّون اليهم بالمودة من دون المؤمنين ثم توعد على ذلك ﴿ ومن يفعل ذلك فليس من الله في سيء ﴾ أي من يرتكب نهي الله في هذا فقد برئ من الله كما قال ﴿ يا أيها الذين آمنوا لا تتخذوا الكافرين أولياء من دون المؤمنين أتريدون أن تجعلوا لله عليكم سلطاناً مبيناً ﴾ وقال تعالى ﴿ يا أيها الذين آمنوا لا تتخذوا اليهود والنصارى أولياء بعضهم أولياء بعض ومن يتولهم منكم فإنه منهم ﴾ وقال تعالى ﴿ يا أيها الذين آمنوا لا تتخذوا عدوي وعدوكم أولياء تلقون اليهم بالمودة ﴾ إلى أن قال ﴿ ومن يفعله منكم فقد ضل سواء السبيل ﴾ وقال تعالى بعد ذكر موالاة المؤمنين للمؤمنين من المهاجرين والأنصار والأعراب ﴿ والذين كفروا بعضهم أولياء بعض إلا تفعلوه تكن فتنة في الأرض وفساد كبير ﴾ وقوله ﴿ إلا أن تتقوا منهم تقاة ﴾ أي إلا من خاف في بعض البلدان أو الأوقات من شرهم فله أن يتقيهم بظاهره لا بباطنه ونيته كما حكاه البخاري عن ابي الدرداء أنه قال إنا لنكشر في وجوه أقوام وقلوبنا تلعنهم وقال الثوري قال ابن عباس رضي الله عنهما ليس التقية بالعمل انما التقية باللسان وكذا رواه العوري عن ابن عباس انما التقية باللسان وكذا قال أبو العالية وأبو الشعثاء والضحاك والربيع بن أنس ويؤيد ما قالوه قول الله تعالى ﴿ من كفر بالله من بعد إيمانه إلا من أُكرِه وقلبه مطمئن بالايمان ﴾ وقال البخاري قال الحسن التقية إلى يوم القيامة ثم قال تعالى ﴿ يحذركم الله نفسه ﴾ أي يحذركم نقمته أي مخالفته وسَطوته في عذابه لمن والى أعداءه وعادى أولياءه

تفسير إبن كثير

Allah Blessed and Exalted prohibited his servants the Believers from standing with the disbelievers [*Kuffar*] and from taking them as associates [*awliya'*, friends or protectors], showing good cheer towards them in friendship in place of Believers. He threatened against this: { Whoever does this has nothing to do with Allah } ; that is, whoever commits Allah's prohibition has separated from Allah, as He has said: { Oh you who have believed! Do not take the disbelievers as associates in place of the Believers; do you want to give Allah clear warrant to act against you? } [*Al-nisaa* 144]. And the Most High said: { Oh you who have believed! Do not take the Jews or the Christians as associates; they are associates of each other; whoever among you turns to them, indeed he is one of them } [*Al-ma'ida* 51]. And the Most High said: { Oh you who have believed! Do not take my enemies and your enemies as associates, extending friendship to them } up until saying: { whoever among you does this has strayed from the sound path } [Al-mumtahana 1]. And the Most High, after reminding the Believers to stand with the *muhajirun*, *Ansar*, and Bedouins who were Believers, said: { Those who have disbelieved, they are associates of each other; do not do this lest there be sedition in the land and great corruption } [Al-anfal 73]. And so His word { Except out of prudence if you fear from them } means: except whoever, in a particular land or particular time, fears harm from them; he may exercise prudence against them outwardly, but not inwardly in intent, just as Al-Bukhari narrated that Abu Al-Dardaa said: We grin in the face of some people but our hearts curse them. Al-Thawri said that Ibn 'Abbas (may Allah be pleased with them both) said: *Taqiyya* [fear, precautionary dissimulation] is not in deed, rather *taqiyya* is in speech. Similarly Al-'Awri narrated from Ibn 'Abbas: Indeed *taqiyya* is in speech. And Abu Al-'Aliya, Abu Al-Shu'athaa, Al-Dahhak, and Al-Rabi' ibn Anas said something similar; and the word of Allah Most High supports what they said: { Whoever disbelieves in Allah after he has believed – except he who has been compelled, and his heart is secure in belief … } [Al-nahl 106]. And Al-Bukhari said that Al-Hasan said: There is *taqiyya* until resurrection day. Then the Most High said: { Allah warns you of Himself } : that is, He warns you of His resentment, that is, His opposition and full control over His punishment for those who stand with His enemies and show enmity towards His associates.

Tafsir Ibn Kathir

قال إبن عباس نهى الله المؤمنين أن يلاطفوا الكفار فيتخذوهم أولياء ... ﴿ إلا أن تتقوا منهم تقاة ﴾ قال معاذ بن جبل ومجاهد كانت التقية في جِدة الاسلام قبل قوة المسلمين فأما اليوم فقد أعز الله الاسلام أن يتقوا من عدوهم قال إبن عباس هو أن يتكلم بلسانه وقلبه مطمئن بالايمان ولا يُقتل ولا يأتي مأثماً وقال الحسن التقية جائزة للاسلام إلى يوم القيامة ولا تقية في القتل وقرأ جابر بن زيد ومجاهد والضحاك ﴿ إلا أن تتقوا منهم تقيّة ﴾ وقيل إن المؤمن إذا كان قائماً بين الكفار فله أن يداريهم باللسان إذا كان خائفاً على نفسه وقلبه مطمئن بالايمان والتقية لا تحل إلا مع خوف القتل أو القطع أو الإيذاء العظيم

تفسير القرطبي

Ibn 'Abbas said: Allah has prohibited the Believers to be nice to disbelievers, taking them as associates [*awliya'*]. … { Except out of prudence if you fear from them [*tuqaa*] } ; Mu'adh ibn Jabal and Mujahid said: *Taqiyya* was part of the inherent power of Islam before the Muslims were strong. Today, however, Allah has strengthened Islam over the need to have to dissimulate from their enemy. Ibn 'Abbas said: This means that one speaks with his tongue while his heart is secure in faith, and he is neither killed nor is guilty of wrongdoing. Al-Hasan said: *Taqiyya* is permissible in Islam until the day of resurrection, but there is no *taqiyya* in killing. Jabir ibn Zaid, Mujahid, and Al-Dahhak recited this part as { except out of prudence from them [*taqiyya*] }. It is said that a Believer, if he resides among the Disbelievers, can be deceptively flattering towards them with his tongue if he fears for himself, as long as his heart is secure in faith. And *taqiyya* is not permitted except out of fear of being killed, maimed, or greatly harmed.

Tafsir Al-Qurtubi

قوله تعالى ﴿ ومن يفعل ذلك ﴾ أي موالاة الكفار في نقل الأخبار اليهم وإظهارهم على عورة المسلمين

تفسير البغوي

The word of the Most High { whoever does this } : that is, standing with disbelievers by conveying news to them or revealing to them the weaknesses of the Muslims.

Tafsir Al-Baghawi

رخص لهم في موالاتهم إذا خافوهم والمراد بتلك الموالاة مخالفة ومعاشرة ظاهرة والقلب مطمئن بالعداوة والبغضاء

تفسير الزمخشري

License for them to associate with them if they fear them; but the purpose of this loyalty is to resist – the intimacy is outward, while the heart is secure in enmity and hatred.

Tafsir Al-Zamakhshari

• • •

$$\text{﴿ فَأَمَّا الَّذِينَ كَفَرُوا فَأُعَذِّبُهُمْ عَذَاباً شَدِيداً فِي الدُّنْيَا وَالآخِرَةِ وَمَا لَهُم مِّن نَّاصِرِينَ ﴾}$$

آل عمران ٥٦

{ And indeed those who have disbelieved I will severely punish, in this world and in the hereafter; and they have none to champion them } *Al 'Imran 56*

﴿ فأما الذين كفروا فأعذّبهم عذاباً شديداً في الدنيا ﴾ بالقتل والسبي والجزية ﴿ والآخرة ﴾ بالنار ﴿ وما لهم من ناصرين ﴾ مانعين منه

تفسير الجلالين

{ And indeed those who have disbelieved I will severely punish, in this world } : with killing, imprisonment, and *jizya*; { And in the hereafter } : with Hellfire; { And they have none to champion them } : None to keep them from it.

Tafsir Al-Jalalain

يعني بالقتل والصلب والسبي والجزية وفي الآخرة بالنار

تفسير القرطبي

Meaning by killing, crucifiction, imprisonment, and *jizya*; and in the next world, by fire.

Tafsir Al-Qurtubi

قوله تعالى ﴿ فأما الذين كفروا ﴾ قيل هم اليهود والنصارى وعذابهم في الدنيا بالسيف والجزية وفي الآخرة بالنار

تفسير ابن الجوزي

The word of the Most High : { And indeed those who have disbelieved } ; it is said these are the Jews and Christians; their punishment in this world is by the sword and *jizya*; and in the hereafter, by fire.

Tafsir Ibn Al-Jawzi

. . .

﴿ وَمَنْ يَبْتَغِ غَيْرَ الْإِسْلَامِ دِينًا فَلَنْ يُقْبَلَ مِنْهُ وَهُوَ فِي الْآخِرَةِ مِنَ الْخَاسِرِينَ ﴾ آل عمران ٨٥

{ Whoever aspires to a religion other than Islam, it will not be accepted of him; and in the hereafter he will be among the losers } Al 'Imran 85

قوله ﴿ ومن يبتغ غير الاسلام ديناً فلن يقبل منه ﴾ نزلت في إثني عشر رجلاً ارتدوا عن الاسلام وخرجوا من المدينة وأتوا مكة كفاراً

تفسير البغوي

His word: { Whoever aspires to a religion other than Islam, it will not be accepted of him } ; this came down regarding twelve men who apostatized from Islam, left Medina, and came to Mecca as disbelievers.

Tafsir Al-Baghawi

﴿ ومن يبتغ غير الاسلام ديناً ﴾ أي غير التوحيد والإنقياد لحكم الله ﴿ فلن يقبل منه وهو في الاخرة من الخاسرين ﴾ الواقعين في الخسران والمعنى أن المعرِض عن الاسلام والطالب لغيره فاقد للنفع واقع في الخسران بإبطال الفطرة السليمة التي فطر الناس عليها وإستدل به على أن الايمان هو الاسلام إذ لو كان غيره لم يقبل والجواب إنه ينفي قبول كل دين يغايره لا قبول كل ما يغايره

تفسير البيضاوي

{ Whoever aspires to a religion other than Islam } : that is, other than asserting one god [tawheed] and compliance with the authority of Allah; { it will not be accepted of him; and in the hereafter he will be among the losers } : those who fall into perdition, the meaning being one who turns away from Islam, and seeks something else, forfeits what is profitable and falls into perdition from having cancelled his innate and sound disposition upon which people are created; and from this it is concluded that belief is Islam, and if it is otherwise, it is not accepted. The response is that there is no acceptance of any religion that contradicts it; nothing that contradicts it is accepted.

Tafsir Al-Baydawi

﴿ ومن يبتغ غير الاسلام ﴾ يعني التوحيد وإسلام الوجه لله أو غير دين محمد عليه السلام

مدارك التنزيل للنسفي

{ Whoever aspires to a religion other than Islam } : that is, *tawheed* and yielding one's intent to Allah, or anything other than Muhammad's religion (peace be upon him).

Al-Nasafi, Madarik Al-tanzil

* * *

﴿ كنتم خير أمة أخرجت للناس تأمرون بالمعروف وتنهون عن المنكر وتؤمنون بالله ﴾
آل عمران ١١٠

{ You all are the best nation that has been sent out to people; you prescribe what is right, prohibit what is wrong, and you believe in Allah } *Al 'Imran* 110

عن أبي هريرة رضي الله عنه ﴿ كنتم خير أمة أخرجت للناس ﴾ قال خير الناس للناس تأتون بهم في السلاسل في أعناقهم حتى يدخلوا في الاسلام

صحيح البخاري كتاب التفسير

Abu Huraira (may Allah be pleased with him) related regarding { You all are the best nation that has been sent out to people } ; he said: The best of people for people, you who bring them with chains around their necks until they enter Islam.

Sahih Al-Bukhari, The book of tafsir

قوله تعالى ﴿ كنتم خير أمة ﴾ الآية قال عكرمة ومقاتل نزلت في إبن مسعود وأبي بن كعب ومعاذ بن جبل وسالم مولى أبي حذيفة وذلك أن مالك بن الضيف ووهب بن يهوذا اليهوديين قالا لهم إن ديننا خير مما تدعونا إليه ونحن خير وأفضل منكم فأنزل الله تعالى هذه الآية

أسباب النزول للواحدي

The word of the Most High: { You all are the best nation } through the end of the verse; 'Ikrama and Muqatil said that this came down in regards to Ibn Mas'ud, Ubayy ibn Ka'b, Mu'adh ibn Jabal, and Salim the freed slave of Abu Hudhaifa. The issue was that Malik ibn Al-Daif and Wahb ibn Yahudha, two Jews, said to them: Our religion is better than what you all are calling us to, and we are better and more virtuous than you. So Allah Most High sent down this verse.

Al-Wahidi, Asbab Al-nuzul

عن إبن عباس قوله ﴿ كنتم خير أمة أخرجت للناس ﴾ يقول تأمرونهم بالمعروف أن يشهدوا أن لا إله إلا الله والإقرار بما أنزل الله وتقاتلونهم عليه و لا إله إلا الله هو أعظم المعروف وتنهونهم عن المنكر والمنكر هو التكذيب وهو أنكرُ المنكر

تفسير الطبري

From Ibn 'Abbas about His word { You all are the best nation that has been sent out to people } ; he said: You prescribe good for them – that they testify that there is no god but Allah, and consent to what Allah has sent down, and you fight them for this; and "There is no god but Allah" is the greatest of good. And you prohibit them from wrongdoing – wrongdoing is denial, which is the wrongest of wrongdoing.

Tafsir Al-Tabari

قال قتادة هم أمة محمد ﷺ لم يؤمر نبي قبله بالقتال فهم يقاتلون الكفار فيدخلونهم في دينهم فهم خير أمة للناس

تفسير البغوي

Qatada said: This is the nation [*ummah*] of Muhammad (SAW) – no prophet before him was ordered to fight; and they fight the disbelievers and drive them into their religion; and they are the best nation unto people.

Tafsir Al-Baghawi

∴

﷽ وَلَقَدْ نَصَرَكُمُ اللَّهُ بِبَدْرٍ وَأَنتُمْ أَذِلَّةٌ فَاتَّقُوا اللَّهَ لَعَلَّكُمْ تَشْكُرُونَ إِذْ تَقُولُ لِلْمُؤْمِنِينَ أَلَن يَكْفِيَكُمْ أَن يُمِدَّكُمْ رَبُّكُم بِثَلَاثَةِ آلَافٍ مِّنَ الْمَلَائِكَةِ مُنزَلِينَ بَلَىٰ إِن تَصْبِرُوا وَتَتَّقُوا وَيَأْتُوكُم مِّن فَوْرِهِمْ هَٰذَا يُمْدِدْكُمْ رَبُّكُم بِخَمْسَةِ آلَافٍ مِّنَ الْمَلَائِكَةِ مُسَوِّمِينَ وَمَا جَعَلَهُ اللَّهُ إِلَّا بُشْرَىٰ لَكُمْ وَلِتَطْمَئِنَّ قُلُوبُكُم بِهِ وَمَا النَّصْرُ إِلَّا مِنْ عِندِ اللَّهِ الْعَزِيزِ الْحَكِيمِ لِيَقْطَعَ طَرَفًا مِّنَ الَّذِينَ كَفَرُوا أَوْ يَكْبِتَهُمْ فَيَنقَلِبُوا خَائِبِينَ ﷽ آل عمران ١٢٣-١٢٧

{ Indeed Allah gave you victory at Badr when you all were miserable and despised, so fear Allah, that perhaps you may be grateful. You said to the Believers: "Is it not enough for you that your Lord support you with three thousand angels sent down?" Yes indeed, if you are steadfast and fear Allah, and they rush out to you, your Lord will support you with five thousand ravaging angels. Allah did this only as good tidings to you, that your hearts might thereby be at ease; there is no victory but from Allah the Mighty, the Wise; that He might cut off a party of those who have disbelieved or hinder them so they turn back in futility } Al 'Imran 123-127

وقوله ﴿ وَمَا جَعَلَهُ اللَّهُ إِلَّا بُشْرَىٰ لَكُمْ وَلِتَطْمَئِنَّ قُلُوبُكُم بِهِ ﴾ أي وما أنزل الله الملائكة وأعلمكم بإنزالها إلا بشارة لكم وتطييباً لقلوبكم وتطميناً وإلا فإنما النصر من عند الله الذي لو شاء لإنتصر من أعدائه بدونكم ومن غير إحتياج إلى قتالكم لهم كما قال تعالى بعد أمره المؤمنين بالقتال ﴿ ذَٰلِكَ وَلَوْ يَشَاءُ اللَّهُ لَانتَصَرَ مِنْهُمْ وَلَٰكِن لِّيَبْلُوَ بَعْضَكُم بِبَعْضٍ وَالَّذِينَ قُتِلُوا فِي سَبِيلِ اللَّهِ فَلَن يُضِلَّ أَعْمَالَهُمْ سَيَهْدِيهِمْ وَيُصْلِحُ بَالَهُمْ وَيُدْخِلُهُمُ الْجَنَّةَ عَرَّفَهَا لَهُمْ ﴾ ولهذا قال هاهنا ﴿ وَمَا جَعَلَهُ اللَّهُ إِلَّا بُشْرَىٰ لَكُمْ وَلِتَطْمَئِنَّ قُلُوبُكُم بِهِ وَمَا النَّصْرُ إِلَّا مِنْ عِندِ اللَّهِ الْعَزِيزِ الْحَكِيمِ ﴾ أي هو ذو العزة التي لا ترام والحكمة في قدره والإحكام ثم قال تعالى ﴿ لِيَقْطَعَ طَرَفًا مِّنَ الَّذِينَ كَفَرُوا ﴾ أي أمركم بالجهاد والجلاد لما له في ذلك من الحكمة في كل تقدير ولهذا ذكر جميع الأقسام الممكنة في الكفار المجاهدين فقال ﴿ لِيَقْطَعَ طَرَفًا ﴾ أي ليهلك أمة ﴿ مِّنَ الَّذِينَ كَفَرُوا أَوْ يَكْبِتَهُمْ ﴾ أي يخزيهم ويردهم بغيظهم لما لم ينالوا منكم ما أرادوا ولهذا قال ﴿ أَوْ يَكْبِتَهُمْ فَيَنقَلِبُوا ﴾ أي يرجعوا ﴿ خَائِبِينَ ﴾ أي لم يحصلوا على ما أملوا

تفسير ابن كثير

His word: { Allah did this only as good tidings to you, that your hearts might thereby be at ease } ; that is, Allah sent down angels and made known to you their coming down only as good news to you, to bring pleasure to your hearts, and as reassurance.

Indeed victory is from Allah, who, if He willed, could have avenged His enemy without you, without need of you fighting them, as the Most High said after ordering the Believers to fight: { And if Allah had willed, He would have avenged himself of them, but rather that some of you might put others of you to the test. And those who are killed in the cause of Allah – their deeds will not be in vain; He will guide them and bestow grace on them, and admit them to the *Jannah* that He has made known to them } [*Muhammad* 4-6]. For this reason He says here: { Allah did this only as good tidings to you, that your hearts might thereby be at ease; there is no victory but from Allah the Mighty, the Wise } ; that is, He is the one with unsurpassed power, and wisdom in His decree and mastery. Then the Most High says: { That He might cut off a portion of those who have disbelieved } ; that is, He has ordered you all to wage *jihad* and fight, this being His widsom in all that is decreed. For this reason He mentions all the possible outcomes regarding the disbelievers to those who wage *jihad*; He says: { That He might cut off a party } ; that is, destroy a nation; { of those who have disbelieved } : that is, disgrace them and send them back in their anger when they did not get from you what they wanted. Here then He says: { Or hinder them so they turn back } ; that is, return; { in futility } : that is, they did not get what they hoped for.

Tafsir Ibn Kathir

وعن الربيع بن أنس قال كان الناس يوم بدر يعرفون قتلى الملائكة ممن قتلوهم بضربٍ فوق الأعناق وعلى البنان مثل سِمة النار قد أُحرق به ذكر جميعه البيهقي رحمه الله وقال بعضهم إن الملائكة كانوا يقاتلون وكانت علامة ضربهم في الكفار ظاهرة لأن كل موضع اصابت ضربتهم اشتعلت النار في ذلك الموضع حتى إن أبا جهل قال لإبن مسعود أنت قتلتَني إنما قتلني الذي لم يصل سناني إلى سُنْبُك فرسِه وإن اجتهدتُ وإنما كانت الفائدة في كثرة الملائكة لتسكين قلوب المؤمنين ولأن الله تعالى جعل أولئك الملائكة مجاهدين إلى يوم القيامة فكل عسكرٍ صبر وإحتسب تأتيهم الملائكة ويقاتلون معهم وقال إبن عباس ومجاهد لم تقاتل الملائكة إلا يوم بدر وفيما سوى ذلك يشهدون ولا تقاتلون إنما يكونون عدداً أو مدداً وقال بعضهم إنما كانت الفائدة في كثرة الملائكة أنهم كانوا يدعون ويسبّحون ويكبّرون الذين يقاتلون يومئذ فعلى هذا لم تقاتل الملائكة يوم بدر وإنما حضروا للدعاء بالتثبيت

تفسير القرطبي

From Al-Rabi' ibn Anas, who said: On the day of Badr, people were aware of the killings of the angels from those they killed by strikes over the necks and the fingertips, like marks of fire they were burned by; Al-Bayhaqi (may Allah have mercy on him) mentions all of them. Some say that the angels indeed fought, and the sign of them striking the disbelievers was clear, because every place they struck a blow it caught on fire, to the point that Abu Jahl said to Ibn Mas'ud: Have you killed me?

I have been killed by someone whose horse was not struck by my arrowhead, but I tried. Indeed the advantage of so many angels was to calm the hearts of the believers, and because Allah Most High made these angels into *mujahideen* until resurrection day. The angels came to every army that was steadfast and sought reward, and they fought with them. Ibn 'Abbas and Mujahid said: The angels only fought on the day of Badr. This can be reconciled by them being present but not fighting; indeed they were in number or as reinforcement. Some say: Indeed the advantage of so many angels is that they were making invocations, saying praises [*tasbih*, "Subhana Allah!"], and boosting those who were fighting that day; in this respect the angels did not fight on the day of Badr, but indeed they were present in invoking affirmation.

Tafsir Al-Qurtubi

﴿ ليقطع طرفاً من الذين كفروا ﴾ ليهلك طائفة منهم بالقتل والأسر وهو ما كان يوم بدر من قتل سبعين وأسر سبعين من رؤساء قريش وصناديده

تفسير الزمخشري

{ That He might cut off a party of those who have disbelieved } : That He might destroy a group of them by killing and imprisonment; and this was what happened on the day of Badr with the killing of seventy and the capturing of seventy of the heads of Quraish and their valiant men.

Tafsir Al-Zamakhshari

* * *

﴿ وَلَا تَهِنُوا وَلَا تَحْزَنُوا وَأَنْتُمُ الْأَعْلَوْنَ إِنْ كُنْتُمْ مُؤْمِنِينَ. إِنْ يَمْسَسْكُمْ قَرْحٌ فَقَدْ مَسَّ الْقَوْمَ قَرْحٌ مِثْلُهُ وَتِلْكَ الْأَيَّامُ نُدَاوِلُهَا بَيْنَ النَّاسِ وَلِيَعْلَمَ اللَّهُ الَّذِينَ آمَنُوا وَيَتَّخِذَ مِنْكُمْ شُهَدَاءَ وَاللَّهُ لَا يُحِبُّ الظَّالِمِينَ. وَلِيُمَحِّصَ اللَّهُ الَّذِينَ آمَنُوا وَيَمْحَقَ الْكَافِرِينَ. أَمْ حَسِبْتُمْ أَنْ تَدْخُلُوا الْجَنَّةَ وَلَمَّا يَعْلَمِ اللَّهُ الَّذِينَ جَاهَدُوا مِنْكُمْ وَيَعْلَمَ الصَّابِرِينَ. وَلَقَدْ كُنْتُمْ تَمَنَّوْنَ الْمَوْتَ مِنْ قَبْلِ أَنْ تَلْقَوْهُ فَقَدْ رَأَيْتُمُوهُ وَأَنْتُمْ تَنْظُرُونَ ﴾ ❊ آل عمران ١٣٩-١٤٣

{ Do not grow weary and do not be saddened while you all have the upper hand, if you are Believers. If injury touches you, similar injury has also touched the other side; We alternate such days between people, so Allah may know those who have believed, and take martyrs from among you; Allah does not love the wrongdoers. And so Allah may put to the test those who have believed, and annihilate the Disbelievers. Or did you all reckon that you would enter *Jannah* while Allah does not yet know those of you who have waged jihad, or know those who are steadfast? You wished for death before you confronted it; now that you are looking, you have seen it } *Al 'Imran* 139-143

﴿ إِنْ يَمْسَسْكُمْ قَرْحٌ فَقَدْ مَسَّ الْقَوْمَ قَرْحٌ مِثْلُهُ ﴾ أي إن كنتم قد أصابكم جراح وقُتل منكم طائفة فقد أصاب أعداءكم قريب من ذلك من قتل وجراح ﴿ وَتِلْكَ الْأَيَّامُ نُدَاوِلُهَا بَيْنَ النَّاسِ ﴾ أي ندِيل عليكم الأعداء تارة وإن كانت العاقبة لكم لما لنا في ذلك من الحكم ولهذا قال تعالى ﴿ وَلِيَعْلَمَ اللَّهُ الَّذِينَ آمَنُوا ﴾ قال ابن عباس في مثل هذا لنرى من يصبر على مناجزة الأعداء ﴿ وَيَتَّخِذَ مِنْكُمْ شُهَدَاءَ ﴾ يعني يقتلون في سبيله ويبذلون مهجهم في مرضاته
تفسير ابن كثير

{ If injury touches you, similar injury has also touched the other side } : that is, if woundings have befallen you and some of you have been killed, similar woundings and killing have befallen your enemies. { We alternate such days between people } : that is, We give the enemies a turn over you, even though the outcome is yours; this is Ours to decree. For this reason the Most High says: { So Allah may know those who have believed } ; Ibn 'Abbas said in a similar regard: So we may see who is steadfast in combating the enemies. { And take martyrs from among you } : meaning that they fight in the cause of Allah and give their heart and soul for His good pleasure.

Tafsir Ibn Kathir

قال ﴿ وَلَا تَهِنُوا وَلَا تَحْزَنُوا ﴾ يا أصحاب محمد يعني ولا تضعفوا بالذي نالكم من عدوكم بأحد من القتل والقروح عن جهاد عدوكم وحربهم ... عن الزهري قال كثر في أصحاب محمد ﷺ القتل والجراح حتى خَلَص إلى كل امرئ منهم البأس فأنزل الله عز وجل القرآن فآسى فيه المؤمنين بأحسن ما آسى به قوماً من المسلمين كانوا قبلهم من الأمم الماضية فقال ﴿ وَلَا تَهِنُوا وَلَا تَحْزَنُوا وَأَنْتُمُ الْأَعْلَوْنَ إِنْ كُنْتُمْ مُؤْمِنِينَ ﴾ إلى قوله ﴿ لَبَرَزَ الَّذِينَ كُتِبَ عَلَيْهِمُ الْقَتْلُ إِلَىٰ مَضَاجِعِهِمْ ﴾ ... وأما قوله ﴿ وَيَمْحَقَ الْكَافِرِينَ ﴾ فإنه يعني به أنه ينقُصهم ويفنيهم ... قال أبو جعفر يعني بذلك جل ثناؤه ﴿ أَمْ حَسِبْتُمْ ﴾ يا معشر أصحاب محمد وظننتم ﴿ أَنْ تَدْخُلُوا الْجَنَّةَ ﴾ وتنالوا كرامة ربكم وشرف المنازل عنده ﴿ وَلَمَّا يَعْلَمِ اللَّهُ الَّذِينَ جَاهَدُوا مِنْكُمْ ﴾ يقول ولما يتبيّن لعبادي المؤمنين المجاهد منكم في سبيل الله على ما أمره به

تفسير الطبري

He says: { Do not grow weary and do not be saddened } : Oh Companions of Muhammad! Meaning: Do not lose heart – because of the killing and injuries your enemy has brought upon you at Uhud – from waging *jihad* and war against your enemy. ... From Al-Zubair, who said: The killing and wounding of Muhammad's (SAW) Companions increased to the point that every man among them fell into distress, and so Allah Mighty and Sublime sent down this portion of the Qur'an, and in it comforted the Believers with the best He had ever comforted a group of Muslims from the nations that had preceeded them; He said: { Do not grow weary and do not be saddened; you are the ones on top, if you are believers } up until His words { ... those who were ordained to be killed would have gone out to their resting places } [Al 'Imran 154]. ... Moreover His word: { Annihilate the disbelievers } ; by this He means reduce them and destroy them. ... Abu Ja'far said: He (may His praise be exalted) means by this: { Or did you all reckon } : Oh band of Muhammad's Companions! Did you envision? { that you would enter *Jannah* } and receive the glory of your Lord and the honor of dwelling places with Him? } while Allah does not yet know those of you who have waged *jihad* } ; He is saying: While it is still being made clear to my servants the Believers who among them is a *mujahid* in the cause of Allah in accordance with what He has ordered him.

Tafsir Al-Tabari

﴿ وَأَنْتُمُ الْأَعْلَوْنَ ﴾ وحالكم انكم أعلى منهم وأغلب لانكم أصبتم منهم يوم بدر أكثر مما اصابوا منكم يوم أحد أو وأنتم الأعلون شأناً لأن قتالكم لله ولإعلاء كلمته وقتالهم للشيطان لإعلاء كلمة الكفر ولأن قتلاكم في الجنة وقتلاهم في النار ... ﴿ وَيَمْحَقَ الْكَافِرِينَ ﴾ يعني ويهلكهم إن كانت الدولة على المؤمنين فليتميز والاستشهاد والتمحيص وغير ذلك مما هو أصلح لهم وإن كانت على الكافرين فليلحقهم ومحو آثارهم ... ﴿ وَقَدْ رَأَيْتُمُوهُ وَأَنْتُمْ تَنْظُرُونَ ﴾ أي رأيتموه معاينين مشاهدين له حين قتل بين أيديكم من قتل من إخوانكم وأقاربكم وشارفتم أن تقتلوا

تفسير الزمخشري

{ You all have the upper hand } : Your situation is such that you are higher than them and more numerous than them, because you attained more of them on the day of Badr than what they attained of you on the day of Uhud. Or: While you are higher in standing, because you fight for Allah so that His word might be raised up, while they fight for Satan so that the word of disbelief might be raised up; and because your dead are in *Jannah* while their dead are in Hellfire. ... { And annihilate the disbelievers } : and destroy them, meaning that if it were the turn of the Believers, it is for discernment, martyrdom, refinement, and other things by which He bestows grace on them; and if it were the turn of the disbelievers, He would have annihilated them and blotted out any remnant of them. ... { Now that you are looking, you have seen it } : that is, you have seen it as spectators and witnesses to it, when those of your brothers and close kin who were killed were killed in front of you, and you vied in honor that you be killed.

Tafsir Al-Zamakhshari

• • •

﴿ وَمَا كَانَ لِنَفْسٍ أَن تَمُوتَ إِلَّا بِإِذْنِ اللَّهِ كِتَابًا مُّؤَجَّلًا وَمَن يُرِدْ ثَوَابَ الدُّنْيَا نُؤْتِهِ مِنْهَا وَمَن يُرِدْ ثَوَابَ الْآخِرَةِ نُؤْتِهِ مِنْهَا وَسَنَجْزِي الشَّاكِرِينَ وَكَأَيِّن مِّن نَّبِيٍّ قَاتَلَ مَعَهُ رِبِّيُّونَ كَثِيرٌ فَمَا وَهَنُوا لِمَا أَصَابَهُمْ فِي سَبِيلِ اللَّهِ وَمَا ضَعُفُوا وَمَا اسْتَكَانُوا وَاللَّهُ يُحِبُّ الصَّابِرِينَ ﴾
آل عمران ١٤٥-١٤٦

{ It is not for any individual to die, except by permission of Allah as ordained at some appointed time. Whoever desires the reward of this world, We will bring of it to him; and whoever desires the reward of the hereafter, We will bring of it to him; We will reward the grateful. And how many prophets have there been, with whom many pious, learned men fought who did not lose heart at what came upon them in the cause of Allah, nor grew weak, nor succumbed? and Allah loves those who are steadfast }

Al 'Imran 145-146

وهذه الآية فيها تشجيع للجبناء وترغيب لهم في القتال فإن الإقدام والإحجام لا ينقص من العمر ... وقيل وكم من نبي قتل بين يديه من أصحابه ربيون كثير وكلام إبن اسحاق في السيرة يقتضي قولاً آخر فإنه قال وكأين من نبي أصابه القتل ومعه ربيون أي جماعات فما وهنوا بعد نبيهم وما ضعفوا عن عدوهم وما استكانوا لما أصابهم في الجهاد عن الله وعن دينهم وذلك الصبر ﴿ والله يحب الصابرين ﴾

تفسير إبن كثير

This verse [145] encourages cowards and rouses in them the desire to fight, since indeed neither courage nor reluctance lessens one's life. ... It is said: How many prophets had pious, learned men from among their companions get killed in front of them? However, what Ibn Ishaq said in his biography [*sirah*] implies a different view; for indeed it says: How many prophets were killed, while pious and learned men were with them, that is, bands of men, but they did not lose heart after what happened to their prophet, or grow weak in the face of their enemy; and they did not succumb to what came upon them in *jihad* for Allah and for their religion [*deen*]. This is what it means to be steadfast, ﴾ And Allah loves those who are steadfast ﴿ .

Tafsir Ibn Kathir

﴿ وسنجزي الشاكرين ﴾ الذين شكروا نعمة الله فلم يشغلهم شيء عن الجهاد

تفسير البيضاوي

﴾ We will reward the grateful ﴿ : those who give thanks for the favors of Allah, and nothing distracts them from *jihad*.

Tafsir Al-Baydawi

﴿ قاتل معه ﴾ فعلى القراءة الأولى يكون المعنى أن كثيراً من الأنبياء قتلوا والذين بقوا بعدهم ما وهنوا في دينهم بل استمروا على جهاد عدوهم ونصرة دينهم

تفسير الرازي

﴾ With whom ... fought ﴿ : according to the first reading the meaning is that many prophets have been killed, and those who remained behind after them did not lose heart in their religion, but rather persevered in *jihad* against their enemy and championing their religion.

Tafsir Al-Razi

﴿ فما وهنوا لما أصابهم في سبيل الله ﴾ فما عجزوا لما نالهم من ألم الجراح الذي نالهم في سبيل الله ولا لقتل من قتل منهم عن حرب أعداء الله ولا نكلوا عن جهادهم ... ﴿ والله يحب الصابرين ﴾ يقول والله يحب هؤلاء وأمثالهم من الصابرين لأمره وطاعته وطاعة رسوله في جهاد عدوه لا من فشل ففرّ عن عدوه ولا من إنقلب على عقبيه فذلّ لعدوه

تفسير الطبري

{ But did not lose heart at what came upon them in the cause of Allah } : they were not thwarted due to the pain of the injuries that came upon them, that came upon them in the cause of Allah, nor were they thwarted, due to the killing of those of them who were killed, from battling Allah's enemies; nor did they shy away from their *jihad*. ... { And Allah loves those who are steadfast } : this is saying that Allah loves these men, and those like them who are steadfast in His orders and in obedience to Him and obedience to His Messenger concerning *jihad* against His enemy, not those who become scared and run away from His enemy, nor those who turn on their heels and cringe towards His enemy.

Tafsir Al-Tabari

. . .

﴿ سَنُلْقِي فِي قُلُوبِ الَّذِينَ كَفَرُوا الرُّعْبَ بِمَا أَشْرَكُوا بِاللَّهِ مَا لَمْ يُنَزِّلْ بِهِ سُلْطَانًا وَمَأْوَاهُمُ النَّارُ وَبِئْسَ مَثْوَى الظَّالِمِينَ وَلَقَدْ صَدَقَكُمُ اللَّهُ وَعْدَهُ إِذْ تَحُسُّونَهُمْ بِإِذْنِهِ حَتَّى إِذَا فَشِلْتُمْ وَتَنَازَعْتُمْ فِي الْأَمْرِ وَعَصَيْتُمْ مِنْ بَعْدِ مَا أَرَاكُمْ مَا تُحِبُّونَ مِنْكُمْ مَنْ يُرِيدُ الدُّنْيَا وَمِنْكُمْ مَنْ يُرِيدُ الْآخِرَةَ ثُمَّ صَرَفَكُمْ عَنْهُمْ لِيَبْتَلِيَكُمْ وَلَقَدْ عَفَا عَنْكُمْ وَاللَّهُ ذُو فَضْلٍ عَلَى الْمُؤْمِنِينَ ﴾ آل عمران ١٥١-١٥٢

{ We shall cast terror into the hearts of those who have disbelieved, because they have ascribed associates to Allah for which He did not send down authority; their dwelling is Hellfire, and miserable is the abode of the oppressors. And Allah was true to his promise to you when by His permission you wiped them out, until you lost heart and quarreled with each other about the issue and disobeyed after He had shown you the things you love; some of you desire this world while some of you desire the hereafter. Then He sent you away from them to test you, but He has forgiven you. And Allah holds abundance for the Believers } Al 'Imran 151-152

قيل قذف الله في قلوب المشركين الخوف يوم أحد فانهزموا إلى مكة من غير سبب ولهم القوة والغلبة وقيل ذهبوا إلى مكة فلما كانوا ببعض الطريق قالوا ما صنعنا شيئاً قتلنا منهم ثم تركناهم ونحن قاهرون ارجعوا فاستأصلوهم فلما عزموا على ذلك ألقى الله الرعب في قلوبهم فأمسكوا

تفسير الزمخشري

It is said that Allah threw fear into the hearts of the idolaters [*mushrikeen*] on the day of Uhud, and they fled towards Mecca for no reason, as they were the ones with strength and the upper hand. It is said they went towards Mecca, and when they had gone some distance, they said: We haven't done anything – we killed a bunch of them and then left them while we were winning; everyone go back and exterminate them! But when they set out to do this, Allah cast terror into their hearts, and they held back.

Tafsir Al-Zamakhshari

ثم بشرهم بأنه سيلقي في قلوب أعدائهم الخوف منهم والذلة لهم بسبب كفرهم وشركهم

تفسير ابن كثير

Then He gave them the good news that He was going to cast fear of them into the hearts of their enemies and make them cringe before them, because of their disbelief [*kufr*] and their ascribing associates [*shirk*].

Tafsir Ibn Kathir

يعني بذلك جل ثناؤه سيلقى الله أيها المؤمنون في قلوب الذين كفروا بربهم وجحدوا نبوة محمد ﷺ ممن حاربكم بأحد الرعب وهو الجزع والهلع بما أشركوا بالله

تفسير الطبري

He (may His praise be exalted) means by this: Allah will cast, oh Believers, into the hearts of those who fought against you at Uhud – who have disbelieved in their Lord and have repudiated the prophethood of Muhammad (SAW) – terror, that is, alarm and dismay, seeing that they have ascribed associates to Allah.

Tafsir Al-Tabari

وأخرج مسلم عن ابي هريرة أن رسول الله ﷺ قال نصرت بالرعب على العدو

الدر المنثور للسيوطي

Muslim reported from Abu Huraira that the Messenger of Allah (SAW) said: I have been made victorious over the enemy by terror.

Al-Suyuti, Al-durr Al-manthur

عن سعد بن ابي وقاص قال رأيت عن يمين رسول الله ﷺ وعن شماله يوم أحد رجلين عليهما ثياب بيض يقاتلان عن رسول الله ﷺ أشدّ القتال وفي رواية عن سعد عليهما ثياب بيض ما رأيتهما قبل ولا بعد يعني جبريل وميكائيل

تفسير القرطبي

From Sa'd ibn Abi Waqqas, who said: On the day of Uhud I saw, to the right of the Messenger of Allah (SAW) and to his left, two men with white garments on, defending the Messenger of Allah (SAW) most fiercefully. In another narration from Sa'd: They had white garments on, and I had never seen them before nor saw them afterwards. These were Jibril and Mika'il.

Tafsir Al-Qurtubi

اعلم أن هذه الآية من تمام ما تقدم ذكره فإنه تعالى ذكر وجوهاً كثيرة في الترغيب في الجهاد وعدم المبالاة بالكفار ومن جملتها ما ذكر في هذه الآية أنه تعالى يلقي الخوف في قلوب الكفار ولا شك أن ذلك مما يوجب إستيلاء المسلمين عليهم ... ﴿ ليبتليكم ﴾ والمراد أنه تعالى لما صرفهم إلى ذلك المكان وتحصنوا به أمرهم هناك بالجهاد والذب عن بقية المسلمين ولا شك أن الإقدام على الجهاد بعد الانهزام وبعد أن شاهدوا في تلك المعركة قتل أقربائهم وأحبائهم هو من أعظم أنواع الابتلاء

تفسير الرازي

Know that this verse is the completion of what preceded His statement here; for indeed the Most High made mention of many ways of arousing desire for *jihad* and showing no concern for the disbelievers [*kuffar*]. What is mentioned in this verse brings together the totality of all these, in that the Most High cast fear into the hearts of the disbelievers. And there is no doubt that this is part of what determines that the Muslims overpower them. ... { To test you } : The aim was that the Most High, when He sent them away to that place, through this they strengthened their position there by *jihad* and in defending the rest of the Muslims. And there is no doubt that courageously undertaking *jihad* after defeat, and after they had witnessed the killing of their kinsfolk and loved ones on that battlefield, was one of the most formidable kinds of ordeals.

Tafsir Al-Razi

* * *

﴿ يَا أَيُّهَا الَّذِينَ آمَنُوا لَا تَكُونُوا كَالَّذِينَ كَفَرُوا وَقَالُوا لِإِخْوَانِهِمْ إِذَا ضَرَبُوا فِي الْأَرْضِ أَوْ كَانُوا غُزًّى لَوْ كَانُوا عِنْدَنَا مَا مَاتُوا وَمَا قُتِلُوا لِيَجْعَلَ اللَّهُ ذَٰلِكَ حَسْرَةً فِي قُلُوبِهِمْ وَاللَّهُ يُحْيِي وَيُمِيتُ وَاللَّهُ بِمَا تَعْمَلُونَ بَصِيرٌ وَلَئِنْ قُتِلْتُمْ فِي سَبِيلِ اللَّهِ أَوْ مُتُّمْ لَمَغْفِرَةٌ مِنَ اللَّهِ وَرَحْمَةٌ خَيْرٌ مِمَّا يَجْمَعُونَ وَلَئِنْ مُتُّمْ أَوْ قُتِلْتُمْ لَإِلَى اللَّهِ تُحْشَرُونَ ﴾ آل عمران ١٥٦-١٥٨

{ Oh you who have believed! Do not be like those who have disbelieved and say to their brothers when they set out in the land or go on raids: "If they had been with us they would not have died and would not have been killed", such that Allah makes this a cause for grief in their hearts; for Allah gives life and brings death, and Allah sees what you all do. And indeed whether you are killed in the cause of Allah, or die, surely forgiveness from Allah and mercy are better than what those people accumulate. And indeed if you die, or are killed, truly unto Allah you are gathered } Al 'Imran 156-158

﴿ يَا أَيُّهَا الَّذِينَ آمَنُوا لَا تَكُونُوا كَالَّذِينَ كَفَرُوا وَقَالُوا لِإِخْوَانِهِمْ ﴾ الآية أي لا تكونوا كالمنافقين الذي ينهون اخوانهم عن الجهاد في سبيل الله ... ﴿ وَاللَّهُ يُحْيِي وَيُمِيتُ ﴾ والله المعجل الموت لمن يشاء من حيث يشاء والمميت من يشاء كلما شاء دون غيره من سائر خلقه وهذا من الله عز وجل ترغيب لعباده المؤمنين على جهاد عدوه والصبر على قتالهم وإخراج هيبتهم من صدورهم وإن قلّ عددهم وكثر عدد أعدائهم وأعداء الله وإعلام منه لهم أن الإماتة والإحياء بيده وأنه لن يموت أحد ولا يقتل إلا بعد فناء أجله الذي كتب له

تفسير الطبري

{ Oh you who have believed! Do not be like those who have disbelieved and say to their brothers ... } and the rest of the verse; that is, do not be like the hypocrites who hold back their brothers from *jihad* in the cause of Allah. ... { For Allah gives life and brings death } : For Allah is the hastener of death upon whoever He wishes, from wherever He wishes; and He is the bringer of death upon whoever He wishes, whenever He wishes; none other than Him from the rest of His creation. This is, from Allah Mighty and Sublime, an arousing of desire in His servants the Believers to wage *jihad* against His enemy, to be steadfast in fighting them, and to cast out from their breasts any anxiety concerning them; even if they are small in number and their enemies and Allah's enemies are great in number. It is a declaration from Him to them that the bringing of death and the giving of life are in His hand, and that no one will die, nor will anyone be killed, until the allotted time ordained for him has come to pass.

Tafsir Al-Tabari

﴿ وَلَئِن قُتِلْتُمْ فِي سَبِيلِ اللَّهِ أَوْ مُتُّمْ لَمَغْفِرَةٌ مِّنَ اللَّهِ وَرَحْمَةٌ خَيْرٌ مِّمَّا يَجْمَعُونَ ﴾ تضمن هذا أن القتل في سبيل الله والموت أيضاً وسيلة إلى نيل رحمة الله وعفوه ورضوانه وذلك خير من البقاء في الدنيا

تفسير ابن كثير

{ And indeed whether you are killed in the cause of Allah, or die, surely forgiveness from Allah and mercy are better than what they accumulate } : this indicates that killing in the cause of Allah, as well as death, are a way to gain the mercy of Allah, His forgiveness, and His good pleasure, and this is better than remaining in this world.

Tafsir Ibn Kathir

﴿ لَإِلَى اللَّهِ تُحْشَرُونَ ﴾ كذّب الكافرين أولاً في زعمهم أن من سافر من اخوانهم أو غزى لو كان في المدينة لما مات ونهى المسلمين عن ذلك لأنه سبب التقاعد عن الجهاد ثم قال لهم ولئن تم عليكم ما تخافونه من الهلاك بالموت والقتل في سبيل الله فإنّ ما تنالونه من المغفرة والرحمة بالموت في سبيل الله خير مما تجمعون من الدنيا ومنافعها لو لم تموتوا وعن إبن عباس رضي الله عنهما خير من طلاع الأرض ذهبةً حمراء

تفسير الزمخشري

{ Truly unto Allah you are gathered } : He refutes the disbelievers first of all in their alleging that whoever of their brothers travelled or went on a raid, even to Medina, would not die. He prohibits the Muslims from doing this, since it would be a reason to refrain from *jihad*. Them He says to them: Even if the demise that you all fear from death and killing in the cause of Allah were to come upon you, surely what you receive in forgiveness and mercy for dying in the cause of Allah is better than what you accumulate in this world and all its gain, were you not to have died. Ibn 'Abbas (may Allah be pleased with both of them) said: Better than all that fills the earth is a piece of gold colored red.

Tafsir Al-Zamakhshari

﴿ وَاللَّهُ يُحْيِي وَيُمِيتُ ﴾ وأيضاً الذي قتل في الجهاد لو أنه ما خرج إلى الجهاد لكان يموت لا محالة فإذا كان لا بد من الموت فلأن يقتل في الجهاد حتى يستوجب الثواب العظيم كان ذلك خيراً له من أن يموت من غير فائدة وهو المراد من قوله ﴿ وَلَئِن قُتِلْتُمْ فِي سَبِيلِ اللَّهِ أَوْ مُتُّمْ لَمَغْفِرَةٌ مِّنَ اللَّهِ وَرَحْمَةٌ خَيْرٌ مِّمَّا يَجْمَعُونَ ﴾

تفسير الرازي

{ For Allah gives life and brings death } : including someone who is killed in *jihad*; if he had not gone out for *jihad*, he still would have inevitably died. If death is unavoidable, then because he is killed in *jihad* in order to be worthy of the great reward, this is better for him than dying uselessly. This is the intended meaning of

His word: { And indeed whether you are killed in the cause of Allah, or die, surely forgiveness from Allah and mercy are better than what those people accumulate }.

Tafsir Al-Razi

ثم قال تعالى ﴿ ولئن قُتلتم في سبيل الله أو متّم لمغفرة من الله ورحمة خير مما يجمعون ﴾ أي إن الموت لكائن لا بد منه فوت في سبيل الله أو قتل خير لو علموا وأيقنوا مما يجمعون من الدنيا التي لها يتأخرون عن الجهاد تخوّف الموت والقتل بما جمعوا من زهرة الدنيا زهادة في الآخرة ﴿ ولئن متم أو قتلتم ﴾ أي ذلك كان ﴿ لإلى الله تُحشرون ﴾ أي إن إلى الله المرجع فلا تغرنّكم الدنيا ولا تغتّروا بها وليكن الجهاد وما رغّبكم الله فيه من ثوابه آثر عندكم منها

السيرة النبوية لإبن هشام ذكر ما أنزل الله عز وجل في أحد من القرآن

Then the Most High said: { And indeed whether you are killed in the cause of Allah, or die, surely forgiveness from Allah and mercy are better than what those people accumulate } ; that is, indeed every being must die, so dying for the cause of Allah or being killed – if only they knew and were assured – is better than what they accumulate in this world, for which they postpone *jihad*, fearing death and killing, due to the splendor of this worldly life which they have accumulated, of little value in the hereafter. { And indeed if you die, or are killed } : whichever of these it is; { Truly unto Allah you are gathered } : that is, indeed the return is to Allah, so let not this world entice you, and do not be enticed by it; but rather let *jihad*, and the desire for reward that Allah has roused in you, be more appealing to you.

Ibn Hisham, Al-sirah Al-nabawiya, Topic section: mention of the portion of the Qur'an that Allah Mighty and Sublime sent down regarding Uhud

* * *

﴿ أَوَلَمَّا أَصَابَتْكُم مُّصِيبَةٌ قَدْ أَصَبْتُم مِّثْلَيْهَا قُلْتُمْ أَنَّىٰ هَـٰذَا قُلْ هُوَ مِنْ عِندِ أَنفُسِكُمْ إِنَّ ٱللَّهَ عَلَىٰ كُلِّ شَىْءٍ قَدِيرٌ وَمَا أَصَابَكُمْ يَوْمَ ٱلْتَقَى ٱلْجَمْعَانِ فَبِإِذْنِ ٱللَّهِ وَلِيَعْلَمَ ٱلْمُؤْمِنِينَ وَلِيَعْلَمَ ٱلَّذِينَ نَافَقُوا۟ وَقِيلَ لَهُمْ تَعَالَوْا۟ قَاتِلُوا۟ فِى سَبِيلِ ٱللَّهِ أَوِ ٱدْفَعُوا۟ قَالُوا۟ لَوْ نَعْلَمُ قِتَالًا لَّٱتَّبَعْنَاكُمْ هُمْ لِلْكُفْرِ يَوْمَئِذٍ أَقْرَبُ مِنْهُمْ لِلْإِيمَانِ يَقُولُونَ بِأَفْوَاهِهِم مَّا لَيْسَ فِى قُلُوبِهِمْ وَٱللَّهُ أَعْلَمُ بِمَا يَكْتُمُونَ ﴾ آل عمران ١٦٥-١٦٧

﴿ And so, when calamity struck you all, even when you had struck twice as much, you say: Where is this from? Say: This is from yourselves. Indeed Allah is powerful over all things. What came upon you, on the day the two groups met, was by Allah's permission, so that He might know the Believers, and so He might know those who were hypocrites, those to whom it was said: "Come and fight in the cause of Allah, or chase away"; they said: "If we knew about fighting, we would follow you". On that day disbelief was nearer to them than belief, as they said with their mouths what was not in their hearts; and Allah knows best what they conceal ﴾ Al 'Imran 165-167

يقول تعالى ﴿ أَوَلَمَّا أَصَابَتْكُم مُّصِيبَةٌ ﴾ وهي ما أصيب منهم يوم أحد من قتل السبعين منهم ﴿ قَدْ أَصَبْتُم مِّثْلَيْهَا ﴾ يعني يوم بدر فإنهم قتلوا من المشركين سبعين قتيلاً وأسروا سبعين أسيراً ﴿ قُلْتُمْ أَنَّىٰ هَـٰذَا ﴾ أي من أين جرى علينا هذا ﴿ قُلْ هُوَ مِنْ عِندِ أَنفُسِكُمْ ﴾ عمر بن الخطاب قال لما كان يوم أحد من العام المقبل عوقبوا بما صنعوا يوم بدر من أخذهم الفداء فقتل منهم سبعون وفر أصحاب رسول الله ﷺ عنه وكسرت رباعيته وهشمت البيضة على رأسه وسال الدم على وجهه فأنزل الله ﴿ أَوَلَمَّا أَصَابَتْكُم مُّصِيبَةٌ قَدْ أَصَبْتُم مِّثْلَيْهَا قُلْتُمْ أَنَّىٰ هَـٰذَا قُلْ هُوَ مِنْ عِندِ أَنفُسِكُمْ ﴾ بأخذكم الفداء ... قال الله عز وجل ﴿ هُمْ لِلْكُفْرِ يَوْمَئِذٍ أَقْرَبُ مِنْهُمْ لِلْإِيمَانِ ﴾ استدلوا به على أن الشخص قد نتقلب به الأحوال فيكون في حال أقرب إلى الكفر وفي حال أقرب إلى الإيمان لقوله ﴿ هُمْ لِلْكُفْرِ يَوْمَئِذٍ أَقْرَبُ مِنْهُمْ لِلْإِيمَانِ ﴾ ثم قال تعالى ﴿ يَقُولُونَ بِأَفْوَاهِهِم مَّا لَيْسَ فِى قُلُوبِهِمْ ﴾ يعني أنهم يقولون القول ولا يعتقدون صحته ومنه قولهم هذا ﴿ لَوْ نَعْلَمُ قِتَالًا لَّٱتَّبَعْنَاكُمْ ﴾

تفسير ابن كثير

The Most High says: ﴿ And so, when calamity struck you all ﴾ : this is what befell them on the day of Uhud when seventy of them were killed; ﴿ even when you had struck twice as much ﴾ : referring to the day of Badr, when indeed they killed seventy of the idolaters [mushrikeen] and took seventy captive; ﴿ you say: Where is this from? ﴾ : that is, from where did this come upon us? ﴿ Say: This is from yourselves }. 'Umar ibn Al-Khattab said: On the day of Uhud the following year, they were punished for what they had done at Badr by accepting ransoms, and seventy of them were killed, and the Messenger of Allah's (SAW) Companions ran away from him. And He broke a front tooth, his helmet was shattered over his head, and blood ran down over his face. And so Allah sent down: { And so, when calamity struck you all, even when you had struck twice as much, you say: Where is this from? Say: This is from yourselves }, due to them having accepted ransom. ... Allah Mighty and Sublime said: { On that day disbelief was nearer to them than belief }: One may conclude from this that people can fluctuate in their condition, being in a state closer to disbelief [*kufr*] or in a state closer to belief [*iman*], based on His word: { On that day disbelief was nearer to them than belief }. Then the Most High said: { They said with their mouths what was not in their hearts }: that is, they said something but did not hold it to be true, and what they said here was along those lines: { If we knew about fighting, we would follow you }.

Tafsir Ibn Kathir

قوله تعالى ﴿ وليعلم المؤمنين ﴾ أي ليطهر إيمان المؤمنين بثبوتهم على ما نالهم ويظهر نفاق المنافقين بفشلهم وقلة صبرهم

تفسير إبن الجوزي

The word of the Most High: { So that He might know the Believers }: that is, so that the belief of the Believers would be manifest by their perseverance through what came upon them, and so that the hypocrisy of the hypocrites would be manifest by their cowardice and lack of steadfastness.

Tafsir Ibn Al-Jawzi

﴿ وليعلم الذين نافقوا ﴾ ﴿ الذين ﴾ ﴿ قيل لهم ﴾ لما انصرفوا عن القتال وهم عبدالله بن أبي وأصحابه ﴿ تعالوا قاتلوا في سبيل الله ﴾ أعداءه ﴿ أو ادفعوا ﴾ عنا القوم بتكثير سوادكم إن لم تقاتلوا

تفسير الجلالين

{ And so He might know those who were hypocrites }: those { to whom it was said: { when they turned away from fighting, these being Abdullah ibn Ubayy and his companions; { "Come and fight in the cause of Allah }: against His enemies; { or chase away" }: the people from us, by increasing the size of your crowd, if you do not fight.

Tafsir Al-Jalalain

قوله تعالى ﴿ هم للكفر يومئذ أقرب منهم للإيمان ﴾ أي بيّنوا حالهم وهتكوا أستارهم وكشفوا عن نفاقهم لمن كان يظن أنهم مسلمون فصاروا أقرب إلى الكفر في ظاهر الحال وإن كانوا كافرين على التحقيق

تفسير القرطبي

The word of the Most High: { On that day disbelief was nearer to them than belief } : that is, they made their condition clear, unmasked their disguises, revealed their hypocrisy to those who thought they were Muslims, and became nearer to disbelief in the most apparent way, but they were actually disbelievers.

Tafsir Al-Qurtubi

* * *

﴿ ولا تحسبن الذين قتلوا في سبيل الله أمواتاً بل أحياء عند ربهم يرزقون فرحين بما آتاهم الله من فضله ويستبشرون بالذين لم يلحقوا بهم من خلفهم ألا خوف عليهم ولا هم يحزنون يستبشرون بنعمة من الله وفضل وأن الله لا يضيع أجر المؤمنين ﴾ آل عمران ١٦٩-١٧١

{ Do not at all deem those who have been killed in the cause of Allah to be dead, but rather alive with their Lord, bestowed with favor; joyful in what Allah has brought them of His abundance, rejoicing over those behind them who have not yet met up with them, that no fear is upon them nor are they sad; rejoicing over grace from Allah and abundance, and that Allah does not squander the reward of the believers } Al 'Imran 169-171

ثم قال لنبيه ﷺ يرغّب المؤمنين في الجهاد ويهوّن عليهم القتل ﴿ ولا تحسبن الذين قتلوا في سبيل الله أمواتاً بل أحياء عند ربهم يرزقون فرحين بما آتاهم الله من فضله ويستبشرون بالذين لم يلحقوا بهم من خلفهم ألا خوف عليهم ولا هم يحزنون ﴾ أي لا تظنّ الذين قتلوا في سبيل الله أمواتاً أي قد أحييتهم فهم عندي يرزقون في روح الجنة وفضلها مسرورون بما آتاهم الله من فضله على جهادهم عنه ويستبشرون بالذين لم يلحقوا بهم من خلفهم أي ويُسرّون بلحوق من لَحِقهم من اخوانهم على ما مضوا عليه من جهادهم ليشركوهم فيما هم

فيه من ثواب الله الذي اعطاهم قد اذهبَ الله عنهم الخوف والحزَن يقول الله تعالى ﴿ يستبشرون بنعمة من الله وفضل وإن الله لا يضيع أجر المؤمنين ﴾ لما عاينوا من وفاء الموعود وعظيم الثواب

السيرة النبوية لإبن هشام ذكر ما أنزل الله عز وجل في أحد من القران

Then He says to His Prophet (SAW), rousing the believers to *jihad* and making it easy for them to kill: { Do not at all deem those who have been killed in the cause of Allah to be dead, but rather alive with their Lord, bestowed with favor; joyful in what Allah has brought them of His abundance, rejoicing over those behind them who have not yet met up with them, that no fear is upon them nor are they sad } : that is, do not at all think that those who have been killed in the cause of Allah are dead, that is, I have made them alive and they are with me, bestowed with bounty in the rest and abundance of *Jannah*; glad at what Allah has brought them of His abundance on account of their *jihad* for Him, and rejoicing over those behind them who have not yet caught up with them, that is, they are happy to meet up with those of their brothers who have caught up with them on account of the *jihad* that they passed through, to share with them in the reward of Allah that Allah has granted them; Allah has driven away fear and sorrow from them. Allah Most High says: { Rejoicing over grace from Allah and abundance, and that Allah does not squander the reward of the believers } , as they have beheld the fulfillment of what was promised; and great is the reward.

Ibn Hisham, *Al-sirah Al-nabawiya*, Topic section: mention of the portion of the Qur'an that Allah Mighty and Sublime sent down regarding Uhud

عن إبن عباس قال قال رسول الله ﷺ لما أُصيب اخوانكم بأحُد جعل الله أرواحهم في جوف طير خُضر ترِد انهار الجنة يأكل من ثمارها وتأوي إلى قناديل من ذهب معلّقة في ظل العرش فلما وجدوا طيب مأكلهم ومشربهم ومقيلهم قالوا من يبلّغ اخواننا عنا أنّا أحياء في الجنة نُرزق لئلاً يزهدوا في الجهاد ولا ينكُلوا عند الحرب فقال الله سبحانه أنا ابلّغهم عنكم قال فأنزل الله ﴿ ولا تحسبنّ الذين قُتلوا في سبيل الله أمواتاً ﴾ إلى آخر الآية

سنن ابي داود كتاب الجهاد

From Ibn 'Abbas, who said: The Messenger of Allah (SAW) said: When your brothers were struck down at Uhud, Allah put their spirits inside green birds that go down to the rivers of *Jannah* to eat of its fruits and retreat to lamps of gold hanging in the shade of the Throne. And when they experience the delight of their food, their drink, and their resting place, they say: Who will tell our brothers about us, that we are alive in *Jannah* bestowed with favor, lest they lose interest in *jihad* and shy away in war? Allah the Exalted said: I will tell them about you. So Allah sent down: { Do not at all deem those who have been killed in the cause of Allah to be dead } up to the end of the verse.

Sunan Abu Dawud, The book of *jihad*

عن مسروق قال سألنا عبدالله عن هذه الآية ﴿ ولا تحسبنَّ الذين قُتلوا في سبيل الله أمواتاً بل أحياءٌ عند ربهم يُرزقون ﴾ قال أما إنا قد سألنا عن ذلك فقال أرواحهم في جوف طير خُضر لها قناديل معلَّقة بالعرش تسرح من الجنة حيث شاءت ثم تأوي إلى تلك القناديل فإطَّلع اليهم ربهم اطّلاعةً فقال هل تشتهون شيئاً قالوا أي شيء نشتهي ونحن نسرح من الجنة حيث شئنا ففعل ذلك بهم ثلاث مرات فلما رأوا أنهم لن يُتركوا من أن يُسألوا قالوا يا رب نريد أن تُردَّ أرواحنا في أجسادنا حتى نقتل في سبيلك مرة أخرى فلما رأى أن ليس لهم حاجة تُركوا

صحيح مسلم كتاب الامارة

From Masruq who said: We asked Abdullah about this verse: { Do not at all deem those who have been killed in the cause of Allah to be dead, but rather alive with their Lord, bestowed with favor } . He said: Indeed we also asked about that, and he said: Their spirits are inside green birds who have lamps hanging from the Throne, and they roam freely in *Jannah* wherever they wish, then retire to the lamps. And their Lord once appeared and looked at them deeply, and said: Is there anything you all desire? They said: What could we desire when we roam freely in *Jannah* wherever we wish? But He did this to them three times, and when they realized that they would not be left alone from being asked, they said: Oh Lord, we want you to return our spirits to our bodies so that we can be killed in your cause once again. And when He saw that they had no needs, they were left alone.

Sahih Muslim, The book of governance

﴿ ولا تحسبن الذين قتلوا في سبيل الله أمواتاً بل أحياء عند ربهم يرزقون ﴾ قيل هم قتلى أحد وقيل شهداء بئر معونة وقيل شهداء بدر وهل سبب ذلك قول من إستشهد وقد دخل الجنة فأكل كل من ثمارها من يبلغ عنا اخواننا أنا في الجنة نرزق لا تزهَدوا في الجهاد فقال الله أنا أبلغ عنكم فنزلت

البحر المحيط لابي حيان

{ Do not at all deem those who have been killed in the cause of Allah to be dead, but rather alive with their Lord, bestowed with favor } : it is said that these are the ones killed at Uhud, or the martyrs at Bi'r Ma'una, or the martyrs at Badr. Can this be attributed to what the ones who were martyred said, having entered *Jannah*, eaten of all its fruit, saying: "Who will tell our brothers about us? That we are in *Jannah* bestowed with favor – Do not forsake *jihad* !" And Allah said: I will tell about you. And so this verse came down.

Abu Hayyan, Al-bahr Al-muhit

عن ابن إسحاق قال قال الله تبارك وتعالى لنبيه محمد ﷺ يرغّب المؤمنين في ثواب الجنة ويهوّن عليهم القتل ﴿ ولا تحسبن الذين قتلوا في سبيل الله أمواتاً بل أحياء عند ربهم يرزقون ﴾ أي قد أحييتهم فهم عندي يرزقون في روح الجنة وفضلها مسرورين بما آتاهم الله من ثواب على جهادهم عنه ..... ﴿ ويستبشرون بالذين لم يلحقوا بهم من خلفهم أن لا خوف عليهم ولا هم يحزنون ﴾ يعني بذلك تعالى ذكره ويفرحون بمن لم يلحق بهم من اخوانهم الذين فارقوهم وهم أحياء في الدنيا على مناهجهم من جهاد أعداء الله مع رسوله لعلمهم بأنهم إن إستشهدوا فلحقوا بهم ... ﴿ لا يضيع أجر المؤمنين ﴾ لا يبطل جزاء أعمال من صدق رسوله وإتبعه وعمل بما جاءه من عند الله

تفسير الطبري

From Ibn Ishaq, who said: Allah Blessed and Exalted said to His Prophet Muhammad (SAW), to rouse in the Believers the desire for the reward of *Jannah*, and to make killing easy for them: { Do not at all deem those who have been killed in the cause of Allah to be dead, but rather alive with their Lord, bestowed with favor } ; that is, I have brought them to life, and they are with me bestowed with favor in the rest and abundance of *Jannah*, delighted in what Allah has granted them of His reward for their *jihad* for Him. ... { Rejoicing over those behind them who have not yet met up with them, that no fear is upon them nor are they sad } ; He (may His remembrance be exalted) means by this: They are joyful for those of their brothers who have not yet caught up with them, those who were separated from them, alive in the world persevering in *jihad* against the enemies of Allah with His Messenger, knowing that if they are martyred, they will meet up with them. ... { Allah does not squander the reward of the Believers } : He does not annul the recompense for the deeds of those who have believed in His Messenger, followed him, and done according to what has come to him from Allah.

Tafsir Al-Tabari

عن إبن عباس رضي الله عنهما قال قال رسول الله ﷺ الشهداء على بارق نهر بباب الجنة في قبة خضراء يخرج عليهم رزقهم من الجنة بكرة وعشياً ... وكأن الشهداء أقسام منهم من تسرح أرواحهم في الجنة ومنهم من يكون على هذا النهر بباب الجنة وقد يحتمل أن يكون منتهى سيرهم إلى هذا النهر فيجتمعون هنالك ويغدى عليهم برزقهم هناك ويراح والله أعلم وقد روينا في مسند الامام أحمد حديثاً فيه البشارة لكل مؤمن بأن روحه تكون في الجنة تسرح فيها أيضاً وتأكل من ثمارها وترى ما فيها من النضرة والسرور وتشاهد ما أعده الله لها من الكرامة وهو بإسناد صحيح عزيز عظيم إجتمع فيه ثلاثة من الأئمة الأربعة أصحاب المذاهب المتبعة ... عن عبد الرحمن بن كعب بن مالك عن أبيه رضي الله عنه قال قال رسول الله ﷺ نسمة المؤمن طائر يعلُق في شجر الجنة حتى يرجعه الله إلى جسده يوم يبعثه قوله يعلق أي يأكل وفي هذا الحديث إن روح المؤمن تكون

على شكل طائر في الجنة وأما أرواح الشهداء فكما تقدم في حواصل طير خضر فهي كالكواكب بالنسبة إلى أرواح عموم المؤمنين فإنها تطير بأنفسها فنسأل الله الكريم المنان أن يميتنا على الإيمان

تفسير إبن كثير

From Ibn 'Abbas (may Allah be pleased with him), who said: The Messenger of Allah (SAW) said: The martyrs are in the radiance of a river by the gate of *Jannah* in a green dome, their bounty sent out to them from *Jannah* day and night. ... It is as if there are several classes of martyrs: there are those whose spirits roam freely in *Jannah*, and those who remain by this river by the gate of *Jannah*; it is also possible that the courses of their lives end at this river, and they gather together there and are nourished of their bounty there, and given rest. But Allah knows best. A *hadith* is narrated to us in the *Musnad* of Imam Ahmad, in which there is the good news for every Believer that his spirit will be in *Jannah*, also roaming freely there, and eating from its fruits, contemplating its richness and delight, and witnessing the honor that Allah has prepared for his spirit. This *hadith* has a great and marvelous authentic chain of narration [*isnad*] – three of the four imams of the established legal schools coincide. ... 'Abd Al-Rahman ibn Ka'b ibn Malik related from his father (may Allah be pleased with him), who said: The Messenger of Allah (SAW) said: A Believer's soul is a bird, held fast in the trees of *Jannah*, until Allah returns him to his body on the day He resurrects him. His saying "held fast in" means "eating from". This *hadith* states that the spirit of a Believer is in the form of a bird in *Jannah*; yet the spirits of martyrs, as was mentioned, are in the crops of green birds, like stars to the rest of the Believers; they fly by themselves. And we ask Allah, the Bountiful, the Benevolent, to have us die firmly in belief.

Tafsir Ibn Kathir

﴿ و يستبشرون ﴾ يسرون بالبشارة ... والآية يدل على أن الإنسان غير الهيكل المحسوس بل هو جوهر مدرك بذاته لا يفنى بخراب البدن ولا يتوقف عليه إدراكه وتألمه والتذاذه ويؤيد ذلك قوله تعالى في آل فرعون ﴿ النار يُعرَضون عليها ﴾ الآية وما روى إبن عباس رضي الله عنهما أنه عليه الصلاة والسلام قال أرواح الشهداء في أجواف طير خضر ترد انهار الجنة وتأكل من ثمارها وتأوي إلى قناديل معلقة في ظل العرش ومن أنكر ذلك ولم ير الروح إلا ريحاً وعرضاً قال هم أحياء يوم القيامة وإنما وصفوا به في الحال لتحققه ودنوّه أو أحياء بالذكر أو بالإيمان وفيها حث على الجهاد وترغيب في الشهادة وبعث على إزدياد الطاعة وإجماد لمن يتمنى لإخوانه مثل ما أنعم عليه وبشرى للمؤمنين بالفلاح

تفسير البيضاوي

﴿ They rejoice ﴾: they delight in the good news. ... This verse is evidence that man is not a framework perceptible by the senses, but rather he is an essence aware of himself, who does not cease to exist upon the destruction of the body; and his consciousness, feeling of pain, and feeling of pleasure do not depend on this. The word of the Most High upholds this regarding the house of Pharaoh: { The fire – they are exposed to it ... } and the rest of the verse [Al-Ghafir 46], as well as what Ibn 'Abbas (may Allah be pleased with them both) related, that He (prayers and peace be upon him) said: The spirits of the martyrs are in the bosoms of green birds, that go down to the rivers of *Jannah* and eat of its fruits, and retreat to lamps hanging in the shade of the Throne. Whoever denies this, and sees the spirit only as a wind or as something fleeting, would say that they will be alive on resurrection day. However they ascribed it forthwith in order to be certain of it, and drew near to them as alive either in memory or in faith. In this there is an exhortation to *jihad* and an arousal of desire for martyrdom, a message towards greater obedience, bestowing of praise on those who desire for their brothers the favor that has been bestowed on them, and to the Believers good tidings of success.

Tafsir Al-Baydawi

﴿ الَّذِينَ اسْتَجَابُوا لِلَّهِ وَالرَّسُولِ مِنْ بَعْدِ مَا أَصَابَهُمُ الْقَرْحُ لِلَّذِينَ أَحْسَنُوا مِنْهُمْ وَاتَّقَوْا أَجْرٌ عَظِيمٌ الَّذِينَ قَالَ لَهُمُ النَّاسُ إِنَّ النَّاسَ قَدْ جَمَعُوا لَكُمْ فَاخْشَوْهُمْ فَزَادَهُمْ إِيمَاناً وَقَالُوا حَسْبُنَا اللَّهُ وَنِعْمَ الْوَكِيلُ فَانْقَلَبُوا بِنِعْمَةٍ مِنَ اللَّهِ وَفَضْلٍ لَمْ يَمْسَسْهُمْ سُوءٌ وَاتَّبَعُوا رِضْوَانَ اللَّهِ وَاللَّهُ ذُو فَضْلٍ عَظِيمٍ ﴾ آل عمران ١٧٢-١٧٤

{ Those who responded to Allah and the Messenger after the injury that befell them; to those of them who do good and fear Allah there is a great reward. Those to whom the people said: "Indeed the people have pulled together against you, so fear them"; this only increased their faith, and they said: "Allah is sufficient for us, a most excellent advocate." So they returned with favor and abundance from Allah, no harm touched them, and they pursued the good pleasure of Allah; and Allah holds great abundance } Al 'Imran 172-174

﴿ والذين ﴾ مبتدأ ﴿ استجابوا لله والرسول ﴾ دعاءه بالخروج للقتال لما أراد أبو سفيان وأصحابه العود وتواعدوا مع النبي ﷺ وأصحابه سوق بدر العام المقبل من يوم أحد ﴿ من بعد ما أصابهم القرح ﴾ بأحد وخبر المبتدأ ﴿ للذين أحسنوا منهم ﴾ بطاعته ﴿ واتقوا ﴾ مخالفته ﴿ أجر عظيم ﴾ هو الجنة

تفسير الجلالين

{ Those } : the subject; { who answered Allah and the Messenger } : His call to go out and fight, when Abu Sufyan and his companions wanted to return, and agreed with the Prophet (SAW) and his Companions to meet at the market in Badr a year after the day of Uhud; { after the injury that befell them } : at Uhud; the predicate is { to those of them who do good } : by obedience to Him; { and fear Allah } : not opposing Him; { there is a great reward } : this is *Jannah*.

Tafsir Al-Jalalain

في قوله ﴿ للذين احسنوا منهم واتقوا أجرٌ عظيم ﴾ وجوه الأول ﴿ احسنوا ﴾ دخل تحته الائتمار بجميع المأمورات وقوله ﴿ واتقوا ﴾ دخل تحته الانتهاء عن جميع المنهيات والمكلف عند هذين الأمرين يستحق الثواب العظيم الثاني احسنوا في طاعة الرسول في ذلك الوقت واتقوا الله في التخلف عن الرسول وذلك يدل على أنه يلزمهم الاستجابة للرسول وإن بلغ الأمر بهم في الجراحات ما بلغ من بعد أن يتمكنوا معه من النهوض الثالث احسنوا فيما أتوا به من طاعة الرسول ﷺ واتقوا إرتكاب شيء من المنهيات بعد ذلك

تفسير الرازي

Concerning His word: { To those of them who do good and fear Allah there is a great reward }, there are several points. The first is that { do good } consists of compliance of all that is ordered; and His word { and fear Allah } consists of refraining from all that is forbidden; anyone bound to these two matters is worthy of the great reward. The second point is that they did good in obedience to the Messenger at that time, and they feared Allah as regards lagging behind the Messenger; and this is evidence that it was necessary for them to respond to the Messenger, even if the order given to them resulted in injuries that came about after they were able to command the upper hand with him. The third point is that they did good in fulfilling obedience to the Messenger, in fear of committing any of what is forbidden after this.

Tafsir Al-Razi

فإن قلت كيف زادهم نعيم أو مقوله إيماناً قلت لما لم يسمعوا قوله وأخلصوا عنده النية والعزم على الجهاد وأظهروا حمية الاسلام كان ذلك أثبت ليقينهم وأقوى لاعتقادهم

تفسير الزمخشري

If you ask: How did being pleased or what the people said increase their faith? I would say: Because they did not listen to what they said, and, in the face of it, stuck to their intention and determination to wage *jihad*. So they attested to the zeal of Islam; this was firmer to their conviction and stronger for their faith.

Tafsir Al-Zamakhshari

عن مجاهد { فانقلبوا بنعمة من الله وفضل } قال الفضل ما اصابوا من التجارة والأجر... { واتبعوا رضوان الله } قال طاعة النبي ﷺ

تفسير الطبري

Mujahid, regarding { So they returned with favor and abundance from Allah }, said: bounty is the goods and the reward they obtained. ... { And they pursued the good pleasure of Allah }; he said: Obedience to the Prophet (SAW).

Tafsir Al-Tabari

* * *

﴿ ربنا وإننا ما وعدتنا على رسلك ولا تخزنا يوم القيامة إنك لا تخلف الميعاد فاستجاب لهم ربهم أني لا أضيع عمل عامل منكم من ذكر أو أنثى بعضكم من بعض فالذين هاجروا وأخرجوا من ديارهم وأوذوا في سبيلي وقاتلوا وقتلوا لأكفرن عنهم سيئاتهم ولأدخلنهم جنات تجري من تحتها الأنهار ثوابا من عند الله والله عنده حسن الثواب ﴾ آل عمران ١٩٤-١٩٥

﴿ "Our Lord, bring us what you promised us by way of your Messengers, and do not disgrace us on the day of resurrection; indeed you do not break promises." And their Lord answered them: Indeed I will not squander the work of any worker among you, male or female; you are of each other; and those who emigrated, who were driven from their homes, made to suffer harm for my cause, who fought and were killed, I will surely expiate their bad deeds, and truly I will admit them to gardens under which rivers flow, as a reward from Allah; and with Allah is the finest reward ﴾ Al 'Imran 194-195

عن عمرو بن دينار عن رجل من ولد أم سلمة عن أم سلمة قالت يا رسول الله لا أسمع الله ذكر النساء في الهجرة فأنزل الله تعالى ﴿ اني لا أضيع عمل عامل منكم من ذكر أو أنثى بعضكم من بعض ﴾

جامع الترمذي كتاب تفسير القرآن

'Amr ibn Diyar related from a man from among the children of Umm Salamah, that Umm Salamah said: Oh Messenger of Allah! I haven't heard Allah mention the women in regards to emigration [hijra]. So Allah Most High sent down: ﴿ Indeed I will not squander the work of any worker among you, male or female; you are of each other ﴾ .

Sunan Al-Tirmidhi, The book of tafsir

﴿ وأخرجوا من ديارهم وأوذوا في سبيلي ﴾ بسبب ايمانهم بالله ومن أجله ﴿ وقاتلوا ﴾ الكفار ﴿ وقتلوا ﴾ في الجهاد

تفسير البيضاوي

﴿ Who were driven from their homes, made to suffer harm for My cause ﴾ : because of their belief in Allah and for His benefit; ﴿ who fought ﴾ : the Disbelievers; ﴾ and were killed ﴾ : in jihad.

Tafsir Al-Baydawi

﴿ وقاتلوا وقُتلوا ﴾ وهذا أعلى المقامات أن يقاتل في سبيل الله فيعقر جواده ويعفَّر وجهه بدمه وترابه

تفسير ابن كثير

{ Who fought and were killed } : this is the highest of ranks – that someone fights in the cause of Allah, his steed is wounded, and his face gets covered in his blood and his dust.

Tafsir Ibn Kathir

وأخرج الحاكم وصححه عن عبدالله بن عمرو قال قال لي رسول الله ﷺ أتعلم أول زمرة تدخل الجنة من أمتي قلت الله ورسوله أعلم قال المهاجرون يأتون يوم القيامة إلى باب الجنة ويستفتحون فتقول لهم الخزنة أوقد حوسبتم قالوا بأي شيء نحاسب وإنما كانت أسيافنا على عواتقنا في سبيل الله حتى متنا على ذلك قال فيفتح لهم فيقيلون فيه أربعين عاماً قبل أن يدخل الناس

الدر المنثور للسيوطي

Hakim related, and confirmed as sound, from Abdullah ibn 'Amr, who said: The Messenger of Allah (SAW) said to me: Do you know who will be the first group of my *ummah* to enter *Jannah*? I said: Allah and His Messenger know better. He said: The Emigrants [*Muhajirun*] will come on resurrection day to the gate of *Jannah*, they will seek admission, and the Keepers will say to them: Have you been reckoned for? They will say: "By what can we be reckoned? Indeed our swords were on our shoulders in the cause of Allah until we died for it." And He said: Then it will be opened for them, and they will take a nap there for forty years before the rest of the people enter.

Al-Suyuti, Al-durr Al-manthur

* * *

Surah 4   Al-nisaa [Women]

﴿ ولا تتمنوا ما فضّل الله به بعضكم على بعض للرجال نصيب مما اكتسبوا وللنساء نصيب مما اكتسبن واسألوا الله من فضله إن الله كان بكل شيء عليما ﴾ النساء ٣٢

{ And do not wish for that with which Allah has favored some of you over others; to men an allotment of what they have earned, and to women an allotment of what they have earned; ask from Allah His abundance; indeed Allah is knower of all things }
Al-nisaa 32

عن مجاهد عن أم سلمة أنها قالت يغزو الرجال ولا يغزو النساء وإنما لنا نصف الميراث فأنزل الله ﴿ ولا تتمنّوا ما فضّل الله به بعضكم على بعضٍ ﴾
جامع الترمذي كتاب تفسير القرآن

Mujahid related that Umm Salamah said: The men go out on raids, but the women don't go out on raids, and we only get half the inheritance! So Allah sent down: { And do not wish for that with which Allah has favored some of you over others } .

Sunan Al-Tirmidhi, The book of tafsir

﴿ للرجال نصيب ﴾ ثواب ﴿ مما اكتسبوا ﴾ بسبب ما عملوا من الجهاد وغيره ﴿ وللنساء نصيب مما اكتسبنَ ﴾ من طاعة أزواجهن وحفظ فروجهن
تفسير الجلالين

{ To men an allotment } : a reward; { of what they have earned } : due to the *jihad* and other things they have done; { and to women an allotment of what they have earned } : from obedience to their husbands and safeguarding their vaginas [*furuj*].

Tafsir Al-Jalalain

عن مجاهد قال قالت أم سلمة يا رسول الله تغزو الرجال ولا نغزو وإنما لنا نصف الميراث فأنزل الله تعالى ﴿ ولا تتنوا ما فضل الله به بعضكم على بعض ﴾ ... عن عكرمة أن النساء سألن الجهاد فقلن وددنا أن الله جعل لنا الغزو فنصيب من الأخر ما يصيب الرجال فأنزل الله تعالى ﴿ ولا تتنوا ما فضل الله بعضكم

على بعض ﴾ وقال قتادة والسدي لما نزل قوله ﴿ للذكر مثل حظ الأنثيين ﴾ قال الرجال إنا لنرجو أن نفضل على النساء بحسناتنا في الآخرة كما فُضِّلنا عليهن في الميراث فيكون أجرنا على الضعف من أجر النساء وقالت النساء إنا لنرجو أن يكون الوزر علينا نصف ما على الرجال في الآخرة كما لنا الميراث على النصف من نصيبهم في الدنيا فأنزل الله تعالى ﴿ ولا تتمنوا ما فضل الله به بعضكم على بعض ﴾

أسباب النزول للواحدي

From Mujahid, who said: Umm Salamah said: Oh Messenger of Allah! The men go out on raids, but we don't go out, and we only get half the inheritance. So Allah Most High sent down: { And do not wish for that with which Allah has favored some of you over others } ... 'Ikrama related that the women asked about *jihad*; they said: We would have liked for Allah to have us go out on raids so we could get the reward the men get; so Allah Most High sent down: { And do not wish for that with which Allah has favored some of you over others } . Qatada and Al-Suddi said: When His word came down: { Males receive the equivalent portion as two females } [Al-nisaa 11], the men said: Indeed we surely hope that we are preferred over women in the hereafter for our good deeds, just as we have been preferred over them in inheritance, so that our reward may be double the reward of women. And the women said: Indeed we surely hope that the burden on us in the hereafter is half of what is on the men, just as we have half the inheritance that they receive in this world. So Allah Most High sent down: { And do not wish for that with which Allah has favored some of you over others } .

Al-Wahidi, Asbab Al-nuzul

أتت واحدة من النساء إلى رسول الله ﷺ فقالت رب الرجال والنساء واحد وأنت الرسول إلينا وإليهم وأبونا آدم وأمنا حواء فما السبب في أن الله يذكر الرجال ولا يذكرنا فنزلت الآية فقالت وقد سبقنا الرجال بالجهاد فما لنا فقال ﷺ إن للحامل منكن أجر الصائم القائم فإذا ضربها الطلق لم يدر ما لها من الأجر فإذا أرضعت كان لها بكل مَصّة أجر إحياء نفس

تفسير الرازي

One of the women came to the Messenger of Allah (SAW) and said: There is one Lord of both men and women, you are the Messenger to us and to them, our father is Adam and our mother is Eve, so then what is the reason that Allah thinks of the men but doesn't think of us? So this verse came down. She said: Men have taken precedence over us in *jihad*, so what is there for us? And He said: Indeed any pregnant woman among you gets the reward of someone who fasts and prays, and whenever labor pains strike her, no one knows what reward she gets; and if she nurses, she gets, for every suck, the reward of bringing a soul to life.

Tafsir Al-Razi

* * *

﴿ يا أيها الذين آمنوا خذوا حذركم فانفروا ثبات أو انفروا جميعاً وإن منكم لمن ليبطئن فإن أصابتكم مصيبة قال قد أنعم الله علي إذ لم أكن معهم شهيداً ولئن أصابكم فضل من الله ليقولن كأن لم تكن بينكم وبينه مودة يا ليتني كنت معهم فأفوز فوزاً عظيماً فليقاتل في سبيل الله الذين يشرون الحياة الدنيا بالآخرة ومن يقاتل في سبيل الله فيقتل أو يغلب فسوف نؤتيه أجراً عظيماً ﴾ النساء ٧١-٧٤

{ Oh you who have believed! Be on guard, then mobilize in squads or mobilize all together. Indeed there are some of you who surely lag behind, and if misfortune comes upon you they say: "Allah has granted me favor in that I was not present with them". But if good fortune from Allah comes upon you, indeed they say – as if there were no fondness between you and them – "Oh how I wish I had been with them, to be victorious in great victory". So then, those who sell this worldly life in exchange for the hereafter, let them fight in the cause of Allah; and whoever fights in the cause of Allah and is either killed or overcomes, We will bring him a great reward } *Al-nisaa 71-74*

فيه خمس مسائل الأولى قوله تعالى ﴿ يا أيها الذين آمنوا خذوا حذركم ﴾ هذا خطاب للمؤمنين المخلصين من أمة محمد ﷺ وأمرٌ لهم بجهاد الكفار والخروج في سبيل الله وحماية الشرع

تفسير القرطبي

There are five points here; the first is the word of the Most High: { Oh you who have believed! Be on guard } ; this is an address to the devoted Believers of Muhammad's (SAW) *ummah*, and a command for them to wage *jihad* on the disbelievers [*kuffar*], to set out in the cause of Allah, and to keep the Islamic laws [*shar'*]

Tafsir Al-Qurtubi

يأمر الله تعالى عباده المؤمنين بأخذ الحذر من عدوهم وهذا يستلزم التأهب لهم بإعداد الأسلحة والعدد وتكثير العدد بالنفير في سبيل الله ﴿ ثُبَاتٍ ﴾ أي جماعة بعد جماعة وفرقة بعد فرقة وسرية بعد سرية ... ﴿ وإن منكم لمن لَيُبَطِّئَنَّ ﴾ قال مجاهد وغير واحد نزلت في المنافقين وقال مقاتل بن حيان ﴿ ليبطئن ﴾ أي ليتخلفن عن الجهاد ويحتمل المراد أنه يتباطأ هو في نفسه ويبطئ غيره عن الجهاد ... ﴿ ومن يقاتل في سبيل

الله فيُقتل أو يغلِب فسوف نؤتيه أجراً عظيماً ﴾ أي كل من قاتل في سبيل الله سواء قتل أو غلب أو سُلِب فله عند الله مثوبة عظيمة وأجر جزيل

تفسير ابن كثير

Allah Most High is commanding His servants the Believers to be on guard against their enemy; this calls for making preparations against them by getting the weapons and count ready, and by boosting the number of those mobilizing in the cause of Allah. { Squads } : that is, group after group, troop after troop, brigade after brigade ... { Indeed there are some of you who surely lag behind } ; Mujahid and others said: This came down in regards to the hypocrites. Muqatil ibn Hayyan said { lag behind } means they stay behind from *jihad*; it is possible that the intended meaning is that they linger behind in themselves, and hold others back from *jihad*. ... { And whoever fights in the cause of Allah and is either killed or overcomes, We will bring him a great reward } : that is, everyone who fights in the cause of Allah, whether he is killed, overcomes, or is plundered – he has, with Allah, a great recompense and a plentiful reward.

Tafsir Ibn Kathir

وهذا حضٌ من الله المؤمنين على جهاد عدوه من أهل الكفر به على أحايينهم غالبين كانوا أو مغلوبين والتهاون بأحوال المنافقين في جهاد من جاهدوا من المشركين وقع جهادهم اياهم مغلوبين كانوا أو غالبين منزلة من الله رفيعة يقول الله لهم جل ثناؤه ﴿ فليقاتل في سبيل الله ﴾ يعني في دين الله والدعاء إليه والدخول فيما أمر به أهل الكفر به

تفسير الطبري

This is an exhortation from Allah to the Believers to wage *jihad* on their enemy – those who hold to disbelief [*kufr*] in Him – at favorable times for them, whether they prevail or are defeated; and to think little of the state of the hypocrites in the *jihad* of the idolaters [*mushrikeen*] who wage *jihad*. Jihad for them became their duty against them whether they were defeated or prevailed, a rank of high prestige from Allah. Allah (may His praise be exalted) says to them: { Let them fight in the cause of Allah } : that is, in the religion of Allah, in calling people to it, and in following what He has ordered for those who hold to disbelief in Him.

Tafsir Al-Tabari

واعلم أنه تعالى عاد بعد الترغيب في طاعة الله وطاعة رسوله إلى ذكر الجهاد الذي تقدم لأنه أشق الطاعات ولأنه أعظم الامور التي بها يحصل تقوية الدين ... ﴿ ومن يقاتل في سبيل الله فيقتل أو يغلب فسوف نؤتيه أجراً عظيماً ﴾ والمعنى من يقاتل في سبيل الله فسواء صار مقتولاً للكفار أو صار غالباً للكفار فسوف نؤتيه

أجراً عظيماً وهو المنفعة الخالصة الدائمة المقرونة بالتعظيم ومعلوم أنه لا واسطة بين هاتين الحالين فإذا كان الأجر حاصلاً على كِلا التقديرين لم يكن عمل أشرف من الجهاد

تفسير الرازي

Know that the Most High, after exhorting obedience to Allah and obedience to His Messenger, returns to the preceding mention of *jihad*, because it is the hardest act of obedience, and because it is the greatest of the undertakings by which the religion [*deen*] is strengthened. ... { And whoever fights in the cause of Allah and is either killed or overcomes, We will bring him a great reward } : the meaning is that whoever fights in the cause of Allah, whether he becomes one killed by the disbelievers or becomes one who overcomes the disbelievers, we will bring him a great reward; this is the clear and enduring advantage tied to glorification. And it is known that there is no middle ground between these two reckonings; and so if the reward is obtained in both ordainments, there is no deed more noble than *jihad*.

Tafsir Al-Razi

عن إبن جريج ﴿ وإن منكم لمن ليبطئن ﴾ قال المنافق يبطئ المسلمين عن الجهاد في سبيل الله ... عن سعيد بن جبير ﴿ فسوف نؤتيه أجراً عظيماً ﴾ يعني جزاء وافراً في الجنة بفعل القاتل والمقتول من المسلمين في جهاد المشركين شريكين في الأجر

الدر المنثور للسيوطي

Ibn Juraij, regarding { Indeed there are some of you who surely lag behind } , said: The hypocrites hold the Muslims back from *jihad* in the cause of Allah ... Sa'id ibn Jubair, regarding { And we will bring them a great reward } : this means abundant recompense in *Jannah*, for He has made the Muslims who kill, as well as those who get killed in *jihad* against the Idolaters, to both share in the reward.

Al-Suyuti, Al-durr Al-manthur

* * *

﴿ وَمَا لَكُمْ لَا تُقَاتِلُونَ فِي سَبِيلِ اللَّهِ وَالْمُسْتَضْعَفِينَ مِنَ الرِّجَالِ وَالنِّسَاءِ وَالْوِلْدَانِ الَّذِينَ يَقُولُونَ رَبَّنَا أَخْرِجْنَا مِنْ هَذِهِ الْقَرْيَةِ الظَّالِمِ أَهْلُهَا وَاجْعَلْ لَنَا مِنْ لَدُنْكَ وَلِيًّا وَاجْعَلْ لَنَا مِنْ لَدُنْكَ نَصِيرًا ﴾ النساء ٧٥

﴿ What is with you all?! that you do not fight in the cause of Allah and of the men, women, and children who have been weakened and oppressed, those who say: Our Lord! Take us out of this city whose people are oppressive, and give us a guardian who comes from you, and give us a champion who comes from you ﴾
Al-nisaa 75

يحرض تعالى عباده المؤمنين على الجهاد في سبيله وعلى السعي في إستنقاذ المستضعفين بمكة من الرجال والنساء والصبيان المتبرمين من المقام بها

تفسير ابن كثير

The Most High is inciting his servants the Believers to wage *jihad* in His cause, and in striving to save the men, women, and children in Mecca who were weakened and oppressed, fed up from having to stay there.

Tafsir Ibn Kathir

اعلم أن المراد منه إنكاره تعالى لتركهم القتال فصار ذلك توكيداً لما تقدم من الأمر بالجهاد وفيه مسائل المسألة الأولى قوله ﴿ وما لكم لا تقاتلون ﴾ يدل على أن الجهاد واجب ومعناه أنه لا عذر لكم في ترك المقاتلة وقد بلغ حال المستضعفين من الرجال والنساء والولدان من المسلمين إلى ما بلغ في الضعف فهذا حث شديد على القتال وبيان العلّة التي لها صار القتال واجباً وهو ما في القتال من تخليص هؤلاء المؤمنين من أيدي الكفرة لأن هذا الجمع إلى الجهاد يجري مجرى فكاك الأسير

تفسير الرازي

Know that the intended meaning here is the Most High refusing for them to abandon fighting, this being an affirmation of the earlier command to wage *jihad*. There are several points here; the first point is His word: ﴿ What is with you all? that you do not fight ﴾ ; this is proof that *jihad* is an obligation. The meaning is that you all have no excuse in abandoning combat. News of the situation of the Muslim men, women, and children who were weakened and oppressed travelled far in their weakness; and this is a severe exhortation to fight, and a declaration of the motive by which fighting became an obligation, this being the rescue of these Believers from the hands of the disbelievers by fighting, since this call to *jihad* was aimed at the release of the captives.

Tafsir Al-Razi

﴿ وإجعل لنا من لدنك نصيراً ﴾ أي من يمنع العدو عنا فإستجاب الله دعوتهم فلما فتح رسول الله ﷺ مكة ولّى عليهم عتاب بن أسيد وجعله الله لهم نصيراً ينصف المظلومين من الظالمين

تفسير البغوي

{ And give us a champion who comes from you } : that is, someone who will keep the enemy away from us. And Allah heard their supplication, and when the Messenger of Allah (SAW) conquered Mecca, He made 'Attab ibn Usaid guardian over them, and Allah made him a champion for them, establishing the rights of the oppressed in the face of the oppressors.

Tafsir Al-Baghawi

* * *

﴿ الذين آمنوا يقاتلون في سبيل الله والذين كفروا يقاتلون في سبيل الطاغوت فقاتلوا أولياء الشيطان إن كيد الشيطان كان ضعيفاً ﴾ النساء ٧٦

{ Those who have believed fight in the cause of Allah, but those who have disbelieved fight in the cause of idols, so fight against the associates of Satan; indeed the guiles of Satan are weak }
Al-nisaa 76

﴿ الذين آمنوا يقاتلون في سبيل الله ﴾ أي في طاعته ﴿ والذين كفروا يقاتلون في سبيل الشيطان ﴾ أي في طاعة الشيطان ﴿ فقاتلوا ﴾ أيها المؤمنون ﴿ أولياء الشيطان ﴾ أي حزبه وجنوده وهم الكفار

تفسير ابن كثير

{ Those who have believed fight in the cause of Allah } : that is, in obedience to Him; { but those who have disbelieved fight in the cause of Satan } : that is, in obedience to Satan; { so fight } : oh Believers! { against the associates of Satan } : that is, his party and his troops, these being the disbelievers [*kuffar*].

Tafsir Ibn Kathir

﴿ وإن كيد الشيطان كان ضعيفاً ﴾ يعني بكيده ما كاد به المؤمنين من تحزيبه أولياءه من الكفار بالله على رسوله وأوليائه أهل الإيمان به يقول فلا تهابوا أولياء الشيطان فإنما هم حزبه وأنصاره وحزب الشيطان أهل وهن وضعف وإنما وصفهم جل ثناؤه بالضعف لأنهم لا يقاتلون رجاء ثواب ولا يتركون القتال خوف عقاب وإنما يقاتلون حميّة أو حسداً للمؤمنين على ما آتاهم الله من فضله والمؤمنون يقاتل من قاتل منهم رجاء العظيم من ثواب الله ويترك القتال إن ترك على خوف من وعيد الله في تركه فهو يقاتل على بصيرة بما له عند الله إن قتل وبما له من الغنيمة والظفر إن سلم والكافر يقاتل على حذر من القتل وإياس من معاد فهو ذو ضعف وخوف

تفسير الطبري

{ Indeed the guiles of Satan are weak } : that is, how he schemes against the Believers by rallying his associates – from among the disbelievers in Allah – against His Messenger and his associates, those who believe in Him. He is saying: Do not be scared of the associates of Satan, for truly they are his party and his helpers, and the party of Satan are a people of frailty and weakness. Indeed He (may His praise be exalted) describes them as weak because they do not fight in the hope of a reward, nor do they fear punishment if they neglect fighting. Indeed they fight out of fervor or envy towards the Believers for what Allah will bring them of His bounty, while the Believers – any one of them who fights, fights in the hope of the greatness of Allah's reward, and neglects fighting, if he neglects it, with the fear of Allah's threat for neglecting it. He fights well-aware of what is his from Allah if he is killed, and the spoils and triumph that are his if he makes it out safely. However, a disbeliever [*kafir*] fights on guard against getting killed, desperate about the hereafter, and so he is a person of weakness and fear.

Tafsir Al-Tabari

واعلم أنه تعالى لما بين وجوب الجهاد بين أنه لا عبرة بصورة الجهاد بل العبرة بالقصد والداعي فالمؤمنون يقاتلون لغرض نصرة دين الله وإعلاء كلمته والكافرون يقاتلون في سبيل الطاغوت وهذه الآية كالدلالة على أن كل من كان غرضه في فعله رضا غير الله فهو في سبيل الطاغوت

تفسير الرازي

Know that the Most High, when He made it clear that *jihad* is an obligation, made it clear that the manner of *jihad* is of no consequence, rather what matters is the intent and the cause. For the Believers fight with the goal of supporting Allah's religion [*deen*] and raising up His word, while the disbelievers fight in the cause of idols. This verse is an indication that whoever does what he does with the goal of satisfying any other besides Allah, he is in the cause of idols.

Tafsir Al-Razi

قوله تعالى ﴿ يقاتلون في سبيل الطاغوت ﴾ الطاغوت هاهنا الشيطان وقال أبو عبيدة الطاغوت هاهنا في معنى جماعة كقوله ﴿ ولحم الخنزير ﴾ معناه ولحم الخنازير

تفسير إبن الجوزي

The word of the Most High: { Fight in the cause of idols } : "idols" [*taghut*] here refers to Satan. Abu 'Ubaida said: "Taghut" here refers to a group, just as in His word: { pig meat } , which means the meat of pigs collectively.

Tafsir Ibn Al-Jawzi

عن إبن عباس قال إذا رأيتم الشيطان فلا تخافوه واحملوا عليه ﴿ إن كيد الشيطان كان ضعيفاً ﴾ قال مجاهد كان الشيطان يتراءى لي في الصلاة فكنت أذكر قول إبن عباس فأحمل عليه فيذهب عني

الدر المنثور للسيوطي

From Ibn 'Abbas, who said: Whenever you all see Satan, do not fear him, but assert this over him: { Indeed the guiles of Satan are weak } . Mujahid said: Satan showed himself to me during prayer, and I remembered what Ibn 'Abbas said, and I asserted this over him, and he left me.

Al-Suyuti, Al-durr Al-manthur

* * *

﴿ أَلَمْ تَرَ إِلَى الَّذِينَ قِيلَ لَهُمْ كُفُّوا أَيْدِيَكُمْ وَأَقِيمُوا الصَّلَاةَ وَآتُوا الزَّكَاةَ فَلَمَّا كُتِبَ عَلَيْهِمُ الْقِتَالُ إِذَا فَرِيقٌ مِنْهُمْ يَخْشَوْنَ النَّاسَ كَخَشْيَةِ اللَّهِ أَوْ أَشَدَّ خَشْيَةً وَقَالُوا رَبَّنَا لِمَ كَتَبْتَ عَلَيْنَا الْقِتَالَ لَوْلَا أَخَّرْتَنَا إِلَى أَجَلٍ قَرِيبٍ قُلْ مَتَاعُ الدُّنْيَا قَلِيلٌ وَالْآخِرَةُ خَيْرٌ لِمَنِ اتَّقَى وَلَا تُظْلَمُونَ فَتِيلًا ﴾

النساء ٧٧

{ Have you not seen those to whom it was said: "Restrain your hands, and observe prayer, and give *zakat*?" Then when fighting was ordained for them, indeed a group of them feared people as they would fear Allah, or with even greater fear; and they said: Our Lord! Why have you ordained fighting for us? If only you would postpone it for us a little while. Say: The enjoyment of this world is little, but the hereafter is better for those who are devout; and you all will not be defrauded so much as a date fiber }

Al-nisaa 77

﴿ وَقَالُوا ﴾ أي جزعاً من الموت ﴿ رَبَّنَا لِمَ كَتَبْتَ عَلَيْنَا الْقِتَالَ لَوْلَا ﴾ هلاَّ ﴿ أَخَّرْتَنَا إِلَى أَجَلٍ قَرِيبٍ قُلْ ﴾ لهم ﴿ مَتَاعُ الدُّنْيَا ﴾ ما يتمتع به فيها أو الاستمتاع بها ﴿ قَلِيلٌ ﴾ آيل إلى الفناء ﴿ وَالْآخِرَةُ ﴾ أي الجنة ﴿ خَيْرٌ لِمَنِ اتَّقَى ﴾ عقاب الله بترك معصيته ﴿ وَلَا تُظْلَمُونَ ﴾ بالتاء والياء تنقصون من أعمالكم ﴿ فَتِيلًا ﴾ قدر قشرة النواة فجاهدوا

تفسير الجلالين

{ And they said } : that is, anxious about death; { Our Lord! Why have you ordained fighting for us? If only you would ... } : Why don't you ...? } postpone it for us a little while. Say: } : to them; { The enjoyment of this world } : what is enjoyed of it or enjoyment of it; { is little } : ends up perishing; { but the hereafter } : that is, *Jannah*; { is better for those who are devout } : fearing Allah's punishment, and so abandon their wrongdoing; { and you all will not be defrauded } : read with a "t" ["*you all* will not be defrauded"] or a "y" ["*they* will not be defrauded"], that is, your deeds will not be minimized; { so much as a date fiber } : the equivalent of the skin on a date pit; so wage *jihad* !

Tafsir Al-Jalalain

كان المؤمنون في إبتداء الاسلام وهم بمكة مأمورين بالصلاة والزكاة وإن لم تكن ذات النصب وكانوا مأمورين بمواساة الفقراء منهم وكانوا مأمورين بالصفح والعفو عن المشركين والصبر إلى حين وكانوا يتحرقون ويودون لو

أمروا بالقتال ليشتفوا من أعدائهم ولم يكن الحال إذ ذلك مناسباً لأسباب كثيرة منها قلة عددهم بالنسبة إلى كثرة عدد عدوهم ومنها كونهم كانوا في بلدهم وهو بلد حرام أشرف بقاع الأرض فلم يكن الأمر بالقتال فيه إبتداء كما يقال فلهذا لم يؤمر بالجهاد إلا بالمدينة لما صارت لهم دار ومنعة وأنصار ومع هذا لما أمروا بما كانوا يودونه جزع بعضهم منه وخافوا مواجهة الناس خوفاً شديداً ... ﴿ ولا تظلمون فتيلاً ﴾ أي من أعمالكم بل توفونها أتم الجزاء وهذه تسلية لهم عن الدنيا وترغيب لهم في الآخرة وتحريض لهم على الجهاد

تفسير ابن كثير

In the beginning of Islam, when the Muslims were in Mecca, they were ordered to observe prayer and give zakat; and they were ordered to support and comfort the poor among them. And they were ordered to be lenient and forgiving of the idolaters [mushrikeen], and to be forbearing with them for a time. But they had a burning desire and wished to be ordered to fight, so that they could satisfy their thirst against their enemies. However, the situation then was not expedient for many reasons, among them their small number against the large number of their enemy, as well as them being in their city, a sacred city, the most noble site on earth, and therefore the order to fight did not occur there in the beginning, as has been said. For this reason they were not ordered to wage *jihad* until they were in Medina, when they had acquired a place for themselves, capability, and helpers [*Ansar*]. In spite of all this, when they were given the order for what they had wished for, some of them became anxious about it, and were intensely afraid to face people. … { And you all will not be defrauded so much as a date fiber } : that is, from your deeds, but you will be recognized for them with the fullest reward. This was to divert their attention from this world, rouse in them a desire for the hereafter, and urge them on to *jihad*.

Tafsir Ibn Kathir

ذكر أن هذه الآية نزلت في قوم من أصحاب رسول الله ﷺ كانوا قد آمنوا به وصدّقوه قبل أن يفرض عليهم الجهاد وقد فرض عليهم الصلاة والزكاة وكانوا يسألون الله أن يفرض عليهم القتال فلما فرض عليهم القتال شقّ عليهم ذلك وقالوا ما أخبر عنهم في كتابه فتأويل قوله ﴿ ألم تر إلى الذين قيل لهم كُفُّوا أيديكم ﴾ ألم تر بقلبك يا محمد فتعلم إلى الذين قيل لهم من أصحابك حين سألوك أن تسأل ربك أن يفرض عليهم القتال ﴿ كفوا أيديكم ﴾ فأمسكوها عن قتال المشركين وحربهم

تفسير الطبري

It is mentioned that this verse came down regarding a group of the Messenger of Allah's (SAW) Companions; they had believed in him and attested to his truth before *jihad* had been made obligatory for them. Prayer and *zakat* had already been made obligatory for them, and they asked Allah to make fighting obligatory for them. But when fighting was made obligatory for them, this troubled them, and they said: He didn't say anything about them in His book. The interpretation of His word: { Have you not seen those to whom it was said: Restrain your hands } is this: Have you not seen, in your heart, oh Muhammad, so as to be aware of those of your Companions to whom it was said, when they asked you to ask your Lord to make fighting obligatory for them: { Restrain your hands } , and so they held back their hands from fighting the idolaters and waging war on them?

Tafsir Al-Tabari

﴿ قل متاع الدنيا قليلٌ ﴾ مذكور لا لأن القوم كانوا منكرين لذلك بل لأجل اسماع الله لهم هذا الكلام مما يهون على القلب أمر هذه الحياة فحينئذ يزول من قلبهم نفرة القتال وحب الحياة ويقدمون على الجهاد بقلب قوي

تفسير الرازي

{ Say: The enjoyment of this world is little } ; this is mentioned, not because people denied it, but rather for Allah to make them hear words that make the affairs of this life easy on the heart; and so at that point the aversion to fighting and love for life left their hearts, and they went forth to *jihad* with fervent hearts.

Tafsir Al-Razi

عن قتادة في الآية قال كان أناس من أصحاب النبي ﷺ وهم يومئذ بمكة قبل الهجرة يسارعون إلى القتال فقالوا للنبي ﷺ ذرنا نتخذ معاول نقاتل بها المشركين وذكر لنا أن عبد الرحمن بن عوف كان فيمن قال ذلك فنهاهم نبي الله ﷺ عن ذلك قال لم أومر بذلك فلما كانت الهجرة وأمروا بالقتال كره القوم ذلك وصنعوا فيه ما تسمعون قال الله تعالى ﴿ قل متاع الدنيا قليل والآخرة خير لمن إتقى ولا تظلمون فتيلاً ﴾

الدر المنثور للسيوطي

From Qadata, who said regarding this verse: Some people from the Prophet's (SAW) Companions, while they were in Mecca before the emigration [*hijra*], were restless to rush into fighting; they said to the Prophet (SAW): Leave us to grab some pickaxes to fight the idolaters with. It was mentioned to us that 'Abd Al-Rahman ibn 'Awf was one of those who said this. But the Prophet of Allah (SAW) forbade them; He said: I have not been ordered to do that. Then after the *hijra*, when they had now been ordered to fight, people were averse to it, and did what you all have heard about already; Allah Most High said: { Say: The enjoyment of this world is little, but the hereafter is better for those who are devout; and you all will not be defrauded so much as a date fiber } .

Al-Suyuti, Al-durr Al-manthur

﴿ فَقَاتِلْ فِي سَبِيلِ اللَّهِ لَا تُكَلَّفُ إِلَّا نَفْسَكَ وَحَرِّضِ الْمُؤْمِنِينَ عَسَى اللَّهُ أَن يَكُفَّ بَأْسَ الَّذِينَ كَفَرُوا وَاللَّهُ أَشَدُّ بَأْسًا وَأَشَدُّ تَنكِيلًا ﴾ النساء ٨٤

{ So fight in the cause of Allah; you are not held accountable except for yourself; and urge the Believers on, that perhaps Allah would hold back the might of those who have disbelieved; Allah is greater in might and more severe in making an example by punishment } *Al-nisaa 84*

﴿ فَقَاتِلْ ﴾ يا محمد ﴿ فِي سَبِيلِ اللَّهِ لَا تُكَلَّفُ إِلَّا نَفْسَكَ ﴾ فلا تهتمّ بتخلفهم عنك المعنى قاتل ولو وحدك فإنك موعود بالنصر ﴿ وَحَرِّضِ الْمُؤْمِنِينَ ﴾ حُثَّهم على القتال ورغبهم فيه ﴿ عَسَى اللَّهُ أَن يَكُفَّ بَأْسَ ﴾ حرب ﴿ الَّذِينَ كَفَرُوا وَاللَّهُ أَشَدُّ بَأْسًا ﴾ منهم ﴿ وَأَشَدُّ تَنكِيلًا ﴾ تعذيباً منهم فقال ﷺ والذي نفسي بيده لأخرجن ولو وحدي فخرج بسبعين راكباً إلى بدر الصغرى فكف الله بأس الكفار بإلقاء الرعب في قلوبهم ومنع أبي سفيان عن الخروج كما تقدم في آل عمران

تفسير الجلالين

{ So fight } : Oh Muhammad; { in the cause of Allah; you are not held accountable except for yourself } : so do not concern yourself that they have stayed behind from you; the meaning is: Fight, even if it is just yourself, for indeed you have been promised victory. { And urge the Believers on } : Stir them up to fight and rouse the desire in them; { that perhaps Allah would hold back the might } : the war; { of those who have disbelieved; Allah is greater in might } : than them; { and more severe in setting an example in punishment } : in torment, compared to them. So He (SAW) said: By Him who holds my soul, surely I will set out, even if it is just me. And He set out with seventy riders to Badr [the lesser or first battle], and Allah held back the might of the disbelievers [*kuffar*] by casting fear into their hearts and preventing Abu Sufyan from setting out, as seen earlier in *surah Al 'Imran*.

Tafsir Al-Jalalain

﴿ وَحَرِّضِ الْمُؤْمِنِينَ ﴾ على القتال إذ ما عليك في شأنهم إلا التحريض

تفسير البيضاوي

{ And urge the Believers on } : to fight; as there is nothing to concern you about them except urging them on.

Tafsir Al-Baydawi

يأمر تعالى عبده ورسوله محمداً ﷺ بأن يباشر القتال بنفسه ومن نكل عنه فلا عليه منه ... ﴿ وحرض المؤمنين ﴾ أي على القتال ورغبهم فيه وشجعهم عليه كما قال لهم ﷺ يوم بدر وهو يسوي الصفوف قوموا إلى جنة عرضها السموات والأرض وقد وردت أحاديث كثيرة في الترغيب في ذلك

تفسير ابن كثير

The Most High is ordering His servant and His Messenger Muhammad (SAW) to engage in fighting by himself, and whoever shies away from him is of no concern to him. ... { And urge the Believers on } : that is, to fight; and rouse in them the desire for it and encourage them in it, as He (SAW) said to them on the day of Badr, while putting the ranks in order: Rise up towards *Jannah*, as broad as the heavens and the earth! Many *hadiths* have been reported on this.

Tafsir Ibn Kathir

قال ابن عطية هذا ظاهر اللفظ إلا أنه لم يجيء في خبر قط أن القتال فُرض عليه دون الأمة مدّة ما فالمعنى والله أعلم أنه خطاب له في اللفظ وهو مثال ما يقال لكل واحد في خاصة نفسه أي أنت يا محمد وكل واحد من أمّتك القول ﴿ فقاتل في سبيل الله لا تكلف إلا نفسك ﴾ ولهذا ينبغي لكل مؤمن أن يجاهد ولو وحده ومن ذلك قول النبي ﷺ والله لأقاتلنهم حتى تنفرد سالِفتي

تفسير القرطبي

Ibn 'Atiyya said: This is expressed clearly, except that nothing was ever said about fighting being made an obligation for him and not for the *ummah*, for any length of time. The meaning – but Allah knows best – is that this is addressed to him as expressed, but what is said is an example for every individual regarding himself in particular, that is: You, oh Muhammad, and everyone in your *ummah* is told: { So fight in the cause of Allah; you are not held accountable except for yourself } . For this reason every Believer is to wage *jihad*, even if by himself; out of this comes what the Prophet (SAW) said: I swear by Allah indeed I will fight them until the sides of my neck come apart. [Sahih Al-Bukhari].

Tafsir Al-Qurtubi

﴿ وأشد تنكيلاً ﴾ يعني نكالاً يعني عقوبة من الكفار ولو لم يطع النبي ﷺ أحداً من الكفار لكفاه الله عز وجل

تفسير مقاتل بن سليمان

{ And more severe in making an example by punishment } : that is, in exemplary punishment, in retribution, compared to the disbelievers; even if the Prophet (SAW) did not yield to any of the disbelievers, Allah Mighty and Sublime would hold them back.

Tafsir Muqatil ibn Sulaiman

• • •

﴿ وَدُّوا لَوْ تَكْفُرُونَ كَمَا كَفَرُوا فَتَكُونُونَ سَوَاءً فَلَا تَتَّخِذُوا مِنْهُمْ أَوْلِيَاءَ حَتَّىٰ يُهَاجِرُوا فِي سَبِيلِ اللَّهِ فَإِن تَوَلَّوْا فَخُذُوهُمْ وَاقْتُلُوهُمْ حَيْثُ وَجَدتُّمُوهُمْ وَلَا تَتَّخِذُوا مِنْهُمْ وَلِيًّا وَلَا نَصِيرًا ۝ إِلَّا الَّذِينَ يَصِلُونَ إِلَىٰ قَوْمٍ بَيْنَكُمْ وَبَيْنَهُم مِّيثَاقٌ أَوْ جَاءُوكُمْ حَصِرَتْ صُدُورُهُمْ أَن يُقَاتِلُوكُمْ أَوْ يُقَاتِلُوا قَوْمَهُمْ ۚ وَلَوْ شَاءَ اللَّهُ لَسَلَّطَهُمْ عَلَيْكُمْ فَلَقَاتَلُوكُمْ ۚ فَإِنِ اعْتَزَلُوكُمْ فَلَمْ يُقَاتِلُوكُمْ وَأَلْقَوْا إِلَيْكُمُ السَّلَمَ فَمَا جَعَلَ اللَّهُ لَكُمْ عَلَيْهِمْ سَبِيلًا ۝ سَتَجِدُونَ آخَرِينَ يُرِيدُونَ أَن يَأْمَنُوكُمْ وَيَأْمَنُوا قَوْمَهُمْ كُلَّ مَا رُدُّوا إِلَى الْفِتْنَةِ أُرْكِسُوا فِيهَا فَإِن لَّمْ يَعْتَزِلُوكُمْ وَيُلْقُوا إِلَيْكُمُ السَّلَمَ وَيَكُفُّوا أَيْدِيَهُمْ فَخُذُوهُمْ وَاقْتُلُوهُمْ حَيْثُ ثَقِفْتُمُوهُمْ وَأُولَٰئِكُمْ جَعَلْنَا لَكُمْ عَلَيْهِمْ سُلْطَانًا مُّبِينًا ﴾ النساء ٨٩-٩١

﴾ They would want you all to disbelieve like they have disbelieved, so that you would be similar; but do not take associates from them until they emigrate in the cause of Allah; but if they turn away, take hold of them and kill them wherever you find them, and take neither associates nor advocates from them, except those who come to a people for which there is an agreement between you and them, or come to you with tightness in their bosoms against fighting you or fighting their people. If Allah had willed, He would have given them power over you and they would have fought you. If they withdraw from you, and do not fight you, but offer you peace, then Allah has not given you cause against them. You will find others who desire to rely on you and rely on their people; every time they are sent back into sedition, they are influenced in it; if they do not withdraw from you, and offer you peace, and hold back their hands, then take them, and kill them wherever you get to them; and these ones – We have given you manifest power over them ﴿ Al-nisaa 89-91

﴿ فَتَكُونُونَ سَوَاءً ﴾ يقول فتكونون كفاراً مثلهم وتستوون أنتم وهم في الشرك بالله ﴿ فَلَا تَتَّخِذُوا مِنْهُمْ أَوْلِيَاءَ حَتَّىٰ يُهَاجِرُوا فِي سَبِيلِ اللَّهِ ﴾ يقول حتى يخرجوا من دار الشرك ويفارقوا أهلها الذين هم بالله مشركون إلى دار الاسلام وأهلها ﴿ فِي سَبِيلِ اللَّهِ ﴾ يعني في ابتغاء دين الله وهو سبيله فيصيروا عند ذلك مثلكم ... عن السدي ﴿ فَإِن تَوَلَّوْا فَخُذُوهُمْ وَاقْتُلُوهُمْ حَيْثُ وَجَدتُّمُوهُمْ ﴾ يقول إذا أظهروا كفرهم فاقتلوهم حيث وجدتموهم

تفسير الطبري

{ So that you would be similar } ; He is saying: So that you would be disbelievers [*kuffar*] like them, and both you and them would be equal in ascribing others to Allah in worship [*shirk*]. { But do not take associates from them until they emigrate in the cause of Allah } ; He is saying: Until they set out from the land of idolatry, and separate from its people – those who idolatrize and ascribe associates to Allah [*mushrikun*] – into the land of Islam and its people. { In the cause of Allah } : that is, seeking after Allah's religion, this being His cause, and thereby become like you all. ... Al-Suddi, regarding { If they turn away, take hold of them and kill them wherever you find them } , said: Whenever they manifest their disbelief, kill them wherever you find them.

Tafsir Al-Tabari

فأنزل الله ﴿ إلا الذين يصلون إلى قوم بينكم وبينهم ميثاق ﴾ فكان من وصل اليهم كان معهم على عهدهم وهذا أنسب لسياق الكلام وفي صحيح البخاري في قصة صلح الحديبية فكان من أحب أن يدخل في صلح قريش وعهدهم ومن أحب أن يدخل في صلح محمد ﷺ وأصحابه وعهدهم وقد روي عن ابن عباس أنه قال نسخها قوله ﴿ فإذا انسلخ الأشهر الحرم فاقتلوا المشركين حيث وجدتموهم ﴾ الآية وقوله ﴿ أو جاءوكم حصرت صدورهم ﴾ الآية هؤلاء أن يقاتلوا قومهم معكم بل هم لا لكم ولا عليكم ﴿ ولو شاء الله لسلطهم عليكم فلقاتلوكم ﴾ أي من لطفه بكم أن كفهم عنكم ... ﴿ كل ما ردوا إلى الفتنة أركسوا فيها ﴾ أي انهمكوا فيها وقال السدي الفتنة ههنا الشرك وحكى ابن جرير عن مجاهد أنها نزلت في قوم من أهل مكة كانوا يأتون النبي ﷺ فيسلمون رياء ثم يرجعون الى قريش فيرتكسون في الأوثان يبتغون بذلك أن يأمنوا ههنا وههنا فأمر بقتالهم إن لم يعتزلوا ويصلحوا ولهذا قال تعالى ﴿ فإن لم يعتزلوكم ويلقوا اليكم السلم ﴾ المهادنة والصلح ﴿ وكفّوا أيديهم ﴾ أي عن القتال ﴿ فخذوهم ﴾ أسرى ﴿ واقتلوهم حيث ثقفتموهم ﴾ أي أين لقيتموهم ﴿ وأولئكم جعلنا لكم عليهم سلطاناً مبيناً ﴾ أي بيناً واضحاً

تفسير ابن كثير

So Allah sent down: { Except those who come to a people for which there is an agreement between you and them } ; whoever came to them was under covenant with them; this is most appropriate for the context of these words. In Sahih Al-Bukhari, regarding the story of the truce of Al-Hudaibiya: whoever wished to enter into truce with Quraish and make a covenant with them, fine; and whoever wished to enter into truce with Muhammad (SAW) and his Companions, and make covenant with them, fine. It is narrated from Ibn 'Abbas, who said: This is abrogated by His word: { But when the sacred months have passed, kill the Idolaters wherever you find them } and the rest of the verse [Al-tawba 5]. And His word: { Or come to you with tightness in their bosoms } and the rest of the verse: tightness against fighting their own people among you; these people are neither for you nor against you. { If Allah had willed, He would have given them power over you and they would have fought you } : that is, out of His kindness towards you, He held them back from you. ... { Every time they are sent back into sedition, they are influenced in it } : that is, they become absorbed in it. Al-Suddi said that "sedition" [*fitnah*] here is idolatry [*shirk*]. Ibn Jarir narrated from Mujahid that this came down regarding some people from Mecca, who would come to the Prophet (SAW) and pretend to yield into Islam, then return to Quraysh and fall back into idols, seeking to be safe on one side as well as on the other side. He ordered that they be fought, if they did not withdraw and make truce, which is why the Most High said: { If they do not withdraw from you, and offer you peace } : a truce and conciliation; { and hold back their hands } : from fighting; { then take them } : captives; { and kill them wherever you get to them } : that is, wherever you face them; { and these ones – we have given you manifest power over them } : that is, clear hostility.

Tafsir Ibn Kathir

﴿ كلما رُدوا إلى الفتنة ﴾ كلما دعاهم قومهم إلى قتال المسلمين ﴿ أُركِسوا فيها ﴾ قلبوا فيها أقبح قلب وأشنعه وكانوا شراً فيها من كل عدو ﴿ حيث ثقفتموهم ﴾ حيث تمكنتم منهم ﴿ سلطاناً مبيناً ﴾ حجة واضحة لظهور عداوتهم وانكشاف حالهم في الكفر والغدر وإضرارهم بأهل الاسلام أو تسلطاً ظاهراً حيث أذنا لكم في قتلهم

تفسير الزمخشري

{ Every time they are sent back into sedition } : every time their people call them to fight the Muslims; { they are influenced in it } : they are disturbed into the most indecent and hideous disturbance, and in this they are the worst of all enemies. { Wherever you get to them } : wherever it is possible for you to get to them. { Manifest power } : Clear affirmation of the disclosure of their enmity, and the revealing of their condition of disbelief and betrayal, and their harm to the people of Islam, or obvious influence, for which we have given you permission to kill them.

Tafsir Al-Zamakhshari

● ● ●

﴿ يَا أَيُّهَا الَّذِينَ آمَنُوا إِذَا ضَرَبْتُمْ فِي سَبِيلِ اللَّهِ فَتَبَيَّنُوا وَلَا تَقُولُوا لِمَنْ أَلْقَى إِلَيْكُمُ السَّلَامَ لَسْتَ مُؤْمِنًا تَبْتَغُونَ عَرَضَ الْحَيَاةِ الدُّنْيَا فَعِنْدَ اللَّهِ مَغَانِمُ كَثِيرَةٌ كَذَلِكَ كُنْتُمْ مِنْ قَبْلُ فَمَنَّ اللَّهُ عَلَيْكُمْ فَتَبَيَّنُوا إِنَّ اللَّهَ كَانَ بِمَا تَعْمَلُونَ خَبِيرًا ﴾ النساء ٩٤

{ Oh you who have believed! Whenever you set forth in the cause of Allah, examine carefully; do not say to those who offer you a greeting of peace: "You are not a Believer", desiring the fleeting gain of this worldly life; for there are abundant spoils with Allah. You were like that before, and Allah favored you; so examine carefully; indeed Allah is well aware of what you do } *Al-nisaa 94*

﴿ وَلَا تَقُولُوا لِمَنْ أَلْقَى إِلَيْكُمُ السَّلَامَ لَسْتَ مُؤْمِنًا ﴾ قَالَ قَالَ ابْنُ عَبَّاسٍ كَانَ رَجُلٌ فِي غُنَيْمَةٍ لَهُ فَلَحِقَهُ الْمُسْلِمُونَ فَقَالَ السَّلَامُ عَلَيْكُمْ فَقَتَلُوهُ وَأَخَذُوا غُنَيْمَتَهُ فَأَنْزَلَ اللَّهُ فِي ذَلِكَ إِلَى قَوْلِهِ ﴿ عَرَضَ الْحَيَاةِ الدُّنْيَا ﴾
صحيح البخاري كتاب التفسير

{ Do not say to those who offer you a greeting of peace: "You are not a Believer" } . Ibn 'Abbas said: A certain man was with a small flock of his, and the Muslims caught up with him. The man said: "Peace upon you" ["*As-salam 'alaikum*"], but they killed him anyway and took his small flock. So Allah sent this down regarding that, up until His word: { the fleeting gain of this worldly life } .

Sahih Al-Bukhari, The book of tafsir

عَنِ ابْنِ عَبَّاسٍ قَالَ مَرَّ رَجُلٌ مِنْ بَنِي سُلَيْمٍ عَلَى نَفَرٍ مِنْ أَصْحَابِ رَسُولِ اللَّهِ ﷺ وَمَعَهُ غَنَمٌ لَهُ فَسَلَّمَ عَلَيْهِمْ قَالُوا مَا سَلَّمَ عَلَيْكُمْ إِلَّا لِيَتَعَوَّذَ مِنْكُمْ فَقَامُوا وَقَتَلُوهُ وَأَخَذُوا غَنَمَهُ فَأَتَوْا بِهَا رَسُولَ اللَّهِ ﷺ فَأَنْزَلَ اللَّهُ تَعَالَى ﴿ يَا أَيُّهَا الَّذِينَ آمَنُوا إِذَا ضَرَبْتُمْ فِي سَبِيلِ اللَّهِ فَتَبَيَّنُوا وَلَا تَقُولُوا لِمَنْ أَلْقَى إِلَيْكُمُ السَّلَامَ لَسْتَ مُؤْمِنًا ﴾
جامع الترمذي كتاب التفسير

From Ibn 'Abbas, who said: A certain man from the Banu Sulaim passed by a group of the Messenger of Allah's (SAW) Companions, and he had a flock of his with him. He greeted them, but they said: He only greeted you all to keep himself safe from you. So they got up, killed him, took his flock, and brought it to the Messenger of Allah (SAW). Then Allah Most High sent down: { Oh you who have believed! Whenever you set forth in the cause of Allah, examine carefully; do not say to those who offer you a greeting of peace: "You are not a Believer" } .

Sunan Al-Tirmidhi, The book of tafsir

﴿ تبتغون ﴾ تطلبون بذلك ﴿ عرض الحياة الدنيا ﴾ متاعها من الغنيمة ﴿ فعند الله مغانم كثيرة ﴾ تغنيكم عن قتل مثله لماله ﴿ كذلك كنتم من قبل ﴾ تعصم دماؤكم وأموالكم بمجرد قولكم الشهادة ﴿ فمنّ الله عليكم ﴾ بالاشتهار بالايمان والاستقامة ﴿ فتبينوا ﴾ أن تقتلوا مؤمناً وافعلوا بالداخل في الاسلام كما فُعل بكم ﴿ إن الله كان بما تعملون خبيراً ﴾ فيجازيكم به

تفسير الجلالين

{ Desiring } : seeking by this; { the fleeting gain of this worldly life } : enjoyment of it in the form of plunder; { for there are abundant spoils with Allah } : that will free you from having to kill someone like this for his wealth. { You were like that before } : your blood and your wealth were safe by simply saying the *shahada*; { and Allah favored you } : with a reputation for your belief and integrity; { so examine carefully } : against killing any Believer or treating someone that has entered Islam as was done to you; { indeed Allah is well aware of what you do } : and He will give you what you are due.

Tafsir Al-Jalalain

وقال الحسن إن أصحاب النبي ﷺ خرجوا يطوفون فلقوا المشركين فهزموهم فشد رجل فتبعه رجل من المسلمين وأراد متاعة فلما غشيه بالسنان قال إني مسلم فكذبه ثم أوجره السنان فقتله وأخذ متاعه وكان قليلاً فرفع ذلك إلى رسول الله فقال قتلته بعدما زعم أنه مسلم فقال يا رسول الله إنما قالها متعوذاً قال فهلا شققت عن قلبه قال لم يا رسول الله قال لتنظر أصادق هو أم كاذب قال وكنت أعلم ذلك يا رسول الله قال ويلك إنك إن لم تكن تعلم ذلك انما كان يبين عنه لسانه قال فما لبث القاتل أن مات فدفن فأصبح وقد وضع إلى جنب قبره قال ثم عادوا لحفروا له وأمكنوا ودفنوه فأصبح وقد وضع إلى جنب قبره مرتين أو ثلاثاً فلما رأوا أن الأرض لا تقبله ألقوه في بعض تلك الشعاب قال وأنزل الله تعالى هذه الآية قال الحسن إن الأرض تجن من هو شر منه ولكن وعظ القوم أن لا يعودوا

اسباب النزول للواحدي

Al-Hasan said: The Prophet's (SAW) Companions went out to walk around, and they met up with some idolaters, and defeated them. One of their men ran off, and one of the Muslims followed him, wanting to get some goods. When his spear was on top of the man, the man said: Truly I am a Muslim! Truly I am a Muslim! But he did not believe him, and stabbed the spear into his mouth, killed him, and took his goods, although there was not much. This was made known to the Messenger of Allah, and He said: You killed him after he claimed to be a Muslim?! The man said: Oh Messenger of Allah, surely he only said it to protect himself. He said: Why didn't you rend his heart? The man said: Why, oh Messenger of Allah? He said: To see whether he was being truthful or lying. The man said: I knew it, oh Messenger of Allah. He said: Woe to you, surely you did not know it – indeed what he said made it clear. After this the killer did not remain around long before he died. He was buried, but in the morning he had been placed over to the side of his grave. So the people came back, dug for him again, did it well, and buried him. But in the morning he had been placed to the side of his grave, two or three more times. When they realized that the earth would not accept him, they threw him into one of the mountain passes. And Allah Most High sent down this verse. Al-Hasan said: Indeed the earth conceals people more evil than him, but this was to admonish people to not repeat this.

Al-Wahidi, Asbab Al-nuzul

﴿ إذا ضربتم في سبيل الله ﴾ يقول إذا سرتم مسيراً لله في جهاد اعدائكم ﴿ فتبينوا ﴾ يقول فتأنوا في قتل من أشكل عليكم أمره فلم تعلموا حقيقة إسلامه ولا كفره ولا تعجلوا فتقتلوا من التبس عليكم أمره ولا تقدموا على قتل أحد إلا على قتل من علمتموه يقيناً حرباً لكم ولله ولرسوله

تفسير الطبري

{ Whenever you set forth in the cause of Allah } ; He is saying: Whenever you march out on a journey for Allah in *jihad* against your enemies. { Examine carefully } ; He is saying: Consider well before killing someone whose situation might not be clear to you, for you do not know the truth about his Islam or his disbelief. Do not be hasty and kill someone whose situation is unclear, and do not proceed to kill anyone except to kill someone who you know for sure is at war with you, with Allah, and with His Messenger.

Tafsir Al-Tabari

▪ ▪ ▪

﴿ لا يَسْتَوِي الْقَاعِدُونَ مِنَ الْمُؤْمِنِينَ غَيْرُ أُولِي الضَّرَرِ وَالْمُجَاهِدُونَ فِي سَبِيلِ اللَّهِ بِأَمْوَالِهِمْ وَأَنْفُسِهِمْ فَضَّلَ اللَّهُ الْمُجَاهِدِينَ بِأَمْوَالِهِمْ وَأَنْفُسِهِمْ عَلَى الْقَاعِدِينَ دَرَجَةً وَكُلًّا وَعَدَ اللَّهُ الْحُسْنَى وَفَضَّلَ اللَّهُ الْمُجَاهِدِينَ عَلَى الْقَاعِدِينَ أَجْرًا عَظِيمًا ﴾ النساء 95

{ Those of the Believers who sit out, other than the impaired, are not on the same level as those who wage jihad in the way of Allah with their wealth and with themselves; Allah has preferred those who wage jihad with their wealth and with themselves by a degree over those who sit it out, but Allah has promised good things to both, although Allah has favored those who wage jihad by a great reward over those who sit it out } Al-nisaa 95

ولما نزلت غزوة بدر قال عبدالله بن جحش وابن مكتوم إنا أعميان يا رسول الله فهل لنا رخصة فنزلت ﴿ لا يستوي القاعدون من المؤمنين غير أولي الضرر ﴾ ... فقوله ﴿ لا يستوي القاعدون من المؤمنين ﴾ كان مطلقاً فلما نزل بوحي سريع ﴿ غير أولي الضرر ﴾ صار ذلك مخرجاً لذوي الأعذار المبيحة لترك الجهاد من العمي والعرج والمرض عن مساواتهم للمجاهدين في سبيل الله بأموالهم وأنفسهم ثم أخبر تعالى بفضيلة المجاهدين على القاعدين ... ﴿ وفضّل الله المجاهدين على القاعدين أجراً عظيماً ﴾ ثم أخبر سبحانه بما فضلهم به من الدرجات في غرف الجنات العاليات ومغفرة الذنوب والزلات وحلول الرحمة والبركات إحساناً منه وتكريماً
تفسير ابن كثير

When the attack on Badr was sent down, 'Abdullah ibn Jahsh and Ibn Maktum said: Indeed we are blind, oh Messenger of Allah, so can we be exempt? So this came down: { Those of the believers who sit out, other than the impaired, are not on the same level } ... His word: { Those of the believers who sit out are not on the same level } is a general reference, but when { other than the impaired } came down in a quick revelation, this became a way out to abandon *jihad* for those with a permissible excuse among the blind, the lame, and the sick, against being treated equally as those who wage *jihad* in the way of Allah with their wealth and with themselves. Then the Most High made known the virtue of the *Mujahideen* over those who sit out. ... { Allah has favored those who wage jihad by a great reward over those who sit it out } ; then the Exalted made known in what way He has favored them, by degrees, in the rooms of the high gardens of paradise, in forgiveness for sins and errors, and the advent of mercy and blessings in benevolence and honor.

Tafsir Ibn Kathir

عن سهل بن سعد الساعدي أنه قال رأيت مروان بن الحكم جالساً في المسجد فأقبلتُ حتى جلستُ إلى جنبه فأخبرنا أن زيد بن ثابت أخبره أن رسول الله ﷺ أملى عليه ﴿ لا يستوي القاعدون من المؤمنين والمجاهدون في سبيل الله ﴾ قال فجاءه ابن أم مكتوم وهو يُملّها عليَّ فقال يا رسول الله لو أستطيع الجهاد لجاهدتُ وكان رجلاً أعمى فأنزل الله تبارك وتعالى على رسوله ﷺ ونحذه على نحذي فثقُلت عليَّ حتى خفتُ أن ترضّ نحذي ثم سُرّي عنه فأنزل الله عز وجل ﴿ غير أولي الضرر ﴾

صحيح البخاري، كتاب الجهاد والسير

From Sahl ibn Sa'd Al-Sa'idi who said: I saw Marwan ibn Al-Hakam sitting in the mosque, so I came to sit alongside him. He told us that Zaid ibn Thabit had told him that the Messenger of Allah (SAW) dictated to him: { Those of the believers who sit out are not on the same level as those who wage *jihad* in the cause of Allah } . He said: And Ibn Umm Maktum came when He was dictating to me, and said: Oh Messenger of Allah, If I could wage *jihad* I would. (He was a blind man.) So Allah Blessed and Exalted sent down revelation to His Messenger, and His thigh was on top of mine, and it got so heavy that I was afraid it would bruise my thigh, but then the revelation was lifted from him once Allah Mighty and Sublime had sent down: { other than the impaired } .

Sahih Al-Bukhari, The book of jihad and campaigns

يعني جل ثناؤه بقوله ﴿ لا يستوي القاعدون من المؤمنين غير أولي الضرر والمجاهدون ﴾ لا يعتدل المتخلفون عن الجهاد في سبيل الله من أهل الإيمان بالله ورسوله المؤثرون الدعة والخفض والقعود في منازلهم على مقاساة حُزونة الأسفار والسير في الأرض ومشقة ملاقاة أعداء الله بجهادهم في ذات الله وقتالهم في طاعة الله إلا أهل العذر منهم بذهاب أبصارهم وغير ذلك من العلَل التي لا سبيل لأهلها للضرر الذي بهم إلى قتالهم وجهادهم في سبيل الله

تفسير الطبري

He (may His praise be exalted), by His word { Those of the believers who sit out, other than the impaired, are not on the same level } , means: Those who belong to the community who believes in Allah and His Messenger, and remain behind from *jihad* in the cause of Allah, do not act rightly – those who take a liking to being friendly, an easy life, and sitting around in their homes over enduring the distress of journeys and campaigns in the land and the hardship of facing Allah's enemies in their *jihad* for the sake of Allah and fighting in obedience to Allah – except those who have an excuse, such as having lost their vision, or other ailment, which due to the impairment they suffer have no way to take up fighting or *jihad* in the cause of Allah.

Tafsir Al-Tabari

والضرر المرض أو العاهة من عمى أو عرج أو زمانة أو نحوها وعن زيد بن ثابت كنت إلى جنب رسول الله ﷺ فغشيته السكينة فوقعت فخذه على فخذي حتى خشيت أن ترضها ثم سُرِّي عنه فقال اكتب فكتبت في كتف

تفسير الزمخشري

"Impairment" is sickness or disabling blindness, lameness, chronic illness, or similar. Zaid ibn Thabit said: I was next to the Messenger of Allah (SAW), and the divine serenity [*sakinah*] came upon him, and his thigh fell upon mine to the point that I feared it would bruise it. Then the revelation was lifted from him, and He said: Write. So I wrote it on a shoulder blade.

Tafsir Al-Zamakhshari

قال الشافعية دلت الأية على أن الإشتغال بالنوافل أفضل من الإشتغال بالنكاح لأن من أقام بالجهاد سقط الفرض عن الباقين فلو أُقيموا عليه كان من النوافل والآية تقتضي تفضيل جميع المجاهدين من مفترض ومن متنفّل على القاعدين والمتنفل بالنكاح قاعد عن الجهاد فثبت أن الإشتغال بالمندوب إليه من الجهاد أفضل من الإشتغال بالنكاح

اللباب في علوم الكتاب لإبن عادل سورة ألنساء فصل الإشتغال بالنوافل أفضل من النكاح

Those of the Shafi'i school have said: This verse substantiates that striving in the supererogatory deeds [*nawafil*; i.e. above and beyond the obligatory] is better than striving in marital relations [*nikah*], because for someone who takes up *jihad*, the remaining obligations are lifted, and even if he were obliged to take it up, it would still count as among the *nawafil*. The verse implies the preferentiality of all *Mujahideen*, whether those who are obliged or those who make the extra effort, over those who sit around; someone who strives in marital relations is still sitting out from *jihad*. It is therefore affirmed that the striving of someone sent out in *jihad* is better than striving in marital relations.

Ibn 'Adil, Al-lubab fi 'Ulum Al-kitab, Surah Al-nisaa, Section: effort in the supererogatory deeds [nawafil] is better than marital relations

قال العلماء أهل الضرر هم أهل الأعذار إذ قد أضرّت بهم حتى منعتهم الجهاد وصح وثبت في الخبر أنه عليه السلام قال قد قفل من بعض غزواته إن بالمدينة رجالاً ما قطعتم وادياً ولا سرتم مسيراً إلا كانوا معكم أولئك قوم حبسهم العذر فهذا يقتضي أن صاحب العذر يعطى أجر الغازي فقيل يحتمل أن يكون أجره مساوياً وفي فضل الله متّسع وثوابه فضل لا إستحقاق فيثيب على النية الصادقة ما لا يثبت على الفعل

تفسير القرطبي

The scholars say: Those who are impaired are those who have an excuse, as it impaires them to the point of preventing them from *jihad*. It is sound and affirmed regarding this statement that He (peace be upon him), as He was returning from one of his raids, said: Indeed in Medina there are some men, that everytime you all crossed through a valley or headed out to advance, those people were with you, this group whose excuses hindered them. And this implies that whoever has an excuse is given the reward of a fighter; it is said: It is possible that his reward is equivalent, for in Allah's bounty there is ample space, and His reward is an unmerited bounty; He rewards for sincere intention what is not affirmed by works.

Tafsir Al-Qurtubi

• • •

﴿ وَإِذَا ضَرَبْتُمْ فِي الْأَرْضِ فَلَيْسَ عَلَيْكُمْ جُنَاحٌ أَن تَقْصُرُوا مِنَ الصَّلَاةِ إِنْ خِفْتُمْ أَن يَفْتِنَكُمُ الَّذِينَ كَفَرُوا إِنَّ الْكَافِرِينَ كَانُوا لَكُمْ عَدُوًّا مُبِينًا وَإِذَا كُنتَ فِيهِمْ فَأَقَمْتَ لَهُمُ الصَّلَاةَ فَلْتَقُمْ طَائِفَةٌ مِنْهُم مَّعَكَ وَلْيَأْخُذُوا أَسْلِحَتَهُمْ فَإِذَا سَجَدُوا فَلْيَكُونُوا مِن وَرَائِكُمْ وَلْتَأْتِ طَائِفَةٌ أُخْرَىٰ لَمْ يُصَلُّوا فَلْيُصَلُّوا مَعَكَ وَلْيَأْخُذُوا حِذْرَهُمْ وَأَسْلِحَتَهُمْ وَدَّ الَّذِينَ كَفَرُوا لَوْ تَغْفُلُونَ عَنْ أَسْلِحَتِكُمْ وَأَمْتِعَتِكُمْ فَيَمِيلُونَ عَلَيْكُم مَيْلَةً وَاحِدَةً وَلَا جُنَاحَ عَلَيْكُمْ إِن كَانَ بِكُمْ أَذًى مِن مَطَرٍ أَوْ كُنتُم مَّرْضَىٰ أَن تَضَعُوا أَسْلِحَتَكُمْ وَخُذُوا حِذْرَكُمْ إِنَّ اللَّهَ أَعَدَّ لِلْكَافِرِينَ عَذَابًا مُهِينًا فَإِذَا قَضَيْتُمُ الصَّلَاةَ فَاذْكُرُوا اللَّهَ قِيَامًا وَقُعُودًا وَعَلَىٰ جُنُوبِكُمْ فَإِذَا اطْمَأْنَنتُمْ فَأَقِيمُوا الصَّلَاةَ إِنَّ الصَّلَاةَ كَانَتْ عَلَى الْمُؤْمِنِينَ كِتَابًا مَوْقُوتًا ﴾ النساء ١٠١-١٠٣

﴿ Whenever you set out in the land, there is no fault on you for shortening prayer, if you fear that those who have disbelieved might entice you; indeed the disbelievers are a clear enemy to you. And whenever you are among the people, and observe prayer for them, let a group observe with you, and take hold of their weapons. And when they prostrate, let them be behind you all, and let another group, who has not yet prayed, pray with you, and let them be on guard and take hold of their weapons. Those who have disbelieved would like you to overlook your weapons and your goods, so they can come down on you in a single swoop. And there is no fault on you, if you are bothered by rain or you are sick, to lay down your weapons; but be on guard; indeed Allah has prepared a humiliating punishment for the disbelievers. And when you have fulfilled the prayer, make remembrance of Allah, standing, sitting, or on your sides; and when you are at ease, observe prayer; indeed prayer is a decree for the Believers at appointed times } *Al-nisaa 101-103*

ثم أخبرهم جل ثناؤه عما عليه أهل الكفر لهم فقال ﴿ إن الكافرين كانوا لكم عدواً مبيناً ﴾ يعني الجاحدون وحدانية الله كانوا لكم عدواً مبيناً يقول عدواً قد أبانوا لكم عداوتهم بمناصبتهم لكم الحرب على إيمانكم بالله وبرسوله وتركم عبادة ما يعبدون من الأوثان والأصنام ومخالفتكم ما هم عليه من الضلالة

تفسير الطبري

Then He (may His praise be exalted) made known to them the situation of the disbelievers with regards to them; He said: { Indeed the disbelievers are a clear enemy to you } , meaning those who repudiate the oneness of Allah are a clear enemy to you. He is saying: An enemy who has clearly showed their enmity to you by their hostility towards you in war because you believe in Allah and in His Messenger, you abandon the idols and images that they worship, and you oppose the delusion that they are in.

Tafsir Al-Tabari

﴿ لا جُناح عليكم إن كان بكم أذى من مطر أو كنتم مرضى أن تضعوا أسلحتكم ﴾ فلا تحملوها وهذا يفيد إيجاب حملها عند عدم العذر وهو أحد قولين للشافعي والثاني أنه سنة ورُجِّح ﴿ وخذوا حذركم ﴾ من العدو أي احترزوا منه ما استطعتم

تفسير الجلالين

{ There is no fault on you, if you are bothered by rain or you are sick, to lay down your weapons } : and not carry them. This makes known the obligation to carry them when there is no excuse, and this is one of two viewpoints of Al-Shafi'i; the second is that this is *sunnah*, and this has greater weight. { But be on guard } : against your enemy, that is, watch out for them as best you can.

Tafsir Al-Jalalain

﴿ ودّ الذين كفروا لو تغفُلون عن أسلحتِكم وأمتِعتِكم فيميلون عليكم ميلة واحدة ﴾ تمنوا أن ينالوا منكم غِرّة في صلاتِكم فيشدون عليكم شدة واحدة وهو بيان ما لأجله أمروا بأخذ الحذر والسلاح

تفسير البيضاوي

{ Those who have disbelieved would like you to overlook your weapons and your goods, so they can come down on you in a single swoop } : they would like to find you oblivious in your prayers, so that they can launch a single attack on you. This makes it clear why people were ordered to take hold of precaution as well as weapons.

Tafsir Al-Baydawi

وإختلف العلماء كيف ينصرفون بعض السجود فقال قوم إذا أتموا مع الامام ركعةً أتموا لأنفسِهم ركعة ثم سلموا وانصرفوا وقد تمت صلاتهم وقال آخرون ينصرفون عن ركعة وإختلف هؤلاء فقال بعضهم إذا صلوا مع الامام ركعة وسلموا فهي تجزئهم وقال آخرون منهم أبو حنيفة بل ينصرفون عن تلك الركعة إلى الحرَس وهو على صلاتهم فيكونون في وجه العدو مكان الطائفة الاخرى التي لم تصل وتأتي تلك طائفة

تفسير إبن الجوزي

Scholars differ – How should people depart from the position of prostration? A group of them say that whenever people complete one prostration with the *imam*, they should complete one prostration for themselves, and they can say the concluding portion [*tasleem*, "As-salam 'alaikum wa-rahmatullah"], depart, and their prayer is complete. Others say they can depart after one prostration, although this group differed: some of them say that if they pray one prostration with the *imam* and say *taslim*, this is profitable for them, while others, including Abu Hanifa, say that they should instead depart from that prostration to assuming the patrol, while still in prayer, so as to face the enemy in the place of the other group that has not yet prayed, and this group can now come.

Tafsir Ibn Al-Jawzi

﴿ إن الله أعد للكافرين عذاباً مهيناً ﴾ يعني الهوان

تفسير مقاتل بن سليمان

{ Indeed Allah has prepared a humiliating punishment for the disbelievers } : that is, disgrace.

Tafsir Muqatil ibn Sulaiman

صلاة الخوف أنواع كثيرة فإن العدو تارةً يكون تجاه القبلة وتارة يكون في غير صوبها والصلاة تارة تكون رُباعية وتارة تكون ثلاثية كالمغرب وتارة تكون ثنائية كالصبح وصلاة السفر ثم تارة يصلون جماعة وتارة يلتحم الحرب فلا يقدرون على الجماعة بل يصلون فرادى مستقبلي القبلة وغير مستقبليها ورجالاً وركباناً ولهم أن يمشوا والحالة هذه ويضربوا الضرب المتتابع في متن الصلاة ... ﴿ وإذا كنتَ فيهم فأقمتَ لهم الصلاة ﴾ أي إذا صليت بهم إماماً في صلاة الخوف ..... يأمر الله تعالى بكثرة الذكر عقيب صلاة الخوف وإن كان مشروعاً مرغباً فيه أيضاً بعض غيرها ولكن ههنا آكد لما وقع فيها من التخفيف في اركانها ومن الرخصة في الذهاب فيها والإياب وغير ذلك مما ليس يوجد في غيرها

تفسير ابن كثير

There are many kinds of fear prayer [salat al-khawf], for indeed at times the enemy is facing the Qibla, and at times they are in another direction. Prayer at times may be four prostrations [rak'a], at times three prostrations like the maghrib prayer, at times two prostrations like the subh prayer and travel prayer. So then at times the people may pray as a group, but at times they may be in the middle of battle and unable to pray as a group, in which case they may pray separately, facing the Qibla or not facing it, on foot or riding. They may, in such a situation, advance and engage in ongoing combat, observing the guidelines of prayer. ... } And whenever you are among the people, and observe prayer for them { : that is, whenever you lead them in prayer as the imam in the fear prayer. ... Allah Most High ordered an abundance of remembrance [dhikr] following the fear prayer, even though this is prescribed and desirable for other prayers as well. Here, however, it is even more asserted, due to the relaxing of the foundations of prayer that occurs here, the license to come and go while observing it, and other things that are not found in other prayers.

Tafsir Ibn Kathir

﴿ وَلَا تَهِنُوا فِي ابْتِغَاءِ الْقَوْمِ إِن تَكُونُوا تَأْلَمُونَ فَإِنَّهُمْ يَأْلَمُونَ كَمَا تَأْلَمُونَ وَتَرْجُونَ مِنَ اللَّهِ مَا لَا يَرْجُونَ وَكَانَ اللَّهُ عَلِيمًا حَكِيمًا ﴾ النساء ١٠٤

{ And do not grow weary in pursuing people; if you all are in pain, indeed they are in pain as you are in pain; but you hope from Allah what they do not hope for; and Allah is knowing, wise } Al-nisaa 104

ونزل لما بعث ﷺ طائفة في طلب أبي سفيان وأصحابه لما رجع من أحد فشكوا الجراحات ﴿ ولا تهنوا ﴾ تضعفوا ﴿ في ابتغاء ﴾ طلب ﴿ القوم ﴾ الكفار لتقاتلوهم ﴿ إن تكونوا تألمون ﴾ تجدون ألم الجراح ﴿ فإنهم يألمون كما تألمون ﴾ أي مثلكم ولا يجبنون عن قتالكم ﴿ وترجون ﴾ أنتم ﴿ من الله ﴾ من النصر والثواب عليه ﴿ ما لا يرجون ﴾ هم فأنتم تزيدون عليهم بذلك فينبغي أن تكونوا أرغب منهم فيه ﴿ وكان الله عليماً ﴾ بكل شيء ﴿ حكيماً ﴾ في صنعه

تفسير الجلالين

This came down when He (SAW) sent out a group to search for Abu Sufyan and his companions after they had returned from Uhud and were complaining about their injuries. { And do not grow weary } : do not grow weak; { in pursuing } : seeking out; { people } : the disbelievers [*kuffar*], so you can fight them; { if you all are in pain } : faced with the pain of injuries; { indeed they are in pain as you are in pain } : that is, just like you, but they do not shrink back from fighting you; { but you hope } : you all; { from Allah } : victory, and the reward in it; { what they do not hope for } : they, but you are superior to them in this, so you ought to be more eager than them for it; { and Allah is knowing } : of everything; { wise } : in what He does.

Tafsir Al-Jalalain

﴿ ولا تهنوا في ابتغاء القوم ﴾ أي لا تضعفوا في طلب عدوكم بل جدوا فيهم وقاتلوهم واقعدوا لهم كل مرصد

تفسير ابن كثير

{ And do not grow weary in pursuing people } : that is, do not grow weak in seeking out your enemy, but rather make every effort regarding them, and fight them, and sit in wait for them at every place of ambush.

Tafsir Ibn Kathir

اعلم أنه تعالى لما ذكر بعض الأحكام التي يحتاج المجاهد إلى معرفتها عاد مرة أخرى إلى الحث على الجهاد فقال ﴿ ولا تهنوا ﴾

تفسير للفيروز آبادي

Know that when the Most High mentioned some of the rulings of which a *Mujahid* needs to be aware, He once again reiterates the exhortation to wage *jihad*, saying: { And do not grow weary } .

Tafsir Fairuz Abadi

قوله ﴿ في ابتغاء القوم ﴾ يعني في إلتماس القوم وطلبهم والقوم هم أعداء الله وأعداء المؤمنين من أهل الشرك بالله

تفسير الطبري

His word: { in pursuing people } means: in searching for people and seeking them out; "people" are the enemies of Allah and the enemies of the Believers, those who have ascribed associates to Allah.

Tafsir Al-Tabari

﴿ إن تكونوا تألمون ﴾ أي ليس ما تكابدون من الألم بالجرح والقتل مختصاً بكم إنما هو أمر مشترك بينكم وبينهم يصيبهم كما يصيبكم ثم إنهم يصبرون عليه ويتشجعون فما لكم لا تصبرون مثل صبرهم مع أنكم أولى منهم بالصبر لأنكم ﴿ ترجون من الله ما لا يرجون ﴾ من إظهار دينكم على سائر الأديان ومن الثواب العظيم في الآخرة

تفسير الزمخشري

{ If you all are in pain } : that is, the pain from injuries and killing that you suffer is not relevant only to you; indeed this is something shared between you and them – it happens to them just like it happens to you. Then indeed they were steadfast through it and were emboldened, so what is with you all that you are not steadfast like they are?! However you ought to be that much more steadfast than them, because { you hope from Allah what they do not hope for } : of your religion being manifest over other religions, and of the great reward in the hereafter.

Tafsir Al-Zamakhshari

فأنتم أيها المؤمنون المقرون بأن لكم في هذا الجهاد ثواباً عظيماً وعليكم في تركه عقاباً عظيماً أولى بأن تكونوا مجدين في هذا الجهاد وهو المراد من قوله تعالى ﴿ وترجون من الله ما لا يرجون ﴾

تفسير الرازي

And you – oh Believers who confess that in *jihad* is a great reward for you, and that in neglecting it is a great punishment – you should be that much more serious in *jihad*. This is the intended meaning of the word of the Most High: { You hope from Allah what they do not hope for } .

Tafsir Al-Razi

عن السدي في الآية قال ... ﴿ وترجون من الله ﴾ يعني الحياة والرزق والشهادة والظفر في الدنيا

الدر المنثور للسيوطي

Al-Suddi said regarding this verse: ... { And you hope from Allah } : that is, life, bountiful favor, martyrdom, and triumph in this world.

Al-Suyuti, Al-durr Al-manthur

﴿ ولا تهنوا في ابتغاء القوم ﴾ يقول لا تضعفوا في ابتغاء القوم أي في طلب المشركين أبي سفيان وأصحابه بعد يوم أحد وذلك أن المسلمين لما أصابتهم الجراحات يوم أحد وكانوا يضعفون عن الخروج إلى الجهاد فأمرهم الله تعالى بأن يظهروا من أنفسهم الجد والقوة وهذا الخطاب لهم ولجميع المسلمين الغزاة إلى يوم القيامة

بحر العلوم للسمرقندي

{ And do not grow weary in pursuing people } ; He is saying: Do not grow weak in pursuing people, that is, regarding Abu Sufyan and his companions seeking out the Idolaters after the day of Uhud. This was when the Muslims received injuries on the day of Uhud and grew too weak to go out and wage *jihad*, Allah Most High ordered them to bring out earnestness and valor in themselves. This was addressed to them and to all Muslim fighters until resurrection day.

Al-Samarqandi, Bahr Al-'ulum

Surah 5   Al-ma'ida [The Tablespread]

$$\text{بسم الله الرحمن الرحيم إِنَّمَا جَزَاءُ الَّذِينَ يُحَارِبُونَ اللَّهَ وَرَسُولَهُ وَيَسْعَوْنَ فِي الْأَرْضِ فَسَادًا أَن يُقَتَّلُوا أَوْ يُصَلَّبُوا أَوْ تُقَطَّعَ أَيْدِيهِمْ وَأَرْجُلُهُم مِّنْ خِلَافٍ أَوْ يُنفَوْا مِنَ الْأَرْضِ ۚ ذَٰلِكَ لَهُمْ خِزْيٌ فِي الدُّنْيَا ۖ وَلَهُمْ فِي الْآخِرَةِ عَذَابٌ عَظِيمٌ ۝ إِلَّا الَّذِينَ تَابُوا مِن قَبْلِ أَن تَقْدِرُوا عَلَيْهِمْ ۖ فَاعْلَمُوا أَنَّ اللَّهَ غَفُورٌ رَّحِيمٌ ۝}$$

المائدة ٣٣-٣٤

} Indeed the recompense of those who war against Allah and His Messenger, and who intend corruption in the land, is that they be slaughtered, or crucified, or their hands and feet cut off on opposite sides, or they be banished from the land; this is their disgrace in this world, and in the hereafter theirs is a great punishment; except those who repent before you take hold of them; and know that Allah is forgiving, merciful } Al-ma'ida 33-34

عن أنس بن مالك رضي الله عنه أن رَهطاً من عُكل ثمانية قدموا على النبي ﷺ فاجتووا المدينة فقالوا يا رسول الله ابغنا رِسْلاً قال ما أجد لكم إلا أن تلحقوا بالذَّود فانطلقوا فشربوا من أبوالها وألبانها حتى صحّوا وسَمِنوا وقتلوا الراعي وإستاقوا الذود وكفروا بعد إسلامهم فأتى الصَّريخ النبي ﷺ فبعث الطلب فما ترجَّل النهار حتى أتي بهم فقطَّع أيديهم وأرجلهم ثم أمر بمسامير فأُحميَت فكحلهم بها وطرحهم بالحرّة يستسقون فما يُسقون حتى ماتوا قال أبو قلابة قتلوا وسرقوا وحاربوا الله ورسوله ﷺ وسعوا في الأرض فساداً

صحيح البخاري كتاب الجهاد والسير

Anas ibn Malik (may Allah be pleased with him) related that a group of eight people from 'Ukl came to where the Prophet (SAW) was, but they found staying in Medina disagreeable, and said: Oh Messenger of Allah, ask some milk for us. He said: You all should just go catch up with the camel herd. So they set off, and drank the camels' urine and milk until they became healthy and put on weight. Then they killed the herdsman, led the herd off, and disbelieved after having been in Islam. Someone cried out and came to the Prophet (SAW) for help, and He sent out a group in pursuit, and the sun had not yet risen by the time they came back with them. He chopped off their hands and their feet, then ordered for some nails, which were heated and smeared over their eyes like eyeliner. And He threw them out into the rocky landscape; they asked for a drink of water but were given none until they died. Abu Qilaba said: Those men killed, stole, warred against Allah and His Messenger (SAW), and intended corruption [*fasad*] in the land.

Sahih Al-Bukhari, The book of jihad and campaigns

ونزل في العرنيين لما قدموا المدينة وهم مرضى فأذن لهم النبي ﷺ أن يخرجوا إلى الإبل ويشربوا من أبوالها وألبانها فلما صحوا قتلوا راعي النبي ﷺ وإستاقوا الإبل ﴿ إنما جزاء الذين يحاربون الله ورسوله ﴾ بمحاربة المسلمين ﴿ ويسعون في الأرض فساداً ﴾ بقطع الطريق ﴿ أن يقتّلوا أو يصلّبوا أو تقطّع أيديهم وأرجلهم من خلاف ﴾ أي أيديهم اليمنى وأرجلهم اليسرى ﴿ أو يُنفوا من الأرض ﴾ أو لترتيب الأحوال فالقتل لمن قتل فقط والصلب لمن قتل وأخذ المال والقطع لمن أخذ ولم يقتل والنفي لمن أخاف فقط قاله ابن عباس وعليه الشافعي وأصح قوليه أن الصلب ثلاثاً بعد القتل وقيل قبله قليلاً ويلحق بالنفي أشبهه في التنكيل من الحبس وغيره ﴿ ذلك ﴾ الجزاء المذكور ﴿ لهم خزيٌ ﴾ ذلّ ﴿ في الدنيا ولهم في الآخرة عذاب عظيم ﴾ هو عذاب النار

تفسير الجلالين

This came down regarding the people from 'Uraynah when they came to Medina, and they were sick, and the Prophet (SAW) gave them permission to go out to the camels and drink their urine and their milk. When they were back in good health, they killed the Prophet's (SAW) herdsman and led the camels off. { Indeed the recompense of those who war against Allah and His Messenger } : by contending against the Muslims; { and who intend corruption in the land } : by impeding travel; { is that they be slaughtered, or crucified, or their hands and feet cut off on opposite sides } : that is, their right hands and their left feet; { or they be banished from the land } . The "or" is to arrange each situation: killing for those who have only killed, crucifixion for those who have killed and taken, dismemberment for those who have taken but have not killed, and banishment for those who are only cause for alarm. Ibn 'Abbas said this, and Al-Shafi'i held the same view; the more correct of his two viewpoints is that crucifiction is to be three days after killing, although some have said shortly before it. Similar exemplary punishments are connected with banishment, such as imprisonment and otherwise. { This } : the stated recompense; { is their disgrace } : humiliation; { in this world, and in the hereafter theirs is a great punishment } : this being the punishment of fire.

Tafsir Al-Jalalain

عن أنس ... فقتلوا راعي رسول الله ﷺ وإستاقوا الذود وكفروا بعد إسلامهم فأتي النبي ﷺ فقطع أيديهم وأرجلهم وسمل أعينهم وتركهم في الحرّة حتى ماتوا فذكر لنا أن هذه الآية نزلت فيهم ﴿ إنما جزاء الذين يحاربون الله ورسوله ﴾ ... حدثنا محمد بن علي بن الحسن بن شقيق قال سمعت أبي يقول أخبرنا أبو حمزة عن عبد الكريم وسئل عن أبوال الإبل فقال حدثني سعيد بن جبير عن المحاربين فقال كان ناس أتوا النبي ﷺ

فقالوا نبايعك عن الاسلام فبايعوه وهم كذبة وليس الاسلام يريدون ثم قالوا إنا نجتوي المدينة فقال النبي ﷺ هذه اللقاح تغدو عليكم وتروح فاشربوا من أبوالها وألبانها قال فبينا هم كذلك إذ جاء الصريخ فصرخ إلى رسول الله ﷺ فقال قتلوا الراعي وساقوا النَّعَم فأمر نبي الله فنودي في الناس أن يا خيل الله اركبي قال فركبوا لا ينتظر فارس فارساً قال فركب رسول الله على أثرهم فلم يزالوا يطلبونهم حتى أدخلوهم مأمنهم فرجع صحابة رسول الله ﷺ وقد أسروا منهم فأتوا بهم النبي ﷺ فأنزل الله ﴿ إنما جزاء الذين يحاربون الله ورسوله ﴾ الآية قال فكان نفيهم أن نفوهم حتى أدخلوهم مأمنهم وأرضهم ونفوهم من أرض المسلمين وقتل نبي الله منهم وصلب وقطع وسمل الأعين قال فما مثَّل رسول الله ﷺ قبل ولا بعد قال ونهى عن المُثْلة وقال لا تمثلوا بشيءٍ قال فكان أنس بن مالك يقول ذلك غير أنه قال أحرقهم بالنار بعد ما قتلهم قال وبعضهم يقول هم ناس من بني سليم ومنهم من عرينة وناس من بجيلة

تفسير الطبري

From Anas ... and they killed the Messenger of Allah's (SAW) herdsman and led the herd away, and disbelieved after they had been in Islam. So they were brought to the Prophet (SAW), and He cut off their hands and feet, gouged out their eyes, and left them out in the rocky landscape until they died. It was mentioned to us that this verse came down regarding them: { Indeed the recompense of those who war against Allah and His Messenger } ... Muhammad ibn 'Ali ibn Al-Hasan ibn Shaqiq related to us and said: I heard my father say: Abu Hamza related to us from 'Abd Al-Karim when he was asked about camel urine; he said: Sa'id ibn Jubair related to me regarding those who war; he said: These were some people who came to the Prophet (SAW) and said: We pledge Islam to you. And they pledged, but they were lying; they did not desire Islam. Then they said: Indeed conditions are hard for us to stay in Medina. The Prophet (SAW) said: The milking camels come and go around you – drink some of their urine and their milk. He [the narrator] said: While they were doing that, the crier came and cried out to the Messenger of Allah (SAW); he said: They have killed the herdsman and stolen the livestock! So the Prophet of Allah gave the order and we called out to the people: Oh steeds of Allah, ride! So they raced off riding, with no horseman even waiting for another; and the Messenger of Allah rode behind them. They did not stop searching for the men until they had gotten them into a secure place. Then the Messenger of Allah's (SAW) companions returned, having captured them, and brought them to the Prophet (SAW). And Allah sent down: { Indeed the recompense of those who war against Allah and His Messenger } and the rest of the verse. Their banishment was that they banished them to a secure place and their own land; so they banished them from the land of the Muslims. But the Prophet of Allah killed some of them, and crucified, and cut off, and gouged out eyes. However the Messenger of Allah (SAW) did not mutilate before or after this. He prohibited mutilation [*muthla*], and said: Do not mutilate by any means. Anas ibn Malik said this, except that he said He burned them with fire after He killed them. Some said these were people from the Banu Sulaim, some from 'Urainah, and some people from Bajilah.

Tafsir Al-Tabari

وفي رواية قال أنس فلقد رأيت أحدهم يكدم الأرض بفيه عطشاً حتى ماتوا وفي البخاري قال جرير بن عبدالله في حديثه فبعثني رسول الله ﷺ في نفر من المسلمين حتى أدركناهم وقد أشرفوا على بلادهم فجئنا بهم إلى رسول الله ﷺ قال جرير فكانوا يقولون الماء ويقول رسول الله ﷺ النار وقد حكى أهل التواريخ والسِّير أنهم قطعوا يدي الراعي ورجليه وغرزوا الشوك في عينيه حتى مات وأُدخل المدينة ميتاً وكان إسمه يسار وكان نوبياً وكان هذا الفعل من المرتدين سنة ست من الهجرة وفي بعض الروايات عن أنس أن رسول الله ﷺ أحرقهم بالنار بعد ما قتلهم ... والمرتد يستحق القتل بنفس الردة دون المحاربة ولا يُنفى ولا تُقطع يده ولا رجله ولا يُخلَّى سبيله بل يقتل إن لم يُسلِم ولا يصلب أيضاً فدل أن ما اشتملت عليه الآية ما عني به المرتدّ

تفسير القرطبي

In one narration, Anas said: I saw one of them biting the ground with his mouth out of thirst until they died. In Al-Bukhari, Jarir ibn 'Abdullah said regarding his hadith: The Messenger of Allah (SAW) sent me out with a group of the Muslims until we caught up with them; they had gotten close to their land. And we brought them to the Messenger of Allah (SAW). Jarir said: They were saying "water" but the Messenger of Allah (SAW) said "fire". The historians and biographers narrated that these people had cut off the hands and feet of the herdsman and driven prongs into his eyes until he died, and he was brought dead into Medina. His name was Yasar and he was Nubian. This act of the apostates was in year six after the hijra. In some of the narrations it is related from Anas that the Messenger of Allah (SAW) burned them with fire after He killed them ... Apostates deserve death due to the apostasy itself – without them having waged war – they are not to be banished nor are their hands or feet to be cut off nor are they to be sent on their way, rather they are to be killed if they do not yield into Islam; nor are they to be crucified. This indicates that the verse encompasses everything that apostates do.

Tafsir Al-Qurtubi

المحاربة هي المضادة والمخالفة وهي صادقة على الكفر وعلى قطع الطريق وإخافة السبيل وكذا الإفساد في الأرض يطلق على أنواع من الشر ... عن عكرمة والحسن البصري قالا ﴿ إنما ... رحيم ﴾ نزلت هذه الآية في المشركين فمن تاب منهم من قبل أن تقدروا عليه لم يكن عليه سبيل وليست تحرز هذه الآية الرجل المسلم من الحد إن قتل أو أفسد في الأرض أو حارب الله ورسوله ثم لحق بالكفار قبل أن يقدروا عليه لم يمنعه ذلك أن يقام عليه الحد الذي أصاب ... عن ابن عباس في قوله ﴿ إنما جزاء الذين يحاربون الله ورسوله ويسعون في الأرض فساداً ﴾ الآية قال كان قوم من أهل الكتاب بينهم وبين النبي ﷺ عهد وميثاق فنقضوا العهد وأفسدوا في الأرض فخير الله رسوله إن شاء يقتل وإن شاء أن يقطع أيديهم وأرجلهم من خلاف ... والصحيح أن هذه الآية عامة في المشركين وغيرهم ممن ارتكب هذه الصفات كما رواه البخاري ومسلم من

حديث ابي قلابة ... ﴿ أن يقتلوا أو يصلبوا أو تقطع أيديهم وأرجلهم من خلاف أو ينفوا من الأرض ﴾ قال إبن ابي طلحة عن إبن عباس في الآية من شهر السلاح في فئة الاسلام وأخاف السبيل ثم ظفر به وقدر عليه فإمام المسلمين فيه بالخيار إن شاء قتله وإن شاء صلبه وإن شاء قطع يده ورجله وكذا قال سعيد بن المسيب ومجاهد وعطاء والحسن البصري وابراهيم النخعي والضحاك

تفسير إبن كثير

"Warring against" means opposition to and conflict with, and this is upheld by disbelief [kufr] and by impeding travel and causing fear along roadways. Similarly, "causing corruption in the land" [ifsad] applies to many kinds of evil. ... From 'Ikrama and Al-Hasan Al-Basri, regarding { Indeed ... merciful } ; they said: This verse came down regarding the idolaters [mushrikeen] – whoever of them repents before you take hold of them, there is no recourse against them; but this verse does not protect a Muslim man from due punishment if he has killed, caused corruption in the land, or warred against Allah and His Messenger, then joins up with the disbelievers [kuffar] before he is caught; this does not prevent carrying out the due punishment that he has incurred. ... Ibn 'Abbas, of His word: { Indeed the recompense of those who war against Allah and His Messenger, and who intend corruption in the land } and the rest of the verse, said: There was a group of the People of the Book who had a pact and agreement between them and the Prophet (SAW), but they broke the pact and caused corruption in the land, so Allah gave His Messenger the choice to kill them if He wished, or to cut off their hands and feet on opposite sides if He wished. ... The correct view, however, is that this verse applies generally to the Idolaters and those other than the Idolaters who commit these sorts of things, as narrated by Al-Bukhari and Muslim in the *hadith* of Abu Qilaba. ... { That they be slaughtered, or crucified, or their hands and feet cut off on opposite sides, or they be banished from the land } ; Ibn Abi Talha related that Ibn 'Abbas said regarding this verse: Whoever unsheaths a weapon among the people of Islam, causes fear along roadways, and is then overcome and caught – the leader [imam] of the Muslims has the choice of killing him if he likes, crucifying him if he likes, or cutting off his hand and foot if he likes; Sa'id ibn Al-Musayyib, Mujahid, 'Ataa, Al-Hasan Al-Basri, Ibrahim Al-Nakh'i, and Al-Dahhak all said this.

Tafsir Ibn Kathir

﴿ انما جزاء الذين يحاربون الله ورسوله ﴾ أي يحاربون أولياءهما وهم المسلمون جعل محاربتهم محاربتهما تعظيماً

تفسير البيضاوي

{ Indeed the recompense of those who war against Allah and His Messenger } : that is, who war against Their associates, these being the Muslims. He made war against the Muslims equivalent to war against the two of Them as a way of exalting Them.

Tafsir Al-Baydawi

قال بعضهم الآية نزلت في أهل الكفر وبيان الحكم فيهم وهو قول الحسن وابي بكر الأصم وقالا لأن الله عز وجل ذكر محاربة الله ورسوله وذكر السعي في الأرض بالفساد وكل كافر قد حارب الله ورسوله وسعى في الأرض بالفساد فللإمام أن يقتلهم بأي أنواع القتل شاء ما دام الحرب فيما بينهم

تفسير الماتريدي

Some have said: This verse came down regarding the Disbelievers, and makes the ruling for them clear; this is what Al-Hasan and Abu Bakr Al-Asm said. Both of them said: Since Allah Mighty and Sublime mentions war against Allah and His Messenger, and mentions the intent to cause corruption [*fasad*] in the land, and every disbeliever wages war on Allah and His Messenger and intends corruption in the land, the *imam* therefore may kill them by any manner of killing he wishes, as long as hostility remains between them.

Tafsir Al-Maturidi

وأما إذا اخذوا المال فقط ولم يقتلوا كما قد يفعله الأعراب كثيراً فإنه يقطع من كل واحد يده اليمنى ورجله اليسرى عند أكثر العلماء كأبي حنيفة وأحمد وغيرهم وهذا معنى قول الله تعالى ﴿ أو تُقطَّع أيديهم وأرجلهم من خلاف ﴾ تقطع اليد التي يبطش بها والرجل التي يمشي عليها وتحسم يده ورجله بالزيت المغلي ونحوه لينحسم الدم فلا يخرج فيفضي إلى تلفه

السياسة الشرعية لإبن تيمية

If people just take property and do not kill – as the Bedouins frequently did – then the right hand and left foot should be cut off of each individual, according to many scholars, like Abu Hanifa, Ahmad, and others. This is the meaning of the word of Allah Most High: { Or their hands and feet cut off on opposite sides } : the hand, used to strike, and the foot, used to walk on, are cut off, and the hand and the foot are finished off with boiling oil or something similar so that bleeding is stopped and does not keep flowing and lead to decay.

Ibn Taymiyya, Al-siyasa Al-shar'iya

﴿ يا أيها الذين آمنوا اتقوا الله وابتغوا إليه الوسيلة وجاهدوا في سبيله لعلكم تفلحون ﴾

المائدة ٣٥

{ Oh you who have believed, fear Allah and seek the means to draw near to Him, and wage jihad in His cause, that perhaps you may be successful } *Al-ma'ida 35*

﴿ يا أيها الذين آمنوا اتقوا الله ﴾ خافوا عقابه بأن تطيعوه ﴿ وابتغوا ﴾ اطلبوا ﴿ إليه الوسيلة ﴾ ما يقرّبكم إليه من طاعته ﴿ وجاهدوا في سبيله ﴾ لإعلاء دينه ﴿ لعلكم تفلحون ﴾ تفوزون

تفسير الجلالين

{ Oh you who have believed, fear Allah } : fear his punishment by obeying Him; { and seek } : pursue; { the means to draw near to Him } : the obedience that affirms you to Him; { and wage *jihad* in His cause } : to exalt His religion; { that perhaps you may be successful } : that you may be victorious.

Tafsir Al-Jalalain

قال أبو جعفر يعني جل ثناؤه بذلك يا أيها الذين صدقوا الله ورسوله فيما أخبرهم ووعد من الثواب وأوعد من العقاب ﴿ اتقوا الله ﴾ يقول أجيبوا الله فيما أمركم ونهاكم بالطاعة له في ذلك وحققوا إيمانكم وتصديقكم ربكم ونبيكم بالصالح من أعمالكم ﴿ وابتغوا إليه الوسيلة ﴾ يقول واطلبوا القربة إليه بالعمل بما يرضيه

تفسير الطبري

Abu Ja'far said: He (may his praise be exalted) means by this: Oh you who have believed in Allah and his Messenger in what He has told them, and the reward He has promised, and the punishment He has threatened; { fear Allah } : He is saying: Comply with Allah in what He has ordered for you and prohibited to you, in obedience to Him regarding these things, and fulfill your faith and your belief in your Lord and your Prophet by your good deeds. { And seek the means to draw near to Him } ; He is saying: Pursue closeness with Him by doing what pleases Him.

Tafsir Al-Tabari

والوسيلة هي التي يتوصل بها إلى تحصيل المقصود والوسيلة أيضاً علم على أعلى منزلة في الجنة وهي منزلة رسول الله ﷺ وداره في الجنة وهي أقرب أمكنة الجنة إلى العرش

تفسير ابن كثير

"Means to draw near" [*waseelah*] is the way in which one advances towards attaining what is desired. *Waseelah* also refers to the highest level in *Jannah*, and this is the

Messenger of Allah's (SAW) level and his abode in *Jannah*. It is the nearest of the places in *Jannah* to the Throne.

Tafsir Ibn Kathir

﴿ وجاهدوا في سبيله لعلكم تُفلحون ﴾ وهذه الآية أية شريفة مشتملة على أسرار روحانية ونحن نشير هاهنا إلى واحد منها وهو أن من يعبد الله تعالى فريقان منهم من يعبد الله لا لغرض سوى الله ومنهم من يعبد لغرض آخر والمقام الأول هو المقام الشريف العالي وإليه الإشارة بقوله ﴿ وجاهدوا في سبيله ﴾ أي من سبيل عبوديته وطريق الإخلاص في معرفته وخدمته والمقام الثاني دون الأول وإليه الإشارة بقوله ﴿ لعلكم تفلحون ﴾ والفلاح إسم جامع للخلاص عن المكروه والفوز بالمحبوب

تفسير الرازي

{ And wage jihad in His cause, that perhaps you may be successful } : This verse is a noble verse, embracing several spiritual mysteries, of which we will indicate one here, namely that those who worship Allah Most High are of two groups. There are those who worship Allah towards no other aim than Allah, and there are those who worship towards another aim. The first stance is the noble and lofty stance, referred to by His word: { And wage jihad in His cause } : that is, in the cause of worshipping Him and pursuing devotion in knowledge of Him and service to Him. The second stance is inferior to the first, referred to by His word: { that perhaps you may be successful } ; success is a term that brings together deliverance from what is aversive and victory through what is desired.

Tafsir Al-Razi

﴿ وجاهدوا في سبيل الله ﴾ يعني في طاعته ويقال جاهدوا العدو ﴿ لعلكم تفلحون ﴾ أي لكي تنجوا من العقوبة وتنالوا الثواب

بحر العلوم للسمرقندي

{ And wage jihad in the cause of Allah } : that is, in obedience to Him; it is said: Wage jihad against the enemy { that perhaps you may be successful } : that is, so that you are delivered from punishment and receive the reward.

Al-Samarqandi, Bahr Al-'ulum

• • •

﴿ لتجدن أشد الناس عداوة للذين آمنوا اليهود والذين أشركوا ولتجدن أقربهم مودة للذين آمنوا الذين قالوا إنا نصارى ذلك بأن منهم قسيسين ورهباناً وأنهم لا يستكبرون ﴾

المائدة ٨٢

{ Truly you will find the Jews and the Idolaters the most severe of people in enmity against those who have believed, and truly you will find those who say "We are Christians" to be the nearest of them in affection to those who have believed; this is because there are priests and monks among them, and because they are not arrogant } *Al-ma'ida 82*

قال آخرون قدم جعفر بن ابي طالب من الحبشة هو وأصحابه ومعهم سبعون رجلاً بعثهم النجاشي وفداً إلى رسول الله ﷺ عليهم ثياب الصوف إثنان وستون من الحبشة وثمانية من أهل الشام وهم بحيرا الراهب وأبرهة وإدريس وأشرف وتمام وقثم ودريد وأيمن فقرأ عليهم رسول الله ﷺ سورة يس إلى آخرها فبكوا حين سمعوا القرآن وآمنوا وقالوا ما أشبه هذا بما كان ينزل على عيسى فأنزل الله تعالى فيهم هذه الآية

اسباب النزول للواحدي

Others said: Ja'far ibn Abi Talib came back from Ethiopia, he and his companions, and with him were seventy men that had been sent by Najashi as a delegation to the Messenger of Allah (SAW), with wool garments on. There were sixty-two from Ethiopia and eight from the people of Sham: Bahira the monk, Abraha, Idris, Ashraf, Tammam, Quthaim, Duraid, and Ayman. And the Messenger of Allah (SAW) recited surah *Ya-Sin* for them until the end. They wept when they heard the Qur'an, and believed, and said: How similar this is to what was sent down to 'Isa. And Allah Most High sent down this verse regarding them.

Al-Wahidi, Asbab Al-nuzul

قوله عن وجل ﴿ لتجدن أشد الناس عداوةً للذين آمنوا اليهود والذين أشركوا ﴾ أي لتجدن يا محمد أشد الناس عداوة لك وللذين آمنوا اليهود وهم يهود بني قريظة وبني النضير وفدك وخيبر كانوا أشد اليهود عداوة للنبي ﷺ وللمسلمين وروي عن رسول الله ﷺ أنه قال ما خلا يهوديان بمسلم إلا هماً بقتله

التفسير الكبير للطبراني

The word of the Mighty and Sublime: { Truly you will find the Jews and the Idolaters the most severe of people in enmity against those who have believed } : that is, truly you, Oh Muhammad, will find the Jews the most severe of people in enmity against you and those who have believed. These are the Jews of Banu Quraidha, Banu Nadir, Fadak, and Khaybar, the worst Jews in enmity against the Prophet (SAW) and the Muslims. It is narrated from the Messenger of Allah (SAW) that He said: Never do two Jews get alone with a Muslim but that they intend to kill him.

Al-Tabarani, Al-tafsir Al-kabir

﴿ لتجدن أشد الناس عداوةً للذين آمنوا اليهود والذين أشركوا ﴾ ما ذلك إلا لأن كفر اليهود كفر عناد وجحود ومباهتة للحق وغمط وتنقص بحملة العلم ولهذا قتلوا كثيراً من الأنبياء حتى هموا بقتل رسول الله ﷺ غير مرة وسموه وسحروه وألّبوا عليه أشباههم من المشركين لعائن الله المتتابعة إلى يوم القيامة ... عن ابي هريرة قال قال رسول الله ﷺ ماخلا يهودي بمسلم قط إلا هم بقتله ... ﴿ ولتجدن أقربهم مودة للذين آمنوا الذين قالوا إنا نصارى ﴾ أي الذين زعموا أنهم نصارى من أتباع المسيح وعلى منهاج إنجيله فيهم مودة للاسلام وأهله في الجملة وما ذلك إلا لما في قلوبهم إذا كانوا على دين المسيح من الرقة والرأفة ... وليس القتال مشروعاً في ملتهم

تفسير ابن كثير

{ Truly you will find the Jews and the idolaters the most severe of people in enmity against those who have believed } : this is only because the disbelief of the Jews is a stubborn and defiant disbelief, defaming the truth, condescending, and cutting down those who transmit knowledge. This is why they killed many of the prophets, to the point of being intent on killing the Messenger of Allah (SAW) more than once; they poisoned him, they bewitched him, and they incited idolaters like them against him. May the neverending curses of Allah be upon them until resurrection day. ... From Abu Huraira, who said: Never does a Jew ever get alone with a Muslim but that he intends to kill him. ... { And truly you will find those who say "We are Christians" to be the nearest of them in affection to those who have believed } : that is, those who claim that they are Christians, among the followers of the Messiah, and who observe their *Injil*. In general they are friendly towards Islam and its people, and this is only because of the gentleness and compassion that is in their hearts whenever they observe the religion of the Messiah. ... And fighting is not prescribed in their religion.

Tafsir Ibn Kathir

﴿ ولتجدن أقربهم مودة للذين آمنوا الذين قالوا إنا نصارى ﴾ لم يرد به جميع النصارى لأنهم في عداوتهم المسلمين كاليهود في قتلهم المسلمين وأسرهم وتخريب بلادهم وهدم مساجدهم وإحراق مصاحفهم لا ولاء ولا كرامة لهم بل الآية فيمن أسلم منهم مثل النجاشي وأصحابه

تفسير البغوي

{ And truly you will find those who say "We are Christians" to be the nearest of them in affection to those who have believed } : He does not mean all Christians by this, since they are at enmity with the Muslims just like the Jews, in killing the Muslims, taking them captive, ruining their land, demolishing their mosques, and burning their copies of the Qur'an. There are no friendly relations or respect towards them. The verse, rather, refers to those of them who yielded into Islam, such as Najashi and his companions.

Tafsir Al-Baghawi

* * *

Surah 7 Al-a'raf [The Heights]

﴿ قَالَ مُوسَىٰ لِقَوْمِهِ اسْتَعِينُوا بِاللَّهِ وَاصْبِرُوا إِنَّ الْأَرْضَ لِلَّهِ يُورِثُهَا مَن يَشَاءُ مِنْ عِبَادِهِ وَالْعَاقِبَةُ لِلْمُتَّقِينَ قَالُوا أُوذِينَا مِن قَبْلِ أَن تَأْتِيَنَا وَمِن بَعْدِ مَا جِئْتَنَا قَالَ عَسَىٰ رَبُّكُمْ أَن يُهْلِكَ عَدُوَّكُمْ وَيَسْتَخْلِفَكُمْ فِي الْأَرْضِ فَيَنظُرَ كَيْفَ تَعْمَلُونَ ﴾ الأعراف ١٢٨-١٢٩

﴿ Musa said to his people: Appeal to Allah for help and be steadfast; indeed the earth belongs to Allah and He bequeaths it to whomever of His servants He wishes; the ultimate outcome belongs to the devout. They said: We have been harmed before you came to us and after you came to us. He said: Perhaps your Lord will destroy your enemy, and afterwards establish you in the land, so that He can see how you fare ﴾ Al-a'raf 128-129

﴿ والعاقبة للمتقين ﴾ فقيل المراد أمر الآخرة فقط وقيل المراد أمر الدنيا فقط وهو الفتح والظفر والنصر على الأعداء وقيل المراد مجموع الأمرين وقوله ﴿ للمتقين ﴾ إشارة إلى أن كل من إتقى الله تعالى وخافه فالله يعينه في الدنيا والآخرة

تفسير الرازي

﴿ The ultimate outcome belongs to the devout ﴾ : it is said that the intended meaning is in the hereafter only. It is also said that the intended meaning is in this world only, this being conquest, triumph, and victory over the enemy. And it is said that the intended meaning is both of them together. His word: ﴿ The devout ﴾ indicates that all who are devout towards Allah Most High, and fear Him – Allah will come to their aid in this world and in the next.

Tafsir Al-Razi

﴿ والعاقبة للمتقين ﴾ قيل النصر والظفر وقيل الدار الآخرة وقيل السعادة والشهادة وقيل الجنة

البحر المحيط لأبي حيان

﴿ The ultimate outcome belongs to the devout ﴾ : it is said that this is victory and triumph; and it is said: the abode of the hereafter; and it is said: happiness and martyrdom; and it is also said: Jannah.

Abu Hayyan, Al-bahr Al-muhit

﴿ والعاقبة للمتقين ﴾ يحتمل وجهين احدهما يريد في الآخرة بالثواب والثاني في الدنيا بالنصر ... ﴿ قال عسى ربكم أن يُهلك عدوكم ﴾ عسى في اللغة طمع وإشفاق قال الحسن عسى من الله واجبة وقال الزجاج عسى من الله يقين

تفسير الماوردي

{ The ultimate outcome belongs to the devout } carries two points of view; one of them is that this means by the reward in the hereafter; the second is that it means by victory in this world. ... { Perhaps your Lord will destroy your enemy } : "Perhaps" in this manner of speech means ambitious desire and fondness. Al-Hasan said: "Perhaps" with Allah is an obligation; and Al-Zajjaj said: "Perhaps" with Allah is certainty.

Tafsir Al-Mawardi

﴿ قال عسى ربكم أن يهلك عدوكم ويستخلفكم في الأرض ﴾ والعسى من الله واجب فوعدهم إهلاك العدو وإستخلافهم في الأرض

تفسير الماتريدي

{ He said: Perhaps your Lord will destroy your enemy, and afterwards establish you in the land } : "Perhaps" with Allah is an obligation, given that He promised them the destruction of the enemy and their establishment in the land.

Tafsir Al-Maturidi

﴿ عسى ربكم أن يهلك عدوكم ﴾ تصريح بما رمز إليه من البشارة قبل وكشف عنه وهو إهلاك فرعون وإستخلافهم بعده في أرض مصر ﴿ فينظر كيف تعملون ﴾ فيرى الكائن منكم من العمل حسنه وقبيحه وشكر النعمة وكفرانها ليجازيكم على حسب ما يوجد منكم

تفسير الزمخشري

{ Perhaps your Lord will destroy your enemy } : this is a declaration of the good news that was indicated earlier, and the revealing of it, this being the destruction of Pharaoh and afterwards establishing them in the land of Egypt. { So that He can see how you fare } : so He can see the good and shameful deeds of those among you, giving thanks for favor or ignoring it, so that He may reward you according to what is found in you.

Tafsir Al-Zamakhshari

ثم بيَّن بقوله ﴿ فينظر كيف تعملون ﴾ ما يجري مجرى الحثِّ له على التمسُّك بطاعة الله

اللباب في علوم الكتاب لإبن عادل

Then He makes clear, by His word { So that He can see how you fare }, what follows in the way of exhorting them to hold firm in obedience to Allah.

Ibn 'Adil, Al-lubab fi 'Ulum Al-kitab

* * *

﴿ والذين كذبوا بآياتنا سنستدرجهم من حيث لا يعلمون ۝ وأملي لهم إنَّ كيدي متين ﴾ الأعراف ١٨٢-١٨٣

{ And those who have denied Our signs – We will get at them little by little from places they do not know; but I will delay for them a little; indeed My guile is solid } Al-a'raf 182-183

قوله تعالى ﴿ والذين كذبوا بآياتنا ﴾ يعني بمحمد والقرآن ﴿ سنستدرجهم ﴾ يعني سنأخذهم بالعذاب ﴿ من حيث لا يعلمون ﴾ يعني من حيث لا يشعرون وقال الكلبي يعني نزين لهم فنهلكهم من حيث لا يعلمون

بحر العلوم للسمرقندي

The word of the Most High: { And those who have denied Our signs } : that is, Muhammad and the Qur'an; { We will get at them little by little } : that is, We will take hold of them by punishment; { from places they do not know } : that is, from where they are not aware. Al-Kalbi said: This means We will grace them and then destroy them from places they do not know.

Al-Samarqandi, Bahr Al-'ulum

﴿ والذين كذبوا بآياتنا سنستدرجهم ﴾ سنستدنيهم إلى الهلاك قليلاً قليلاً وأصل الاستدراج الإستصعاد أو الاستنزال درجة بعد درجة ﴿ من حيث لا يعلمون ﴾ ما نزيد بهم وذلك أن نتواتر عليهم النعم فيظنوا أنها لطف من الله تعالى بهم فيزدادوا بطراً وإنهماكاً في الغي حتى يحق عليهم كلمة العذاب

تفسير البيضاوي

{ And those who have denied Our signs, We will get at them little by little } : We will draw them closer to destruction little by little; the basis of getting at little by little is making something go up or down step by step. { From places they do not know } : Whatever We desire for them; and this by way of steady ease for them so that they think it is kindness from Allah Most High, although they will grow in being presumptuous and preoccupied in error, until the pronouncement of punishment comes to pass for them.

Tafsir Al-Baydawi

﴿ والذين كذبوا بآياتنا سنستدرجهم من حيث لا يعلمون ﴾ قال عطاء سنمكر بهم من حيث لا يعلمون وقيل نأتيهم من مأمنهم كما قال ﴿ فأتاهم الله من حيث لم يحتسبوا ﴾

تفسير البغوي

{ And those who have denied Our signs, We will get at them little by little from places they do not know } ; 'Ataa said: We will deceive them from places they do not know. It is said: We will come to them in their place of safety, as He says: { Allah came to them from where they did not reckon } [Al-hashr 2].

Tafsir Al-Baghawi

قوله تعالى ﴿ سنستدرجهم ﴾ قال الخليل بن أحمد سنطوي أعمارهم في اغترار منهم وقال أبو عبيدة الاستدراج أن يتدرج إلى الشيء في خُفية قليلاً قليلاً ولا يهجم عليه

تفسير ابن الجوزي

The word of the Most High: { We will get at them little by little } ; Al-Khalil ibn Ahmad said: We will bring their lives to an end with them being deluded. Abu 'Ubaida said: "Get at little by little" means gradually progessing towards something stealthily little by little, without making an open attack on it.

Tafsir Ibn Al-Jawzi

وأما قوله ﴿ وَأُمْلِي لَهُمْ ﴾ فمعناه أني أبقيهم في الدنيا مع إصرارهم على الكفر ولا أعاجلهم بالعقوبة لأنهم لا يفوتونني ولا يعجزونني وهذا معنى قوله ﴿ إِنَّ كَيْدِي مَتِينٌ ﴾ لأن كيده هو عذابه وسماه كيداً لنزوله بالعباد من حيث لا يشعرون

تفسير الرازي

Now then His word: { But I will delay for them a little } ; the meaning is: I will keep them in this world, with their insistence on disbelieving, and I will not hasten on them with punishment, since they have not eluded Me nor frustrated Me. This is the meaning of His word: { Indeed My guile is solid } , since His guile is His punishment; and He calls it "guile" because it comes upon people from where they are not aware.

Tafsir Al-Razi

وأخرج أبو الشيخ عن السدي ﴿ وَأُمْلِي لَهُمْ إِنَّ كَيْدِي مَتِينٌ ﴾ يقول كُفَّ عنهم وأخرهم على رَسَلِهِم إن مكري شديد ثم نسخها الله فأنزل الله ﴿ فَاقْتُلُوا الْمُشْرِكِينَ حَيْثُ وَجَدْتُمُوهُمْ ﴾ الآية

الدر المنثور للسيوطي

Abu Al-Shiekh related from Al-Suddi regarding { But I will delay for them a little } : He is saying: Cease from them and let them remain a little while in their ease; indeed My deceipt is severe. Then Allah abrogated this when Allah sent down: { Kill the idolaters wherever you find them } and the rest of the verse [Al-tawba 5].

Al-Suyuti, Al-durr Al-manthur

• • •

Surah 8 Al-anfal [The Spoils]

﴿ يَسْأَلُونَكَ عَنِ الْأَنْفَالِ قُلِ الْأَنْفَالُ لِلَّهِ وَالرَّسُولِ فَاتَّقُوا اللَّهَ وَأَصْلِحُوا ذَاتَ بَيْنِكُمْ وَأَطِيعُوا اللَّهَ وَرَسُولَهُ إِنْ كُنْتُمْ مُؤْمِنِينَ ﴾ الأنفال ١

﴿ **They ask you about the spoils; say: The spoils are for Allah and the Messenger, so fear Allah and set things right between you all, and obey Allah and His Messenger, if you are Believers** ﴾ *Al-anfal 1*

عن عطاء ﴿ يسألونك عن الأنفال ﴾ قال هي ما شذَّ من المشركين إلى المسلمين بغير قتال من عبد أو أمة أو متاع أو نفل فهو للنبي ﷺ يصنع فيه ما شاء

تفسير الطبري

'Ataa, regarding ﴿ They ask you about the spoils ﴾, said: This is whatever is separated from the idolaters [*mushrikeen*] for the Muslims without fighting, including slaves, servant girls, goods, or loot; it is for the Prophet (SAW) for him to do with it what He wishes.

Tafsir Al-Tabari

عن مصعب بن سعد عن أبيه قال أخذ ابي من الخمس سيفاً فأتى به النبي ﷺ فقال هَبْ لي هذا فأبى فأنزل الله عز وجل ﴿ يسألونك عن الانفال قال الانفال لله والرسول ﴾

صحيح مسلم كتاب الجهاد والسير

Mus'ab ibn Sa'd related from his father, who said: My father took a sword from the fifth of the spoils, brought it to the Prophet (SAW) and said: Give this to me. But He refused; and Allah Mighty and Sublime sent down: ﴿ They ask you about the spoils; say: The spoils are for Allah and the Messenger ﴾.

Sahih Muslim, The book of jihad and campaigns

عن سعد بن ابي وقاص قال لما كان يوم بدر قُتل أخي عمير وقتلت سعيد بن العاص فأخذت سيفه وكان يسمى ذا الكيفة فأتيت به النبي ﷺ قال إذهب فاطرحه في القبض قال فرجعت وبي ما لا يعلمه إلا الله من قتل أخي وأخذ سلبي فما جاوزت إلا قريباً حتى نزلت سورة الأنفال فقال لي رسول الله ﷺ نحذ سيفك

اسباب النزول للواحدي

From Sa'd ibn Abi Waqqas, who said: On the day of Badr, my brother 'Umair was killed, and I killed Sa'id ibn Al-'As; I took his sword, which was called the Patched One, and brought it to the Prophet (SAW). He said: Go and throw it with everything that has been collected. So I went back, feeling something only Allah knows from the killing of my brother and the taking of my loot. And I had only gone off a short distance when surah *Al-anfal* was sent down; and the Messenger of Allah (SAW) said to me: Go get your sword!

Al-Wahidi, Asbab Al-nuzul

ثم قال ﴿ وأطيعوا الله ورسوله إن كنتم مؤمنين ﴾ والمعنى أنه تعالى نهاهم عن مخالفة حكم الرسول

تفسير الرازي

The He says: { And obey Allah and His Messenger, if you are Believers } ; the meaning is that the Most High prohibited them from contradicting the Messenger's decision.

Tafsir Al-Razi

وأخرج إبن جرير عن الضحاك قال هي في قراءة إبن مسعود يسئلونك الأنفال

الدر المنثور للسيوطي

Ibn Jarir reported from Al-Dahhak, who said: Part of the way Ibn Mas'ud recited it was "They ask you *for* the spoils".

Al-Suyuti, Al-durr Al-manthur

• • •

﴿ كَمَا أَخْرَجَكَ رَبُّكَ مِنْ بَيْتِكَ بِالْحَقِّ وَإِنَّ فَرِيقًا مِنَ الْمُؤْمِنِينَ لَكَارِهُونَ يُجَادِلُونَكَ فِي الْحَقِّ بَعْدَمَا تَبَيَّنَ كَأَنَّمَا يُسَاقُونَ إِلَى الْمَوْتِ وَهُمْ يَنْظُرُونَ وَإِذْ يَعِدُكُمُ اللَّهُ إِحْدَى الطَّائِفَتَيْنِ أَنَّهَا لَكُمْ وَتَوَدُّونَ أَنَّ غَيْرَ ذَاتِ الشَّوْكَةِ تَكُونُ لَكُمْ وَيُرِيدُ اللَّهُ أَنْ يُحِقَّ الْحَقَّ بِكَلِمَاتِهِ وَيَقْطَعَ دَابِرَ الْكَافِرِينَ ﴾ الأنفال ٥-٧

{ As your Lord sent you out from your house with the truth, and indeed a group of the Believers was averse to it, disputing with you regarding the truth after it was made clear, as if they were being led out to death while looking at it; and Allah promised you all one of the two groups, to be yours, and you desired that the group without any prowess be yours, but Allah wanted to accomplish the truth by His words and cut off any remnant of disbelievers } *Al-anfal 5-7*

﴿ وَيُرِيدُ اللَّهُ أَنْ يُحِقَّ الْحَقَّ بِكَلِمَاتِهِ ﴾ أي هو يريد أن يجمع بينكم وبين الطائفة التي لها الشوكة والقتال ليظفركم بهم وينصركم عليهم ويظهر دينه ويرفع كلمة الاسلام ويجعله غالباً على الأديان وهو أعلم بعواقب الأمور وهو الذي يدبركم بحسن تدبيره وإن كان العباد يحبون خلاف ذلك فيما يظهر لهم كقوله تعالى ﴿ كُتِبَ عَلَيْكُمُ الْقِتَالُ وَهُوَ كُرْهٌ لَكُمْ وَعَسَى أَنْ تَكْرَهُوا شَيْئًا وَهُوَ خَيْرٌ لَكُمْ وَعَسَى أَنْ تُحِبُّوا شَيْئًا وَهُوَ شَرٌّ لَكُمْ ﴾ ... وغيرهم من علمائنا ... قالوا لما سمع رسول الله ﷺ بأبي سفيان مقبلاً من الشام ندب المسلمين اليهم وقال هذه عير قريش فيها أموالهم فاخرجوا إليها لعل الله أن ينفلكموها

تفسير ابن كثير

{ But Allah wanted to accomplish the truth } : that is, He wanted to bring you all together with the group that had prowess and fighting ability, in order to have you prevail over them, give you victory over them, manifest His religion [deen], raise the word of Islam, and make it surpass other religions. He knows best how things will turn out, and He is the one who plans for you in the best of His planning, even if people desire what is contrary to this from what is made apparent to them, as the word of the Most High says: { Fighting is ordained for you, being something you dislike; but perhaps you dislike something that is good for you, and perhaps you like something that is bad for you } {*Al-baqara* 216}. ... Others of our scholars ... say: When the Messenger of Allah (SAW) heard that Abu Sufyan had headed out from Sham, He charged the Muslims to go out to them, saying: This is the caravan of Quraysh carrying their wealth – so go out to it, that perhaps Allah might give the spoils to you all.

Tafsir Ibn Kathir

﷽ يجادلونك في ألحق ﴾ في إيثارك الجهاد بإظهار ألحق لإيثارهم تلقي العير عليه

تفسير البيضاوي

{ Disputing with you regarding the truth } : regarding your preference for *jihad* to manifest the truth, against their preference for capturing the caravan instead.

Tafsir Al-Baydawi

﴿ و ﴾ أذكر ﴿ إذ يعدكم الله إحدى الطائفتين ﴾ العير أو النفير ﴿ أنها لكم وتودّون ﴾ تريدون ﴿ أن غير ذات الشوكة ﴾ أي البأس والسلاح وهي العير ﴿ تكون لكم ﴾ لقلة عَددها وعُددها بخلاف النفير ﴿ ويريد الله أن يُحقّ ألحق ﴾ يظهره ﴿ بكلماته ﴾ السابقة بظهور الاسلام ﴿ ويقطع دابر الكافرين ﴾ آخرهم بالإستئصال فأمركم بقتال النفير

تفسير الجلالين

{ And } : remember; { Allah promised you all one of the two groups } : the caravan or the band of troops; { to be yours, and you desired } : you wanted; { that the group without prowess } : that is, without might or weapons, this being the caravan; { to be yours } : due to its being small and poorly outfitted, in contrast to the band of troops; { but Allah wanted to accomplish the truth } : make it manifest; { by His words } : His prior words, by bringing Islam into plain view; { and cut off any renmant of disbelievers } : the last of them, by eradication, and so He ordered you to fight the band of troops.

Tafsir Al-Jalalain

﴿ كأنما يُساقون إلى الموت وهم ينظرون ﴾ فإن معناه كأن هؤلاء الذين يجادلونك في لقاء العدو من كراهتهم للقائهم إذا دُعوا إلى لقائهم للقتال يساقون إلى الموت ... ﴿ ويقطع دابر الكافرين ﴾ يقول يريد أن يجبّ أصل الجاحدين توحيد الله وقد بيَّنا فيما مضى معنى دابر وأنه المتأخر وأن معنى قطعه الإتيان على الجميع منهم

تفسير الطبري

{ As if they were being led out to death while looking at it } ; indeed the meaning is: As if those who disputed with you about facing the enemy – out of their aversion to facing them, when they are called to face them and fight – were being led out to death. ... { And cut off any remnant of disbelievers } ; He is saying that He wants to put an end to the lineage of those who reject the oneness of Allah [*tawhid*]; and we have clarified the meaning of "remnant" earlier, that it is anything left behind, and that the meaning of "cut off" is to come down upon all of them.

Tafsir Al-Tabari

﴿ وهم ينظرون ﴾ كناية عن الجزْم والقطع ومنه قوله عليه السلام من نفى ابنه وهو ينظر إليه أي يعلم أنه ابنه

تفسير الرازي

{ While looking at it } : an allusion to getting cut short and getting cut off, along the lines of what He (peace be upon him) said: "Whoever banishes his son while looking at him"; that is, aware that he is his son.

Tafsir Al-Razi

﴿ وهم ينظرون ﴾ لأن أشد حال من يساق إلى الموت أن يكون ناظراً إليه وعالماً به وعلى قول ابن زيد كأنما يساقون إلى الموت حين يُدعون إلى الاسلام لكراهتهم إياه

تفسير ابن الجوزي

{ While looking at it } : because the toughest situation for someone being led to death is that he sees it and is aware of it. Ibn Zaid said: As if they were being led out to death when they were called to Islam, due to their aversion to it.

Tafsir Ibn Al-Jawzi

عن السدي في قوله ﴿ كما أخرجك ربك من بيتك بالحق ﴾ قال خروج النبي ﷺ إلى بدر ﴿ وإن فريقاً من المؤمنين لكارهون ﴾ قال لطلب المشركين ﴿ يجادلونك في الحق بعدما تبين ﴾ انك لا تصنع إلا ما أمرك الله به ﴿ كأنما يساقون إلى الموت ﴾ حين قيل هم المشركون

الدر المنثور للسيوطي

Al-Suddi, regarding His word: { As your Lord sent you out from your house with the truth }, said: The departure of the Prophet (SAW) towards Badr. { Indeed a group of the Believers was averse to it } ; he said: Averse to seeking out the idolaters. { Disputing with you regarding the truth after it was made clear } : in that you only do what Allah has commanded you. { As if they were being led out to death } : when it was said: Those are the idolaters.

Al-Suyuti, Al-durr Al-manthur

∙ ∙ ∙

﷽ إِذْ تَسْتَغِيثُونَ رَبَّكُمْ فَاسْتَجَابَ لَكُمْ أَنِّي مُمِدُّكُم بِأَلْفٍ مِّنَ الْمَلَائِكَةِ مُرْدِفِينَ وَمَا جَعَلَهُ اللَّهُ إِلَّا بُشْرَىٰ وَلِتَطْمَئِنَّ بِهِ قُلُوبُكُمْ وَمَا النَّصْرُ إِلَّا مِنْ عِندِ اللَّهِ إِنَّ اللَّهَ عَزِيزٌ حَكِيمٌ إِذْ يُغَشِّيكُمُ النُّعَاسَ أَمَنَةً مِّنْهُ وَيُنَزِّلُ عَلَيْكُم مِّنَ السَّمَاءِ مَاءً لِّيُطَهِّرَكُم بِهِ وَيُذْهِبَ عَنكُمْ رِجْزَ الشَّيْطَانِ وَلِيَرْبِطَ عَلَىٰ قُلُوبِكُمْ وَيُثَبِّتَ بِهِ الْأَقْدَامَ إِذْ يُوحِي رَبُّكَ إِلَى الْمَلَائِكَةِ أَنِّي مَعَكُمْ فَثَبِّتُوا الَّذِينَ آمَنُوا سَأُلْقِي فِي قُلُوبِ الَّذِينَ كَفَرُوا الرُّعْبَ فَاضْرِبُوا فَوْقَ الْأَعْنَاقِ وَاضْرِبُوا مِنْهُمْ كُلَّ بَنَانٍ ذَٰلِكَ بِأَنَّهُمْ شَاقُّوا اللَّهَ وَرَسُولَهُ وَمَن يُشَاقِقِ اللَّهَ وَرَسُولَهُ فَإِنَّ اللَّهَ شَدِيدُ الْعِقَابِ ﴾ الأنفال ٩-١٣

{ You all appealed to your Lord for help, and He answered you: "I will support you with a thousand angels coming one after the other". Allah did this only as good tidings, and so that your hearts might be at ease; there is no victory except from Allah; indeed Allah is mighty, wise. Behold He covered you with slumber as a means of safety from Him, and sent down water from heaven on you to purify you with it, to remove the filth of Satan from you, to strengthen your hearts, and affirm your feet by it. For your Lord has made known to the angels: Indeed I am with you, so affirm those who have believed; I shall cast terror into the hearts of those who have disbelieved, so strike over the necks and strike off all their fingertips. This is because they have antagonized Allah and His Messenger; whoever antagonizes Allah and His Messenger – indeed Allah is severe in punishment } Al-anfal 9-13

عمر بن الخطاب قال نظر نبي الله ﷺ إلى المشركين وهم ألف وأصحابه ثلاثمائة وبضعة عشر رجلاً فإستقبل نبي الله ﷺ القبلة ثم مدَّ يديه وجعل يهتف بربه اللهم أنجز لي ما وعدتني اللهم آتني ما وعدتني اللهم إن تُهلك هذه العصابة من أهل الاسلام لا تُعبد في الأرض فما زال يهتف بربه مادّاً يديه مستقبل القبلة حتى سقط رداؤه من منكبيه فأتاه أبو بكر فأخذ رداءه فألقاه على منكبيه ثم إلتزمه من ورائه فقال يا نبي الله كفاك مناشدتك ربك فإنه سينُجز لك ما وعدك فأنزل الله ﴿ إِذْ تَسْتَغِيثُونَ رَبَّكُمْ فَإِسْتَجَابَ لَكُمْ أَنِّي مُمِدُّكُم بِأَلْفٍ مِّنَ الملائكة مُردِفِينَ ﴾ فأمدَّهم الله بالملائكة
جامع الترمذي كتاب تفسير القرآن

'Umar ibn Al-Khattab said: The Prophet of Allah (SAW) looked towards the idolaters – there were a thousand of them, while his Companions were only three hundred and ten-something men – and the Prophet of Allah (SAW) faced the *Qibla*, then stretched out his hands and began to cry out to his Lord: Oh Allah! Accomplish what you have promised me! Oh Allah! Bring about what you have promised me! Oh Allah! If you destroy this group of those in Islam, you will not be worshipped anywhere on earth! He did not stop crying out to his Lord, with his hands stretched out, facing the Qibla, until his garment fell off his shoulders. And Abu Bakr grabbed his garment and threw it back on his shoulders, then hung onto him from behind, and said: Oh Prophet of Allah! You've implored your Lord enough; surely He will accomplish for you what He has promised. Then Allah sent down: { You all appeal to your Lord for help, and He answered you: "I will support you with a thousand angels coming one after the other" } . And Allah supported them with the angels.

Sunan Al-Tirmidhi, The book of tafsir

وقوله ﴿ لِيُطَهِّرَكُم بِهِ ﴾ أي من حدث أصغر أو أكبر وهو تطهير الظاهر ﴿ وَيُذْهِبَ عَنكُمْ رِجْزَ الشَّيْطَانِ ﴾ أي من وسوسة أو خاطر سيئ وهو تطهير الباطن

تفسير ابن كثير

His word: { To purify you with it } : that is, from any bodily function, large or small; this is outer purification. { To remove the filth of Satan from you } : that is, whispering and evil notions; this is inner purification.

Tafsir Ibn Kathir

﴿ وَمَا جَعَلَهُ اللَّهُ ﴾ أي الإمداد ﴿ إِلَّا بُشْرَىٰ ﴾ إلا بشارة لكم بالنصر ﴿ وَلِتَطْمَئِنَّ بِهِ قُلُوبُكُمْ ﴾ فيزول ما بها من الوجل لقلتكم وذلتكم ... ﴿ وَلِيَرْبِطَ عَلَىٰ قُلُوبِكُم ﴾ بالوثوق على لطف الله بهم ﴿ وَيُثَبِّتَ بِهِ الْأَقْدَامَ ﴾ أي بالمطر حتى لا تسوخ في الرمل أو بالربط على القلوب حتى ثبت في المعركة

تفسير البيضاوي

{ Allah did this } : that is, the reinforcements; { only as good tidings } : only as good news to you of the victory; { and so that your hearts might be at ease } : and the alarm in them due to your small numbers and your humiliation might be dispelled. ... { To strengthen your hearts } : by the assurance of Allah's favor to them; { and affirm your feet by it } : that is, by the rain, so that they would not slip in the sand, or to strengthen hearts so that they would be affirmed on the battleground.

Tafsir Al-Baydawi

عن علي رضي الله عنه قال كان رسول الله ﷺ يصلي تلك الليلة ليلة بدر ويقول اللهم إن تهلك هذه العصابة لا تُعبد وأصابهم تلك الليلة مطر شديد فذلك قوله ﴿ وَيُثَبِّتَ بِهِ الْأَقْدَامَ ﴾

الدر المنثور للسيوطي

From 'Ali (may Allah be pleased with him), who said: The Messenger of Allah (SAW) was praying that night, the night of Badr, saying: Oh Allah! If you destroy this troop, you will not be worshipped. And an intense rain came upon them that night; this is His word: { and affirm your feet by it }.

Al-Suyuti, Al-durr Al-manthur

قال مالك بلغني أن جبريل عليه السلام قال للنبي ﷺ كيف فيكم أهل بدر قال خيارنا قال أنهم كذلك فينا فدل هذا على أن شرف المخلوقات ليس بالذوات وإنما هو بالأفعال فللملائكة أفعالها الشريفة من المواظبة على التسبيح الدائم ولنا أفعالنا بالإخلاص بالطاعة وبتفاضل الطاعات بتفضيل الشرع لها وأفضلها الجهاد وأفضل الجهاد يوم بدر لأن بناء الإسلام كان عليه ودل خروج النبي ﷺ ليلقى العير على جواز النفير للغنيمة لأنها كسب حلال وهو يرد ما كره مالك من ذلك إذ قال ذلك قتال على الدنيا وما جاء أن من قاتل لتكون كلمة الله هي العليا فهو في سبيل الله دون من يقاتل للغنيمة

تفسير القرطبي

Malik said: It was made known to me that Jibril (peace be upon him) asked the Prophet (SAW): What do you think of those of you at Badr? He said: The best of us. Jibril said: Indeed it is likewise with us. This subtantiates that the glory of the created beings is not in their own selves; rather it is in deed. For the honorable deeds of the angels are to persevere in giving continuous praise, while our deeds are devotion to obedience. Acts of obedience rival for precedence in their preference to the divine law in them; the best of these is *jihad*, and the best *jihad* was on the day of Badr, because Islam was established there. The fact that the Prophet (SAW) went out to meet the caravan substantiates the permissibility of mobilizing to take plunder, since this is lawful gain. This refutes Malik's dislike of it, when he said that this is only fighting for worldly gain, and when he stated that whoever fights so that the word of Allah be the utmost, he is in the cause of Allah, except those who fight for plunder.

Tafsir Al-Qurtubi

يقول تعالى ذكره لم يجعل الله إرداف الملائكة بعضها بعضاً وتتابعها بالمصير إليكم أيها المؤمنون مدداً لكم إلا بشرى لكم أي بشارة لكم تبشركم بنصر الله إياكم على أعدائكم ﴿ وَلِتَطْمَئِنَّ بِهِ قُلُوبُكُمْ ﴾ يقول ولتسكن قلوبكم بمجيئها إليكم وتوقنَ بنصرة الله لكم ... عن القاسم قال قال رسول الله ﷺ إني لم أبعث لأعذِّب بعذاب الله إنما بعثت لضرب الأعناق وشدّ الوثاق ... قال أبو جعفر والصواب من القول في ذلك أن يقال أن الله أمر

المؤمنين معلِّمهم كيفية قتل المشركين وضربهم بالسيف أن يضربوا فوق الأعناق منهم والأيدي والأرجل وقوله ﴿ فوق الأعناق ﴾ محتمل أن يكون مراداً بالرؤوس ومحتمل أن يكون مراداً له من فوق جلدة الأعناق ... وأما قوله ﴿ واضربوا منهم كل بنان ﴾ فإن معناه واضربوا أيها المؤمنون من عدوكم كل طرف ومَفصِل من أطراف أيديهم وأرجلهم ... ﴿ ذلك بأنهم ﴾ هذا الفعل من ضرب هؤلاء الكفرة فوق الأعناق وضرب كل بنان منهم جزاء لهم بشقاقهم الله ورسوله وعقاب لهم عليه ومعنى قوله ﴿ شاقّوا الله ورسوله ﴾ فارقوا أمر الله ورسوله وعصوهما وأطاعوا أمر الشيطان ومعنى قوله ﴿ ومن يشاقق الله رسوله ﴾ ومن يخالف أمر الله وأمر رسوله وفارق طاعتهما

تفسير الطبري

He (may His remembrance be exalted) says: Allah sent the succession of angels, continuously one after the other destined for you, oh Believers, as reinforcement for you, only as good tidings to you, that is, to bring you the good news of Allah's victory for you over your enemies. { So that your hearts might be at ease } ; He is saying: So your hearts will be still by them coming to you, and be certain of Allah's support to you ... From Qasim, who said: The Messenger of Allah (SAW) said: Indeed I have not been sent forth to punish with Allah's punishment, rather I have been sent forth to strike people's necks [darb al-a'naq] and tighten shackles. ... Abu Ja'far said: The accurate way to say this is to say that Allah has commanded the Believers, instructing them in the manner of killing the idolaters [mushrikun] and striking them with the sword – that they should strike over their necks, and their hands and feet. His word { Over the necks } implies that the intent is their heads, and implies that the target is above the skin of the neck. ... Moreover His word { And strike off all their fingertips } : Indeed the meaning of this is: Strike, oh Believers, on your enemy, all the tips and joints off the ends of their hands and feet. ... { This is because } : striking these Disbelievers over the necks and striking off all their fingertips is their recompense for antagonizing Allah and His Messenger, and their punishment for it. The meaning of His word: { They have antagonized Allah and His Messenger } is that they have departed from the command of Allah and His Messenger, have disobeyed both of them, and have obeyed the command of Satan. The meaning of His word { Whoever antagonizes Allah and His Messenger } is: Whoever opposes the command of Allah and the command of His Messenger and departs from obedience to both of them.

Tafsir Al-Tabari

وفي قوله ﴿ فاضربوا فوق الأعناق ﴾ قولان الأول أن ما فوق العنق هو الرأس فكان هذا أمراً بإزالة الرأس عن الجسد والثاني أن قوله ﴿ فاضربوا فوق الأعناق ﴾ أي فاضربوا الأعناق ثم قال ﴿ واضربوا منهم كل بنان ﴾ يعني الأطراف من اليدين والرجلين ثم اختلفوا فمنهم من قال المراد أن يضربوهم كم شاؤوا لأن ما فوق العنق هو الرأس وهو أشرف الأعضاء والبنان عبارة عن أضعف الأعضاء فذكر الأشرف والأخس تنبيهاً على

كل الأعضاء ومنهم من قال بل المراد إما القتل وهو ضرب ما فوق الأعناق أو قطع البنان لأن الأصابع هي الآلات في أخذ السيوف والرماح وسائر الأسلحة فإذا قطع بنانهم عجزوا عن المحاربة

تفسير الرازي

Regarding His word: { So strike over the necks } there are two viewpoints; the first is that what is over the neck is the head, and this was a command to eliminate the head from the body; the second is that His word: { So strike over the necks } means "So strike the necks". Then He says: { And strike off all their fingertips }, meaning the tips of the hands and feet. Then a difference in opinion arose; some said that the intended meaning is for them to strike them however they wish, since what is above the neck is the head, and this is the most honorable of the bodily members, while "fingertips" is an expression for the weakest members; mentioning the most honorable and the most dishonorable is indicative of all of the members. Some said that rather the intended meaning is either killing, that is, striking what is above the neck, or cutting off the fingertips, since the fingers are the tools used to take hold of swords, spears, and other weapons, and if their fingertips are cut off they are prevented from combat.

Tafsir Al-Razi

{ فاضربوا فوق الأعناق } أي الرؤوس { واضربوا منهم كل بنانٍ } أي أطراف اليدين والرجلين فكان الرجل يقصد ضرب رقبة الكافر فتسقط قبل أن يصل إليه سيفه ورماهم ﷺ بقبضة من حصى فلم يبق مشرك إلا دخل في عينيه منها شيء فهُزموا

تفسير الجلالين

{ So strike over the necks } : that is, the heads; { and strike off all their fingertips } : that is, the ends of their hands and feet. A man would aim to strike the head of a disbeliever, and it would fall off even before his sword reached it. And He (SAW) threw a handful of pebbles at them, and there wasn't a single idolater who did not get some in their eyes; and they were defeated.

Tafsir Al-Jalalain

{ فوق الأعناق } أراد أعالي الأعناق التي هي المذابح لأنها مفاصل فكان إيقاع الضرب فيها حزاً وتطييراً للرؤوس وقيل أراد الرؤوس لأنها فوق الأعناق

تفسير الزمخشري

{ Over the necks } : He means the uppermost part of the necks, the part where slaughterings are made, since there are joints there; a blow there separates the head and sends it flying. It is said: He means the head, as it is over the neck.

Tafsir Al-Zamakhshari

• • •

﴿ يا أيها الذين آمنوا إذا لقيتم الذين كفروا زحفاً فلا تولوهم الأدبار ومن يولهم يومئذ دبره إلا متحرفاً لقتال أو متحيزاً إلى فئة فقد باء بغضب من الله ومأواه جهنم وبئس المصير فلم تقتلوهم ولكن الله قتلهم وما رميت إذ رميت ولكن الله رمى وليبلي المؤمنين منه بلاءً حسناً إن الله سميع عليم ﴾ الأنفال ١٥-١٧

{ Oh you who have believed, whenever you face the Disbelievers advancing, do not turn your rears to them. Whoever turns his rear to them on that day, except to move around to fight or take sides with a squad, he has incurred the wrath of Allah; and his dwelling is Hell, a miserable fate. And you all did not kill them, but Allah killed them; you did not hurl when you hurled, but Allah hurled, so that He might put the Believers to the test with a suitable ordeal from Him; indeed Allah is hearing, knowing } *Al-anfal 15-17*

﴿ ومن يولّهم يومئذ ﴾ أي يوم لقائهم ﴿ دبره إلا متحرّفاً ﴾ منعطفاً ﴿ لقتال ﴾ بأن يريهم الفرّة مكيدة وهو يريد الكرّة ﴿ أو متحيّزاً ﴾ منضماً ﴿ إلى فئة ﴾ جماعة من المسلمين يستنجد بها ﴿ فقد باء ﴾ رجع ﴿ بغضب من الله ومأواه جهنم وبئس المصير ﴾ المرجع هي وهذا مخصوص بما إذا لم يزد الكفار على الضعف ﴿ فلم تقتلوهم ﴾ ببدر بقوّتكم ﴿ ولكن الله قتلهم ﴾ بنصره إياكم ﴿ وما رميت ﴾ يا محمد أعين القوم ﴿ إذ رميت ﴾ بالحصى لأن كفاً من الحصى لا يملأ عيون الجيش الكثير برمية بشر ﴿ ولكن الله رمى ﴾ بإيصال ذلك اليهم فعل ذلك ليقهر الكافرين ﴿ وليبلي المؤمنين منه بلاء ﴾ عطاء ﴿ حسناً ﴾ هو الغنيمة ﴿ إن الله سميع ﴾ لأقوالهم ﴿ عليم ﴾ بأحوالهم

تفسير الجلالين

{ Whoever turns his rear to them on that day } : that is, the day of facing them; { except to move around } : to change direction; { to fight } : by making it look like he is escaping while actually intending a surprise attack; { or take sides } : joining up with; { with a squad } : seeking assistance from another group of Muslims; { he has incurred } : brought about; { the wrath of Allah; and his dwelling is Hell, a miserable fate } : this end; and this is relevant as long as the disbelievers are not more than double in number. { And you all did not kill them } : at Badr, by your own strength; { but Allah killed them } : by His aid to you; { you did not hurl } : Oh Muhammad, at people's eyes; { when you hurled } : the pebbles – because a handful of pebbles thrown by someone can not fill the eyes of a large army; { but Allah hurled } : by making it reach them; He did this to gain victory over the disbelievers; { so that He might put the Believers to the test with a suitable ordeal from Him } : a gift; { suitable } : this is the spoils; { indeed Allah is hearing } : of what they say; { knowing } : of their circumstances.

Tafsir Al-Jalalain

يقول إذا تدانيتم وتعاينتم فلا تَفِرّوا عنهم ولا تعطوهم أدباركم حرّم الله ذلك على المؤمنين حين فرض عليهم الجهاد وقتال الكفار

تفسير القرطبي

He is saying: Whenever you get close to each other and catch sight of each other, do not run away from them, and do not give them your rears. Allah prohibited this to the Believers when *jihad* and fighting the disbelievers [*kuffar*] were made obligatory for them.

Tafsir Al-Qurtubi

﴿ فلا تُولّوهم الأدبار ﴾ يقول فلا تولوهم ظهورهم فتنهزموا عنهم ولكن اثبتوا لهم فإن الله معكم عليهم

تفسير الطبري

{ Do not turn your rears to them } ; He is saying: Do not turn your backs on them, so that you are defeated and put to flight from them, but be firm towards them, for indeed Allah is with you against them.

Tafsir Al-Tabari

عن أبي المثنى العبدي سمعت السدوسي يعني إبن الخصاصية وهو بشير بن معبد قال أتيت النبي ﷺ لأبايعه فإشترط علي شهادة أن لا إله إلا الله وأن محمداً عبده ورسوله وأن أقيم الصلاة وأن أؤدي الزكاة وأن أحج حجة الإسلام وأن أصوم شهر رمضان وأن أجاهد في سبيل الله فقلت يا رسول الله أمّا اثنتان فوالله ما أطيقهما الجهاد فإنهم زعموا أنه من ولي الدبر فقد باء بغضب من الله فأخاف إن حضرت ذلك خشعت نفسي وكرهت الموت والصدقة فوالله ما لي إلا غُنَيمة وعشر ذَود هن رَسل أهلي وحمولتهم فقبض رسول الله ﷺ يده ثم حرّك يده ثم قال فلا جهاد ولا صدقة فبم تدخل الجنة إذاً فقلت يا رسول الله أنا أبايعك فبايعته عليهن كلهن

تفسير إبن كثير

Abu Al-Muthanna Al-'Abdi related: I heard Al-Sadusi, that is, Ibn Al-Khasasiya, Bashir ibn Ma'bad, say: I came to the Prophet (SAW) to pledge allegiance to him, and He imposed the conditions to bear witness that there is no god but Allah, that Muhammad is His servant and His Messenger, that I observe prayer, that I give *zakat*, that I perform the *hajj* of Islam, that I fast in the month of Ramadan, and that I wage *jihad* in the cause of Allah. And I said: Oh Messenger of Allah, two of these I swear by Allah I am unable to bear: *jihad*, for people allege that whoever turns his back has incurred the wrath of Allah, but I'm afraid that if I undertake this, my soul will be brought down, for I dislike death; and as for giving charity, I swear by Allah the only thing I have is a small herd and ten of my family's herd that they have carried along. And the Messenger of Allah (SAW) grabbed his hand, jerked it around, then said: No *jihad* and no charity – so by what then will you enter *Jannah*?! I said: "Oh Messenger of Allah, I pledge to you"; and I pledged to all of it.

Tafsir Ibn Kathir

يعلم تبارك وتعالى أن النصر ليس على كثرة العدد ولا بلبس اللأمة والعُدَد وإنما النصر من عنده تعالى كما قال تعالى ﴿ كم من فئة قليلة غلبت فئة كثيرة بإذن الله والله مع الصابرين ﴾ ثم قال تعالى لنبيه ﷺ أيضاً في شأن القبضة من التراب التي حصت بها وجوه الكافرين يوم بدر حين خرج من العريش بعد دعائه وتضرعه واستكانته فرماهم بها وقال شاهت الوجوه ثم أمر أصحابه أن يصدقوا الحملة إثرها ففعلوا فأوصل الله تلك الحصاء إلى أعين المشركين فلم يبق أحد منهم إلا ناله منها ما شغله عن حاله ولهذا قال تعالى ﴿ وما رميت إذ رميت ولكن الله رمى ﴾ أي هو الذي بلغ ذلك إليهم وكبتهم بها لا أنت

تفسير ابن كثير

The Blessed and Exalted is making known that victory is not in large numbers, nor in putting on armor, nor in reinforcements. Rather victory is from the Most High, as the Most High says: { How many small groups have overcome large groups by the permission of Allah; and Allah is with the steadfast } [Al-baqara 249]. Then the Most High also says to His Prophet (SAW) regarding the handful of soil that He hurled at the disbelievers' faces on the day of Badr, when He came out of the shack after his invocation, supplication, and yielding. He threw the handful at them and said: May their faces be disfigured. Then He ordered his Companions to affirm the campaign after this, and they did so. And Allah made that throw reach the eyes of the Idolaters, and there wasn't a single one of them who did not get hit with some of it and was distracted from what they were doing. For this reason the Most High says: { You did not hurl when you hurled, but Allah hurled } : that is, He is the one who made it reach them and hindered them with it, not you.

Tafsir Ibn Kathir

عن زيد مولى رسول الله ﷺ عن أبيه عن جده أنه سمع رسول الله يقول من قال استغفر الله الذي لا إله إلا هو الحي القيوم وأتوب إليه غفر له وإن كان فر من الزحف

الدر المنثور للسيوطي

Zaid, the freed slave of the Messenger of Allah (SAW), related from his father, that his grandfather heard the Messenger of Allah say: Whoever says "I seek forgiveness from Allah, He of who there is no god but Him, the Living, the Everlasting, and I repent unto Him" – he will be forgiven, even if he ran away from advancing with the army.

Al-Suyuti, Al-durr Al-manthur

* * *

﴿ قَل لِّلَّذِينَ كَفَرُوا إِن يَنتَهُوا يُغْفَرْ لَهُم مَّا قَدْ سَلَفَ وَإِن يَعُودُوا فَقَدْ مَضَتْ سُنَّتُ الْأَوَّلِينَ ۞ وَقَاتِلُوهُمْ حَتَّىٰ لَا تَكُونَ فِتْنَةٌ وَيَكُونَ الدِّينُ كُلُّهُ لِلَّهِ فَإِنِ انتَهَوْا فَإِنَّ اللَّهَ بِمَا يَعْمَلُونَ بَصِيرٌ ۞
الأنفال ٣٨-٣٩

{ Say to those who have disbelieved that if they cease, they will be forgiven for what has preceded, but if they return, the way of the forefathers has passed. So fight them until there is no more sedition and religion is all for Allah; and if they cease, then indeed Allah is aware of what they do } Al-anfal 38-39

يقول تعالى لنبيه محمد ﷺ ﴿ قل للذين كفروا إن ينتهوا ﴾ أي عما هم فيه من الكفر والمشاقّة والعناد ويدخلوا في الاسلام والطاعة والإنابة يغفر لهم ما قد سلف أي من كفرهم وذنوبهم وخطاياهم اياهم كما جاء في الصحيح من حديث ابي وائل عن ابن مسعود رضي الله عنه أن رسول الله ﷺ قال من أحسن في الاسلام لم يؤاخذ بما عمل في الجاهلية ومن أساء في الاسلام أُخِذَ بالأول والآخر وفي الصحيح أيضاً أن رسول الله ﷺ قال الاسلام يَجُبُّ ما قبله والتوبة تجب ما كان قبلها

تفسير ابن كثير

The Most High is saying to His Prophet Muhammad (SAW): { Say to those who have disbelieved that if they cease } : that is, from the disbelief, antagonism, and stubborn opposition that they are in, and enter into Islam, obedience, and repentance, they are forgiven for what has preceded, that is, of their disbelief, their offenses, and their sins, as recorded in the *Sahih* [Al-Bukhari and Muslim] from a hadith of Abu Wa'il, from Ibn Mas'ud (may Allah be pleased with him), that the Messenger of Allah (SAW) said: Whoever does good in Islam will not be held accountable for what he did during the age of ignorance [*jahiliya*], but whoever does bad in Islam will be taken by both the former and latter deeds. It is also related in the *Sahih* that the Messenger of Allah (SAW) said: Islam puts an end to whatever came before it, and repentance puts an end to whatever came before it.

Tafsir Ibn Kathir

﴿ قل للذين كفروا ﴾ كابي سفيان وأصحابه ﴿ إن ينتهوا ﴾ عن الكفر وقتال النبي ﷺ ﴿ يُغفر لهم ما قد سلف ﴾ من أعمالهم ﴿ وإن يعودوا ﴾ إلى قتاله ﴿ فقد مضت سُنَّت الأولين ﴾ أي سنتنا فيهم بالإهلاك فكذا نفعل بهم

تفسير الجلالين

{ Say to those who have disbelieved } : like Abu Sufyan and his companions; { that if they cease } : from their disbelief and from fighting the Prophet (SAW); { they will be forgiven for what has preceded } : of their deeds; { but if they return } : to fighting him; { the way of the forefathers has passed } : that is, our course of conduct of destruction concerning them, and we will do likewise with these people.

Tafsir Al-Jalalain

قوله تعالى ﴿ وقاتلوهم حتى لا تكون فتنة ﴾ أي قاتلوا كفار مكة حتى لا يكون شرك وقيل حتى لا يكون كافر بغير عهدٍ لأن الفتنة إنما تكون بأن يُترك الكفار بلا عهد فإن الكافر بغير عهد يكون عزيزاً في نفسه يدعو الناس إلى دينه ويجوز أن يكون المراد بالفتنة كل ما يودّي إلى الفساد وقوله تعالى ﴿ ويكون الدين كله لله ﴾ أي وتكون الطاعة كلها لله فتجتمع الناس على دين الاسلام

التفسير الكبير للطبراني

The word of the Most High: { So fight them until there is no more sedition [*fitnah*] } : that is, fight the disbelievers [*kuffar*] in Mecca until there is no more idolatry [*shirk*]. It is said: Until there remains no disbeliever that is not held under a covenant; for surely sedition occurs by leaving the disbelievers without covenant. Indeed a disbeliever that is not under covenant becomes emboldened within himself to call people to his religion. It is permissible to consider as sedition anything that leads to corruption. And the word of the Most High: { And religion is all for Allah } : that is, obedience is all to Allah, and people all agree on the religion of Islam.

Al-Tabarani, Al-tafsir Al-kabir

﴿ وقاتلوهم حتى لا تكون فتنة ﴾ أي شرك وقال أبو العالية بلاء وقال الربيع حتى لا يفتن مؤمن عن دينه ﴿ ويكون الدين ﴾ التوحيد خالصاً ﴿ كله لله ﴾ عز وجل ليس فيه شرك ويخلع ما دونه من الأنداد وقال قتادة حتى يقال لا إله إلا الله عليها قاتل نبي الله واليها دعا

تفسير الثعلبي

{ So fight them until there is no more sedition } : that is, idolatry [*shirk*]. Abu Al-'Aliya said: affliction; Rabi' said: until no Believer is enticed away from his religion. { And religion } : asserting one god [*tawheed*] with devotion; { is all for Allah } : Mighty and Sublime, with no other associated to Him [*shirk*] and eradicating any equal to Him. Qatada said: Until "There is no god but Allah" is declared ["*La ilaha illa Allah*"]; the Prophet of Allah fought for this and called people to this.

Tafsir Al-Tha'labi

﴿ وقاتلوهم حتى لا تكون فتنة ﴾ إلى أن لا يوجد فيهم شرك قط ﴿ ويكون الدين كله لله ﴾ ويضمحلّ عنهم كل دين باطل ويبقى فيهم دين الاسلام وحده ﴿ فإن انتهوا ﴾ عن الكفر وأسلموا ﴿ فإن الله بما يعملون بصير ﴾ يثيبهم على توبتهم وإسلامهم وقرئ ﴿ تعملون ﴾ بالتاء فيكون المعنى فإن الله بما تعلمون من الجهاد في سبيله والدعوة إلى دينه والإخراج من ظلمة الكفر إلى نور الاسلام ﴿ بصير ﴾ يجازيكم عليه أحسن الجزاء

تفسير الزمخشري

{ So fight them until there is no more sedition } : until no idolatry whatsoever is found in them; { and religion is all for Allah } : and every vain religion is eradicated from them, and only the religion of Islam remains among them. { And if they cease } : from disbelief, and yield into Islam; { then indeed Allah is aware of what they do } : He rewards them for their repentance and their Islam; this can also be read as { what you do } making the meaning: Then indeed Allah is aware of what you do – your *jihad* in His cause, calling people [*da'wah*] into His religion, and driving them from the obscurity of disbelief into the light of Islam; { aware } : He will reward you with the finest reward.

Tafsir Al-Zamakhshari

قال القاضي إنه تعالى أمر بقتالهم ثم بين العلّة التي بها أوجب قتالهم فقال ﴿ حتى لا تكون فتنة ﴾ ويخلص الدين الذي هو دين الله من سائر الاديان

تفسير الرازي

Al-Qadi said: Indeed the Most High ordered that they be fought, and then He made clear the reason by which He made it obligatory to fight them; He said: { Until there is no more sedition } and the religion which is Allah's religion is safe from all other religions.

Tafsir Al-Razi

* * *

﴿ وَاعْلَمُوا أَنَّمَا غَنِمْتُم مِّن شَيْءٍ فَأَنَّ لِلَّهِ خُمُسَهُ وَلِلرَّسُولِ وَلِذِي الْقُرْبَى وَالْيَتَامَى وَالْمَسَاكِينِ وَابْنِ السَّبِيلِ إِن كُنتُمْ آمَنتُم بِاللَّهِ وَمَا أَنزَلْنَا عَلَى عَبْدِنَا يَوْمَ الْفُرْقَانِ يَوْمَ الْتَقَى الْجَمْعَانِ وَاللَّهُ عَلَى كُلِّ شَيْءٍ قَدِيرٌ ﴾ الأنفال ٤١

{ So know that whatever you all take as spoils, indeed one-fifth of it is for Allah, for His Messenger, for the kinsman, orphans, the poor, and the journeyer, if you have believed in Allah and what We sent down to our servant on the day of the criterion, the day the two bands faced each other; and Allah is powerful over all things } *Al-anfal 41*

يبين تعالى تفصيل ما شرعه مخصصاً لهذه الأمة الشريفة من بين سائر الأمم المتقدمة بإحلال الغنائم والغنيمة هي المال المأخوذ من الكفار بإيجاف الخيل والركاب والفيء ما أخذ منهم بغير ذلك كالأموال التي يصالحون عليها أو يتوفون عنها ولا وارث لهم والجزية والخراج ونحو ذلك ... ﴿ وَاعْلَمُوا أَنَّمَا غَنِمْتُم مِّن شَيْءٍ فَأَنَّ لِلَّهِ خُمُسَهُ ﴾ توكيد لتخميس كل قليل وكثير حتى الخيط والمخيط.

تفسير ابن كثير

The Most High is making clear the details of what He has prescribed especially for this noble nation [*ummah*], apart from the other former nations, by making spoils lawful. Spoils [*ghanima*] are the wealth that is taken from the disbelievers [*kuffar*], by spurring on the horses and riding camels; plunder or loot [*fai'*] is what is taken from them by other means, such as the property that they make a truce with, or leave behind after they die with no heirs, as well as the protection tax [*jizya*], land tax [*kharaj*], and other related things. ... { So know that whatever you take as spoils, indeed one-fifth of it is for Allah } : this stresses that a fifth of everything must be allotted – small or large, even a needle and thread.

Tafsir Ibn Kathir

اعلم أنه تعالى لما أمر بالمقاتلة في قوله ﴿ وَقَاتِلُوهُمْ ﴾ وكان من المعلوم أن عند المقاتلة قد تحصل الغنيمة لا جَرَمَ ذكر الله تعالى حكم الغنيمة.

تفسير الرازي

Know that the Most High, when He ordered fighting by His word { So fight them } , and it was known that spoils would be had from fighting, of course the Most High mentioned the ruling concerning the spoils.

Tafsir Al-Razi

عن عطاء في قوله عز وجل ﴿ واعلموا أنما غنمتم من شيء فأن لله خمسه وللرسول ولذي القربى ﴾ قال خُمُس الله وخمس رسوله واحد كان رسول الله ﷺ يحمل منه ويعطي منه ويضعه حيث شاء ويصنع به ما شاء

سنن النسائي كتاب قسم الفيء

'Ataa, regarding the word of the Mighty and Sublime: { So know that whatever you all take as spoils, indeed one-fifth of it is for Allah, for His Messenger, for the kinsman }, said: The fifth for Allah and the fifth for His Messenger are the same; the Messenger of Allah would use some to get riding animals, He would give some of it away, He would set it aside wherever He wished, and He would do with it whatever He wished.

Sunan Al-Nasa'i, The book of dividing up the plunder

واختلف أهل العلم في مصرف الفيء بعد رسول الله ﷺ فقال قوم هو للأئمة بعده وللشافعي فيه قولان احدهما للمقاتلة الذين أُثبتَت أساميهم في ديوان الجهاد لأنهم القائمون مقام النبي ﷺ في إرهاب العدو

تفسير البغوي

Scholars disagreed concerning dealing out the plunder after the time of the Messenger of Allah. A group of them said it should be for the leaders [imams] after him. Al-Shafi'i had two points of view; one of them is that it should be for the fighters whose names have been confirmed in the register of *jihad*, since they rose up in place of the Prophet (SAW) to terrorize the enemy.

Tafsir Al-Baghawi

* * *

﴿ يَا أَيُّهَا الَّذِينَ آمَنُوا إِذَا لَقِيتُمْ فِئَةً فَاثْبُتُوا وَاذْكُرُوا اللَّهَ كَثِيرًا لَعَلَّكُمْ تُفْلِحُونَ وَأَطِيعُوا اللَّهَ وَرَسُولَهُ وَلَا تَنَازَعُوا فَتَفْشَلُوا وَتَذْهَبَ رِيحُكُمْ وَاصْبِرُوا إِنَّ اللَّهَ مَعَ الصَّابِرِينَ ﴾
الأنفال ٤٥-٤٦

{ Oh you who have believed! Whenever you come upon a squad, be firm and make much remembrance of Allah, that perchance you may be successful. And obey Allah and His Messenger, and do not argue such that you lose your wind and your dominance recedes; and be steadfast; indeed Allah is with those who are steadfast. } *Al-anfal 45-46*

﴿ وَاذْكُرُوا اللَّهَ كَثِيرًا ﴾ يقول وادعوا الله بالنصر عليهم والظفر بهم وأشعروا قلوبكم وألسنتكم ذكره ﴿ لَعَلَّكُمْ تُفْلِحُونَ ﴾ يقول كيما تنجحوا فتظفروا بعدوكم ويرزقكم الله النصر والظفر عليهم

تفسير الطبري

{ Make much remembrance of Allah } ; He is saying: Call upon Allah for victory over them and to triumph over them, and admonish your hearts and tongues to make remembrance of Him. { That perchance you may be successful } ; He is saying: In order to succeed and triumph over your enemy, that Allah would bountifully bestow you with victory and triumph over them.

Tafsir Al-Tabari

﴿ إِذَا لَقِيتُمْ فِئَةً فَاثْبُتُوا وَاذْكُرُوا اللَّهَ كَثِيرًا ﴾ وقال قتادة إفترض الله جل وعز ذكره على عباده أشغلَ ما يكونون عند الضِراب بالسيوف

تفسير القرطبي

{ Whenever you come upon a squad, be firm and make much remembrance of Allah } ; Qatada said: Allah Sublime and Mighty prescribed remembrance of Him [*dhikr*] for His servants as what they are to be most occupied in when striking with their swords.

Tafsir Al-Qurtubi

هذا تعليم من الله تعالى لعباده المؤمنين آداب اللقاء وطريق الشجاعة عند مواجهة الأعداء فقال ﴿ يا أيها الذين آمنوا إذا لقيتم فئة فاثبتوا ﴾ ثبت في الصحيحين عن عبدالله بن ابي أوفى أن رسول الله ﷺ إنتظر في بعض أيامه التي لقي فيها العدو حتى إذا مالت الشمس قام فيهم فقال يا أيها الناس لا تتنوا لقاء العدو واسألوا الله العافية فإذا لقيتموهم فاصبروا واعلموا أن الجنة تحت ظلال السيوف ثم قام النبي ﷺ وقال اللهم منزل الكتاب ومجري السحاب وهازم الاحزاب اهزمهم وانصرنا عليهم

تفسير ابن كثير

This is instruction from Allah Most High to His servants the Believers about how to act in a confrontation, and how to find courage when facing enemies, for He says: { Oh you who have believed! Whenever you come upon a squad, be firm } . It is affirmed in the Two *Sahihs* [Al-Bukhari and Muslim] from Abdullah ibn Abi Awfa, that the Messenger of Allah (SAW), on one of the days on which He faced the enemy, waited until the sun declined, got up among them, and said: Oh people! Do not wish to face the enemy, and ask Allah for good health; but whenever you face them, be steadfast, and know that *Jannah* is under the shades of the swords. Then the Prophet (SAW) got up and said: Oh Allah! He who sends down the Book, makes the clouds advance, and defeats the Confederates, defeat them and grant us victory over them!

Tafsir Ibn Kathir

﴿ وأطيعوا الله ورسوله ﴾ في سائر ما يأمر به لأن الجهاد لا ينفع إلا مع التمسك بسائر الطاعات

تفسير الرازي

{ And obey Allah and His Messenger } : in the other things that He has ordered, because *jihad* is not profitable except with adherence to the rest of the acts of obedience.

Tafsir Al-Razi

﴿ واصبروا ﴾ لقتال عدوكم ﴿ إن الله مع الصابرين ﴾ يعني في النصر للمؤمنين على الكافرين بذنوبهم وبعملهم

تفسير مقاتل بن سليمان

{ And be steadfast } : in fighting your enemy; { indeed Allah is with those who are steadfast } : that is, in victory for the Believers over the disbelievers, due to their offenses and their deeds.

Tafsir Muqatil ibn Sulaiman

﴿ وتذهب ريحكم ﴾ ... والريح هاهنا كناية عن نفاذ الأمر وجريانه على المراد تقول العرب هبت ريح فلان إذا أقبل أمره على ما يريد. قال قتادة وابن زيد هو ريح النصر لم يكن نصر قط إلا بريح يبعثها الله عز وجل تضرب وجوه العدو ومنه قول النبي ﷺ نُصرتُ بالصَبا وأُهلكتْ عادٌ بالدَبور

تفسير البغوي

{ Such that you lose your wind } ... "Wind" here is an allusion to executing a matter and following through with the intent; the Arabs say "So-and-so's wind has risen up" when he gets what he wants. Qatada and Ibn Zaid said: This refers to the wind of victory; never has there ever been victory except by a wind that Allah Mighty and Sublime sends forth to strike the faces of the enemy. Along these lines the Prophet (SAW) said: I have been made victorious by the *saba* [easterly wind] and the people of 'Ad were destroyed by the *dabur* [westerly wind].

Tafsir Al-Baghawi

فأمر تعالى بالثبات عند قتال الأعداء والصبر على مبارزتهم فلا يفروا ولا ينكلوا ولا يجبنوا وأن يذكروا الله في تلك الحال ولا ينسوه بل يستعينوا به ويتوكلوا عليه ويسألوه النصر على أعدائهم وأن يطيعوا الله ورسوله في حالهم ذلك فما أمرهم الله تعالى به أتمروا وما نهاهم عنه انزجروا ولا يتنازعوا فيما بينهم أيضاً فيختلفوا فيكون سبباً لتخاذلهم وفشلهم ﴿ وتذهب ريحكم ﴾ أي قوتكم وحدتكم وما كنتم فيه من الإقبال ﴿ واصبروا إن الله مع الصابرين ﴾ وقد كان للصحابة رضي الله عنهم في باب الشجاعة والائتمار بما أمرهم الله ورسوله به وإمتثال ما أرشدهم إليه ما لم يكن لأحد من الأمم والقرون قبلهم ولا يكون لأحد ممن بعدهم فإنهم ببركة الرسول ﷺ وطاعته فيما أمرهم فتحوا القلوب والأقاليم شرقاً وغرباً في المدة اليسيرة مع قلة عددهم بالنسبة إلى جيوش سائر الاقاليم من الروم والفرس والترك والصقالبة والبربر والحبوش وأصناف السودان والقبط وطوائف بني آدم قهروا الجميع حتى علت كلمة الله وظهر دينه على سائر الأديان وامتدت الممالك الاسلامية في مشارق الأرض ومغاربها في أقل من ثلاثين سنة فرضي الله عنهم وأرضاهم أجمعين وحشرنا في زمرتهم إنه كريم وهاب

تفسير ابن كثير

The Most High ordered perseverance when fighting enemies and steadfastness in combating them. People are not to flee, not shy away, and not grow cowardly; they are to make remembrance of Allah under these circumstances and not forget Him, but rather invoke His aid, trust in Him, and ask Him for victory over their enemies; they are to obey Allah and His Messenger when they are in this situation, deliberating on what Allah Most High has ordered them, and guarding restraint against what He has forbidden them. Nor are they to quarrel with each other, or differ, such that this leads to their frailty and failure; { such that you lose heart } : that is, your strength and vitality, and the enthusiasm you feel. { And be steadfast; indeed Allah is with those who are steadfast } : the Companions (may Allah be pleased with them) – in their courage and deliberation in what Allah and His Messenger ordered, and observance of what He guided them towards – had what no other nation or generation before them had, or any after them will have. Indeed, by the blessing of the Messenger (SAW) and obedience to him in what Allah had ordered them, they opened hearts as well as territories east and west in a brief span of time, in spite of their small number compared to the armies of the other territories – the Romans, Persia, the Turks, the Slavs, the Berbers, the Ethiopians, the different classes in Sudan, the Copts, and all factions of mankind; they conquered all of them, until the word of Allah rose high and His religion [deen] was manifest above all other religions. The Islamic empires spread out to the eastern and western regions of the earth in less than thirty years. So then may Allah be pleased with them and give pleasure to them all, and gather us up among their league; indeed He is generous, granting.

Tafsir Ibn Kathir

* * *

﴿ إِنَّ شَرَّ الدَّوَابِّ عِنْدَ اللَّهِ الَّذِينَ كَفَرُوا فَهُمْ لَا يُؤْمِنُونَ الَّذِينَ عَاهَدْتَ مِنْهُمْ ثُمَّ يَنْقُضُونَ عَهْدَهُمْ فِي كُلِّ مَرَّةٍ وَهُمْ لَا يَتَّقُونَ فَإِمَّا تَثْقَفَنَّهُمْ فِي الْحَرْبِ فَشَرِّدْ بِهِمْ مَنْ خَلْفَهُمْ لَعَلَّهُمْ يَذَّكَّرُونَ ﴾
الأنفال ٥٥-٥٧

{ Truly the worst of animals in the sight of Allah are those who have disbelieved, for they have not believed. Those of them with whom you have made a pledge but then they broke their pledge every time, not being devout. If indeed you get to them in warfare, use them to drive away those who come after them, that perchance they might be reminded } *Al-anfal 55-57*

﴿ فَهُمْ لَا يُؤْمِنُونَ ﴾ يقول فهم لا يصدّقون رسل الله ولا يقرّون بوحيه وتنزيله ... ﴿ فَإِمَّا تَثْقَفَنَّهُمْ فِي الْحَرْبِ فَشَرِّدْ بِهِمْ مَنْ خَلْفَهُمْ لَعَلَّهُمْ يَذَّكَّرُونَ ﴾ أي نكّل بهم من وراءهم لعلهم يعقلون

تفسير الطبري

{ For they have not believed } ; He is saying: They do not accept the messengers of Allah and do not attest to His revelation and inspiration. ... { If indeed you get to them in warfare, use them to drive away those who come after them } : that is, make an example of them to those who come after them, that perhaps they might understand.

Tafsir Al-Tabari

أخبر تعالى أن شرّ ما دبّ على وجه الأرض هم الذين كفروا فهم لا يؤمنون الذين كلما عاهدوا عهداً نقضوه وكلما أكدوه بالإيمان نكثوه ﴿ وهم لا يتقون ﴾ أي لا يخافون من الله في شيء ارتكبوه من الآثام ﴿ فإما تثقفنّهم في الحرب ﴾ أي تغلبهم وتظفر بهم في حرب ﴿ فشرّد بهم من خلفهم ﴾ أي نكّل بهم قاله ابن عباس والحسن البصري والضحاك والسدي وعطاء الخراساني وابن عيينة ومعناه غلظ عقوبتهم وأثخنهم قتلاً ليخاف من سواهم من الأعداء من العرب وغيرهم ويصيروا لهم عبرة ﴿ لعلهم يذكّرون ﴾ وقال السدي يقول لعلهم يحذرون أن ينكثوا فيصنع بهم مثل ذلك

تفسير ابن كثير

The Most High is making it known that the worst of what crawls on the face of the earth are those who have disbelieved, since they do not believe; those who, every time they make a covenant, break it, and every time they affirm it with oaths, they violate it. { Not being devout } : that is, they have no fear of Allah of any of the sins they have committed. { If indeed you get to them in warfare } : that is, you overcome them and triumph over them in warfare; { use them to drive away those who come after them } : that is, make an example by punishing them severly; Ibn 'Abbas, Al-Hasan Al-Basri, Al-Dahhak, Al-Suddi, 'Ataa Al-Kurasani, and Ibn 'Uyaina all said this. The meaning of this is: Make their punishment harsh and massacre them, so that those Arab and other enemies like them will fear, and it will serve as an example to them. { That perchance they might be reminded } ; Al-Suddi said: He is saying that perchance they will be careful not to break any pacts and have something similar done to them.

Tafsir Ibn Kathir

﴿ إن شر الدواب عند الله ﴾ أي في حكمه وعلمه من حصلت له صفتان الصفة الأولى الكافر الذي يكون مستمراً على كفره مصراً عليه لا يتغير عنه البتّة الصفة الثانية أن يكون ناقضاً للعهد على الدوام ... اعلم أنه تعالى تارة يرشد رسوله إلى الرفق واللطف في آيات كثيرة منها قوله ﴿ وما أرسلناك إلا رحمة للعالمين ﴾ ومنها قوله ﴿ فاعفُ عنهم واستغفر لهم وشاورهم في الأمر ﴾ وتارة يرشد إلى التغليظ والتشديد كما في هذه الآية وذلك لأنه تعالى لما ذكر الذين ينقضون عهدهم في كل مرة بين ما يجب أن يعاملوا به

تفسير الرازي

{ Truly the worst of animals in the sight of Allah } : that is, in His judgment and awareness concerning those befallen with two attributes: the first attribute is that a disbeliever [kafir], someone who persists in his disbelief and is fixed on it, can not change from it whatsoever; the second is that he perpetually breaks covenants. ... Know that the Most High at times guides His Messenger to gentleness and kindness in numerous verses, including: { We have only sent you as a mercy to the worlds } [Al-anbiyaa 107], and: { So pardon them, and seek forgiveness for them, and consult with them regarding the issue } [Al 'Imran 159]. But sometimes His guidance is to exert harshness and severity, as in this verse; this is because the Most High, when He mentions those who break their covenant every time, makes it clear how they must be treated.

Tafsir Al-Razi

﴿ وَلَا يَحْسَبَنَّ الَّذِينَ كَفَرُوا سَبَقُوا إِنَّهُمْ لَا يُعْجِزُونَ وَأَعِدُّوا لَهُم مَّا اسْتَطَعْتُم مِّن قُوَّةٍ وَمِن رِّبَاطِ الْخَيْلِ تُرْهِبُونَ بِهِ عَدُوَّ اللَّهِ وَعَدُوَّكُمْ وَآخَرِينَ مِن دُونِهِمْ لَا تَعْلَمُونَهُمُ اللَّهُ يَعْلَمُهُمْ وَمَا تُنفِقُوا مِن شَيْءٍ فِي سَبِيلِ اللَّهِ يُوَفَّ إِلَيْكُمْ وَأَنتُمْ لَا تُظْلَمُونَ وَإِن جَنَحُوا لِلسَّلْمِ فَاجْنَحْ لَهَا وَتَوَكَّلْ عَلَى اللَّهِ إِنَّهُ هُوَ السَّمِيعُ الْعَلِيمُ ﴾ الأنفال ٥٩-٦١

{ Let not those who have disbelieved reckon that they have gotten away; indeed they can not frustrate. Prepare for them whatever you are able of force and tethers of steeds, so that you can terrify Allah's enemy and your enemy with it, as well as others besides them that you do not know but that Allah knows; and anything you spend in the cause of Allah will be paid back to you, and you will not be oppressed. And if they incline to peace, then incline to it; and rely on Allah, indeed He is the one who hears, the one who knows } Al-anfal 59-61

يقول تعالى لنبيه ﴿ لا تحسبنّ ﴾ يا محمد ﴿ الذين كفروا سبقوا ﴾ أي فاتونا فلا نقدر عليهم بل هم تحت قهر قدرتنا وفي قبضة مشيئتنا فلا يعجزوننا ... ثم أمر تعالى بإعداد آلات الحرب لمقاتلتهم حسب الطاقة والإمكان والإستطاعة ... عقبة بن عامر يقول سمعت رسول الله ﷺ يقول وهو على المنبر ﴿ وأعدّوا لهم ما استطعتم من قوة ﴾ ألا إن القوة الرمي ألا إن القوة الرمي
تفسير ابن كثير

The Most High is saying to His Prophet (SAW): { Do not reckon } : Oh Muhammad; { that those who have disbelieved have gotten away } : that is, that they have eluded Us and that We can not catch them; rather they are subjugated to our power and the grasp of our will, and they will not frustrate Us. ... Then the Most High ordered the preparation of instruments of war to fight against them according to their strength, possibility, and capability. ... 'Uqba ibn 'Amir said: I heard the Messenger of Allah (SAW) say, while He was at the pulpit: Prepare for them whatever you are able of force – Is not shooting indeed force? Is not shooting indeed force?

Tafsir Ibn Kathir

﴿ وأعدّوا لهم ﴾ لقتالهم ﴿ ما استطعتم من قوة ﴾ قال ﷺ هي الرمي رواه مسلم ﴿ ومن رباط الخيل ﴾ مصدر بمعنى حبسها في سبيل الله ﴿ تُرهبون ﴾ تخوّفون ﴿ به عدو الله وعدوّكم ﴾ أي كفار مكة ﴿ وآخرين من دونهم ﴾ أي غيرهم وهو المنافقون أو اليهود ﴿ لا تعلمونهم الله يعلمهم وما تنفقوا من شيء في سبيل الله يوفَّ

اليكم ﴾ جزاؤه ﴿ وانتم لا تُظلمون ﴾ تنقصون منه شيئاً ﴿ وإن جنحوا ﴾ مالوا ﴿ للسَّلْم ﴾ بكسر السين وفتحها الصلح ﴿ فاجنَحْ لها ﴾ وعاهدهم قال إبن عباس هذا منسوخ بآية السيف وقال مجاهد مخصوص بأهل الكتاب إذ نزلت في بني قريظة ﴿ وتوكل على الله ﴾ ثق به ﴿ إنه هو السميع ﴾ للقول ﴿ العليم ﴾ بالفعل

تفسير الجلالين

{ Prepare for them } : to fight them; { whatever you are able of force } : He (SAW) said: This is archery (narrated by Muslim); { and tethers of steeds } : a verbal noun meaning to hold them for the cause of Allah; { so you can terrify } : fill with fear; { Allah's enemy and your enemy by it } : that is, the disbelievers of Mecca; { as well as others besides them } : that is, other than them, these being the hypocrites or the Jews; { that you do not know but that Allah knows; and anything you spend in the cause of Allah will be paid back to you } : its reward; { and you will not be oppressed } : lack any of it. { And if they incline } : lean towards; { to peace} : conciliation; { then incline to it } : make a pact with them; Ibn 'Abbas said: This is abrogated by the sword verse [Al-tawba 5]. Mujahid said: This is just for the People of the Book, having come down regarding the Banu Quraiza. { And rely on Allah } : trust in Him; { indeed He is the one who hears } : what is said; { the one who knows } : what is done.

Tafsir Al-Jalalain

عن عقبة بن عامر أن رسول الله ﷺ قرأ هذه الآية على المنبر ﴿ واعدوا لهم ما استطعتم من قوة ﴾ قال ألا إن القوة الرمي ثلاث مرات ألا إن الله سيفتح لكم الأرض وستكفون المؤنة فلا يَعجزَنَّ أحدكم أن يلهو بأسهمه

جامع الترمذي كتاب تفسير القرآن

'Uqba ibn 'Amir related that the Messenger of Allah (SAW) recited this verse at the pulpit: { Prepare for them whatever you are able of force } and said: Is not shooting indeed force? – three times – Will not Allah indeed open up the land for you, and you will have enough supplies? So let none of you neglect practicing with his arrows.

Sunan Al-Tirmidhi, The book of tafsir of the Qur'an

﴿ واعدوا لهم ما استطعتم من قوة ومن رباط الخيل ترهبون به عدو الله وعدوكم وآخرين من دونهم لا تعلمونهم الله يعلمهم وما تنفقوا من شيء في سبيل الله يُوَفَّ اليكم وأنتم لا تظلمون ﴾ لما إتفق في قصة بدر أن قصدوا الكفار بلا تكميل آلة ولا عُدَّة وأمره تعالى بالتشريد وبنبذ العهد للناقضين كان ذلك سبباً للأخذ في قتاله والتآلؤ عليه فأمره تعالى للمؤمنين بإعداد ما قدروا عليه من القوة للجهاد والإعداد الأرصاد وعلّق ذلك بالإستطاعة لطفاً منه تعالى والمخاطبون هم المؤمنين والضمير في ﴿ لهم ﴾ عائد على الكفار المتقدّمي الذكر وهم المأمور بحربهم في ذلك الوقت ويعمّ من بعده

البحر المحيط لأبي حيان

{ Prepare for them whatever you are able of force and tethers of steeds, so that you can terrify Allah's enemy and your enemy with it, as well as others besides them that you do not know but that Allah knows; and anything you spend in the cause of Allah will be paid back to you, and you will not be oppressed } . When it came to pass in the account of Badr that they had set their sights on the disbelievers without a complete array of tools or gear, and the Most High ordered them to drive away the violators and disregard the pact with them, this became reason to engage in fighting them and join forces against them. So the Most High ordered the Believers to prepare whatever they could of force for *jihad* and set aside preparations, and made this conditional to their capability as an act of kindness from Him Most High. Those being addressed are the Believers, and the pronoun { for them } denotes the disbelievers [*kuffar*] referred to earlier, those against whom war was ordered at that time, although it became universal after this.

Abu Hayyan, Al-bahr Al-muhit

﴿ تُرهبون به عدو الله وعدوّكم ﴾ يعني تُخيفون به عدو الله وعدوّكم من اليهود وقريش وكفار العرب ﴿ وآخرين من دونكم ﴾ يعني فارس والروم قاله السدي وقيل الجنّ وهو اختيار الطبري وقيل المراد بذلك كل من لا تعرف عداوته

تفسير القرطبي

{ So you can terrify Allah's enemy and your enemy with it } : that is, so you can frighten the Jews, the Quraish, and the Disbelievers among the Arabs who are Allah's enemy and your enemy; { as well as others besides them } : that is, Persia and the Romans; Al-Suddi said this. It is also said: The genies [*jinn*]; this was Al-Tabari's preference. It is also said: The intended meaning of this is anyone whose enmity is not known.

Tafsir Al-Qurtubi

قال إبن زيد في قوله ﴿ واخرين من دونهم لا تعلمونهم الله يعلمهم ﴾ قال هؤلاء المنافقون لا تعلمونهم لأنهم معكم يقولون لا إله إلا الله ويغزون معكم وقال آخرون هم قوم من الجنّ قال أبو جعفر والصواب من القول في ذلك أن يقال إن الله أمر المؤمنين بإعداد الجهاد وآلة الحرب وما يتقوّون به على جهاد عدوه وعدوهم من المشركين من السلاح والرمي وغير ذلك ورباط الخيل

تفسير الطبري

Ibn Zaid, regarding His word { As well as others besides them that you do not know but that Allah knows } , said: These are the hypocrites that you do not recognize, because they are with you, they say "There is no god but Allah", and they go on raids with you. Others said that this refers to a group of the genies [jinn]. Abu Ja'far said: The correct view regarding this is to say: Indeed Allah has ordered the Believers to prepare jihad, instruments of war, and whatever weapons, archery, other things, and tethers of steeds they can strengthen themselves with in order to wage jihad on His enemy and their enemy the idolaters [mushrikeen].

Tafsir Al-Tabari

فقال ﴿ ترهبون به عدو الله وعدوكم ﴾ وذلك أن الكفار إذا علموا كون المسلمين متأهبين للجهاد ومستعدين له مستكملين لجميع الأسلحة والآلات خافوهم وذلك الخوف يفيد أموراً كثيرة أولها أنهم لا يقصدون دخول دار الاسلام وثانيها أنه إذا إشتد خوفهم فربما التزموا من عند أنفسهم جزية وثالثها أنه ربما صار ذلك داعياً لهم إلى الإيمان ورابعها أنهم لا يعينون سائر الكفار وخامسها أن يصير ذلك سبباً لمزيد الزينة في دار الاسلام
تفسير الرازي

And He says: { So you can terrify Allah's enemy and your enemy with it } ; this is because the disbelievers [kuffar], whenever they are aware of the presence of the Muslims geared up for jihad, prepared for it, fully outfitted with all kinds of weapons and instruments, they will be fearful, and this fear is advantageous for many reasons. The first is that they will not try to enter Islamic territory; the second is that if their fear becomes intense, perhaps they will take it upon themselves to give *jizya*; the third is that perhaps this will become a motive for them to believe; the fourth is that they will not aid other disbelievers; the fifth is that this will become a reason for greater glory in the land of Islam.

Tafsir Al-Razi

قوله تعالى ﴿ وإن جنحوا للسلم فاجنح لها ﴾ معناه فإن مالت بني قريظة إلى الصلح فمل اليهم وصالحهم فكان هذا قبل نزول براءة ثم نُسخ بقوله ﴿ فاقتلوا المشركين حيث وجدتموهم ﴾ وبقوله ﴿ قاتلوا الذين لا يؤمنون بالله ﴾
التفسير الكبير للطبراني

The word of the Most High: { If they incline to peace, then incline to it } : the meaning is: If the Jews of the Banu Quraiza are inclined towards a truce, then incline to them as well and make peace with them. However this was before "Absolution" [surah Al-tawha] was sent down, after which it was abrogated by His word: { Kill the Idolaters wherever you find them } [Al-tawba 5], and by His word: { Fight those who do not believe in Allah } [Al-tawba 29].

Al-Tabarani, Al-tafsir Al-kabir

وعن إبن عباس رضي الله عنه أن الآية منسوخة بقوله تعالى ﴿ قاتلوا الذين لا يؤمنون بالله ﴾ وعن مجاهد بقوله ﴿ فاقتلوا المشركين حيث وجدتموهم ﴾ والصحيح أن الأمر موقوف على ما يرى فيه الإمام صلاح الإسلام وأهله من حرب أو سلم وليس بحتم أن يقاتلوا أبداً أو يجابوا إلى الهدنة أبداً

تفسير الزمخشري

Ibn 'Abbas (may Allah be pleased with him) related that this verse is abrogated by the word of the Most High: { Fight those who do not believe in Allah } , and according to Mujahid, by His word: { Kill the Idolaters wherever you find them } . The correct view is that the issue depends on what the leader [*imam*] finds of benefit to Islam and its people between either war or peace; there is no obligation to either always fight or to always make a way towards peace.

Tafsir Al-Zamakhshari

وأخرج عبد الرزاق وإبن المنذر والنحاس في ناسخه وأبو الشيخ عن قتادة رضي الله عنه في قوله ﴿ وإن جنحوا للسلم ﴾ أي الصلح ﴿ فأجنَحْ لها ﴾ قال كانت قبل براءة وكان النبي يوادع الناس إلى أجل فإما أن يسلموا وإما أن يقاتلهم ثم نسخ ذلك في براءة فقال ﴿ فاقتلوا المشركين حيث وجدتموهم ﴾ وقال ﴿ وقاتلوا المشركين كافة ﴾ نبذ إلى كل ذي عهد عهده وأمره أن يقاتلهم حتى يقولوا لا إله إلا الله ويسلموا وإن لا يقبلوا منهم إلا ذلك وكل عهد كان في هذه السورة وغيرها وكل صلح يصالح به المسلمون المشركين يتواعدون به فإن براءة جاءت بنسخ ذلك فأمر بقتالهم قبلها على كل حال حتى يقولوا لا إله إلا الله

الدر المنثور للسيوطي

'Abd Al-Razzaq, Ibn Al-Mundhir, and Al-Nahhas, and Abu Al-Shiekh from Qatada (may Allah be pleased with him), regarding His word: { And if they incline to peace } : that is, conciliation; { then incline to it } : he said: This was before "Absolution" [surah *Al-tawba*], when the Prophet would make peace with people for a certain period of time, then either they yielded into Islam or He would fight them. This was then abrogated in the *Absolution*; He said: { Kill the Idolaters wherever you find them } [*Al-tawba* 5] and He said: { So fight the Idolaters completely } [*Al-tawba* 36], which dispensed with the pacts of anyone with a pact, and He ordered him to fight them until they said "There is no god but Allah" ["*La ilaha illa Allah*"] and yielded into Islam, and for them not to accept anything from them except this. Every pact in this *surah* and others, and every truce that the Muslims had made with the idolaters [*mushrikun*] in mutual promise to each other – the *Absolution* [surah *Al-tawba*] brought abrogation to this, and He ordered that they be fought for it in all situations until they say "*La ilaha illa Allah*".

Al-Suyuti, Al-durr Al-manthur

وقد إختُلف في هذه الآية هل هي منسوخة أم لا فقال قتادة وعكرمة نسخها ﴿ فاقتلوا المشركين حيث وجدتموهم ﴾ ﴿ وقاتلوا المشركين كافة ﴾ وقالا نسخت براءة كل موادعة حتى يقولوا لا إله إلا الله إبن عباس الناسخ لها ﴿ فلا تهنوا وتدعوا إلى السلم ﴾ وقيل ليست بمنسوخة بل أراد قبول الجزية من أهل الجزية وقد صالح أصحاب رسول الله ﷺ في زمن عمر بن الخطاب رضي الله عنه ومن بعده من الأئمة كثيراً من بلاد العجم على ما اخذوه منهم وتركوهم على ما هم فيه وهم قادرون على استئصالهم

تفسير القرطبي

There is difference in opinion regarding this verse – it is abrogated or not? Qatada and 'Ikrama say that the following abrogates it: { And kill the idolaters wherever you find them } [Al-tawba 5] and { And fight the Idolaters completely } [Al-tawba 36]. The two of them say that "Absolution" [surah Al-tawba] abrogated all peacemaking, until people say "There is no god but Allah" ["La ilaha illa Allah"]. Ibn 'Abbas said that { So do not grow weary and make a call to peace } [Muhammad 35] is what abrogates it. It is also said that this verse is not abrogated, but rather He has called for jizya to be taken from the people of jizya. The Messenger of Allah's (SAW) Companions made truces, at the time of 'Umar ibn Al-Khattab (may Allah be pleased with him) and numerous leaders [imams] after him, in non-Arab lands, based on what they took from them, and they let them keep what they had, being capable nonetheless of getting rid of them.

Tafsir Al-Qurtubi

▪ ▪ ▪

﴿ يا أيها النبي حرض المؤمنين على القتال إن يكن منكم عشرون صابرون يغلبوا مائتين وإن يكن منكم مائة يغلبوا ألفاً من الذين كفروا بأنهم قوم لا يفقهون ۞ الآن خفف الله عنكم وعلم أن فيكم ضعفاً فإن يكن منكم مائة صابرة يغلبوا مائتين وإن يكن منكم ألف يغلبوا ألفين بإذن الله والله مع الصابرين ﴾ الأنفال ٦٥-٦٦

{ Oh Prophet! Incite the Believers to fight; if there are twenty steadfast among you, that they would overcome two hundred, and if there are a hundred among you, that they would overcome a thousand of those who have disbelieved, since they are a people who do not comprehend. Now Allah has given you all relief, and is aware that there is weakness in you; so if there are a hundred steadfast among you, that they would overcome two hundred; and if there are a thousand, that they would overcome two thousand; and Allah is with those who are steadfast } Al-anfal 65-66

يقول تعالى ذكره لنبيه محمد ﷺ ﴿ يا أيها النبي حرض المؤمنين على القتال ﴾ حُثَّ متبعيك ومصدقيك على ما جئتهم به من ألحق على قتال من أدبر وتولى عن ألحق من المشركين

تفسير الطبري

He (may His remembrance be exalted) is saying to His Prophet Muhammad (SAW): Rouse those who follow you and have believed you in the truth I have brought to them regarding the duty to fight the idolaters [mushrikeen] who have turned away and renounced the truth.

Tafsir Al-Tabari

﴿ يا أيها النبي حرض المؤمنين على القتال ﴾ أي حثهم أو ذمرهم عليه ولهذا كان رسول الله ﷺ يحرض على القتال عند صفهم ومواجهة العدو كما قال لأصحابه يوم بدر حين أقبل المشركون في عَدَدهم وعُدَدهم قوموا إلى جنة عرضها السموات والأرض فقال عمير بن الحمام عرضها السموات والأرض فقال رسول الله ﷺ نعم فقال بخ بخ فقال ما يحملك على قولك بخ بخ قال رجاء أن أكون من أهلها قال فإنك من أهلها فتقدم الرجل فكسر جفن سيفه وأخرج تمرات فجعل يأكل منهن ثم ألقى بقيتهن من يده وقال لئن أنا حييت حتى آكلهن إنها لحياة طويلة ثم تقدم فقاتل حتى قتل رضي الله عنه

تفسير ابن كثير

{ Oh Prophet! Incite the Believers to fight } : that is, rouse them or urge them on towards it. For this reason the Messenger of Allah (SAW) urged fighting when they were lined up and facing the enemy, as He said to his Companions on the day of Badr when the Idolaters were advancing with their numbers and their reinforcements: Rise up towards *Jannah*, as broad as the heavens and the earth! And 'Umair ibn Al-Hammam said: As broad as the heavens and the earth?! The Messenger of Allah (SAW) said: Yes. And 'Umair said: Excellent! Excellent! He said: What makes you say Excellent Excellent? 'Umair said: I hope to be among its people. He said: Indeed you are among its people. So the man went ahead, broke the sheath of his sword, and took out some dates and started to eat them. Then he tossed the rest of them from his hand, and said: If I live to eat them, truly it was a long life. Then he pressed ahead, and fought until he was killed (may Allah be pleased with him).

Tafsir Ibn Kathir

﴿ يا أيها النبي حرض المؤمنين على القتال ﴾ بالغ في حثهم عليه

تفسير البيضاوي

{ Oh Prophet! Incite the Believers to fight } : Do your utmost to rouse them to it.

Tafsir Al-Baydawi

وكان هذا يوم بدر قَرَنَ على الرجل من المؤمنين قتال عشرة من الكافرين فثقلت على المؤمنين وضجّوا فخفّف الله الكريم عنهم وأنزل ﴿ الآن خفف الله عنكم وعلم أن فيكم ضعفاً ﴾ أي في الواحد عن قتال عشرة والمائة عن قتال الألف

تفسير الثعلبي

This was on the day of Badr when every man among the Believers was made to fight ten disbelievers [*kuffar*]. This weighed heavily on the Believers, and they cried out, so Allah the Most Generous gave them relief, and sent down: { Now Allah has given you all relief, and is aware that there is weakness in you } : that is, for one man to fight ten, or a hundred to fight a thousand.

Tafsir Al-Tha'labi

عن إبن أنس رضي الله عنهما لما نزلت ﴿ إن يكن منكم عشرون صابرون يغلبوا مائتين ﴾ فكُتب عليهم أن لا يفرَّ واحد من عشرة فقال سفيان غير مرة أن لا يفرَّ عشرون من مائتين ثم نزل ﴿ الآن خفَّف الله عنكم ﴾ الآية فكتب أن لا يفر مائة من مائتين

صحيح البخاري كتاب التفسير

Ibn 'Abbas (may Allah be pleased with them both) related that when { If there are twenty steadfast among you, that they would overcome two hundred } came down, it was decreed for them that one man should not run away from ten. Sufyan said, more than once, that twenty should not run away from two hundred. Then: { Now Allah has given you all relief } and the rest of the verse came down, and He decreed that one hundred not run away from two hundred.

Sahih Al-Bukhari, The book of tafsir

عن إبن عباس رضي الله عنهما قال لما نزلت ﴿ إن يكون منكم عشرون صابرون يغلبوا مائتين ﴾ شَقَّ ذلك على المسلمين حين فُرض عليهم أن لا يفرَّ واحد من عشرة لجاء التخفيف فقال ﴿ الآن خفَّف الله عنكم وعلم أن فيكم ضعفاً فإن يكن منكم مائة صابرة يغلبوا مائتين ﴾ قال فلما خفف الله عنهم من العِدَّة نقص من الصبر بقدر ما خُفِّف عنهم

صحيح البخاري كتاب التفسير

From Ibn 'Abbas (may Allah be pleased with them both), who said: When { If there are twenty steadfast among you, that they would overcome two hundred } came down, this was very hard on the Muslims, when it was made obligatory on them that one man not run away from ten. So the "relief" came and He said: { Now Allah has given you all relief, and is aware that there is weakness in you; so if there are a hundred steadfast among you, that they would overcome two hundred } . Ibn 'Abbas said: And when Allah relieved the number for them, steadfastness diminished by the same degree to which it had been lightened for them.

Sahih Al-Bukhari, The book of tafsir

* * *

﴿ مَا كَانَ لِنَبِيٍّ أَن يَكُونَ لَهُ أَسْرَىٰ حَتَّىٰ يُثْخِنَ فِى ٱلْأَرْضِ تُرِيدُونَ عَرَضَ ٱلدُّنْيَا وَٱللَّهُ يُرِيدُ ٱلْآخِرَةَ وَٱللَّهُ عَزِيزٌ حَكِيمٌ ﴾ الأنفال ٦٧

{ It is not for a prophet to take captives until he has wreaked havoc on the land; you desire the fleeting gain of this world but Allah desires the hereafter; and Allah is mighty, wise } Al-anfal 67

قال إبن إسحاق فقال ﴿ ما كان لنبي ﴾ أي قبلك ﴿ أن يكون له أسرى ﴾ من عدوه ﴿ حتى يُثخن في الأرض ﴾ أي يُثخن عدوّه حتى ينفيه من الأرض ﴿ تريدون عرض الدنيا ﴾ أي المتاع الفداء بأخذ الرجال ﴿ والله يريد الآخرة ﴾ أي قتلهم لظهور الدين الذي تريدون إظهاره أي والذي تُدرَك به الآخرة

السيرة النبوية لإبن هشام ذكر نزول سورة الأنفال

Ibn Ishaq said: And He said { It is not for a prophet } : that is, before you; { to take captives } : from among his enemy; { until he has wreaked havoc on the land } : that is, wreaked havoc on his enemy until he drives them out of the land; { you desire the fleeting gain of this world } : that is, goods, ransom for capturing men; { but Allah desires the hereafter } : that is, that they be killed so that the religion [deen] you desire to be manifest may be manifest, that is, that by which the hereafter is attained.

Ibn Hisham, Al-sirah Al-nabawiya, Topic section: mention of the sending down of surah Al-anfal

عن عبدالله بن مسعود قال لما كان يوم بدر وجيءَ بالاسارى قال رسول الله ﷺ ما تقولون في هؤلاء الأسارى فذكر في الحديث قصة فقال رسول الله ﷺ لا ينفلتنَّ منهم أحد إلا بفداء أو ضرب عنق قال عبدالله بن مسعود فقلت يا رسول الله إلا سهيل بن بيضاء فإني قد سمعته يذكر الاسلام قال فسكت رسول الله ﷺ قال فما رأيتُني في يوم أخوف أن تقع عليَّ حجارة منه في ذلك اليوم قال حتى قال رسول الله ﷺ إلا سهيل بن بيضاء قال ونزل القرآن بقول عمر ﴿ وما كان لنبي أن يكون له أسرى حتى يُثخن في الأرض ﴾ إلى آخر الآيات

جامع الترمذي كتاب تفسير القرآن

From Abdullah ibn Mas'ud, who said: On the day of Badr, when the captives were brought out, the Messenger of Allah (SAW) said: What do you all say about these captives? So he [Abdullah] related an account. The Messenger of Allah (SAW) said: Let none of them go free without a ransom or a blow to the neck. I said: Oh Messenger of Allah, except Suhail ibn Baydaa, for indeed I heard him mention Islam. And the Messenger of Allah (SAW) was silent. I have never seen myself on any day more afraid that stones would fall on me from the sky than that day, until the Messenger of Allah (SAW) finally said: Except Suhail ibn Baydaa. And that portion of the Qur'an came down according to what 'Umar said: { It is not for a prophet to take captives until he has wreaked havoc on the land } until the end of the verses.

Sunan Al-Tirmidhi, The book of tafsir

ونزل لما أخذوا الفداء من أسرى بدر ﴿ ما كان لنبي أن يكون ﴾ بالتاء والياء ﴿ له أسرى حتى يثخن في الأرض ﴾ يبالغ في قتل الكفار ﴿ تريدون ﴾ أيها المؤمنون ﴿ عرض الدنيا ﴾ حُطامها بأخذ الفداء ﴿ والله يريد ﴾ لكم ﴿ الآخرة ﴾ أي ثوابها بقتلهم ﴿ والله عزيز حكيم ﴾ وهذا منسوخ بقوله ﴿ فإما مناً بعد وإما فداء ﴾

تفسير الجلالين

This came down when they took ransom from the captives at Badr. { It is not for a prophet to take } : read with a "t" or a "y"; { captives until he has wreaked havoc on the land } : done his utmost to kill the disbelievers; { you desire } : oh Believers; { the fleeting gain of this world } : its scraps, by taking ransoms; { but Allah desires } : for you all; { the hereafter } : that is, the reward there for killing them; { and Allah is mighty, wise } . This was abrogated by His word: { Afterwards either an act of kindness or ransom } [Muhammad 4].

Tafsir Al-Jalalain

﴿ حتى يثخن في الأرض ﴾ يقول حتى يبالغ في قتل المشركين فيها ويقهرهم غلبة وقسراً ... عن سعيد بن جبير في قوله ﴿ ما كان لنبي أن يكون له أسرى حتى يثخن في الأرض ﴾ قال إذا أسرتموهم فلا تفادوهم حتى تثخنوا فيهم القتل

تفسير الطبري

{ Until he has wreaked havoc on the land } ; He is saying: Until he has given his utmost to kill the idolaters in it, and has won victory over them by domination and subjugation. ... Sa'id ibn Jubair, regarding His word { It is not for a prophet to take captives until he has wreaked havoc on the land } , said: Whenever you all take them captive, do not ransom them until you have massacred them by killing.

Tafsir Al-Tabari

﴿ والله عزيز ﴾ يغلب أولياءه على أعدائه ﴿ حكيم ﴾ يعلم ما يليق بكل حال ويخصه بها ... والآية دليل على أن الأنبياء عليهم الصلاة والسلام يجتهدون وأنه قد يكون خطأ ولكن لا يقرون عليه

تفسير البيضاوي

{ And Allah is mighty } : He gives His associates victory over His enemies; { wise } : He knows what is suitable in every situation, and He apportions it. ... This verse is evidence that the prophets (prayers and peace upon them) make a diligent effort, and that a mistake may arise, but they do not linger in it.

Tafsir Al-Baydawi

هذا حكم آخر من أحكام الجهاد ومعنى ﴿ ما كان ﴾ ما صح وما إستقام والإمتحان كثرة القتل وإشاعته من الثخانة التي هي الغلظ والكثافة والمعنى فيه تذليل الكفر وإضعافه وإعزاز الاسلام وإظهاره بإشاعة القتل في الكفرة
تفسير النيسابوري

This is an additional ruling among the rulings for *jihad*; the meaning of { it is not ... } : it is not proper and not correct. "Wreaking havoc" is plentiful killing, and spreading it heavily in harshness and intensity; the intent is to degrade disbelief and weaken it, and to strengthen Islam and make it manifest, by spreading killing among the disbelievers.

Tafsir Al-Nisaburi

* * *

﴿ إِنَّ الَّذِينَ آمَنُوا وَهَاجَرُوا وَجَاهَدُوا بِأَمْوَالِهِمْ وَأَنْفُسِهِمْ فِي سَبِيلِ اللَّهِ وَالَّذِينَ آوَوْا وَنَصَرُوا أُولَٰئِكَ بَعْضُهُمْ أَوْلِيَاءُ بَعْضٍ وَالَّذِينَ آمَنُوا وَلَمْ يُهَاجِرُوا مَا لَكُمْ مِنْ وَلَايَتِهِمْ مِنْ شَيْءٍ حَتَّىٰ يُهَاجِرُوا وَإِنِ اسْتَنْصَرُوكُمْ فِي الدِّينِ فَعَلَيْكُمُ النَّصْرُ إِلَّا عَلَىٰ قَوْمٍ بَيْنَكُمْ وَبَيْنَهُمْ مِيثَاقٌ وَاللَّهُ بِمَا تَعْمَلُونَ بَصِيرٌ وَالَّذِينَ كَفَرُوا بَعْضُهُمْ أَوْلِيَاءُ بَعْضٍ إِلَّا تَفْعَلُوهُ تَكُنْ فِتْنَةٌ فِي الْأَرْضِ وَفَسَادٌ كَبِيرٌ وَالَّذِينَ آمَنُوا وَهَاجَرُوا وَجَاهَدُوا فِي سَبِيلِ اللَّهِ وَالَّذِينَ آوَوْا وَنَصَرُوا أُولَٰئِكَ هُمُ الْمُؤْمِنُونَ حَقًّا لَهُمْ مَغْفِرَةٌ وَرِزْقٌ كَرِيمٌ وَالَّذِينَ آمَنُوا مِنْ بَعْدُ وَهَاجَرُوا وَجَاهَدُوا مَعَكُمْ فَأُولَٰئِكَ مِنْكُمْ ﴾
الأنفال ٧٢-٧٥

{ **Indeed those who have believed, and emigrated, and waged jihad with their wealth and with themelves in the cause of Allah, and those who have given shelter and aid, these are associates of each other; and those who have believed but have not emigrated, you** owe no guardianship to them in anything until they emigrate, although if they turn to you for aid under the religion, then you are obliged to aid, except against people with whom you have an agreement; and Allah is well aware of what you do. But those who have disbelieved, they are associates of each other; should you not do this there will be sedition in the land and great corruption. But those who have believed, and emigrated, and waged jihad in the cause of Allah, and those who have given shelter and aid – those truly are the Believers; theirs is forgiveness and abundant bounty. And those who have believed afterwards, and emigrated, and waged jihad with you, they are of you } *Al-anfal 72-75*

ذكر تعالى أصناف المؤمنين وقسمهم إلى مهاجرين خرجوا من ديارهم وأموالهم وجاؤوا لنصر الله ورسوله وإقامة دينه وبذلوا أموالهم وأنفسهم في ذلك وإلى أنصار وهم المسلمون من أهل المدينة إذ ذاك آووا إخوانهم المهاجرين في منازلهم وواسوهم في أموالهم ونصروا الله ورسوله بالقتال معهم فهؤلاء ﴿ بعضهم أولياء بعضٍ ﴾ ... لما ذكر تعالى حكم المؤمنين في الدنيا عطف بذكر مالهم في الآخرة فأخبر عنهم بحقيقة الإيمان كما تقدم في أول السورة وأنه سبحانه سيجازيهم بالمغفرة والصفح عن الذنوب إن كانت وبالرزق الكريم وهو الحسن الكثير الطيب الشريف وهو دائم مستمر أبداً لا ينقطع ولا ينقضي ولا يسأم ولا يمل لحسنه وتنوعه

تفسير ابن كثير

The Most High mentions categories of the Believers and divides them into the Emigrants [*Muhajirun*], who left their homes and their wealth and came to support Allah and His Messenger and to establish His religion, and who gave their wealth and themselves in this, and the Helpers [*Ansar*], these being the Muslims among the people of Medina at the time, who provided lodging in their homes for their brothers the *Muhajirun*, comforted them with their wealth, and supported Allah and His Messenger by fighting with them; truly these { are associates of each other } . ... When the Most High mentioned the decree for the Believers in this world, He turned to mentioning their estate in the hereafter, declaring the genuineness of their belief as in the beginning of this *surah*, and how He the Exalted will reward them with forgiveness, pardon for their sins, if any, and with generous bounty, this being abundant, delightful, and honorable goodness. This is everlasting and endures forever; it does not cease nor does it subside; one does not grow weary or bored, due to its delight and diverse variety.

Tafsir Ibn Kathir

﴿ إلا تفعلوه ﴾ أي تولي المسلمين وقمع الكفار ﴿ تكن فتنة في الأرض وفساد كبير ﴾ بقوة الكفر وضعف الاسلام

تفسير الجلالين

{ Should you not do this } : that is, join forces with the Muslims and stifle the disbelievers; { there will be sedition in the land and great corruption } : from the power of disbelief and the weakness of Islam.

Tafsir Al-Jalalain

﴿ والذين كفروا بعضهم أولياء بعضٍ ﴾ ظاهره إثبات الموالاة بينهم كقوله تعالى في المسلمين ﴿ أولئك بعضهم أولياء بعض ﴾ ومعناه نهى المسلمين عن موالاة الذين كفروا ومواريثهم وإيجاب مباعدتهم ومصارمتهم وإن كانوا أقارب وأن يتركوا يتوارثون بعضهم بعضاً ثم قال ﴿ إلّا تفعلوه ﴾ أي إلا تفعلوا ما أمرتكم به من تواصل المسلمين وتولي بعضهم بعضاً حتى في التوارث تفضيلاً لنسبة الاسلام على نسبة القرابة ولم تقطعوا العلائق بينكم وبين الكفار ولم تجعلوا قرابتهم كلا قرابة تحصل فتنة في الأرض ومفسدة عظيمة لأن المسلمين ما لم يصيروا يداً واحدة على الشرك كان الشرك ظاهراً والفساد زائداً

تفسير الزمخشري

{ But those who have disbelieved, they are associates of each other } : evidence for the support among them makes this clear, like the word of the Most High regarding the Muslims: { These are associates of each other } ; the meaning is that He has prohibited the Muslims from supporting those who have disbelieved or granting them inheritance, as well as an obligation to separate from them and show hostility towards them, even if they are their relatives; and they are to abandon inheritance among each other. Then He says: { Should you not do this } ; that is, should you not do what I have ordered you – joining up with the Muslims and turning away from each other even in inheritance, in preference to the ties of Islam over the ties of family – and you do not sever relations between you all and the disbelievers, and you do not treat family ties with them as if there were none, then there will be sedition [*fitnah*] in the land and great cause for corruption, because as long as the Muslims do not form a single power against idolatry [*shirk*], idolatry will persist and corruption will increase.

Tafsir Al-Zamakhshari

﴿ تكن فتنة في الأرض وفساد كبير ﴾ فالفتنة في الأرض قوة الكفر والفساد الكبير ضعف الاسلام ﴿ والذين آمنوا وهاجروا وجاهدوا في سبيل الله والذين آووا ونصروا أولئك هم المؤمنون حقاً ﴾ لا مرية ولا ريب في ايمانهم قيل حققوا إيمانهم بالهجرة والجهاد وبذل المال في الدين ﴿ لهم مغفرة ورزق كريم ﴾ في الجنة

تفسير البغوي

{ There will be sedition in the land and great corruption } : sedition in the land is disbelief gaining strength, and great corruption is Islam becoming weak. { But those who have believed, and emigrated, and waged jihad in the cause of Allah, and those who have given shelter and aid – those truly are the Believers } : there is no disputing and no doubt concerning their belief; it is said: They have proven their belief by emigration and *jihad* and by giving wealth for the religion; { theirs is forgiveness and abundant bounty } : in *Jannah*.

Tafsir Al-Baghawi

▪ ▪ ▪

Surah 9   Al-tawba [Repentance]
or   Al-bara'a [Absolution]

عن سعيد بن جبير قال قلت لإبن عباس سورة التوبة قال التوبة هي الفاضحة
صحيح البخاري كتاب التفسير

From Sa'id ibn Jubair, who said: I asked Ibn 'Abbas about Surah Al-tawba. He said: Al-tawba is the heinous and scandalous one [Al-fadiha].

Sahih Al-Bukhari, The book of tafsir

قال عبدالله بن عباس سألت علي بن ابي طالب لم لم يُكتب في براءة بسم الله الرحمن الرحيم قال لأن بسم الله الرحمن الرحيم أمان وبراءة نزلت بالسيف ليس فيها أمان
تفسير القرطبي

'Abdullah ibn 'Abbas said: I asked 'Ali ibn Abi Talib why *"Bismillah Al-Rahman Al-Rahim"* was not written in surah *Al-bara'a*. He said: Because *"Bismillah Al-Rahman Al-Rahim"* is security [*aman*; safety and protection], and *Al-bara'a* came down by the sword; there is no security in it.

Tafsir Al-Qurtubi

﴿ بَرَاءَةٌ مِنَ اللَّهِ وَرَسُولِهِ إِلَى الَّذِينَ عَاهَدْتُمْ مِنَ الْمُشْرِكِينَ فَسِيحُوا فِي الْأَرْضِ أَرْبَعَةَ أَشْهُرٍ وَاعْلَمُوا أَنَّكُمْ غَيْرُ مُعْجِزِي اللَّهِ وَأَنَّ اللَّهَ مُخْزِي الْكَافِرِينَ وَأَذَانٌ مِنَ اللَّهِ وَرَسُولِهِ إِلَى النَّاسِ يَوْمَ الْحَجِّ الْأَكْبَرِ أَنَّ اللَّهَ بَرِيءٌ مِنَ الْمُشْرِكِينَ وَرَسُولُهُ فَإِنْ تُبْتُمْ فَهُوَ خَيْرٌ لَكُمْ وَإِنْ تَوَلَّيْتُمْ فَاعْلَمُوا أَنَّكُمْ غَيْرُ مُعْجِزِي اللَّهِ وَبَشِّرِ الَّذِينَ كَفَرُوا بِعَذَابٍ أَلِيمٍ إِلَّا الَّذِينَ عَاهَدْتُمْ مِنَ الْمُشْرِكِينَ ثُمَّ لَمْ يَنْقُصُوكُمْ شَيْئًا وَلَمْ يُظَاهِرُوا عَلَيْكُمْ أَحَدًا فَأَتِمُّوا إِلَيْهِمْ عَهْدَهُمْ إِلَى مُدَّتِهِمْ إِنَّ اللَّهَ يُحِبُّ الْمُتَّقِينَ فَإِذَا انْسَلَخَ الْأَشْهُرُ الْحُرُمُ فَاقْتُلُوا الْمُشْرِكِينَ حَيْثُ وَجَدْتُمُوهُمْ وَخُذُوهُمْ وَاحْصُرُوهُمْ وَاقْعُدُوا لَهُمْ كُلَّ مَرْصَدٍ فَإِنْ تَابُوا وَأَقَامُوا الصَّلَاةَ وَآتَوُا الزَّكَاةَ فَخَلُّوا سَبِيلَهُمْ إِنَّ اللَّهَ غَفُورٌ رَحِيمٌ ﴾ التوبة ١-٥

{ There is absolution, from Allah and his Messenger, regarding the Idolaters with whom you made covenant; so travel in the land for four months, but know that you can not frustrate Allah and that Allah brings disgrace on the disbelievers. And a proclamation from Allah and His Messenger to people on the day of the greater pilgrimage – that Allah is absolved from the Idolaters, as is His Messenger; so if you all repent, this is better for you; but if you turn away, then know that you can not frustrate Allah. And give news to the disbelievers of a painful punishment, except the Idolaters with whom you made covenant and who have since not let you down in anything nor supported anyone against you – complete their covenant with them until their time is up; indeed Allah loves the devout. But when the sacred months have passed, kill the idolaters wherever you find them, and take hold of them, and bring them under siege, and sit in wait for them at every place of ambush; but if they turn in repentance, and observe prayer, and bring *zakat*, then let them go on their way; indeed Allah is forgiving, merciful } *Al-tawba* 1-5

﴿ وأن الله مُخزِي الكافرين ﴾ مذلُّهم في الدنيا بالقتل وفي الآخرة بالنار

تفسير الجلالين

{ And that Allah brings disgrace on the disbelievers } : debasing them in this world by killing, and in the hereafter by fire.

Tafsir Al-Jalalain

﴿ وأن الله مُخزِي الكافرين ﴾ قال إبن عباس بالقتل في الدنيا والعذاب في الآخرة وقال الزجاج هذا ضمان من الله عز وجل لنصرة المؤمنين على الكافرين والإخزاء والإذلال مع إظهار الفضيحة والعار والخزي والنكال الفاضح

تفسير الرازي

{ And that Allah brings disgrace on the disbelievers} ; Ibn 'Abbas said: By killing in this world and punishment in the hereafter. Al-Zajjaj said: This is a guarantee from Allah Mighty and Sublime to support the Believers against the disbelievers, and to put them to shame and humiliate them by displaying scandal, infamy, contempt, and disgraceful exemplary punishment.

Tafsir Al-Razi

﴿ وعلموا أنكم غير معجزي الله وأن الله مخزي الكافرين ﴾ بعد هذه الآية ﷺ فلم يعاهد النبي أحداً من الناس

تفسير مقاتل بن سليمان

{ But know that you can not frustrate Allah and that Allah brings disgrace on the disbelievers } : The Prophet (SAW) did not enter into an agreement with anyone after this verse.

Tafsir Muqatil ibn Sulaiman

فأمر الله نبيه إذا انسلخ المحرم أن يضع السيف فيمن لم يكن بينه وبين نبي الله ﷺ عهد يقتلهم حتى يدخلوا في الإسلام وأمر بمن كان له عهد إذا انسلخ أربعة من يوم النحر أن يضع فيهم السيف أيضاً يقتلهم حتى يدخلوا في الاسلام ... ﴿ فاقتلوا المشركين ﴾ يقول فاقتلوهم ﴿ حيث وجدتموهم ﴾ يقول حيث لقيتموهم من الأرض في الحرم وغير الحرم في الأشهر الحرم وغير الأشهر الحرم ﴿ وخذوهم ﴾ يقول وأسروهم ﴿ وإحصروهم ﴾ يقول وامنعوهم من التصرّف في بلاد الاسلام ودخول مكة ﴿ وأقعدوا لهم كل مرصَد ﴾ يقول واقعدوا لهم بالطلب لقتلهم أو أسْرهم ﴿ كل مرصد ﴾ يعني كل طريق ومرقَب

تفسير الطبري

Allah ordered His Prophet that when the month of Muharram had passed, that he should put the sword on whoever did not have a covenant with the Prophet of Allah (SAW), and kill them until they entered into Islam; and He ordered that with whoever did have a covenant, four [months] after the day of sacrifice [*yawm al-nahr*/*'Eid al-adha*, in the month of *Dhu Al-hijjah*] he should put the sword on them as well, and kill them until they enter Islam ... { Kill the idolaters } : that is, kill them; { wherever you find them } : that is, wherever on earth you face them, in the sacred sanctuary and other places, in the sacred months and in other months; { and take hold of them } : that is, take them captive; { and bring them under siege } : that is, prohibit them from moving freely in the territory of Islam, and from entering Mecca; { and sit in wait for them at every place of ambush } : that is, sit in wait for them, seeking to kill them or take them captive; "every place of ambush" meaning every road and lookout.

Tafsir Al-Tabari

قوله تعالى ﴿ فاقتلوا المشركين ﴾ عام في كل مشرك لكن السنة خصت منه ما تقدم بيانه في سورة البقرة من إمرأة وراهب وصبي وغيرهم ... واعلم أن مطلق قوله ﴿ فاقتلوا المشركين ﴾ يقتضي جواز قتلهم بأي

وجه كان إلا أن الأخبار وردت بالنهي عن المثلة ومع هذا فيجوز أن يكون الصديق رضي الله عنه حين قتل أهل الردة بالإحراق بالنار وبالحجارة وبالرمي من رؤوس الجبال والتنكيس في الآبار تعلّق بعموم الآية ... فقال الحسين بن الفضل نسخت هذه كل آية في القرآن فيها ذكر الاعراض والصبر على أذى الأعداء ... في هذا دليل على جواز اغتيالهم قبل الدعوة

تفسير القرطبي

The word of the Most High { Kill the idolaters } is for all idolaters in general, although the *sunnah* makes a distinction for women, monks, children, and others that have been made known in *surah Al-baqara* ... And know that His unrestricted word { Kill the idolaters } implies the permissibility to kill them in any manner, except that the prohibition against mutilation has been made known. Notwithstanding, it is permissible for Al-Siddiq (may Allah be pleased with him) to have adhered to the generality of the verse when he killed those who had apostatized by burning them with fire, by stones, by shooting from the mountaintops, or by turning people upside-down into wells. ... Al-Husain ibn Al-Fadl said that this verse abrogates all the verses in the Qur'an which mention turning away from or forbearance over the harm of the enemy. ... Here it is substantiated that it is permissible to assassinate them before any invitation [*da'wah*; i.e. to Islam].

Tafsir Al-Qurtubi

وقوله ﴿ وخذوهم ﴾ أي وأسروهم إن شئتم قتلاً وإن شئتم أسراً وقوله ﴿ وأحصُروهم واقعدوا لهم كل مرصد ﴾ أي لا تكتفوا بمجرد وجدانكم لهم بل اقصدوهم بالحصار في معاقلهم وحصونهم والرصد في طرقهم ومسالكهم حتى تضيقوا عليهم الواسع وتضطروهم إلى القتل أو الاسلام ... ثم إختلف المفسرون في آية السيف هذه فقال الضحاك والسدي هي منسوخة بقوله تعالى ﴿ فإما منا بعد وإما فداء ﴾ وقال قتادة بالعكس

تفسير ابن كثير

His word: { And take hold of them } : that is, capture them, killing if you like, or taking prisoner if you like. And His word: { And bring them under seige, and sit in wait for them at every place of ambush } : that is, do not settle for merely having strong feelings towards them, but rather aim to blockade them in their strongholds and ramparts, and by lying in wait on their roads and passageways, until you constrict their open spaces and compel them either to getting killed or to Islam ... Then the expositors differed regarding this verse of the sword; Al-Dahhak and Al-Suddi said: This is abrogated by the word of the Most High: { Afterwards either an act of kindness or ransom } [*Muhammad* 4]. Qatada said the opposite.

Tafsir Ibn Kathir

قوله تعالى ﴿ وعلموا أنكم غير معجزي الله ﴾ أي وإن أُجِّلتم هذه الأربعة الأشهر فلن تفوتوا الله ... واختلف علماء الناسخ والمنسوخ في هذه الآية على ثلاثة أقوال أحدها أن حكم الأسارى كان وجوب قتلهم ثم نُسخ بقوله ﴿ فإما منّاً بعد وإما فداءً ﴾ قاله الحسن وعطاء في آخرين والثاني بالعكس وأنه كان الحكم في الأسارى أنه لا يجوز قتلهم صبراً وإنما يجوز المن أو الفداء بقوله ﴿ فإما منّاً بعد وإما فداء ﴾ ثم نُسخ بقوله ﴿ فاقتلوا المشركين ﴾ قاله مجاهد وقتادة والثالث أن الآيتين مُحكمتان والأسير إذا حصل في يد الإمام فهو مخيّر إن شاء منّ عليه وإن شاء فاداه وإن شاء قتله صبراً أي ذلك رأى فيه المصلحة للمسلمين فعل هذا قول جابر بن زيد وعليه عامة الفقهاء وهو قول الإمام أحمد

تفسير ابن الجوزي

His word: { But know that you can not frustrate Allah } : that is, indeed you have been deferred these four months, but you can not elude Allah. ... The scholars of verses that abrogate and are abrogated differ regarding this verse, into three points of view. The first is that the ruling for captives is for them to be killed, but this was abrogated by: { Afterwards either an act of kindness or ransom } ; this is what Al-Hasan and 'Ataa said. The second is the opposite, that the ruling for captives is that they are not permitted to be killed as captives, although acts of kindness or ransoming are permitted, in accordance with His word: { Afterwards either an act of kindness or ransom } ; then this was abrogated by His word: { And kill the idolaters } ; this is what Mujahid and Qatada said. The third point of view is that both verses are firm: the prisoner, when he falls into the hands of the leader, the leader has the choice – if he wishes he may show kindness to him, if he wishes he may ransom him, or if he wishes, kill him as captive; whatever he finds to be in the best interest of the Muslims, he may do. This is what Jabir ibn Zaid said, and in general the legal scholars agree; it is also what Imam Ahmad said.

Tafsir Ibn Al-Jawzi

روي عن أنس قال لما توفي رسول الله ﷺ ارتدّت العرب كافة فقال عمر يا أبا بكر أتريد أن نقاتل العرب كافة فقال أبو بكر إنما قال رسول الله ﷺ إذا شهدوا أن لا إله إلا الله وأن محمداً رسول الله وأقاموا الصلاة وآتوا الزكاة منعوني دماءهم وأموالهم والله لو منعوني عَناقاً مما كانوا يعطون رسول الله ﷺ قاتلتهم عليه قال عمر فلما رأيت رأي أبي بكر قد شرح عرفت أنه ألحق

تفسير الماتريدي

It is narrated from Anas that he said: When the Messenger of Allah (SAW) passed away, all the Arabs apostatized. And 'Umar said: Oh Abu Bakr, do you want us to fight all the Arabs?! Abu Bakr said: Indeed the Messenger of Allah (SAW) said: If they testify that there is no god but Allah and that Muhammad is the Messenger of Allah, observe prayer, and give *zakat*, they have kept their blood and their wealth safe from me. I swear by Allah that if they withheld from me even a young she-goat that they had given to the Messenger of Allah (SAW), I would fight them for it! 'Umar said: When I saw Abu Bakr's attitude and how he had been laid bare, I knew that it was true.

Tafsir Al-Maturidi

قوله تعالى ﴿ فإذا انسلخ الأشهر الحرم ﴾ يقول إذا مضى الأشهر التي جعلتها أجلهم ﴿ فاقتلوا المشركين حيث وجدتموهم ﴾ في الحل والحرم يعني المشركين الذين لا عهد لهم بعد ذلك الأجل ويقال إن هذه الآية ﴿ فاقتلوا المشركين حيث وجدتموهم ﴾ نسخت سبعين آية في القرآن من الصلح والعهد والكف مثل قوله ﴿ قل لستُ عليكم بوكيل ﴾ وقوله ﴿ لستَ عليهم بمصيطر ﴾ وقوله ﴿ فأعرض عنهم ﴾ وقوله ﴿ لكم دينكم ولي دينِ ﴾ وما سوى ذلك من الآيات التي نحو هذا صارت كلها منسوخة بهذه الآية

بحر العلوم للسمرقندي

The word of the Most High: { But when the sacred months have passed } ; He is saying: When the months that you have appointed a time for them come to an end; { kill the idolaters wherever you find them } : in non-sacred or sacred occasions; that is, the idolaters with whom there is no covenant, after this period of time. It is said that this verse: { Kill the idolaters wherever you find them } abrogated seventy verses in the Qur'an about truces, covenants, and restraint, for example His word: { Say: I am not a guardian over you } [Al-an'am 66], and His word: { You are not master over them } [Al-ghashiya 22], and His Word: { So turn away from them } [Al-nisaa 63], and His Word: { You all have your religion and I have mine } [Al-kafirun 6], and similar verses that are like these – all of them have been abrogated by this verse.

Al-Samarqandi, Bahr Al-'ulum

﴿ فاقتلوا المشركين ﴾ أمر بقتال المشركين نخرج الأمر بذلك بلفظ اقتلوا على جهة التشجيع وتقوية النفس أي هكذا يكون أمركم معهم وهذه الآية نسخت كل موادعة في القرآن أو مهادنة وما جرى مجرى ذلك وهي على ما ذكر مائة آية وأربع عشرة آية

تفسير ابن عطية

{ Kill the idolaters } : He ordered the idolaters to be fought, and the order was related by saying "Kill" as a means of encouragement and strengthening the individual, that is: This is your order concerning them. This verse abrogated all peacemaking and truce-making in the Qur'an, as well as whatever followed in its course. According to what has been mentioned this amounts to one hundred fourteen verses.

Tafsir Ibn 'Atiyya

قال الحسين بن الفضل فنسخت هذه الآية كل آية في القرآن فيها ذكر الاعراض على أذى الأعداء وقال الضحاك والسدي وعطاء قوله ﴿ فاقتلوا المشركين ﴾ منسوخة بقوله ﴿ فإما مَنّاً بعد وإما فداءً ﴾ وقال قتادة بل هي ناسخة لقوله ﴿ فإما مناً بعد وإما فداء ﴾ والصحيح أن حكم هذه الآية ثابت وأنها غير منسوخة إحداهما بصاحبتها لأن المنّ والقتل والفداء لم يزل من حكم رسول الله ﷺ فهم من أول حاربهم وهو يوم بدر ويدلّ عليه قوله تعالى ﴿ وخذوهم ﴾ والأخذ هو الأسر والأسر إنما يكون للقتل أو الفداء والدليل عليه أيضاً قول عطاء قال أتى النبي ﷺ بأسير يقال له أبو أمامة وهو سيد اليمامة فقال له النبي ﷺ يا أبا أمامة أيها أحب إليك أعتقك أو أفاديك أو أقتلك أو تسلم فقال إن تعتق تعتق عظيماً وإن تفاد تفاد عظيماً وإن تقتل تقتل عظيماً وأما أن أسلم فلا والله لا أسلم أبداً قال فإني أعتقتك فقال إني أشهد أن لا إله إلا الله وأشهد أنك رسوله

تفسير الثعلبي

Al-Husain ibn Al-Fadl said: This verse abrogated every verse in the Qur'an that mentions turning away from harming enemies. Al-Dahhak, Al-Suddi, and 'Ataa said that His word: { And kill the idolaters } is abrogated by His word: { Afterwards either an act of kindness or ransom } [*Muhammad* 4]. But Qatada said: Rather this abrogates His word: { Afterwards either an act of kindness or ransom } . The correct answer is that the ruling of this verse stands firm, and that neither of the two is abrogated by the other, since acts of kindness, killing, and ransoming have not ceased from the Messenger of Allah's (SAW) ruling, coming from the first time He engaged them in battle, this being the day of Badr. Evidence for this is the word of the Most High: { And take hold of them } : taking hold is taking captive, and taking captive is either for killing or for ransoming. What 'Ataa said is also evidence of this; he said: The Prophet (SAW) brought a prisoner called Abu Umama; he was the chief of Al-Yamama. The Prophet (SAW) said to him: Oh Abu Umama, which do you most prefer – that I set you free, I ransom you, I kill you, or you yield into Islam? And He replied: If you set me free, you are setting a great man free; if you ransom, you are ransoming a great man; if you kill, you are killing a great man; but as for me yielding into Islam, no, I swear by Allah I will never yield into Islam. He said: Indeed I am setting you free. And He said: Indeed I bear witness that there is no god but Allah, and I bear witness that you are His Messenger.

Tafsir Al-Tha'labi

﴿ كَيْفَ يَكُونُ لِلْمُشْرِكِينَ عَهْدٌ عِنْدَ اللَّهِ وَعِنْدَ رَسُولِهِ إِلَّا الَّذِينَ عَاهَدْتُمْ عِنْدَ الْمَسْجِدِ الْحَرَامِ فَمَا اسْتَقَامُوا لَكُمْ فَاسْتَقِيمُوا لَهُمْ إِنَّ اللَّهَ يُحِبُّ الْمُتَّقِينَ كَيْفَ وَإِنْ يَظْهَرُوا عَلَيْكُمْ لَا يَرْقُبُوا فِيكُمْ إِلًّا وَلَا ذِمَّةً يُرْضُونَكُمْ بِأَفْوَاهِهِمْ وَتَأْبَى قُلُوبُهُمْ وَأَكْثَرُهُمْ فَاسِقُونَ ﴾ التوبة ٧-٨

{ How can there be a covenant from Allah and from His Messenger towards the idolaters, except those with whom you made covenant at the Sacred Mosque? As long as they are straightfoward with you, be straightforward with them; indeed Allah loves the devout. How then? If they prevail over you, they will observe neither covenant nor safeguard with you; they please you with their mouths but their hearts refuse; and most of them are depraved } Al-tawba 7-8

يبين تعالى حكمته في البراءة من المشركين نظرته اياهم أربعة أشهر ثم بعد ذلك السيف المُرهَف أين ثقفوا ... يقول تعالى محرضاً للمؤمنين على معاداتهم والتبري منهم ومبيناً أنهم لا يستحقون أن يكون لهم عهد لشركهم بالله تعالى وكفرهم برسول الله ﷺ

تفسير ابن كثير

Allah Most High displays His wisdom in the absolution from the idolaters [mushrikeen], and His granting a delay to them for four months; then after this, a sharp sword wherever they are found. ... The Most High says this to incite the Believers in enmity towards them and refusal to have anything to do with them, and to make it clear to them that they are not worthy that any pacts should be made with them, due to their ascribing associates [shirk] to Allah Most High and their disbelief in the Messenger of Allah (SAW).

Tafsir Ibn Kathir

﴿ كيف ﴾ يكون لهم عهد ﴿ وإن يظهروا عليكم ﴾ يظفروا بكم ﴿ لا يرقُبوا ﴾ يراعوا ﴿ فيكم إلاًّ ﴾ قرابة ﴿ ولا ذمة ﴾ عهداً بل يؤذيكم ما استطاعوا وجملة الشرط حال ﴿ يُرضونكم بأفواههم ﴾ بكلامهم الحسن ﴿ وتأبى قلوبهم ﴾ الوفاء به ﴿ وأكثرهم فاسقون ﴾ ناقضون للعهد

تفسير الجلالين

{ How then? } : can there be a covenant with them? { If they prevail over you } : triumph over you; { they will observe } : abide by; { with you neither covenant } :

kinship relationship; { nor safeguarding [*dhimma*] } : pact, but rather they will harm you as much as they can (the conditional phrase "if they" refers to this situation); { they please you with their mouths } : with their pleasant speech; { but their hearts refuse } : to be loyal to it; { and most of them are depraved } : violators of covenants.

Tafsir Al-Jalalain

﴿ يرضونكم بأفواههم ﴾ فإنه يقول يعطونكم بألسنتهم من القول خلاف ما يضمرونه لكم في نفوسهم من العداوة والبغضاء ﴿ وتأبى قلوبهم ﴾ أي تأبى عليهم قلوبهم أن يذعنوا لكم بتصديق ما يبدونه لكم بألسنتهم يحذر جل ثناؤه أمرهم المؤمنين ويشحذهم على قتلهم واجتياحهم حيث وجدوا من أرض الله وألا يقصروا في مكروههم بكل ما قدروا عليه

تفسير الطبري

{ They please you with their mouths } ; indeed He is saying: With their tongues they give you words that are contrary to the enmity and hostility that they conceal from you within themselves. { But their hearts refuse } : that is, their hearts refuse to concede to you by confirming what they have shown you with their tongues. He (may His praise be exalted) is warning the Believers about them, and sharpening them to kill them and ravage them wherever they are found on Allah's earth, and to not be negligent in loathing them to the fullest extent that they are able.

Tafsir Al-Tabari

* * *

﴿ وَإِن نَّكَثُوٓاْ أَيْمَٰنَهُم مِّنۢ بَعْدِ عَهْدِهِمْ وَطَعَنُواْ فِى دِينِكُمْ فَقَٰتِلُوٓاْ أَئِمَّةَ ٱلْكُفْرِ إِنَّهُمْ لَآ أَيْمَٰنَ لَهُمْ لَعَلَّهُمْ يَنتَهُونَ ﴾ التوبة ١٢

{ And if they break their oaths after having made their covenant, and defame your religion, then fight the leaders of disbelief – for indeed they have no oaths – that perhaps they might cease }
Al-tawba 12

يقول تعالى وإن نكث المشركون الذين عاهدتموهم على مدة معينة أيمانهم أي عهودهم ومواثيقهم ﴿ وطعنوا في دينكم ﴾ أي عابوه وانتقصوه ومن ههنا أخذ قتل من سب الرسول صلوات الله وسلامه عليه أو من طعن في دين الاسلام

تفسير ابن كثير

The Most High is saying that if the idolaters, those with whom you made covenant for a specific period, break their oaths, their covenants, or their agreements, { and defame your religion } , that is, slander it and undermine it. From this it can be taken that whoever slanders the Messenger (may the prayers and peace of Allah be upon him), or whoever defames the religion of Islam, is to be killed.

Tafsir Ibn Kathir

﴿ وطعنوا في دينكم ﴾ يقول وقدحوا في دينكم الاسلام فثلبوه وعابوه ﴿ فقاتلوا أئمة الكفر ﴾ يقول فقاتلوا رؤساء الكفر بالله ﴿ إنهم لا أيمان لهم ﴾ يقول إن رؤساء الكفر لا عهد لهم ﴿ لعلهم ينتهون ﴾ لكي ينتهوا عن الطعن في دينكم والمظاهرة عليكم

تفسير الطبري

{ And defame your religion } ; He is saying: And vilify Islam, your religion [*deen*], and defile it, and slander it; { then fight the leaders of disbelief } ; He is saying: Fight the heads of disbelief in Allah; { for indeed they have no oaths } ; He is saying: Indeed the heads of disbelief have no covenant; { that perhaps they might cease } : so that they will stop defaming your religion and manifesting against you.

Tafsir Al-Tabari

﴿ وَطَعَنُوا فِي دِينِكُمْ ﴾ يقال طعنه بالرمح يطعنه وطعن بالقول السيء يطعن قال الليث وبعضهم يقول يطعن بالرمح ويطعن بالقول فيفرق بينهما والمعنى أنهم عابوا دينكم وقدحوا فيه ثم قال ﴿ فَقَاتِلُوا أَئِمَّةَ الْكُفْرِ ﴾ أي متى فعلوا ذلك فافعلوا هذا

تفسير الرازي

{ And defame [*ta'anu*, i.e. stab] your religion } ; it can be said that someone "stabs" with a spear, and also "stabs" with malicious speech. Al-Laith said: Some of them said stabs with a spear or stabs in speech, and distinguishes between the two; but the meaning is that they slander your religion and vilify ["pierce"] it. Then He says: { Then fight the leaders of disbelief } : that is, when they do that, do this.

Tafsir Al-Razi

استدلّ بعض العلماء بهذه الآية على وجوب قتل كل من طعن في الدين إذ هو كافر والطعن أن ينسب إليه ما لا يليق به أو يعترض بالإستخفاف على ما هو من الدين لما ثبت من الدليل القطعي على صحة أصوله وإستقامة فروعه

تفسير القرطبي

Some scholars have reached the conclusion from this verse that it is obligatory to kill anyone who defames the religion, as he is a disbeliever [*kafir*]. And defaming ["stabbing"] means attributing to it what is not befitting of it, or making belittling objections against matters of the religion, when the veracity of their foundation and the integrity of their rulings have been affirmed by definitive evidence.

Tafsir Al-Qurtubi

* * *

﴿ اَلَا تُقَاتِلُونَ قَوْمًا نَكَثُوا أَيْمَانَهُمْ وَهَمُّوا بِإِخْرَاجِ الرَّسُولِ وَهُمْ بَدَءُوكُمْ أَوَّلَ مَرَّةٍ أَتَخْشَوْنَهُمْ فَاللَّهُ أَحَقُّ أَنْ تَخْشَوْهُ إِنْ كُنْتُمْ مُؤْمِنِينَ ۞ قَاتِلُوهُمْ يُعَذِّبْهُمُ اللَّهُ بِأَيْدِيكُمْ وَيُخْزِهِمْ وَيَنْصُرْكُمْ عَلَيْهِمْ وَيَشْفِ صُدُورَ قَوْمٍ مُؤْمِنِينَ ۞ وَيُذْهِبْ غَيْظَ قُلُوبِهِمْ وَيَتُوبُ اللَّهُ عَلَى مَنْ يَشَاءُ وَاللَّهُ عَلِيمٌ حَكِيمٌ ﴾

التوبة ١٣-١٥

{ Shall you not fight a people who have broken their oaths and were intent on expelling the Messenger, and started with you the first time? Do you fear them? For Allah is more worthy that you should fear Him, if you are Believers. Fight them; Allah will punish them by your hands and disgrace them, and will give you the victory over them, and will heal the bosoms of a believing people. And He will drive out the fury from their hearts; for Allah turns towards who He wishes; and Allah is knowing, wise }

Al-tawba 13-15

ثم قال حاضاً المسلمين على جهاد المشركين ﴿ أَلَا تُقَاتِلُونَ قَوْمًا نَكَثُوا أَيْمَانَهُمْ ﴾ نقضوا عهودهم ﴿ وَهَمُّوا بِإِخْرَاجِ الرَّسُولِ ﴾ محمد ﷺ من مكة ﴿ وَهُمْ بَدَءُوكُمْ ﴾ بالقتال ﴿ أَوَّلَ مَرَّةٍ ﴾ يعني يوم بدر

تفسير الثعلبي

Then He says, exhorting the Muslims to *jihad* against the idolaters [*mushrikeen*]: { Shall you not fight a people who have broken their oaths } : violating their covenants; { and were intent on expelling the Messenger } : Muhammad (SAW), from Mecca; { and started with you } : in fighting; { the first time } : referring to the day of Badr.

Tafsir Al-Tha'labi

﴿ قَاتِلُوهُمْ يُعَذِّبْهُمُ اللَّهُ ﴾ يقتلهم ﴿ بِأَيْدِيكُمْ وَيُخْزِهِمْ ﴾ ويذلّهم بالأسر والقهر ﴿ وَيَنْصُرْكُمْ عَلَيْهِمْ وَيَشْفِ صُدُورَ قَوْمٍ مُؤْمِنِينَ ﴾ بما فُعل بهم هم بن خزاعة ﴿ وَيُذْهِبْ غَيْظَ قُلُوبِهِمْ ﴾ كربها ﴿ وَيَتُوبُ اللَّهُ عَلَى مَنْ يَشَاءُ ﴾ بالرجوع إلى الاسلام كأبي سفيان ﴿ وَاللَّهُ عَلِيمٌ حَكِيمٌ ﴾

تفسير الجلالين

{ Fight them; Allah will punish them } : He will kill them; { by your hands and disgrace them } : and will humilliate them by imprisonment and subjugation; { and will give you the victory over them, and will heal the bosoms of a believing people } : for what was done to them; these were the Banu Khuza'a. { And He will drive out the fury from their hearts } : the distress in them; { for Allah turns towards who He wishes } : when they return to Islam, such as Abu Sufyan; { and Allah is knowing, wise } .

Tafsir Al-Jalalain

وقوله ﴿ أتخشونهم فالله أحق أن تخشوه إن كنتم مؤمنين ﴾ يقول تعالى لا تخشوهم واخشون فأنا أهل أن يخشى العباد من سطوتي وعقوبتي فبيدي الأمر وما شئت كان ومالم أشأ لم يكن ثم قال تعالى عزيمة على المؤمنين وبياناً لحكمته فيما شرع لهم من الجهاد مع قدرته على إهلاك الأعداء بأمر من عنده ﴿ قاتلوهم يعذبهم الله بأيديكم ويخزهم وينصركم عليهم ويشف صدور قوم مؤمنين ﴾ وهذا عام في المؤمنين كلهم وقال مجاهد وعكرمة والسدي في هذه الآية ﴿ ويشف صدور قوم مؤمنين ﴾ يعني خزاعة

تفسير ابن كثير

His word: { Do you fear them? For Allah is more worthy that you should fear Him, if you are Believers } ; the Most High is saying: Do not fear them, but fear me, for I am more fit to be feared by people for my power and my punishment. The matter is in my hand, whatever I desire comes to be, and whatever I do not desire does not come to be. Then the Most High said, firm in intent with the Believers and declaring His wisdom in the *jihad* that He prescribed for them, notwithstanding His power to destroy the enemies by His command: { Fight them; Allah will punish them by your hands and disgrace them, and will give you the victory over them, and will heal the bosoms of a believing people } . This applies generally to all Believers, although Mujahid, 'Ikrama, and Al-Suddi, in regards to this verse: { and will heal the bosoms of a believing people } , said that it refers to the Khuza'a.

Tafsir Ibn Kathir

قوله تعالى ﴿ قاتلوهم ﴾ أمر ﴿ ويعذبهم الله ﴾ جوابه وهو جزم بمعنى المجازاة والتقدير إن تقاتلوهم يعذبهم الله بأيديكم ويخزهم وينصركم عليهم ويشف صدور قوم مؤمنين ﴾ ويذهب غيظ قلوبهم ﴾ دليل على أن غيظهم كان قد إشتد وقال مجاهد يعني خزاعة حلفاء رسول الله ﷺ

تفسير القرطبي

The word of the Most High: { Fight them } : a command; { Allah will punish them } : its fulfillment; and this is a declaration meaning punishment in retribution. The reckoning is: If you fight them, Allah will punish them by your hands and disgrace them, and will give you the victory over them, and will heal the bosoms of a believing people. { And He will drive out the fury from their hearts } : evidence that their fury had become severe. Mujahid said: This refers to the Khuza'a, allies of the Messenger of Allah (SAW).

Tafsir Al-Qurtubi

اعلم أنه تعالى لما قال في الآية الأولى ﴿ ألا تقاتلون قوماً ﴾ ذكر عقيبه سبعة أشياء كل واحد منها يوجب إقدامهم على القتال ثم إنه تعالى في هذه الآية أعاد الأمر بالقتال وذكر في ذلك القتال خمسة أنواع من الفوائد كل واحد منها يعظم موقعه إذا إنفرد بها فكيف إذا اجتمعت فأولها قوله ﴿ يعذبهم الله بأيديكم ﴾ وفيه مباحث البحث

الأول أنه تعالى سمى ذلك عذاباً وهو حق فإنه تعالى يعذب الكافرين فإن شاء عجله في الدنيا وإن شاء أخره إلى الآخرة البحث الثاني أن المراد من هذا التعذيب القتل تارة والأسر أخرى واغتنام الأموال ثالثاً

تفسير الرازي

Know that the Most High, when He said in the prior verse: { Shall you not fight a people } , He subsequently mentioned seven things, each of which makes it obligatory for them to be valiant in fighting. Then indeed the Most High, in this verse, reiterates the command to fight, and mentions five kinds of advantages regarding this fighting, each of which extols its occurrence if taken separately, so how much more then if they are taken together. The first of these is His word: { Allah will punish them by your hands } ; and here there are several points to consider. The first point is that the Most High calls this "punishment", it being a certainty; for indeed the Most High punishes the disbelievers, hastening it in this world if He wishes, or delaying it to the hereafter if He wishes. The second point is that the intent of this punishment is sometimes to kill, other times to take captive, and yet other times to seize wealth.

Tafsir Al-Razi

ولما وبخهم الله على ترك القتال جرّد لهم الأمر به فقال ﴿ قاتلوهم ﴾ ووعدهم ليثبت قلوبهم ويصحح نياتهم أنه يعذبهم بأيديهم قتلاً ويخزيهم أسراً ويوليهم النصر والغلبة عليهم ﴿ ويشف صدور ﴾ طائفة من المؤمنين وهم خزاعة قال إبن عباس رضي الله عنه هم بطون من اليمن وسبأ قدموا مكة فأسلموا فلقوا من أهلها أذى شديداً فبعثوا إلى رسول الله ﷺ يشكون إليه فقال أبشروا فإن لفَرَج قريب ﴿ ويذهب غيظ ﴾ قلوبكم لما لقيتم منهم من المكروه وقد حصّل الله لهم هذه المواعيد كلها فكان ذلك دليلاً على صدق رسول الله ﷺ وصحة نبوته

تفسير الزمخشري

When Allah admonished them about abandoning fighting, He got right to the point with them about the command; He said: { Fight them }. And He promised them – to affirm their hearts and make their intentions right – that He would punish them with killing by their hands, would disgrace them with imprisonment, and would empower them with victory and subjugation over them. { And will heal the bosoms } : of a group of the Believers, these being the Khuza'a; Ibn 'Abbas (may Allah be pleased with him) said: These were a clan from Yemen and Saba' who came to Mecca, yielded into Islam, and met with severe harm from their people. They let the Messenger of Allah (SAW) know about this, complaining to him, and He said: Rejoice, for indeed relief is near. { And He will drive out the fury } from your hearts, when you faced unpleasantness from them. And Allah made every one of these promises come true for them, and this is proof of the Messenger of Allah's (SAW) authenticity and the veracity of his prophethood.

Tafsir Al-Zamakhshari

∗ ∗ ∗

﴿ أَمْ حَسِبْتُمْ أَنْ تُتْرَكُوا وَلَمَّا يَعْلَمِ اللَّهُ الَّذِينَ جَاهَدُوا مِنْكُمْ وَلَمْ يَتَّخِذُوا مِنْ دُونِ اللَّهِ وَلَا رَسُولِهِ وَلَا الْمُؤْمِنِينَ وَلِيجَةً وَاللَّهُ خَبِيرٌ بِمَا تَعْمَلُونَ ﴾ التوبة ١٦

{ Or do you suppose that you will be overlooked, given that Allah knows those of you who have waged jihad, and have not taken as close associates any other besides Allah, His Messenger, and the Believers? Allah is well aware of what you do } *Al-tawba 16*

يقول تعالى ذكره للمؤمنين الذين أمرهم بقتال هؤلاء المشركين الذين نقضوا عهدهم الذي بينهم وبينه بقوله ﴿ قاتلوهم يعذبهم الله بأيديكم ﴾ الآية حاضاً على جهادهم أم حسبتم أيها المؤمنون أن يتركم الله بغير محنة يمتحنكم بها وبغير إختبار يختبركم به فيعرف الصادق منكم في دينه من الكاذب فيه ﴿ ولمَّا يعلم الله الذين جاهدوا ﴾ يقول أحسبتم أن تتركوا بغير إختبار يعرف به أهل ولايته المجاهدين منكم في سبيله من المضيعين أمر الله في ذلك المفرِّطين

تفسير الطبري

He (may His remembrance be exalted) is saying to the Believers – those who He ordered to fight the Idolaters who broke the covenant they had between them and Him, by His word: { Fight them; Allah will punish them by your hands } through the rest of the verse – He is saying this to incite them to their *jihad*: Or do you suppose, oh Believers, that Allah will overlook you without a trial by which to test you all, or without an examination by which to examine you, that He might know who among you is genuine in his religion apart from those who are false in it? { Given that Allah knows those of you who have waged jihad } ; He is saying: Do you all suppose that you will be overlooked without an examination by which to make known those who are under His sovereignty, those among you who wage *jihad* in His cause, apart from those who squander Allah's command, those who neglect it?

Tafsir Al-Tabari

يقول تعالى ﴿ أم حسبتم ﴾ أيها المؤمنون ﴿ أن تتركم مهملين لا نختبركم بأمور يظهر فيها أهل العزم الصادق من الكاذب ولهذا قال ﴿ ولما يعلم الله الذين جاهدوا منكم ولم يتخذوا من دون الله ولا رسوله ولا المؤمنين وليجةً ﴾ أي بطانة ودخيلة بل هم في الظاهر على النصح لله ورسوله فإكتفى بأحد القسمين عن الآخر كما قال الشاعر وما أدري إذا يممت أرضاً أريد الخير أيهما يليني وقد قال تعالى في الآية الأخرى ﴿ أَلَمْ أَحَسِبَ الناس أن يُتْرَكوا أن يقولوا آمنا وهم لا يُفتَنون ولقد فتنَّا الذي من قبلهم فليعلمنَّ الله الذين صدقوا وليعلمن الكاذبين ﴾ وقال تعالى ﴿ أم حسبتم أن تدخلوا الجنة ﴾ وقال تعالى ﴿ ما كان الله ليذَر المؤمنين على ما أنتم

عليه حتى يميز الخبيث من الطيب وما كان الله ليُطلعكم على الغيب ﴾ والحاصل أنه تعالى لما شرع لعباده الجهاد بين أن له فيه حكمة وهو إختبار عبيده من يطيعه ممن يعصيه وهو تعالى العالم بما كان وما يكون وما لم يكن لو كان كيف كان يكون فيعلم الشيء قبل كونه ومع كونه على ما هو عليه لا إله إلا هو ولا رب سواه ولا رادّ لما قدّره وأمضاه

تفسير ابن كثير

The word of the Most High: { Or do you suppose }, oh Believers, that We will leave you overlooked, and not test you with things by which those with genuine intent are manifest apart from liars? For this reason He says: { Given that Allah knows those of you who have waged jihad, and have not taken as close associates any other besides Allah, His Messenger, and the Believers }, that is, inwardly and outwardly, but indeed they are clearly faithful to Allah and to His Messenger. He is only satisfied with one of these two categories over the other, as the poet said: And I know not, if I head out to a certain land desiring good, which of the two is near to me. Moreover the Most High says in another verse: { Do people think that they will be left alone – because they say "We have believed" – and they will not be put to the test? Indeed We tested those who came before them; so that Allah might surely know those who are genuine, and know those who are false } [Al-'ankabut 2-3]. And the Most High said: { Or did you suppose that you would enter *Jannah*? } [Al 'Imran 142]. And the Most High said: { It is not for Allah to leave the Believers the way you all are, until He distinguishes the harmful from the good; and it is not for Allah to show you the unknown } [Al 'Imran 179]. To summarize, the Most High, when He prescribed *jihad* for His servants, He demonstrated His wisdom in this, this being the testing of His servants – those who obey Him from those who disobey Him. And He is Most High, the One who knows what has been, what is to come, and what was not, if it had been, how it would have been. He knows things before they exist, and when they exist, how they will be; there is no god but Him, no lord His equal, and none who can deter what He has decreed and executed.

Tafsir Ibn Kathir

قوله تعالى ﴿ أم حسبتم ﴾ أظننتم ﴿ أن تُتركوا ﴾ قيل هذا خطاب للمنافقين وقيل للمؤمنين الذين شقّ عليهم القتال فقال أم حسبتم أن تتركوا فلا تؤمروا بالجهاد ولا تُمتحنوا ليظهر الصادق من الكاذب

تفسير البغوي

The word of the Most High: { Or do you suppose } : Or do you think? { that you will be overlooked } ; it is said that this is addressed to hypocrites, and it is also said it is to the Believers, those who were troubled by fighting; He said: Do you all suppose that you would be overlooked, that you would not be ordered to wage *jihad*, that you would not be put to the test to show who is genuine and who is false?

Tafsir Al-Baghawi

﴿ وَلَمَّا يَعْلَمِ اللهُ ﴾ أي ولم تجاهدوا فليعلم الله وجود ذلك منكم وقد كان يعلم غيباً فأراد إظهار ما علم ليجازي على العمل

تفسير ابن الجوزي

{ Given that Allah knows } : that is, you all have not waged *jihad*, and Allah is aware that this is your case; He knew it when it was concealed, but wanted to manifest what He knew in order to give reward for deeds.

Tafsir Ibn Al-Jawzi

* * *

﴿ أَجَعَلْتُمْ سِقَايَةَ الْحَاجِّ وَعِمَارَةَ الْمَسْجِدِ الْحَرَامِ كَمَنْ آمَنَ بِاللهِ وَالْيَوْمِ الْآخِرِ وَجَاهَدَ فِي سَبِيلِ اللهِ لَا يَسْتَوُونَ عِنْدَ اللهِ وَاللهُ لَا يَهْدِي الْقَوْمَ الظَّالِمِينَ الَّذِينَ آمَنُوا وَهَاجَرُوا وَجَاهَدُوا فِي سَبِيلِ اللهِ بِأَمْوَالِهِمْ وَأَنْفُسِهِمْ أَعْظَمُ دَرَجَةً عِنْدَ اللهِ وَأُولَٰئِكَ هُمُ الْفَائِزُونَ ﴾ التوبة ١٩-٢٠

{ Do you reckon that giving pilgrims water to drink or upkeep of the Sacred Mosque is like those who have believed in Allah and the last day and have waged jihad in the cause of Allah? They are not equal in the sight of Allah; and Allah does not guide those who oppress. Those who have believed, and have gone out and waged jihad in the cause of Allah with their wealth and with themselves, are a degree greater in the sight of Allah; and those are the victorious ones } *Al-tawba 19-20*

عن زيد بن سلام أنه سمع أبا سلام قال حدثني النعمان بن بشير قال كنت عند منبر رسول الله ﷺ فقال رجل ما أبالي أن لا أعمل عملاً بعد الاسلام إلا أن أسقي الحاج وقال آخر ما أبالي أن لا أعمل عملاً بعد الاسلام إلا

أن أعمرُ المسجد الحرام وقال آخر الجهاد في سبيل الله أفضل مما قلتم فزجرهم عمر وقال لا ترفعوا أصواتكم عند منبر رسول الله ﷺ وهو يوم الجمعة ولكن إذا صليتُ الجمعة دخلت فاستفتيتهُ فيما اختلفتم فيه فأنزل الله عز وجل ﴿ أجعلتم سقاية الحاج وعِمارة المسجد الحرام كمن آمن بالله واليوم الآخر ﴾ الآية إلى آخرها

صحيح مسلم كتاب الامارة

Zaid ibn Sallam related that he heard Abu Sallam say: Al-Nu'man ibn Bashir related to us, saying: I was at the pulpit of the Messenger of Allah (SAW), and a certain man said: I don't care if I don't do any deed after entering Islam except giving pilgrims water to drink. Another man said: I don't care if I don't do any deed after entering Islam except upkeep of the Sacred Mosque. Still another man said: *Jihad* in the cause of Allah is better than what you all have said. But 'Umar scolded them and said: Don't raise your voices near the pulpit of the Messenger of Allah (SAW) on a Friday! However when I had prayed the Friday prayer, I went in to ask his ruling regarding the issue you all had disagreed about. And Allah Mighty and Sublime sent down: { Do you reckon that giving pilgrims water to drink or upkeep of the Sacred Mosque is like someone who has believed in Allah and the last day } up until the end of the verse.

Sahih Muslim, The book of governance

وهذا قضاء من الله بين فِرَق المفتخرين الذين إفتخر احدهم بالسقاية والأخر بالسدانة والآخر بالإيمان بالله والجهاد في سبيله يقول ذكره تعالى إن الذين آمنوا بالله صدقوا بتوحيده من المشركين وهاجروا دور قومهم وجاهدوا المشركين في دين الله بأموالهم وأنفسهم أعظم درجة عند الله وأرفع منزلة عنده من سقاة الحاج وعمار المسجد الحرام وهم بالله مشركون ﴿ وأولئك ﴾ يقول وهؤلاء الذين وصفنا صفتهم أنهم آمنوا وهاجروا وجاهدوا ﴿ وهم الفائزون ﴾ بالجنة الناجون من النار

تفسير الطبري

This is a legal judgment from Allah between a group of boasters, one of whom took pride in giving pilgrims water to drink, another in custodianship, and another in belief in Allah and *jihad* in His cause. He (may His praise be exalted) says that those of the Idolaters who have believed in Allah and have attested to His oneness, who have emigrated from the homes of their people, and who wage *jihad* against the Idolaters in the religion of Allah with their wealth and with themselves, they are of greater status with Allah and of higher standing with Him than those who give pilgrims water or those who take care of the Sacred Mosque, while still being Idolaters against Allah. { Those } ; He is saying: These, whose distinguishing virtue we have described as belief, emigration, and *jihad*; { are the victorious ones } : in *Jannah,* those who are saved from Hellfire.

Tafsir Al-Tabari

∎ ∎ ∎

﴿ يَا أَيُّهَا الَّذِينَ آمَنُوا لَا تَتَّخِذُوا آبَاءَكُمْ وَإِخْوَانَكُمْ أَوْلِيَاءَ إِنِ اسْتَحَبُّوا الْكُفْرَ عَلَى الْإِيمَانِ وَمَن يَتَوَلَّهُم مِّنكُمْ فَأُولَٰئِكَ هُمُ الظَّالِمُونَ ۝ قُلْ إِن كَانَ آبَاؤُكُمْ وَأَبْنَاؤُكُمْ وَإِخْوَانُكُمْ وَأَزْوَاجُكُمْ وَعَشِيرَتُكُمْ وَأَمْوَالٌ اقْتَرَفْتُمُوهَا وَتِجَارَةٌ تَخْشَوْنَ كَسَادَهَا وَمَسَاكِنُ تَرْضَوْنَهَا أَحَبَّ إِلَيْكُم مِّنَ اللَّهِ وَرَسُولِهِ وَجِهَادٍ فِي سَبِيلِهِ فَتَرَبَّصُوا حَتَّىٰ يَأْتِيَ اللَّهُ بِأَمْرِهِ ۗ وَاللَّهُ لَا يَهْدِي الْقَوْمَ الْفَاسِقِينَ ۝

التوبة ٢٣-٢٤

﴿ Oh you who have believed! Do not take your fathers and your brothers as associates if they prefer disbelief over belief; whoever of you concerns himself with them – indeed these are the wrongdoers. Say: If your fathers, your sons, your brothers, your wives, your kinsfolk, the wealth you have acquired, the downturn in business that you fear, and the dwellings that please you, are more beloved to you than Allah and His Messenger and jihad in His cause, then be on the lookout until Allah brings His command; and Allah does not guide the dissolute ﴾ *Al-tawba 23-24*

﴿ ومساكن ترضونها أحب اليكم من الله ورسوله وجهاد في سبيله ﴾ فقعدتم لأجله عن الهجرة والجهاد ﴿ فتربَّصوا ﴾ انتظروا ﴿ حتى يأتي الله بأمره ﴾ تهديد لهم

تفسير الجلالين

﴿ And the dwellings that please you, are more beloved to you than Allah and His Messenger and jihad in His cause ﴾ : and for this you have abstained from emigrating and *jihad*; ﴿ then be on the lookout ﴾ : wait; ﴿ until Allah brings His command ﴾ : this is a threat to them.

Tafsir Al-Jalalain

قال الكلبي لما أمر رسول الله ﷺ بالهجرة إلى المدينة جعل الرجل يقول لأبيه وأخيه وإمرأته إنا قد أمرنا بالهجرة فمنهم من يسرع الى ذلك ويعجبه ومنهم من يتعلق به زوجته وعياله وولده فيقولون ناشدناك الله أن تدعنا إلى غير شيء فنضيع فيرقّ فيجلس معهم ويدع الهجرة فنزل قول الله تعالى ﴿ يا أيها الذين آمنوا لا تتخذوا آباءكم واخوانكم ﴾ الآية ونزل في الذين يخلفوا بمكة ولم يهاجروا قوله تعالى ﴿ قل إن كان اباءكم ﴾ إلى قوله ﴿ فتربصوا حتى يأتي الله بأمره ﴾ يعني القتال وفتح مكة

اسباب النزول للواحدي

Al-Kalbi said: When the Messenger of Allah (SAW) ordered emigration [*hijra*] to Medina, men began to say to their fathers and their brothers and their women: Indeed we have been ordered to emigrate. Some of them hastened to it and liked it, while for some of them, their wives, family, and children hung on to them and said: We beg you by Allah not to leave us to nothing that we should be ruined! They felt pity and remained with them, and refrained from emigrating. And so the word of Allah Most High came down: { Oh you who have believed! Do not take your fathers and your brothers as associates } and the rest of the verse. And this word of the Most High came down concerning those who stayed behind in Mecca and did not emigrate: { Say: If your fathers ... } up until His word: { the be on the lookout until Allah brings His command } : that is, for fighting and the conquest of Mecca.

Al-Wahidi, Asbab Al-nuzul

﴿ أحب اليكم ﴾ من الهجرة إلى الله ورسوله من دار الشرك ومن جهاد في سبيله يعني في نصرة دين الله الذي ارتضاه

تفسير الطبري

{ More beloved to you } : than emigrating for Allah and His Messenger out of the land of idolatry [*shirk*], and *jihad* in His cause, that is, to uphold Allah's religion [*deen*] that He is satisfied with.

Tafsir Al-Tabari

﴿ ومساكن ترضونها أحب اليكم من الله ورسوله وجهاد في سبيله ﴾ الحب الإختياري دون الطبيعي فإنه لا يدخل تحت التكليف في التحفظ عنه ﴿ فتربَّصوا حتى يأتي الله بأمره ﴾ جواب ووعيد والأمر عقوبة عاجلة أو آجلة

تفسير البيضاوي

{ And the dwellings that please you, are more beloved to you than Allah and His Messenger and jihad in His cause } : intentional love, not that which comes naturally, for indeed it does not fall within the bestowing of an obligation regarding having reservations about it. { Then be on the lookout until Allah brings His command } : a consequence and a threat; the matter being punishment sooner or later.

Tafsir Al-Baydawi

وأخرج أحمد والبخاري عن عبدالله بن هشام رضي الله عنه قال كنا مع رسول الله ﷺ وهو آخذ بيد عمر بن الخطاب رضي الله عنه فقال والله لأنت يا رسول الله أحب إلي من كل شيء إلا من نفسي فقال النبي ﷺ لا يؤمن أحدكم حتى أكون أحب إليه من نفسه

الدر المنثور للسيوطي

Ahmad and Al-Bukhari both related from Abdullah ibn Hisham (may Allah be pleased with him), who said: We were with the Messenger of Allah (SAW), and He was holding the hand of 'Umar ibn Al-Khattab (may Allah be pleased with him). 'Umar said: I swear by Allah, you, oh Messenger of Allah, are more beloved to me than anything except myself. Then the Prophet (SAW) said: None of you truly believes until I am more beloved to him than even himself.

Al-Suyuti, Al-dur Al-manthur

* * *

﴿ لقد نصركم الله في مواطن كثيرة ويوم حنين إذ أعجبتكم كثرتكم فلم تغن عنكم شيئا وضاقت عليكم الأرض بما رحبت ثم وليتم مدبرين ثم أنزل الله سكينته على رسوله وعلى المؤمنين وأنزل جنودا لم تروها وعذب الذين كفروا وذلك جزاء الكافرين ﴾ التوبة ٢٥-٢٦

{ Indeed Allah granted you victory in many territories, and on the day of Hunayn, when you relished your abundance, although it was of no use to you, for the land grew narrow to you even as it became spacious, then you turned away in retreat. Then Allah sent down His reaffirming tranquility over His Messenger and over the Believers, and He sent down troops which you did not see, and punished those who disbelieved; and this is the recompense of the disbelievers } *Al-tawba 25-26*

قال ابن جريج عن مجاهد هذه أول آية نزلت من براءة يذكر تعالى للمؤمنين فضله عليهم وإحسانه لديهم في نصره إياهم في مواطن كثيرة من غزواتهم مع رسوله وأن ذلك من عنده تعالى وبتأييده وتقديره لا بعددهم ولا بعُددهم ونبهم على أن النصر من عنده سواء قل الجمع أو كثر فإن يوم حنين أعجبتهم كثرتهم ومع هذا ما أجدى ذلك عنهم شيئاً فولوا مدبرين إلا القليل منهم مع رسول الله ﷺ ثم أنزل نصره وتأييده على رسوله وعلى المؤمنين الذين معه كما سنبينه إن شاء تعالى مفصلاً ليعلمهم أن النصر من عنده تعالى وحده وبإمداده وإن قل الجمع فكم من فئة قليلة غلبت فئة كبيرة بإذن الله والله مع الصابرين

تفسير ابن كثير

Ibn Juraij related from Mujahid that this is the first verse that came down in this *surah* in which the Most High mentions to the Believers His favor over them and His benevolence with them in granting them victory in the many places where they went on attacks with His Messenger. Moreover this is from Him Most High, by His support and decree, not by their numbers or their reinforcements; and He points out to them that the victory is from Him whether the unit is small or large. Indeed on the day of Hunayn they relished their abundance, however this was not at all of any advantage to them, as they turned away in retreat, all but a few of them with the Messenger of Allah (SAW). Then He sent down His victory and His support over His Messenger and over the Believers who were with him – as we will clarify in detail, Allah Most High willing – to let them know that the victory is from Him Most High alone and by His provision, even if the unit is small. How many small groups have overcome large groups by the permission of Allah? And Allah is with those who are steadfast.

Tafsir Ibn Kathir

﴿ ثم أنزل الله سكينته ﴾ طمأنينته ﴿ على رسوله وعلى المؤمنين ﴾ فردّوا إلى النبي ﷺ لما ناداهم العباس بإذنه وقاتلوا ﴿ وأنزل جنوداً لم تروها ﴾ ملائكة ﴿ وعذّب الذين كفروا ﴾ بالقتل والأسر ﴿ وذلك جزاء الكافرين ﴾

تفسير الجلالين

{ Then Allah sent down his reaffirming tranquility [*sakinah*] } : reassuring serenity; { over His Messenger and over the Believers } : and they turned back to the Prophet (SAW) when 'Abbas called them by his permission, and they fought; { and He sent down troops which you did not see } : angels; { and punished those who disbelieved } : with killing and imprisonment; { and this is the recompense of the disbelievers } .

Tafsir Al-Jalalain

عن السدي ﴿ وعذب الذين كفروا ﴾ يقول قتلهم بالسيف ... عن سعيد ﴿ وعذب الذين كفروا ﴾ قال بالهزيمة والقتل ... قال إبن زيد في قوله ﴿ وعذب الذين كفروا وذلك جزاء الكافرين ﴾ قال من بقي منهم

تفسير الطبري

Al-Suddi, regarding { And punished those who disbelieved }, said: He killed them by the sword. ... Sa'id, regarding { And punished those who disbelieved }, said: by utter defeat and killing. ... Ibn Zaid, regarding His word: { And punished those who disbelieved; and this is the recompense of the disbelievers }, said: Whoever is left of them.

Tafsir Al-Tabari

والمعنى لا تجدون موضعاً تستصلحونه لهربكم إليه ونجائكم لفرط الرعب فكأنها ضاقت عليكم ﴿ ثم وليتم مدبرين ﴾ ثم انهزمتم ﴿ سكينته ﴾ رحمته التي سكنوا بها وآمنوا ﴿ وعلى المؤمنين ﴾ الذين انهزموا وقيل هم الذين ثبتوا مع رسول الله ﷺ حين وقع الهرب ﴿ وأنزل جنوداً ﴾ يعني الملائكة وكانوا ثمانية آلاف وقيل خمسة آلاف وقيل ستة عشر ألفاً ﴿ وعذب الذين كفروا ﴾ بالقتل والأسر وسبي النساء والذراري

تفسير الزمخشري

The meaning is that you all did not find a place that you deemed suitable to flee towards or to escape past the terror, as it grew narrow around you; { then you turned away in retreat }: then you were defeated. { His reaffirming tranquility }: His mercy by which they became calm and felt safe; { and over the Believers }: those who had been defeated; it is said that this refers to those who remained firm with the Messenger of Allah (SAW) when the fleeing occurred. { Then Allah sent down troops }: that is, the angels; and there were eight thousand of them; some say five thousand, and some say sixteen thousand. { And punished those who disbelieved }: by killing and imprisonment, and by capturing the women and children.

Tafsir Al-Zamakhshari

﴿ يا أيها الذين آمنوا إنما المشركون نجس فلا يقربوا المسجد الحرام بعد عامهم هذا وإن خفتم عيلة فسوف يغنيكم الله من فضله إن شاء إن الله عليم حكيم فاتلوا الذين لا يؤمنون بالله ولا باليوم الآخر ولا يحرمون ما حرم الله ورسوله ولا يدينون دين الحق من الذين أوتوا الكتاب حتى يعطوا الجزية عن يد وهم صاغرون ﴾ التوبة ٢٨-٢٩

{ Oh you who have believed! Indeed the idolaters are filthy, so let them not come near the Sacred Mosque after this year of theirs; and if you fear poverty, Allah will make you rich from His abundance if He wishes; Indeed Allah is knowing, wise. Fight those who do not believe in Allah nor in the last day and who do not forbid what Allah and His Messenger have forbidden and who do not profess the religion of truth – from among those to whom the book was given – until they give *jizya* from their hands and they are abased } Al-tawba 28-29

يقول تعالى ذكره للمؤمنين به وبرسوله وأقرّوا بوحدانيته ما المشركون إلا نجس واختلف أهل التأويل في معنى النجس وما السبب الذي من أجله سماهم بذلك فقال بعضهم سماهم بذلك لأنهم يُجنبون فلا يغتسلون فقال هم نجس ولا يقربوا المسجد الحرام لأن أُجنب لا ينبغي له أن يدخل المسجد ... عن معمر في قوله ﴿ إنما المشركون نجس ﴾ لا أعلم قتادة إلا قال النجس الجنابة وبه عن معمر قال وبلغني أن النبي ﷺ لقي حذيفة وأخذ النبي ﷺ بيده فقال حذيفة يا رسول الله إني جنب فقال إن المؤمن لا يَنجُس ..... وقال آخرون معنى ذلك ما المشركون إلا رجس خنزير أو كلب

تفسير الطبري

He (may His remembrance be exalted) is saying to those who believe in Him and in His Messenger and affirm His oneness: idolaters [*mushrikun*] are nothing but filthy. Expositors differ as to the meaning of "filthy" and the reason why He calls them such. Some say: He calls them such because they become sexually impure, and they do not wash. He is saying: They are filthy, so let them not come near the Sacred Mosque, because someone who is sexually impure [*junub*] ought not to enter the mosque. ... Mu'amar, regarding His word: { Indeed the idolaters are filthy }, related: I only know that Qatada said "filth" means sexual impurity; Mu'amar moreover said: I heard that the Prophet (SAW) met up with Hudhaifa, and the Prophet (SAW) took hold of his hand, and Hudhaifa said: Oh Messenger of Allah! But I am sexually impure. He replied: Indeed a Believer does not get filthy. ... Others say that the meaning of this is that idolaters are nothing but pig or dog filth.

Tafsir Al-Tabari

﴿ قاتلوا الذين لا يؤمنون بالله ولا باليوم الاخر ﴾ وإلا لآمنوا بالنبي ﷺ ﴿ ولا يحرمون ما حرم الله ورسوله ﴾ كالخمر ﴿ ولا يدينون دين ألحق ﴾ الثابت الناسخ لغيره من الأديان وهو دين الاسلام ﴿ من الذين ﴾ بيان للذين ﴿ أوتوا الكتاب ﴾ أي اليهود والنصارى ﴿ حتى يعطوا الجزية ﴾ الخراج المضروب عليهم كل عام ﴿ عن يد ﴾ حال أي منقادين أو بأيديهم لا يوكلون بها ﴿ وهم صاغرون ﴾ أذلاء منقادون لحكم الاسلام

تفسير الجلالين

{ Fight those who do not believe in Allah nor in the last day } : otherwise they would have believed in the Prophet (SAW); { and who do not forbid what Allah and His Messenger have forbidden } : like fermented drinks; { and who do not profess the religion of truth } : the unshakable one, the one that abrogates any other religion, this being the religion of Islam; { from among those } : declaring to those; { to whom the book was given } : that is, the Jews and the Christians; { until they give the *jizya* } : the tribute appointed for them every year; { from their hands } : that is, yieldingly, with their own hands, not by someone else on their behalf; { and they are abased } : shamed and yielded to the authority of Islam.

Tafsir Al-Jalalain

﴿ قاتلوا الذين لا يؤمنون بالله ولا باليوم الأخر ولا يحرمون ما حرم الله ورسوله ولا يدينون دين ألحق من الذين أوتوا الكتاب حتى يعطوا الجزية عن يد وهم صاغرون ﴾ فهم في نفس الأمر لما كفروا بمحمد ﷺ لم يبق لهم إيمان صحيح بأحد من الرسل ولا بما جاؤوا به وإنما يتبعون آراءهم وأهواءهم وآباءهم فيما هم فيه لا لأنه شرع الله ودينه لأنهم لو كانوا مؤمنين بما بأيديهم إيماناً صحيحاً لقادهم ذلك إلى الإيمان بمحمد ﷺ لأن جميع الأنبياء بشروا به وأمروا باتباعه فلما جاء وكفروا به وهو أشرف الرسل علم أنهم ليسوا متمسكين بشرع الأنبياء الأقدمين لأنهم من عند الله بل لحظوظهم وأهوائهم فلهذا لا ينفعهم ايمانهم ببقية الأنبياء وقد كفروا بسيدهم وأفضلهم وخاتمهم وأكملهم ولهذا قال ﴿ قاتلوا الذين لا يؤمنون بالله ولا باليوم الأخر ولا يحرمون ما حرم الله ورسوله ولا يدينون دين ألحق من الذين أوتوا الكتاب ﴾ وهذه الآية الكريمة نزلت أول الأمر بقتال أهل الكتاب بعدما تمهدت أمور المشركين ودخل الناس في دين الله أفواجاً واستقامت جزيرة العرب أمر الله ورسوله بقتال أهل الكتابين اليهود والنصارى وكان ذلك في سنة تسع ولهذا تجهز رسول الله ﷺ لقتال الروم ودعا الناس إلى ذلك وأظهره لهم ... وقوله ﴿ حتى يعطوا الجزية ﴾ أي إن لم يسلموا ﴿ عن يد ﴾ أي عن قهر لهم وغلبة ﴿ وهم صاغرون ﴾ أي ذليلون حقيرون مهانون فلهذا لا يجوز إعزاز أهل الذمة ولا رفعهم على المسلمين بل هم أذلاء صَغَرَة أشقياء كما جاء في صحيح مسلم عن ابي هريرة رضي الله عنه أن النبي ﷺ قال لا تبدؤوا اليهود والنصارى بالسلام وإذا لقيتم احدهم في طريق فاضطروه إلى أضيقه ولهذا إشترط عليهم أمير المؤمنين عمر بن الخطاب رضي الله عنه تلك الشروط المعروفة في إذلالهم وتصغيرهم وتحقيرهم

تفسير إبن كثير

{ Fight those who do not believe in Allah nor in the last day and who do not forbid what Allah and His Messenger have forbidden and who do not profess the religion of truth – from among those to whom the book was given – until they give the jizya from their hands and they are abased } : and they are in the same situation they were when they disbelieved in Muhammad (SAW); they no longer have any true belief in any of the messengers, nor in what they have brought. Indeed they follow after their own opinions, their desires, and what their forefathers did, not because this was Allah's prescribed law or His religion. If they were Believers with true belief in what was among them, this would have guided them to belief in Muhammad (SAW), since all the prophets gave the good news about him, and ordered that He be followed. When He came, however, and they disbelieved in him, although He was the most honorable of the messengers, He knew that they did not hold fast to the prescribed law of the earlier prophets which was from Allah, but rather to their good fortunes and desires. As such their belief in the rest of the prophets was of no use to them, as they had disbelieved in their lord, the best of them, their completion and the most perfect of them. For this reason He says: { Fight those who do not believe in Allah nor in the last day and who do not forbid what Allah and His Messenger have forbidden and who do not profess the religion of truth – from among those to whom the book was given } . This noble verse came down as the first command to fight the People of the Book after the issues of the idolaters [*mushrikeen*] were settled and people entered into Allah's religion in droves, and the Arabian peninsula was put in order. Allah and His Messenger ordered the people of the two books – Jews and Christians – to be fought, and this was in the ninth year. For this reason the Messenger of Allah (SAW) prepared himself to fight Rome, and He called the people to this and made it known to them. ... His word: { until they give jizya } : that is, if they have not yielded into Islam; { from their hands } : that is, under their compulsion and subjugation; { and they are abased } : that is, humiliated, miserable, and scorned. For this reason it is not permissible to esteem those held under safeguard [*dhimma*], nor elevate them above the Muslims; rather they are shamed, abased, and wretched, as related in Sahih Muslim from Abu Huraira (may Allah be pleased with him), that the Prophet (SAW) said: Do not initiate greetings with Jews or Christians, and whenever you meet one of them on a road, force him to its narrowest part. This is why the Leader of the Faithful 'Umar ibn Al-Khattab (may Allah be pleased with him) imposed these well-known conditions on them – to shame them, abase them, and make them miserable.

Tafsir Ibn Kathir

﴿ وهم صاغرون ﴾ أي ذليلون حقيرون مهانون فلهذا لا يجوز إعزاز أهل الذمة ولا رفعهم على المسلمين بل هم أذلاء صغرة أشقياء كما جاء في صحيح مسلم عن ابي هريرة رضي الله عنه أن النبي ﷺ قال لا تبدؤوا اليهود والنصارى بالسلام وإذا لقيتم احدهم في طريق فاضطروه إلى أضيقه ولهذا اشترط عليهم أمير المؤمنين عمر بن الخطاب رضي الله عنه تلك الشروط المعروفة في إذلالهم وتصغيرهم وتحقيرهم وذلك مما رواه الأئمة الحفاظ من رواية عبد الرحمان بن غنم الأشعري قال كتبت لعمر بن الخطاب رضي الله عنه حين صالح نصارى من أهل الشام

بسم الله الرحمان الرحيم هذا كتاب لعبد الله عمر أمير المؤمنين من نصارى مدينة كذا وكذا إنكم لما قدمتم علينا سألناكم الأمان لأنفسنا وذرارينا وأموالنا وأهل ملتنا وشرطنا لكم على أنفسنا أن لا نحدث في مدينتنا ولا فيما حولها ديراً ولا كنيسة ولا قلّاية ولا صومعة راهب ولا نجدد ما خرب منها ولا نحيي ما كان منها خططاً للمسلمين وأن لا نمنع كنائسنا أن ينزلها أحد من المسلمين في ليل ولا نهار وأن نوسع ابوابها للمارة وابن السبيل وأن ننزل من مر بنا من المسلمين ثلاثة أيام نطعمهم ولا نؤوي في كنائسنا ولا منازلنا جاسوساً ولا نكتم غشّاً للمسلمين ولا نعلم اولادنا القرآن ولا نظهر شركاً ولا ندعو إليه أحداً ولا نمنع أحداً من ذوي قراباتنا الدخول في الاسلام إن أرادوه وأن نوقّر المسلمين وأن نقوم لهم من مجالسنا إن ارادوا الجلوس ولا نتشبه بهم في شيء من ملابسهم في قَلَنْسُوَة ولا عمامة ولا نعلين ولا فرق شعر ولا نتكلم بكلامهم ولا نكتني بكناهم لا نركب السروج ولا نتقلد السيوف ولا نتخذ شيئاً من السلاح ولا نحمله معنا ولا ننقش خواتمنا بالعربية ولا بنيع الخمور وأن نجزّ مقاديم رؤوسنا وأن نلزم زينا حيثما كنا وأن نشد الزنانير على أوساطنا وأن لا نظهر الصليب على كنائسنا وأن لا نظهر صلبنا ولا كتبنا في شيء من طرق المسلمين ولا أسواقهم ولا نضرب نواقيسنا في كنائسنا إلا ضرباً خفيفاً وأن لا نرفع أصواتنا بالقراءة في كنائسنا في شيء من حضرة المسلمين ولا نخرج شعانين ولا باعوثاً ولا نرفع أصواتنا مع موتانا ولا نظهر النيران معهم في شيء من طرق المسلمين ولا أسواقهم ولا نجاورهم بموتانا ولا نتخذ من الرقيق ما جرى عليه سهام المسلمين وأن نرشد المسلمين ولا نطلع عليهم في منازلهم قال فلما أتيت عمر بالكتاب زاد فيه ولا نضرب أحداً من المسلمين شرطنا لكم ذلك على أنفسنا وأهل ملتنا وقبلنا عليه الأمان فإن نحن خالفنا في شيء مما شرطناه ووظفناه على أنفسنا فلا ذمة لنا وقد حل لكم منا ما يحل من أهل معاندة والشقاق

تفسير ابن كثير

{ And they are abased } [Al-tawba 29]: that is, humiliated, miserable, and scorned. For this reason it is not permissible to esteem those who are under safeguard [dhimma], nor elevate them above the Muslims; rather, they are shamed, abased, and wretched, as reported in Sahih Muslim from Abu Huraira (may Allah be pleased with him), that the Prophet (SAW) said: Do not initiate greetings with Jews or Christians, and whenever you meet one of them on a road, force him to its narrowest part. This is why the Leader of the Faithful 'Umar ibn Al-Khattab (may Allah be pleased with him) imposed these well-known conditions on them – to shame them, abase them, and make them miserable. This is what the leading scholars of hadith preservation narrated from 'Abd Al-Rahman ibn Ghanm Al-Ash'ari, who said: I wrote down the following for 'Umar ibn Al-Khattab (may Allah be pleased with him) when he made a truce with the Christians of Sham:

In the name of Allah the Merciful the Compassionate. This is a document to the servant of Allah 'Umar, Leader of the Faithful, from the Christians of such-and-such city. Indeed when you [the Muslims] came to us, we requested security from you for ourselves, our children, our property, and followers of our religion. And we have imposed upon ourselves to you the condition that we will not renovate any monastery, church, bishop's residence, or hermitage for monks in our city, nor in the surrounding area; neither will we restore any of these that has been damaged, or set them up for anything that could be used to plot against the Muslims. And we will not prevent any Muslim from staying in our churches, night or day, and we will open their doors to anyone passing through or journeying. And we will host any Muslims who come by us, for three days, and we will provide their meals. And we will not give lodging in our churches or homes to any spies, nor will we conceal any deception or betrayal from the Muslims. We will not teach our children the Qur'an, we will not manifest any shirk nor call anyone to it, nor will we prevent any of our kinsfolk from entering into Islam, if they desire it. We will treat the Muslims with great respect, and we will get up from where we are sitting if they wish to sit. And we will not imitate them in any of their clothing, headpieces, turbans, sandals, or the way they part their hair. We will not speak as they speak, and we will not use their *kunya*. We will not ride on saddles, and we will not wear swords nor will we take hold of any kind of weapon or carry one with us. We will not engrave our seals in Arabic, and we will not sell alcoholic drinks. We will shave the front of our heads, stick to our adornments wherever we are, and keep belts around our waists. We will not display the cross on our churches, and we will not display our crosses or our books on absolutely any of the Muslim paths or their marketplaces. We will not ring our bells in our churches except a gentle ring, and we will not raise our voices during recitation in our churches if there are at all any Muslims around. And we will not bring out palm branches or Easter litany, nor will we raise our voices for our dead or display fires for them on absolutely any of the Muslim paths or their marketplaces, and we will not put our dead in their vicinity. And we will not take any slaves upon whom have fallen Muslim arrows [i.e. captured by Muslims]. We will guide the Muslims and we will not intrude on them in their homes.

He [Al-Ash'ari] said: When I had brought the document to 'Umar, he added: We will not beat any of the Muslims. We have imposed to you all these conditions, upon ourselves and the followers of our religion, and we have accepted safety in return for it. And if we fail to keep anything of what we have imposed and designated on ourselves and promised to you, we are no longer under safeguard [dhimma], and you are permitted to do to us what is permitted for those who are obstinate and rebelious.

Tafsir Ibn Kathir (Pact of 'Umar)

فلما كثر الفتح وإنتشر الاسلام خرجوا وتأمروا كأبي هريرة وغيره وما قعدوا ثم قيل الأسباب التي يطلب بها الرزق ستة أنواع أعلاها كسب نبينا محمد ﷺ قال جُعل رزقي تحت ظل رمحي وجعل الذِّلة والصَّغار على من خالف أمري خرجه الترمذي وصححه فجعل الله رزق نبيه ﷺ في كسبه لفضله وخصه بأفضل أنواع الكسب وهو أخذ الغَلَبَة والقهر لشرفه

تفسير القرطبي

When victory increased and Islam spread, they went out and dominated – like Abu Huraira and others – and did not desist. Then, it is said, the reasons for which bounty was sought were of six kinds, the greatest of which is the gain of our prophet Muhammad (SAW), who said: I have been made to prosper under the shadow of my spear; and disgrace and cringing for whoever goes against my orders. Al-Tirmidhi related this and considered it sound [*sahih*]. And Allah made the livelihood of His Prophet (SAW) to be in gaining for his bounty, and He gave him special favor through the best kind of gain – using subjugation and force for his glory.

Tafsir Al-Qurtubi

اعلم أنه تعالى لما ذكر حكم المشركين في إظهار البراءة عن عهدهم وفي إظهار البراءة عنهم في أنفسهم وفي وجوب مقاتلتهم ... ذكر بعده حكم أهل الكتاب وهو أن يقاتلوا إلى أن يعطوا الجزية فحينئذ يقرون على ما هم عليه بشرائط ... وفي الآية مسائل المسألة الأولى اعلم أنه تعالى ذكر أن أهل الكتاب إذا كانوا موصوفين بصفات أربعة وجبت مقاتلتهم إلى أن يسلموا أو إلى أن يعطوا الجزية فالصفة الاولى أنهم لا يؤمنون بالله ... والصفة الثانية من صفاتهم أنهم لا يؤمنون باليوم الآخر واعلم أن المنقول عن اليهود والنصارى إنكار البعث الجسماني فكأنهم يميلون إلى البعث الروحاني ... الصفة الثالثة من صفاتهم قوله تعالى ﴿ ولا يحرمون ما حرم الله ورسوله ﴾ وفيه وجهان الأول أنهم لا يحرمون ما حرم في القرآن وسنة الرسول والثاني قال أبو روق لا يعملون بما في التوراة والانجيل بل حرفوهما وأتوا بأحكام كثيرة من قبل أنفسهم الصفة الرابعة قوله ﴿ ولا يدينون دين الحق من الذين اوتوا الكتاب ﴾ يقال فلان يدين بكذا إذا إتخذه ديناً فهو معتقده فقوله ﴿ ولا يدينون دين الحق ﴾ أي لا يعتقدون في صحة دين الاسلام الذي هو الدين الحق

تفسير الرازي

Know that the Most High, when He mentioned the ruling for the idolaters by declaring absolution from the covenant with them and by declaring absolution from them within themselves, and the necessity of fighting them ... after this He mentioned the ruling for the People of the Book – that they are to be fought until they give *jizya*, and then they may remain in the situation they were in, provided certain conditions are met. ... In this verse there are several points; the first point: Know that the Most High has mentioned that the People of the Book are characterized by four qualities that make it necessary to fight them until they yield into Islam or until they give *jizya*.

The first quality is that they do not believe in Allah ... The second quality is that they do not believe in the last day; know that denial of bodily resurrection is related from the Jews and Christians, as they favor a resurrection in the spirit. ... The third quality is the word of the Most High: { who do not forbid what Allah and His Messenger have forbidden } ; here there are two veiwpoints: the first is that they do not forbid what had been forbidden in the Qur'an and in the Messenger's way of life [*sunnah*], and the second is what Abu Rawq said, in that they do not know what is in the Torah and the *Injil*, but rather they have misconstrued both of these and have brought many rulings that come merely from themselves. The fourth quality is His word: { who do not profess the religion of truth – from among those to whom the book was given } . It is said that someone "professes" something when he embraces it as a religion and becomes a firm believer in it. His word: { who do not profess the religion of truth } : that is, they do not firmly believe in the veracity of the religion of Islam, that which is the true religion.

Tafsir Al-Razi

* * *

﴿ وقالت اليهود عزير ابن الله وقالت النصارى المسيح ابن الله ذلك قولهم بأفواههم يضاهؤن قول الذين كفروا من قبل قاتلهم الله أنى يؤفكون ﴾ التوبة ٣٠

{ The Jews say that 'Uzair is the son of Allah and the Christians say that the Messiah is the son of Allah; this is what they say with their mouths, following what those who disbelieved before them said; may Allah fight them, how deluded they are } *Al-tawba* 30

وهذا إغراء من الله تعالى للمؤمنين على قتال الكفار من اليهود والنصارى لمقالتهم هذه المقالة الشنيعة والفرية على الله تعالى

تفسير ابن كثير

This is incitement from Allah Most High for the Believers to fight the Jews and Christians who are disbelievers [*kuffar*], due to this statement of theirs, this abominable and astounding statement against Allah Most High.

Tafsir Ibn Kathir

﴿ قاتلهم الله ﴾ أي هم أحقاء بأن يقال لهم هذا تعجباً من شناعة قولهم كم يقال لقوم ركبوا شنعاء قاتلهم الله ما أعجب فعلهم

تفسير الزمخشري

{ May Allah fight them } : that is, it is befitting for this to be said to them in astonishment at the abomination of what they say, as it is said to people who perpetrate an atrocious act: "May Allah fight them! How astonishing are their actions!"

Tafsir Al-Zamakhshari

عن إبن عباس رضي الله عنهما في قوله ﴿ قاتلهم الله ﴾ قال لعنهم الله وكل شيء في القرآن قتل فهو لعن

الدر المنثور للسيوطي

Ibn 'Abbas (may Allah be pleased with him), regarding His word { May Allah fight them } , said: May Allah curse them; everything in the Qur'an that is "kill" is a curse.

Al-Suyuti, Al-dur Al-manthur

* * *

﴿ هو الذي أرسل رسوله بالهدى ودين الحق ليظهره على الدين كله ولو كره المشركون ﴾

التوبة ٣٣

{ It is He who has sent His Messenger with guidance and the religion of truth, to make it prevail over all religion, even if the idolaters dislike this } Al-tawba 33

﴿ هو الذي أرسل رسوله بالهدى ودين الحق ﴾ فالهدى هو ما جاء به من الاخبارات الصادقة والإيمان الصحيح والعلم النافع ودين الحق هي الاعمال الصالحة الصحيحة النافعة في الدنيا والآخرة ﴿ ليظهره على الدين كله ﴾ أي على سائر الأديان كما ثبت في الصحيح عن رسول الله ﷺ أنه قال إن الله زوى لي الأرض مشارقها ومغاربها وسيبلغ ملك أمتي ما زويَ لي منها ... عن تميم الداري رضي الله عنه قال سمعت رسول الله ﷺ يقول ليبلغن هذا الأمر ما بلغ الليل والنهار ولا يترك الله بيت مدر ولا وبر إلا أدخله هذا الدين يعز عزيزاً ويذل ذليلاً بعز عزيز أو بذل ذليل عزاً يعز الله به الاسلام وذلاً يذل الله به الكفر

تفسير إبن كثير

{ It is He who has sent His Messenger with guidance and the religion of truth } ; guidance is the genuine communications, sound belief, beneficial knowledge that He brought, and the religion of truth [*deen al-haqq*] is good, genuine, and beneficial deeds in this world and the next. { To make it prevail over all religion } : that is, over all other religions, as affirmed in the *Sahih* [Sahih Muslim] from the Messenger of Allah (SAW), who said: Indeed Allah compressed the earth together for me to see its eastern and westernmost points; and the dominion of my *ummah* will extend to what was compressed together for me. ... From Tamim Al-Dari (may Allah be pleased with him), who said: I heard the Messenger of Allah (SAW) say: This affair will spread out as far as night and day spread out, and Allah will not leave a house of mud or animal hair without bringing this religion into it, fortifying the mighty and disgracing the disgraced by the might of the mighty or the disgrace of the disgraced, might by which Allah fortifies Islam, and disgrace by which Allah disgraces disbelief.

Tafsir Ibn Kathir

يقول تعالى ذكره الله الذي يأبى إلا إتمام دينه ولو كره ذلك جاحدوه ومنكروه الذي أرسل رسوله محمداً ﷺ بالهدى يعني ببيان فرائض الله على خلقه وجميع اللازم لهم وبدين الحق وهو الاسلام

تفسير الطبري

He (may His remembrance be exalted) is saying: Allah is the one who refuses anything other than the realization of His religion – even if those who controvert and deny it dislike this – the One who has sent His Messenger Muhammad (SAW) with guidance, that is, declaring Allah's obligations on His creation and all that is required of them, and with the religion of truth, this being Islam.

Tafsir Al-Tabari

قال الشافعي رحمه الله فقد أظهر الله رسوله ﷺ على الأديان كلها بأن أبان لكل من سمعه أنه ألحق وما خالفه من الأديان باطل وقال وأظهره بأن جماع الشرك ديانان دين أهل الكتاب ودين أُمّيين فقهر رسول الله ﷺ الاميين حتى دانوا بالاسلام طوعاً وكرهاً وقتل أهل الكتاب وسبى حتى دان بعضهم بالاسلام وأعطى بعضهم الجزية صاغرين وجرى عليهم حكمه فهذا ظهوره على الدين كله والله أعلم

تفسير البغوي

Al-Shafi'i (may Allah have mercy on him) said: Allah made His Messenger (SAW) prevail over all religions by demonstrating to all who heard him that He was true, and whatever religion contradicted him was false. He said: He made him prevail by the fact that idolatry [*shirk*] encompasses two religions: the religion of the People of the

Book and the religion of the illiterate [i.e. who have no books]. And the Messenger of Allah (SAW) conquered the illiterates until they professed Islam willingly or under compulsion, and He killed the People of the Book and took prisoners until some of them professed Islam and others of them gave *jizya*, being abased, and his authority came over them. This is how He prevailed over all religion. And Allah knows best.

Tafsir Al-Baghawi

* * *

﴿ إِنَّ عِدَّةَ الشُّهُورِ عِندَ اللَّهِ اثْنَا عَشَرَ شَهْرًا فِي كِتَابِ اللَّهِ يَوْمَ خَلَقَ السَّمَاوَاتِ وَالْأَرْضَ مِنْهَا أَرْبَعَةٌ حُرُمٌ ذَٰلِكَ الدِّينُ الْقَيِّمُ فَلَا تَظْلِمُوا فِيهِنَّ أَنفُسَكُمْ وَقَاتِلُوا الْمُشْرِكِينَ كَافَّةً كَمَا يُقَاتِلُونَكُمْ كَافَّةً وَاعْلَمُوا أَنَّ اللَّهَ مَعَ الْمُتَّقِينَ ﴾ التوبة ٣٦

{ Indeed the number of months for Allah is twelve months, in the decree of Allah, the day He created the heavens and the earth; four of them are sacred; this is the proper religion, so do not wrong yourselves in these months. And fight the idolaters completely just as they fight you completely; and know that Allah is with the devout } Al-tawba 36

في قوله ﴿ كَافَّةً ﴾ قولان الأول أن يكون المراد قاتلوهم بأجمعهم مجتمعين على قتالهم كما يقاتلونكم على هذه الصفة يريد تعاونوا وتناصروا على ذلك ولا تخاذلوا ولا تتقاطعوا وكونوا عباد الله مجتمعين متوافقين في مقاتلة الأعداء والثاني قال إبن عباس قاتلوهم بكليتهم ولا تحابوا بعضهم بترك القتال كما أنهم يستحلون قتال جميعكم ... ﴿ قَاتِلُوا الْمُشْرِكِينَ كَافَّةً ﴾ إباحة قتالهم في جميع الأشهر ومن الناس من يقول المقاتلة مع الكفار محرمة بدليل قوله ﴿ مِنْهَا أَرْبَعَةٌ حُرُمٌ ذَٰلِكَ الدِّينُ الْقَيِّمُ فَلَا تَظْلِمُوا فِيهِنَّ أَنفُسَكُمْ ﴾ أي فلا تظلموا فيهن أنفسكم باستحلال القتال والغارة فيهن وقد ذكرنا هذه المسألة في سورة البقرة في تفسير قوله ﴿ يَسْأَلُونَكَ عَنِ الشَّهْرِ الْحَرَامِ قِتَالٍ فِيهِ ﴾

تفسير الرازي

Regarding His word: { Completely } there are two points of view; the first is that the intended meaning is: Fight all of them, being joined together in fighting them, just as they fight you this way. He means to say: Support each other, uphold each other towards this end, do not grow weak or separate from each other, and be servants of Allah, united and in agreement in combatting the enemies. The second point of view is what Ibn 'Abbas said: Fight them in their entirety, and do not be biased against some of them by neglecting to fight, just as they have found it lawful to fight all of you. ... { And fight the idolaters completely } : permission to fight them in all months. Some people might say: Battle with the disbelievers [kuffar] is prohibited as shown in His word: { Four of them are sacred; this is the proper religion, so do not wrong yourselves in these months } : that is, do not wrong yourselves in these months by making fighting and assaulting lawful in these months. However, we have mentioned this issue in *Surah Al-baqara* in the explanation of His word: { They ask you about the sacred months – is there fighting during them? } [Al-baqara 217].

Tafsir Al-Razi

﴿ واعلموا أن الله مع المتقين ﴾ بشارة وضمان لهم بالنصرة بسبب تقواهم

تفسير البيضاوي

{ And know that Allah is with the devout } : glad tidings and assurance to them of assistance due to their devotion.

Tafsir Al-Baydawi

﴿ واعلموا أن الله مع المتقين ﴾ فإن معناه واعلموا أيها المؤمنون بالله انكم إن قاتلتم المشركين كافة واتقيتم الله فأطعتموه فيما أمركم ونهاكم ولم تخالفوا أمره فتعصوه كان الله معكم على عدوكم وعدوه من المشركين ومن كان الله معه لم يغلبه شيء لأن الله مع من اتقاه نخافه وأطاعه فيما كلفه من أمره ونهيه

تفسير الطبري

{ And know that Allah is with the devout } ; the meaning is indeed: And know, oh you who believe in Allah, that if you fight the idolaters completely, and fear Allah and obey Him in what He has ordered you and prohibited to you, and you do not oppose His orders and disobey Him, then Allah is with you against your enemy and His enemy the Idolaters. And whoever Allah is with, nothing will overcome him, because Allah is with those who are devout towards Him and fear Him and obey Him in the orders and prohibitions He has required.

Tafsir Al-Tabari

﴿ يَا أَيُّهَا الَّذِينَ آمَنُوا مَا لَكُمْ إِذَا قِيلَ لَكُمُ انْفِرُوا فِي سَبِيلِ اللَّهِ اثَّاقَلْتُمْ إِلَى الْأَرْضِ أَرَضِيتُم بِالْحَيَاةِ الدُّنْيَا مِنَ الْآخِرَةِ فَمَا مَتَاعُ الْحَيَاةِ الدُّنْيَا فِي الْآخِرَةِ إِلَّا قَلِيلٌ إِلَّا تَنْفِرُوا يُعَذِّبْكُمْ عَذَابًا أَلِيمًا وَيَسْتَبْدِلْ قَوْمًا غَيْرَكُمْ وَلَا تَضُرُّوهُ شَيْئًا وَاللَّهُ عَلَى كُلِّ شَيْءٍ قَدِيرٌ ﴾ التوبة ٣٨-٣٩

{ Oh you who have believed, what is with you all? Whenever it is said to you: "Mobilize in the cause of Allah", you sink down to the ground; Are you pleased with the life of this world over the hereafter? But how little is the enjoyment of the life of this world compared to the hereafter. If you do not mobilize, He will punish you painfully, that He might substitute other people, and you can not harm Him at all; Allah has power to do all things }

Al-tawba 38-39

ونزل لما دعا ﷺ الناس إلى غزوة تبوك وكانوا في عسرة وشدّة حرّ فشقّ عليهم ﴿ يَا أَيُّهَا الَّذِينَ آمَنُوا مَا لَكُمْ إِذَا قِيلَ لَكُمُ انْفِرُوا فِي سَبِيلِ اللَّهِ اثَّاقَلْتُمْ ﴾ ... أي تباطأتم ومِلتم عن الجهاد ﴿ إِلَى الْأَرْضِ ﴾ والقعود فيها والاستفهام للتوبيخ ﴿ أَرَضِيتُم بِالْحَيَاةِ الدُّنْيَا ﴾ ولذاتها ﴿ مِنَ الْآخِرَةِ ﴾ أي بدل نعيمها ... ﴿ إِلَّا تَنْفِرُوا ﴾ تخرجوا ما النبي ﷺ للجهاد ﴿ يُعَذِّبْكُمْ عَذَابًا أَلِيمًا ﴾ مؤلماً ﴿ وَيَسْتَبْدِلْ قَوْمًا غَيْرَكُمْ ﴾ أي يأت بهم بدلكم ... ﴿ وَلَا تَضُرُّوهُ ﴾ أي الله أو النبي ﷺ ﴿ شَيْئًا ﴾ بترك نصره فإن الله ناصر دينه ﴿ وَاللَّهُ عَلَى كُلِّ شَيْءٍ قَدِيرٌ ﴾ ومنه نصر دينه ونبيه

تفسير الجلالين

This came down when He (SAW) called the people to the attack on Tabuk, but they were going through hardship and intense heat, and it was burdensome for them. { Oh you who have believed, what is with you all? Whenever it is said to you: "Mobilize in the cause of Allah", you sink down } ... that is, you become sluggish and are averse to jihad; { to the ground } : and sitting there (the questioning is meant as a scolding); { Are you pleased with the life of this world } : and its delights; { compared to the hereafter? } : that is, instead of its bliss? ... { If you do not mobilize } : set out with the Prophet (SAW) for jihad; { He will punish you painfully } : grievously; { that He might substitute other people } : that is, that He might bring them instead of you ... { And you can not harm Him } : that is, Allah or the Prophet; { at all } : by abandoning support of Him, for indeed Allah can uphold His religion; { Allah has power to do all things } : and He can champion his religion and His Prophet.

Tafsir Al-Jalalain

﴿ يا أيها الذين آمنوا ما لكم ﴾ الآية فيها حتٌ من الله سبحانه لأصحاب رسول الله ﷺ على غزوة تبوك وذلك أن رسول الله ﷺ لما رجع من الطائف أمر بالجهاد لغزوة الروم وذلك في زمان عسرة من الناس وجدب من البلاد وشدة من الحر فأحرقت النخل وطابت الثمار وعظم على الناس غزوة الروم وأحبوا الظلال والمقام في المسكن والمال فشقّ عليهم الخروج إلى القتال وكان رسول الله ﷺ قلَّ ماخرج في غزوة إلا كنّى عنها وورّى بغيرها إلا غزوة تبوك لبُعد شقتها وكثرة العدو ليتأهب الناس وأمرهم بالجهاد وأخبرهم بالذي يريد فلما علم الله تثاقل الناس أنزل الله تعالى ﴿ يا أيها الذين آمنوا مالكم ﴾ ... ﴿ أرضيتم بالحياة الدنيا من الآخرة ﴾ أي أرضيتم الدنيا ودعتها عِوَضًا من نعيم الآخرة وثوابها ﴿ فما متاع الحياة الدنيا في الآخرة إلا قليل ﴾ ثم أوعدهم على ترك الجهاد

تفسير الثعلبي

{ Oh you who have believed, what is with you all? } and the rest of the verse; in it is an urging from Allah the Exalted to the Messenger of Allah's (SAW) Companions towards the attack on Tabuk. This is because the Messenger of Allah (SAW), when He returned from Ta'if, ordered *jihad* to make an attack on the Romans. This was during a time of hardship for people, and drought in the land, and intense heat; the date palms had become parched and the fruits were ripe, and it was distressing for people to attack the Romans, as they preferred the shade, remaining at home, and their earnings. Thus it was burdensome on them to set out to fight. So the Messenger of Allah (SAW) minimized it – He went out on an attack only by alluding to it and making a play on words, calling it something other than the attack on Tabuk, to put away the hardship and the large number of the enemy, so that people would get ready, then He ordered them to *jihad* and announced his intention. But when Allah became aware of people's sluggishness, Allah Most High sent down: { Oh you who have believed, what is with you all? } ... { Are you pleased with the life of this world over the hereafter? } : that is, are you all pleased with this world and its good feeling instead of the bliss of the hereafter and its reward? { But how little is the enjoyment of the life of this world compared to the hereafter. } Then He threatened them against neglecting *jihad*.

Tafsir Al-Tha'labi

وقد روي عن إبن عباس والحسن وعكرمة قالوا نُسخ قوله ﴿ إلا تنفروا يعذبكم عذاباً أليماً ﴾ بقوله ﴿ وما كان المؤمنون لينفروا كافة ﴾ وقال أبو سليمان الدمشقي ليس هذا من المنسوخ إذ لا تنافي بين الآيتين وإنما حكم كل آية قائم في موضعها

تفسير إبن الجوزي

It is related from Ibn 'Abbas, Al-Hasan, and 'Ikrama, who said: This word of His: { If you do not mobilize, He will punish you painfully } was abrogated by His word: { It is not for all of the Believers to mobilize } [Al-tawba 122]. But Abu Sulaiman Al-Dimashqi said: This is not abrogated; there is no mutual contradiction between the two verses, but rather the ruling of each verse stands in its particular instance.

Tafsir Ibn Al-Jawzi

﴿ وَلَا تَضُرُّوهُ شَيْئًا ﴾ أي ولا تضروا الله شيئاً بتوليكم عن الجهاد ونكولكم وتثاقلكم عنه ﴿ وَاللَّهُ عَلَى كُلِّ شَيْءٍ قَدِيرٌ ﴾ أي قادر على الإنتصار من الأعداء بدونكم

تفسير إبن كثير

{ And you can not harm Him at all } : that is, you all can not harm Allah at all by turning away from *jihad* and by retreating and sinking down from it; { Allah has power to do all things } : that is, He is capable of victory over the enemies without you.

Tafsir Ibn Kathir

. . .

﴿ انْفِرُوا خِفَافًا وَثِقَالًا وَجَاهِدُوا بِأَمْوَالِكُمْ وَأَنْفُسِكُمْ فِي سَبِيلِ اللَّهِ ذَلِكُمْ خَيْرٌ لَكُمْ إِنْ كُنْتُمْ تَعْلَمُونَ ﴾ التوبة ٤١

{ **Mobilize, light or heavy, and wage jihad with your wealth and with yourselves in the cause of Allah; this is better for you, if you only knew** } *Al-tawba 41*

﴿ انْفِرُوا خِفَافًا وَثِقَالًا ﴾ نشاطاً وغير نشاط وقيل أقوياء وضعفاء أو أغنياء وفقراء وهي منسوخة بآية ﴿ لَيْسَ عَلَى الضُّعَفَاءِ ﴾ ﴿ وَجَاهِدُوا بِأَمْوَالِكُمْ وَأَنْفُسِكُمْ فِي سَبِيلِ اللَّهِ ذَلِكُمْ خَيْرٌ لَكُمْ إِنْ كُنْتُمْ تَعْلَمُونَ ﴾ أنه خير لكم فلا تثاقلوا

تفسير الجلالين

{ Mobilize, light or heavy } : with vitality or without vitality; it is also said: strong or weak, rich or poor; but this is abrogated by the verse: { There is no blame on the weak } [*Al-tawba* 91]. { And wage jihad with your wealth and with yourselves in the cause of Allah; this is better for you, if you only knew } : that it is better for you; so do not sink down from it.

Tafsir Al-Jalalain

﴿ انفِروا خِفافاً ثِقالاً ﴾ الآيةَ ﴿ الآيةُ أمرٌ اللهُ تعالى بالنفيرِ العامِ مع رسولِ اللهِ ﷺ عامَ غزوةِ تبوكَ لقتالِ أعداءِ اللهِ من الرومِ الكفرةِ من أهلِ الكتابِ وحتمَ على المؤمنينَ في الخروجِ معه على كلِ حالٍ في المنشطِ والمكرهِ والعسرِ واليسرِ فقالَ ﴿ انفِروا خِفافاً وثِقالاً ﴾ قالَ عليُ بنُ زيدٍ عن أنسٍ عن أبي طلحةَ كهولاً وشباباً ما سمعَ اللهُ عذرَ أحدٍ ... وقد رويَ عن ابنِ عباسٍ ومحمدِ بنِ كعبٍ وعطاءٍ الخرسانيِّ وغيرهم أن هذه الآيةِ منسوخةٌ بقولِه تعالى ﴿ فلولا نفر من كلِّ فرقةٍ منهم طائفةٌ ﴾ ... وقالَ السديُ قولَه ﴿ انفِروا خِفافاً ثِقالاً ﴾ يقولُ غنياً وفقيراً وقوياً وضعيفاً فجاءه رجلٌ يومئذٍ زعموا أنه المقدادُ وكانَ عظيماً سميناً فشكى إليه وسألَه أن يأذنَ له فأبى فنزلت يومئذٍ ﴿ انفِروا خِفافاً ثِقالاً ﴾ فلما نزلت هذه الآيةِ اشتدَ على الناسِ فنسخَها اللهُ فقالَ ﴿ ليسَ على الضعفاءِ ولا على المرضى ولا على الذينَ لا يجدونَ ما ينفقونَ حرجٌ إذا نصحوا للهِ ورسولِه ﴾ ... ﴿ وجاهدوا بأموالِكم وأنفسِكم في سبيلِ اللهِ ذلكم خيرٌ لكم إن كنتم تعلمونَ ﴾ أي هذا خيرٌ لكم في الدنيا والآخرةِ لأنكم تغرمونَ في النفقةِ قليلاً فيغنمكم اللهُ أموالَ عدوِكم في الدنيا مع ما يدخرُ لكم من الكرامةِ في الآخرةِ كما قالَ النبيُ ﷺ تكفلَ اللهُ للمجاهدِ في سبيله إن توفاه أن يدخلَه الجنةَ أو يردَه إلى منزلِه بما نالَ من أجرٍ أو غنيمةٍ ولهذا قالَ اللهُ تعالى ﴿ كُتبَ عليكمُ القتالُ وهو كرهٌ لكم وعسى أن تكرهوا شيئاً وهو خيرٌ لكم وعسى أن تحبوا شيئاً وهو شرٌ لكم واللهُ يعلمُ وأنتم لا تعلمونَ ﴾ ومن هذا القبيلِ ما رواه الإمامُ أحمدُ حدثنا محمدُ بنُ أبي عديٍ عن حميدٍ عن أنسٍ أن رسولَ اللهِ ﷺ قالَ لرجلٍ أسلِم قال أجدُني كارهاً قال أسلم وإن كنتَ كارهاً

تفسيرُ ابنِ كثيرٍ

{ Mobilize, light or heavy } and the rest of the verse: Allah Most High ordered general mobilization with the Messenger of Allah (SAW) in the year of the attack on Tabuk, to fight the enemies of Allah the Romans, the Disbelievers from among the People of the Book. He commanded the Believers to set out with him under all circumstances, whether energized or coerced, in hardship or in ease; He said: { Mobilize, light or heavy } . 'Ali ibn Zaid related from Anas, who related from Abu Talha: Elderly or young; he did not hear of Allah excusing anyone. … It is narrated from Ibn 'Abbas, Muhammad ibn Ka'b, 'Ataa Al-Kurasani, and others, that this verse was abrogated by His word: { If a small group from among each band were not to mobilize } [Al-tawba 122]. … Al-Suddi, regarding His word { Mobilize, light or heavy } , said: rich or poor, strong or weak. A certain man came to him on that day – they allege it was Miqdad, a very large and overweight man – and complained to him and asked him to excuse him, but He refused, and that day { Mobilize, light or heavy } came down. But when this verse came down, it got very hard for people, and so Allah abrogated it and said: { There is no blame on the weak, on the sick, or on those who do not have anything to spend, if they are sincere towards Allah and His Messenger } [Al-tawba 91]. … { And wage jihad with your wealth and with yourselves in the cause of Allah; this is better for you, if you only knew } : in other words, this is better for you in this world and the next, since you might have to spend a little, but Allah will grant you the wealth of your enemy in this world as well as the honor that He reserves for you in the hereafter, as the Prophet (SAW) said: Allah pledges to whoever wages *jihad* in

His cause, that if He brings death upon him, He will admit him into *Jannah*, or else He will return him to his home with the reward or spoils that he will have received. For this reason Allah Most High said: { Fighting is ordained for you, being something you dislike; but perhaps you dislike something that is good for you, and perhaps you like something that is bad for you; and Allah knows but you do not know } [*Al-baqara* 216]. Similar to this is what Imam Ahmad narrated: Muhammad ibn Abi 'Adi related to us from Humaid, from Anas, that the Messenger of Allah (SAW) said to a man: Yield into Islam! He said: I find myself averse to it. He said: Yield into Islam, even if you are averse to it.

Tafsir Ibn Kathir

﴿ جاهدوا بأموالكم وأنفسكم في سبيل الله ذلكم خير لكم إن كنتم تعلمون ﴾ يقول تعالى ذكره للمؤمنين به وبرسوله من أصحاب رسول الله ﷺ جاهدوا أيها المؤمنون الكفار بأموالكم فانفقوها في مجاهدتهم على دين الله الذي شرعه لكم حتى ينقادوا لكم فيدخلوا فيه طوعاً أو كرهاً أو يعطوكم الجزية عن يد صغاراً إن كانوا أهل الكتاب أو تقتلوهم

تفسير الطبري

{ Wage jihad with your wealth and with yourselves in the cause of Allah; this is better for you, if you only knew } ; He (may His remembrance be exalted) is saying to those of the Messenger of Allah's (SAW) Companions who believe in Him and in His Messenger: Wage *jihad*, oh Believers, against the disbelievers [*kuffar*] with your wealth – spend it to strive in *jihad* against them for the religion of Allah, that which He has prescribed for you, until they yield to you and enter into it willingly or under compulsion, or they give you *jizya* out of their hands, being abased, if they are of the People of the Book, otherwise you kill them.

Tafsir Al-Tabari

* * *

﷽ لَا يَسْتَأْذِنُكَ الَّذِينَ يُؤْمِنُونَ بِاللَّهِ وَالْيَوْمِ الْآخِرِ أَن يُجَاهِدُوا بِأَمْوَالِهِمْ وَأَنفُسِهِمْ وَاللَّهُ عَلِيمٌ بِالْمُتَّقِينَ ﷽ التوبة ٤٤

{ Those who believe in Allah and in the last day do not seek your permission to stay back from waging jihad with their wealth and with themselves; and Allah knows the devout } *Al-tawba 44*

﴿ الَّذِينَ يُؤْمِنُونَ بِاللَّهِ وَالْيَوْمِ الْآخِرِ أَن يُجَاهِدُوا بِأَمْوَالِهِمْ وَأَنفُسِهِمْ ﴾ لِأَنَّهُمْ يَرَوْنَ الْجِهَادَ قُرْبَةً وَلَمَّا نَدَبَهُمْ إِلَيْهِ بَادَرُوا وَامْتَثَلُوا

تفسير ابن كثير

{ Those who believe in Allah and in the last day ... from waging *jihad* with their wealth and with themselves } : because they see *jihad* as an act of devotion, so when He charged them with it, they hastened to comply.

Tafsir Ibn Kathir

﴿ لَا يَسْتَأْذِنُكَ ﴾ لَيْسَ عَادَةَ الْمُؤْمِنِينَ أَن يَسْتَأْذِنُوكَ فِي أَن يُجَاهِدُوا وَكَانَ الْخُلَّصُ مِنَ الْمُهَاجِرِينَ وَالْأَنْصَارِ يَقُولُونَ لَا نَسْتَأْذِنُ النَّبِيَّ أَبَداً وَلَنُجَاهِدَنَّ أَبَداً مَعَهُ بِأَمْوَالِنَا وَأَنفُسِنَا وَمَعْنَى ﴿ أَن يُجَاهِدُوا ﴾ فِي أَن يُجَاهِدُوا أَو كَرَاهَةَ أَن يُجَاهِدُوا ﴿ وَاللَّهُ عَلِيمٌ بِالْمُتَّقِينَ ﴾ شَهَادَةٌ لَهُم بِالِانْتِظَامِ فِي زُمْرَةِ الْمُتَّقِينَ وَعِدَةٌ لَهُم بِأَجْزَلِ الثَّوَابِ

تفسير الزمخشري

{ Do not seek your permission } : It is not usual for Believers to ask your permission to stay back from waging *jihad*; the sincere Emigrants [*Muhajireen*] and Ansar said: We will never ask permission of the Prophet to stay back; we will always wage *jihad* with him with our wealth and with ourselves. And the meaning of { from waging jihad } is: from waging *jihad* or aversion to waging *jihad*. { And Allah knows the devout } : testifying to them of the steadiness concerning the group of the devout, and a pledge to them of the most generous reward.

Tafsir Al-Zamakhshari

﴿ والله عليم بالمتقين ﴾ يقول والله ذو علم بمن خافه فاتقاه بأداء فرائضه وإجتناب معاصيه والمسارعة إلى طاعته في غزو عدوه وجهادهم بماله ونفسه وغير ذلك من أمره ونهيه

تفسير الطبري

{ And Allah knows the devout } ; He is saying: And Allah is aware of those who fear Him and are devoted to Him in carrying out His obligations, and avoiding wrongdoings against Him, and in hastening to obey Him by attacking His enemy and waging *jihad* on them with their wealth and with themselves, as well as other things He has ordered and prohibited.

Tafsir Al-Tabari

قوله تعالى ﴿ لا يستأذنك الذين يؤمنون بالله ﴾ قال إبن عباس هذا تعيير للمنافقين حين استأذنوا في القعود قال الزجاج أعلم الله عز وجل نبيَّه ﷺ أن علامة النفاق في ذلك الوقت الإستئذان

تفسير إبن الجوزي

The word of the Most High: { Those who believe in Allah ... do not seek your permission } ; Ibn 'Abbas said: This is a rebuke to the hypocrites when they sought permission to sit it out. Al-Zajjaj said: Allah Mighty and Sublime made it known to His Prophet (SAW) that the sign of hypocrisy at that time was seeking such permission.

Tafsir Ibn Al-Jawzi

عن إبن عباس رضي الله عنهما في قوله ﴿ لا يستأذنك الذين يؤمنون بالله واليوم الآخر ﴾ الآيتين قال هذا تفسير للمنافقين حين استأذنوا في القعود عن الجهاد بغير عذر وعذر الله المؤمنين فقال ﴿ فإذا استأذنوك لبعض شأنهم فأذن لمن شئت منهم ﴾

الدر المنثور للسيوطي

Ibn 'Abbas (may Allah be pleased with them both), of His word: { Those who believe in Allah and in the last day do not seek your permission } (both verses), said: This makes it clear to the hypocrites when they sought permission to sit out from *jihad* without an excuse, and Allah excused the Believers, saying: { Whenever they seek permission for some issue of theirs, give permission to whomever of them you wish } [Al-nur 62].

Al-Suyuti, Al-durr Al-manthur

* * *

﴿ وَمِنْهُمْ مَنْ يَقُولُ ائْذَنْ لِي وَلَا تَفْتِنِّي أَلَا فِي الْفِتْنَةِ سَقَطُوا وَإِنَّ جَهَنَّمَ لَمُحِيطَةٌ بِالْكَافِرِينَ ﴾ التوبة ٤٩

{ **And there are some among them who say: "Grant me leave and do not beguile me". Have they not fallen into beguilement? Surely Hell surrounds the disbelievers** } *Al-tawba 49*

عن مجاهد في قول الله ﴿ ائْذَنْ لِي وَلَا تَفْتِنِّي ﴾ قال قال رسول الله ﷺ اغزوا تبوك تغنموا بنات الأصفر ونساء الروم ... ﴿ وَمِنْهُمْ مَنْ يَقُولُ ائْذَنْ لِي وَلَا تَفْتِنِّي ﴾ قال هو رجل من المنافقين يقال له جد بن قيس فقال له رسول الله ﷺ العام نغزو بني الأصفر ونتخذ منهم سراري ووصفاناً فقال أي رسول الله ائذن لي ولا تفتني إن لم تأذن لي افتتنت ووقعت فغضب فقال الله ﴿ أَلَا فِي الْفِتْنَةِ سَقَطُوا وَإِنَّ جَهَنَّمَ لَمُحِيطَةٌ بِالْكَافِرِينَ ﴾

تفسير الطبري

From Mujahid, regarding the word of Allah { Grant me leave and do not beguile me } , said: The Messenger of Allah (SAW) said: Attack Tabuk and take the daughters of the Yellow Ones [i.e. blondes] and the Roman women as booty. ... { And there are some among them who say: Grant me leave and do not beguile me } : This was a man from among the hypocrites, called Jadd ibn Qais, and the Messenger of Allah (SAW) said to him: This year we are attacking the Yellow Ones and taking mistresses and servant girls from them. He replied: Oh Messenger of Allah, grant me leave and don't tempt me; if you don't grant me leave I will be tempted and fall. But He became angry and then Allah said: { Have they not fallen into beguilement? Surely Hell surrounds the disbelievers }.

Tafsir Al-Tabari

﴿ وَمِنْهُمْ مَنْ يَقُولُ ائْذَنْ لِي ﴾ في التخلف ﴿ وَلَا تَفْتِنِّي ﴾ وهو الجد بن قيس قال له النبي ﷺ هل لك في جلاد بني الأصفر فقال إني مغرم بالنساء وأخشى إن رأيت نساء بني الأصفر أن لا اصبر عنهن فأفتن قال تعالى ﴿ أَلَا فِي الْفِتْنَةِ سَقَطُوا ﴾ بالتخلف وقرئ ﴿ سَقَطَ ﴾ ﴿ وَإِنَّ جَهَنَّمَ لَمُحِيطَةٌ بِالْكَافِرِينَ ﴾ لا محيص لهم عنها

تفسير الجلالين

{ And there are some among them who say: Grant me leave } : to stay behind; { and do not beguile me } : this was Jadd ibn Qais; the Prophet (SAW) asked him: Do you have it in you to fight the Yellow Ones? He replied: Indeed I am infatuated with women, and I am afraid that if I saw the women of the Blondes, I wouldn't be able to hold back from them and I would be tempted. The Most High said: { Have they not fallen into beguilement? } : by staying behind; also read as "Has he not fallen". { Surely Hell surrounds the disbelievers } : there is no way out of it for them.

Tafsir Al-Jalalain

﴿ ومنهم من يقول ائذن لي ﴾ يعني المنافقين من يقول ائذن لي في التخلف ﴿ ولا تفتني ﴾ يعني ولا توقعني في الفتنة ثم قال الله تعالى ﴿ ألا في الفتنة سقطوا ﴾ يعني في الكفر والنفاق وقعوا ﴿ وإن جهنم لمحيطة بالكافرين ﴾ يعني جعلت جهنم للكافرين

بحر العلوم للسمرقندي

{ And there are some among them who say: Grant me leave } : that is, the hypocrites, who say: Grant me leave to stay behind; { and do not beguile me } : that is, do not cause me to fall into temptation; then Allah Most High said: { Have they not fallen into beguilement? } : that is, they have fallen into disbelief and hypocrisy; { Surely Hell surrounds the Disbelievers } : that is, Hell was made for the disbelievers [kuffar].

Al-Samarqandi, Bahr Al-'ulum

• • •

﴿ قل هل تربصون بنا إلا إحدى الحسنيين ونحن نتربص بكم أن يصيبكم الله بعذاب من عنده أو بأيدينا فتربصوا إنا معكم متربصون ﴾ التوبة ٥٢

{ Say: Do you all await anything for us other than one of two wonderful things? We also await for Allah to come upon you with punishment, from Him, or at our hands; so wait, indeed we wait with you } Al-tawba 52

يقول تعالى ذكره لنبيه محمد ﷺ قل يا محمد لهؤلاء المنافقين الذين وصفت لك صفتهم وبيَّنت لك أمرهم هل تنتظرون بنا إلا إحدى الخلَّتين اللتين هما أحسن من غيرهما إما ظفراً بالعدو وفتحاً لنا بغلبتناهم ففيها الاجر والغنيمة والسلامة وإما قتلاً من عدونا لنا ففيه الشهادة والفوز بالجنة والنجاة من النار وكلتاهما مما نحب ولا نكره ونحن نتربص بكم أن يصيبكم الله بعذاب من عنده

تفسير الطبري

He (may His remembrance be exalted) is saying to His Prophet Muhammad (SAW): Say, oh Muhammad, to these hypocrites, whose qualities I described to you and whose matter I made clear to you: Do you all expect us to get anything other than one of the two outcomes which are finer than anything else? Either triumph over the enemy and victory for us to subjugate them – and in this the reward, the spoils, and security; or our enemy killing us – and in this martyrdom, winning *Jannah* in victory, and safety from Hellfire. Both of these are things we love and do not despise, and we wait with you for Allah to bring His punishment upon you.

Tafsir Al-Tabari

اعلم أن هذا هو الجواب الثاني عن فرح المنافقين بمصائب المؤمنين وذلك لأن المسلم إذا ذهب إلى الغزو فإن صار مغلوباً مقتولاً فاز بالاسم الحسن في الدنيا والثواب العظيم الذي اعده الله للشهداء في الآخرة وإن صار غالباً فاز في الدنيا بالمال الحلال والاسم الجميل وهي الرجولية والشوكة والقوة وفي الآخرة بالثواب العظيم
تفسير الزمخشري

Know that this is the second rebuttal to the hypocrites rejoicing at the misfortunes of the Believers, this being because a Muslim, whenever he sets out on an attack, if he is overcome and is killed, he gains the victory with a good reputation in this world and the great reward that Allah has prepared for martyrs in the hereafter. But if he overcomes, he gains the victory in this world with lawful wealth and a fine reputation, this being manhood, valor, and strength, and in the hereafter with the great reward.

Tafsir Al-Zamakhshari

. . .

﴿ يا أيها النبي جاهد الكفار والمنافقين واغلظ عليهم ومأواهم جهنم وبئس المصير ﴾ التوبة ٧٣

{ Oh Prophet! Wage jihad on the disbelievers and the hypocrites, and be harsh to them; their dwelling is Hell, a miserable fate }
Al-tawba 73

﴿ جاهد الكفار والمنافقين ﴾ قال بيده فإن لم يستطع فليكفهرّ في وجهه وقال ابن عباس أمره الله تعالى بجهاد الكفار بالسيف والمنافقين باللسان وأذهب الرفق عنهم وقال الضحاك جاهد الكفار بالسيف وأغلظ على المنافقين بالكلام وهو مجاهدتهم وعن مقاتل والربيع مثله فقال الحسن وقتادة مجاهدتهم إقامة الحدود عليهم وقد يقال إنه لا منافاة بين هذه الأقوال لأنه تارة يؤاخذهم بهذا وتارة بهذا بحسب الأحوال والله أعلم
تفسير ابن كثير

{ Wage jihad on the disbelievers and the hypocrites } ; He is saying: By his hand, or if He is unable, then at least let him have a menacing face. Ibn 'Abbas said: Allah Most High ordered him to wage *jihad* on the disbelievers [*kuffar*] with the sword, and on the hypocrites by words and by removing kindness towards them. Al-Dahhak said: Wage *jihad* on the disbelievers with the sword, and be harsh to the hypocrites in speech; this is how to strive in *jihad* against them. Muqatil and Rabi' said something similar. Al-Hasan and Qatada said: Striving in *jihad* against them is observing the prescribed punishments [*hudud*] for them. It can be said that there is no inconsistency among these statements, since at times He punishes them in one way, and at times the other way, according to the situation. And Allah knows best.

Tafsir Ibn Kathir

﴿ يا أيها النبي جاهد الكفار ﴾ بالسيف ﴿ والمنافقين ﴾ باللسان والحجة ﴿ وأغلظ عليهم ﴾ بالانتهار والمقت
تفسير الجلالين

{ Oh Prophet! Wage jihad on the disbelievers } : with the sword; { and the hypocrites } : with words and with arguments; { and be harsh to them } : by rebukes and hatred.

Tafsir Al-Jalalain

يقول تعالى ذكره يا أيها النبي جاهد الكفار بالسيف والمنافقين والسلاح واختلف أهل التأويل في صفة الجهاد الذي أمر الله نبيه به في المنافقين فقال بعضهم أمره بجهادهم باليد واللسان وبكل ما أطاق جهادهم به ... وقال آخرون بل أمره بجهادهم باللسان ... وقوله ﴿ وأغلظ عليهم ﴾ يقول تعالى ذكره واشدد عليهم بالجهاد والقتال والإرعاب
تفسير الطبري

He (may His remembrance be exalted) is saying: Oh Prophet! Wage *jihad* on the disbelievers with the sword and with weapons, and on the hypocrites. Expositors differ regarding the nature of *jihad* that Allah ordered His Prophet to wage on the hypocrites. Some of them say: He ordered him to wage *jihad* on them with the hand, with the tongue, and with anything by which He is capable of waging *jihad* on them. ... Others say, rather, that He ordered him to wage *jihad* on them with words. ... His word: { And be harsh to them } ; He (may His remembrance be exalted) is saying: And be severe against them with *jihad*, fighting, and terror.

Tafsir Al-Tabari

﴿ جاهد الكفار ﴾ بالسيف ﴿ والمنافقين ﴾ بالحجّة ﴿ وأغلظ عليهم ﴾ في الجهادين جميعاً ولا تحابهم وكل من وقف منه على فساد في العقيدة فهذا الحكم ثابت فيه يجاهد بالحجة وتستعمل معه الغلظة ما أمكن منها وعن إبن مسعود إن لم يستطع بيده فبلسانه فإن لم يستطع فليكفهر في وجهه فإن لم يستطع فبقلبه يريد الكراهة والبغضاء والتبرأ منه وقد حمل الحسن جهاد المنافقين على إقامة الحدود عليهم إذا تعاطوا أسبابها

تفسير الزمخشري

{ Wage jihad on the disbelievers } : with the sword; { and the hypocrites } : with arguments; { and be harsh to them } : in both kinds of *jihad*; do not show favoritism. Anyone who becomes aware of corruption in doctrine among them, this is the ruling, and it is firm regarding them; *jihad* is waged against them with arguments, and harshness is employed as much as possible. Ibn Mas'ud said: If one is unable with his hands, then with his tongue; if he is unable, then at least with a menacing face; if he is still unable, then in his heart. He means aversion, hatred, and refusal to have anything to do with them; Al-Hasan associated *jihad* against hypocrites with carrying out the prescribed punishments against them whenever they give reason for it.

Tafsir Al-Zamakhshari

فيه مسألتان الاولى قوله تعالى ﴿ يا أيها النبي جاهد الكفار ﴾ الخطاب للنبي ﷺ وتدخل فيه أُمّته من بعده قيل المراد جاهد بالمؤمنين الكفارَ وقال إبن عباس أمر بالجهاد مع الكفار بالسيف ومع المنافقين باللسان وشدّة الزجر والتغليظ وروي عن إبن مسعود أنه قال جاهد المنافقين بيدك فإن لم تستطع فبلسانك فإن لم تستطع فاكْفَهِرّ في وجوههم وقال الحسن جاهد المنافقين بإقامة الحدود عليهم وباللسان واختاره قتادة وكانوا أكثر من يصيب الحدود ... الثانية قوله تعالى ﴿ وأغلظ عليهم ﴾ الغِلَظ نقيض الرأفة وهي شدة القلب على إحلال الأمر بصاحبه وليس ذلك في اللسان فإن النبي ﷺ قال إذا زنت أمة أحدكم فليجلدها الحدّ ولا يُثرّب عليها ومنه قوله تعالى ﴿ ولو كنت فظّاً غليظ القلب لانفضّوا من حولك ﴾

تفسير القرطبي

Here there are two points: the first is that the word of the Most High { Oh Prophet! Wage jihad on the disbelievers } is addressed to the Prophet, but his *ummah* is included after him; the intended meaning is: Wage *jihad*, by way of the Believers, on the disbelievers. Ibn 'Abbas said: He ordered *jihad* on disbelievers with the sword and on hypocrites with words, severe rebukes, and coarseness. It is narrated from Ibn Mas'ud, who said: Wage *jihad* on the hypocrites with your hands, and if you are unable, then with your tongue, and if you are still unable, then give them menacing looks. Al-Hasan said: Wage *jihad* on the hypocrites by carrying out the prescribed punishments on them, and with words – Qatada held this view – and they were the ones upon whom most punishments were brought. ... The second point is the word of the Most High: { And be harsh to them } ; harshness is the opposite of compassion, and this means tightening one's heart against lifting an order that applies to someone. This is not through words; indeed the Prophet (SAW) said: Whenever a servant girl of one you adulterates, let him whip her as prescribed, not rebuke her. And along these lines is the word of the Most High: { If you had only had a coarse and harsh heart, they would have disbanded from around you } [Al 'Imran 159].

Tafsir Al-Qurtubi

* * *

﴿ فرح المخلفون بمقعدهم خلاف رسول الله وكرهوا أن يجاهدوا بأموالهم وأنفسهم في سبيل الله وقالوا لا تنفروا في الحر قل نار جهنم أشد حرا لو كانوا يفقهون فليضحكوا قليلا وليبكوا كثيرا جزاء بما كانوا يكسبون فإن رجعك الله إلى طائفة منهم فاستأذنوك للخروج فقل لن تخرجوا معي أبدا ولن تقاتلوا معي عدوا إنكم رضيتم بالقعود أول مرة فاقعدوا مع الخالفين ﴾ التوبة ٨١-٨٣

{ Those who stayed behind were glad to have sat out behind the Messenger of Allah, and were adverse to waging *jihad* in the cause of Allah with their wealth and with themselves; they said: "Do not mobilize in the heat". Say: The fire of Hell is hotter; if only they could comprehend. So let them laugh little and weep much, in recompense for what they have brought upon themselves. And if Allah brings you back to a group of them, and they ask you permission to set out, then say: You all will never set out with me, and you will never fight an enemy with me; indeed it pleased you to sit it out the first time, so sit it out with those who stay behind } Al-tawba 81-83

يقول تعالى ذاماً للمنافقين المتخلفين عن صحابة رسول الله ﷺ في غزوة تبوك وفرحوا بقعودهم بعد خروجه ﴿ وكرهوا أن يجاهدوا ﴾ معه ﴿ بأموالهم وأنفسهم في سبيل الله وقالوا ﴾ أي بعضهم لبعض ﴿ لا تنفروا في الحر ﴾ وذلك أن الخروج في غزوة تبوك كان في شدة الحر عند طيب الظلال والثمار فلهذا قالوا ﴿ لا تنفروا في الحر ﴾ قال الله تعالى لرسوله ﷺ ﴿ قل ﴾ لهم ﴿ نار جهنم ﴾ التي تصيرون إليها بمخالفتكم ﴿ أشد حراً ﴾ مما فررتم منه من الحر بل أشد حراً من النار

تفسير ابن كثير

The Most High is saying, as a rebuke to the hypocrites who stayed behind from the Messenger of Allah's (SAW) Companions in the attack on Tabuk, and were glad about sitting it out after He set out: { And were adverse to waging jihad } : with him; { in the cause of Allah with their wealth and with themselves; they said: } : that is, to each other; { Do not mobilize in the heat } : this was because the campaign to attack Tabuk was during a time of intense heat, when shade and fruit were pleasing, and for this reason they said: { Do not mobilize in the heat } . Allah Most High said to His Messenger (SAW): { Say: } : to them; { the fire of Hell } : to where you all are headed because of your dissent; { is hotter } : that the heat you have run away from; it is even hotter than fire.

Tafsir Ibn Kathir

اعلم أن هذا نوع آخر من قبائح أعمال المنافقين وهو فرحهم بالقعود وكراهتهم الجهاد

تفسير الرازي

Know that this is yet another kind of the shameful deeds of the hypocrites, this being their joy from sitting it out, and their aversion to *jihad*.

Tafsir Al-Razi

عن ابن عباس في قوله ﴿ فليضحكوا قليلاً ﴾ قال الدنيا قليل فليضحكوا فيها ما شاؤوا فإذا انقطعت الدنيا وصاروا إلى الله تعالى استأنفوا بكاء لا ينقطع أبداً

الدر المنثور للسيوطي

Ibn 'Abbas, regarding His word { So let them laugh little } , said: This worldly life is little, so let them laugh as much as they wish in it, and when this world comes to an end and they go to Allah Most High, they will carry on with weeping that never ends.

Al-Suyuti, Al-durr Al-manthur

وقوله ﴿ إلى طائفة ﴾ يقتضي عندي أن المراد رؤوسهم والمتبوعون وعليها وقع التشديد بأنها لا تخرج ولا تقاتل عدواً وكرر معنى قتال العدو لأنه عظم الجهاد وموضع بارقة السيوف التي تحتها الجنة

تفسير إبن عطية

His word: { To a group } implies, in my view, that the meaning is their leaders and chiefs; the emphasis falls on them since they have not set out nor fought against any enemy. He reiterates the meaning of fighting the enemy since He extols *jihad* and the scene of the gleaming of swords, swords under which *Jannah* lies.

Tafsir Ibn 'Atiyya

* * *

﴿ وَإِذَا أُنزِلَتْ سُورَةٌ أَنْ آمِنُوا بِاللَّهِ وَجَاهِدُوا مَعَ رَسُولِهِ اسْتَأْذَنَكَ أُولُو الطَّوْلِ مِنْهُمْ وَقَالُوا ذَرْنَا نَكُن مَّعَ الْقَاعِدِينَ رَضُوا بِأَن يَكُونُوا مَعَ الْخَوَالِفِ وَطُبِعَ عَلَىٰ قُلُوبِهِمْ فَهُمْ لَا يَفْقَهُونَ لَٰكِنِ الرَّسُولُ وَالَّذِينَ آمَنُوا مَعَهُ جَاهَدُوا بِأَمْوَالِهِمْ وَأَنفُسِهِمْ وَأُولَٰئِكَ لَهُمُ الْخَيْرَاتُ وَأُولَٰئِكَ هُمُ الْمُفْلِحُونَ أَعَدَّ اللَّهُ لَهُمْ جَنَّاتٍ تَجْرِي مِن تَحْتِهَا الْأَنْهَارُ خَالِدِينَ فِيهَا ذَٰلِكَ الْفَوْزُ الْعَظِيمُ ﴾ التوبة ٨٦-٨٩

{ Whenever a surah is sent down to "Believe in Allah and wage *jihad* with His Messenger", the well-off among them seek exemption from you, and say: Let us alone, so we can be with those who sit it out. It pleases them to be with the women who stay behind, and their hearts have been sealed over, and so they do not comprehend. But the Messenger and those who have believed with him, and have waged *jihad* with their wealth and with themselves – they will have delights and they are the successful ones. Allah has prepared for them gardens under which rivers flow, living forever there; this is the great victory } Al-tawba 86-89

يقول تعالى منكراً وذاماً للمتخلفين عن الجهاد الناكلين عنه مع القدرة عليه ووجود السعة والطول واستأذنوا الرسول في القعود وقالوا ﴿ ذَرْنَا نَكُن مَّعَ الْقَاعِدِينَ ﴾ ورضوا لأنفسهم بالعار والقعود في البلد مع النساء وهن الخوالف بعد خروج الجيش فإذا وقع الحرب كانوا أجبن الناس وإذا كان أمن كانوا أكثر الناس كلاماً كما قال تعالى عنهم في الآية الاخرى ﴿ فإذا جاء الخوف رأيتهم ينظرون إليك تدور أعينهم كالذي يُغشى عليه من الموت فإذا ذهب الخوف سلقوكم بألسنة حداد ﴾ أي علت ألسنتهم بالكلام الحاد القوي في الأمن وفي الحرب أجبن شيء ... ﴿ وطُبع على قلوبهم ﴾ أي بسبب نكولهم عن الجهاد والخروج مع الرسول في سبيل الله ﴿ فهم لا يفقهون ﴾ أي لا يفهمون ما فيه صلاح لهم فيفعلوه ولا ما فيه مضرة لهم فيجتنبوه

تفسير ابن كثير

The Most High is speaking as a way to renounce and rebuke those who stay behind from *jihad*, those who shy away from it even though they have the ability, and the means and the competency are there. They seek permission from the Messenger to sit it out, and say: { Let us alone, so we can be with those who sit it out } . They are content to bring shame upon themselves and to sit it out where they are with the women, those who stay behind after the army has set out. Whenever war breaks out, they are the most cowardly of people, but whenever there is a state of safety, they are the ones who talk the most, as the Most High said about them in another verse: { Whenever fear comes, you see them looking at you rolling their eyes like someone whose death looms over him; but when fear departs, they slash you with sharp tongues } [Al-ahzab 19] , that is, their tongues become lofty with sharp and strong words in safe times, but in war they are the most cowardly things. ... { Their hearts have been sealed over } : that is, because they have shied away from *jihad* and from setting out with the Messenger in the cause of Allah; { and so they do not comprehend } : that is, they do not understand what is good for them so that they might do it, and what is harmful to them, so that they might avoid it.

Tafsir Ibn Kathir

﴿ لكن الرسول والذين آمنوا معه جاهدوا بأموالهم وأنفسهم وأولئك لهم الخيرات ﴾ في الدنيا والآخرة ﴿ وأولئك هم المفلحون ﴾ أي الفائزون

تفسير الجلالين

{ But the Messenger and those who have believed with him, and have waged *jihad* with their wealth and with themselves – they will have delights } : in this world and the next; { and they are the successful ones } : that is, the victorious ones.

Tafsir Al-Jalalain

* * *

﷽ لَيْسَ عَلَى الضُّعَفَاءِ وَلَا عَلَى الْمَرْضَى وَلَا عَلَى الَّذِينَ لَا يَجِدُونَ مَا يُنْفِقُونَ حَرَجٌ إِذَا نَصَحُوا لِلَّهِ وَرَسُولِهِ مَا عَلَى الْمُحْسِنِينَ مِنْ سَبِيلٍ وَاللَّهُ غَفُورٌ رَحِيمٌ وَلَا عَلَى الَّذِينَ إِذَا مَا أَتَوْكَ لِتَحْمِلَهُمْ قُلْتَ لَا أَجِدُ مَا أَحْمِلُكُمْ عَلَيْهِ تَوَلَّوْا وَأَعْيُنُهُمْ تَفِيضُ مِنَ الدَّمْعِ حَزَنًا أَلَّا يَجِدُوا مَا يُنْفِقُونَ ﷽

التوبة ٩١-٩٢

{ There is no blame on the weak, on the sick, or on those who do not have anything to spend, if they are sincere towards Allah and His Messenger; there is no course of action against those who do good; and Allah is forgiving, merciful. And there is nothing against those who, when they came to you for you to give them mounts, you said: "I have nothing for you to ride on"; and they turned away, their eyes overflowing with tears of sadness but that they could find something to spend } *Al-tawba 91-92*

ثم بين تعالى الأعذار التي لا حرج على من قعد معها عن القتال فذكر منها ما هو لازم للشخص لا ينفك عنه وهو الضعف في التركيب الذي لا يستطيع معه الجلاد في الجهاد ومنه العمى والعرج ونحوهما ولهذا بدأ به ومنه ما هو عارض بسبب مرض عنّ له في بدنه شغله عن الخروج في سبيل الله وبسبب فقره لا يقدر على التجهيز للحرب فليس على هؤلاء حرج إذا قعدوا ونصحوا في حال قعودهم ولم يرجفوا بالناس ولم يثبطوهم وهم محسنون في حالهم هذا

تفسير ابن كثير

The Most High then clarifies the excuses for which there is no blame on those who sit out from fighting as a result. Of these He mentions those which are permanent and always with a person, these being weakness of composure which do not permit fighting in *jihad*, including blindness, lameness, and others similar to these two; for this reason He begins with such. There are also those who turn away due to illnesses that arise in their bodies and prevent them from setting out in the cause of Allah, or those who due to their poverty are unable to prepare for war. There is no blame on such people if they sit out and are sincere in having to sit it out, and do not spread rumors about people or hold them back, and do good in the situation they are in.

Tafsir Ibn Kathir

يقول تعالى ذكره ليس على أهل الزمانة وأهل العجز عن السفر والغزو ولا على المرضى ولا على من لا يجد نفقة يتبلغ بها إلى مغزاه حرج وهو الإثم يقول ليس عليهم إثم إذا نصحوا الله ورسوله في مغيبهم عن الجهاد مع رسول الله ﷺ ﴿ ما على المحسنين من سبيل ﴾ يقول ليس على من أحسن فنصح لله ورسوله في تخلفه عن رسول الله ﷺ عن جهاد معه لعذر يعذر به طريق يتطرّق عليه فيعاقب من قبله ... ﴿ وأعينهم تفيض من الدمع حَزَنًا ﴾ وهم يبكون من حزن على أنهم لا يجدون ما ينفقون ويتحملون به للجهاد في سبيل الله

تفسير الطبري

He (may His remembrance be exalted) is saying: There is no blame, that is, sin, on those with chronic illness, those unable to travel and go on an attack, nor on the sick, nor on those who have nothing to spend towards going on an attack. He is saying: There is no sin on them provided they are sincere towards Allah and His Messenger concerning their absence from *jihad* with the Messenger of Allah (SAW). { There is no course of action against those who do good } ; He is saying: There is no action to deal with or punishment on their part for those who do good and are sincere towards Allah and His Messenger concerning staying behind from the Messenger of Allah (SAW) and from *jihad* with him, because of an excuse that they present against being able to undertake it. ... { Their eyes overflowing with tears of sadness } : they cry out of sadness for not having anything to spend or take upon themselves for *jihad* in the cause of Allah.

Tafsir Al-Tabari

اعلم أنه تعالى لما بين الوعيد في حق من يوهم العذر مع أنه لا عذر له ذكر أصحاب الأعذار الحقيقية وبين أن تكليف الله تعالى بالغزو والجهاد عنهم ساقط

تفسير الرازي

Know that the Most High, when He clarified the threat regarding those who act like they have an excuse when they have no excuse, He mentioned those who have genuine excuses, and made it clear that the obligation from Allah Most High to go on attacks and *jihad* was cancelled for them.

Tafsir Al-Razi

• • •

﴿ إِنَّ اللَّهَ اشْتَرَىٰ مِنَ الْمُؤْمِنِينَ أَنْفُسَهُمْ وَأَمْوَالَهُمْ بِأَنَّ لَهُمُ الْجَنَّةَ يُقَاتِلُونَ فِي سَبِيلِ اللَّهِ فَيَقْتُلُونَ وَيُقْتَلُونَ وَعْدًا عَلَيْهِ حَقًّا فِي التَّوْرَاةِ وَالْإِنْجِيلِ وَالْقُرْآنِ وَمَنْ أَوْفَىٰ بِعَهْدِهِ مِنَ اللَّهِ فَاسْتَبْشِرُوا بِبَيْعِكُمُ الَّذِي بَايَعْتُمْ بِهِ وَذَٰلِكَ هُوَ الْفَوْزُ الْعَظِيمُ ﴾ التوبة ١١١

{ Indeed Allah has bought, from the Believers, their lives and their wealth, so that *Jannah* may be theirs; they fight in the cause of Allah, and kill and are killed, a promise of truth on Him in the Torah, the Injil, and the Qur'an. And who is more faithful to His covenant than Allah? So rejoice over the deal that you have pledged to; this is the great victory } *Al-tawba* 111

يقول تعالى ذكره إن الله ابتاع من المؤمنين أنفسهم وأموالهم بالجنة وعداً عليه حقاً يقول وعدهم الجنة جل ثناؤه وعداً عليه حقاً أن يوفي لهم به في كتبه المنزّلة التوراة والإنجيل والقرآن إذا هم وفوا بما عاهدوا الله فقاتلوا في سبيله ونصرة دينه أعداءه فقتلوا وقُتلوا

تفسير الطبري

He (may His remembrance be exalted) is saying: Indeed Allah has purchased from the Believers their lives and their wealth in exchange for *Jannah*, a promise of truth on Him. He is saying that He (may His praise be exalted) has promised them *Jannah*, a promise of truth on Him, that He will fulfill it for them, in His revealed books the Torah, *Injil*, and Qur'an, if they live up to what they have contracted with Allah, and fight His enemies in His cause and to uphold His religion, and kill and are killed.

Tafsir Al-Tabari

﴿ بِأَنَّ لَهُمُ الْجَنَّةَ ﴾ قال سعيد بن جبير يعني الجنة وهذا الكلام مجاز معناه أن الله تعالى أمرهم بالجهاد بأنفسهم وأموالهم ليجازيهم بالجنة فعبّر بالشراء لما فيه من عوض ومعوض فصار معناه ولأن حقيقة الشراء لما لا يملكه المشتري

تفسير الماوردي

{ So that *Jannah* may be theirs } ; Sa'id ibn Jubair said: He means *Jannah*, and the way of speaking here is figurative; the meaning is that Allah Most High has ordered them to wage *jihad* with their lives and with their wealth, in order that He may reward them with *Jannah*. He expresses this as a purchase because in it there is compensation as well as one who is compensated, and so this is its meaning; because a true purchase involves something the buyer does not possess.

Tafsir Al-Mawardi

يخبر تعالى أنه عاوض عباده المؤمنين عن أنفسهم وأموالهم إذا بذلوها في سبيله بالجنة وهذا من فضله وكرمه وإحسانه فإنه قبل العوض عما يملكه بما تفضل به على عبيده المطيعين له ولهذا قال الحسن البصري وقتادة بايعهم والله فأغلى ثمنهم وقال شمر بن عطية ما من مسلم إلا والله عز وجل في عنقه بيعة وفي بها أو مات عليها ثم تلا هذه الآية ولهذا يقال من حمل في سبيل الله بايع الله أي قبل هذا العقد ووفى به ... ﴿ يقاتلون في سبيل الله فيقتلون ويُقتلون ﴾ أي سواء قتلوا أو قتلوا أو إجتمع لهم هذا وهذا فقد وجبت لهم الجنة ... وقوله ﴿ ومن أوفى بعهده من الله ﴾ فإنه لا يخلف الميعاد هذا كقوله ﴿ ومن أصدق من الله حديثاً ﴾ ﴿ ومن أصدق من الله قيلاً ﴾ ولهذا قال ﴿ فاستبشروا ببَيعكم الذي بايعتم به وذلك هو الفوز العظيم ﴾ أي فليستبشر من قام بمقتضي هذا العقد ووفى بها العهد بالفوز العظيم والنعيم المقيم

تفسير إبن كثير

The Most High is making known to His servants the Believers that He compensates them for their lives and their wealth – whenever they sacrifice them in His cause – with *Jannah*. This comes out of His abundance, generosity, and goodness, for indeed He has accepted to compensate with what He already possesses, for what He has been gracious with towards His servants, those who are obedient to Him. For this reason Hasan Al-Basri and Qatada said: He has pledged to them, by Allah! And has raised their valuable price! And Shimr ibn 'Atiyya said: There is no Muslim – I swear by Allah Mighty and Sublime – that does not have a deal on his neck which he either lives up to or dies in. Then he recited this verse. For this reason it is said that whoever undertakes to be part of the cause of Allah has pledged to Allah, that is, they have accepted this contract and have lived up to it. ... { They fight in the cause of Allah, and kill and are killed } : that is, whether they kill or are killed, or both happen to them, *Jannah* is certainly theirs. ... His word: { And who is more faithful to His covenant then Allah? } : indeed He does not go back on this promise, as His word says: { Who is truer than Allah in word? } [Al-nisaa 87], and: { Who is truer than Allah in speech? } [Al-nisaa 122]. Therefore then His word: { So rejoice over the deal that you have pledged to; this is the great victory } : that is, whoever has carried out the requirements of this contract, and has lived up to the covenant, let them rejoice in the great victory and the everlasting bliss.

Tafsir Ibn Kathir

اعلم أنه تعالى لما شرع في شرح فضائح المنافقين وقبائحهم لسبب تخلفهم عن غزوة تبوك فلما تم ذلك الشرح والبيان وذكر أقسامهم وفرع على كل قسم ما كان لائقاً به عاد إلى بيان فضيلة الجهاد وحقيقته فقال ﴿ إن الله إشترى من المؤمنين أنفسهم وأموالهم ﴾ ... ﴿ يقاتلون في سبيل الله فيقتلون ويقتلون ﴾ ومنهم من قال كل أنواع الجهاد داخل فيه بدليل الخبر الذي روياه عن عبدالله بن رواحة وأيضاً فالجهاد بالحجة والدعوة إلى دلائل التوحيد أكمل آثاراً من القتال ولذلك قال ﷺ لعلي رضي الله عنه لأن يهدي الله على يدك رجلاً خير

لك مما طلعت عليه الشمس ولأن الجهاد بالمقاتلة لا يحسن أثرها إلا بعد تقديم الجهاد بالحجة وأما الجهاد بالحجة فإنه غني عن الجهاد بالمقاتلة ... الأمر بالقتال والجهاد هو موجود في جميع الشرائع

تفسير الرازي

Know that the Most High, when He prescribed the ruling in explaining the scandal of the hypocrites and their shameful deeds as a result of them staying behind from the attack on Tabuk, finished the explanation and the declaration, mentioned the different categories among them, and went over what was fitting for each group, He then returned to declaring the excellence of *jihad* and its true nature; He said: { Indeed Allah has bought, from the Believers, their lives and their wealth } . ... { They fight in the cause of Allah, and kill and are killed } : among them there are those who say that all types of *jihad* fall under this, as evidenced by the information we related from Abdullah ibn Rawaha and others, and also by the fact that *jihad* by way of arguments and calling people [*da'wah*] to the proofs of the oneness of Allah [*tawheed*] leaves a more complete mark than fighting, and for this reason He (SAW) said to 'Ali (may Allah be pleased with him): Allah guiding someone by your hand is better for you than all that the sun rises upon. Since *jihad* by combat does not make its mark well except after bringing forward *jihad* by arguments, *jihad* by arguments indeed dispenses with *jihad* by combat. ... The command to fight and to wage *jihad* is found in all divinely prescribed systems.

Tafsir Al-Razi

﴿ وعداً عليه حقاً في التوراة والانجيل والقران ﴾ إخبار من الله تعالى أن هذا كان في هذه الكتب فأن الجهاد ومقاومة الأعداء أصله من عهد موسى عليه السلام

تفسير القرطبي

{ A promise of truth on Him in the Torah, the Injil, and the Qur'an } : Allah Most High making it known that this was in these books, that He established *jihad* and combatting enemies since the time of Musa [Moses] (peace be upon him).

Tafsir Al-Qurtubi

﴿ فاستبشروا ببيعكم الذي بايعتم به وذلك هو الفوز العظيم ﴾ قال قتادة ثامنهم وأغلى ثمنهم وقال الحسن أسمعوا بيعة ربحة باع الله بها كل مؤمن والله ما على وجه الأرض مؤمن إلا دخل في هذه البيعة

تفسير الثعلبي

{ So rejoice over the deal that you have pledged to; this is the great victory } ; Qatada said: He has bargained with them and has raised their valuable price. Al-Hasan said: Have they heard of a transaction, a dividend which Allah has pledged to every Believer? I swear by Allah, there is no Believer on the face of the earth that has not entered into this transaction.

Tafsir Al-Tha'labi

عن أبي هريرة قال قال رسول الله ﷺ من سل سيفه في سبيل الله فقد بايع الله

الدر المنثور للسيوطي

From Abu Huraira, who said: The Messenger of Allah (SAW) said: Whoever unsheaths his sword in the cause of Allah has pledged to Allah.

Al-Suyuti, Al-durr Al-manthur

* * *

﴿ مَا كَانَ لِلنَّبِيِّ وَالَّذِينَ آمَنُوا أَن يَسْتَغْفِرُوا لِلْمُشْرِكِينَ وَلَوْ كَانُوا أُولِي قُرْبَى مِن بَعْدِ مَا تَبَيَّنَ لَهُمْ أَنَّهُمْ أَصْحَابُ الْجَحِيمِ ﴾ التوبة ١١٣

{ It is not for the Prophet nor those who have believed to seek forgiveness for idolaters – even if they are blood relatives – after it has been made clear to them that they are the inhabitants of Hell } *Al-tawba* 113

عن علي قال سمعت رجلاً يستغفر لأبويه وهما مشركان فقلت له أتستغفر لأبويك وهما مشركان فقال أوليس إستغفر إبراهيم لأبيه وهو مشرك فذكرتُ ذلك للنبي ﷺ فنزلت ﴿ مَا كَانَ لِلنَّبِيِّ وَالَّذِينَ آمَنُوا أَن يَسْتَغْفِرُوا لِلْمُشْرِكِينَ ﴾

جامع الترمذي كتاب تفسير القرآن

From 'Ali, who said: I heard a man seeking forgiveness for his parents, they being idolaters. And I said to him: Are you seeking forgiveness for your parents, they being idolaters? He replied: And did not Ibrahim seek forgiveness for his father, he being an idolater? So I mentioned this to the Prophet (SAW), and this came down: { It is not for the Prophet nor those who have believed to seek forgiveness for idolaters }.

Sunan Al-Tirmidhi, The book of tafsir

عن سعيد بن مسيب عن أبيه قال لما حضرتْ أبا طالب الوفاة دخل عليه النبي ﷺ وعنده أبو جهل وعبدالله بن ابي أمية فقال النبي ﷺ أي عمّ قل لا إله إلا الله أُحاجّ لك بها عند الله فقال أبو جهل وعبدالله بن ابي أمية يا أبا طالب أترغب عن ملة عبد المطلب فقال النبي ﷺ لأستغفرنّ لك ما لم أُنهَ عنك فنزلت ﴿ ما كان للنبي والذين آمنوا أن يستغفروا للمشركين ولو كانوا أولي قربى من بعد ما تبين لهم أنهم أصحاب الجحيم ﴾
صحيح البخاري كتاب التفسير

Sa'id ibn Musayyib related from his father, who said: When death was close for Abu Talib, the Prophet (SAW) went in to see him, and Abu Jahl and Abdullah ibn Abi Umayya were with him. The Prophet (SAW) said: Oh uncle! Say: There is no god but Allah ["La ilaha illa Allah"], that I might make a case for you with Allah. And Abu Jahl and Abdullah ibn Abi Umayya said: Oh Abu Talib! Do you wish to turn away from the religion of 'Abd Al-Mutallib? And the Prophet (SAW) said: Truly I will seek forgiveness for you as long as it is not prohibited to do this for you. But then this came down: { It is not for the Prophet nor those who have believed to seek forgiveness for idolaters – even if they are blood relatives – after it has been made clear to them that they are the inhabitants of Hell }.

Sahih Al-Bukhari, The book of tafsir

ونزل في استغفاره ﷺ لعمّه ابي طالب واستغفار بعض الصحابة لأبويه المشركين ﴿ ما كان للنبي والذين آمنوا أن يستغفروا للمشركين ولو كانوا أولي قربى ﴾ ذوي قرابة ﴿ من بعد ما تبين لهم أنهم أصحاب الجحيم ﴾ النار بأن ماتوا على الكفر
تفسير الجلالين

This came down because of Him (SAW) seeking forgiveness for his uncle Abu Talib, and because of some of the Companions seeking forgiveness for their idolater parents: { It is not for the Prophet nor those who have believed to seek forgiveness for idolaters – even if they are blood relatives } : those with family ties; { after it has been made clear to them that they are the inhabitants of Hell } : Hellfire, because they died in disbelief.

Tafsir Al-Jalalain

إن النبي ﷺ أراد أن يستغفر لأمه فنهاه الله عز وجل عن ذلك
تفسير ابن كثير

Indeed the Prophet (SAW) wanted to seek forgiveness for his mother, but Allah Mighty and Sublime forbade him to do that.

Tafsir Ibn Kathir

• • •

﴿ وَمَا كَانَ الْمُؤْمِنُونَ لِيَنفِرُوا كَافَّةً فَلَوْلَا نَفَرَ مِن كُلِّ فِرْقَةٍ مِّنْهُمْ طَائِفَةٌ لِّيَتَفَقَّهُوا فِي الدِّينِ وَلِيُنذِرُوا قَوْمَهُمْ إِذَا رَجَعُوا إِلَيْهِمْ لَعَلَّهُمْ يَحْذَرُونَ ﴾ التوبة ١٢٢

{ It is not for all of the Believers to mobilize; if a small band from among each group were not to mobilize, in order to gain knowledge in religion, and make their people aware, when they return to them, that perchance they might take caution }

Al-tawba 122

أن الله نهى بهذه الآية المؤمنين به أن يخرجوا في غزو وجهاد وغير ذلك من أمورهم ويدعوا رسول الله ﷺ وحيداً ولكن عليهم إذا سرّى رسول الله سرية أن ينفر معها من كل قبيلة من قبائل العرب وهي الفرقة

تفسير الطبري

By this verse Allah prohibited the Believers in Him to set out on attacks or *jihad* or other matters of theirs, and leave the Messenger of Allah (SAW) alone. Rather, it was their obligation, whenever the Messenger of Allah sent out troops, that some of each tribe among the Arabs mobilized with it; this being the "group".

Tafsir Al-Tabari

هذا بيان من الله تعالى لما أراد من نفير الأحياء مع رسول الله ﷺ في غزوة تبوك فإنه قد ذهبت طائفة من السلف إلى أنه كان يجب النفير على كل مسلم إذا خرج رسول الله ﷺ ولهذا قال تعالى ﴿ انفروا خفافاً وثقالاً ﴾ وقال ﴿ ما كان لأهل المدينة ومن حولهم من الاعراب ﴾ قال فنسخ ذلك بهذه الآية وقد يقال إن هذا بيان لمراده تعالى من نفير الأحياء كلها وشرذمة من كل قبيلة إن لم يخرجوا كلهم ليتفقه الخارجون مع رسول الله بما ينزل من الوحي عليه وينذروا قومهم إذا رجعوا اليهم بما كان من أمر العدو فيجتمع لهم الأمران في هذا النفير المعين ﷺ وبعده تكون الطائفة النافرة من الحي إما للتفقه وإما للجهاد فإنه فرض كفاية على الأحياء وقال علي بن أبي طلحة عن ابن عباس في الآية ﴿ وما كان للمؤمنين لينفروا كافة ﴾ يقول ما كان المؤمنون لينفروا جميعاً ويتركوا النبي ﷺ وحده ﴿ فلولا نفر من كل فرقة منهم طائفة ﴾ يعني عصبة يعني السرايا ولا يسيروا إلا بإذنه فإذا رجعت السرايا وقد أنزل بعدهم قرآن تعلمه القاعدون مع النبي ﷺ وقالوا إن الله قد أنزل على نبيكم قرآناً وقد تعلمناه فتمكث السرايا يتعلمون ما أنزل الله على نبيهم بعدهم ويبعث سرايا أخرى فذلك قوله ﴿ ليتفقهوا في الدين ﴾

تفسير ابن كثير

This is a declaration from Allah Most High, when He desired all communities to mobilize with the Messenger of Allah (SAW) for the attack on Tabuk. Indeed a group of the forefathers held the view that it was obligatory for every Muslim to mobilize whenever the Messenger of Allah (SAW) set out, which is why the Most High said: { Mobilize, light or heavy } [Al-tawba 41], and He said: { It is not for the people of Medina and those of the Bedouins around them ... } [Al-tawba 120]. They said that this, however, was abrogated by the present verse, and it could be said that the intent of Allah Most High in this declaration is the mobilization of all communities, a group from each tribe if all of them do not set out, so that those who set out with the Messenger of Allah could gain knowledge in religion from the revelation that came down to him, and then warn their people when they returned to them concerning the affairs of the enemy. In this way both issues would be accomplished by this assigned mobilization. After him (SAW), a group would mobilize from a given community, to either gain knowledge in religion or to wage *jihad*, for indeed this is a collective duty on all communities. 'Ali ibn Abi Talha related from Ibn 'Abbas, regarding the verse: { It is not for all of the Believers to mobilize } ; he said: It is not for the all the Believers to mobilize, and leave the Prophet (SAW) alone; if a small group from among each band were not to mobilize } : namely, a small contingent, that is, the troops, and they are not to advance except by his permission. When these troops returned – and in the meantime a portion of the Qur'an had been sent down – those who remained behind with the Prophet (SAW) would have learned it; they would say: Indeed Allah has sent down on your Prophet a portion of the Qur'an, and we have learned it. So the troops would stay and learn what Allah had sent down on their Prophet in the meantime, and He would send out other troops; this is His word: { In order to gain knowledge in religion } .

Tafsir Ibn Kathir

أن رسول الله ﷺ كان إذا بعث بعثاً بعد غزوة تبوك وبعد ما أنزل في المتخلفين من الآيات الشداد إستبق المؤمنون عن آخرهم إلى النفير وانقطعوا جميعاً عن إستماع الوحي والتفقه في الدين فأمروا أن ينفر من كل فرقة منهم طائفة إلى الجهاد ويبقى أعقابهم يتفقهون حتى لا ينقطعوا عن التفقه الذي هو الجهاد الأكبر لأن الجدال بالحجة أعظم أثراً من الجلاد بالسيف

تفسير الزمخشري

The Messenger of Allah (SAW), whenever He sent forth a mission after the attack on Tabuk, and after the verses of severity that were sent down concerning those who stayed behind – the Believers would try to get ahead of each other in mobilizing, and they all became disengaged from hearing the revelation and gaining knowledge in religion [*deen*]. So they were ordered that a small band from each group should mobilize for *jihad*, and those behind them should stay and gain knowledge, so that they would not become disengaged from gaining knowledge, which is the greater *jihad*, since debating with arguments has a greater effect than fighting with the sword.

Tafsir Al-Zamakhshari

المعنى أنه لا يجوز للمؤمنين أن ينفروا بكليتهم إلى الغزو والجهاد بل يجب أن يصيروا طائفتين تبقى طائفة في خدمة الرسول وتنفر طائفة أخرى إلى الغزو وذلك لأن الاسلام في ذلك الوقت كان محتاجاً إلى الغزو والجهاد وقهر الكفار وأيضاً كانت التكاليف تحدث والشرائع تنزل وكان بالمسلمين حاجة إلى من يكون مقيماً بحضرة الرسول عليه السلام فيتعلم تلك الشرائع ويحفظ تلك التكاليف ويبلغها إلى الغائبين

تفسير الرازي

The meaning is that it is not permissible for the Believers to mobilize in their entirety for attacks and *jihad*, but rather they are to form two groups. One group stays to serve the Messenger, and the other group mobilizes to attack. This is because at that time Islam was in need of attacking and *jihad*, and conquering the disbelievers, but ordinances were also coming to pass, and divinely prescribed laws were being sent down, and the Muslims were in need of people to remain present with the Messenger (peace be upon him) and learn these laws and guard these ordinances, and then to communicate them to those who were absent.

Tafsir Al-Razi

* * *

﴿ يَا أَيُّهَا الَّذِينَ آمَنُوا قَاتِلُوا الَّذِينَ يَلُونَكُم مِّنَ الْكُفَّارِ وَلْيَجِدُوا فِيكُمْ غِلْظَةً وَاعْلَمُوا أَنَّ اللَّهَ مَعَ الْمُتَّقِينَ ﴾ التوبة ١٢٣

{ Oh you who have believed! Fight the disbelievers who are near to you, and may they find harshness in you; and know that Allah is with the devout } *Al-tawba* 123

فيه أنه سبحانه عرفهم كيفية الجهاد وأن الإبتداء بالأقرب فالأقرب من العدو

تفسير الطبري

In this the Exalted is stipulating the manner of *jihad*, which is to begin with those nearest, that is, the nearest enemies.

Tafsir Al-Tabari

فالغلظة كالشدة والغلظة كالضغطة والغلظة كالسخطة ونحوه ﴿ وأغلظ عليهم ﴾ ﴿ ولا تهنوا ﴾ وهو يجمع الجرأة والصبر على القتال وشدة العداوة والعنف في القتل والأسر ومنه ﴿ ولا تأخذكم بهما رأفةٌ في دين الله ﴾

تفسير الزمخشري

"Harshness" is like forcefulness, and harshness is like pressure, and harshness is like indignation, as for example: { And be harsh to them } [Al-tawba 73], and: { And do not grow weary } [Al 'Imran 139]. This brings together boldness, steadfastness in fighting, intensity of enmity, and violence in killing and capturing, along the lines of: { And let not any compassion for the two of them take hold of your hearts in the religion of Allah } [Al-nur 2].

Tafsir Al-Zamakhshari

أمر الله تعالى المؤمنين أن يقاتلوا الكفار أولاً فأولاً فالأقرب فالأقرب إلى حوزة الاسلام ولهذا بدأ رسول الله ﷺ بقتال المشركين في جزيرة العرب فلما فرغ منهم وفتح الله عليه مكة والمدينة والطائف واليمن واليمامة وهجر وخيبر وحضرموت وغير ذلك من أقاليم جزيرة العرب ودخل الناس من سائر العرب في دين الله أفواجاً شرع في قتال أهل الكتاب فتجهز لغزو الروم الذين هم أقرب الناس إلى جزيرة العرب وأولى الناس بالدعوة إلى الاسلام لكونهم أهل الكتاب فبلغ تبوك ثم رجع لاجل جهد الناس وجدب البلاد وضيق الحال وكان ذلك سنة تسع من هجرته عليه السلام

ثم إشتغل في ألسنة العاشر بحجته حجة الوداع ثم عاجلته ألمنية صلوات الله وسلامه عليه بعد الحجة بأحد وثمانين يوماً فاختاره الله لما عنده وقام بالأمر بعده وزيره وصديقه وخليفته أبو بكر رضي الله عنه وقد مال الدين ميلة كاد أن ينحفل فثبته الله تعالى به فوطد القواعد وثبت الدعائم ورد شارد الدين وهو راغم ورد أهل الردة إلى الاسلام وأخذ الزكاة ممن منعها من الطغام وبين ألحق لمن جهله وأدى عن الرسول ما حمله ثم شرع في تجهيز الجيوش الاسلامية إلى الروم عبدة الصلبان وإلى الفرس عبدة النيران ففتح الله ببركة سفارته البلاد وأرغم أنف كسرى وقيصر ومن أطاعهما من العباد وأنفق كنوزهما في سبيل الله كما أخبر بذلك رسول الإله

وكان تمام الأمر على يدي وصيه من بعده وولي عهده الفاروق الأواب شهيد المحراب ابي حفص عمر بن الخطاب فأرغم الله به أنوف الكفرة الملحدين وقمع الطغاة والمنافقين وإستولى على الممالك شرقاً وغرباً وحملت إليه خزائن الأموال من سائر الاقاليم بعداً وقرباً ففرقها على الوجه الشرعي والسبيل المرضي

ثم لما مات شهيداً وقد عاش حميداً أجمع الصحابة من المهاجرين والأنصار على خلافة أمير المؤمنين ابي عمرو عثمان بن عفان شهيد الدار فكسا الاسلام بجلاله رياسة حلة سابغة وأمدت في سائر الاقاليم على رقاب العباد حجة الله البالغة وظهر الاسلام في مشارق الأرض ومغاربها وعلت كلمة الله وظهر دينه وبلغت الأمة الحنيفية من أعداء الله غاية مآربها فكلما علوا أمة انتقلوا إلى من بعدهم ثم الذين يلونهم من العتاة الفجار إمتثالاً لقوله تعالى ﴿ يا أيها الذين آمنوا قاتلوا الذين يلونكم من الكفار ﴾ وقوله تعالى ﴿ وليجدوا فيكم غلظة ﴾ أي وليجد الكفار منكم غلظة عليهم ﴿ قاتلكم لهم فإن المؤمن الكامل هو الذي يكون رفيقاً لأخيه المؤمن غليظاً على عدوه الكافر

تفسير ابن كثير

Allah Most High ordered the believers to fight the disbelievers [*kuffar*] first, and the nearest ones first, that is, those nearest to the land of Islam. For this reason the Messenger of Allah (SAW) began by fighting the idolaters [*mushrikun*] in the Arabian peninsula. When He finished with them, and Allah gave him victory over Mecca, Medina, Ta'if, Yemen, Al-yamama, Hajr, Khaybar, Hadramawt, and other territories of the Arabian peninsula, and people from among the rest of the Arabs entered into the religion [*deen*] of Allah in droves, He set out to fight the People of the Book. He got ready to raid the Romans, the people nearest to the Arabian peninsula, and the first people to be called to Islam, since they were a people of the book. He reached Tabuk but then turned back due to the weariness of the people, drought in the land, and tight circumstances. This was in the ninth year after his (peace be upon him) emigration [*hijra*].

Then in the tenth year He became occupied with his pilgrimage, the farewell pilgrimage; then the end came upon him (may the prayers and peace of Allah be upon him) eighty-one days after the pilgrimage; Allah preferred for him to be with what He had for him. And after him, his adviser, friend, and caliph Abu Bakr (may Allah be pleased with him) took command. And the *deen* fell under attack and was almost dissipated, except that Allah Most High affirmed it by him, and he fortified the foundations and affirmed the supports. He brought back, being compelled to, those who wandered from the *deen*, and brought back to Islam those who had apostatized. He took *zakat* from those abject people who had banned it, and manifested the truth to those who were unaware of it. And he carried out for the Messenger what He had imparted to him. Then he set out to prepare the Islamic armies against the Romans, the cross worshippers, and the Persians, the fire worshippers. And Allah by a blessing gave him victory over the land in his mission, and brought down Khosrow and Caesar, as well as those people who obeyed the two of them. And he spent their treasures in the cause of Allah, as the Messenger of God had told.

The matter was brought to completion at the hands of his successor after him, the one who followed his time in power, Al-Faruq the Ever-repentant, martyred in the prayer niche, Abu Hafs 'Umar ibn Al-Khattab. Allah disgraced the heretical Disbelievers, quashed the tyrants and the hypocrites, and appropriated kingdoms east and west. And the storehouses of riches from the rest of the territories, near and far, were brought to him, and he divided them up lawfully and agreeably.

Then when he died a martyr, having lived a praiseworthy life, the Companions from among the Emigrants [*muhajirun*] and the *Ansar* agreed to the caliphate of the Leader of the Faithful Abu 'Amr 'Uthman ibn 'Affan, martyr of the abode. And by his majesty he clothed Islam amply with authority, and the remaining territories were furnished, over peoples' necks, with the full proof of Allah. And Islam was manifest in the eastern and western regions of the earth; and the word of Allah was raised up and his *deen* made manifest. And the true *ummah* attained the utmost of its aims from the enemies of Allah; every time they surpassed a nation, they moved on to whoever was next, and then to the wantonly haughty who were close to them, following the word of the Most High: { Oh you who have believed, fight the disbelievers who are near to you } and the word of the Most High: { And may they find harshness in you } ; that is, may the Disbelievers find harshness from you in your fighting them. Indeed the full Believer is he who is a companion to his believing brother but harsh to his disbelieving enemy.

Tafsir Ibn Kathir

مسألة قال ويقاتل كل قوم من يليهم من العدو
الأصل في هذا قوله الله تعالى ﴿ يا أيها الذين آمنوا قاتلوا الذين يلونكم من الكفار ﴾ ولأن الأقرب أكثر ضرراً وفي قتاله دفع ضرره عن المقابل له وعمن وراءه والإشتغال بالبعيد عنه يمكّنه من انتهاز الفرصة في المسلمين لاشتغالهم عنه

المغني لإبن قدامة كتاب الجهاد

His [Al-Khiraqi] statement: They fight any of the enemy who are near to them.

The basis for this is the word of Allah Most High: { Oh you who have believed! Fight the disbelievers who are near to you } , since the nearest are the most harmful, and fighting them drives back their harm from those who face them as well as from those who are behind them; but engaging with those far away will enable them to seize the opportunity against the Muslims due to them being distracted from them.

Ibn Qudama, Al-mughni, The book of jihad

* * *

Surah 10 (The prophet) Yunus

﴿ وَلَوْ شَاءَ رَبُّكَ لَآمَنَ مَنْ فِي الْأَرْضِ كُلُّهُمْ جَمِيعًا أَفَأَنْتَ تُكْرِهُ النَّاسَ حَتَّى يَكُونُوا مُؤْمِنِينَ وَمَا كَانَ لِنَفْسٍ أَنْ تُؤْمِنَ إِلَّا بِإِذْنِ اللَّهِ وَيَجْعَلُ الرِّجْسَ عَلَى الَّذِينَ لَا يَعْقِلُونَ ﴾ يونس ٩٩-١٠٠

{ And if your Lord wished, everyone on earth would have believed, all of them; so then will you compel people until they become Believers? No one believes, except by the permission of Allah; and He brings depravity on those who have no sense } *Yunus* 99-100

قال القاضي أبو محمد فهذا التأويل الآية عليه محكمة أي أدع وقاتل من خالفك وإيمان من آمن مصروف إلى المشيئة وقالت فرقة المعنى أفأنت تُكره الناس بالقتال حتى يدخلوا في الإيمان وزعمت أن هذه الآية في صدر الاسلام وأنها منسوخة بآية السيف

تفسير إبن عطية

Al-Qadi [judge] Abu Muhammad said: This interpretation of the verse has been decreed on, that is: Call and fight those who oppose you, but the belief of whoever believes is left to free will. Another group said that the meaning is: So then will you compel people by fighting them, until they enter into belief? But they allege that this verse was at the onset of Islam, and that it was abrogated by the verse of the sword.

Tafsir Ibn ʿAtiyya

قوله تعالى ﴿ أفأنت تُكره الناس ﴾ قال المفسرون منهم مقاتل هذا منسوخ بآية السيف والصحيح أنه ليس هاهنا نسخ لأن الإكراه على الإيمان لا يصح لأنه عمل القلب

تفسير إبن الجوزي

The word of the Most High: { So then will you compel people } ; the expositors, among them Muqatil, said that this is abrogated by the verse of the sword. However the correct view is that there is no abrogation here, since compulsion to belief is not genuine, because this is a work of the heart.

Tafsir Ibn Al-Jawzi

• • •

Surah 16   Al-nahl [The bees]

﴿ وَإِذَا بَدَّلْنَا آيَةً مَكَانَ آيَةٍ وَاللَّهُ أَعْلَمُ بِمَا يُنَزِّلُ قَالُوا إِنَّمَا أَنْتَ مُفْتَرٍ بَلْ أَكْثَرُهُمْ لَا يَعْلَمُونَ ﴾ النحل ١٠١

{ And whenever We substitute one verse in place of another – and Allah knows best what He sends down – they say: Indeed you are just a fabricator; but most of them do not know } *Al-nahl* 101

﴿ وَإِذَا بَدَّلْنَا آيَةً مَكَانَ آيَةٍ ﴾ بِنَسْخِهَا وَإِنْزَالِ غَيْرِهَا لِمَصْلَحَةِ الْعِبَادِ ﴿ وَاللَّهُ أَعْلَمُ بِمَا يُنَزِّلُ ﴾ أَيِ الْكُفَّارُ لِلنَّبِيِّ ﷺ ﴿ إِنَّمَا أَنْتَ مُفْتَرٍ ﴾ كَذَّابٌ تَقُولُهُ مِنْ عِنْدِكَ ﴿ بَلْ أَكْثَرُهُمْ لَا يَعْلَمُونَ ﴾ حَقِيقَةَ الْقُرْآنِ وَفَائِدَةَ النَّسْخِ
تفسير الجلالين

{ And whenever we substitute one verse in place of another } : by abrogating it and sending down one different from it for the benefit of people; { and Allah knows best what He sends down – they say } : that is, the disbelievers [*kuffar*] to the Prophet (SAW): { Indeed you are just a fabricator } : a liar, who makes it up yourself; { but most of them do not know } : the truth about the Qur'an and the benefit of abrogation.

Tafsir Al-Jalalain

• • •

﴿ ثُمَّ إِنَّ رَبَّكَ لِلَّذِينَ هَاجَرُوا مِنْ بَعْدِ مَا فُتِنُوا ثُمَّ جَاهَدُوا وَصَبَرُوا إِنَّ رَبَّكَ مِنْ بَعْدِهَا لَغَفُورٌ رَحِيمٌ ﴾ النحل ١١٠

{ Then indeed your Lord, towards those who emigrated after they were made to endure trial, and waged *jihad* and were steadfast, indeed after that your Lord is forgiving, merciful } *Al-nahl* 110

قال قتادة ذكر لنا أنه لما أنزل الله تعالى قبل هذه الآية أن أهل مكة لا يقبل منهم اسلامهم حتى يهاجروا كتب بها أهل المدينة إلى أصحابهم من أهل مكة فلما جاءهم ذلك خرجوا فلحقهم المشركون فردّوهم فنزلت ﴿ ألم أحَسِب الناس أن يُتركوا أن يقولوا آمنا وهم لا يُفتنون ﴾ فكتبوا بها اليهم فتبايعوا بينهم على أن يخرجوا فإن لحقهم المشركون من أهل مكة قاتلوهم حتى ينجوا ويلحقوا بالله فأدركهم المشركون فقاتلوهم فمنهم من قُتل ومنهم من نجا فأنزل الله عز وجل ﴿ ثم إن ربك للذين هاجروا من بعد ما فُتنوا ثم جاهدوا وصبروا ﴾

اسباب النزول للواحدي

Qatada said: It was mentioned to us that when Allah Most High sent down, prior to this verse, that Islam would not be accepted from the people of Mecca until they emigrated, the people of Medina wrote to their companions in Mecca concerning this. When they got word of this, they left, but the Idolaters caught up with them and brought them back. And this came down: { Alif, Lam, Mim. Have people reckoned that they will be left alone if they say "We have believed", and will not be put to the test? } [Al-'ankabut 1-2]; and they wrote to them concerning this. So they pledged to each other that they would set out, and if the Idolaters from Mecca caught up with them, they would fight them until they were either safe or joined Allah. The Idolaters reached them, and they fought them, and some were killed and some made it safely; and Allah Mighty and Sublime sent down: { Then indeed your Lord, towards those who emigrated after they were made to endure trial, and waged jihad and were steadfast ... } .

Al-Wahidi, Asbab Al-nuzul

قوله تعالى ﴿ ثم إن ربك للذين هاجروا من بعد ما فتنوا ثم جاهدوا وصبروا ﴾ هذا كله في عمّار والمعنى وصبروا على الجهاد

تفسير القرطبي

The word of the Most High: { Then indeed your Lord, towards those who emigrated after they were made to endure trial, and waged jihad and were steadfast } : all of this concerns forbearance in suffering, and the meaning is: they were steadfast in jihad.

Tafsir Al-Qurtubi

يقول تعالى ذكره ثم إن ربك يا محمد للذين هاجروا من ديارهم ومساكنهم وعشائرهم من المشركين وانتقلوا عنهم إلى ديار أهل الاسلام ومساكنهم وأهل ولايتهم من بعد ما فتنهم المشركون الذين كانوا بين أظهرهم قبل هجرتهم عن دينهم ثم جاهدوا المشركين بعد ذلك بأيديهم وبألسنتهم بالبراءة منهم ومما يعبدون من دون الله وصبروا على جهادهم ﴿ إن ربك من بعدها لغفور رحيم ﴾ يقول إن ربك من بعد فعلتهم هذه لهم لغفور

تفسير الطبري

He (may His remembrance be exalted) is saying: Then indeed your Lord, Oh Muhammad, towards those who emigrated from their homes and their dwellings and their kinsmen among the idolaters, and moved from them into the homes of the people of Islam, their dwellings, and those who were their associates, after the Idolaters had put them to the test, those who were among them before they emigrated from their religion, who afterwards waged *jihad* on the Idolaters with their hands, the sword, and their tongues, being absolved from them and from what they worship other than Allah, and were steadfast in their *jihad*, { indeed after that your Lord is forgiving, merciful } ; He is saying: Indeed your Lord, after they did all this to them, surely will be forgiving towards them.

Tafsir Al-Tabari

* * *

﴿ ادعُ إلى سبيل ربك بالحكمة والموعظة الحسنة وجادلهم بالتي هي أحسن إنّ ربك هو أعلم بمن ضلّ عن سبيله وهو أعلم بالمهتدين وإن عاقبتم فعاقبوا بمثل ما عوقبتم به ولئن صبرتم لهو خير للصابرين ﴾ النحل ١٢٥-١٢٦

{ Call to the cause of your Lord with wisdom and fitting exhortation, and dispute with them in what is best; indeed your Lord knows better those who have strayed from His cause, and He knows better those who have been guided. But if you punish, then punish in the same way by which you have been punished, although if you are forbearing, it is better for those who are forbearing } *Al-nahl* 125-126

أبي بن كعب قال لما كان يوم أحد أُصيبَ من الأنصار أربعة وستون رجلاً فمن المهاجرين ستة فيهم حمزة فمثّلوا بهم فقالت الأنصار لئن أصبنا منهم يوماً مثل هذا لنُربينَّ عليهم قال فلما كان يوم فتح مكة فأنزل الله ﴿ وإن عاقبتم فعاقبوا بمثل ما عوقبتم به ولئن صبرتم لهم خير للصابرين ﴾ فقال رجل لا قريش بعد اليوم فقال رسول الله ﷺ كُفّوا عن القوم إلا أربعة

جامع الترمذي كتاب تفسير القرآن

Ubayy ibn Ka'b said: On the day of Uhud, sixty-four *Ansar* men were befallen, six of whom were from those who had emigrated, among them Hamza; and they mutilated them. The Ansar said: If we get to any of them on a day like this, surely we will do even more to them! And on the day of the conquest of Mecca, Allah sent down: { But if you punish, then punish in the same way by which you have been punished, although if you are forbearing, it is better for those who are forbearing } . A certain man said: There will be no more Quraish after today. But the Messenger of Allah (SAW) said: Leave the people, except four.

Sunan Al-Tirmidhi, The book of tafsir

﴿ أدع ﴾ الناس يا محمد ﷺ ﴿ إلى سبيل ربك ﴾ دينه ﴿ بالحكمة ﴾ بالقرآن ﴿ والموعظة الحسنة ﴾ مواعظة أو القول الرقيق ﴿ وجادلهم بالتي ﴾ أي المجادلة التي ﴿ هي أحسن ﴾ كالدعاء إلى الله بآياته والدعاء إلى حججه ﴿ ان ربك هو أعلم ﴾ أي عالم ﴿ بمن ضل عن سبيله وهو أعلم بالمهتدين ﴾ فيجازيهم وهذا قبل الأمر بالقتال ونزل لما قتل حمزة ومثل به فقال ﷺ وقد رآه لأمثلنّ بسبعين منهم مكانك ﴿ وإن عاقبتم فعاقبوا بمثل ما عوقبتم به ولئن صبرتم ﴾ عن الإنتقام ﴿ لهو ﴾ أي الصبر ﴿ خير للصابرين ﴾ فكفّ ﷺ وكفّر عن يمينه رواه البزار

تفسير الجلالين

{ Call } : people, Oh Muhammad (SAW); { to the cause of your Lord } : His religion [*deen*]; { with wisdom } : with the Qur'an; { and fitting exhortation } : preaching or tender words; { and dispute with them in } : that is, making the case for; { what is best } : like invoking Allah for His signs or invoking his authoritative arguments; { Indeed your Lord knows better } : that is, He is aware; { those who have strayed from His cause, and He knows better those who have been guided } : so He may reward them. This was before the command to fight, and came down when Hamza was killed and mutilated. The Messenger of Allah (SAW) – after seeing him – said: Surely I will mutilate seventy of them in your place. { But if you punish, then punish in the same way by which you have been punished, although if you are forbearing } : against taking revenge; { it is better } : forbearance; { for those who are forbearing } . So He (SAW) held back and made amends for what He swore. Al-Bazzar narrated this.

Tafsir Al-Jalalain

قال المفسرون إن المسلمين لما رأوا ما فعل المشركون بقتلاهم يوم أحد من تبقير البطون وقطع المذاكير والمثلة السيئة قالوا حين رأوا ذلك لئن أظفرنا الله سبحانه وتعالى عليهم لنزيدنّ على صنيعهم ولنمثلنّ بهم مثلة لم يمثلها أحد من العرب بأحد قط ولنفعلن ولنفعلن ولنفعلن ووقف رسول الله ﷺ على عمه حمزة وقد جدعوا أنفه وأذنه وقطعوا مذاكيره وبقروا بطنه وأخذت هند بنت عتبة قطعة من كبده فمضغتها ثم استرطتها لتأكلها فلم تثبت

في بطنها حتى رمت بها فبلغ ذلك نبي الله ﷺ فقال أما إنها لو أكلتها لم تدخل النار أبداً حمزة أكرم على الله من أن يدخل شيئاً من جسده النار فلما نظر رسول الله ﷺ إلى حمزة نظر لم ينظر قط إلى شيء كان أوجع لقلبه منه فقال رحمة الله عليك انك ما علمت كنت وصولاً للرحم فعالاً للخيرات ولولا حزن من بعدك عليك لأمثلنّ بسبعين منهم مكانك فأنزل الله تعالى ﴿ وإن عاقبتم فعاقبوا بمثل ما عوقبتم به ﴾ الآية فقال النبي ﷺ بل نصبر وأمسك عما أراد وكفر عن يمينه

اسباب النزول للواحدي

The expositors say: Indeed the Muslims, when they saw what the idolaters had done to their dead on the day of Uhud by way of ripping open bellies, cutting off male members, and savage mutilation, said when they saw this: If Allah Most High and Exalted gives us victory over them, surely we will do even more than they have done, and we will mutilate them like no Arab has ever mutilated another Arab, and indeed we will do this and we will do that. And the Messenger of Allah (SAW) stopped beside his uncle Hamza – they had cut off his nose and ears and severed his member and ripped open his belly. Hind bint 'Utba had taken a piece of his liver, chewed it, gulped it down to eat it, but it would not stay in her belly so she threw it up. The Prophet of Allah (SAW) got word of this and He said: As for her, indeed if she had eaten it, she would never enter Hellfire; Hamza is too honorable to Allah for any part of his body to enter Hellfire. And when the Messenger of Allah (SAW) saw Hamza, He saw something more agonizing to his heart than anything He had ever seen, and He said: May the mercy of Allah be on you, indeed from what I know you were true to the ties of kinship, accomplished in good deeds, and were it not for the grief for you of those who remained after you, truly I would mutilate seventy of them in your place. But Allah Most High sent down: { But if you punish, then punish in the same way by which you have been punished } and the rest of the verse, and the Prophet (SAW) said: And so we will be forbearing. And He took back what He wished for, and made amends for what He swore.

Al-Wahidi, Asbab Al-nuzul

والقول الثاني أن هذا كان قبل الأمر بالسيف والجهاد حين كان المسلمون قد أمروا بالقتال مع من يقاتلهم ولا يبدؤوا بالقتال

تفسير الرازي

The second thing that is said is that this was before the command to take up swords and *jihad*, when the Muslims had been ordered to fight those who fought them, not to initiate fighting.

Tafsir Al-Razi

قال إبن زيد في قوله ﴿ وإن عاقبتم فعاقبوا بمثل ما عوقبتم به ﴾ قال أمرهم الله أن يعفوا عن المشركين فأسلم رجال لهم منعة فقالوا يا رسول الله لو أذن الله لنا لانتصرنا من هؤلاء الكلاب فنزل القرآن ﴿ وإن عاقبتم فعاقبوا بمثل ما عوقبتم به ولئن صبرتم لهو خيرٌ للصابرين ﴾ واصبر أنت يا محمد ولا تكن في ضيق ممن ينتصر وما صبرك إلا بالله ثم نسخ هذا وأمره بجهادهم فهذا كله منسوخ

تفسير الطبري

Ibn Zaid, regarding His word: { But if you punish, then punish in the same way by which you have been punished } , said: Allah ordered them to excuse the Idolaters, but some tough men yielded into Islam and said: Oh Messenger of Allah, if Allah gave us permission we would take revenge on these dogs! Then the full portion of Qur'an came down: { But if you punish, then punish in the same way by which you have been punished, although if you are forbearing, it is better for those who are forbearing } : and you be forbearing too, Oh Muhammad, and do not worry about who will take revenge; only by Allah can you be forbearing. Then this was abrogated and He ordered him to wage *jihad* on them. And all of this is abrogated.

Tafsir Al-Tabari

. . .

Surah 17   Al-israa [The Night Journey]
or   Bani Isra'il [Children of Israel]

﴿ مَنِ اهْتَدَى فَإِنَّمَا يَهْتَدِي لِنَفْسِهِ وَمَن ضَلَّ فَإِنَّمَا يَضِلُّ عَلَيْهَا وَلَا تَزِرُ وَازِرَةٌ وِزْرَ أُخْرَى وَمَا كُنَّا مُعَذِّبِينَ حَتَّى نَبْعَثَ رَسُولاً ﴾ الإسراء ١٥

{ He who is guided is indeed guided for his own benefit, but he who goes astray indeed goes astray against himself; no burdened soul can bear the burden of another. And We are not punishers until We send forth a messenger } Al-israa 15

﴿ من إهتدى فإنما يهتدي لنفسه ﴾ لأن ثواب اهتدائه له ﴿ ومن ضل فإنما يضل عليها ﴾ لأن إثمه عليها ﴿ ولا تزر ﴾ نفس ﴿ وازرة ﴾ آثمة أي لا تحمل ﴿ وزر ﴾ نفس ﴿ أخرى ﴾ وما كنا معذبين ﴿ أحداً ﴾ حتى نبعث رسولاً ﴾ يبيّن له ما يجب عليه

تفسير الجلالين

{ He who is guided is indeed guided for his own benefit } : since the reward of his guidance belongs to him; { but he who goes astray indeed goes astray against himself } : since his sin is on him; { no burdened soul } : sinful soul; { can bear } : carry; { the burden } : of another soul; { And We are not punishers } : of anyone; { until We send forth a messenger } : to make it clear to them what they are obliged to do.

Tafsir Al-Jalalain

﴿ وما كنا معذبين حتى نبعث رسولاً ﴾ إن الله تبارك ليس يعذب أحداً حتى يسبق إليه من الله خبراً ويأتيه من الله بيّنة وليس معذباً أحداً إلا بذنبه

تفسير الطبري

{ And We are not punishers until We send forth a messenger } : Indeed Allah Most Blessed does not punish anyone until he [the messenger] reaches him first with a declaration from Allah, and comes to him with affirmation from Allah; and He does not punish anyone except for their sins.

Tafsir Al-Tabari

﴿ وما كنا معذبين حتى نبعث رسولاً ﴾ إقامة للحجة وقطعاً للعذر وفيه دليل على أن ما وَجَبَ وَجَبَ بالسمع لا بالعقل

تفسير البغوي

{ And We are not punishers until We send forth a messenger } : to establish the argument and put an end to excuses, and there is proof here that what is obligatory is obligatory due to it being heard, not due to reasoning.

Tafsir Al-Baghawi

ومعنى ﴿ حتى نبعث رسولاً ﴾ أي حتى نُبيّن ما به نعذّب وما من أجله نُدخل الجنة

تفسير ابن الجوزي

The meaning of: { Until We send forth a messenger } : that is, until We make clear what We punish for, and what We admit into *Jannah* for.

Tafsir Ibn Al-Jawzi

* * *

﴿ ولا تقتلوا النفس التي حرم الله إلا بالحق ومن قُتل مظلوماً فقد جعلنا لوليه سلطاناً فلا يسرف في القتل إنه كان منصوراً ﴾ الإسراء ٣٣

{ And do not kill the soul that Allah has forbidden, except with just cause; whoever is killed wrongly, we have given authority to his heir; but let one not go to extremes in killing, for indeed he will be aided } Al-israa 33

﴿ ولا تقتلوا النفس التي حرم الله إلا بالحق ﴾ وإنا والله ما تعلم بحلّ دم امرىء مسلم إلا بإحدى ثلاث إلا رجلاً قتل متعمداً فعليه القَوَد أو زنى بعد إحصانه فعليه الرجم أو كفر بعد اسلامه فعليه القتل

تفسير الطبري

{ And do not kill the soul that Allah has forbidden, except with just cause } ; By Allah indeed we know of nothing that makes the blood of a Muslim man lawful except one of three things: a man who kills intentionally – retaliation is due him; someone who adulterates after being married – he is to be stoned; and someone who disbelieves after being in Islam – he is to be killed.

Tafsir Al-Tabari

عن الضحاك رضي الله عنه في قوله ﴿ ولا تقتلوا النفس التي حرم الله إلا بالحق ﴾ الآية قال كان هذا بمكة والنبي ﷺ بها وهو أول شيء نزل من القرآن في شأن القتل كان المشركون من أهل مكة يغتالون أصحاب النبي ﷺ فقال من قتلكم من المشركين فلا يحملنّكم قتله إياكم على أن تقتلوا له أباً أو أخاً وأحداً من عشيرته وإن كانوا مشركين فلا تقتلوا إلا قاتلكم وهذا قبل أن تنزل براءة وقبل أن يؤمروا بقتال المشركين

الدر المنثور للسيوطي

Al-Dahhak (may Allah be pleased with him), regarding His word { And do not kill the soul that Allah has forbidden, except with just cause } and the rest of the verse, said: This was in Mecca when the Prophet (SAW) was there, and was the first thing in the Qur'an to come down in regards to killing. The idolaters [*mushrikun*] in Mecca were murdering the Prophet's (SAW) Companions and He said: Whoever of the idolaters kills one of you all, do not let his killing you make you kill his father or brother or any other of his relatives, even if they are idolaters – do not kill anyone except the one who kills one of you. But this was before the "Absolution" [Surah *Al-tawba*] came down, and before they were ordered to kill the idolaters.

Al-Suyuti, Al-durr Al-manthur

■ ■ ■

Surah 21 Al-anbiyaa [The Prophets]

إِنَّ فِي هَذَا لَبَلَاغًا لِقَوْمٍ عَابِدِينَ وَمَا أَرْسَلْنَاكَ إِلَّا رَحْمَةً لِلْعَالَمِينَ قُلْ إِنَّمَا يُوحَى إِلَيَّ أَنَّمَا إِلَهُكُمْ إِلَهٌ وَاحِدٌ فَهَلْ أَنْتُمْ مُسْلِمُونَ فَإِنْ تَوَلَّوْا فَقُلْ آذَنْتُكُمْ عَلَى سَوَاءٍ وَإِنْ أَدْرِي أَقَرِيبٌ أَمْ بَعِيدٌ مَا تُوعَدُونَ ۞ الأنبياء ١٠٦- ١٠٩

{ Indeed in this there is a proclamation for people who worship; We have only sent you as a mercy to the worlds; Say: Indeed it has been revealed to me that your god is one god, so do you all yield? And if they turn away, then say: I have informed you all equally, but I do not know if what you are promised is near or far }
Al-anbiyaa 106-109

وقوله تعالى { وَمَا أَرْسَلْنَاكَ إِلَّا رَحْمَةً لِلْعَالَمِينَ } يخبر الله تعالى أن الله جعل محمداً ﷺ رحمة للعالمين أي أرسله رحمة لهم كلهم فمن قبل هذه الرحمة وشكر هذه النعمة سعد في الدنيا والآخرة ومن ردها وجحدها خسر في الدنيا والآخرة ... يقول تعالى آمراً رسوله صلوات الله وسلامه عليه أن يقول للمشركين { إِنَّمَا يُوحَى إِلَيَّ أَنَّمَا إِلَهُكُمْ إِلَهٌ وَاحِدٌ فَهَلْ أَنْتُمْ مُسْلِمُونَ } أي متبعون على ذلك مستسلمون منقادون له ... { فَإِنْ تَوَلَّوْا } أي تركوا ما دعوتهم إليه { فَقُلْ آذَنْتُكُمْ عَلَى سَوَاءٍ } أي أعلمتكم أني حرب لكم كما أنكم حرب لي بريء منكم كما أنكم برآء مني
تفسير ابن كثير

The word of the Most High: { We have only sent you as a mercy to the worlds } : Allah Most High is making known that Allah has made Muhammad (SAW) a mercy to the worlds, that is, He has sent him as a mercy to them all; whoever accepts this mercy and gives thanks for this favor will be happy in this world and the next, but whoever refutes it and rejects it is lost in this world and the next. ... The Most High says, as a command to His Messenger (may the prayers and peace of Allah be upon him), for him to say to the Idolaters: { Indeed it has been revealed to me that your god is one god, so do you all yield? ["Are you all Muslims?"] } : that is, do you follow this, surrender, and obey Him? ... { And if they turn away } : that is, neglect what you have called them to, { then say: I have informed you all equally } : that is, I have declared to you that I am at war with you as you are at war with me, and I am absolved from you as you are absolved from me.
Tafsir Ibn Kathir

﴿ فإن تولوا ﴾ عن ذلك ﴿ فقل آذنتكم ﴾ أعلمتكم بالحرب ﴿ على سواء ﴾ حال من الفاعل والمفعول أي مستوين في علمه لا أستبدّ به دونكم لتتأهبوا ﴿ وإن ﴾ ما ﴿ أدري أقريب أم بعيد ما توعَدون ﴾ من العذاب أو القيامة المشتملة عليه وإنما يعلمه الله

تفسير الجلالين

{ And if they turn away } : from this; { then say: I have informed you all } : I have declared war on you; { equally } : a circumstancial clause for both subject and object, that is, you are all equally aware; I will not proceed independently without you, so that you can get ready; { But } : I do not; { know if what you are promised is near or far } : in terms of punishment or the resurrection that includes this; indeed Allah knows this.

Tafsir Al-Jalalain

فقل لهم قد آذنتكم على سواء يقول أعلمهم أنك وهم على علم من أن بعضكم لبعض حرب لا صلح بينكم ولا سلم

تفسير الطبري

Then say to them: I have informed you all equally. He is saying: Make it known to them that you and them are aware that you are at war with each other; there is neither reconciling nor peace between you.

Tafsir Al-Tabari

Surah 22   Al-hajj [The Pilgrimage]

$$\text{﴿ أُذِنَ لِلَّذِينَ يُقَاتَلُونَ بِأَنَّهُمْ ظُلِمُوا وَإِنَّ اللَّهَ عَلَىٰ نَصْرِهِمْ لَقَدِيرٌ الَّذِينَ أُخْرِجُوا مِن دِيَارِهِم بِغَيْرِ حَقٍّ إِلَّا أَن يَقُولُوا رَبُّنَا اللَّهُ وَلَوْلَا دَفْعُ اللَّهِ النَّاسَ بَعْضَهُم بِبَعْضٍ لَّهُدِّمَتْ صَوَامِعُ وَبِيَعٌ وَصَلَوَاتٌ وَمَسَاجِدُ يُذْكَرُ فِيهَا اسْمُ اللَّهِ كَثِيرًا وَلَيَنصُرَنَّ اللَّهُ مَن يَنصُرُهُ إِنَّ اللَّهَ لَقَوِيٌّ عَزِيزٌ الَّذِينَ إِن مَّكَّنَّاهُمْ فِي الْأَرْضِ أَقَامُوا الصَّلَاةَ وَآتَوُا الزَّكَاةَ وَأَمَرُوا بِالْمَعْرُوفِ وَنَهَوْا عَنِ الْمُنكَرِ وَلِلَّهِ عَاقِبَةُ الْأُمُورِ ﴾ الحج ٣٩-٤١}$$

{ Permission has been given to those who fight, because they have been oppressed; indeed Allah is truly able to give them victory. Those who have been driven from their homes for no reason except that they say "Allah is our Lord"; and if Allah had not driven people away, some by means of others, then monasteries, churches, synagogues, and mosques in which the name of Allah is mentioned much, would have been ruined; truly Allah champions those who champion Him; indeed Allah is strong, mighty. Those who, if we establish them in the land, observe prayer, bring *zakat*, and prescribe what is right and prohibit what is wrong; and to Allah belongs the conclusion of all matters } *Al-hajj* 39-41

عن ابن عباس قال لما أُخرج النبي ﷺ من مكة قال أبو بكر أخرجوا نبيهم ليهلكنَّ فأنزل الله ﴿ أُذِنَ لِلَّذِينَ يُقَاتَلُونَ بِأَنَّهُمْ ظُلِمُوا وَإِنَّ اللَّهَ عَلَىٰ نَصْرِهِمْ لَقَدِيرٌ ﴾ الآية فقال أبو بكر لقد علمت أنه سيكون قتال

جامع الترمذي كتاب تفسير القرآن

From Ibn 'Abbas, who said: When the Prophet (SAW) was driven out of Mecca, Abu Bakr said: They have driven out their Prophet surely to their own destruction. And Allah sent down: { Permission has been given to those who fight, because they have been oppressed; indeed Allah is truly able to give them victory } and the rest of the verse. And Abu Bakr said: Then I knew that there would be fighting.

Sunan Al-Tirmidhi, The book of tafsir

﴿ أذن للذين يقاتلون ﴾ أي للمؤمنين أن يقاتلوا وهذه أول آية نزلت في الجهاد ﴿ بأنهم ﴾ أي بسبب أنهم ﴿ ظُلِموا ﴾ لظلم الكافرين إياهم ﴿ وإن الله على نصرهم لقدير ﴾ وهم ﴿ الذين اخرجوا من ديارهم بغير حق في الإخراج ما أخرجوا ﴾ ﴿ إلا أن يقولوا ﴾ أي بقولهم ﴿ ربنا الله ﴾ وحده وهذا القول حق فالإخراج به إخراج بغير حق ... ﴿ ولينصرنَّ الله من ينصره ﴾ أي ينصر دينه

تفسير الجلالين

{ Permission has been given to those who fight } : that is, to the Believers that fight; this was the first verse to come down concerning *jihad*; { because they } : that is, for the reason that; { they have been oppressed } : by the oppresssion of the Disbelievers towards them; { indeed Allah is truly able to give them victory } : "them" being { those who have been driven from their homes for no reason } : for them being driven out – they were not driven out { except that they say } : that is, for them saying { Allah is our Lord } alone; but this saying is true, and therefore being driven out for it means being driven out unduly ... { Truly Allah champions those who champion Him } : that is, who champion His religion [*deen*].

Tafsir Al-Jalalain

﴿ وإن الله على نصرهم لقدير ﴾ وقد فعل وإنما شرع تعالى الجهاد في الوقت الأليق به لأنهم لما كانوا بمكة كان المشركون أكثر عدداً فلو أمر المسلمين وهم أقل من العشر بقتال الباقين لشق عليهم ... فلما بغى المشركون وأخرجوا النبي ﷺ من بين أظهرهم وهموا بقتله وشردوا أصحابه شذر مذر فذهب منهم طائفة إلى الحبشة وآخرون إلى المدينة فلما استقروا بالمدينة ووافاهم رسول الله ﷺ واجتمعوا عليه وقاموا بنصره وصارت لهم دار إسلام ومعقلاً يلجؤون إليه شرع الله جهاد الأعداء فكانت هذه الآية أول ما نزل في ذلك

تفسير ابن كثير

{ Indeed Allah is truly able to give them victory } : and He did so. Indeed the Most High prescribed *jihad* at the most suitable time for it, because when they were in Mecca, the idolaters were more numerous, and if He had ordered the Muslims – who were less than a tenth – to fight the rest of them, this would have been very hard on them. ... But when the idolaters became oppressive, and drove the Prophet (SAW) from among them, and were intent on killing him, and forced his Companions out in all directions, a group of them went off to Ethiopia, and others to Medina. When they settled in Medina and the Messenger of Allah (SAW) showed up to meet them, and they all gathered together to support him, and this became a territory of Islam for them and a stronghold in which they could find refuge, then Allah prescribed *jihad* against the enemies. This verse was the first to come down concerning this.

Tafsir Ibn Kathir

عن محمد بن إسحاق المطلبي وكان رسول الله ﷺ قبل بيعة العقبة لم يؤذن له في الحرب ولم تُحَلَّل له الدماء إنما يؤمر بالدعاء إلى الله والصبر على الأذى والصفح عن الجاهل وكانت قريش قد اضطهدت من اتّبعه من المهاجرين حتى فتنوهم عن دينهم ونفوهم من بلادهم فهم من بين مفتون في دينه ومن بين معذَّب في أيديهم وبين هارب في البلاد فراراً منهم منهم من بأرض الحبشة ومنهم من بالمدينة وفي كل وجه

فلما عتت قريش على الله عز وجل وردوا عليه ما ارادهم به من الكرامة وكذّبوا نبيه ﷺ وعذّبوا ونفوا من عبَده ووحَّده وصدق نبيه وإعتصم بدينه أذن الله عز وجل لرسوله ﷺ في القتال والامتناع والإنتصار ممن ظلمهم وبغى عليهم فكانت أول آية أُنزلت في إذنه في الحرب واحلاله له الدماء والقتال لمن بغى عليهم فيما بلغني عن عروة بن الزبير وغيره من العلماء قول الله تبارك وتعالى ﴿ الحج ٣٩-٤١ ﴾ أي إني انما أحللت لهم القتال لأنهم ظُلموا ولم يكن لهم ذنب فيما بينهم وبين الناس إلا أن يعبدوا لله وأنهم إذا ظهروا أقاموا الصلاة وآتوا الزكاة وأمروا بالمعروف ونهوا عن المنكر يعني النبي ﷺ وأصحابه رضي الله عنهم أجمعين

ثم أنزل الله تبارك وتعالى عليه ﴿ وقاتلوهم حتى لا تكون فتنة ﴾ أي حتى لا يُفتن مؤمن عن دينه ﴿ ويكون الدين لله ﴾ أي حتى يعبد الله لا يعبد معه غيره

السيرة النبوية لإبن هشام نزول الأمر لرسول الله ﷺ في القتال

From Muhammad ibn Ishaq Al-Mutallabi: The Messenger of Allah (SAW), before the Pledge of 'Aqaba, was not given permission to wage war, and bloodshed was not permitted to him; rather He was ordered to make supplication to Allah, to bear insult patiently, and to be lenient with the ignorant. And the Quraysh persecuted the emigrants [*muhajirun*] who followed him, to the point of drawing them away from their religion and banishing them from their land. So they were either drawn away from their religion, punished at their [Quraish's] hands, or fled from their land to escape from them – some went to the land of the Ethiopians, some to Medina, and in every direction.

And when the Quraish became arrogant towards Allah High and Exalted, refused the esteem that He desired for them, accused His Prophet (SAW) of lying, and punished and banished those who worshipped Him, who ascribed oneness to Him, believed His prophet, and held strong to their religion, then Allah Mighty and Sublime gave His Messenger (SAW) permission to fight, desist from, and overcome those who oppressed them and treated them wrongly. The first verse that was sent down regarding His permission to wage war, make bloodshed permissible, and fight those who wronged them, as far as what I found out from 'Urwa ibn Al-Zubair and other scholars besides him, was the word of Allah Blessed and Exalted { *Al-hajj* 39-41} . This is to say: Indeed I have made fighting permissible for them because they have been oppressed, and they are guilty of no wrong between the people and them except that they worship Allah, and because whenever they present themselves, they observe prayer, bring *zakat*, prescribe what is right and prohibit what is wrong, that is, the Prophet (SAW) and his Companions (may Allah be pleased with them all).

Then Allah Blessed and Exalted sent down to him { And fight them until there is no more sedition } ; that is, until no believer is enticed away from his religion { And religion belongs to Allah } ; that is, until Allah is worshipped and no other than Him is worshipped. [Al-baqara 193]

Ibn Hisham, Al-sirah Al-nabawiya, Topic section: the order to fight coming down to the Messenger (SAW)

عن إبن جريج قوله ﴿ ولولا دفع الله الناس بعضهم ببعض ﴾ دفع المشركين بالمسلمين وقال آخرون معنى ذلك ولولا القتال والجهاد في سبيل الله ... ﴿ ولينصرن الله من ينصره ﴾ يقول تعالى ذكره وليعينّ الله من يقاتل في سبيله لتكون كلمته العليا على عدوه فنصر الله عبده معونته إياه ونصر العبد ربه جهاده في سبيله لتكون كلمته العليا

تفسير الطبري

Ibn Juraij, regarding His word { And if Allah had not driven people away, some by means of others } : Allah drove the idolaters away by means of the Muslims. Others say that the meaning here is: If it were not for fighting and *jihad* in the cause of Allah ... { Truly Allah champions those who champion Him } ; He (may His remembrance be exalted) is saying: Truly Allah comes to the aid of those who fight in His cause so that His word is the utmost over His enemy. Allah champions His servants by His assistance to them, and a servant champions his Lord by his *jihad* in His cause so that His word is the utmost.

Tafsir Al-Tabari

﴿ وَالَّذِينَ هَاجَرُوا فِي سَبِيلِ اللَّهِ ثُمَّ قُتِلُوا أَوْ مَاتُوا لَيَرْزُقَنَّهُمُ اللَّهُ رِزْقًا حَسَنًا وَإِنَّ اللَّهَ لَهُوَ خَيْرُ الرَّازِقِينَ ﴾ الحج ٥٨

{ And those who left home for the cause of Allah, then were killed or died, truly Allah will bestow bountiful favor on them; and indeed Allah - He is the best of those who bestow favor } Al-hajj 58

يخبر تعالى عمن خرج مهاجراً في سبيل الله ابتغاء مرضاته وطلباً لما عنده وترك الأوطان والأهلين والخلان وفارق بلاده في الله ورسوله ونصرة لدين الله ثم قتلوا أي في الجهاد أو ماتوا أي حتف أنفهم أي من غير قتال على فرشهم فقد حصلوا على الأجر الجزيل والثناء الجميل

تفسير ابن كثير

The Most High is informing concerning those who set out to emigrate in the cause of Allah, intent on His good pleasure and seeking after what is His, leaving behind homelands, kinsfolk, and dear friends, breaking off from their land for Allah and His Messenger and to uphold Allah's religion, and are then killed, either in *jihad* or a natural death on their mats without having fought – they have gained abundant reward and excellent praise.

Tafsir Ibn Kathir

يقول تعالى ذكره والذين فارقوا أوطانهم وعشائرهم فتركوا ذلك في رضا الله وطاعته وجهاد أعدائه ثم قتلوا أو ماتوا وهم كذلك ﴿ ليرزقنهم الله ﴾ يوم القيامة في جناته

تفسير الطبري

He (may His remembrance be exalted) is saying: Those who broke off from their homelands and kinsfolk, and left that behind for the pleasure of Allah, obedience to Him, and *jihad* against His enemies, and then are killed or die, as such: { truly Allah will bestow bountiful favor on them } on resurrection day, in His gardens.

Tafsir Al-Tabari

روي عن طوائف من أصحاب رسول الله ﷺ ورضي عنهم قالوا يا نبي الله هؤلاء الذين قتلوا قد علمنا ما أعطاهم الله من الخير ونحن نجاهد معك كما جاهدوا فما لنا إن متنا معك فأنزل الله هاتين الآيتين

تفسير الزمخشري

It is narrated from certain groups of the Messenger of Allah's (SAW) Companions (may Allah be pleased with them), who said: Oh Prophet of Allah, these who have been killed – we know the bounty that Allah has given them, but as for us, we wage *jihad* with you as they waged *jihad*; what is there for us if we die with you? And so Allah sent down these two verses [58 and 59].

Tafsir Al-Zamakhshari

﴿ والذين هاجروا في سبيل الله ثم قتلوا ﴾ في الجهاد ﴿ أو ماتوا ليرزقنهم الله رزقاً حسناً ﴾ الجنة ونعيمها وإنما سوى بين من قتل في الجهاد ومن مات حتف أنفه في الوعد لاستوائهما في القصد وأصل العمل

تفسير البيضاوي

{ And those who left home for the cause of Allah, then were killed } : in *jihad*; { or died, truly Allah will bestow bountiful favor on them } : *Jannah* and its bliss. Indeed those who were killed in *jihad* and those who died a natural death were put on the same level of the promise, as both are equal in intent and the starting point for the deed.

Tafsir Al-Baydawi

* * *

﴿ وجاهدوا في الله حق جهاده هو اجتباكم وما جعل عليكم في الدين من حرج ملة أبيكم إبراهيم هو سماكم المسلمين من قبل وفي هذا ليكون الرسول شهيداً عليكم وتكونوا شهداء على الناس فأقيموا الصلاة وآتوا الزكاة واعتصموا بالله هو مولاكم فنعم المولى ونعم النصير ﴾ الحج ٧٨

{ And wage jihad for Allah as is due His *jihad*; He has selected you all and has not given you any uneasiness in religion; the religion of your father Ibrahim; He called you the Muslims beforehand and in the present, so that the Messenger would be a witness to you and that you would be witnesses to people; so observe prayer, and bring *zakat*, and hold fast to Allah; He is your Lord, a most excellent Lord and a most excellent champion } *Al-hajj* 78

وقوله ﴿ وجاهدوا في الله حق جهاده ﴾ أي بأموالكم وألسنتكم وأنفسكم كما قال تعالى ﴿ اتقوا الله حق تُقاته ﴾ وقوله ﴿ هو إجتباكم ﴾ أي يا هذه الأمة الله اصطفاكم واختاركم على سائر الأمم وفضلكم وشرفكم وخصكم بأكرم رسول وأكمل شرع ﴿ وما جعل عليكم في الدين من حرج ﴾ أي ما كلفكم ما لا تطيقون وما ألزمكم بشيء يشق عليكم إلا جعل الله لكم فرجاً ومخرجاً

تفسير ابن كثير

His word: { And wage jihad for Allah as is due His jihad } : that is, with your wealth, your tongues, and yourselves, as the Most High said: { Fear Allah as is due fear of Him } [Al 'Imran 102]. And His word: { He has selected you all } ; that is: Oh nation! [*ummah*], Allah has picked you, He has chosen you over the rest of the nations, and has preferred you, distinguished you, and endowed you with the most honorable Messenger and the most perfect prescribed system of laws. { And has not given you any uneasiness in religion } : that is, He has not imposed on you what you can not bear, and has not obliged you to anything that is hard on you, without Allah providing relief for you and a way out of it.

Tafsir Ibn Kathir

﴿ وجاهدوا ﴾ أمر بالغزو وبمجاهدة النفس والهوى وهو الجهاد الأكبر عن النبي ﷺ أنه رجع من بعض غزواته فقال رجعنا من الجهاد الأصغر إلى الجهاد الأكبر

تفسير الزمخشري

{ And wage jihad } : A command to go on attacks and strive in *jihad* against one's self and against passions; this is the greater *jihad* [*al-jihad al-akbar*]. The Prophet (SAW), returning from one of his attacks, said: We have returned from the lesser *jihad* to the greater *jihad*.

Tafsir Al-Zamakhshari

ويكون تأويل قوله ﴿ وجاهدوا في الله حق جهاده ﴾ و ﴿ حق تقاته ﴾ حقه الذي إحتمل وسعكم وبنيتكم وطاعتكم كقوله ﴿ فاتقوا الله ما استطعتم ﴾ فيكون هذا تفسيراً لقوله ﴿ حق تقاته ﴾ و ﴿ حق جهاده ﴾ ثم يحتمل قوله ﴿ وجاهدوا في الله ﴾ أي جاهدوا أنفسكم في شهوتها وأمانيها أو جاهدوا أعداء الله في دفع الوسواس والمحاربة معهم

تفسير الماتريدي

The interpretation of { And wage jihad for Allah as is due His *jihad* } and { as is due fear of Him } [Al 'Imran 102]: What is due Him is that which implies your capacity, your innate disposition, and your obedience, as in His word: { So fear Allah as best you can } [Al-taghabun 16]. And this is the explanation of His word: { as is due fear of Him } and { as is due His jihad } ; then this implies His word: { And wage jihad for Allah } : that is, wage *jihad* on yourselves against your desires and ambitions, or wage *jihad* on the enemies of Allah in driving away the Tempter and in battling them.

Tafsir Al-Maturidi

قوله تعالى ﴿ وجاهدوا في الله حق جهاده ﴾ قيل عنى به جهاد الكفار وقيل هو إشارة إلى إمتثال جميع ما أمر الله به والانتهاء عن كل ما نهى الله عنه أي جاهدوا أنفسكم في طاعة الله وردّها عن الهوى وجاهدوا الشيطان في ردّ وسوسته والظَّلَمَة في ردّ ظلمهم والكافرين في ردّ كفرهم قال إبن عطية وقال مقاتل وهذه الآية منسوخة بقوله تعالى ﴿ فاتقوا الله ما استطعتم ﴾ وكذا قال هبة الله إن قوله ﴿ حق جهده ﴾ وقوله في الآية الاخرى ﴿ حق تقاته ﴾ منسوخ بالتخفيف إلى الإستطاعة في هذه الأوامر ولا حاجة إلى تقدير النسخ فإن هذا هو المراد من أول الحكم لأن ﴿ حق جهاده ﴾ ما إرتفع عنه الحرج وقد روى سعيد بن المسيب قال قال رسول الله ﷺ خير دينكم أيسره وقال أبو جعفر النحاس وهذا مما لا يجوز أن يقع فيه نسخ لأنه واجب على الانسان كما روى حيوة بن شريح يرفعه إلى النبي ﷺ قال المجاهد من جاهد نفسه لله عز وجل

تفسير القرطبي

The word of the Most High: { And wage jihad for Allah as is due His *jihad* } : it is said that by this He means *jihad* against the disbelievers [*kuffar*]; and it is said that this refers to compliance with everything Allah has ordered and cessation of everything that Allah has forbidden; that is: Wage *jihad* on yourselves by obeying Allah and warding off your passions, wage *jihad* on Satan by warding off his tempting whispers, on oppressors by warding off their oppression, and on the disbelievers by warding off their disbelief. Ibn 'Atiyya said, and Muqatil said: This verse is abrogated by the word of the Most High: { So fear Allah as best you can } [Al-taghabun 16]; likewise HibatAllah said: Indeed His word { as is due His *jihad* } and His word in the other verse { as is due fear of Him } are abrogated by the "relief" to be just what one is capable of concerning these orders, and there is no need to presume abrogation. This then is the intended meaning of the first ruling, since uneasiness is not eliminated from { as is due His *jihad* } . Sa'id ibn Al-Musayyib narrated that the Messenger of Allah (SAW) said: The best part of your religion [*deen*] is the easiest part. And Abu Ja'far Al-Nahhas said: This belongs to that for which abrogation is not permissible, since it is a man's obligation; as Haywa ibn Shuraih narrated, directly from the Prophet (SAW), who said: A *mujahid* is one who wages *jihad* on himself for Allah Mighty and Sublime.

Tafsir Al-Qurtubi

﴿ هو اجتباكم ﴾ يقول هو اختاركم لدينه واصطفاكم لحرب أعدائه والجهاد في سبيله

تفسير الطبري

{ He has selected you all } ; He is saying: He has chosen you for His religion and picked you out to wage war on His enemies and *jihad* in His cause.

Tafsir Al-Tabari

﴿ هو اجتباكم ﴾ ومعناه أن التكليف تشريف من الله تعالى للعبد فلما خصكم بهذا التشريف فقد خصكم بأعظم التشريفات واختاركم لخدمته والإشتغال بطاعته فأي رتبة أعلى من هذا وأي سعادة فوق هذا

تفسير الرازي

{ He has selected you all } ; the meaning of this is that assigning this obligation is how Allah Most High honors His servants, for He has endowed you with the greatest of honors, and has chosen you for His service and to be preoccupied with obeying Him. Indeed what prestige is higher than this? And what happiness is above it?

Tafsir Al-Razi

* * *

Surah 25   Al-furqan [The Criterion]

﴿ فلا تطع الكافرين وجاهدهم به جهاداً كبيراً ﴾ الفرقان ٥٢

﴿ **So do not obey the disbelievers, but wage *jihad* against them with it in a great *jihad*** ﴾ Al-furqan 52

﴿ فلا تُطع الكافرين ﴾ في هواهم ﴿ وجاهدهم به ﴾ أي القرآن ﴿ جهاداً كبيراً ﴾

تفسير الجلالين

﴿ So do not obey the disbelievers ﴾ : in their whims; ﴿ but wage *jihad* on them with it ﴾ : that is, the Qur'an; ﴿ in a great *jihad* ﴾ .

Tafsir Al-Jalalain

قال ابن عباس قوله ﴿ فلا تطع الكافرين وجاهدهم به ﴾ قال بالقرآن ... قال ابن زيد في قوله ﴿ وجاهدهم به جهاداً كبيراً ﴾ قال الإسلام وقرأ ﴿ وأغلظ عليهم ﴾ وقرأ ﴿ وليجدوا فيكم غلظة ﴾ وقال هذا الجهاد الكبير

تفسير الطبري

Ibn 'Abbas, regarding His word ﴿ So do not obey the disbelievers, but wage *jihad* on them with it ﴾ , said: With the Qur'an. ... Ibn Zaid, regarding His word ﴿ But wage *jihad* on them with it in a great *jihad* ﴾ , said: Islam. And then he recited: ﴿ And be harsh to them ﴾ [Al-tahrim 9], and he recited: ﴿ And may they find harshness in you ﴾ [Al-tawba 12], and then he said: This is the great *jihad*.

Tafsir Al-Tabari

﴿ وجاهدهم به جهاداً كبيراً ﴾ فقال بعضهم المراد بذل الجهد في الأداء والدعاء وقال بعضهم المراد القتال وقال آخرون كلاهما والأقرب الأول لأن السورة مكية والأمر بالقتال ورد بعد الهجرة بزمان وإنما قال ﴿ جهاداً كبيراً ﴾ لأنه لو بعث في كل قرية نذيراً لوجب على كل نذير مجاهدة قريته فاجتمعت على رسول الله تلك المجاهدات وكثر جهاده من اجل ذلك وعظم فقال له ﴿ وجاهدهم ﴾ بسبب كونك نذير كافة القرى ﴿ جهاداً كبيراً ﴾ جامعاً لكل مجاهدة

تفسير الرازي

{ But wage *jihad* on them with it in a great *jihad* } ; some say that the meaning is to exert effort in carrying out one's duty and in making invocations, some say that the meaning is to fight, and others say both. The closest is the first, since this *surah* is from Mecca, and the command to fight came a certain time after the emigration [*hijra*]. Indeed He says: { In a great *jihad* } because if He sent forth someone to warn every village, He would oblige every warner to strive in *jihad* on his village, so all these strivings came together in the Messenger of Allah, and for this reason his *jihad* became greater and was exalted. So He says to him: { But wage *jihad* on them } : since you are to warn all villages; { in a great *jihad* } : that brings together all individual strivings in *jihad*.

Tafsir Al-Razi

Surah 29   Al-'ankabut [The Spider]

﴿ من كان يرجوا لقاء الله فإن أجل الله لآت وهو السميع العليم ومن جاهد فإنما يجاهد لنفسه إن الله لغني عن العالمين ﴾ العنكبوت ٥-٦

﴿ Whoever hopes in meeting Allah, indeed Allah comes with certainty; for He is the one who hears, the one who knows. And whoever wages *jihad*, indeed he wages *jihad* for himself; truly Allah is rich above any need for the worlds ﴾ Al-'ankabut 5-6

﴿ ومن جاهد فإنما يجاهد لنفسه ﴾ يقول ومن يجاهد عدوه من المشركين فإنما يجاهد لنفسه لأن يفعل ذلك ابتغاء الثواب من الله على جهاده والهرب من العقاب

تفسير الطبري

﴿ And whoever wages *jihad*, indeed he wages *jihad* for himself ﴾ ; He is saying: Whoever wages *jihad* against his enemy the Idolaters, indeed he wages *jihad* for himself, since he does this fixed on the reward from Allah for his *jihad* and escape from punishment.

Tafsir Al-Tabari

﴿ ومن جاهد فإنما يجاهد لنفسه ﴾ أي ومن جاهد في الدين وصبر على قتال الكفار وأعمال الطاعات فإنما يسعى لنفسه أي ثواب ذلك كله له ولا يرجع إلى الله نفعٌ من ذلك

تفسير القرطبي

﴿ And whoever wages *jihad*, indeed he wages *jihad* for himself ﴾ ; that is, whoever wages *jihad* in religion, and is steadfast in fighting the disbelievers [*kuffar*] and in acts of obedience, indeed he strives for himself, that is, all the reward for that is his, and no benefit from it goes to Allah.

Tafsir Al-Qurtubi

﴿ ومن جاهد فإنما يجاهد لنفسه ﴾ له ثوابه و الجهاد هو الصبر على الشدة ويكون ذلك في الحرب وقد يكون على مخالفة النفس

تفسير البغوي

{ And whoever wages *jihad*, indeed he wages *jihad* for himself } : the reward goes to him; and "jihad" is being steadfast in rigor; this is in warfare, or perhaps in opposing one's self.

Tafsir Al-Baghawi

﴿ ومن جاهد فإنما يجاهد لنفسه ﴾ يقول من يعمل الخير فإنما يعمل لنفسه يقول انما أعمالهم لأنفسهم

تفسير مقاتل بن سليمان

{ And whoever wages *jihad*, indeed he wages *jihad* for himself } ; He is saying: Whoever does good, indeed he does it for himself; He is saying: Indeed his deeds are for himself.

Tafsir Muqatil ibn Sulaiman

• • •

﴿ والذين جاهدوا فينا لنهدينهم سبلنا وإن الله لمع المحسنين ﴾ العنكبوت ٦٩

{ But those who wage *jihad* for Us, truly We will guide them in our ways; indeed Allah is surely with those who do good }
Al-'ankabut 69

لما فرغ من التقرير والتقريع ولم يؤمن الكفار سلّى قلوب المؤمنين بقوله ﴿ والذين جاهدوا فينا لنهدينّهم سبلنا ﴾ أي من جاهد بالطاعة هداه سبل الجنة

تفسير الرازي

When He had finished with the affirmations and rebukes, and the disbelievers [*kuffar*] still had not believed, He comforted the hearts of the Believers with His words: { But those who wage *jihad* for us, truly We will guide them in our ways } : that is, those who wage *jihad* out of obedience, He will guide them in the paths to *Jannah*.

Tafsir Al-Razi

قوله تعالى ﴿ والذين جاهدوا فينا ﴾ أي جاهدوا الكفار فينا أي في طلب مرضاتنا وقال السدي وغيره إن هذه الآية نزلت قبل فرض القتال قال إبن عطية فهي قبل الجهاد العرفي وإنما هو جهاد عام في دين الله وطلب مرضاته قال الحسن بن ابي الحسن الآية في العبّاد وقال إبن عباس وابراهيم بن أدهم هي في الذين يعملون بما يعلمون وقد قال ﷺ من عمل بما علم علّمه الله ما لم يعلم

تفسير القرطبي

The word of the Most High: { But those who wage *jihad* for Us } : that is, who wage *jihad* against the Disbelievers for Us, seeking our good pleasure. Al-Suddi and others said: This verse came down before fighting was made obligatory. Ibn 'Atiyya said: This was before routine *jihad*; indeed it is general *jihad* in Allah's religion [*deen*], seeking His good favor. Al-Hasan ibn Abi Al-Hasan said: This verse refers to the devout. Ibn 'Abbas and Ibrahim ibn Adham said: This refers to those who do what they know; He (SAW) said: Whoever does what he knows – Allah will teach him what he does not know.

Tafsir Al-Qurtubi

قوله تعالى ﴿ والذين جاهدوا فينا لنهدينّهم سبلنا ﴾ أي الذين جاهدوا الكفار لابتغاء مرضاتنا لنهدينهم سبلنا إلى الجنة أي لنوفقنّهم لإصابة الطريق المستقيمة وقيل معناه والذين قاتلوا لأجلنا اعداءنا لنهدينهم سبيل الشهادة والمغفرة

التفسير الكبير للطبراني

The word of the Most High: { But those who wage *jihad* for Us, truly We will guide them in our ways } : that is, those who wage *jihad* on the Disbelievers, intent on our good pleasure, truly We will guide them in our ways into *Jannah*, that is, We will bring them to success in reaching the straight path. It is also said that the meaning is: But those who fight our enemies for our sake, truly We will guide them in the way to martyrdom and forgiveness.

Al-Tabarani, Al-tafsir Al-kabir

· · ·

Surah 33   Al-ahzab [The Confederates]

﴿ قل لن ينفعكم الفرار إن فررتم من الموت أو القتل وإذا لا تمتعون إلا قليلا ﴾
الأحزاب ١٦

﴿ **Say: Running away will be of no use to you if you run away from death or killing, and even if so, you will be granted only brief enjoyment** ﴾ *Al-ahzab* 16

ثم أخبرهم أن فرارهم ذلك لا يؤخر آجالهم ولا يطول اعمارهم بل ربما كان ذلك سبباً في تعجيل أخذهم غِرّة ولهذا قال تعالى ﴿ وإذا لا تُمتَّعُنَ إلا قليلاً ﴾ أي بعد هربكم وفراركم

تفسير ابن كثير

Then He lets them know that their running away like that will not postpone their appointed moment, nor will it prolong their lives, but rather may be a reason for hastening their being taken unexpectedly; for this reason the Most High says: ﴿ And even if so, you will be granted only brief enjoyment ﴾ .

Tafsir Ibn Kathir

أمر الله تعالى نبيه في هذه الآية أن يخاطبهم بتوبيخ فأعلمهم بأن الفرار لا ينجيهم من القدر وأعلمهم أنهم لا يتمتعون في تلك الأوطان كثيراً بل تنقطع أعمارهم في يسير من المدة

تفسير ابن عطية

In this verse Allah Most High orders His Prophet to address them with rebuke, and let them know that running away will not save them from destiny, and to let them know that they will not be granted much enjoyment in those lands, but that their lives will be cut off within a trivial period of time.

Tafsir Ibn 'Atiyya

يقول تعالى ذكره لنبيه محمد ﷺ ﴿ قل ﴾ يا محمد لهؤلاء الذين يستأذنونك في الإنصراف عنك ويقولون إن بيوتنا عورة ﴿ لا ينفعكم الفرار إن فررتم من الموت أو القتل ﴾ يقول لأن ذلك أو ما كتب الله منهما وأصل اليكم بكل حال كرهتم أو احببتم ﴿ وإذاً لا تمتعون إلا قليلاً ﴾ يقول وإذا فررتم من الموت أو القتل لم يزد فراركم ذلك في أعماركم وآجالكم بل انما تمتعون في هذه الدنيا إلى الوقت الذي كتب لكم ثم يأتيكم ما كتب لكم وعليكم

تفسير الطبري

He (may his remembrance be exalted) is saying to His Prophet Muhammad (SAW): { Say } : Oh Muhammad, to these who have sought permission from you to turn back from you, and say "Indeed our houses are exposed" : { Running away will be of no use to you if you run away from death or killing } . He is saying: Because of this, or what Allah has decreed of either of them and what He has established for you in all circumstances, whether you like it or dislike it. { And even so, you will be granted only brief enjoyment } ; He is saying: If you run away from death or killing, this will not add anything to your lifetime or your appointed moment, but rather you will be granted enjoyment in this world only until the time that has been decreed for you, and then what has been decreed for you and required of you will come upon you.

Tafsir Al-Tabari

﴿ قل لن ينفعكم الفرار إن فررتم من الموت أو القتل ﴾ فإنه لا بد لكل شخص من حتف النف أو قتل في وقت معين سبق به القضاء وجرى عليه القلم

تفسير البيضاوي

{ Say: running away will be of no use to you if you run away from death or killing } : indeed every individual must face a natural death or be killed, at the specific time that has been decreed beforehand and over which the pen has written.

Tafsir Al-Baydawi

* * *

﴿ من المؤمنين رجال صدقوا ما عاهدوا الله عليه فمنهم من قضى نحبه ومنهم من ينتظر وما بدلوا تبديلا ﴾ الاحزاب ٢٣

{ **Among the Believers are men who were true to what they pledged to Allah, among them are those who consummated their release from life, and among them are those who wait, and have not at all wavered** } *Al-ahzab 23*

عن أنس رضي الله عنه قال غاب عمي أنس بن النضر عن قتال بدر فقال يا رسول الله غبت عن أول قتال قاتلتَ المشركين لئن الله أشهدني قتال المشركين ليرينَّ الله ما اصنع فلما كان يوم أحد وانكشف المسلمون قال اللهم إني اعتذر إليك مما صنع هؤلاء يعني اصحابه وأبرأ إليك مما صنع هؤلاء يعني المشركين ثم تقدم فاستقبله

سعد بن معاذ فقال يا سعد بن معاذ الجنة وربِّ النضر إني أجد ريحها من دون أحُد قال سعد فما استطعتُ يا رسول الله ما صنع قال أنس فوجدنا به بِضعاً وثمانين ضربة بالسيف أو طعنة برمح أو رَمية بسهم ووجدناه قد قُتل وقد مثَّل به المشركون فما عرفه أحد إلا أختهُ ببنانه قال أنس كنا نرى أو نظن أن هذه الآية نزلت فيه وفي أشباهه ﴿ من المؤمنين رجال صدقوا ما عاهدوا الله عليه ﴾ إلى آخر الآية

صحيح البخاري، كتاب الجهاد والسِيَر

From Anas (may Allah be pleased with him), who said: My uncle Anas ibn Al-Nadr was absent at the battle of Badr. And he said: Oh Messenger of Allah, I was absent at the first battle you fought against the Idolaters; if Allah would have me be present to fight the Idolaters, truly Allah would see what I can do. On the day of Uhud, when the Muslims were overcome and fled, he said: Oh Allah! Truly I apologize to you for what these men have done (meaning his companions), and I denounce to you what these men have done (meaning the Idolaters). Then he went forward, and Sa'd ibn Mu'adh met up with him, and he said: Oh Sa'd ibn Mu'adh, *Jannah*! I swear by Al-Nadr's Lord, indeed I can smell its aroma from in front of Uhud. Sa'd said: I was not able, oh Messenger of Allah, to do what he did. Anas said: We found on him eighty-something strikes from swords, stabs from lances, or pierces from arrows. And we found him to have been killed and brutalized by the idolaters, and no one recognized him except his sister, by his fingertips. Anas said: We believed or reckoned that this verse came down regarding him and regarding those like him: { Among the Believers are men who were true to what they pledged to Allah } until the end of the verse.

Sahih Al-Bukhari, The book of jihad and campaigns

﴿ من المؤمنين رجال صدقوا ما عاهدوا الله عليه ﴾ من الثبات مع النبي ﷺ ﴿ فمنهم من قضى نَحْبَه ﴾ مات أو قُتل في سبيل الله ﴿ ومنهم من ينتظر ﴾ ذلك ﴿ وما بدَّلوا تبديلاً ﴾ في العهد بخلاف حال المنافقين

تفسير الجلالين

{ Among the Believers are men who were true to what they pledged to Allah } : in remaining firm with the Prophet (SAW); { among them are those who consummated their release from life } : they died or were killed in the cause of Allah; { and among them are those who wait } : for this; { and have not at all wavered } : in the covenant, in contrast to the situation with the hypocrites.

Tafsir Al-Jalalain

قول تعالى ذكره ﴿ من المؤمنين ﴾ بالله ورسوله ﴿ رجال صدقوا ما عاهدوا الله عليه ﴾ يقول أوفوا بما عاهدوه عليه من الصبر على البأساء والضرَّاء وحين البأس ﴿ فمنهم من قضى نحبه ﴾ يقول فمنهم من فرغ من العمل الذي كان نذره لله وأوجبه له على نفسه فإستشهد بعض يوم بدر وبعض يوم أحد وبعض في غير ذلك من

المواطن ﴿ ومنهم من ينتظر ﴾ قضاءه والفراغ منه كما قضى من مضى منهم على الوفاء لله بعهده والصبر من الله والظفر على عدوه والنحب النذر في كلام العرب

تفسير الطبري

The word of Him whose remembrance is exalted: ﴿ Among the Believers ﴾ : in Allah and His Messenger; ﴿ are men who were true to what they pledged to Allah ﴾. He is saying: They fulfilled the steadfastness in combat and adversity that they had pledged to Him, and at the moment of valor, ﴿ among them were those who consummated their release from life ﴾ ; He is saying: Among them were those who completed the work which they had vowed to Allah, and which they had made their personal obligation to Him. Some were martyred on the day of Badr, some on the day of Uhud, and some in other places. ﴿ And among them are those who wait ﴾ : To fulfill it and to complete it, just as those who have gone before them fulfilled their loyalty to Allah in their pledge. Steadfastness is from Allah, and the victory is over His enemy. "Release from life" is a vow in the way the Arabs spoke.

Tafsir Al-Tabari

نذر رجال من الصحابة أنهم إذا لقوا حرباً مع رسول الله ﷺ ثبتوا وقاتلوا حتى يستشهدوا وهم عثمان بن عفان وطلحة بن عبيد الله وسعيد بن زيد بن عمرو بن نفيل وحمزة ومصعب بن عمير وغيرهم رضي الله عنهم ﴿ فمنهم من قضى نحبه ﴾ يعني حمزة ومصعباً ﴿ ومنهم من ينتظر ﴾ يعني عثمان وطلحة وفي الحديث من أحب أن ينظر إلى شهيد يمشي على وجه الأرض فلينظر إلى طلحة فإن قلت ما قضاء النحب قلت وقع عبارة عن الموت لأن كل حي لا بد له من أن يموت فكأنه نذر لازم في رقبته فإذا مات فقد قضى نحبه أي نذره وقوله ﴿ فمنهم من قضى نحبه ﴾ يحتمل موته شهيداً ويحتمل وفاءه بنذره من الثبات مع رسول الله ﷺ

تفسير الزمخشري

Some men among the Companions made a vow that, if they faced war alongside the Messenger of Allah (SAW), they would remain firm and fight until they were martyred. These were 'Uthman ibn 'Affan, Talha ibn 'Ubaid Allah, Sa'id ibn Zaid ibn 'Amr ibn Nufail, Hamza, Mus'ab ibn 'Umair, and others (may Allah be pleased with them). ﴿ And among them are those who consummated their release from life ﴾ : that is, Hamza and Mus'ab; ﴿ and among them are those who wait ﴾ : that is, 'Uthman and Talha; the *hadith* says: Whoever desires to see a martyr walking on the face of the earth, let him look at Talha. And if you should ask: What is "consummation of release from life"?, I would say an expression for death, because every living being must die, and as if it were a vow, it is required of him. If he dies, he has consummated his release from life, that is, his vow; and His word ﴿ And among them are those who consummated their release from life ﴾ implies their death as martyrs, and implies loyalty to their vow to stay firm with the Messenger of Allah (SAW).

Tafsir Al-Zamakhshari

∙ ∙ ∙

﴿ وردَّ اللهُ الذين كفروا بغيظهم لم ينالوا خيراً وكفى اللهُ المؤمنينَ القتالَ وكان اللهُ قوياً عزيزاً وأنزل الذين ظاهروهم من أهل الكتاب من صياصيهم وقذف في قلوبهم الرعب فريقاً تقتلون وتأسرون فريقاً وأورثكم أرضهم وديارهم وأموالهم وأرضاً لم تطؤوها وكان اللهُ على كل شيء قديراً ﴾ الاحزاب ٢٥-٢٧

﴾ Allah turned back those who disbelieved, in their fury, and they gained nothing; and Allah spared the believers from fighting; indeed Allah is strong, mighty. And He made those of the People of the Book who supported them come down from their bastions, and flung terror into their hearts; you killed some, and you took some captive. And He bequeathed to you their land, their homes, their property, and land you have not walked on; and Allah has power to do all things ﴿ Al-ahzab 25-27

﴿ وردَّ الله الذين كفروا ﴾ يعني الأحزاب

تفسير البيضاوي

﴾ Allah turned back those who disbelieved ﴿ : that is, the Confederates.

Tafsir Al-Baydawi

يقول تعالى مخبراً عن الأحزاب لما أجلاهم عن المدينة بما أرسل عليهم من الريح والجنود الإلهية ولولا أن الله جعل رسوله رحمة للعالمين لكانت هذه الريح عليهم أشد من الريح العقيم التي أرسلها على عاد ولكن قال تعالى ﴿ وما كان الله ليعذّبهم وأنت فيهم ﴾ فسلط عليهم هواء فرق شملهم كما كان سبب اجتماعهم من الهوى وهم أخلاط من قبائل شتى احزاب وآراء فناسب أن يرسل عليهم الهواء الذي فرق جماعتهم وردهم خائبين خاسرين بغيظهم وحنقهم ولم ينالوا خيراً لا في الدنيا مما كان في أنفسهم من الظفر والمغنم ولا في الآخرة بما تحملوه من الآثام في مبارزة الرسول ﷺ بالعداوة وهمهم بقتله وإستئصال جيشه ومن هم بشيء وصدق همه بفعله فهو في الحقيقة كفاعله ... فلما أيده الله تعالى ونصره وكبت الأعداء وردهم خائبين بأخسر صفقة ورجع رسول الله ﷺ إلى المدينة مؤيداً منصوراً ووضع الناس السلاح فبينما رسول الله ﷺ يغتسل من وعثاء تلك المرابطة في بيت أم سلمة رضي الله عنها إذ تبدى له جبريل عليه الصلاة والسلام معتجراً بعمامة من استبرق على بغلة عليها قطيفة من ديباج فقال أوضعت السلاح يا رسول الله ﷺ قال ﷺ نعم قال لكن الملائكة لم تضع

أسلحتها وهذا الآن رجوعي من طلب القوم ثم قال إن الله تبارك وتعالى يأمرك أن تنهض إلى بني قريظة وفي رواية فقال له عذيرك من مقاتل أوضعت السلاح قال نعم قال لكنا لم نضع اسلحتنا بعد أنهض إلى هؤلاء قال ﷺ أين قال بني قريظة فإن الله تعالى أمرني أن أزلزل عليهم فنهض رسول الله ﷺ من فوره وأمر الناس بالمسير إلى نبي قريظة وكانت على أميال من المدينة وذلك بعد صلاة الظهر

تفسير ابن كثير

The Most High is informing about the Confederates, how He drove them away from Medina with the wind and divine armies that He sent against them. If Allah had not made His Messenger a mercy to the worlds, this wind would have been even more severe on them than the barren wind that He sent against 'Ad; however the Most High said: { Surely it is not for Allah to punish them while you are among them } [Al-anfal 33]. And He empowered a wind against them that scattered their members as they had gathered together out of their liking. They were a mixture of tribes of a variety of parties and opinions, and so it was fitting for Him to send against them this wind that scattered their gatherings and sent them back frustrated, lost in their fury and their rage, having received nothing of good – neither the victory and spoils that they had longed for in this life, nor in the hereafter due to the sins that they had borne by fighting the Messenger (SAW) in enmity, and intending to kill him and eradicate his army. Whoever is intent on doing something and believes that his intent will be realized, is in reality just like someone who actually does it. … When Allah Most High came to his aid, championed him, held back the enemies, and sent them back frustrated in the worst kind of loss, the Messenger of Allah (SAW) returned to Medina championed and victorious, and the people laid down their weapons. And while the Messenger of Allah (SAW) was washing himself from the exertion of stationing the troops, in the house of Umm Salama (may Allah be pleased with her), behold Jibril (prayers and peace upon him) appeared to him with a gold-embroidered turban on his head and covering his face, riding a mule covered by a plush silk cloth. He said: Have you laid down the weapons, oh Messenger of Allah? He (SAW) replied: Yes. And Jibril said: But the angels have not laid down their weapons, and just now I am returning from pursuing people. Then he said: Indeed Allah Most Blessed and Exalted commands you to make haste towards the Banu Qurayza. In another narration he said to him: What an excuse of a fighter you are! Have you laid down the weapons? He replied: Yes. And Jibril said: But we have not yet laid down our weapons – Make haste towards them! He said: Where? Jibril said: Banu Qurayza; indeed Allah Most High has ordered me to shake them up. So the Messenger of Allah (SAW) made haste immediately and ordered people to advance towards Banu Quraiza, who were several miles from Medina. This was after the midday [dhuhr] prayer.

Tafsir Ibn Kathir

أي عاونوهم من أهل الكتاب وهم بنو قريظة من صياصيهم من قلاعهم وقذف في قلوبهم الرعب حتى سلموا أنفسهم للقتل واولادهم ونسائهم للسبي فريقاً تقتلون وهم الرجال وتأسرون فريقاً وهم الصبيان والنسوان

تفسير الرازي

That is, { those of the People of the Book } : who came to their aid, these being the Banu Quraiza, { from their bastions } : from their strongholds, { and flung terror into their hearts } : until they gave themselves over to being killed, and their women and children to being taken captive; { you killed some } : the men, { and you took some captive } : the women and children.

Tafsir Al-Razi

﴿ وقذف في قلوبهم الرعب ﴾ قال قتادة بصنيع جبريل بهم

تفسير الماوردي

{ And flung terror into their hearts } ; Qatada said: From what Jibril did to them.

Tafsir Al-Mawardi

. . .

﴿ لئن لم ينته المنافقون والذين في قلوبهم مرض والمرجفون في المدينة لنغرينك بهم ثم لا يجاورونك فيها إلا قليلاً ملعونين أينما ثقفوا أخذوا وقتلوا تقتيلاً سنة الله في الذين خلوا من قبل ولن تجد لسنة الله تبديلاً ﴾ الاحزاب ٦٠-٦٢

{ Indeed if the hypocrites, and those with sickness in their hearts, and those who spread lies in Medina, do not cease, surely We will incite you against them, then they will only be your neighbors there a little longer. They are cursed; wherever they can be reached, they will be taken and fiercely slaughtered. The way of Allah for those who came before; and you will not find the way of Allah to be altered } *Al-ahzab 60-62*

ثم قال تعالى متوعداً للمنافقين وهم الذين يظهرون الإيمان ويبطنون الكفر ﴿ والذين في قلوبهم مرض ﴾ قال عكرمة وغيره هم الزناة ههنا ﴿ والمُرجِفون في المدينة ﴾ يعني الذين يقولون جاء الأعداء وجاءت الحروب وهو كذب وافتراء لئن لم ينتهوا عن ذلك فيرجعون إلى الحق ﴿ لنُريِّنَك بهم ﴾ قال علي بن أبي طلحة عن إبن عباس أي لنسلطنك عليهم وقال قتادة لنحرشنك بهم وقال السدي لنعلمنك بهم ﴿ ثم لا يجاورونك فيها ﴾ أي في المدينة ﴿ إلا قليلاً ملعونين ﴾ حال منهم في مدة اقامتهم في المدينة مدة قريبة مطرودين مبعدين ﴿ أين ما ثُقِفوا ﴾ أي وجدوا ﴿ أخذوا ﴾ لذاتهم وقلتهم ﴿ وقتِّلوا تقتيلاً ﴾ ثم قال تعالى ﴿ سنة الله في الذين خلوا من قبل ﴾ أي هذه سنته في المنافقين إذا تمردوا على نفاقهم وكفرهم ولم يرجعوا عما هم فيه أن أهل الإيمان يسلطون عليهم ويقهرونهم

تفسير إبن كثير

Then the Most High declares a threat to the hypocrites, these being people who display belief but harbor disbelief; { and those with sickness in their hearts } : 'Ikrama and others said that here these are adulterers; { and those who spread lies in Medina } : that is, those who say "The enemies have come" or "Warfare has come" – these being lies and fabrications – if they do not cease from this and turn back to the truth; { surely We will incite you against them } : 'Ali ibn Abi Talha related from Ibn 'Abbas: "Surely we will give you authority over them", and Qatada said: "Surely We will rouse you up against them", and Al-Suddi said: "We will notify you about them"; { then they will only be your neighbors there } : that is, in Medina; { a little longer. They are cursed } : their situation as long as they stay in Medina – they will soon be forced out and banished. { Wherever they can be reached } : that is, found; { they will be taken } : because of who they are and their small number; { and fiercely slaughtered } . Then the Most High says: { The way [*sunnah*] of Allah for those who came before } : that is, this is His course of action regarding the hypocrites whenever they obstinately rebel in their hypocrisy and disbelief and do not turn away from what they are in – that the Believers are given authority over them and conquer them.

Tafsir Ibn Kathir

عن عطاء رضي الله عنه في قوله ﴿ والذين في قلوبهم مرض ﴾ قال كانوا مؤمنين وكان في أنفسهم أن يزنوا

الدر المنثور للسيوطي

'Ataa (may Allah be pleased with him), regarding His word { And those with sickness in their hearts } , said: These were Believers, but they had it in themselves to adulterate.

Al-Suyuti, Al-durr Al-manthur

﴿ والذين في قلوبهم مرض ﴾ قوم كان فيهم ضعف إيمان وقلة ثبات عليه وقيل هم الزناة وأهل الفجور من قوله تعالى ﴿ فيطمع الذي في قلبه مرض ﴾ ﴿ والمرجفون ﴾ ناس كانوا يرجفون بأخبار السوء عن سرايا رسول الله ﷺ فيقولون هزموا وقتلوا وجرى عليهم كيت وكيت فيكسرون بذلك قلوب المؤمنين

تفسير الزمخشري

{ And those with sickness in their hearts } : people who were weak in belief and scarcely able to remain firm in it; it is also said that these are those who adulterate and those given to prostitution, from the word of the Most High: { Such that those with sickness in their hearts might desire } [Al-ahzab 32]. { And those who spread lies } : people who would spread bad reports about the Messenger of Allah's (SAW) troops, saying that they had been defeated and killed and that such and such had befallen them – breaking the hearts of the Believers.

Tafsir Al-Zamakhshari

أي في ذلك القليل الذي يجاورونك فيه يكونون ملعونين مطرودين من باب الله وبابك وإذا خرجوا لا ينفكّون عن المذلة ولا يجدون ملجأ بل أينما يكونون يطلبون ويؤخذون ويقتلون

تفسير الرازي

That is, in that brief time that they are your neighbors, they are cursed, forced out of the domain of Allah and your domain; and if they leave they will not be able to break free from the disgrace, and they will not find refuge, but rather wherever they are, they will be sought out, taken, and killed.

Tafsir Al-Razi

﴿ أينما ثقفوا ﴾ يقول حيثما لُقوا من الأرض اخذوا وقتلوا لكفرهم بالله تقتيل

تفسير الطبري

{ Wherever they can be reached } ; He is saying: Wherever on earth they are met up with, they are taken and fiercely killed for their disbelief in Allah.

Tafsir Al-Tabari

﴿ أينما ثقفوا اخذوا وقتلوا تقتيلاً ﴾ فهذا فيه معنى الأمر بقتلهم وأخذهم أي هذا حكمهم إذا كانوا مقيمين على النفاق والإرجاف

تفسير القرطبي

{ Wherever they can be reached, they will be taken and fiercely slaughtered } : this is the meaning of the command to kill them and take them, that is, this is the ruling whenever they persist in hypocrisy and false rumors.

Tafsir Al-Qurtubi

﴿ لنغرينك ﴾ يا محمد ﴿ بهم ﴾ يقول لنحملنك على قتلهم ﴿ ثم لا يجاورونك فيها إلا قليلاً ﴾ ونجعلهم ﴿ ملعونين أينما ثقفوا ﴾ فأوجب لهم اللعنة على كل حال اينما وجدوا وادركوا ﴿ اخذوا وقتلوا تقتيلاً ﴾ يقول خذوهم واقتلوهم قتالاً فانتهوا عن ذلك مخافة القتل

تفسير مقاتل بن سليمان

{ We will incite you } : Oh Muhammad; { against them } ; He is saying: We will make you kill them; { then they will only be your neighbors there a little longer } ; and We will make them { cursed; wherever they can be reached } : and so He imposed a curse on them in every situation, wherever they are found or overtaken. { They will be taken and fiercely slaughtered } ; He is saying: Take hold of them and devastate them with killing. So then these people stopped doing those things out of fear of being killed.

Tafsir Muqatil ibn Sulaiman

قال قتادة ذُكر لنا أن المنافقين أرادوا أن يظهروا لما في قلوبهم من النفاق فأوعدهم الله في هذه الآية فكتموه

تفسير الثعلبي

Qatada said: It was mentioned to us that the hypocrites wanted to show the hypocrisy in their hearts, but Allah threatened them in this verse and so they kept it hidden.

Tafsir Al-Tha'labi

Surah 47   Muhammad

﴿ ذَلِكَ بِأَنَّ الَّذِينَ كَفَرُوا اتَّبَعُوا الْبَاطِلَ وَأَنَّ الَّذِينَ آمَنُوا اتَّبَعُوا الْحَقَّ مِن رَّبِّهِمْ كَذَلِكَ يَضْرِبُ اللَّهُ لِلنَّاسِ أَمْثَالَهُمْ فَإِذَا لَقِيتُمُ الَّذِينَ كَفَرُوا فَضَرْبَ الرِّقَابِ حَتَّى إِذَا أَثْخَنتُمُوهُمْ فَشُدُّوا الْوَثَاقَ فَإِمَّا مَنًّا بَعْدُ وَإِمَّا فِدَاءً حَتَّى تَضَعَ الْحَرْبُ أَوْزَارَهَا ذَلِكَ وَلَوْ يَشَاءُ اللَّهُ لَانتَصَرَ مِنْهُمْ وَلَكِن لِّيَبْلُوَ بَعْضَكُم بِبَعْضٍ وَالَّذِينَ قُتِلُوا فِي سَبِيلِ اللَّهِ فَلَن يُضِلَّ أَعْمَالَهُمْ ﴾ محمد ٣-٤

{ This is because those who have disbelieved have followed after futility, and because those who have believed have followed the truth from their Lord; thus Allah puts forth to people their parables. So whenever you face those who have disbelieved, strike the necks until you have thoroughly brought them down; and tighten the shackles. Afterwards either an act of kindness or ransom, until the war puts down its burdens. Such it is; and if Allah had willed, He would have avenged Himself of them, but rather that some of you might put others of you to the test. And those who are killed in the cause of Allah – their deeds will not be in vain } *Muhammad 3-4*

يقول تعالى مرشداً للمؤمنين إلى ما يعتمدونه في حروبهم مع المشركون ﴿ فَإِذَا لَقِيتُمُ الَّذِينَ كَفَرُوا فَضَرْبَ الرِّقَابِ ﴾ أي إذا واجهتموهم فاحصدوهم حصداً بالسيف ﴿ حَتَّى إِذَا أَثْخَنتُمُوهُمْ ﴾ أي أهلكتموهم قتلاً ﴿ فَشُدُّوا الْوَثَاقَ ﴾ الأسارى الذين تأسرونهم ثم أنتم بعد إنقضاء الحرب وإنفصال المعركة مخيرون في أمرهم إن شئتم مننتم عليهم فأطلقتم أساراهم مجاناً وإن شئتم فاديتموهم بمال تأخذونه منهم

تفسير ابن كثير

The Most High says this to the Believers as guidance toward how they should reckon in their wars with the idolaters [*mushrikun*]. { So whenever you face those who have disbelieved, strike the necks } : that is, whenever you face them, harvest them completely by the sword. { Until you have thoroughly brought them down } : that is, until you have ravaged them by killing. { And tighten the shackles } : the prisoners who you have taken captive. Then, after the war has ceased and the battle has disengaged, you may choose regarding their affair – if you like, you may show kindness to them and freely release their prisoners, or if you like, you may ransom them for a price you take from them.

Tafsir Ibn Kathir

فقال ﴿ فَإِذَا لَقِيتُمُ الَّذِينَ كَفَرُوا ﴾ من مشركي العرب بتوحيد الله تعالى ﴿ فَضَرْبَ الرِّقَابِ ﴾ يعني الأعناق ﴿ حَتَّى إِذَا أَثْخَنْتُمُوهُمْ ﴾ يعني قهرتموهم بالسيف وظهرتم عليهم ﴿ فَشُدُّوا الْوَثَاقَ ﴾ يعني الأسر ﴿ فَإِمَّا مَنًّا بَعْدُ ﴾ يعني عتقاً بعد الأسر فيمن عليهم ﴿ وَإِمَّا فِدَاءً ﴾ يقول فيفتدي نفسه بماله ليقوى به المسلمون على المشركين ثم نسختها آية السيف في براءة وهي قوله ﴿ فاقتلوا المشركين حيث وجدتموهم ﴾ يعني مشركي العرب ﴿ حتى تضع الحرب أوزارها ﴾ يعني ترك الشرك حتى لا يكون في العرب مشرك وأمر ألا يقبل منهم إلا الاسلام ثم إستأنف فقال ﴿ ذلك ﴾ يقول هذا أمر الله في المن والفداء حدثنا عبدالله قال حدثني أبي قال حدثني الهذيل قال قال مقاتل إذا أسلمت العرب وضعت الحرب أوزارها وقال في سورة الصف ﴿ فأيَّدنا الذين آمنوا على عدوهم فأصبحوا ظاهرين ﴾ بمحمد حين أسلمت العرب

تفسير مقاتل بن سليمان

He says: { So whenever you face those who have disbelieved } : among the Arabs who idolatrize against the oneness of Allah Most High ; { strike the necks } : that is, the neck in general; { until you have thoroughly brought them down } : that is, overpowered them by the sword and prevailed over them; { and tighten the shackles } : that is, imprisonment. { Afterwards either an act of kindness } : that is, release after being taken captive; { or ransom } : He is saying: He may use his wealth to ransom himself, so that with it the Muslims can be strengthened over the Idolaters. Then the verse of the sword in the "Absolution" *surah* abrogated it, this being His word: { Kill the idolaters wherever you find them } [Al-tawba 5] , that is, the Idolaters among the Arabs. { Until the war puts down its burdens } : that is, they abandon idolatry [*shirk*] until there are no more Idolaters among the Arabs; He orders that nothing but Islam be accepted from them. Then He continues and says: { Such it is } ; He is saying that this is a command from Allah for acts of kindness or ransom. Abdullah related to us, saying: My father related to me, from Al-Hudhail, from Muqatil, who said: When the Arabs yield into Islam, the war puts down its burdens. And He says in *surah Al-saff*: { We came to the aid of those who believed, against their enemy, and they became the ones who prevailed } [Al-saff 14] : by way of Muhammad, when the Arabs yielded into Islam.

Tafsir Muqatil ibn Sulaiman

قوله تعالى ﴿ فَإِذَا لَقِيتُمُ الَّذِينَ كَفَرُوا فَضَرْبَ الرِّقَابِ ﴾ أي إذا لقيتموهم في القتال فاضربوا رقابهم أي اقتلوهم والمعنى فاضربوا الرقاب ضرباً ... وعن ابن عباس قال هذه الآية منسوخة بقوله ﴿ فاقتلوا المشركين حيث وجدتموهم ﴾ وإليه ذهب أبو حنيفة وقال لا يجوز المنّ على الأسير ولا الفداء بالمال ولا بغير المال من الأسارى ولا يُباع السبي من أهل الحرب ... ولم يختلف أهل التفسير في أن التوبة نزلت بعد سورة محمد ﷺ ولا خلاف بين العلماء في جواز قتل الأسير وجواز قِسمة الأسارى بين المسلمين إذا لم يكن الأسارى من العرب وانما اختلفوا في جواز المنّ عليهم في مفاداتهم بالمال أو النفس ... وقال ابن عباس

معنى قوله ﴿ حتى تضع الحرب أوزارها ﴾ أي حتى لا يبقى أحدٌ من المشركين وقال مجاهد حتى لا يكون دين إلا الاسلام ... ومعنى الآية اتخِنوا المشركين بالقتل والأسر حتى يظهر الاسلام على الأديان كلها

التفسير الكبير للطبراني

The word of the Most High: { So whenever you face those who have disbelieved, strike the necks } : that is, whenever you face them in battle, strike their necks, that is, kill them; the meaning is "strike the necks hard." ... Ibn 'Abbas said: This verse is abrogated by His word: { Kill the idolaters wherever you find them } [Al-tawba 5]. This was the position taken by Abu Hanifa, who said: Acts of kindness to prisoners are not permitted, nor is ransom with wealth or anything else from the prisoners; and captives from the warring party are not to be sold. ... The expositors did not disagree that *Al-tawba* came down after surah *Muhammad* (SAW); and there is no disagreement among scholars concerning the permissibility of killing a prisoner or the permissibility of distributing the prisoners among the Muslims, whenever there are no prisoners from the Arabs. However, they did disagree regarding the permissibility of acts of kindness towards them in releasing them in return for money or them offering up themselves. ... Ibn 'Abbas said: The meaning of His word { Until the war puts down its burdens } is: Until none of the idolaters are left; Mujahid said: Until there is no religion but Islam. ... The meaning of this verse, therefore, is: Exhaust the idolaters by killing and imprisonment until Islam prevails over all religions.

Al-Tabarani, Al-tafsir Al-kabir

ثم قال ﴿ حتى تضع الحرب أوزارها ﴾ روي عن إبن عباس أنه قال حتى تترك الكفار إشراكها ويوحدوا الرب تبارك وتعالى حتى لا يبقى إلا مسلم أو مسالم يعني في ذمة المسلمين الذين يعطون الجزية وعن سعيد إبن جبير قال ﴿ حتى تضع الحرب أوزارها ﴾ قال خروج عيسى عليه السلام يكسر الصليب فيلقى الذئب الغنم فلا يأخذها ولا تكون عداوة بين إثنين وهكذا قال مجاهد

بحر العلوم للسمرقندي

Then He said: { Until the war puts down its burdens } ; it is narrated from Ibn 'Abbas that he said: Until the disbelievers [*kuffar*] stop associating others in worship, and they assert the oneness of the Lord Blessed and Exalted; until only Muslims and peaceable people remain, meaning under obligation to be safeguarded [*dhimma*] by the Muslims – those who give *jizya*. Sa'id ibn Jubair, regarding { Until the war puts down its burdens } , said: The coming of 'Isa (peace be upon him) to break the cross, when the wolf encounters the flock but does not seize it, and there is no more enmity between two; Mujahid said something similar.

Al-Samarqandi, Bahr Al-'ulum

قوله تعالى ﴿ فضرب الرقاب ﴾ إغراء والمعنى فاقتلوهم لأن الأغلب في موضع القتل ضرب العنق ﴿ حتى إذا أثخنتموهم ﴾ أي أكثرتم فيهم القتل ... قوله تعالى ﴿ حتى تضع الحرب أوزارها ﴾ قال ابن عباس حتى لا يبقى أحد من المشركين وقال مجاهد حتى لا يكون دين إلا دين الاسلام وقال سعيد بن جبير حتى يخرج المسيح وقال الفراء حتى لا يبقى إلا مسلم أو مسالم وفي معنى الكلام قولان احدهما حتى يضع أهل الحرب سلاحهم ... والثاني حتى تضع حربكم وقتالكم أوزار المشركين وقبائح أعمالهم بأن يسلموا ولا يعبدوا إلا الله ذكره الواحدي

تفسير ابن الجوزي

The word of the Most High { Strike the necks } : an urging; the meaning is: Kill them; since the most likely location to kill is to decapitate [*darb al-'unuq*, i.e. striking the neck]. { Until you have thoroughly brought them down } : that is, until you have made ample killing among them ... The word of the Most High: { Until the war puts down its burdens } ; Ibn 'Abbas said: Until none of the Idolaters are left. Mujahid said: Until there is no religion but the religion of Islam. Sa'id ibn Jubair said: Until the Messiah comes. Al-Farra said: Until only Muslims and peaceable people remain. Regarding the meaning of these words there are two points of view; one of them is: Until those waging war have put down their weapons. ... The second is: Until your waging of war and fighting have put down the burdens of the Idolaters and the abominations of their deeds, by them yielding into Islam and worshipping only Allah. Al-Wahidi mentioned this.

Tafsir Ibn Al-Jawzi

قوله تعالى ﴿ فإذا لقيتم الذين كفروا فضرب الرقاب ﴾ لما ميّز بين الفريقين أمر بجهاد الكفار قال ابن عباس الكفار المشركون عبدة الأوثان وقيل كل من خالف دين الاسلام من مشرك أو كتابي إذا لم يكن صاحب عهد ولا ذمّة ذكره الماوردي ... ﴿ فضرب الرقاب ﴾ مصدر قال الزجاج أي فاضربوا الرقاب ضرباً وخص الرقاب بالذكر لأن القتل أكثر ما يكون بها وقيل اقصدوا ضرب الرقاب وقال فضرب الرقاب ولم يقل فاقتلوهم لأن في العبارة بضرب الرقاب من الغلظة والشدة ما ليس في لفظ القتل لما فيه من تصوير القتل بأشنع صورة وهو حز العنق وإطارة العضو الذي هو رأس البدن وعلوّهُ وأوجهُ أعضائه ... ﴿ حتى تضع الحرب أوزارها ﴾ قال مجاهد وابن جبير هو خروج عيسى عليه السلام وعن مجاهد أيضاً أن المعنى حتى لا يكون دين إلا دين الاسلام فيسلم كل يهودي ونصراني وصاحب ملة

تفسير القرطبي

The word of the Most High: { So whenever you face those who have disbelieved, strike the necks } : when He distinguished between the two groups, He ordered *jihad* to be waged on the disbelievers. Ibn 'Abbas said: The idolatrizing disbelievers are idol-worshippers. And it is said: Any idolater or Person of the Book who opposes the religion of Islam, if they are under neither covenant nor obligation to be safeguarded [*dhimma*]; Al-Mawardi mentioned this. ... { Strike the necks } ; Al-Zajjaj said: That is, strike the necks hard. He makes specific mention of necks since most killing occurs in this manner. It is said: Aim to strike the necks. And He said: "strike the necks" rather than saying "kill them", because the expression "strike the necks" carries harshness and intensity not found in simply stating "kill", since in this way killing can be portrayed in the most heinous manner, this being nicking the neck and sending the member flying, the main part of the body, its highest point and the most honorable of its members. ... { Until the war puts down its burdens } ; Mujahid and Ibn Jubair said: This is the coming of 'Isa (peace be upon him); Mujahid also said that the meaning is: Until there is no religion but the religion of Islam, and every Jew, Christian, and adherent of any religion yields into Islam.

Tafsir Al-Qurtubi

﴿ وإذا لقيتم الذين كفروا فضرب الرقاب ﴾ مصدر بدل من اللفظ بفعله أي فاضربوا رقابهم أي اقتلوهم وعبر بضرب الرقاب أن الغالب في القتل أن يكون بضرب الرقبة ﴿ حتى إذا أثخنتموهم ﴾ أكثرتم فيهم القتل

تفسير الجلالين

{ So whenever you face those who have disbelieved, strike the necks } : the object, substituting for it by stating the action, namely, strike their necks, that is, kill them. And by "strike the necks" He expressed that most killing is to be done by striking the neck. { Until you have thoroughly brought them down } : until you have made ample killing among them.

Tafsir Al-Jalalain

﴿ وَيَقُولُ الَّذِينَ آمَنُوا لَوْلَا نُزِّلَتْ سُورَةٌ فَإِذَا أُنْزِلَتْ سُورَةٌ مُحْكَمَةٌ وَذُكِرَ فِيهَا الْقِتَالُ رَأَيْتَ الَّذِينَ فِي قُلُوبِهِمْ مَرَضٌ يَنْظُرُونَ إِلَيْكَ نَظَرَ الْمَغْشِيِّ عَلَيْهِ مِنَ الْمَوْتِ فَأَوْلَى لَهُمْ طَاعَةٌ وَقَوْلٌ مَعْرُوفٌ فَإِذَا عَزَمَ الْأَمْرُ فَلَوْ صَدَقُوا اللَّهَ لَكَانَ خَيْرًا لَهُمْ ﴾ محمد ٢٠-٢١

{ Those who have believed say: "Were that a surah would be sent down"; but when a surah that is firm was sent down, and fighting was mentioned in it, you saw those with sickness in their hearts look at you with the look of someone whose death is looming over them; it would have been worthier of them to obey and say good things. Then when the matter was decided, if they had remained true to Allah it would have been better for them } *Muhammad 20-21*

يقول تعالى مخبراً أن المؤمنين أنهم تمنوا شرعية الجهاد فلما فرضه الله عز وجل وأمر به نكل عنه كثير من الناس
تفسير ابن كثير

The Most High is reporting about the Believers, how they were hoping that *jihad* would be prescribed, but when Allah Mighty and Sublime made it an obligation, and commanded it, many people shied away from it.

Tafsir Ibn Kathir

﴿ وَيَقُولُ الَّذِينَ آمَنُوا ﴾ طلباً للجهاد ﴿ لَوْلَا ﴾ هلا ﴿ نُزِّلَتْ سُورَةٌ ﴾ فيها ذكر الجهاد ﴿ فَإِذَا أُنْزِلَتْ سُورَةٌ مُحْكَمَةٌ ﴾ أي لم ينسخ منها شيء ﴿ وَذُكِرَ فِيهَا الْقِتَالُ ﴾ أي طلبه ﴿ رَأَيْتَ الَّذِينَ فِي قُلُوبِهِمْ مَرَضٌ ﴾ أي شك وهم المنافقون ﴿ يَنْظُرُونَ إِلَيْكَ نَظَرَ الْمَغْشِيِّ ﴾ المغمى ﴿ عَلَيْهِ مِنَ الْمَوْتِ ﴾ خوفاً منه وكراهية له أي فهم يخافون من القتال ويكرهونه
تفسير الجلالين

{ Those who have believed say } : seeking *jihad*; { Were that } : Why is there not; { a surah would be sent down } : that mentions *jihad*; { but when a surah that is firm was sent down } : that is, nothing in it has been abrogated; { and fighting was mentioned in it } : that is, a call to it; { you saw those with sickness in their hearts } : that is, doubt – these are the hypocrites; { look at you with the look of someone whose death is looming over them } : fainting, fearful of it and averse towards it, that is, they are fearful of fighting and are averse towards it.

Tafsir Al-Jalalain

يقول تعالى ذكره ويقول الذين صدّقوا الله ورسوله هلّا نزلت سورة من الله تأمرنا بجهاد أعداء الله من الكفار ﴿ فإذا أُنزِلت سورة مُحكمة ﴾ يعني أنها محكمة بالبيان والفرائض ... عن قتادة قوله ﴿ ويقول الذين آمنوا لولا نزّلت سورة فإذا أنزلت سورة محكمة وذُكر فيها القتال ﴾ قال كل سورة ذُكر فيها الجهاد فهي محكمة وهي أشدّ القرآن على المنافقين

تفسير الطبري

He (may His remembrance be exalted) is saying: Those who have believed in Allah and His Messenger say: Why hasn't a surah come down from Allah that orders us to wage *jihad* on the disbelievers [*kuffar*], the enemies of Allah? } But when a surah that is firm was sent down { : that is, firm in declaration and obligation. ... Qatada, regarding His word { Those who have believed say: "Were that a surah would be sent down"; but when a surah that is firm was sent down, and fighting was mentioned in it } , said: Every *surah* in which *jihad* is mentioned is firm, and is the most severe of what is in the Qur'an against hypocrites.

Tafsir Al-Tabari

كانوا يدعون الحرص على الجهاد ويتمنونه بألسنتهم ويقولون ﴿ لولا نزلت سورة ﴾ في معنى الجهاد ﴿ فإذا أنزلت ﴾ وأمروا فيها بما تمنوا وحرصوا عليه كأعوا وشق عليهم ... ﴿ الذين في قلوبهم مرض ﴾ هم الذين كانوا على حرف غير ثابتي الأقدام ... ﴿ فلو صدقوا الله ﴾ فيما زعموا من الحرص على الجهاد أو فلو صدقوا في إيمانهم وواطأت قلوبهم فيه ألسنتهم

تفسير الزمخشري

They were invoking aspirations for *jihad*, and wanted it with their tongues, saying: { Were that a surah would be sent down } : meaning *jihad*; { but when a surah was sent down } : and in it they were ordered to carry out what they had wanted and aspired to, they groveled around and it was agonizing for them ... { Those with sickness in their hearts } : those who wavered and were not on firm footing ... { If they had remained true to Allah } : regarding the aspirations they alleged they had for *jihad*, or if they had remained true to their tongues concerning their belief and the soft voices in their hearts regarding it.

Tafsir Al-Zamakhshari

وقولهم ﴿ لولا نزلت سورة ﴾ المراد منه سورة فيها تكليف بمحن المؤمن والمنافق ثم إنه تعالى أنزل سورة فيها القتال فإنه أشق تكليف

تفسير الرازي

Their words: { Were that a surah would be sent down } : the intended meaning is a *surah* with an assignment to put the Believers and the hypocrites to the test. Indeed the Most High then sent down a *surah* with fighting in it, since this is truly the most difficult assignment.

Tafsir Al-Razi

﴿ رأيت الذين في قلوبهم مرض ﴾ أي شك ونفاق ... ﴿ فلو صدقوا الله ﴾ أي في الايمان والجهاد ﴿ لكان خيراً لهم ﴾ من المعصية والمخالفة

تفسير القرطبي

{ You saw those with sickness in their hearts } : that is, doubt and hypocrisy. ... { If they had remained true to Allah } : that is, regarding belief and *jihad*; { it would have been better for them } : than rebelling and objecting.

Tafsir Al-Qurtubi

﴿ رأيت الذين في قلوبهم مرض ﴾ يعني المنافقين ﴿ ينظرون إليك ﴾ شزراً بتحديق شديد كراهية منهم للجهاد وجبناً عن لقاء العدو

تفسير البغوي

{ You saw those with sickness in their hearts } : that is, the hypocrites; { look at you } : warily, staring intently, averse to *jihad,* and fainthearted to face the enemy.

Tafsir Al-Baghawi

قوله تعالى ﴿ فإذا عزم الأمر ﴾ قال الحسن جَدَّ الأمر وقال غيره جد رسول الله ﷺ وأصحابه في الجهاد ولَزِمَ فرضُ القتال

تفسير ابن الجوزي

The word of the Most High: { Then when the matter was decided } ; Al-Hasan said: When the matter got serious. Others have said: The Messenger of Allah (SAW) and his Companions strived earnestly in *jihad*, and the obligation to fight was imperative.

Tafsir Ibn Al-Jawzi

* * *

﴿ وَلَنَبْلُوَنَّكُمْ حَتَّى نَعْلَمَ الْمُجَاهِدِينَ مِنكُمْ وَالصَّابِرِينَ وَنَبْلُوَ أَخْبَارَكُمْ ﴾ محمد ٣١

{ **Surely We will put you all to the test so We can know those among you who wage *jihad*, and those who are steadfast; and We will test your reports** } *Muhammad* 31

﴿ وَلَنَبْلُوَنَّكُمْ ﴾ نختبركم ﴿ بالجهاد وغيره ﴾ ﴿ حَتَّى نَعْلَمَ ﴾ علم ظهور ﴿ الْمُجَاهِدِينَ مِنكُمْ وَالصَّابِرِينَ ﴾ في الجهاد وغيره ﴿ وَنَبْلُوَ ﴾ نظهر ﴿ أَخْبَارَكُمْ ﴾ من طاعتكم وعصيانكم في الجهاد وغيره

تفسير الجلالين

{ **Surely We will put you all to the test** } : We will test you with *jihad* and in other ways; { **so We can know** } : with clear knowledge; { **those among you who wage jihad, and those who are steadfast** } : in *jihad* and other things; { **and We will test** } : We will make clear; { **your reports** } : concerning your obedience and disobedience in *jihad* and other things.

Tafsir Al-Jalalain

يقول تعالى ذكره لأهل الإيمان به من أصحاب رسول الله ﷺ ﴿ وَلَنَبْلُوَنَّكُمْ ﴾ أيها المؤمنون بالقتل وجهاد أعداء الله ﴿ حَتَّى نَعْلَمَ الْمُجَاهِدِينَ مِنكُمْ ﴾ يقول حتى نعلم حزبي وأوليائي أهل الجهاد في الله منكم وأهل الصبر على قتال أعدائه فيظهر ذلك لهم ويعرف ذوو البصائر منكم في دينه من ذوي الشكّ والحَيرة فيه وأهل الايمان من أهل النفاق ونبلو أخباركم فنعرف الصادق منكم من الكاذب

تفسير الطبري

He (may His remembrance be exalted) is saying to those of the Messenger of Allah's (SAW) Companions who believe in Him: { **Surely We will put you all to the test** } : oh Believers, with killing and *jihad* against the enemies of Allah. { **So We can know those among you who wage jihad** } ; He is saying: So We can know who my party is, and my associates, those of you who wage *jihad* for Allah and those who are steadfast in fighting His enemies. And so He will make this clear to them, and those of you who show insight in their religion [*deen*] will be distinguished from those who doubt and are perplexed in it, those who believe from those who are hypocrites; and We will test your reports, so that We may know who among you is genuine from who is a liar.

Tafsir Al-Tabari

﴿ وَلَنَبْلُوَنَّكُمْ ﴾ بالأمر بالجهاد وسائر التكاليف الشاقة ﴿ حتى نعلم المجاهدين منكم والصابرين ﴾ على مشاقه

تفسير البيضاوي

{ Surely We will put you all to the test } : by ordering *jihad* and the other burdensome obligations; { So We can know those among you who wage jihad, and those who are steadfast } : in their hardships.

Tafsir Al-Baydawi

﴿ وَلَنَبْلُوَنَّكُمْ ﴾ ولنعاملنكم معاملة المختبر بأن نأمركم بالجهاد والقتال ﴿ حتى نعلم المجاهدين منكم والصابرين ﴾ أي علم الوجود يريد حتى يتبين المجاهد والصابر على دينه من غيره ﴿ ونبلوا أخباركم ﴾ أي نظهرها ونكشفها بإباء من يأبى القتال ولا يصبر على الجهاد

تفسير البغوي

{ Surely We will put you all to the test } : and surely We will deal with you in the way those who are tested are dealt with, by ordering you to wage *jihad* and fight; { so We can know those among you who wage *jihad*, and those who are steadfast } : that is, to find out, meaning: So it can become clear who wages *jihad* and is steadfast in his religion from those who are not; { and We will test your reports } : that is, We will make them clear and expose them by way of the refusal of those who refuse to fight and are not steadfast in *jihad*.

Tafsir Al-Baghawi

قال ابراهيم بن الأشعث كان الفضل إذا قرأ هذه الآية بكى وقال اللهم لا تبلنا فإنك إن بلوتنا هتكت أستارنا وفضحتنا

تفسير الثعلبي

Ibrahim ibn Al-Ash'ath said: Al-Fadl, whenever he recited this verse, would weep and say: Oh Allah! Put us not to the test, for indeed if you put us to the test, you will expose our pretexts and bring shame upon us.

Tafsir Al-Tha'labi

﴿ إِنَّ الَّذِينَ كَفَرُوا وَصَدُّوا عَن سَبِيلِ اللَّهِ ثُمَّ مَاتُوا وَهُمْ كُفَّارٌ فَلَن يَغْفِرَ اللَّهُ لَهُمْ فَلَا تَهِنُوا وَتَدْعُوا إِلَى السَّلْمِ وَأَنتُمُ الْأَعْلَوْنَ وَاللَّهُ مَعَكُمْ وَلَن يَتِرَكُمْ أَعْمَالَكُمْ ﴾ محمد ٣٤-٣٥

{ Indeed those who have disbelieved and obstruct the cause of Allah, and then die, they are the disbelievers and Allah will not forgive them. So do not grow weary and make a call to peace when you are the ones on top; Allah is with you and will not defraud you of your works } *Muhammad 34-35*

يقول تعالى ذكره فلا تضعفوا أيها المؤمنون بالله عن جهاد المشركين وتجبُنوا عن قتالهم

تفسير الطبري

He (may His remembrance be exalted) is saying: Do not be weary, oh Believers in Allah, of *jihad* against the idolaters [*mushrikeen*], or lose courage in fighting them.

Tafsir Al-Tabari

قال الزجاج منع الله المسلمين أن يدعوا الكفار إلى الصلح وأمرهم بحربهم حتى يسلموا

التفسير الكبير للطبراني

Al-Zajjaj said: Allah prohibited the Muslims from calling the disbelievers [*kuffar*] to a truce, but ordered them to wage war on them until they yielded into Islam.

Al-Tabarani, Al-tafsir Al-kabir

وفي هذه الآية دليل على أن أيدي المسلمين إذا كانت عالية على المشركين لا ينبغي لهم أن يجيبوهم إلى الصلح لأن فيه ترك الجهاد

بحر العلوم للسمرقندي

In this verse is proof that the hands of the Muslims, whenever they are raised over the idolaters – there is no need for them to respond to them with a truce, since this implies abandoning *jihad*.

Al-Samarqandi, Bahr Al-'ulum

واختلف العلماء في حكمها فقيل إنها ناسخة لقوله تعالى ﴿ وإن جنحوا للسلم فاجنح لها ﴾ لأن الله تعالى منع من الميل إلى الصلح إذا لم يكن بالمسلمين حاجة إلى الصلح وقيل منسوخة بقوله تعالى ﴿ وإن جنحوا للسلم فاجنح لها ﴾ وقيل هي محكمة والآيتان نزلتا في وقتين مختلفي الحال وقيل إن قوله ﴿ وإن جنحوا للسلم فاجنح لها ﴾ مخصوص في قوم بأعيانهم والاخرى عامة فلا يجوز مهادنة الكفار إلا عند الضرورة وذلك إذا عجزنا عن مقاومتهم لضعف المسلمين

تفسير القرطبي

Scholars differ with respect to its ruling; it is said that this abrogates the word of the Most High: { And if they incline to peace, then incline to it } [Al-anfal 61], since Allah Most High prohibited an inclination towards truce if the Muslims were not in need of a truce. It is also said that it is itself abrogated by the word of the Most High: { And if they incline to peace, then incline to it } ; it is said: this is firm. Both these verses came down in two times of differing circumstances. It is said: Indeed His word { And if they incline to peace, then incline to it } was a special case for a specific group, while the other verse is general. It is not permissible to conclude a truce with the disbelievers except when necessary, this being whenever we are prevented from combatting them due to the weakness of the Muslims.

Tafsir Al-Qurtubi

∗ ∗ ∗

Surah 48   Al-fath [The Victory]

﴿ قُلْ لِلْمُخَلَّفِينَ مِنَ الْأَعْرَابِ سَتُدْعَوْنَ إِلَىٰ قَوْمٍ أُولِي بَأْسٍ شَدِيدٍ تُقَاتِلُونَهُمْ أَوْ يُسْلِمُونَ فَإِنْ تُطِيعُوا يُؤْتِكُمُ اللَّهُ أَجْرًا حَسَنًا وَإِنْ تَتَوَلَّوْا كَمَا تَوَلَّيْتُمْ مِنْ قَبْلُ يُعَذِّبْكُمْ عَذَابًا أَلِيمًا ﴾ الفتح ١٦

﴿ Say to those of the Bedouins who stayed behind: You will be called to a people of great might, you will fight them or they will yield; and if you obey, Allah will grant you a fine reward, but if you turn away as you turned away before, He will punish you painfully ﴾ Al-fath 16

﴿ تُقَاتِلُونَهُمْ أَوْ يُسْلِمُونَ ﴾ يعني شرع لكن جهادهم وقتالهم فلا يزال مستمراً عليهم ولكم النصرة عليهم أو يسلمون فيدخلون في دينكم بلا قتال بل بإختيار ثم قال عز وجل ﴿ فإن تطيعوا ﴾ أي تستجيبوا وتنفروا في الجهاد وتؤدوا الذي عليكم فيه
تفسير ابن كثير

﴿ You will fight them or they will yield ﴾ : that is, *jihad* against them and fighting them is prescribed for you, unceasingly, your continuous obligation; and you are to either gain victory over them or they yield [*yuslimun*, i.e. become Muslims] and enter into your religion without fighting but by choice. Then the Mighty and Sublime says: ﴿ And if you obey ﴾ : that is, if you respond, and mobilize for *jihad*, and carry out your duty concerning this.

Tafsir Ibn Kathir

ومعنى ﴿ يسلمون ﴾ ينقادون
تفسير الزمخشري

The meaning of ﴿ they yield ﴾ is: they comply.

Tafsir Al-Zamakhshari

﴿ تقاتلونهم أو يسلمون ﴾ معناه تقاتلوهم أن يكون منهم الاسلام
التفسير الكبير للطبراني

﴿ You will fight them or they will yield ﴾ : this means you fight them to get *islam* ["yielding"] from them.

Al-Tabarani, Al-tafsir Al-kabir

﴿ تقاتلونهم أو يسلمون ﴾ هذا حكم من لا يؤخذ منهم الجزية وهو معطوف على تقاتلونهم أي يكون أحد الأمرين إما المقاتلة وإما الاسلام لا ثالث لهما

تفسير القرطبي

{ You will fight them or they will yield } : this is the ruling for those from whom *jizya* is not taken. This is coupled with "You will fight them", that is, one of the two options will hold – either fighting, or Islam; there is no third option besides these two.

Tafsir Al-Qurtubi

والظاهر أن هؤلاء المقاتلون ليسوا ممن تؤخذ منهم الجزية إذ لم يذكر هنا إلا القتال أو الاسلام ومذهب ابي حنيفة رحمه الله تعالى ورضي عنه أن الجزية لا تقبل من مشركي العرب ولا من المرتدين وليس إلا الإسلام أو القتل

البحر المحيط لابي حيان

It is clear that the ones being fought are not those from whom *jizya* is taken, since here only fighting or Islam are mentioned. The teaching of Abu Hanifa (may Allah Most High have mercy on him and be pleased with him) is that *jizya* is not accepted from Idolaters among the Arabs nor from apostates; it is only Islam or be killed.

Abu Hayyan, Al-bahr Al-muhit

﴿ يعذّبكم عذاباً أليماً ﴾ يعني وجيعاً وذلك عذاب النار على عصيانكم إياه وتركّكم جهادهم وقتالهم مع المؤمنين

تفسير الطبري

{ He will punish you painfully } : that is, grievously; this punishment is Hellfire, because of your disobedience to Him and your neglecting to wage *jihad* on them and fight them along with the Believers.

Tafsir Al-Tabari

* * *

﴿ لَيْسَ عَلَى الْأَعْمَى حَرَجٌ وَلَا عَلَى الْأَعْرَجِ حَرَجٌ وَلَا عَلَى الْمَرِيضِ حَرَجٌ وَمَنْ يُطِعِ اللَّهَ وَرَسُولَهُ يُدْخِلْهُ جَنَّاتٍ تَجْرِي مِنْ تَحْتِهَا الْأَنْهَارُ وَمَنْ يَتَوَلَّ يُعَذِّبْهُ عَذَابًا أَلِيمًا ﴾ الفتح ١٧

{ There is no blame on the blind, no blame on the lame, no blame on the sick. Whoever obeys Allah and His Messenger, He will admit him into gardens below which flow rivers, but whoever turns away, He will punish him painfully } Al-fath 17

﴿ لَيْسَ عَلَى الْأَعْمَى حَرَجٌ وَلَا عَلَى الْأَعْرَجِ حَرَجٌ وَلَا عَلَى الْمَرِيضِ حَرَجٌ ﴾ في ترك الجهاد

تفسير الجلالين

{ There is no blame on the blind, no blame on the lame, no blame on the sick } : for abstaining from *jihad*.

Tafsir Al-Jalalain

ثم ذكر تعالى الأعذار في ترك الجهاد فمنها لازم كالعمى والعرج المستمر وعارض كالمرض الذي يطرأ أياماً ثم يزول فهو في حال مرضه ملحق بذوي الأعذار اللازمة حتى يبرأ ثم قال تبارك وتعالى مرغباً في الجهاد وطاعة الله ورسوله ﴿ وَمَنْ يُطِعِ اللَّهَ وَرَسُولَهُ يُدْخِلْهُ جَنَّاتٍ تَجْرِي تَحْتَهَا الْأَنْهَارُ وَمَنْ يَتَوَلَّ ﴾ أي ينكل عن الجهاد ويقبل على المعاش ﴿ يُعَذِّبْهُ عَذَابًا أَلِيمًا ﴾ في الدنيا بالمذلة وفي الآخرة بالنار والله تعالى أعلم

تفسير ابن كثير

Then the Most High mentions the excuses for abstaining from *jihad*; among them permanent conditions such as blindness or persistent lameness, and passing conditions that appear for a few days and then cease. In the latter case, as long as he is sick, one may join those with permanent excuses until he recovers. Then the Most Blessed and Exalted said, rousing desire for *jihad* and obedience to Allah and His Messenger: { Whoever obeys Allah and His Messenger, He will admit him into gardens below which flow rivers, but whoever turns away } : that is, shies away from *jihad*, occupying himself in his livelihood, { He will punish him painfully } : by humiliation in this world, and by Hellfire in the next. And Allah Most High knows best.

Tafsir Ibn Kathir

نفى الحرج عن هؤلاء من ذوي العاهات في التخلف عن الغزو

تفسير الزمخشري

This removes any blame from those with disabilities regarding staying behind from going on attacks.

Tafsir Al-Zamakhshari

بين من يجوز له التخلف وترك الجهاد وما بسببه يجوز ترك الجهاد وهو ما يمنع من الكر والفر وبين ذلك ببيان ثلاثة اصناف الأول ﴿ الأعمى ﴾ فإنه لا يمكنه الإقدام على العدو والطلب ولا يمكنه الاحتراز والهرب والأعرج كذلك والمريض كذلك وفي معنى الأعرج الأقطع والمقعد بل ذلك أولى بأن يعذر ومن به عرج لا يمنعه من الكر والفر لا يعذر وكذلك المرض القليل الذي لا يمنع من الكر والفر كالطحال والسعال إذ به يضعف وبعض أوجاع المفاصل لا يكون عذراً

تفسير الرازي

This clarifies who is permitted to stay behind and abstain from *jihad*, and the reasons for which it is permissible to abstain from *jihad*. This is anything that prevents attacking and retreating, and this is made clear by stating three categories. The first is { the blind }, for indeed they can not attack or pursue the enemy, and they can not be on the lookout or flee. The lame are similar, as are the sick. Lameness implies those who are amputees or crippled, indeed that is even more reason for them to have an excuse. Those with a lameness that does not prevent them from attacking and retreating have no excuse, and similarly for those with light sickness that does not prevent attacking and retreating, such as disease of the spleen or a cough, if they are merely weakened by it; nor do certain joint pains warrant an excuse.

Tafsir Al-Razi

﴿ ومن يتول يعذبه عذاباً أليماً ﴾ إذ الترهيب هاهنا أنفع من الترغيب

تفسير البيضاوي

{ But whoever turns away, He will punish him painfully } : Since in this case a threat is more effective than rousing desire.

Tafsir Al-Baydawi

• • •

﴿ لَقَدْ رَضِيَ اللَّهُ عَنِ الْمُؤْمِنِينَ إِذْ يُبَايِعُونَكَ تَحْتَ الشَّجَرَةِ فَعَلِمَ مَا فِي قُلُوبِهِمْ فَأَنْزَلَ السَّكِينَةَ عَلَيْهِمْ وَأَثَابَهُمْ فَتْحًا قَرِيبًا وَمَغَانِمَ كَثِيرَةً يَأْخُذُونَهَا وَكَانَ اللَّهُ عَزِيزًا حَكِيمًا ﴾ الفتح ١٨-١٩

{ Allah was pleased with the Believers, when they pledged allegiance to you under the tree, and knew what is in their hearts, so He sent down peaceful reassurance upon them and rewarded them with an impending victory, and many spoils for them to take; and Allah is mighty, wise } *Al-fath 18-19*

﴿ لقد رضي الله عن المؤمنين إذ يبايعونك ﴾ بالحديبية ﴿ تحت الشجرة ﴾ هي سَمُرة وهم ألف وثلاثمائة أو الكثر ثم بايعهم على أن يناجزوا قريشاً وأن لا يفرّوا وعلى الموت ﴿ فعلم ﴾ الله ﴿ ما في قلوبهم ﴾ من الصدق والوفاء ﴿ فأنزل السكينة عليهم وأثابهم فتحاً قريباً ﴾ هو فتح خيبر بعد انصرافهم من الحديبية
تفسير الجلالين

{ Allah was pleased with the Believers, when they pledged allegiance to you } : at Hudaibiyya; { under the tree } : it was an acacia; and there were one thousand three hundred of them, or more; He took a pledge there from them that they would fight against the Quraysh, and that they would not run away, and to die. { And knew } : Allah; { what was in their hearts } : the sincerity and loyalty; { so He sent down peaceful reassurance [*sakinah*] upon them and rewarded them with an impending victory } : this was the victory at Khaibar after they had left Hudaibiyya.
Tafsir Al-Jalalain

فكان الناس يقولون بايعهم رسول الله ﷺ على الموت فكان جابر بن عبدالله يقول إن رسول الله ﷺ لم يبايعنا على الموت ولكنه بايعنا على أن لا نفرّ
تفسير الطبري

People said that the Messenger of Allah (SAW) took from them a pledge that they would die; but Jabir ibn Abdullah said: The Messenger of Allah (SAW) did not take our pledge to die – He took our pledge not to run away.
Tafsir Al-Tabari

﴿ فنزل السكينة ﴾ وهي الطمأنينة ﴿ عليهم وأثابهم فتحاً قريباً ﴾ وهو ما أجرى الله عز وجل على أيديهم من الصلح بينهم وبين أعدائهم وما حصل بذلك من الخير العام المستمر المتصل بفتح خيبر وفتح مكة ثم سائر البلاد والأقاليم عليهم وما حصل لهم من العز والنصر والرفعة في الدنيا والآخرة ولهذا قال تعالى ﴿ ومغانم كثيرة يأخذونها وكان الله عزيزاً حكيماً ﴾
تفسير ابن كثير

{ So He sent down peaceful reassurance } : peace of mind; { upon them, and rewarded them with an impending victory } : this was the conciliation that Allah Mighty and Sublime brought about between them and their enemies, and the generally good and continuous things that resulted from this and followed one after the other, like the victory at Khaibar, the conquest of Mecca, and then the rest of the territories and surrounding areas, as well as the might, triumph, and glory they gained in this world and the next. This is why the Most High said: { And many spoils for them to take; and Allah is mighty, wise } .

Tafsir Ibn Kathir

... ثم فتح العموص حصن إبن ابي الحقيق فأصاب منه سبايا منهم صفية بنت حيي بن أخطب جاء بلال بها وبأخرى معها فمرّ بهما على قتلى من يهود فلما رأتهم التي مع صفية صاحت وصكت وجهها وحثت التراب على رأسها فلما رآها رسول الله ﷺ قال أعزبوا عني هذه الشيطانة وأمر بصفية فحيزت خلفه وألقى عليها رداءه فعرف المسلمون أن رسول الله ﷺ اصطفاها لنفسه

تفسير البغوي

... Al-'Ammous gained victory over the fortress of Ibn Abi Al-Haqiq and took captives from it, among them Safiya bint Huyay ibn Akhtab. Bilal brought her, and another with her, and passed with the two of them over some of the Jews who had been killed. And when the one who was with Safiya saw them, she cried out and struck her face and threw dirt all over her head. When the Messenger of Allah (SAW) saw her, he said: Get this devil away from me! And he ordered for Safiya, and she got up behind him, and he threw his garment over her; and the Muslims knew that the Messenger of Allah (SAW) had chosen her for himself.

Tafsir Al-Baghawi

* * *

﴿ محمد رسول الله والذين معه أشداء على الكفار رحماء بينهم ﴾ الفتح ٢٩

{ **Muhammad is the messenger of Allah, and those who are with him are severe against the disbelievers but merciful with each other** } *Al-fath 29*

﴿ محمد رسول الله والذين معه أشداء على الكفار رحماء بينهم ﴾ يقول تعالى ذكره محمد رسول الله وأتباعه من أصحابه الذين هم معه على دينه أشداء على الكفار غليظة عليهم قلوبهم قليلة بهم رحمتهم ﴿ رحماء بينهم ﴾ يقول رقيقة قلوب بعضهم لبعض لينة أنفسهم لهم هينة عليهم لهم

تفسير الطبري

{ Muhammad is the messenger of Allah, and those who are with him are severe against the disbelievers but merciful with each other } ; He (may His remembrance be exalted) is saying: Muhammad is the messenger of Allah, and his followers from among his Companions, those who are with him in his religion [deen], are severe against the disbelievers [kuffar], their hearts harsh towards them and their mercy meager towards them. { Merciful with each other } : He is saying: Their hearts tender towards each other, their souls delicate towards them and at ease towards them.

Tafsir Al-Tabari

والمعنى أنهم يغلظون على من خالف دينهم ويتراحمون فيما بينهم
تفسير البيضاوي

The meaning is that they are harsh on whoever opposes their religion but merciful to each other regarding what is between them.

Tafsir Al-Baydawi

معنى الآية ﴿ أشداء على الكفار ﴾ أي غلاظٌ عليهم كالأسد على فريسته لا تأخذهم فيهم رأفة ﴿ رحماء بينهم ﴾ متعاطفون متوادّون بعضهم لبعض كالوالد مع الولد
اللباب في علوم الكتاب لإبن عادل

The meaning of the verse { Severe against the disbelievers } : that is, harsh to them like a lion on its prey, with no compassion taking hold of them regarding them; { merciful with each other } : sympathetic to each other, friendly towards each other, like a father with a child.

Ibn 'Adil, Al-lubab fi 'Ulum Al-kitab

﴿ والذين معه أشداء على الكفار ﴾ أي والذين معه من المؤمنين أشداء على الكفار غلاظ عليهم والأشداء جمع الشديد وهو قوي في دين الله تعالى القوي على أعداء الله كانوا لا يميلون إلى الكفار لقرابة ولا غيرها بل اظهروا لهم العداوة في الدين وكانوا على الكفار كالاسد على فرسه
التفسير الكبير للطبراني

{ And those who are with him are severe against the disbelievers } : that is, those Believers who are with him are severe against the disbelievers, harsh on them; "severe" means strong in the religion of Allah Most High, strong against the enemies of Allah. They do not incline towards the disbelievers, relatives or otherwise, but instead make enmity clear to them in the religion; they are towards disbelievers like a lion towards its prey.

Al-Tabarani, Al-tafsir Al-kabir

Surah 49 Al-hujarat [The Chambers]

﴿ وَإِن طَائِفَتَانِ مِنَ الْمُؤْمِنِينَ اقْتَتَلُوا فَأَصْلِحُوا بَيْنَهُمَا فَإِن بَغَتْ إِحْدَاهُمَا عَلَى الْأُخْرَى فَقَاتِلُوا الَّتِي تَبْغِي حَتَّى تَفِيءَ إِلَى أَمْرِ اللَّهِ فَإِن فَاءَتْ فَأَصْلِحُوا بَيْنَهُمَا بِالْعَدْلِ وَأَقْسِطُوا إِنَّ اللَّهَ يُحِبُّ الْمُقْسِطِينَ ﴾ الحجرات 9

{ If two groups of Believers get into a fight with each other, make things right between them; if one of them oppresses the other, then fight the one that is oppressive until they come back around to the commands of Allah; if they come back around, make things right between them fairly, and act justly; indeed Allah loves those who act justly } Al-hujarat 9

عن أنس بن مالك قال قيل للنبي ﷺ لو أتيتَ عبدالله بن أبي قال فإنطلق إليه وركب حماراً وانطلق المسلمون وهي أرض سبخة فلما أتاه النبي ﷺ قال إليك عني فوالله لقد آذاني نَتْنُ حمارك قال فقال رجل من الأنصار والله لحمار رسول الله ﷺ أطيب ريحاً منك قال فغضب لعبدالله رجل من قومه قال فغضب لكل واحد منهما أصحابه قال فكان بينهم ضرب بالجريد وبالأيدي وبالنعال قال فبلغنا أنها نزلت فيهم ﴿ وإن طائفتان من المؤمنين اقتتلوا فأصلحوا بينهما ﴾

صحيح مسلم كتاب الجهاد والسير

From Anas ibn Malik, who said: Someone said to the Prophet (SAW): You should go see Abdullah ibn Ubay. So He set out to see him, riding on a donkey, and the Muslims set out, and it was salty land. When the Prophet (SAW) got there, Abdullah said: Stay away from me! I swear by Allah the stench of your donkey is making me sick. And a man from the *Ansar* said: And I swear by Allah the Messenger of Allah's (SAW) donkey smells better than you! Then a man from Abdullah's people defended him. The companions of these two men each defended their man, and between them there were blows with palm branches, hands, and sandals. He [the narrator] said: We found out that this came down regarding them: { If two groups of Believers get into a fight with each other, make things right between them } .

Sahih Muslim, The book of jihad and campaigns

عن إبن عمر رضي الله عنهما أتاه رجلان في فتنة إبن الزبير فقالا إن الناس قد ضُيِّعوا وأنت إبن عمر وصاحب النبي ﷺ فما يمنعك أن تخرج فقال يمنعني أن الله حرَّم دم أخي فقالا ألم يقل الله ﴿ وقاتلوهم حتى لا تكون فتنة ﴾ فقال قاتلنا حتى لم تكن فتنة وكان الدين لله وانتم تريدون أن تقاتلوا حتى تكون فتنة ويكون الدين لغير الله وزاد عثمان بن صالح عن إبن وهب قال أخبرني فلان وحيوة بن شريح عن بكر بن عمرو المعافري أن بكير بن عبدالله حدثه عن نافع أن رجلاً أتى إبن عمر فقال يا أبا عبد الرحمان من حملك على أن تحجّ عاماً وتعتمر عاماً وتترك الجهاد في سبيل الله عز وجل وقد علمتَ ما رغّب الله فيه قال يا إبن أخي بُنِي الاسلام على خمس إيمان بالله ورسوله والصلاة الخمس وصيام رمضان وأداء الزكاة وحج البيت قال يا أبا عبد الرحمان ألا تسمع ما ذكَر الله في كتابه ﴿ وإن طائفتان من المؤمنين اقتتلوا فأصلحوا بينهما ﴾ إلى أمر الله ﴿ قاتلوهم حتى لا تكون فتنة ﴾ قال فعلنا على عهد رسول الله ﷺ وكان الاسلام قليلاً فكان الرجل يُفتن في دينه إما قتلوه وإما يعذّبوه حتى كثُر الاسلام فلم تكن فتنة قال فما قولك في علي وعثمان قال أما عثمان فكأنّ الله عفا عنه وأما أنتم فكرهتم أن تعفوا عنه وأما علي فإبن عم رسول الله ﷺ وخَتَنه وأشار بيده فقال هذا بيته حيث ترون

صحيح البخاري كتاب التفسير

Ibn 'Umar (may Allah be pleased with them both) related that two men came to him during the sedition of Ibn Al-Zubair, and said: The people have been abandoned, and you are the son of 'Umar and a Companion of the Prophet (SAW), so what prevents you from going out? He said: What prevents me is that Allah has prohibited the blood of my brother. The two men said: Did Allah not say: { So fight them until there is no more sedition } ? [Al-anfal 39] Ibn 'Umar said: We did fight until there was no more sedition and religion was all for Allah, but you all want to fight until there is sedition and religion is for other than Allah. 'Uthman Ibn Salih added, by way of Ibn Wahab, who said: So-and-so, as well as Haiwa ibn Suraih, told me from Bikr ibn 'Amr Al-Ma'afiri that Bukair ibn Abdullah related to him from Nafi' that a certain man came to Ibn 'Umar and said: Oh Abu 'Abd Al-Rahman, what made you perform pilgrimage [hajj] one year and the lesser pilgrimage ['umrah] one year, and give up jihad in the cause of Allah Mighty and Sublime, when you know how much Allah rouses the desire for it? He replied: Oh nephew, Islam was built on five things – belief in Allah and His Messenger, the five prayers, fasting in Ramadan, giving zakat, and pilgrimage to the House. The man said: Oh Abu 'Abd Al-Rahman, have you not heard what Allah mentioned in His book: { If two groups of Believers get into a fight with each other, make things right between them } up to Allah's command: { Fight them until there is no more sedition } ? He replied: We did this during the time of the Messenger of Allah (SAW), when Islam was small, and men were put to the test in their religion – they would either kill you or torment you – until Islam grew and there was no more sedition. The man said: And what do you say about 'Ali and 'Uthman? He replied: Well 'Uthman, it looks like Allah has forgiven him, although you all were averse to forgiving him; and as for

'Ali, he was the Messenger of Allah's (SAW) cousin and his brother-in-law. And he pointed with his hand and said: That is his house where you are looking.

Sahih Al-Bukhari, The book of tafsir

عن أبي مالك في قوله ﴿ وإن طائفتان من المؤمنين اقتتلوا فأصلحوا بينهما ﴾ قال رجلان اقتتلا فغضب لذا قومه ولذا قومه فاجتمعوا حتى اضَّربوا بالنعال حتى كاد يكون بينهم قتال فأنزل الله هذه الآية

تفسير الطبري

Abu Malik, regarding His word { If two groups of Believers get into a fight with each other, make things right between them } , said: Two men got into a fight, and the people of the one man defended him, and the people of the other defended him, and they got piled up to the point of hitting each other with sandals, until there was almost a battle between them. So Allah sent down this verse.

Tafsir Al-Tabari

وذكر سعيد بن جبير أن الأوس والخزرج بينهما قتال بالسعف والنعال فأنزل الله تعالى هذه الآية فأمر بالصلح بينهما وقال السدي كان رجل من الأنصار يقال له عمران كانت له إمرأة تدعى أم زيد وإن المرأة ارادت أن تزور أهلها فحبسها زوجها وجعلها في عُلِيّة له لا يدخل عليها أحد من أهلها وإن المرأة بعثت إلى أهلها فجاء قومها وأنزلوها لينطلقوا بها وإن الرجل كان قد خرج فإستعان أهل الرجل فجاء بنو عمه ليحولوا بين المرأة وبين أهلها فتدافعوا واجتلدوا بالنعال فنزلت فيهم الآية فبعث اليهم رسول الله ﷺ وأصلح بينهم وفاؤوا إلى أمر الله تعالى

تفسير إبن كثير

Sa'id ibn Jubair mentioned that there was a fight between the Aws and the Khazraj with palm branches and sandals, and so Allah Most High sent down this verse, and ordered conciliation between them. Al-Suddi said: There was a man from the *Ansar* called 'Imran, who had a woman called Umm Zaid. The woman wanted to visit her family, but her husband locked her in an upper room of his where no one from her family could enter in to see her. So the woman sent word to her family, and her people came and got her down to take her away. The man had left, so the man's family sought assistance, and his cousins came to intervene between the woman and her family. They pushed each other and struck each other with sandals, and so this verse came down concerning them. And the Messenger of Allah (SAW) sent someone out, and he made things right between them. So they came back around to the command of Allah Most High.

Tafsir Ibn Kathir

* * *

﴿ قَالَتِ الْأَعْرَابُ آمَنَّا قُلْ لَمْ تُؤْمِنُوا وَلَكِنْ قُولُوا أَسْلَمْنَا وَلَمَّا يَدْخُلِ الْإِيمَانُ فِي قُلُوبِكُمْ وَإِنْ تُطِيعُوا اللَّهَ وَرَسُولَهُ لَا يَلِتْكُمْ مِنْ أَعْمَالِكُمْ شَيْئًا إِنَّ اللَّهَ غَفُورٌ رَحِيمٌ إِنَّمَا الْمُؤْمِنُونَ الَّذِينَ آمَنُوا بِاللَّهِ وَرَسُولِهِ ثُمَّ لَمْ يَرْتَابُوا وَجَاهَدُوا بِأَمْوَالِهِمْ وَأَنْفُسِهِمْ فِي سَبِيلِ اللَّهِ أُولَئِكَ هُمُ الصَّادِقُونَ ﴾

الحجرات ١٤-١٥

{ The Bedouins say: "We have believed"; say: "You have not believed, but say rather: 'We have yielded'; for indeed belief has not entered your hearts; but if you obey Allah and His Messenger, He will not minimize any of your works; indeed Allah is forgiving, merciful." Truly the Believers are those who have believed in Allah and His Messenger, then have no misgivings, and wage *jihad* in the cause of Allah with their wealth and with themselves; these are the true ones } *Al-hujarat 14-15*

وقد روي عن سعيد بن جبير ومجاهد وإبن زيد أنهم قالوا في قوله تبارك وتعالى ﴿ ولكن قولوا أسلمنا ﴾ أي إستسلمنا خوف القتل والسبي ... وقوله تعالى ﴿ إنما المؤمنون ﴾ أي إنما المؤمنون الكمّل ﴿ الذين آمنوا بالله ورسوله ثم لم يرتابوا ﴾ أي لم يشكوا ولا تزلزلوا بل ثبتوا على حال واحدة وهي التصديق المحض ﴿ وجاهدوا بأموالهم وأنفسهم في سبيل الله ﴾ أي وبذلوا مهجهم ونفائس أموالهم في طاعة الله ورضوانه

تفسير إبن كثير

It is narrated from Sa'id ibn Jubair, Mujahid, and Ibn Zaid that they said regarding the word of the Blessed and Exalted: { But say rather: 'We have yielded [*aslamna*]' } ; they said: In other words, "we have surrendered out of fear of being killed or imprisoned". ... The word of the Most High: { Truly the Believers } : that is, truly the perfect Believers; { are those who have believed in Allah and His Messenger, then have no misgivings } : that is, they have no doubts and are not shaken up, but rather remain firm upon a single state of affairs, this being unadulterated belief. { And wage *jihad* in the cause of Allah with their wealth and with themselves } : that is, they freely give their lives and their most valuable wealth in obedience to Allah and His good pleasure.

Tafsir Ibn Kathir

﴿ إنما المؤمنون ﴾ أي الصادقون في إيمانهم كما صرح به بعد ﴿ الذين آمنوا بالله ورسوله ثم لم يرتابوا ﴾ لم يشكوا في الإيمان ﴿ وجاهدوا بأموالهم وأنفسهم في سبيل الله ﴾ لجهادهم يظهر بصدق إيمانهم ﴿ أولئك هم الصادقون ﴾ في إيمانهم لا من قالوا آمنا ولم يوجد منهم غير الإسلام

تفسير الجلالين

{ Truly the Believers } : that is, those who are sincere in their belief, as He makes it clear in the following; { are those who have believed in Allah and His Messenger then have no misgivings } : have not doubted regarding belief; { and wage *jihad* in the cause of Allah with their wealth and with themselves } : their *jihad* attests to the sincerity of their belief; { these are the true ones } : in their belief; not those who say "We have believed", when there is nothing from them but their yielding [*islam*].

Tafsir Al-Jalalain

عن الزهري ﴿ قالت الأعراب آمنا قل لم تؤمنوا ولكن قولوا أسلمنا ﴾ قال إن الإسلام الكلمة والإيمان العمل ... وأخبرهم أن المؤمنين الذين آمنوا بالله ورسوله ثم لم يرتابوا وجاهدوا بأموالهم وأنفسهم في سبيل الله أولئك هم الصادقون صدّقوا إيمانهم بأعمالهم فمن قال منهم أنا مؤمن فقد صدق قال وأما من قال إنتحل الإيمان بالكلام ولم يعمل فقد كذب وليس بصادق ... قال ابن زيد وقرأ قول الله ﴿ قل لم تؤمنوا ولكن قولوا أسلمنا ﴾ استسلمنا دخلنا في السلم وتركنا المحاربة والقتال بقولهم لا إله إلا الله وقال رسول الله ﷺ أمرت أن أقاتل الناس حتى يقولوا لا إله إلا الله فإذا قالوا لا إله إلا الله عصموا مني دماءهم وأموالهم إلا بحقها وحسابهم على الله ... ﴿ وجاهدوا بأموالهم وأنفسهم في سبيل الله ﴾ يقول جاهدوا المشركين بإنفاق أموالهم وبذل مُهجهم في جهادهم على ما أمرهم الله به من جهادهم وذلك سبيله لتكون كلمة الله العليا وكلمة الذين كفروا السفلى

تفسير الطبري

Al-Zuhri, of { The Bedouins say: "We have believed"; say: "You have not believed, but say rather: 'We have yielded' } , said: Indeed Islam is what is said, but belief is what is done. ... He is letting them know that Believers, those who have believed in Allah and His Messenger, then have no misgivings, and wage *jihad* in the cause of Allah with their wealth and with themselves – those are the sincere ones, the ones who have attested to their belief by their deeds. Whoever among them says "I am a Believer" ought to be sincere; He says: Although anyone who professes belief with words but does not act on it, he is a liar and not being truthful. ... Ibn Zaid, reciting the word of Allah { Say: "You have not believed, but say rather: 'We have yielded' } , said: 'We have surrendered, we have entered into a state of peace, and have abandoned combat and fighting', by them saying "There is no god but Allah" ["*La ilaha illa Allah*"]. The Messenger of Allah (SAW) said: I have been ordered to fight people until they say "There is no god but Allah", and if they say " There is no god but Allah", their blood and their property are made unlawful to us, except when these are due, and their reckoning is with Allah. ... { And wage *jihad* in the cause of Allah with their wealth and with themselves } ; He is saying: They wage *jihad* on the Idolaters [*Mushrikeen*] by spending their wealth and by freely giving their lives in *jihad* according to the *jihad* that Allah has ordered them; and this is His cause, so that the word of Allah be the utmost, and the word of those who have disbelieved be the lowest.

Tafsir Al-Tabari

﴿ وجاهدوا ﴾ يجوز أن يكون المجاهد منويّاً وهو العدو المحارب أو الشيطان أو الهوى

تفسير الزمخشري

{ And wage jihad } : It is permissible for a *Mujahid* to be intent on any worthwile goal, this being an enemy in combat, Satan, or one's passions.

Tafsir Al-Zamakhshari

عن أنس عن النبي ﷺ قال الاسلام علانية والايمان في القلب ثم يشير بيده إلى صدره ثلاث مرات ويقول التقوى ههنا التقوى ههنا

الدر المنثور للسيوطي

Anas related from the Prophet (SAW), who said: Islam is an outward declaration but belief is in the heart. Then He pointed with his hand to his chest three times, saying: Reverence is here, reverence is here.

Al-Suyuti, Al-durr Al-manthur

* * *

Surah 57   Al-hadid [Iron]

﴿ وما لكم ألّا تنفقوا في سبيل الله ولله ميراث السماوات والأرض لا يستوي منكم من أنفق من قبل الفتح وقاتل أولئك أعظم درجة من الذين أنفقوا من بعد وقاتلوا وكلاً وعد الله الحسنى والله بما تعملون خبير ﴾ الحديد ١٠

﴿ And what is with you all, that you do not spend for the cause of Allah, when the inheritance of the heavens and the earth is Allah's? Those of you who spent before the conquest, and fought, are not on the same level – they are a degree above those who spent and fought afterwards; but Allah has promised good things to both; and Allah is mindful of what you do ﴾ Al-hadid 10

﴿ وما لكم ألّا تنفقوا في سبيل الله ولله ميراث السماوات والأرض ﴾ أي أنفقوا ولا تخشوا فقراً وإقلالاً فإن الذي أنفقت في سبيله هو مالك السموات والأرض وبيده مقاليدهما وعنده خزائنهما وهو مالك العرش بما حوى وهو القائل ﴿ وما أنفقتم من شيء فهو يخلفه وهو خير الرازقين ﴾ وقال ﴿ ما عندكم ينفد وما عند الله باق ﴾ فمن توكل على الله أنفق ولم يخش من ذي العرش إقلالاً وعلم أن الله سيخلفه عليه وقوله تعالى ﴿ لا يستوي منكم من أنفق من قبل الفتح وقاتل ﴾ أي لا يستوي من هذا ومن لم يفعل كفعله وذلك أن قبل فتح مكة كان الحال شديداً فلم يكن حينئذ يؤمن إلا الصديقون وأما بعد الفتح فإنه ظهر الاسلام ظهوراً عظيماً ودخل الناس في دين الله أفواجاً

تفسير ابن كثير

﴿ And what is with you all, that you do not spend for the cause of Allah, when the inheritance of the heavens and the earth is Allah's? ﴾ ; that is: Spend, and do not be afraid of poverty or scarcity; indeed whatever you spend in His cause, He is Master over the heavens and the earth, in His hands are the keys to their power, and with Him are their coffers. He reigns on the Throne and all that it encompasses, and He is the one who said: ﴿ You do not spend a thing but that He will repay it, and He is the best of bountiful providers ﴾ [Al-saba' 39], and He said: ﴿ What is yours comes to an end, but what is Allah's endures ﴾ [Al-nahl 96]. So then, whoever trusts in Allah spends, and does not fear scarcity from the One on the Throne, and he knows that Allah will repay it. And the word of the Most High: ﴿ Those of you who spent before the conquest, and fought, are not on the same level } : in other words, this, and those who did not do this, are not equal. This is because before the conquest of Mecca, the situation was dire, and there were no Believers at the time except the righteous. But after the conquest, Islam was powerfully manifested, and people entered into Allah's religion in droves.

Tafsir Ibn Kathir

ثم بين فضل من سبق بالانفاق في سبيل الله والجهاد فقال ﴿ لا يستوي منكم من أنفق من قبل الفتح ﴾ يعني فتح مكة في قول أكثر المفسرين

تفسير البغوي

Then He declares the superiority of those who spent first in the cause of Allah and in *jihad*; He says: { Those of you who spent before the conquest } : this refers to the conquest of Mecca according to what most expositors say.

Tafsir Al-Baghawi

﴿ وما لكم ألا تنفقوا ﴾ في أن لا تنفقوا ﴿ ولله ميراث السماوات والأرض ﴾ يرث كل شيء فيهما لا يبقى منه باق لأحد من مال وغيره يعني وأي غرض لكم في ترك الإنفاق في سبيل الله والجهاد مع رسول الله مهلككم فوارث أموالكم وهو من أبلغ البعث على الانفاق في سبيل الله

تفسير الزمخشري

{ And what is with you all, that you do not spend } : regarding that you do not spend; { when the inheritance of the heavens and the earth is Allah's? } : He inherits everything that is in them; nothing remains that He owes anyone, money or otherwise. The meaning is: What is your intent in neglecting to spend in the cause of Allah and wage *jihad* with the Messenger of Allah, the One who destroys you and is heir to your wealth?; it is He who has made known the call to spend in the cause of Allah.

Tafsir Al-Zamakhshari

∙ ∙ ∙

﴿ وَالَّذِينَ آمَنُوا بِاللَّهِ وَرُسُلِهِ أُولَٰئِكَ هُمُ الصِّدِّيقُونَ وَالشُّهَدَاءُ عِندَ رَبِّهِمْ لَهُمْ أَجْرُهُمْ وَنُورُهُمْ وَالَّذِينَ كَفَرُوا وَكَذَّبُوا بِآيَاتِنَا أُولَٰئِكَ أَصْحَابُ الْجَحِيمِ ﴾ الحديد ١٩

{ Those who have believed in Allah and His Messenger – those are the righteous ones and the martyrs unto their Lord; their reward is theirs, and their light; but those who have disbelieved and accused our signs of being false – those are the associates of Hell } Al-hadid 19

عن مجاهد قال كل مؤمن شهيد ثم تلا ﴿ والذين آمنوا بالله ورسوله أولئك هم الصدقين والشهداء ﴾
المصنف لعبد الرزاق كتاب الجهاد

From Mujahid, who said: Every believer is a martyr [*shaheed*, i.e. witness]. Then he recited: { Those who have believed in Allah and His Messenger – those are the righteous ones and the martyrs }

'Abd Al-Razzaq, the Musannaf, The book of jihad

﴿ والشهداء ﴾ فيه قولان الأول أنه عطف على الآية الأولى والتقدير إن الذين آمنوا بالله ورسوله هم الصديقون وهم الشهداء قال مجاهد كل مؤمن فهو صديق وشهيد وتلا هذه الآية جذا القول اختلفوا في أنه لم سمي كل مؤمن شهيد فقال بعضهم لأن المؤمنين هم الشهداء عند ربهم على العباد في أعمالهم والمراد أنهم عدول الآخرة الذي تقبل شهادتهم وقال الحسن السبب في هذا الإسم أن كل مؤمن فإنه يشهد كرامة ربه وقال الأصم كل مؤمن شهيد لأنه قائم لله تعالى بالشهادة فيما تعبدهم به من وجوب الإيمان ووجوب الطاعات وحرمة الكفر والمعاصي وقال أبو مسلم قد ذكرنا أن الصديق نعت لمن كثر منه الصدق وجمع صدقاً إلى صدق في الإيمان بالله تعالى ورسوله فصاروا بذلك شهداء على غيرهم القول الثاني أن قوله ﴿ والشهداء ﴾ ليس عطفاً على ما تقدم بل هو مبتدأ وخبره قوله ﴿ عند ربهم ﴾ أو يكون ذلك صفة وخبره هو قوله ﴿ لهم أجرهم ﴾ وعلى هذا القول اختلفوا في المراد من الشهداء فقال الفراء والزجاج هم الأنبياء لقوله تعالى ﴿ فكيف إذا جئنا من كل أمة بشهيد وجئنا بك على هؤلاء شهيداً ﴾ وقال مقاتل ومحمد بن جرير الشهداء هم الذين استشهدوا في سبيل الله وروي عن النبي ﷺ أنه قال ما تعُدّون الشهداء فيكم قالوا إن المقتول فقال إن شهداء أمتي إذا لقليل ثم ذكر أن المقتول شهيد والمبطون شهيد والمطعون شهيد

تفسير الرازي

{ And the martyrs } ; regarding this there are two points of view. The **first** is that it is tied to the other verse, and may be reckoned as: Indeed those who have believed in Allah and His Messenger are the righteous ones and they are the martyrs [*shuhadaa*, witnesses]. Mujahid said: Every Believer is righteous and a martyr; and he recited this verse. These words have been affirmed but there is disagreement as to why every Believer is called a martyr. Some say because Believers are witnesses to their Lord against people regarding their deeds, the meaning being that they are the upright ones in the hereafter that follows their martyrdom [*shahada*, i.e. testimony]. Al-Hasan said: The reason for this designation is that every Believer is indeed witness to the glory of their Lord. Al-Asm said: All Believers are martyrs because they stand before Allah Most High giving witness to the obligations of belief and acts of obedience and the prohibition of disbelief and rebellion which subject them to Him. Abu Muslim said: We have mentioned that "righteous" [*siddiq*] characterizes someone whose sincerity has increased and who adds sincerity upon sincerity in belief in Allah Most High and His Messenger, and as such becomes a martyr above others. The **second** point of view is that His word: { And the martyrs } is not tied to what precedes it, but rather that it is the subject and its predicate is His word { unto their Lord } , or this could be an adjective and the predicate His word { their reward is theirs } . Based on this there is disagreement as to the meaning of "martyrs"; Al-Farra and Al-Zajjaj said: This refers to the prophets, according to His word: { So how, since we bring a witness [*shaheed*] from every nation, and We have brought you as a witness against them? } [*Al-nisaa* 41]. Muqatil and Muhammad ibn Jarir said: Martyrs [*shuhadaa*, witnesses] are those who are martyred [*istashhadu*, i.e. give witness] in the cause of Allah. It is narrated from the Prophet (SAW) that He said: Who do you all think are the martyrs among you? They said: Someone who gets killed. And He said: Indeed in that case there would only be a few martyrs in my *ummah*. Then He mentioned that someone who gets killed is a martyr, and someone stricken by abdominal sickness is a martyr, and someone stricken by plague is a martyr.

Tafsir Al-Razi

وقيل ﴿ والشهداء عند ربهم ﴾ مبتدأ وخبر والمراد به الأنبياء من قوله ﴿ فكيف إذا جئنا من كل أمة بشهيد ﴾ أو الذين استشهدوا في سبيل الله

تفسير البيضاوي

It is said that: { The martyrs [*shuhadaa*, witnesses] unto their Lord } is a subject and predicate, the meaning being the prophets, according to His word: { So how, since we bring a witness [*shaheed*] from every nation? } [*Al-nisaa* 41], or those who have been martyred in the cause of Allah.

Tafsir Al-Baydawi

عن عمرو بن ميمون الجهني قال جاء رجل للنبي ﷺ فقال يا رسول الله أرأيت إن شهدت أن لا إله إلا الله وأنك رسول الله وصليت الصلوات الخمس وأديت الزكاة وصمت رمضان وقمته فمن أنا قال من الصديقين والشهداء

الدر المنثور للسيوطي

'Amr ibn Maimun Al-Juhani said: A certain man came to the Prophet (SAW) and said: Oh Messenger of Allah, have you seen that I have borne witness that there is no god but Allah and that you are the Messenger of Allah, I have prayed the five prayers, given *zakat*, fasted Ramadan and gotten up to pray during it, so who do I belong to? He said: To the righteous ones and the martyrs.

Al-Suyuti, Al-durr Al-manthur

• *Surah 58 Al-mujadilah [The Complaining Woman]* •

﴿ إِنَّ الَّذِينَ يُحَادُّونَ اللَّهَ وَرَسُولَهُ أُولَئِكَ فِي الْأَذَلِّينَ كَتَبَ اللَّهُ لَأَغْلِبَنَّ أَنَا وَرُسُلِي إِنَّ اللَّهَ قَوِيٌّ عَزِيزٌ لَا تَجِدُ قَوْمًا يُؤْمِنُونَ بِاللَّهِ وَالْيَوْمِ الْآخِرِ يُوَادُّونَ مَنْ حَادَّ اللَّهَ وَرَسُولَهُ وَلَوْ كَانُوا آبَاءَهُمْ أَوْ أَبْنَاءَهُمْ أَوْ إِخْوَانَهُمْ أَوْ عَشِيرَتَهُمْ أُولَئِكَ كَتَبَ فِي قُلُوبِهِمُ الْإِيمَانَ وَأَيَّدَهُمْ بِرُوحٍ مِنْهُ وَيُدْخِلُهُمْ جَنَّاتٍ تَجْرِي مِنْ تَحْتِهَا الْأَنْهَارُ خَالِدِينَ فِيهَا رَضِيَ اللَّهُ عَنْهُمْ وَرَضُوا عَنْهُ أُولَئِكَ حِزْبُ اللَّهِ أَلَا إِنَّ حِزْبَ اللَّهِ هُمُ الْمُفْلِحُونَ ﴾ المجادلة ٢٠-٢٢

﴿ Indeed those who oppose Allah and His Messenger – they are among the most miserable. Allah has decreed: "Surely I will overcome, me and my messengers"; indeed Allah is strong, mighty. You will not find people who believe in Allah and the last day to be affectionate towards anyone who opposes Allah and His Messenger, even if they are their fathers, or their sons, or their brothers, or their kinsfolk; These – He has written belief upon their hearts, and He upholds them with a spirit of His; and He will admit them into gardens below which rivers flow, there for eternity. Allah is pleased with them, and they are pleased with Him; they are the party of Allah; is it not indeed the party of Allah who are the prosperous ones? ﴾ *Al-mujadilah 20-22*

﴿ إِنَّ الَّذِينَ يُحَادُّونَ ﴾ يُخَالِفُونَ ﴿ اللَّهَ وَرَسُولَهُ أُولَئِكَ الْأَذَلِّينَ ﴾ المغلوبين ﴿ كَتَبَ اللَّهُ ﴾ في اللوح المحفوظ أو قضى ﴿ لَأَغْلِبَنَّ أَنَا وَرُسُلِي ﴾ بالحجة أو السيف ﴿ إِنَّ اللَّهَ قَوِيٌّ عَزِيزٌ ﴾ ﴿ لَا تَجِدُ قَوْمًا يُؤْمِنُونَ بِاللَّهِ وَالْيَوْمِ الْآخِرِ يُوَادُّونَ ﴾ يصادقون ﴿ مَنْ حَادَّ اللَّهَ وَرَسُولَهُ وَلَوْ كَانُوا ﴾ أي المحادون ﴿ آبَاءَهُمْ ﴾ أي المؤمنين ﴿ أَوْ أَبْنَاءَهُمْ أَوْ إِخْوَانَهُمْ أَوْ عَشِيرَتَهُمْ ﴾ بل يقصدونهم بالسوء ويقاتلونهم على الإيمان كما وقع لجماعة من الصحابة رضي الله عنهم

تفسير الجلالين

﴿ Indeed those who oppose ﴾ : act in opposition to; ﴿ Allah and His Messenger – they are among the most miserable ﴾ : the conquered. ﴿ Allah has written ﴾ : on the Preserved Tablet, or has decreed; ﴿ "Surely I will overcome, me and my messengers" ﴾ : by arguments or the sword; { indeed Allah is strong, mighty } . { You will not find people who believe in Allah and the last day to be affectionate } : make friends; { towards anyone who opposes Allah and His Messenger, even if they } : that is, the ones being shown affection; { are their fathers } : that is, of the Believers; { or their sons, or their brothers, or their kinsfolk } : but rather, they seek harm on them and fight against them over belief, as a group of the Companions (may Allah be pleased with them) had to do.

Tafsir Al-Jalalain

يقول تعالى مخبراً الكفار المعاندين المحادين لله ورسوله يعني الذين هم في حد والشرع في حد أي مجانبون للحق مشاقون له هم في ناحية والهدى في ناحية ﴿ أولئك في الأذلين ﴾ أي في الأشقياء المبعدين المطرودين عن الصواب الأذلين في الدنيا والآخرة ﴿ كتب الله لأغلبن أنا ورسلي ﴾ أي قد حكم وكتب في كتابه الأول وقدره الذي لا يخالف ولا يمانع ولا يبدل بأن النصرة له ولكتابه ورسوله وعباده المؤمنين في الدنيا والآخرة ... ﴿ ولو كانوا آباءهم ﴾ نزلت في أبي عبيدة قتل أباه يوم بدر ﴿ أو أبناءهم ﴾ في الصديق همّ يومئذ بقتل ابنه عبد الرحمن ﴿ أو اخوانهم ﴾ في مصعب بن عمير قتل أخاه عبيد بن عمير يومئذ ﴿ أو عشيرتهم ﴾ في عمر قتل قريباً له يومئذ أيضاً وفي حمزة وعلي وعبيدة بن الحارث قتلوا عتبة وشيبة والوليد بن عتبة يومئذ فالله أعلم قلت ومن هذا القبيل حين إستنشار رسول الله المسلمين في أسارى بدر فأشار الصديق بأن يفادوا فيكون ما يؤخذ منهم قوة للمسلمين وهم بنو العم والعشيرة ولعل الله تعالى أن يهديهم وقال عمر لا أرى ما رأى يا رسول الله هل تمكنني من فلان قريب لعمر فأقتله وتمكن علياً من عقيل وتمكن فلاناً من فلان ليعلم الله أنه ليست في قلوبنا موادة للمشركين

تفسير ابن كثير

The Most High is informing about the disbelievers [*kuffar*], stubborn and opposed to Allah and His Messenger, that is, those who are on one edge while divine law is on another edge, that is, those who avoid the truth and antagonize it – they are on one side and guidance is on another side. { They are among the most miserable } : that is, wretched, excluded, cast out from what is right, most miserable in this world and the next. { Allah has decreed: "Surely I will overcome, me and my messengers" } : that is, He has prescribed and written in His foremost book, and it has been decreed by Him who can not be contradicted, resisted, or changed, that victory belongs to Him, His book, His Messenger, and His servants the Believers, in this world and the next. ... { Even if they are their fathers } : this came down regarding Abu 'Ubaida, who killed his father on the day of Badr; { or their sons } : regarding Al-Siddiq, who intended that day to kill his son 'Abd Al-Rahman; { or their brothers } : regarding Mus'ab ibn 'Umair, who killed his brother 'Ubaid ibn 'Umair on that day; { or their kinsfolk } : regarding 'Umar, who killed a relative of his on that day as well, and regarding Hamza, 'Ali, and 'Ubaida ibn Al-Harith, who killed 'Utba, Shayba, and Al-Walid ibn 'Utba on that day. But Allah knows best. Something similar was when the Messenger of Allah consulted with the Muslims concerning the captives of Badr. Al-Siddiq advised that they should be ransomed, and that what was collected in exchange for them could be to strengthen the Muslims; the captives included cousins and kinsfolk, and perhaps Allah Most High would guide them. But 'Umar said: I'm not thinking what he is thinking, oh Messenger of Allah – will you place So-and-so, a relative of 'Umar's, in my hands, so I can kill him? And give 'Aqil to 'Ali, and give So-and-so to So-and-so? Let Allah know that there is no affection in our hearts towards the idolaters [*mushrikeen*].

Tafsir Ibn Kathir

يعني جل ثناؤه بقوله ﴿ لا تجد قوماً يؤمنون بالله واليوم الآخر يوادّون من حادّ الله ورسوله ﴾ لا تجد يا محمد قوماً يصدّقون الله ويقرّون باليوم الآخر يوادون من حاد الله ورسوله وشاقّهما وخالف أمر الله ونهيه ... ﴿ ألا إن حزب الله ﴾ يقول ألا إن جند الله وأولياءه ﴿ هم المُفلحون ﴾ يقول هم الباقون المنجَحون بادراكهم ما طلبوا والتمسوا ببيعتهم في الدنيا وطاعتهم ربهم

تفسير الطبري

He (may His praise be exalted), by His word: { You will not find people who believe in Allah and the last day to be affectionate towards anyone who opposes Allah and His Messenger }, means: You, oh Muhammad, will not find people who believe Allah and attest to the last day to be affectionate towards anyone who opposes Allah and His Messenger, antagonizes the two of Them, and is against what Allah has commanded and forbidden. ... { Is it not indeed the party of Allah } ; He is saying: Are not indeed Allah's army and His associates; { who are the prosperous ones? } ; He is saying: They are the enduring ones, the ones who have been made successful by attaining what they desired, seeking after their pledge in this life, and obeying their Lord.

Tafsir Al-Tabari

﴿ أولئك حزب الله ﴾ جنده وأنصار دينه ﴿ ألا إن حزب الله هم المفلحون ﴾ الفائزون بخير الدارين عن النبي ﷺ من قرأ سورة المجادلة كتب من حزب الله يوم القيامة

تفسير البيضاوي

{ They are the party of Allah } : His army, and those who uphold His religion; { Is it not indeed the party of Allah who are the prosperous ones? } : the victorious ones by the best of the two dwellings. The Prophet (SAW) said: Whoever recites surah *Al-mujadilah* is decreed to be part of the party of Allah on resurrection day.

Tafsir Al-Baydawi

Surah 59 Al-hashr [The Gathering]

﷽ سَبَّحَ لِلَّهِ مَا فِي السَّمَاوَاتِ وَمَا فِي الْأَرْضِ وَهُوَ الْعَزِيزُ الْحَكِيمُ هُوَ الَّذِي أَخْرَجَ الَّذِينَ كَفَرُوا مِنْ أَهْلِ الْكِتَابِ مِنْ دِيَارِهِمْ لِأَوَّلِ الْحَشْرِ مَا ظَنَنتُمْ أَن يَخْرُجُوا وَظَنُّوا أَنَّهُم مَّانِعَتُهُمْ حُصُونُهُم مِّنَ اللَّهِ فَأَتَاهُمُ اللَّهُ مِنْ حَيْثُ لَمْ يَحْتَسِبُوا وَقَذَفَ فِي قُلُوبِهِمُ الرُّعْبَ يُخْرِبُونَ بُيُوتَهُم بِأَيْدِيهِمْ وَأَيْدِي الْمُؤْمِنِينَ فَاعْتَبِرُوا يَا أُولِي الْأَبْصَارِ وَلَوْلَا أَن كَتَبَ اللَّهُ عَلَيْهِمُ الْجَلَاءَ لَعَذَّبَهُمْ فِي الدُّنْيَا وَلَهُمْ فِي الْآخِرَةِ عَذَابُ النَّارِ ذَٰلِكَ بِأَنَّهُمْ شَاقُّوا اللَّهَ وَرَسُولَهُ وَمَن يُشَاقِّ اللَّهَ فَإِنَّ اللَّهَ شَدِيدُ الْعِقَابِ ﴿الحشر ١-٤﴾

{ Let all that is in the heavens and in the earth glorify Allah, for He is mighty and wise. It is He who drove away from their dwellings those of the People of the Book who disbelieved, at the first gathering; you did not think that they would leave, and they thought that their fortifications would guard them from Allah, but Allah came to them from where they did not reckon, and flung terror into their hearts so that they destroyed their houses by their own hands and the hands of the Believers; so take heed, you who can see. If Allah had not decreed that they vacate, He would have punished them in this world, and the punishment of Hellfire is theirs in the hereafter. This because they antagonized Allah and His Messenger, and whoever antagonizes Allah, indeed Allah is severe in punishment } Al-hashr 1-4

{ هو الذي أخرج الذين كفروا من أهل الكتاب } يعني يهود بني النضير قاله ابن عباس ومجاهد والزهري وغير واحد كان رسول الله ﷺ لما قدم المدينة هادنهم وأعطاهم عهداً وذمة على أن لا يقاتلهم ولا يقاتلوه فنقضوا العهد الذي كان بينهم وبينه فأحل الله بهم بأسه الذي لا مرد له وأنزل عليهم قضاءه الذي لا يصد فأجلاهم النبي ﷺ وأخرجهم من حصونهم الحصينة التي ما طمع فيها المسلمون وظنوا هم أنها ما نعتهم من بأس الله فما أغنى عنهم من الله شيئاً وجاءهم من الله ما لم يكن ببالهم وسيّرهم رسول الله ﷺ وأجلاهم من المدينة
تفسير ابن كثير

{ It is He who drove away from their dwellings those of the People of the Book who disbelieved } : that is, the Jews of Banu Nadir; Ibn 'Abbas, Mujahid, Al-Zuhri, and more than one other said this. The Messenger of Allah (SAW), when He came to Medina, made a truce with them and gave them a covenant and safeguarding [dhimma] under the terms that He would not fight them and they would not fight him. But they broke the covenant that was between them and him, so Allah released on them His might from which there is no turning away, and sent down on them His judgment that can not be obstructed. The Prophet (SAW) forced them out and drove them from their fortified fortresses that the Muslims had never even wished for. And they thought that the fortresses would hold them against the might of Allah, but it was of no use against Allah. And so what they did not envision came upon them from Allah, and the Messenger of Allah (SAW) made them march and forced them out of Medina.

Tafsir Ibn Kathir

﴿ وقذف في قلوبهم الرعب ﴾ بقتل سيدهم كعب بن الأشرف

تفسير البغوي

{ And flung terror into their hearts } : by killing their leader Ka'b ibn Al-Ashraf.

Tafsir Al-Baghawi

قوله تعالى ﴿ وقذف في قلوبهم الرعب ﴾ قال أهل اللغة الرعب الخوف الذي يستوعب الصدر أي يملؤه وقذفه إثباته فيه

تفسير الرازي

The word of the Most High: { And flung terror into their hearts } ; linguists say that "terror" [ru'b] is fear that extends over the chest, that is, fills it; and flinging it affixes it there.

Tafsir Al-Razi

﴿ ذلك بأنهم شاقّوا الله ورسوله ﴾ يقول تعالى ذكره هذا الذي فعل الله بهؤلاء اليهود ما فعل بهم في اخراجهم من ديارهم وقذف في قلوبهم من المؤمنين وجعل لهم في الآخرة عذاب النار بما فعلوا هم في الدنيا من مخالفتهم الله ورسوله في أمره ونهيه وعصيانهم ربهم فيما أمرهم به من إتباع محمد ﷺ

تفسير الطبري

{ This because they antagonized Allah and His Messenger } ; He (may His remembrance be exalted) is saying: This is what Allah did to these Jews, driving them from their homes, flinging things into their hearts from the Believers, and giving them the punishment of Hellfire in the hereafter because of how they opposed Allah and

His Messenger in this world concerning His orders and prohibitions, and rebelled against their Lord regarding how He ordered them to follow Muhammad (SAW).

Tafsir Al-Tabari

﴿ ذلك بأنهم شاقوا الله ورسوله ومن يشاقّ الله ﴾ يعني خالفوا الله ورسوله في الدين ويقال عادوا الله ورسوله

بحر العلوم للسمرقندي

{ This is because they antagonized Allah and His Messenger, and whoever antagonizes Allah } : that is, opposes Allah and His Messenger in religion; it is also said: shows enmity towards Allah and His Messenger.

Al-Samarqandi, Bahr Al-ʿulum

﴿ بأنهم شاقوا الله ﴾ وقد سبق بيان الآية الأنفال ١٣ و محمد ٣٢ قال القاضي أبي يعلى فقد دلت هذه الآية على جواز مصالحة أهل الحرب على الجلاء من ديارهم من غير سبي ولا إسترقاق ولا جزية ولا دخول في ذمة وهذا حكم منسوخ إذا كان في المسلمين قوة على قتالهم لأن الله تعالى أمر بقتال الكفار حتى يسلموا أو يؤدّوا الجزية وإنما يجوز هذا الحكم إذا عجز المسلمون عن مقاومتهم فلم يقدروا على ادخالهم في الاسلام أو الذمة فيجوز لهم حينئذ مصالحتهم على الجلاء من بلادهم

تفسير إبن الجوزي

{ This is because they antagonized Allah } : the explanations of *Al-anfal* 13 and *Muhammad* 32 have already preceded. Al-Qadi [judge] Abu Ya'la said: This verse is evidence that it is permissible to make conciliation with the other party in warfare with the stipulation of them vacating their homes, with no captives, no taking of slaves, no *jizya*, and no entering into a safeguarding agreement [*dhimma*]. However this ruling is abrogated whenever the Muslims have the power to fight them, because Allah Most High ordered that the disbelievers [*kuffar*] be fought until they yield into Islam or give *jizya*. Nevertheless this ruling is permitted whenever the Muslims are prevented from combatting them and are unable to make them enter into Islam or *dhimma*; in this instance it is permissible to make conciliation with them, with the stipulation of them departing from their land.

Tafsir Ibn Al-Jawzi

• • •

Surah 60 Al-mumtahana [The Examined Woman]

﴿ يَا أَيُّهَا الَّذِينَ آمَنُوا لَا تَتَّخِذُوا عَدُوِّي وَعَدُوَّكُمْ أَوْلِيَاءَ تُلْقُونَ إِلَيْهِم بِالْمَوَدَّةِ وَقَدْ كَفَرُوا بِمَا جَاءَكُم مِّنَ الْحَقِّ يُخْرِجُونَ الرَّسُولَ وَإِيَّاكُمْ أَن تُؤْمِنُوا بِاللَّهِ رَبِّكُمْ إِن كُنتُمْ خَرَجْتُمْ جِهَادًا فِي سَبِيلِي وَابْتِغَاءَ مَرْضَاتِي تُسِرُّونَ إِلَيْهِم بِالْمَوَدَّةِ وَأَنَا أَعْلَمُ بِمَا أَخْفَيْتُمْ وَمَا أَعْلَنتُمْ وَمَن يَفْعَلْهُ مِنكُمْ فَقَدْ ضَلَّ سَوَاءَ السَّبِيلِ ﴾ الممتحنة ١

﴿ Oh you who have believed! Do not take my enemy and your enemy as associates, extending friendship to them, as they have disbelieved in the truth that has come to you, and have driven away the Messenger and you all, because you believe in Allah your Lord; if you have set out to wage *jihad* for my cause, seeking after my good pleasure, being cordial towards them in secret, while I know better what you hide and what you declare openly; and whoever among you does this has strayed from the sound path ﴾

Al-mumtahana 1

ويعني بقوله تعالى ذكره ﴿ إن كنتم خرجتم جهاداً في سبيلي ﴾ إن كنتم خرجتم من دياركم فهاجرتم منها إلى مهاجركم للجهاد في طريقي الذي شرعته لكم وديني الذي أمرتكم به وإلتماس مرضاتي

تفسير الطبري

He (may His remembrance be exalted) means by His word: ﴿ If you have set out to wage jihad for My cause ﴾ : If you have set out from your homes, and have emigrated from them to the places of your emigration for *jihad* in my path that I have prescribed for you, in My religion that I have ordered you to, and seeking my good pleasure.

Tafsir Al-Tabari

علي رضي الله عنه يقول بعثني رسول الله ﷺ أنا والزبير والمقداد فقال انطلقوا حتى تأتوا روضة خاخ فإن بها ظعينة معها كتاب فخذوه منها قال فانطلقنا تعادى بنا خيلنا حتى اتينا الروضة فإذا نحن بالظعينة قلنا لها أخرجي الكتاب قالت ما معي كتاب فقلنا لتُخرجنَّ الكتاب أو لنُلقينَّ الثياب قال فأخرجته من عقاصها فأتينا به رسول

الله ﷺ فإذا فيه من حاطب بن ابي بلتعة إلى ناس بمكة من المشركين يخبرهم ببعض أمر رسول الله ﷺ فقال رسول الله ﷺ يا حاطب ما هذا قال يا رسول الله لا تعجل علي إني كنت امرأ ملصقاً في قريش يقول كنت حليفاً ولم أكن من أنفسها وكان من معك من المهاجرين من لهم قرابات يحمون أهليهم وأموالهم فأحببت إذ فاتني ذلك من النسب فيهم أن أتخذ عندهم يداً يحمون قرابتي ولم أفعله إرتداداً عن ديني ولا رضًا بالكفر بعد الاسلام فقال رسول الله ﷺ أما إنه قد صدقكم فقال عمر يا رسول الله دعني اضرب عنق هذا المنافق فقال إنه قد شهد بدراً وما يُدريك لعل الله اطَّلع على من شهد بدراً قال اعملوا ما شئتم فقد غفرتُ لكم فأنزل الله السورة ﴿ يا أيها الذين آمنوا لا تتخذوا عدوي وعدوكم أولياء تُلقون اليهم بالمودة ﴾ إلى قوله ﴿ فقد ضَلَّ سواء السبيل ﴾

صحيح البخاري كتاب المغازي

'Ali (may Allah be pleased with him) said: The Messenger of Allah (SAW) sent me out, me and Zubair and Miqdad, and said: Head out until you get to Rawda Khakh; surely there is a lady there with a letter – take it from her. 'Ali said: So we set out with our steeds sprinting until we reached Rawda. And indeed we found the lady, and we said to her: Hand over the letter. She said: I don't have any letter. And we said: Surely you will hand over the letter, or we'll strip you! So she took it out of her braids, and we brought it back to the Messenger of Allah (SAW). And it was from Hatib ibn Abi Balta'a to some of the Idolaters of Mecca, telling them about some of what the Messenger of Allah (SAW) was up to. The Messenger of Allah (SAW) said: Oh Hatib, what is this? He said: Oh Messenger of Allah, don't be hasty with me, indeed I was a man joined with the Quraysh, I was an ally, but I was not one of them; and all the Emigrants who were with you are kinsfolk to them who guard their households and their wealth; I wanted to do them a favor so they would guard my relatives, seeing that I don't have any kinsfolk among them; I didn't do it to apostatize from my religion or because I was pleased by disbelief after being in Islam. The Messenger of Allah (SAW) said: Indeed he is being sincere. But 'Umar said: Oh Messenger of Allah, let me decapitate this hypocrite! He said: Indeed he was present at Badr, and who knows, perhaps Allah is well aware of who was present at Badr, and said: Do whatever you all wish, for I have forgiven you. And Allah sent down the surah: { Oh you who have believed! Do not take My enemy and your enemy as associates, extending friendship to them } up until His word: { has strayed from the sound path }.

Sahih Al-Bukhari, The book of military raids

﴿ يا أيها الذين آمنوا لا تتخذوا عدوي وعدوكم أولياء تلقون إليهم بالمودة وقد كفروا بما جاءكم من الحق ﴾ يعني المشركين والكفار الذين هم محاربون لله ولرسوله وللمؤمنين الذين شرع الله عداوتهم ومصارمتهم ونهى أن يتخذوا أولياء وأصدقاء وأخلاء كما قال تعالى ﴿ يا أيها الذين آمنوا لا تتخذوا اليهود والنصارى أولياء بعضهم أولياء بعض ومن يتولهم منكم فإنه منهم ﴾ ... وقال تعالى ﴿ لا يتخذ المؤمنون الكافرين أولياء من دون المؤمنين

ومن يفعل ذلك فليس من الله في شيء إلا أن تتقوا منهم تقاة ويحذركم الله نفسه ﴾ ولهذا قبل رسول الله ﷺ عُذر حاطب لما ذكر أنه إنما فعل ذلك مصانعة لقريش لأجل ما كان له عندهم من الأموال والأولاد

تفسير ابن كثير

{ Oh you who have believed! Do not take My enemy and your enemy as associates, extending friendship to them, as they have disbelieved in the truth that has come to you } : that is, the Idolaters and the Disbelievers, those who war against Allah and His Messenger and the Believers, those to whom Allah has prescribed enmity and hostility, and has prohibited them to be taken as associates, friends, and intimates, as the Most High said: { Oh you who have believed! Do not take Jews or Christians as associates; they are associates of each other; whoever among you associates with them is indeed one of them } [Al-ma'ida 51]. … And the Most High said: { Let not the Believers take Disbelievers as associates in place of Believers, for whoever does this has nothing to do with Allah, except out of prudence if you fear from them; Allah warns you of Himself } [Al 'Imran 28]; for this reason the Messenger of Allah (SAW) accepted Hatib's excuse, when he mentioned that indeed he had done what he did, going along with the Quraysh, because of the property and children he had there with them.

Tafsir Ibn Kathir

من حقوق الله تعالى أن لا يمايل من المشركين ذا قربى ولا يحابي في نصرة دين الله ذا مودة فإن حق الله أوجب ونصرة دينه ألزم قال الله تعالى ﴿ يا أيها الذين آمنوا لا تتخذوا عدوي وعدوكم أولياء تلقون إليهم بالمودة وقد كفروا بما جاءكم من الحق ﴾ الآية

الأحكام السلطانية والولايات الدينية للماوردي الباب الرابع في تقليد الإمارة على الجهاد

It is part of duty to Allah Most High that one not be sympathetic to a relative from among the Idolaters, nor side with a friend while upholding the religion of Allah; indeed duty to Allah is more incumbent, and upholding His religion [deen] is more binding. Allah Most High has said: { Oh you who have believed! Do not take my enemy and your enemy as associates, extending friendship to them, as they have disbelieved in the truth that has come to you } and the rest of the verse.

Al-Mawardi, Ahkam Al-sultaniya, Chapter 4: On appointing position of authority (an emirate) over jihad

■   ■   ■

﴿ لَا يَنْهَاكُمُ اللَّهُ عَنِ الَّذِينَ لَمْ يُقَاتِلُوكُمْ فِي الدِّينِ وَلَمْ يُخْرِجُوكُم مِّن دِيَارِكُمْ أَن تَبَرُّوهُمْ وَتُقْسِطُوا إِلَيْهِمْ إِنَّ اللَّهَ يُحِبُّ الْمُقْسِطِينَ إِنَّمَا يَنْهَاكُمُ اللَّهُ عَنِ الَّذِينَ قَاتَلُوكُمْ فِي الدِّينِ وَأَخْرَجُوكُم مِّن دِيَارِكُمْ وَظَاهَرُوا عَلَىٰ إِخْرَاجِكُمْ أَن تَوَلَّوْهُمْ وَمَن يَتَوَلَّهُمْ فَأُولَٰئِكَ هُمُ الظَّالِمُونَ ﴾ الممتحنة ٨-٩

{ Allah does not forbid you all from those who have not fought against you in religion, nor driven you from your homes, that you treat them kindly and act justly towards them; indeed Allah loves those who act justly. But indeed Allah forbids you from taking as associates those who have fought against you in religion, driven you from your homes, and supported driving you out; and whoever takes them as associates, those are the wrongdoers }
Al-mumtahana 8-9

أسماء إبنة ابي بكر رضي الله عنهما قالت أتتني أمي راغبة في عهد النبي ﷺ فسألتُ النبي ﷺ آصِلُها قال نعم قال إبن عيينة فأنزل الله تعالى فيها ﴿ لا ينهاكم الله عن الذين لم يقاتلونكم في الدين ﴾
صحيح البخاري كتاب الأدب

Asmaa bint Abi Bakr (may Allah be pleased with them both) said: My mother came to me, in need, during the time of the Prophet (SAW). So I asked the Prophet (SAW): Can I be kind to her? He said: Yes. Ibn 'Uyaina said: Then Allah Most High sent down concerning her: { Allah does not forbid you all from those who have not fought against you in religion } .
Sahih Al-Bukhari, The book of manners

وقوله تعالى ﴿ لا ينهاكم الله عن الذين لم يقاتلوكم في الدين ولم يُخرجوكم من دياركم ﴾ أي لا ينهاكم عن الاحسان إلى الكفرة الذين لا يقاتلونكم في الدين كالنساء والضعفة منهم ﴿ أن تبرّوهم ﴾ أي تحسنوا اليهم ﴿ وتُقسطوا اليهم ﴾ أي تعدلوا ... وقوله تعالى ﴿ إنما ينهاكم الله عن الذين قاتلوكم في الدين وأخرجوكم من دياركم وظاهروا على إخراجكم أن تولَّوهم ﴾ أي إنما ينهاكم عن موالاة هؤلاء الذين ناصبوكم بالعداوة فقاتلوكم وأخرجوكم وعاونوا على إخراجكم ينهاكم الله عز وجل موالاتهم ويأمركم بمعاداتهم ثم أكد الوعيد على موالاتهم فقال ﴿ ومن يتولَّهم فأولئك هم الظالمون ﴾
تفسير إبن كثير

The word of the Most High: { Allah does not forbid you all from those who have not fought against you in religion, nor driven you from your homes } : that is, He does not forbid you from doing good to Disbelievers that do not fight against you because of religion, like women and the weak among them; { that you treat them kindly } : that is, do good to them; { and act justly towards them } : that is, to be fair. ... The word of the Most High: { But indeed Allah forbids you from taking as associates those who have fought against you in religion, driven you from your homes, and supported driving you out } : that is, indeed He forbids you all from standing with these people, the ones who are hostile towards you in enmity, have fought against you, have driven you out, and have advocated driving you out; Allah Mighty and Sublime forbids you from standing with them, and He orders you to be hostile towards them. Then He emphasized the threat against standing with them, and said: { Whoever takes them as associates, those are the wrongdoers } .

Tafsir Ibn Kathir

إبن وهب قال قال إبن زيد وسألته عن قول الله عز وجل ﴿ لا ينهاكم الله ﴾ الآية فقال هذا قد نسخه القتال أمروا أن يرجعوا اليهم بالسيوف ويجاهدوهم بها يضربونهم وضرب الله لهم أجل أربعة أشهر إما المذابحة وإما الاسلام

تفسير الطبري

Ibn Wahb said: Ibn Zayd said, when I asked him about the word of Allah Mighty and Sublime { Allah does not forbid you all } up to the rest of the verse; he said: This has been abrogated; fighting abrogated it. People were ordered to turn back to them with swords, and wage *jihad* on them with the swords, striking them. Allah fixed a time for them of four months – either slaughter or Islam.

Tafsir Al-Tabari

عن قتادة ﴿ لا ينهاكم الله عن الذين لم يقاتلوكم في الدين ﴾ نسختها ﴿ فاقتلوا المشركين حيث وجدتموهم ﴾

الدر المنثور للسيوطي

Qatada said that { Allah does not forbid you all from those who have not fought against you in religion } was abrogated by { Kill the idolaters wherever you find them } [Al-tawba 5].

Al-Suyuti, Al-durr Al-manthur

* * *

Surah 61 Al-saff [The Ranks]

﴿ إِنَّ اللَّهَ يُحِبُّ الَّذِينَ يُقَاتِلُونَ فِي سَبِيلِهِ صَفًّا كَأَنَّهُم بُنْيَانٌ مَّرْصُوصٌ ﴾ الصف ٤

{ Indeed Allah loves those who fight in His cause lined up in ranks, as if they were a firmly packed structure } *Al-saff 4*

يقول تعالى ذكره للقائلين لو علمنا أحب الأعمال إلى الله لعملناه حتى نموت ﴿ إن الله ﴾ أيها القوم ﴿ يحب الذين يقاتلون في سبيله ﴾ كأنهم يعني في طريقه ودينه الذي دعا إليه ﴿ صفاً ﴾ يعني بذلك أنهم يقاتلون أعداء الله مصطفين

تفسير الطبري

He (may His remembrance be exalted) is addressing those who say: If we knew what deeds Allah loves most we would do them until we died. { Indeed Allah } : Oh people! { loves those who fight in His cause } : meaning in His path and His religion [*deen*], that which He has called them to; { in ranks } : meaning that they fight Allah's enemies lined up in formation.

Tafsir Al-Tabari

وقال الكرماني المقصود من الآية في هذه الترجمة قوله ﴿ آخرها ق صفاً كأنهم بنيان مرصوص ﴾ لأن الصف في القتال من العمل الصالح قبل القتال

فتح الباري لإبن حجر العسقلاني كتاب الجهاد

Al-Kirmani said: The intended meaning in this explanation is His word at the end of it: { As if they were a firmly packed structure } , because lining up to fight is a good deed done before fighting.

Ibn Hajar Al-Asqalani, Fath Al-Bari, The book of jihad

فهذا إخبار من الله تعالى بمحبته عباده المؤمنين إذا صفوا مواجهين لأعداء الله في حومة الوغى يقاتلون في سبيل الله من كفر بالله لتكون كلمة الله هي العليا ودينه هو الظاهر العالي على سائر الأديان

تفسير ابن كثير

This is Allah making known His love for His servants the Believers whenever they line up facing Allah's enemies in the heat of battle, fighting in the cause of Allah against those who have disbelieved in Allah, so that the word of Allah be the utmost, and His religion the most highly manifest over other religions.

Tafsir Ibn Kathir

* * *

﴿ هو الذي أرسل رسوله بالهدى ودين الحق ليظهره على الدين كله ولو كره المشركون يا أيها الذين آمنوا هل أدلكم على تجارة تنجيكم من عذاب أليم تؤمنون بالله ورسوله وتجاهدون في سبيل الله بأموالكم وأنفسكم ذلكم خير لكم إن كنتم تعلمون يغفر لكم ذنوبكم ويدخلكم جنات تجري من تحتها الأنهار ومساكن طيبة في جنات عدن ذلك الفوز العظيم وأخرى تحبونها نصر من الله وفتح قريب وبشر المؤمنين ﴾ الصف ٩-١٣

{ It is He who has sent His Messenger with guidance and the religion of truth, to make it manifest over all religion, even if the idolaters dislike it. Oh you who have believed! Shall I attest to you all of a transaction that will deliver you from painful punishment? That you believe in Allah and His Messenger, and wage *jihad* in the cause of Allah with your wealth and with yourselves; this is better for you, if only you knew. He will forgive your sins and will admit you into gardens below which rivers flow and pleasant dwelling places in gardens of Eden; this is the great victory. And other things that you love – support from Allah and impending victory. So give the good news to the Believers! } *Al-saff* 9-13

تقدم في حديث عبدالله بن سلام أن الصحابة رضي الله عنهم أرادوا أن يسألوا رسول الله ﷺ عن أحب الأعمال إلى الله عز وجل ليفعلوه فأنزل الله تعالى هذه السورة ومن جملتها هذه الآية ﴿ يا أيها الذين آمنوا هل أدلكم على تجارة تنجيكم من عذاب أليم ﴾ ثم فسر هذه التجارة العظيمة التي لا تبور التي هي محصلة

للمقصود ومزيلة للمحذور فقال تعالى ﴿ تؤمنون بالله ورسوله وتجاهدون في سبيل الله بأموالكم وأنفسكم ذلك خيرٌ لكم إن كنتم تعلمون ﴾ أي من تجارة الدنيا والكد لها والتصدي لها وحدها ثم قال تعالى ﴿ يغفر لكم ذنوبكم ﴾ أي إن فعلتم ما أمرتكم به ودللتكم عليه غفرت لكم الزلات وأدخلتكم الجنات والمساكن الطيبات والدرجات العاليات ولهذا قال تعالى ﴿ ويُدخلكم جنات تجري من تحتها الانهار ومساكن طيبة في جنات عدن ذلك الفوز العظيم ﴾ ثم قال تعالى ﴿ وأخرى تحبونها ﴾ أي وأزيدكم على ذلك زيادة تحبونها وهي ﴿ نصرٌ من الله وفتح قريب ﴾ أي إذا قاتلتم في سبيله ونصرتم دينه تكفل الله بنصركم قال الله تعالى ﴿ يا أيها الذين آمنوا إن تنصروا الله ينصركم ويثبّت أقدامكم ﴾ وقال تعالى ﴿ ولينصرنّ الله من ينصره إن الله لقوي عزيز ﴾ وقوله تعالى ﴿ وفتح قريب ﴾ أي عاجل فهذه الزيادة هي خير الدنيا موصول بنعيم الآخرة لمن أطاع الله ورسوله ونصر الله ودينه ولهذا قال تعالى ﴿ وبشير المؤمنين ﴾

تفسير ابن كثير

It has been mentioned earlier, in a hadith of Abdullah ibn Salam, that the Companions (may Allah be pleased with them) wanted to ask the Messenger of Allah (SAW) about the deeds most pleasing to Allah Mighty and Sublime, so they could do them. And so Allah Most High sent down this surah, which includes this verse: { Oh you who have believed! Shall I attest to you all of a transaction that will deliver you from painful punishment? } . Then He expounds on this great transaction that does not fail, that brings one to what he seeks after and does away with peril; the Most High says: { That you believe in Allah and His Messenger, and wage jihad in the cause of Allah with your wealth and with yourselves; this is better for you, if only you knew } : that is, better than the commerce of this life, laboring for it, and being occupied only with this. Then the Most High says: { He will forgive your sins } : that is: If you do what I have commanded you and that of which I have attested to you, I will forgive your errors and I will admit you into the gardens and the dwellings of pleasant delights, degrees of the greatest heights. For this reason the Most High says: { He will admit you into gardens below which rivers flow and pleasant dwelling places in gardens of Eden; this is the great victory } . Then the Most High says: { And other things that you love } : that is: I will add even more to this for you, a bonus that you will love, this being { support from Allah and impending victory } . In other words, if you all fight in His cause and uphold His religion, Allah will promise to support you; Allah Most High said: { Oh you who have believed! If you uphold Allah He will uphold you, and affirm your feet } [Muhammad 7], and the Most High said: { Truly Allah champions those who champion Him; indeed Allah is strong, mighty } [Al-hajj 40]. Regarding the word of the Most High: { Impending victory } ; that is, swift; and this bonus is the best of this world, continuing on to the bliss of the hereafter, for whoever obeys Allah and His Messenger and upholds Allah and His religion. This is why the Most High says: { So give the good news to the Believers! }

Tafsir Ibn Kathir

يقول تعالى ذكره الله الذي أرسل رسوله محمداً بالهدى ودين الحق يعني ببيان الحق ودين الحق يعني وبدين الله وهو الاسلام وقوله ﴿ لِيُظْهِرَهُ عَلَى الدِّينِ كُلِّهِ ﴾ يقول ليظهر دينه الحق الذي أرسل به رسوله على كل دين سواه وذلك عند نزول عيسى إبن مريم وحين تصير الملة واحدة فلا يكون دين غير الاسلام ... ﴿ وَبَشِّرِ المُؤْمِنِينَ ﴾ يقول تعالى ذكره لنبيه محمد ﷺ وبشر يا محمد المؤمنين بنصر الله إياهم على عدوهم وفتح عاجل لهم

تفسير الطبري

He (may His remembrance be exalted) is saying: Allah is He who has sent His Messenger Muhammad with guidance and the religion of truth [deen al-haqq], that is, by declaring the truth and the religion of truth, that is, the religion of Allah, this being Islam. His word: { To make it manifest over all religion } ; He is saying: To make His religion of truth manifest, the one He sent His Messenger with, over all other religion, this being when 'Isa ibn Maryam comes down, and when there is only one religion, and no other religion but Islam. ... { So give the good news to the Believers! } ; He (may His remembrance be exalted) is saying to His Prophet Muhammad (SAW): So give the good news, Oh Muhammad, to the Believers, of Allah's support for them against their enemy, and of the swift victory to be theirs.

Tafsir Al-Tabari

﴿ هُوَ الَّذِي أَرْسَلَ رَسُولَهُ بِالهُدَى ﴾ بالقرآن أو المعجزة ﴿ وَدِينِ الحَقِّ ﴾ والملة الحنيفية ﴿ لِيُظْهِرَهُ عَلَى الدِّينِ كُلِّهِ ﴾ ليغلبه على جميع الأديان ﴿ وَلَوْ كَرِهَ المُشْرِكُونَ ﴾ لما فيه من محض التوحيد وإبطال الشرك ... ﴿ تُؤْمِنُونَ بِاللهِ وَرَسُولِهِ وَتُجَاهِدُونَ فِي سَبِيلِ اللهِ بِأَمْوَالِكُمْ وَأَنْفُسِكُمْ ﴾ إستئناف مبين للتجارة وهو الجمع بين الايمان والجهاد المؤدي إلى كمال عزهم والمراد به الأمر وانما جيء بلفظ الخبر ايذاناً بأن ذلك مما لا يترك ﴿ ذَلِكُمْ خَيْرٌ لَكُمْ ﴾ يعني ما ذكر من الايمان والجهاد ﴿ إِنْ كُنْتُمْ تَعْلَمُونَ ﴾ إن كنتم من أهل العلم إذ الجاهل لا يعتد بفعله

تفسير البيضاوي

{ It is He who has sent His Messenger with guidance } : with the Qur'an or miracles; { and the religion of truth } : the true religion; { to make it manifest over all religion } : to make it triumph over all religions; { even if the idolaters dislike it } : because of the purity, oneness, and refutation of idolatry that there is in it. ... { That you believe in Allah and His Messenger, and wage *jihad* in the cause of Allah with your wealth and with yourselves } : a clear continuation of the transaction, this being the integration of belief and the *jihad* that leads to the perfection of their glory. The meaning is a command; indeed it came in the form of an announcement to indicate that it is something that can not be neglected. { This is better for you } : that is, the belief and *jihad* that have been mentioned; { if only you knew } : if you are of those who know, since someone who is ignorant does not consider what he does.

Tafsir Al-Baydawi

﴿ ودين أحق ﴾ الملة الحنفية ﴿ ليظهره ﴾ ليعليه ﴿ على الدين كله ﴾ على جميع الأديان المخالفة له ولعمري لقد فعل فما بقي دين من الأديان إلا وهو مغلوب مقهور بدين الاسلام وعن مجاهد إذا نزل عيسى لم يكن في الأرض إلا دين الاسلام

تفسير الزمخشري

{ The religion of truth } : the true religion; { to make it manifest } : to raise it; { over all religion } : over all religions in opposition to it; I swear by my life this is now done! For not a single religion has remained that has not been overcome and conquered by the religion of Islam. Mujahid said: When 'Isa comes down there will be nothing on earth but the religion of Islam.

Tafsir Al-Zamakhshari

﴿ على تجارة ﴾ هي التجارة بين أهل الايمان وحضرة الله تعالى كما قال تعالى ﴿ إن الله إشترى من المؤمنين أنفسهم وأموالهم بأن لهم الجنة ﴾

تفسير الرازي

{ Of a transaction } : this is the transaction between those who believe and Allah Most High and Excellent, as the Most High says: { Indeed Allah has bought, from the Believers, their lives and their wealth, so that *Jannah* may be theirs } [Al-tawba 111]

Tafsir Al-Razi

قوله تعالى ﴿ يا أيها الذين آمنوا هل أدلكم على تجارة ﴾ قال مقاتل نزلت في عثمان بن مظعون وذلك أنه قال لرسول الله ﷺ لو أذنت لي فطلّقتُ خولة وترهّبت واختصيت وحرمت اللحم ولا أنام بليل أبداً ولا أُفطر بنهار أبداً فقال رسول الله ﷺ إن من سنتي النكاح ولا رهبانية في الاسلام انما رهبانية أمتي الجهاد في سبيل الله وخصاء أمتي الصوم ولا تحرّموا طيبات ما أحلّ الله لكم ومن سنتي أنام وأقوم وأفطر وأصوم فمن رغب عن سنتي فليس مني فقال عثمان والله لوددتُ يا نبي الله أي التجارات أحب إلى الله فأتَّجر فيها فنزلت

تفسير القرطبي

The word of the Most High: { Oh you who have believed! Shall I attest to you all of a transaction } ; Muqatil said: This came down regarding 'Uthman ibn Madh'un. This was because he said to the Messenger of Allah (SAW): If only you would give me permission, I would divorce Khawlah, become a monk, get castrated, and prohibit meat, and I would not ever sleep at night or break fast during the day. But the Messenger of Allah (SAW) said: Truly it is my way of life [*sunnah*] to have marital relations, and there is no monasticism in Islam; indeed the monasticism of my *ummah* is *jihad* in the cause of Allah, and the castration of my *ummah* is fasting; and do not forbid the delights that Allah has made permissible for you; and it is my way of life to sleep and then arise, break fast, and fast; and whoever turns away from my way of life is not of me. Then 'Uthman said: I swear by Allah, I wish, oh Prophet of Allah, for whatever transaction is most pleasing to Allah, and I will make the deal for it. And so the verse came down.

Tafsir Al-Qurtubi

فدلَّهم الله سبحانه فقال ﴿ تؤمنون بالله ورسوله وتجاهدون في سبيل الله ﴾ الآية فأبتلوا بذلك يوم أحد ففرّوا عن رسول الله ﷺ حين صرع وشجّ في وجهه وكسرت رباعيته فنزلت هذه الآية يعيّرهم ترك الوفاء

تفسير الثعلبي

So Allah the Exalted attested to them, and said: { That you believe in Allah and His Messenger, and wage *jihad* in the cause of Allah } and the rest of the verse. The people prompted this on the day of Uhud, running away from the Messenger of Allah (SAW) when He was knocked down and his face fractured and his front tooth broke. So this verse came down and He reproached them against abandoning allegiance.

Tafsir Al-Tha'labi

قوله تعالى ﴿ هل أدلكم على تجارة ﴾ قال المفسرون نزلت هذه الآية حين قالوا لو علمنا أي الأعمال أحب إلى الله لعملنا به أبداً فدلَّهم الله على ذلك وجعله بمنزلة التجارة لمكان ربحهم فيه

تفسير ابن الجوزي

The word of the Most High: { Shall I attest to you all of a transaction } ; the expositors say that this verse came down when the people said: If only we knew what deeds are most pleasing to Allah, we would do them always. And so Allah attested to them concerning this, and gave it the status of a transaction due to the gain present in it.

Tafsir Ibn Al-Jawzi

ثم قال ﴿ هو الذي أرسل رسوله ﴾ محمداً ﷺ ﴿ بالهدى ودين الحق ﴾ يعني الاسلام يعني دين محمد ﷺ ﴿ ليظهره على الدين كله ﴾ يعني الأديان كلها ففعل الله هذا تعالى ذلك وأظهر دين محمد ﷺ على أهل كل دين حين قتلهم فأدوا إليه الجزية مثل قوله ﴿ فأيّدنا الذين آمنوا على عدوهم فأصبحوا ظاهرين ﴾ ﴿ ولو كره المشركون ﴾ من العرب يعني كفار قريش لما نزلت هذه الآية ﴿ إن الله يحب الذين يقاتلون في سبيله صفاً كأنهم بنيان مرصوص ﴾ قال بعضهم يا رسول الله فما لنا من الأجر إذا جاهدنا في سبيل

الله فأنزل الله تعالى ﴿ يَا أَيُّهَا الَّذِينَ آمَنُوا هَلْ أَدُلُّكُمْ عَلَى تِجَارَةٍ تُنجِيكُم مِّنْ عَذَابٍ أَلِيمٍ ﴾ يعني وجيع فقال المسلمون والله لو علمنا ما هذه التجارة لأعطينا فيها الأموال والأولاد والأهلين فبين الله لهم ما هذه التجارة يعني التوحيد

تفسير مقاتل بن سليمان

Then He said: { It is He who has sent His Messenger } : Muhammad (SAW); { with guidance and the religion of truth } : namely, Islam, that is, Muhammad's (SAW) religion; { to make it manifest over all religion } : that is, all religions. And Allah in fact did this, may He be exalted, and He made Muhammad's (SAW) religion triumph over the adherents of every religion, when He killed them and they gave him *jizya*, as in His word: { We came to the aid of those who believed, against their enemy, and they became the ones who prevailed } [*Al-saff* 14]. { Even if the Idolaters dislike it } : among the Arabs, that is, the disbelievers [*kuffar*] of Quraish, when this verse came down: { Indeed Allah loves those who fight in His cause lined up in ranks, as if they were a firmly packed structure } [*Al-saff* 4]. Some of them said: Oh Messenger of Allah, what reward do we get if we wage *jihad* in the cause of Allah? So Allah Most High sent down: { Oh you who have believed! Shall I attest to you all of a transaction that will deliver you from painful punishment? } : that is, grievous; and the Muslims said: By Allah, if only we knew what this transaction was, we would give our wealth, our children, and our kinsfolk. So Allah made clear to them what this transaction was, namely, asserting one god [*tawheed*, unification].

Tafsir Muqatil ibn Sulaiman

﴿ وَبَشِّرِ الْمُؤْمِنِينَ ﴾ يا محمد بالنصر في الدنيا والجنة في الآخرة ثم حضَّهم على نصرة الدين وجهاد المخالفين

تفسير البغوي

{ So give the good news to the Believers! } : oh Muhammad, of the victory in this world and of *Jannah* in the next, then urge them on to upholding the religion and *jihad* against those who oppose.

Tafsir Al-Baghawi

• • •

• Surah 63   Al-munafiqun [The Hypocrites] •

﴿ إِذَا جَاءَكَ الْمُنَافِقُونَ قَالُوا نَشْهَدُ إِنَّكَ لَرَسُولُ اللَّهِ وَاللَّهُ يَعْلَمُ إِنَّكَ لَرَسُولُهُ وَاللَّهُ يَشْهَدُ إِنَّ الْمُنَافِقِينَ لَكَاذِبُونَ اتَّخَذُوا أَيْمَانَهُمْ جُنَّةً فَصَدُّوا عَن سَبِيلِ اللَّهِ إِنَّهُمْ سَاءَ مَا كَانُوا يَعْمَلُونَ ذَلِكَ بِأَنَّهُمْ آمَنُوا ثُمَّ كَفَرُوا فَطُبِعَ عَلَى قُلُوبِهِمْ فَهُمْ لَا يَفْقَهُونَ وَإِذَا رَأَيْتَهُمْ تُعْجِبُكَ أَجْسَامُهُمْ وَإِن يَقُولُوا تَسْمَعْ لِقَوْلِهِمْ كَأَنَّهُمْ خُشُبٌ مُسَنَّدَةٌ يَحْسَبُونَ كُلَّ صَيْحَةٍ عَلَيْهِمْ هُمُ الْعَدُوُّ فَاحْذَرْهُمْ قَاتَلَهُمُ اللَّهُ أَنَّى يُؤْفَكُونَ ﴾ المنافقون ١-٤

﴿ If the hypocrites come to you and say: "We bear witness that you are indeed the Messenger of Allah"; surely Allah knows that you are His Messenger, and Allah bears witness that the hypocrites are truly liars. They take their oaths to cover up, and obstruct the cause of Allah; indeed what they were doing was evil. This was because they believed and then disbelieved, and their hearts have been sealed over, and so they do not comprehend. Whenever you see them, their bodies look good to you, and if they speak, you hear their words, as if they were solid wooden beams; they reckon that every shout is against them; they are the enemy, so beware of them; may Allah fight them, how they are deceived! ﴾ Al-munafiqun 1-4

وَهُمْ مِن شَأْنِهِمْ أَنَّهُمْ كَانُوا فِي الْبَاطِنِ لَا يَأْلُونَ الْإِسْلَامَ وَأَهْلَهُ خَبَالًا فَحَصَلَ بِهَذَا الْقَدْرِ ضَرَرٌ كَبِيرٌ عَلَى كَثِيرٍ مِنَ النَّاسِ وَلِهَذَا قَالَ تَعَالَى ﴿ فَصَدُّوا عَن سَبِيلِ اللَّهِ إِنَّهُمْ سَاءَ مَا كَانُوا يَعْمَلُونَ ﴾
تفسير ابن كثير

It is inherent in their condition that they inwardly never let up on madness towards Islam and its people, and to this extent bring about great harm upon many people. For this reason the Most High said: ﴿ And obstruct the cause of Allah; indeed what they were doing was evil ﴾.

Tafsir Ibn Kathir

عن قتادة في قوله ﴿ ذلك بأنهم آمنوا ثم كفروا فطبع على قلوبهم ﴾ قال أقروا بلا إله إلا الله وأن محمداً رسول الله وقلوبهم تأبى ذلك

الدر المنثور للسيوطي

From Qatada, concerning His word { This was because they believed and then disbelieved, and their hearts have been sealed over } , said: They declared that "There is no god but Allah and that Muhammad is the Messenger of Allah", but their hearts refused this.

Al-Suyuti, Al-dur Al-manthur

﴿ يحسَبون كل صَيحة ﴾ تصاح كنداء في العسكر وإنشاد ضالة ﴿ عليهم ﴾ لما في قلوبهم من الرعب أن ينزل فيهم ما يبيح دماءهم ﴿ هم العدو فاحذروهم ﴾ فإنهم يفشون سرك للكفار ﴿ قاتلهم الله ﴾ أهلكهم ﴿ أنى يؤفكون ﴾ كيف يصرفون عن الإيمان بعد قيام البرهان

تفسير الجلالين

{ They reckon that every shout } : that is shouted, such as a battle cry or a search for a stray animal; { is against them } : due to the terror in their hearts that something will come down regarding them that will make their blood lawful; { they are the enemy, so beware of them } : indeed they spill your secrets to the Disbelievers; { may Allah fight them } : may He destroy them! { How they are deceived! } : How can they turn away from belief, after the clear evidence has been brought?

Tafsir Al-Jalalain

قوله تعالى ﴿ قاتلهم الله أنى يؤفكون ﴾ أي لعنهم الله وأخزاهم وأحلهم محلَّ مَن يقاتله عدواً قاهراً له ﴿ أنى يؤفكون ﴾ أي يُصرَفون من الحق إلى الباطل

التفسير الكبير للطبراني

The word of the Most High: { May Allah fight them; how they are deceived! } : that is, may Allah curse them, disgrace them, and substitute them for others who oppose Him as His oppressive enemy. { How they are deceived! } : that is, how they have been turned away from the truth to vanity.

Al-Tabarani, Al-tafsir Al-kabir

* * *

Surah 64   Al-taghabun [Mutual gain and loss]

﴿ يَا أَيُّهَا الَّذِينَ آمَنُوا إِنَّ مِنْ أَزْوَاجِكُمْ وَأَوْلَادِكُمْ عَدُوًّا لَكُمْ فَاحْذَرُوهُمْ وَإِنْ تَعْفُوا وَتَصْفَحُوا وَتَغْفِرُوا فَإِنَّ اللَّهَ غَفُورٌ رَحِيمٌ ﴾ التغابن ١٤

{ Oh you who have believed! Indeed among your wives and your children are enemies of yours, so beware of them; but if you pardon, and are forbearing, and forgive, indeed Allah is forgiving, merciful } Al-taghabun 14

﴿ يا أيها الذين آمنوا إن من أزواجكم وأولادكم عدواً لكم فاحذروهم ﴾ أن تطيعوهم في التخلف عن الخير كالجهاد والهجرة فإن سبب نزول الآية الإطاعة في ذلك

تفسير الجلالين

{ Oh you who have believed! Indeed among your wives and your children are enemies of yours, so beware of them } : beware of complying with them in falling behind on good deeds like *jihad* and emigration [*hijra*]; the reason for this verse coming down was such compliance.

Tafsir Al-Jalalain

يقول تعالى ذكره يا أيها الذين صدّقوا الله ورسوله ﴿ إن من أزواجكم وأولادكم عدواً لكم ﴾ يصدّونكم عن سبيل الله ويبطئونكم عن طاعة الله ﴿ فاحذروهم ﴾ أن تقبلوا منهم ما يأمرونكم به من ترك طاعة الله وذُكر أن هذه الآية نزلت في قوم كانوا أرادوا الاسلام والهجرة فثبّطهم عن ذلك أزواجهم واولادهم

تفسير الطبري

He (may His remembrance be exalted) is saying: Oh you who have believed in Allah and His Messenger! { indeed among your wives and your children are enemies to you } who hinder you from the cause of Allah and hold you back from obedience to Allah. { So beware of them } : that you do not consent with them in the neglect of obedience to Allah that they have asked of you. It is mentioned that this verse came down in regards to a group of people who desired Islam and emigration but their wives and children prevented them from it.

Tafsir Al-Tabari

إن من الأزواج أزواجاً يعادين بعولتهنّ ويخاصمنهم ويجلبن عليهم ومن الأولاد أولاداً يعادون آباءهم ويعقّونهم ويجرّعونهم الغصص والأذى ﴿ فاحذروهم ﴾ الضمير للعدو أو للازواج والأولاد جميعاً أي لما علمتم أن هؤلاء لا يخلون من عدو فكونوا منهم على حذر ولا تأمنوا غوائلهم وشرهم

تفسير الزمخشري

Indeed there are some wives who act in hostility by their groaning, who quarrel with the men and trouble them, and there are some children who act in hostility towards their fathers, are disobedient to them, and make them choke on agony and distress. { So beware of them } : "them" refers to the enemy, or to all wives and children, that is, when you are aware that they are not without enemies among them. So be on guard against them, and do not feel like you are safe from their aggravations and their evil.

Tafsir Al-Zamakhshari

قال عكرمة عن إبن عباس وهؤلاء الذين منعهم أهلهم عن الهجرة لما هاجروا ورأوا الناس قد فقهوا في الدين هموا أن يعاقبوا أهليهم الذين منعوهم فأنزل الله تعالى ﴿ وإن تعفوا وتصفحوا وتغفروا فإن الله غفور رحيم ﴾

اسباب النزول للواحدي

'Ikrama related from Ibn 'Abbas that these people were those whose households prevented them from emigrating; when they did emigrate and saw that people had come to greater knowledge of the religion, they resolved to punish those of their households who had prevented them; but Allah Most High sent down: { But if you pardon, and are forbearing, and forgive, indeed Allah is forgiving, merciful } .

Al-Wahidi, Asbab Al-nuzul

• • •

Surah 66   Al-tahrim [Prohibition]

﴿ قَدْ فَرَضَ اللَّهُ لَكُمْ تَحِلَّةَ أَيْمَانِكُمْ وَاللَّهُ مَوْلَاكُمْ وَهُوَ الْعَلِيمُ الْحَكِيمُ ﴾ التحريم ٢

{ Allah has ordained for you all the dissolution of your oaths }
Al-tahrim 2

﴿ قد فرض الله لكم تحلة أيمانكم ﴾ تحليل اليمين كفارتها أي إذا أحببتم استباحة المحلوف عليه
تفسير القرطبي

{ Allah has ordained for you all the dissolution of your oaths } : An oath is dissolved by making expiation for it.

Tafsir Al-Qurtubi

﴿ قد فرض الله لكم تحلة أيمانكم ﴾ فيه وجهان أحدهما قد بيّن الله لكم المخرج من أيمانكم الثاني قد قدر الله لكم الكفارة في الحنث في ايمانكم
تفسير الماوردي

{ Allah has ordained for you all the dissolution of your oaths } . There are two points of view; one of them is: Allah has made the way out of your oaths clear to you; the second is: Allah has decreed for you expiation for the perjury in your oaths.

Tafsir Al-Mawardi

﴿ يَا أَيُّهَا النَّبِيُّ جَاهِدِ الْكُفَّارَ وَالْمُنَافِقِينَ وَاغْلُظْ عَلَيْهِمْ وَمَأْوَاهُمْ جَهَنَّمُ وَبِئْسَ الْمَصِيرُ ﴾ التحريم 9

{ **Oh Prophet! Wage *jihad* on the disbelievers and the hypocrites, and be harsh to them; their dwelling is Hell, a miserable fate** }
Al-tahrim 9

﴿ يا أيها النبي جاهد الكفار ﴾ بالسيف ﴿ والمنافقين ﴾ باللسان والحجة ﴿ وأغلظ عليهم ﴾ بالانتهار والمقت

تفسير الجلالين

{ Oh Prophet! Wage jihad on the disbelievers } : with the sword; { and the hypocrites } : with words and with arguments; { and be harsh to them } : with rebuke and animosity.

Tafsir Al-Jalalain

يقول تعالى ذكره لنبيه محمد ﷺ ﴿ يا أيها النبي جاهد الكفار ﴾ بالسيف ﴿ والمنافقين ﴾ بالوعيد واللسان ... عن قتادة قال أمر الله نبيه عليه الصلاة والسلام أن يجاهد الكفار بالسيف ويغلظ على المنافقين بالحدود

تفسير الطبري

He (may His remembrance be exalted) is saying to His Prophet Muhammad (SAW): { Oh Prophet! Wage jihad on the disbelievers } : with the sword; { and the hypocrites } : with threats and with the tongue. ... Qadata said: Allah ordered His Prophet (prayers and peace upon him) to wage *jihad* on the disbelievers [*kuffar*] with the sword, and to be harsh on the hypocrites with the prescribed punishments [*hudud*].

Tafsir Al-Tabari

﴿ يا أيها النبي جاهد الكفار والمنافقين ﴾ ذكر المنافقين مع أن لفظ الكفار يتناول المنافقين ﴿ وأغلظ عليهم ﴾ أي شدد عليهم والمجاهدة قد تكون بالقتال وقد تكون بالحجة تارة باللسان وتارة بالسنان وقيل جاهدهم بإقامة الحدود عليهم لأنهم هم المرتكبون الكبائر لأن أصحاب الرسول عصموا منها

تفسير الرازي

{ Oh Prophet! Wage jihad on the disbelievers and the hypocrites } : He mentions the hypocrites even though saying "disbelievers" encompasses hypocrites; { and be harsh to them } : that is, exert pressure on them. Striving in *jihad* may be by fighting, or by arguments, at times with words and at times with spearheads. It is said: Wage *jihad* on them by observing the prescribed punishments for them, since they are the ones who commit grave sins, because the Messenger's Companions have been preserved from them.

Tafsir Al-Razi

قوله تعالى ﴿ يا أيها النبي جاهد الكفار والمنافقين وأغلظ عليهم ﴾ فيه مسألة واحدة وهو التشديد في دين الله فأمره أن يجاهد الكفار بالسيف والمواعظ الحسنة والدعاء إلى الله

تفسير القرطبي

The word of the Most High: { Oh Prophet! Wage jihad on the disbelievers and the hypocrites, and be harsh to them } ; there is one point to be made, and this is severity in Allah's religion [*deen*]; He has ordered him to wage *jihad* on the disbelievers by the sword, by suitable admonitions, by calling them to Allah.

Tafsir Al-Qurtubi

▪ ▪ ▪

• Surah 73   Al-muzzammil [The Enshrouded One] •

﴿ وَاصْبِرْ عَلَىٰ مَا يَقُولُونَ وَاهْجُرْهُمْ هَجْرًا جَمِيلًا ﴾ المزمل ١٠

{ Be forbearing with what they say, and refrain from them nicely } Al-muzzammil 10

﴿ واصبر على ما يقولون وأهجرهم هجراً جميلاً ﴾ براءة نسخت ما ههنا أمر بقتالهم حتى يشهدوا أن لا إله إلا الله وأن محمداً رسول الله لا يقبل منهم غيرها

تفسير الطبري المزمل ١٠

{ Be forbearing with what they say, and refrain from them nicely } ; an absolution that abrogates what is here is the command to fight them until they bear witness that there is no god but Allah, and that Muhammad is the Messenger of Allah; nothing is to be accepted from them other than this.

Tafsir Al-Tabari, Al-muzzammil 10

﴿ إِنَّ رَبَّكَ يَعْلَمُ أَنَّكَ تَقُومُ أَدْنَىٰ مِن ثُلُثَيِ اللَّيْلِ وَنِصْفَهُ وَثُلُثَهُ وَطَائِفَةٌ مِّنَ الَّذِينَ مَعَكَ وَاللَّهُ يُقَدِّرُ اللَّيْلَ وَالنَّهَارَ عَلِمَ أَن لَّن تُحْصُوهُ فَتَابَ عَلَيْكُمْ فَاقْرَءُوا مَا تَيَسَّرَ مِنَ الْقُرْآنِ عَلِمَ أَن سَيَكُونُ مِنكُم مَّرْضَىٰ وَآخَرُونَ يَضْرِبُونَ فِي الْأَرْضِ يَبْتَغُونَ مِن فَضْلِ اللَّهِ وَآخَرُونَ يُقَاتِلُونَ فِي سَبِيلِ اللَّهِ فَاقْرَءُوا مَا تَيَسَّرَ مِنْهُ وَأَقِيمُوا الصَّلَاةَ وَآتُوا الزَّكَاةَ وَأَقْرِضُوا اللَّهَ قَرْضًا حَسَنًا وَمَا تُقَدِّمُوا لِأَنفُسِكُم مِّنْ خَيْرٍ تَجِدُوهُ عِندَ اللَّهِ هُوَ خَيْرًا وَأَعْظَمَ أَجْرًا وَاسْتَغْفِرُوا اللَّهَ إِنَّ اللَّهَ غَفُورٌ رَّحِيمٌ ﴾ المزمل ٢٠

{ Indeed your Lord knows that you all are up for close to two-thirds of the night, half of it, a third of it, and a group of those who are with you; but Allah decrees the night and the daytime; He knows that you can not keep track, and has turned to you, so recite what is easy of the Qur'an; He knows that there will be sick ones among you, and others go around the land seeking

Allah's bounty, and still others fight in the cause of Allah, so recite what is easy of it; and observe prayer, give zakat, and lend a good loan to Allah; whatever good things you put forth for yourselves, you will surely find better things with Allah, and the greatest rewards; so seek the forgivness of Allah, indeed Allah is forgiving, merciful } *Al-muzzammil 20*

﴿ وآخرون يقاتلون في سبيل الله ﴾ يقول وآخرون أيضاً منكم يجاهدون العدو فيقاتلونهم في نصرة دين الله فرحمكم الله نخفف عنكم ووضع عنكم فرض قيام الليل

تفسير الطبري

{ And still others fight in the cause of Allah } ; He is saying: And there are others of you as well, who wage *jihad* against the enemy and fight to uphold Allah's religion; Allah will have mercy on you, make it easy on you, and unburden you of the obligation to get up for prayer at night.

Tafsir Al-Tabari

سَوَّى الله تعالى في هذه الآية بين درجة المجاهدين والمكتسبين المال الحلال للنفقة على نفسه وعياله والاحسان والافضال فكان هذا دليلاً على أن كسب المال بمنزلة الجهاد لأنه جمعه مع الجهاد في سبيل الله وروي ابراهيم عن علقمة قال قال رسول الله ﷺ ما من جالب يجلب طعاماً من بلد إلى بلد فيبيعه بسعر يومه إلا كانت منزلته عند الله منزلة الشهداء

تفسير القرطبي

In this verse Allah Most High places the status of *Mujahideen* on the same level with those who engage in lawful earnings with which to spend on themselves and their households, doing good, and granting favors. This is evidence that acquiring earnings carries the same status as *jihad*, since He mentions it together with *jihad* in the cause of Allah. Ibrahim relates that 'Alqama said: The Messenger of Allah (SAW) said: Anyone who brings food from one land to another and sells it for the price of his daily needs – his status in the sight of Allah is as the status of the martyrs.

Tafsir Al-Qurtubi

وقوله تعالى ﴿ أن سيكون منكم مرضى وآخرون يضربون في الأرض يبتغون من فضل الله وآخرون يقاتلون في سبيل الله ﴾ أي علم أن سيكون من هذه الامة ذوو أعذار في ترك قيام الليل من مرضى لا يستطيعون ذلك ومسافرين في الأرض يبتغون من فضل الله في المكاسب والمتاجر وآخرون مشغولين بما هو الأهم في حقهم من الغزو في سبيل الله وهذه الآية بل السورة كلها مكية ولم يكن القتال شرع بعد فهي من أكبر دلائل النبوة لأنه من باب الإخبار بالمغيبات المستقبلة

تفسير ابن كثير

The word of the Most High: { That there will be sick ones among you, and others go around the land seeking Allah's good favor, and still others fight in the cause of Allah } : that is, He knows that in this *ummah* there will be those with excuses for not getting up at night to pray, including sick people who are unable to do this, people travelling in the land seeking Allah's bounty in profitable earnings and commerce, and others who are occupied in their most important duty of going on attacks in the cause of Allah. This verse, indeed the entire surah, is from Mecca, although fighting had not yet been prescribed – and this is one of the greatest proofs of the prophethood, in that it makes known divine secrets yet to come.

Tafsir Ibn Kathir

عن عمر بن الخطاب قال ما من حال يأتيني عليه الموت بعد الجهاد في سبيل الله أحب إليّ من أن يأتيني وأنا بين شعبتي رحلي ألتمس من فضل الله ثم تلا هذه الآية

الدر المنثور للسيوطي

From 'Umar ibn Al-Khattab, who said: There is no manner that I would more rather have death come upon me – besides *jihad* in the cause of Allah – than it should come upon me while I am between the two limbs of my saddle, seeking Allah's bounty. Then He recited this verse.

Al-Suyuti, Al-durr Al-manthur

. . .

• ## Surah 88   Al-ghashiya [The Enveloping]   •

﴿ فَذَكِّرْ إِنَّمَا أَنتَ مُذَكِّرٌ لَّسْتَ عَلَيْهِم بِمُصَيْطِرٍ إِلَّا مَن تَوَلَّىٰ وَكَفَرَ فَيُعَذِّبُهُ اللَّهُ الْعَذَابَ الْأَكْبَرَ ﴾

الغاشية ٢١-٢٤

{ So inform, for indeed you are an informer, you are not lord over them; except that whoever turns away and disbelieves, Allah will punish him with the greatest punishment } Al-ghashiya 21-24

﴿ فَيُعَذِّبُهُ اللَّهُ الْعَذَابَ الْأَكْبَرَ ﴾ وهي جهنم العذاب الدائم عذابها وإنما قال ﴿ الْأَكْبَرَ ﴾ لأنهم عذبوا في الدنيا بالجوع والقَحْط والأَسر وقتل ودليل هذا التأويل قراءة ابن مسعود ﴿ إِلَّا مَن تَوَلَّىٰ وَكَفَرَ فَإِنَّهُ يُعَذِّبُهُ اللَّهُ ﴾ وقيل هو إستثناء متصل والمعنى لست بِمُسَلَّط إلا على من تولى وكفر فأنت مسلط عليه بالجهاد والله يعذبه بعد ذلك العذاب الأكبر فلا نسخ في الآية على هذا التقدير وروي أن عليّاً أُتِي برجل إرتد فاستتابه ثلاثة أيام فلم يعاود الاسلام فضرب عنقه وقرأ ﴿ إِلَّا مَن تَوَلَّىٰ وَكَفَرَ ﴾

تفسير القرطبي

{ Allah will punish him with the greatest punishment } : this being Hellfire, the punishment of which is everlasting. Indeed He said { greatest } because they were punished in this world with hunger, drought, imprisonment, and killing. Evidence for this interpretation is the recitation of Ibn Mas'ud: { Except that whoever turns away and disbelieves, indeed Allah will punish him } . It is said that this is an adjoining exception, the meaning being: You are not charged to be a ruler, except over those who turn away and disbelieve; over these you are a ruler by *jihad*, and Allah will punish them afterwards with the greatest punishment. There is no abrogation in this verse by this reckoning. It is narrated that a certain man who had apostatized was brought to 'Ali, and he gave him three days to repent, but he did not come back to Islam, so he decapitated him, and recited: { except that whoever turns away and disbelieves } .

Tafsir Al-Qurtubi

﴿ فيعذبه الله العذاب الأكبر ﴾ يعني عذاب الآخرة وقيل متصل فإن جهاد الكفار وقتلهم تسلط وكأنه أوعدهم بالجهاد في الدنيا وعذاب النار في الآخرة وقيل هو إستثناء من قوله ﴿ فذكّر ﴾ أي فذكّر إلا من تولى وأصر فإستحق العذاب الأكبر

تفسير البيضاوي

{ Allah will punish him with the greatest punishment } : that is, the punishment of the hereafter. This is said in connection, for indeed *jihad* against the disbelievers [*kuffar*] and killing them is what dominates, as He is threatening them with *jihad* in this world and the punishment of fire in the next. It is said that this is an exception linked to His word { So inform } ; that is, "So inform, except those who turn away and insist, for they are deserving of the greatest punishment".

Tafsir Al-Baydawi

The Messenger of Allah ﷺ

أبو سعيد الخدري رضي الله عنه حدثه قال قيل يا رسول الله أي الناس أفضل فقال رسول الله ﷺ مؤمن يجاهد في سبيل الله بنفسه وماله قالوا ثم من قال مؤمن في شِعب من الشعاب يتقي الله ويدع الناس من شره

صحيح البخاري كتاب الجهاد والسِّيَر

Abu Sa'id Al-Khudri said: Someone said: Oh Messenger of Allah, who are the best people? And the Messenger of Allah (SAW) said: Believers who wage *jihad* in the cause of Allah with themselves and their wealth. They said: And then who? He said: Believers on one of the mountain passes who fear Allah and spare people their evil.

Sahih Al-Bukhari, *The book of jihad and campaigns*

قال عبدالله بن مسعود رضي الله عنه سألت رسول الله ﷺ قلت يا رسول الله أي العمل أفضل قال الصلاة على ميقاتها قلت ثم أي قال ثم بِرّ الوالدين قلت ثم أي قال الجهاد في سبيل الله فسكتُّ عن رسول الله ﷺ ولو استزدته لزادني

صحيح البخاري كتاب الجهاد والسِّيَر

Abdullah ibn Mad'ud (may Allah be pleased with him) said: I asked the Messenger of Allah (SAW) and said: What deed is best? He said: Prayer at its appointed times. I said: Then what? He said: Benevolent devotion [*birr*] to parents. I said: Then what? He said: *Jihad* in the cause of Allah. Then I stopped asking the Messenger of Allah (SAW); but if I had sought more of him, He would have given me more.

Sahih Al-Bukhari, *The book of jihad and campaigns*

عن عبدالله بن عبد الرحمان بن ابي حسين أن رسول الله ﷺ قال ... كل ما يلهو به الرجل المسلم باطلٌ إلا رميه بقوسه وتأديبه فرسه وملاعبته أهله فإنهن من الحق

جامع الترمذي كتاب فضائل الجهاد

Abdullah ibn 'Abd Al-Rahman ibn Abi Husain related that the Messenger of Allah (SAW) said: . . . Every amusement in which a Muslim man engages is futile, except shooting his bow, training his horse, and playing with the women of his household; for these bring full reward.

Sunan Al-Tirmidhi, *The virtues of jihad*

يجب الحج على المرأة إذا كانت حرة بالغة عاقلة مستطيعة لها محرم يخرج معها فالحج للمرأة مكان الجهاد للرجل

أحكام النساء لإبن الجوزي الباب الثالث والأربعون في ذكر الحج

Pilgrimage [*hajj*] is obligatory for a woman provided she is free, has reached maturity, is of sound mind, able, and she has a non-marriageable relative [*mahram*] to go with her. Indeed *hajj* is for a woman like *jihad* for a man.

Ibn Al-Jawzi, Ahkam Al-nisaa, Chapter forty-three: regarding pilgrimage [hajj]

عن عائشة أم المؤمنين رضي الله عنها قالت استأذنتُ النبي ﷺ في الجهاد فقال جهادكن الحج

صحيح البخاري كتاب الجهاد والسير

From 'Aishah, mother of the believers (may Allah be pleased with her), who said: I asked permission of the Prophet (SAW) to do *jihad*, but He said: *Jihad* for you women is the *hajj*.

Sahih Al-Bukhari, The book of jihad and campaigns

عن جندب بن سفيان أن رسول الله ﷺ كان في بعض المشاهد وقد دميَت إصبعه فقال هل انتِ إلا إصبع دميتِ وفي سبيل الله ما لقيتِ

صحيح البخاري كتاب الجهاد والسير

Jundub ibn Sufyan related that the Messenger of Allah (SAW) was on one of the attacks, and his finger bled; and He said: Are you not but a finger that has bled, and that which you have faced is for the cause of Allah?

Sahih Al-Bukhari, The book of jihad and campaigns

عن ابي موسى رضي الله عنه قال جاء رجل إلى النبي ﷺ فقال الرجل يقاتل للمغنم والرجل يقاتل للذكر والرجل يقاتل ليُرى مكانه فمن في سبيل الله قال من قاتل لتكون كلمة الله هي العُليا فهو في سبيل الله

صحيح البخاري كتاب الجهاد والسير

From Abu Musa (may Allah be pleased with him), who said: A man came to the Prophet (SAW) and said: One man fights to plunder, another fights for fame, and another fights to show off; which of them is in the cause of Allah? He said: Whoever fights for the word of Allah to be the utmost, he is in the cause of Allah.

Sahih Al-Bukhari, The book of jihad and campaigns

عن عبيد بن عمير عن أبيه قال سئل رسول الله ﷺ ما الاسلام قال طيب الكلام وإطعام الطعام وإفشاء السلام قيل وأي الاسلام أفضل قال من سَلِمَ الناسُ من يده ولسانه قيل فأي الصلاة أفضل قال طول القيام قيل فأي الصدقة أفضل قال جهد المقل قيل فأي الايمان أفضل قال الصبر والسماحة قيل فأي الجهاد أفضل قال من عُقر جوَاده و أُهريق دمُه قيل فأي الرقاب أفضل قال أغلاها ثمناً

تنبيه الغافلين للسمرقندي باب فضل الغزو والجهاد

'Ubaid ibn 'Umair related from his father, who said: The Messenger of Allah (SAW) was asked: What is Islam? He said: Pleasant speech, giving food to eat, and spreading peace. Someone said: And what Islam is the best? He said: The one from whose hand and tongue people are safe. Someone said: And what prayer is the best? He said: Standing for a long time. Someone said: And what charity is the best? An attentive look. Someone said: And what faith is the best? He said: Forbearance and tolerance. Someone said: And what jihad is the best? He said: Whoever's horse is hamstrung and his blood is spilled. Someone said: And what necks are the best? He said: The ones worth the highest price.

Al-Samarqandi, Tanbih Al-ghafilin, Section: The excellence of conquest and jihad

عن ابي هريرة عن النبي ﷺ قال قال سليمان بن داود لأطوفن الليلة على سبعين إمرأة تحمل كل إمرأة فارساً يجاهد في سبيل الله فقال له صاحبه إن شاء الله فلم يقل ولم تحمل شيئاً إلا واحداً ساقطاً إحدى شقّيه فقال النبي ﷺ لو قالها لجاهدوا في سبيل الله

صحيح البخاري كتاب أحاديث الأنبياء

Abu Huraira related that the Prophet (SAW) said: Sulaiman ibn Dawud said: Indeed I will go around to seventy women tonight, and each of them will get pregnant with a horseman to wage *jihad* in the cause of Allah. And his companion said: "If Allah wills" [*In shaa Allah*]. But Sulaiman did not say this, and the women did not bear a thing except for one child, maimed on one side. The Prophet (SAW) said: If he had said it, they would have fought in the cause of Allah.

Sahih Al-Bukhari, The book of the sayings of the prophets

أبو هريرة رضي الله عنه يقول قال النبي ﷺ من احتبس فرساً في سبيل الله إيماناً بالله وتصديقاً بوعده فإن شِبعه ورِيَّه وروثه وبوله في ميزانه يوم القيامة

صحيح البخاري كتاب الجهاد والسير

Abu Huraira (may Allah be pleased with him) said: The Prophet (SAW) said: Whoever holds a horse in the cause of Allah, with faith in Allah and believing in His promise, indeed what the horse has eaten its fill of, and the water it has been given, and its dung, and its urine, will be weighed in his favor on resurrection day.

Sahih Al-Bukhari, The book of jihad and campaigns

عن أبي هريرة أن رسول الله ﷺ قال فُضّلت على الأنبياء بستٍ أعطيتُ جوامع الكلم ونصرت بالرعب وأحلَّت لي الغنائم وجُعلت لي الأرض طهوراً ومسجداً وأُرسلت إلى الخلق كافّة وخُتم بي النبيون

صحيح مسلم كتاب المساجد ومواضع الصلاة

Abu Huraira related that the Messenger of Allah (SAW) said: I have been favored over other prophets in six things: I have been given clear and concise words, I have been made victorious by terror, the spoils of war have been made permissible for me, the earth has been made pure for me and has been made a mosque [*masjid*, place of worship], I have been sent to all creation, and by me the prophets have been sealed.

Sahih Muslim, The book of mosques and places of prayer

جابر بن عبدالله أن النبي ﷺ قال أُعطيتُ خمساً لم يُعطهن أحد قبلي نصرت بالرعب مسيرة شهر وجُعلت لي الأرض مسجداً وطهوراً فأيما رجل من أمتي أدركته الصلاة فليصلِّ وأحلت لي المغانم ولم تحلّ لأحد قبلي وأعطيت الشفاعة وكان النبي يُبعث إلى قومه خاصة وبُعثتُ إلى الناس عامة

صحيح البخاري كتاب التيمم

Jabir ibn Abdullah related that the Prophet (SAW) said: I have been given five things that have not been given to anyone before me: I have been made victorious by terror up to a distance of one month; the earth has been made a mosque for me, as well as pure, so that any man of my *ummah* may pray when it comes upon him; taking war spoils has been made permissible for me, although it was not permissible for anyone before me; it has been given to me to act as intercessor; and any given prophet would be sent forth specifically to his people, but I have been sent forth to all people.

Sahih Al-Bukhari, The book of tayammum [rubbing with dust]

عن جابر قال قال رسول الله ﷺ أُمِرْتُ أن أقاتل الناس حتى يقولوا لا إله إلا الله فإذا قالوا لا إله إلا الله عصموا مني دماءَهم وأموالهم إلا بحقها وحسابُهم على الله ثم قرأ ﴿ فذكِّرْ إنما أنت مذكِّر لست عليهم بمسيطر ﴾

صحيح مسلم كتاب الإيمان

From Jabir, who said: The Messenger of Allah (SAW) said: I have been ordered to fight people until they say "There is no god but Allah" ["*La ilaha illa Allah*"]; and if they say "There is no god but Allah", their blood and their property are safe from me, except when these are due; and their reckoning is with Allah. Then He recited: { So inform; indeed you are someone who informs; you do not hold authority over them } [Al-ghashiya 21-22]

Sahih Muslim, The book of belief

عن أنس بن مالك قال قال رسول الله ﷺ أُمِرْتُ أن أقاتل الناس حتى يقولوا لا إله إلا الله فإذا قالوها وصلوا صلاتنا واستقبلوا قبلتنا وذبحوا ذبيحتنا فقد حرُمَت علينا دماؤهم وأموالهم إلا بحقها وحسابهم على الله

صحيح البخاري كتاب الصلاة

From Anas ibn Malik, who said: The Messenger of Allah (SAW) said: I have been ordered to fight people until they say "There is no god but Allah"; and if they say it, and pray our prayers, and face towards our *Qibla*, and sacrifice like we sacrifice, then their blood and their property become unlawful to us, except when these are due; and their reckoning is with Allah.

Sahih Al-Bukhari, The book of prayer

عن أنس قال قال رسول الله ﷺ أُمِرْتُ أن أقاتل الناس حتى يشهدوا أن لا إله إلا الله وأن محمداً عبده ورسوله وأن يستقبلوا قبلتنا وأن يأكلوا ذبيحتنا وأن يصلوا صلاتنا فإذا فعلوا ذلك حرُمَت علينا دماؤهم وأموالهم إلا بحقها لهم ما للمسلمين وعليهم ما على المسلمين

سنن أبي داود كتاب الجهاد

From Anas, who said: The Messenger of Allah (SAW) said: I have been ordered to fight people until they bear witness that there is no god but Allah ["*La ilaha illa Allah*"] and that Muhammad is His servant and His Messenger, and that they face towards our *Qibla*, eat in the way we sacrifice, and pray our prayers. If they do this, their blood and their property become unlawful to us, except when these are due. What the Muslims have is theirs, and the duties of the Muslims are theirs as well.

Sunan Abu Dawud, The book of jihad

عن أبي هريرة قال قال النبي ﷺ الساعي على الأرملة والمسكين كالمجاهد في سبيل الله أو القائم الليل الصائم النهار

صحيح البخاري كتاب النفقات

From Abu Huraira, who said: The Prophet (SAW) said: He who cares for a widow or a poor person is like a *Mujahid* in the cause of Allah or someone who gets up at night [to pray] and fasts during the day.

Sahih Al-Bukhari, The book of expenditures

عن ابي هريرة عن النبي ﷺ قال من مات ولم يغزُ ولم يحدّث نفسه بغزوٍ مات على شُعبة نفاق

سنن النسائي كتاب الجهاد

Abu Huraira related from the Prophet (SAW), who said: Whoever dies without having gone out on an attack or having talked to himself about attacking, has died on a limb of hypocrisy.

Sunan Al-Nasa'i, The book of jihad

عن ابي سعيد الخدري قال كان رسول الله ﷺ عام تبوك يخطب الناس وهو مسند ظهره إلى راحلته فقال ألا أخبركم بخير الناس وشر الناس إنّ من خير الناس رجلاً عمل في سبيل الله على ظهر فرسه أو على ظهر بعيره أو على قدمه حتى يأتيه الموت وإن من شر الناس رجلاً فاجراً يقرأ كتاب الله لا يرعوي إلى شيء منه

سنن النسائي كتاب الجهاد

From Abu Sa'id Al-Khudri, who said: The Messenger of Allah (SAW) was addressing the people in the year of Tabuk, leaning his back against his riding camel, and he said: Shall I not make known to you all who are the best of people and the worst of people? Indeed among the best of people is a man who is occupied in the cause of Allah on the back of his horse or on the back of his camel or on foot, until he dies. And indeed among the worst of people is a lecherous man who reads the book of Allah but does not refrain from anything as a result.

Sunan Al-Nasa'i, The book of jihad

عن ابي هريرة قال قال رسول الله ﷺ لا يجتمع غبار في سبيل الله ودخان جهنم في منخري مسلم ولا يجتمع الشُحّ والايمان في قلب رجل مسلم

سنن النسائي كتاب الجهاد

From Abu Huraira, who said: The Messenger of Allah (SAW) said: The dust raised up in the cause of Allah and the smoke of Hellfire will never mix in the nostrils of a Muslim; stinginess and belief will never mix in the heart of a Muslim man.

Sunan Al-Nasa'i, The book of jihad

عن ابي هريرة أن رسول الله ﷺ قال لا يجتمع كافر وقاتله في النار أبداً

صحيح مسلم كتاب الامارة

From Abu Huraira, who said: The Messenger of Allah (SAW) said: A disbeliever and his killer will never join each other in Hellfire.

Sahih Muslim, The book of governance

عن ابي أمامة الباهلي قال جاء رجل إلى النبي ﷺ فقال أرأيت رجلاً غزا يلتمس الأجر والذكر ما له فقال رسول الله ﷺ لا شيء له فأعادها ثلاث مرات يقول له رسول الله لا شيء له ثم قال إن الله لا يقبل من العمل إلا ما كان له خالصاً وابتُغي به وجهه

سنن النسائي كتاب الجهاد

From Abu Umama Al-Bahili, who said: A man came to the Prophet (SAW) and said: What do you think of a man who goes out to attack seeking reward and fame; what will be his? And the Messenger of Allah (SAW) said: He will have nothing. And He repeated it three times, the Messenger of Allah (SAW) saying to him: He will have nothing. Then He said: Indeed Allah does not accept any deed except that which is for Him alone and that by which His face is sought.

Sunan Al-Nasa'i, The book of jihad

عن أنس قال قال رسول الله ﷺ جاهدوا بأيديكم وألسنتكم وأموالكم

سنن النسائي كتاب الجهاد

From Anas who said: The Messenger of Allah (SAW) said: Wage *jihad* with your hands, your tongues, and your wealth.

Sunan Al-Nasa'i, The book of jihad

عن طارق بن شهاب وهذا حديث ابي بكر قال أول من بدأ بالخطبة يوم العيد قبل الصلاة مروان فقام إليه رجل فقال الصلاة قبل الخطبة فقال قد تُرك ما هنالك فقال أبو سعيد أما هذا فقد قضى ما عليه سمعتُ رسول الله ﷺ يقول من رأى منكم منكراً فليغيِّره بيده فإن لم يستطع فبلسانه فإن لم يستطع فبقلبه وذلك أضعف الايمان

صحيح مسلم كتاب الإيمان

From Tariq ibn Shihab, a hadith of Abu Bakr, who said: The first person who began on the day of festival ['eid] with the address [khutbah] before prayer was Marwan.

And a man stood up to him and said: Prayer is before the *khutbah*. But he said: That has been abandoned. And Abu Sa'id remarked: Indeed this man has complied with his obligation; I heard the Messenger of Allah (SAW) say: Whoever of you sees wrongdoing, let him change it with his hand, but if he can not, then with his tongue, and if he can not, then with his heart, although this is the weakest of belief.

Sahih Muslim, The book of belief

عن عبدالله بن مسعود أن رسول الله ﷺ قال ما من نبي بعثه الله في أمةٍ قبلي إلا كان له من أمته حواريون وأصحاب يأخذون بسنته ويقتدون بأمره ثم إنها تخلُف من بعدهم خلوف يقولون ما لا يفعلون ويفعلون ما لا يؤمَرون فمن جاهدهم بيده فهو مؤمن ومن جاهدهم بلسانه فهو مؤمن ومن جاهدهم بقلبه فهو مؤمن وليس وراء ذلك من الإيمان حبة خردل

صحيح مسلم كتاب الإيمان

Abdullah ibn Mas'ud related that the Messenger of Allah (SAW) said: There is no prophet sent forth to people by Allah before me who did not have apostles and companions that adhered to his way of life [*sunnah*] and followed the example of what he ordered. Then indeed after them came successors who said what they did not do and did what they were not ordered to do. So whoever wages *jihad* against them with his hand, he is a Believer; and whoever wages *jihad* against them with his tongue, he is a Believer; and whoever wages *jihad* against them in his heart, he is a Believer; but besides this there is not even a mustard seed's worth of belief.

Sahih Muslim, The book of belief

عن الصعب بن جثامة رضي الله عنهم قال مر بي النبي ﷺ بالأبواء أو بودان وسئل عن أهل الدار يبيَّتون من المشركين فيُصاب من نسائهم وذراريهم قال هم منهم

صحيح البخاري كتاب الجهاد والسير

From Sa'b ibn Juthama (may Allah be pleased with them), who said: The Prophet (SAW) passed by me either at Abwaa' or at Waddan, and He was being asked about the people of the land – could the idolaters [*mushrikun*] be attacked by surprise at night but maybe some of their women and children would be struck? He said: They belong to them.

Sahih Al-Bukhari, The book of jihad and campaigns

قوله هم منهم أي في الحكم تلك الحالة وليس المراد إباحة قتلهم بطريق القصد اليهم بل المراد إذا لم يُمكن الوصول إلى الآباء إلا بوطء الذّرّية فإذا أُصيبوا لاختلاطهم بهم جاز قتلُهم

فتح الباري لإبن حجر العسقلاني كتاب الجهاد

His words "they belong to them" : that is, in this condition regarding the command. The intended meaning is not permission to kill them on purpose; rather the meaning is that, if the fathers can not be reached except by treading on the women and children, and if they are struck due to being intermingled with them, then killing them is permitted.

Ibn Hajar Al-Asqalani, Fath Al-Bari, The book of jihad

عن أنس بن مالك قال قال رسول الله ﷺ ثلاثة من أصل الايمان الكف عمن قال لا إله إلا الله ولا تكفّره بذنب ولا تخرجه من الاسلام بعمل والجهاد ماضٍ منذ بعثني الله إلى أن يقاتل آخر أمتي الدجال لا يُبطله جور جائر ولا عدل عادل والايمان بالأقدار

سنن ابي داود كتاب الجهاد

From Anas ibn Malik who said: The Messenger of Allah (SAW) said: Three things lie at the root of belief: To desist from someone who says "There is no god but Allah"; that you do not accuse him of disbelief for any sin; and that you do not force him out of Islam for anything he does. And *jihad* will transpire from the time Allah has sent me forth until the last of my *ummah* fight the Imposter Messiah [*Dajjal*]. No tyrant's tyranny nor any just man's justice will annul this; belief rests on things preordained.

Sunan Abu Dawud, The book of jihad

عن ابي هريرة قال قال رسول الله ﷺ الجهاد واجب عليكم مع كل أمير براً كان أو فاجراً والصلاة واجبة عليكم خلف كل مسلم براً كان أو فاجراً وإن عمل الكبائر والصلاة واجبة على كل مسلم براً كان أو فاجراً وإن عمل الكبائر

سنن ابي داود كتاب الجهاد

From Abu Huraira, who said: The Messenger of Allah (SAW) said: *Jihad* is obligatory on you all with every leader, whether he be righteous [*barr*] or immoral [*fajir*]; prayer is incumbent on you following after every Muslim, righteous or immoral, even if he has committed grave sins [*kaba'ir*]; and prayer is obligatory over every Muslim, righteous or immoral, even if he has committed grave sins.

Sunan Abu Dawud, The book of jihad

عن عبادة بن الصامت قال قال رسول الله ﷺ عليكم بالجهاد في سبيل الله تبارك وتعالى فإنه باب من أبواب الجنة يذهب الله به الهم والغم

مسند أحمد، حديث عبادة بن الصامت رضي الله عنه

From 'Ubada ibn Al-Samit, who said: The Messenger of Allah (SAW) said: You all are obliged to *jihad* in the cause of Allah Blessed and Exalted, for indeed it is one of the gates into *Jannah*; with it Allah drives away distress and gloom.

Musnad Ahmad, The hadith of 'Ubada ibn Al-Samit (may Allah be pleased with him)

عن أبي أمامة أن رسول الله ﷺ قال عليكم بالجهاد في سبيل الله فإنه باب من أبواب الجنة يذهب الله به الغش وألهم

المصنف لعبد الرزاق كتاب الجهاد

Abu Umama related that the Messenger of Allah (SAW) said: You all are obliged to *jihad* in the cause of Allah; for indeed it is one of the gates into *Jannah*; with it Allah drives away deception and distress.

'Abd Al-Razzaq, the Musannaf, The book of jihad

عن أبي هريرة أن رسول الله ﷺ قال تكفّل الله لمن جاهد في سبيله لا يخرجه إلا الجهاد في سبيله وتصديق كلماته بأن يدخله الجنة أو يرجعه إلى مسكنه الذي خرج منه مع ما نال من أجرٍ أو غنيمة

صحيح البخاري كتاب التوحيد

Abu Huraira related that the Messenger of Allah (SAW) said: Allah pledges to whoever wages *jihad* in His cause – who has not been motivated to go out except for *jihad* in His cause and belief in His words – that He will admit him into *Jannah* or He will return him to the home he left with the reward or booty he will have received.

Sahih Al-Bukhari, The book of unification (oneness)

عن أبي ذر عن النبي ﷺ قيل أي الأعمال خير قال إيمان بالله وجهاد في سبيله قيل فأي الرقاب أفضل قال أغلاها ثمناً وأنفَسها عند أهلها قال أفرأيتَ إن لم استطع بعض العمل قال فتُعين ضائعاً أو تصنع لأخرق قال أفرأيت إن ضَعُفت قال تدع الناس من الشر فإنها صدقة تصدّق بها على نفسك

الأدب المفرد للبخاري كتاب الرعاية

Abu Dharr related from the Prophet (SAW) that someone asked: What deeds are best? He said: Belief in Allah and *jihad* in His cause. Someone said: And what necks [i.e.

slaves] are best? He said: The most costly and esteemed of them among their people. Abu Dharr said: And what do you think if I am unable to do certain deeds? He said: Then you should look after someone in trouble or do some work for someone who is not competent. He said: And what do you think if I should become weak? He said: You should spare people your worst; for indeed this is charity that you grant yourself.

Al-Bukhari, Al-adab Al-Mufrad, The book of looking after people

عن خريم بن فاتك قال قال رسول الله ﷺ من أنفق نفقة في سبيل الله كُتبت له بسبعمائة ضِعف

جامع الترمذي كتاب فضائل الجهاد

From Khuraim ibn Fatik, who said: The Messenger of Allah (SAW) said: Whoever expends an expenditure in the cause of Allah, this is inscribed to him seven hundred times over.

Sunan Al-Tirmidhi, The book of virtues of jihad

عن إبن عباس قال سمعت رسول الله ﷺ يقول عينان لا تمسُّهما النار عين بكت من خشية الله وعين باتت تحرس في سبيل الله

جامع الترمذي كتاب فضائل الجهاد

From Ibn 'Abbas, who said: I heard the Messenger of Allah (SAW) say: Hellfire will not touch two kinds of eyes – an eye that weeps out of fear of Allah, and an eye that keeps watch at night for the cause of Allah.

Sunan Al-Tirmidhi, The book of virtues of jihad

عن أنس قال قال رسول الله ﷺ القتل في سبيل الله يكفِّر كل خطيئة فقال جبريل إلا الدين فقال النبي ﷺ إلا الدين

جامع الترمذي كتاب فضائل الجهاد

From Anas, who said: The Messenger of Allah (SAW) said: Killing in the cause of Allah atones for every sin. But Jibril said: Except debt. And so the Prophet (SAW) said: Except debt.

Sunan Al-Tirmidhi, The book of virtues of jihad

عن معاذ بن جبل عن النبي ﷺ قال من سأل الله القتل في سبيله صادقاً من قلبه أعطاه الله أجر الشهيد
جامع الترمذي كتاب فضائل الجهاد

Mu'adh ibn Jabal related from the Prophet (SAW), who said: Whoever asks of Allah to be killed in His cause, sincerely from his heart, Allah will give him the reward of a martyr.

Sunan Al-Tirmidhi, The book of virtues of jihad

عن ابي هريرة قال مر رجلٌ من أصحاب رسول الله ﷺ بشعب فيه عُيَينة من ماء عذبة فأعجبته لطيبها فقال لو اعتزلت الناس فأقمت في هذا الشعب ولن أفعل حتى استأذن رسول الله ﷺ فذكر ذلك لرسول الله ﷺ فقال لا تفعل فإن مقام أحدكم في سبيل الله أفضل من صلاته في بيته سبعين عاماً ألا تحبون أن يغفر الله لكم ويُدخلكم الجنة اغزوا في سبيل الله مَن قاتل في سبيل الله فُواق ناقة وجبت له الجنة
جامع الترمذي كتاب فضائل الجهاد

From Abu Huraira who said: One of the men from among the Messenger of Allah's (SAW) Companions passed through a mountain pass in which there was a small freshwater spring that delighted him by how nice it was; he said: If only I could seclude myself from people and stay in this mountain pass; but I won't do it until I ask permission from the Messenger of Allah (SAW). So he mentioned this to the Messenger of Allah (SAW), but He said: Don't do it, for indeed the position of any of you in the cause of Allah is better than seventy years of him praying in his house; do you all not wish to be forgiven by Allah and to be brought into *Jannah*? Go out on raids for the cause of Allah!; whoever fights in the cause of Allah for the time that lapses between two milkings of a camel, *Jannah* is indispensably his.

Sunan Al-Tirmidhi, The book of virtues of jihad

قال إبن اسحاق ولما أصبح رسول الله ﷺ إنصرف عن الخندق راجعاً إلى المدينة والمسلمون ووضعوا السلاح فلما كانت الظهر أتى جبريل عليه السلام كما حدثني الزهري معتجراً بعمامة من استبرق على بغلة عليها رحالة عليها قطيفة من ديباج فقال أو قد وضعت السلاح يا رسول الله قال نعم فقال جبريل فما وضعت الملائكة السلاح بعد وما رجعتُ الآن إلا من طلب القوم إن الله عز وجل يأمرك يا محمد بالمسير إلى بني قريظة فإني عامدٌ اليهم فُزلزل بهم
السيرة النبوية لإبن هشام غزوة بني قريظة في سنة خمس

Ibn Ishaq said: When the Messenger of Allah (SAW) arose in the morning, He and the Muslims set out from Khandaq [The Trench] to return to Medina, and they laid down their weapons. But at midday, Jibril (peace be upon him) came to him – as Al-Zuhri related to me – with a gold-embroidered turban on his head and covering his face, riding a mule with a saddle covered by a plush silk cloth. And he said: So you have laid down the weapons then, oh Messenger of Allah? He said: Yes. And Jibril said: But the angels have not yet laid down weapons, and the only thing I have returned from now is pursuit of people. Indeed Allah Mighty and Sublime orders you, oh Muhammad, to advance towards the Banu Qurayza; for indeed I am headed firmly towards them to shake them up.

Ibn Hisham, Al-sirah Al-nabawiya, Topic section: the raid on the Banu Qurayza in year five

قال إبن اسحاق ثم استنزلوا فحبسهم رسول الله ﷺ في دار إبنة الحارث إمرأة من بني النجار ثم خرج رسول الله ﷺ إلى التي هي سوقها اليوم نخندق بها خنادق ثم بعث إليهم فضرب أعناقهم في تلك الخنادق يُخرَج بهم إليه أرسالاً وفيهم عدو الله حيي بن أخطب وكعب بن أسد رأس القوم وهم ستمائة أو سبعمائة المكثِّر لهم يقول كانوا من الثمانمائة إلى التسعمائة وقد قالوا لكعب بن أسد وهم يُذهَب بهم إلى رسول الله ﷺ أرسالاً يا كعب ما ترى ما يصنع بنا فقال كعب في كل موطن لا تعقلون ألا ترون الداعي لا ينزع وأنه من ذُهِب به منكم لا يرجع هو والله القتل فلم يزل ذلك الدأب حتى فرغ منهم رسول الله ﷺ

تاريخ الطبري سنة ٥ غزوة بني قريظة

Ibn Ishaq said: Then they [the Banu Quraiza] were called down and the Messenger of Allah (SAW) held them in the house of Al-Harith's daughter, a woman of the Banu Al-Najjar. Then the Messenger of Allah (SAW) went out to the market in Medina, the one which is still its market today, and dug trenches in it. Then He sent for them, and struck their necks [beheaded them] in these trenches, they being brought out to him in groups. Among them was the enemy of Allah, Huyayy ibn Akhtab, and Ka'b ibn Asad, the leader of the tribe. There were six or seven hundred of them; the one with the most ominous report of them said that there were eight to nine hundred. And while they were being taken in groups to the Messenger of Allah (SAW), they said to Ka'b ibn Asad: Oh Ka'b, what do you think He's going to do to us?! And Ka'b said: You all don't ever get it! Don't you see that the one who is summoning us does not dismiss anyone, and that every one of you who is taken away does not come back? By God this means killing! And the affair went on until the Messenger of Allah (SAW) had finished with them.

Tarikh Al-Tabari [Al-Tabari's History], Year five, Section: The attack on the Banu Quraiza

عن أنس أن رسول الله ﷺ غزا خيبر فصلينا عندها صلاة الغداة بغلس فركب نبي الله ﷺ وركب أبو طلحة وأنا رديف ابي طلحة فأجرى نبي الله ﷺ في زقاق خيبر وإن ركبتي لتمس نخذ نبي الله ﷺ ثم حسر الإزار عن نخذه حتى إني لأنظر إلى بياض نخذ نبي الله ﷺ فلما دخل القرية قال الله أكبر خربت خيبر إنا إذا نزلنا بساحة قوم فساء صباح المنذَرين قالها ثلاثاً قال وخرج القوم الى أعمالهم فقالوا محمد قال عبد العزيز وقال بعض أصحابنا والخميس يعني الجيش قال فأصبناها عنوةً فجُمع السبي فجاء دحية فقال يا نبي الله اعطني جارية من السبي قال اذهب نخذ جارية فأخذ صفية بنت حُيي فجاء رجل إلى النبي ﷺ فقال يا نبي الله اعطيت دحية صفية بنت حيي سيدة قريظة والنضير لا تصلح إلا لك قال ادعوه بها فجاء بها فلما نظر إليها النبي ﷺ قال خذ جارية من السبي غيرها قال فأعتقها النبي ﷺ وتزوجها

صحيح البخاري كتاب الصلاة

Anas related: The Messenger of Allah (SAW) raided Khaibar, and we prayed the dawn prayer while it was still dark. The Prophet of Allah (SAW) rode in and Abu Talha rode in and I rode behind Abu Talha. And the Prophet of Allah (SAW) came down the road through Khaybar, and my knee was touching the Prophet of Allah's (SAW) thigh. Then He pulled up his waist wrap from his thigh until I saw the whiteness of the Prophet of Allah's (SAW) thigh. And when He entered the town, He said: *Allahu akbar*, Khaybar is ruined! Indeed when we descend onto a people, the morning gets bad for those who have been warned! He said this three times. The people set out to begin work, but said: It's Muhammad! 'Abd Al-'Aziz and some of our companions said: And the five-fold squad; that is, the army. We overtook the town forcefully and the captives were gathered. Then Dihya came and said: Oh Prophet of Allah, give me a young maid from among the captives. And He said: Go and take a young maid. So he took Safiyah bint Huyay. Then a man came to the Prophet (SAW) and said: Oh Prophet of Allah, to Dihya you gave Safiyah bint Huyay, a noble lady of the Qurayza and Al-Nadir clans, but she is not suitable for anyone except you. He said: Call him to bring her. And he came with her. And when the Prophet (SAW) saw her, He said: Take another young maid from the captives besides her. And the Prophet (SAW) freed her and married her.

Al-Bukhari, Sahih Al-Bukhari, The book of prayer

قال عبدالله بن عمرو يا رسول الله أخبرني عن الجهاد والغزو فقال يا عبدالله بن عمرو إن قاتلت صابراً محتسباً بعثك الله صابراً محتسباً وإن قاتلت مرائياً مكاثراً بعثك الله مرائياً مكاثراً يا عبدالله بن عمرو على أي حال قاتلت أو قُتلت بعثك الله على تلك الحال

سنن ابي داود كتاب الجهاد

Abdullah ibn 'Amr said: Oh Messenger of Allah, tell me about *jihad* and going on raids [*ghazw*]. And He said: Oh Abdullah ibn 'Amr, if you fight being steadfast, intent on the reward, Allah will resurrect you being steadfast, intent on the reward; but if you fight hypocritically, vying for greatness, then Allah will resurrect you as a hypocrite, vying for greatness; oh Abdullah ibn 'Amr, in whatever situation you fight or are killed, that is how Allah will resurrect you.

Sunan Abu Dawud, The book of jihad

عن عبدالله بن ابي قتادة عن ابي قتادة أنه سمعه يحدث عن رسول الله ﷺ أنه قام فيهم فذكر لهم أن الجهاد في سبيل الله والايمان بالله أفضل الأعمال فقام رجل فقال يا رسول الله أرأيت إن قُتلتُ في سبيل الله تُكفَّر عني خطاياي فقال له رسول الله ﷺ نعم إن قتلت في سبيل الله وأنت صابر محتسب مُقبل غير مدبر ثم قال رسول الله ﷺ كيف قلتَ قال أرأيت إن قتلت في سبيل الله أتُكفر عني خطاياي فقال رسول الله ﷺ نعم وأنت صابر محتسب مقبل غير مدبر إلا أَلدَين فإن جبريل عليه السلام قال لي ذلك
صحيح مسلم كتاب الإمارة

Abdullah ibn Abu Qatada related from Abu Qatada that he heard him relate from the Messenger of Allah (SAW), that He got up among them and mentioned to them that *jihad* in the cause of Allah, and belief in Allah, were the best deeds. And a man got up and said: Oh Messenger of Allah, do you reckon if I am killed in the cause of Allah, my sins will be atoned for? The Messenger of Allah (SAW) said to him: Yes; if you are killed in the cause of Allah having been steadfast, intent on the reward, advancing and not retreating. Then the Messenger of Allah (SAW) said: What was it that you asked? The man said: Do you reckon that if I am killed in the cause of Allah, will my sins be atoned for? And the Messenger of Allah (SAW) said: Yes; having been steadfast and intent on the reward, advancing and not retreating; except for any debt – indeed Jibril (peace be upon him) told me that.

Sahih Muslim, The book of governance

عن عبد الكريم الجزري قال جاء رجلٌ إلى النبي ﷺ فقال إني رجل جبان لا أطيق لقاء العدو فقال ألا أدّلك على جهاد لا قتال فيه فقال بلى يا رسول الله قال عليك بالحج والعمرة
المصنف لعبد الرزاق كتاب الجهاد

From 'Abd Al-Karim Al-Jazari, who said: A certain man came to the Prophet (SAW) and said: Indeed I am a fainthearted man and I can not bear to face the enemy. And He said: Shall I not attest to you of a *jihad* in which there is no fighting? The man said: Oh yes, Messenger of Allah. He said: You are obliged to the *hajj* and the *'umrah*.

'Abd Al-Razzaq, the Musannaf, The book of jihad

عن محمد بن طلحة أن رجلاً جاء النبي ﷺ فقال يا رسول الله إني أريد الغزو وقد جئتك أستشيرك قال هل لك أمّ قال نعم قال الزمْها فإن الجنة عند رجلها ثم الثانية ثم الثالثة كذلك

المصنف لعبد الرزاق كتاب الجهاد

Muhammad ibn Talha related that a certain man came to the Prophet (SAW) and said: Oh Messenger of Allah, indeed I want to go on a raid, and so I have come to you to ask your advice. He said: Do you have a mother? The man said: Yes. He said: Stay close to her, for indeed *Jannah* is at her feet. Then a second time, and then similarly a third time.

'Abd Al-Razzaq, the Musannaf, The book of jihad

عن مالك بن حمزة عن أبيه عن جده قال قال لنا رسول الله ﷺ يوم بدر من رأى المشركين أن أكثبوكم فارموهم بالنبل ولا تسُلّوا السيوف حتى يغشوكم

المصنف لعبد الرزاق كتاب الجهاد

Malik ibn Hamza related from his father, from his grandfather, who said: The Messenger of Allah (SAW) said to us on the day of Badr: Whoever sees the idolaters [*mushrikun*] get near to you all, shoot arrows at them but do not draw your swords until they are on top of you.

'Abd Al-Razzaq, the Musannaf, The book of jihad

عن مالك بن حمزة بن أبي أسيد الساعدي عن أبيه عن جده قال قال رسول الله ﷺ يوم بدر إذا أكثبوكم فارموهم بالنّبل ولا تسُلّوا السيوف حتى يغشوكم

سنن أبي داود كتاب الجهاد

Malik ibn Hamza ibn Abi Usaid Al-Sa'idi related from his father, from his grandfather, who said: The Messenger of Allah (SAW) said on the day of Badr: When they get close to you all, shoot arrows at them but do not draw your swords until they are on top of you.

Sunan Abu Dawud, The book of jihad

عن زيد بن أسلم أن رسول الله ﷺ قال لأصحابه ذات يوم وهو مستقبل العدو ولا يقاتل أحد منكم فعمد رجل منهم فرمى العدو وقاتلهم فقتلوه فقيل للنبي ﷺ إستُشهد فلان فقال أبعدما نهيت عن القتال قالوا نعم قال لا يدخل الجنة عاصٍ

المصنف لعبد الرزاق كتاب الجهاد

Zayd Ibn Aslam related that the Messenger of Allah (SAW) said to his Companions one day while confronting the enemy: Let none of you fight. But a certain man among them proceeded to shoot at the enemy and fight, and they killed him. And it was mentioned to the Prophet (SAW) that so-and-so had been martyred. He said: After I prohibited fighting?! They said: Yes. He said: No one who disobeys enters *Jannah*.

'Abd Al-Razzaq, the Musannaf, The book of jihad

عن إبن عمر قال نهى رسول الله ﷺ أن يسافرَ بالقرآن إلى أرض العدو مخافة أن يناله العدو

المصنف لعبد الرزاق كتاب الجهاد

Ibn 'Umar related that the Messenger of Allah (SAW) prohibited traveling with the Qur'an into enemy land, out of fear that the enemy might get hold of it.

'Abd Al-Razzaq, the Musannaf, The book of jihad

عن عبدالله بن عمر رضي الله عنهما أن رسول الله ﷺ نهى أن يسافرَ بالقرآن إلى أرض العدو

صحيح البخاري كتاب الجهاد والسِيَر

Ibn 'Umar related that the Messenger of Allah (SAW) prohibited traveling with the Qur'an into enemy land, out of fear that the enemy might get hold of it.

Sahih Al-Bukhari, The book of jihad and campaigns

قوله وقد سافر النبي ﷺ وأصحابه في أرض العدو وهم يعلمون القران أشار البخاري بذلك أنّ المراد بالنهي عن السفر بالقران السفر بالمصحف خشية أن يناله العدو لا السفر بالقران نفسه

فتح الباري لإبن حجر العسقلاني كتاب الجهاد

His words "The Prophet (SAW) would travel with his Companions in enemy land knowing the Qur'an" : Al-Bukhari is indicating by this that the intent of the prohibition on traveling with the Qur'an was traveling with a copy of the Qur'an [*musHaf*] out of fear that the enemy would get hold of it, not traveling with the Qur'an itself.

Ibn Hajar Al-Asqalani, Fath Al-Bari, The book of jihad

علقمة بن شهاب القشيري قال قال رسول الله ﷺ من لم يدرك الغزو معي فليغزُ في البحر فإن أجر يوم في البحر كأجر شهر في البَرّ وإن القتل في البحر كالقتلين في البر وإن المائد في السفينة كالمتشحّط في دمه وإن خيار شهداء أمتي أصحاب الكَفّ قالوا وما أصحاب الكف يا رسول الله قال قوم تكفّأ بهم في مراكبهم في سبيل الله

المصنف لعبد الرزاق كتاب الجهاد

'Alqama ibn Shihab Al-Qushairi said: The Messenger of Allah (SAW) said: Whoever has not experienced going on an attack with me, let him go out to attack at sea, for indeed the reward of one day at sea is like the reward of one month on land; and indeed killing at sea is like two killings on land; and indeed one who sways in a boat is like one who is immersed in his blood; and indeed the best of the martyrs of my *ummah* are the ones in the core [lower deck]. The people asked: And what are the ones in the core, oh Messenger of Allah? He said: The people who make their ships tilt and tip over for the cause of Allah.

'Abd Al-Razzaq, the Musannaf, The book of jihad

عن بن جريج قال أخبرني رجل من أهل المدينة أن راية النبي ﷺ كانت تكون بيضاء ولواءه أسود

المصنف لعبد الرزاق كتاب الجهاد

From Ibn Juraij, who said: One of the men from Medina told me that the Prophet's (SAW) banner was white, and his flag [under the banner] was black.

'Abd Al-Razzaq, the Musannaf, The book of jihad

عن جعفر بن محمد عن أبيه قال كان إسم جارية النبي ﷺ خضرة وحماره يعفر وناقته القصواء وبغلته الشهباء وسيفه ذا الفقار

المصنف لعبد الرزاق كتاب الجهاد

Ja'far ibn Muhammad related from his father, who said: The name of the Prophet's (SAW) maidservant was Khadirah ["Grassy"]; his donkey, Ya'fur; his she-camel, Al-Qaswaa ["Snipped ear"]; his she-mule, Al-Shahbaa ["Gray"]; and his sword, Dhu Al-Faqar ["Having a spinal column"].

'Abd Al-Razzaq, the Musannaf, The book of jihad

عن عبد القدوس قال سمعت الحسن قال قال رسول الله ﷺ على النساء ما على الرجال إلا الجمعة والجنائز والجهاد

المصنف لعبد الرزاق كتاب الجهاد

From 'Abd Al-Quddus, who said: I heard Al-Hasan say: The Messenger of Allah said: Women are obliged to do what men are obliged to do, except for the Friday assembly, funerals, and *jihad*.

'Abd Al-Razzaq, the Musannaf, The book of jihad

عن الحسن عن النبي ﷺ قال أردية الغزاة السيوف

المصنف لعبد الرزاق كتاب الجهاد

Al-Hasan related from the Prophet (SAW), who said: The garments of attackers are their swords.

'Abd Al-Razzaq, the Musannaf, The book of jihad

عن الشعبي قال لما قدم عدي بن حاتم الكوفة أتيناه في نفر من فقهاء أهل الكوفة فقلنا له حدّثنا ما سمعت من رسول الله ﷺ فقال أتيتُ النبي ﷺ فقال يا عدي بن حاتم أسلم تسلم قلت وما الإسلام فقال تشهد أن لا إله إلا الله وإني رسول الله وتؤمن بالأقدار كلها خيرها وشرها حلوها ومرها

سنن ابن ماجه كتاب المقدمة

From Al-Sha'bi who said: When 'Adi ibn Hatim came to Kufa, we went to see him with a group of the legal scholars of Kufa and said to him: Tell us about what you heard from the Messenger of Allah (SAW). And he said: I went to the Prophet (SAW) and He said: Oh 'Adi ibn Hatim, yield [to Islam] and be safe. I said: And what is Islam? He said: You bear witness that there is no god but Allah and that I am the Messenger of Allah; and you believe in all that is preordained – the good and bad of it, the sweet and bitter of it.

Sunan Ibn Majah, The book of introduction

عمر بن عبد العزيز كتب إلى عامل من عماله أنه بلغنا أن رسول الله ﷺ كان إذا بعث سرية يقول لهم اغزوا بإسم الله في سبيل الله تقاتلون من كفر بالله لا تغُلّوا ولا تغدِروا ولا تمثّلوا ولا تقتلوا وليداً وقل ذلك لجيوشك وسراياك إن شاء الله واسلام عليك

موطأ مالك كتاب الجهاد

'Umr ibn 'Abd Al-'Aziz wrote to one of his governors: We have been made aware that the Messenger of Allah (SAW), whenever He sent out a detachment, said to them: Attack in the name of Allah and in the cause of Allah, fighting whoever disbelieves in Allah; do not steal from the spoils, do not deceive, do not mutilate, and do not kill children; tell this to your armies and your detachments, Allah willing, and peace be upon you.

Muwatta Malik, The book of jihad

عن إبن عباس قال قال رسول الله ﷺ يوم الفتح فتح مكة لا هجرة ولكن جهاد ونية وإذا استُنفرتم فانفروا

سنن ابي داود كتاب الجهاد

From Ibn 'Abbas who said: The Messenger of Allah (SAW) said at the conquest of Mecca: There is no emigration [*hijra*], but rather *jihad* and determination; so whenever you all are called to mobilize, then mobilize.

Sunan Abu Dawud, The book of jihad

عن عبدالله بن السعدي رضي الله عنه قال قال رسول الله ﷺ لا تنقطع الهجرة ما قوتل العدو

بلوغ المرام الإبن حجر كتاب الجهاد

From Abdullah ibn As-Sa'di (may Allah be pleased with him), who said: The Messenger of Allah (SAW) said: Emigration [*hijra*] will not cease as long as the enemy is fought.

Ibn Hajar, Bulugh Al-maram, The book of jihad

عن ابي أمامة أن رجلاً قال يا رسول الله ائذن لي في السياحة قال النبي ﷺ إن سياحة أمتي الجهاد في سبيل الله تعالى

سنن ابي داود كتاب الجهاد

Abu Umama related that a certain man said: Oh Messenger of Allah, give me permission to go on an excursion. The Prophet (SAW) said: The excursion of my *ummah* is *jihad* in the cause of Allah Most High.

Sunan Abu Dawud, The book of jihad

عن عبد الخبير بن ثابت بن قيس بن شماس عن أبيه عن جده قال جاءت إمرأة إلى النبي ﷺ يقال لها أم خلاد وهي منتقبة تسأل عن ابنها وهو مقتول فقال لها بعض أصحاب النبي ﷺ جئتِ تسألين عن ابنك وأنت منتقبة فقالت إن أُرزأ ابني فلن أُرزأ حيائي فقال رسول الله ﷺ ابنك له أجر شهيدين قالت ولِمَ ذاك يا رسول الله قال لأنه قتله أهل الكتاب

سنن ابي داود كتاب الجهاد

'Abd Al-Khabir ibn Thabit ibn Qais ibn Shammas related from his father, from his grandfather, who said: A woman known as Umm Khallad came to the Prophet (SAW), veiled, seeking her son who had been killed. Some of the Prophet's (SAW) Companions said to her: Have you come veiled to seek your son? She said: If I am deprived of my son I will not be deprived of my modesty. And the Messenger of Allah (SAW) said: Your son has the reward of two martyrs. She said: And why is that, oh Messenger of Allah? He said: Because the People of the Book killed him.

Sunan Abu Dawud, The book of jihad

عن عبدالله بن مسعود قال قال رسول الله ﷺ عجب ربنا من رجل غزا في سبيل الله فإنهزم يعني أصحابه فعلم ما عليه فرجع حتى أُهريقَ دمه فيقول الله تعالى لملائكته انظروا إلى عبدي رجع رغبةً فيما عندي وشفقةً مما عندي حتى أهريق دمه

سنن ابي داود كتاب الجهاد

From Abdullah ibn Mas'ud who said: The Messenger of Allah (SAW) said: Our Lord marvels at any man who goes out on a raid in the cause of Allah, then whose companions flee, but he knows what he must do, so he goes back until his blood is shed. And Allah Most High says to His angels: Look at my servant, who went back, desiring what I have to give, and fearful of what I administer, until his blood was shed.

Sunan Abu Dawud, The book of jihad

عن المهلب بن ابي صفرة قال أخبرني من سمع النبي ﷺ يقول إن بُيِّتّم فليكن شعاركم حم لا يُنصَرون

سنن ابي داود كتاب الجهاد

From Muhallab ibn Abi Sufra who said: Someone told me who heard the Prophet (SAW) say: If you are attacked by surprise at night, let your rallying cry be *"Ha-mim"* [surah *Fussilat*]; they will not be made victorious.

Sunan Abu Dawud, The book of jihad

عن أنس أن النبي ﷺ كان يغيز عند صلاة الصبح وكان يتسمع فإذا سمع أذاناً أمسك وإلا أغاز

سنن ابي داود كتاب الجهاد

Anas related that the Prophet (SAW) would stage attacks at the time of the morning prayer and listen; if He heard a call to prayer He would hold back, otherwise He would attack.

Sunan Abu Dawud, The book of jihad

عن عمرو أنه سمع جابراً أن رسول الله ﷺ قال الحرب خُدعة

سنن ابي داود كتاب الجهاد

'Amr related that he heard Jabir relate that the Messenger of Allah (SAW) said: War is deceit.

Sunan Abu Dawud, The book of jihad

عن ابي هريرة رضي الله عنه قال سمّى النبي ﷺ الحرب خدعة

صحيح البخاري كتاب الجهاد والسِيَر

From Abu Huraira (may Allah be pleased with him), who said: The Prophet (SAW) called war deceit.

Sahih Al-Bukhari, The book of jihad and campaigns

عن سهل بن معاذ الجهني عن أبيه قال نزلنا على حصن سنان بأرض الروم مع عبدالله بن عبد الملك فضيّق الناس المنازل وقطع الطريق فقال معاذ أيها الناس إنا غزونا مع رسول الله ﷺ غزوة كذا وكذا فضيق الناس الطريق فبعث النبي ﷺ منادياً فنادى من ضيق منزلاً أو قطع طارق فلا جهاد له

مسند أحمد حديث معاذ بن أنس الجهني رضي الله تعالى عنه

Sahl ibn Mu'adh Al-Juhani related from his father, who said: We descended upon the stronghold of Sinan, in Roman territory, with Abdullah ibn 'Abd Al-Malik, but the people confined the encampments and blocked the road. And Mu'adh said: Oh people! Indeed we went out on such-and-such a raid with the Messenger of Allah (SAW), and the people confined the road, so the Prophet (SAW) sent out a herald who announced: There is no *jihad* for anyone who confines an encampment or cuts off a road.

Musnad Ahmad, The hadith of Mu'adh ibn Anas Al-Juhani (may Allah be pleased with him)

عن أبي المثنى العبدي قال سمعت السدوسي يعني إبن الخصاصية قال أتيت النبي ﷺ لأبايعه قال فإشترط علي شهادة ألا إله إلا الله وأن محمداً عبده ورسوله وأن أقيم الصلاة وأن أؤدي الزكاة وأن أحج حجة الاسلام وأن أصوم شهر رمضان وأن أجاهد في سبيل الله فقلت يا رسول الله أما اثنتان فوالله ما أطيقهما الجهاد والصدقة فانهم زعموا أنه من ولي الدبر فقد باء بغضب من الله فأخاف إن حضرت تلك جشعت نفسي وكرهت الموت والصدقة فوالله ما لي إلا غُنَيْمة وعشر ذود هن رَسَل أهلي وحمولتهم قال فقبض رسول الله ﷺ يده ثم حرّك يده ثم قال فلا جهاد ولا صدقة فلم تدخل الجنة إذاً قلت يا رسول الله أنا أبايعك قال فبايعت عليهن كلهن

مسند أحمد حديث بشير بن الخصاصية السدوسي رضي الله عنه

From Abu Al-Muthanna Al-'Abdi who said: I heard Al-Sadusi, that is, Ibn Al-Khasasiya, say: I came to the Prophet (SAW) to pledge allegiance to him, and He imposed the conditions that I bear witness that there is no god but Allah, that Muhammad is His servant and His Messenger, that I observe prayer, that I give *zakat*, that I perform the *hajj* of Islam, that I fast in the month of Ramadan, and that I wage *jihad* in the cause of Allah. And I said: Oh Messenger of Allah, two of these I swear by Allah I am unable to bear – *jihad* and giving charity; but people allege that whoever turns his back has incurred the wrath of Allah [*Al-anfal* 16]. I'm afraid that if I undertake this, my soul will be unwilling, for I dislike death; and as for charity, I swear by Allah the only thing I have is a small herd and ten of my family's herd that they have carried along. And the Messenger of Allah (SAW) grabbed his hand, jerked it around, then said: No *jihad* and no charity – so you're not going to *Jannah* then?! I said: Oh Messenger of Allah, I pledge to you. He said: Then you have pledged to all of it.

Musnad Ahmad, The hadith of Bashir ibn Al-Khasasiya (may Allah be pleased with him)

عن إبن عباس قال بينا رسول الله ﷺ في بيت بعض نسائه إذ وضع رأسه فنام فضحك في منامه فلما إستيقظ قالت له إمرأة من نسائه لقد ضحكت في منامك فما أضحكك قال أعجب من ناس من أمتي يركبون هذا البحر هَوْلَ العدو ويجاهدون في سبيل الله فذكر لهم خيراً كثيراً

مسند أحمد مسند عبدالله بن العباس بن عبد المطلب عن النبي ﷺ.

From Ibn 'Abbas who said: While the Messenger of Allah (SAW) was in the house of some of his women, He lay his head down and slept. And He laughed while he was sleeping. When He awoke, one of his women said to him: You were laughing in your sleep – what made you laugh? He said: The most wonderful people of my *ummah* set out on the sea in fear and anticipation of the enemy, waging *jihad* in the cause of Allah. And He spoke to them of many good things.

Musnad Ahmad, The narrations of Abdullah ibn Al-'Abbas ibn 'Abd Al-Muttalib from the Prophet (SAW)

عن الحكم قال سمعت أبا عمر الصيني عن ابي الدرداء أنه إذا كان نزل به ضيفٌ قال يقول له أبو الدرداء مقيم فنسرح أو ظاعن فنعلف قال فإن قال له ظاعن قال له ما أجد لك شيئاً خيراً من شيء أمرنا به رسول الله ﷺ قلنا يا رسول الله ذهب الأغنياء بالأجر يحجون ولا نحج ويجاهدون ولا نجاهد وكذا وكذا فقال رسول الله ﷺ ألا أدلكم على شيء إن أخذتم به جئتم من أفضل ما يجيء به أحد منهم أن تكبّروا الله أربعاً وثلاثين وتسبّحوه ثلاثاً وثلاثين تحمّدوه ثلاثاً وثلاثين في دبر كل صلاة

مسند أحمد مسند عبدالله بن العباس بن عبد المطلب عن النبي ﷺ.

From Al-Hakim, who said: I heard Abu 'Umar Al-Sini relate from Abu Al-Dardaa, that whenever a guest came to him, Abu Al-Dardaa said to him: "Staying?" – in which case we would leave – or "Departing?" – in which case we would feed the animals. If the guest said to him "departing", he would say to him: I find nothing better for you than something that the Messenger of Allah (SAW) ordered us to do; we said: Oh Messenger of Allah, the rich take the reward – they do *hajj* and we do not do *hajj*, they wage *jihad* and we do not wage *jihad*, and so on. And the Messenger of Allah (SAW) said: Shall I not attest to you all of something, that if you take hold of it, you will have something better than any of them have? That is if you make Allah great [say "*Allahu Akbar*"] thirty-four times, and exalt Him ["*Subhana Allah*"] thirty-three times, and glorify Him ["*Al-hamdu Lillah*"] thirty-three times at the end of every prayer.

Musnad Ahmad, The narrations of Abdullah ibn Al-'Abbas ibn 'Abd Al-Muttalib from the Prophet (SAW)

عن شداد بن أوس قال ثنتان حفظتهما عن رسول الله ﷺ قال إن الله كتب الإحسان على كل شيء فإذا قتلتم فاحسنوا القِتلة وإذا ذبحتم فاحسنوا الذبح وليُحدّ أحدكم شفرته فليُرح ذبيحته

صحيح مسلم كتاب الصيد والذبائح وما يؤكل من الحيوان

From Shaddad ibn Aws, who said: I've kept in mind two things that the Messenger of Allah (SAW) said: Indeed Allah has ordained for things to be done well, so whenever you kill, make it a good killing, and whenever you sacrifice, make it a good sacrifice; and let each of you sharpen his blade, to make it amenable for what is being sacrificed.

Sahih Muslim, The book of hunting, slaughtering, and what animals may be eaten

عن ابي الدرداء رضي الله عنه قال قال النبي ﷺ ألا أنبّئكم بخير أعمالكم وأزكاها عند مليككم وأرفعها في درجاتكم وخير لكم من إنفاق الذهب والورِق وخير لكم من أن تلقوا عدوّكم فتضربوا أعناقهم ويضربوا أعناقكم قولوا بلى قال ذكر الله تعالى

جامع الترمذي كتاب الدعوات

From Abu Al-Dardaa (may Allah be pleased with him), who said: The Prophet (SAW) said: Shall I not inform you all of the best of your deeds, the purest of them in the sight of your Sovereign, the highest of them in your standing, better for you than spending gold and silver, and better for you than meeting your enemy and striking off their heads and them striking off your heads? The people said: Yes indeed! He said: Remembrance [*dhikr*] of Allah Most High.

Sunan Al-Tirmidhi, The book of supplications

عن زيد بن أسلم أن رسول الله ﷺ قال من غير دينه فاضربوا عنقه

موطأ مالك كتاب الأقضية

Zaid ibn Aslam related that the Messenger of Allah (SAW) said: Whoever changes his religion – decapitate him [*idribu 'unuqahu*, strike his neck].

Muwatta Malik, The book of judgments

عن اسامة بن شريك قال قال رسول الله ﷺ أيما رجل خرج يُفرّق بين أمتي فاضربوا عنقه

سنن النسائي كتاب تحريم الدم

From Usama ibn Sharik who said: The Messenger of Allah (SAW) said: Any man who goes out to cause division among my *ummah* – decapitate him.

Sunan Al-Nasa'i, The book of the prohibition of bloodshed

عن عكرمة قال أُتِيَ عليّ رضي الله عنه بزنادقة فأحرقهم فبلغ ذلك إبن عباس فقال لو كنت أنا لم أحرقهم لنهي رسول الله ﷺ ولقتلتُهم لقول رسول الله ﷺ من بدّل دينه فاقتلوه

صحيح البخاري كتاب استتابة المرتدين والمعاندين وقتالهم

From 'Ikrama, who said: Some nonbelievers [*zanadiqa*] were brought to 'Ali, and he burned them. News of this reached Ibn 'Abbas, and he said: If it were me, I would not have burned them, since the Messenger of Allah (SAW) prohibited that; I would have just killed them based on what the Messenger of Allah (SAW) said: Whoever changes his religion – kill him.

Sahih Al-Bukhari, The book of seeking the repentance of apostates and the obstinate, and fighting against them

عن عرفجة قال سمعت رسول الله ﷺ يقول إنه ستكون هنات وهنات فمن أراد أن يفرّق أمر هذه الأمة وهي جميع فاضربوه بالسيف كائناً من كان

صحيح مسلم كتاب الإمارة

'Arfaja said: I heard the Messenger of Allah (SAW) say: Indeed this and that will arise, so whoever desires to cause division in the affairs of this *ummah*, when it is united, strike him with the sword, whoever he is.

Sahih Muslim, The book of governance

عن عفرجة بن شريح قل قال النبي ﷺ إنها ستكون بعدي هنات وهنات وهنات ورفع يديه فمن رأيتموه يريد تفريق أمر أمة محمد ﷺ وهم جميع فاقتلوه كائناً من كان من الناس

سنن النسائي كتاب تحريم الدم

From 'Arfaja ibn Shuraih, who said: The Prophet (SAW) said: Indeed this, that, and other things will arise after me – and He raised his hands – so whoever you see wanting to cause division in the affairs of Muhammad's (SAW) *ummah* when they are united – kill him, whoever he is from among the people.

Sunan Al-Nasa'i, The book of the prohibition of bloodshed

عن عطية القرظي قال عُرِضنا على النبي ﷺ يوم قريظة فكان من أنبت قُتل ومن لم ينبت خُلّيَ سبيله فكنت ممن لم ينبت نخلى سبيلي

جامع الترمذي كتاب السير

From 'Atiya Al-Quradhi who said: We were brought before the Prophet (SAW) on the day of Quraidha (Quraiza), and anyone who had sprouted [i.e. pubic hair] was killed, but anyone who had not yet sprouted was sent on his way. I was among those who had not sprouted, so I was sent on my way.

Sunan Al-Tirmidhi, The book of campaigns

عن عطية القرظي قال لما كان يوم قريظة جعل رسول الله ﷺ من أنبت ضرب عنقه فكنت فيمن لم ينبت فعرضت على رسول الله ﷺ فخلى عني

المحلى لإبن حزم بلوغ الغلام والجارية

From 'Atiya Al-Quradhi who said: On the day of Quraidha, the Messenger of Allah (SAW) had everyone who had sprouted get decapitated; I was among those who had not yet sprouted, so I was sent on my way from the Messenger of Allah (SAW) and He left me alone.

Ibn Hazm, Muhalla, Section: puberty for boys and girls

...فكشفوا عانتي فوجدوها لم تنبت فجعلوني في السبي

سنن أبي داود كتاب الحدود

"... They exposed my pubic area ['ana] and found that it had not yet sprouted, so they put me with the prisoners."

Sunan Abu Dawud, The book of legal punishments [hudud]

عن أبي هريرة رضي الله عنه قال قال رسول الله صلى الله عليه وآله وسلم أكثروا ذكر هاذم اللذات الموت

مختصر منهاج القاصدين لإبن قدامة باب ما جاء في فضل ذكر الموت

From Abu Huraira (may Allah be pleased with him), who said: The Messenger of Allah (may Allah pray over him and his household and salute him) said: Think more about the Slasher of Pleasures – death.

Ibn Qudama, Mukhtasar Minhaj Al-Qasideen, Section: Regarding the merit in remembering death

وقد روي عن عبدالله بن عمر رضي الله عنهما قال أخذ رسول الله صلى الله عليه وآله وسلم بمنكبي فقال كن في الدنيا كأنك غريب أو عابر سبيل

مختصر منهاج القاصدين لإبن قدامة باب ما جاء في فضل ذكر الموت

It was narrated from Abdullah ibn 'Umar (may Allah be pleased with them both), who said: The Messenger of Allah (may Allah pray over him and his household and salute him) grabbed my shoulder and said: Be in this world as a stranger or someone passing through.

Ibn Qudama, Mukhtasar Minhaj Al-Qasideen, Section: Regarding the merit in remembering death

عن إبن عمر أنه قال كنت مع رسول الله ﷺ فجاءه رجلٌ من الأنصار فسلم على النبي ﷺ ثم قال يا رسول الله أي أمنؤمنين أفضل قال أحسنهم خُلُقاً قال فأي المؤمنين أكيس قال أكثرهم للموت ذكراً وأحسنهم لما بعده إستعداداً أولئك الأكياس

سنن إبن ماجه كتاب الزهد

Ibn 'Umar related, saying: We were with the Messenger of Allah (SAW), and a man from the *Ansar* came, greeted the Prophet (SAW), then said: Oh Messenger of Allah, which Believers are the best? He said: Those of them with the best morals. The man said: And which Believers are the keenest? He said: The ones who remember death the most, and the ones who best prepare for what comes after it; those are the keenest.

Ibn Majah, Sunan Ibn Majah, The book of abstinence

عن عبادة بن الصامت عن النبي ﷺ قال من أحب لقاء الله أحب الله لقاءه ومن كره لقاء الله كره الله لقاءه قالت عائشة أو بعض أزواجه إنا لنكره الموت قال ليس ذاك ولكن المؤمن إذا حضره الموت بُشِّر برضوان الله وكرامته فليس شيءٌ أحب إليه مما أمامه فأحب لقاء الله وأحب الله لقاءه

صحيح البخاري كتاب الرقاق

'Ubada ibn Al-Samit related from the Prophet (SAW), who said: Whoever loves to encounter Allah, Allah loves to encounter him; and whoever dislikes encountering Allah, Allah dislikes encountering him. 'Aishah or one of his other wives said: But indeed we dislike death. He said: It's not that; but a Believer, whenever death approaches, is given the good tidings of Allah's favor and honor, and there is nothing he loves more than what is before him; for he loves encountering Allah and Allah loves encountering him.

Sahih Al-Bukhari, The book of tenderness

عن عائشة رضي الله عنها قالت يا رسول الله نرى الجهاد أفضل العمل أفلا نجاهد قال لكن أفضل الجهاد حج مبرور

صحيح البخاري كتاب الجهاد والسِيَر

From 'Aishah (may Allah be pleased with her), who said: Oh Messenger of Allah, we find *jihad* to be the best deed; should we not wage *jihad*? He said: Actually the best *jihad* is the accepted pilgrimage [*hajj mabrur*].

Sahih Al-Bukhari, The book of jihad and campaigns

عائشة قالت قلت يا رسول الله ألا نخرج فنجاهد معك فإني لا أرى عملاً في القرآن أفضل من الجهاد قال لا ولكن أحسن الجهاد وأجمله حج البيت حج مبرور

سنن النسائي كتاب مناسك الحج

'Aishah said: Oh Messenger of Allah, Shall we not go out and wage *jihad* with you? For indeed I see no better deed in the Qur'an then *jihad*. He said: No, actually the best and most beautiful *jihad* is pilgrimage [*hajj*] to the House, the *hajj mabrur*.

Sunan Al-Nasa'i, The book of hajj rituals

عن أبي هريرة أن رسول الله ﷺ قال العمرة إلى العمرة كفارة لما بينهما والحج المبرور ليس له جزاء إلا الجنة

صحيح مسلم كتاب الحج

Abu Huraira related that the Messenger of Allah (SAW) said: The *'umrah* pilgrimage is expiation for what comes between it and another *'umrah*, and the accepted pilgrimage [*hajj mabrur*] has only *Jannah* as a reward.

Sahih Muslim, The book of hajj

قوله ﷺ والحج المبرور ليس له جزاء إلا الجنة الأصح الأشهر أن المبرور هو الذي لا يخالطه إثم مأخوذ من البر وهو الطاعة وقيل هو المقبول ومن علامة القبول أن يرجع خيراً مما كان ولا يعاود المعاصي وقيل هو الذي لا رياء فيه وقيل الذي لا يعقبه معصية

المنهاج بشرح صحيح مسلم للنووي

His (SAW) words: "The *hajj mabrur* has only *Jannah* as a reward." The most correct and well known is that the "accepted" [*mabrur*] is that which is not accompanied by wrongdoing that takes away from sincere devotion, that is, obedience; it is said that it is accepted, one of the indications of acceptance being that one returns better than he was, and does not turn again to misdeeds; and it is said that it is that in which there is no hypocrisy; and it is said that which is not followed by misdeeds.

Al-Nawawi, Al-minhaj bi Sharh Sahih Muslim

معاذ بن جبل أنه سمع رسول الله ﷺ يقول من قاتل في سبيل الله فواق ناقة فقد وجبت له الجنة ومن سأل الله القتل من نفسه صادقاً ثم مات أو قُتل فإن له أجر شهيد زاد إبن المصفى من هنا ومن جُرح جُرحاً في سبيل الله أو نُكب نَكبة فإنها تجيء يوم القيامة كأغزر ما كانت لونها لون الزعفران وريحها ريح المسك ومن خَرج به خُراج في سبيل الله فإن عليه طابع الشهداء

سنن أبي داود كتاب الجهاد

Mu'adh ibn Jabal related that he heard the Messenger of Allah (SAW) say: Whoever fights in the cause of Allah for the time that lapses between two milkings of a camel, *Jannah* is indispensably his. And whoever sincerely asks of Allah to be killed, and then dies or is killed, his is the reward of a martyr. (From here Ibn Musaffa adds: And whoever is injured with a wound in the cause of Allah or made to suffer misfortune, it will come on the day of resurrection more copious than what it was, its color the color of saffron and its scent the scent of musk; and whoever receives a painful ulcer in the cause of Allah, indeed the seal of the martyrs is upon him.)

Sunan Abu Dawud, The book of jihad

قال المغيرة بن شعبة أخبرنا نبينا ﷺ عن رسالة ربنا من قُتل منا صار إلى الجنة وقال عمر للنبي ﷺ أليس قَتلانا في الجنة وقتلاهم في النار قال بلى

فتح الباري لإبن حجر العسقلاني كتاب الجهاد

Al-Mughira ibn Shu'ba said: Our Prophet (SAW) related to us the message of our Lord – whoever of us is killed goes to *Jannah*. And 'Umar asked the Prophet (SAW): Are not those of us who got killed now in *Jannah*, and those of them who got killed now in Hellfire? He said: Yes indeed.

Ibn Hajar Al-Asqalani, Fath Al-Bari, The book of jihad

أبو هريرة يقول سمعت رسول الله ﷺ يقول لقد عجِب ربنا عز وجل من قوم يقادون إلى الجنة في السلاسل

سنن ابي داود كتاب الجهاد

Abu Huraira said: I heard the Messenger of Allah (SAW) say: Indeed our Lord will marvel at people who are led to *Jannah* in chains.

Sunan Abu Dawud, The book of jihad

عن ابي هريرة رضي الله عنه عن النبي ﷺ قال عجِب الله من قوم يدخلون الجنة في السلاسل

صحيح البخاري كتاب الجهاد والسِيَر

Abu Huraira (may Allah be pleased with him) related from the Prophet (SAW), who said: Allah will marvel at people who enter *Jannah* in chains.

Sahih Al-Bukhari, The book of jihad and campaigns

قال إبن الجوزي معناه أنهم أُسِروا وقُيِّدوا فلما عرفوا صحة الاسلام دخلوا طوعاً فدخلوا الجنة فكان الاكراه على الأسر والتقييد هو السبب الأول وكأنه أطلق على الاكراه التسلسُل ولما كان هو السبب في دخول الجنة أقام المسبِّب مقامَ السبب وقال الطيبي ويحتمل أن يكون المراد بالسلسلة الجذب الذي يجذبه الحقُّ مَن خلَّص من عباده من الضلالة إلى الهدى ومن الهبوط في مهاوي الطبيعة إلى العروج للدراجات العُلى لكن الحديث في تفسير آل عمران يدل على أنه على الحقيقة ونحوه ما أخرجه الطبراني من طريق ابي الطفيل رفعه رأيت ناساً من أمتي يُساقون إلى الجنة في السلاسل كَرهاً قلتُ يا رسول الله من هم قال قوم من العَجَم يسبيهم المهاجرون فيُدخلونهم في الإسلام مُكرَهين

فتح الباري لإبن حجر العسقلاني كتاب الجهاد

Ibn Jawzi said: The meaning is that they will be taken captive and bound, and when they become aware of the truth of Islam, they enter willingly, and enter *Jannah*. Compelling the prisoner and binding him is the primary cause, as if giving chains to coercion, and considering that this is the cause for entering *Jannah*, he who brought about the cause established the high standing of the cause. Al-Tibi said: This implies that the intended meaning of chains is the attraction that the truth draws to Him who rescues his servants from error into guidance, from falling into the depths of natural disposition to rising to the highest degrees. Yet the *hadith* in the *tafsir* of *surah Al 'Imran* makes it clear that the following is correct, and similarly what Al-Tabarani has recorded by way of Abu Al-Tufail directly from Muhammad: I saw some people of my *ummah* being taken to *Jannah* in chains under coercion. I said: Oh Messenger of Allah, who were they? He said: Some of the non-Arabs, who the *muhajirun* took captive and made them enter Islam by force.

Ibn Hajar Al-Asqalani, Fath Al-Bari, The book of jihad

عن ابي هريرة رضي الله عنه أن رسول الله ﷺ قال يضحك الله إلى رجلين يقتل احدهما الآخر يدخلان الجنة يقاتل هذا في سبيل الله فيُقتل ثم يتوب الله على القاتل فيُستشهَد

صحيح البخاري كتاب الجهاد والسِيَر

Abu Huraira (may Allah be pleased with him) related that the Messenger of Allah (SAW) said: Allah chuckles at two men, one of who kills the other, and both of them enter *Jannah* – one of them fights in the cause of Allah and is killed, then Allah turns towards the killer in forgiveness and he is made to become a martyr.

Sahih Al-Bukhari, The book of jihad and campaigns

عن عمرو بن عبسة قال أتيت النبي ﷺ فقلت يا رسول الله أي الجهاد أفضل قال من أُهريق دمه وعُقر جواده

سنن إبن ماجه كتاب الجهاد

From 'Amr ibn 'Abasa who said: I came to the Prophet (SAW) and said: Oh Messenger of Allah, what *jihad* is the best? He said: Someone whose blood is spilled and his steed gets injured.

Sunan Ibn Majah, The book of jihad

زيد بن خالد رضي الله عنه أن رسول الله ﷺ قال من جهّز غازياً في سبيل الله فقد غزا ومن خلف غازياً في سبيل الله بخير فقد غزا

صحيح البخاري كتاب الجهاد والسِيَر

Zaid ibn Khalid related that the Messenger of Allah (SAW) said: Whoever prepares a fighter in the cause of Allah has himself fought, and whoever takes good care of the affairs of a fighter in the cause of Allah has himself fought.

Sahih Al-Bukhari, The book of jihad and campaigns

عن حديث عائشة كل حدثني طائفة من الحديث قالت كان النبي ﷺ إذا أراد أن يخرج أقرع بين نسائه فأيتهن يخرج سهمها خرج بها النبي ﷺ فأقرع بيننا في غزوة غزاها فخرج فيها سهمي فخرجتُ مع النبي ﷺ بعد ما أُنزل الحجاب

صحيح البخاري كتاب الجهاد والسِيَر

In a hadith of 'Aishah, who said: The Prophet (SAW), whenever He wanted to set out, would cast lots among his women, and whichever of them whose arrow fell, the

Prophet (SAW) would set out with her. He cast lots between us on one of the raids He went on, and my arrow fell, and so I set out with the Prophet (SAW); this was after the *hijab* verse had been sent down.

Sahih Al-Bukhari, The book of jihad and campaigns

عن عبدالله بن عمر رضي الله عنهما أن رسول الله ﷺ قال تقاتلون اليهود حتى يختبئ احدهم وراء الحجر فيقول يا عبد الله هذا يهوديٌ ورائي فاقتله

صحيح البخاري كتاب الجهاد والسِير

'Abdullah ibn 'Umar (may Allah be pleased with them both) related that the Messenger of Allah (SAW) said: You all will fight the Jews, to the point that one of them will hide himself behind a rock, and it will say: Oh servant of Allah! It's a Jew behind me, so kill him!

Sahih Al-Bukhari, The book of jihad and campaigns

عن ابي هريرة رضي الله عنه عن رسول الله ﷺ قال لا تقوم الساعة حتى تقاتلوا اليهود حتى يقول الحجر وراءه اليهودي يا مسلم هذا يهودي ورائي فاقتله

صحيح البخاري كتاب الجهاد والسير

Abu Huraira (may Allah be pleased with him) related from the Messenger of Allah (SAW), who said: The hour will not come until you all fight the Jews, to the point that a rock with a Jew behind it will say: Oh Muslim! It's a Jew behind me, so kill him!

Sahih Al-Bukhari, The book of jihad and campaigns

قال أبو هريرة رضي الله عنه قال رسول الله ﷺ لا تقوم الساعة حتى تقاتلوا الترك صغار الأعين حُمر الوجوه ذُلف الأنوف كأنّ وجوههم المجانّ المطرّقة ولا تقوم الساعة حتى تقاتلوا قوماً نعالهم الشعر

صحيح البخاري كتاب الجهاد والسير

Abu Huraira (may Allah be pleased with him) said: The Messenger of Allah (SAW) said: The hour will not come until you fight the Turks – small eyes, red faces, and turned-up noses, like their faces were hammered-out shields; and the hour will not come until you fight people whose sandals are made of hair.

Sahih Al-Bukhari, The book of jihad and campaigns

عن خالد بن معدان أن عمير بن الأسود العنسي حدثه أنه أتى عبادة بن الصامت وهو نازل في ساحل حمص وهو في بناء له ومعه أمّ حرام قال عمير فحدثتنا أمّ حرام أنها سمعت النبي ﷺ يقول أول جيش من أمّتي يغزون البحر قد أوجبوا قالت أم حرام قلت يا رسول الله أنا فيهم قال انتِ فيهم ثم قال النبي ﷺ أول جيش من أمّتي يغزون مدينة قيصر مغفور لهم فقلت أنا فيهم يا رسول الله قال لا

صحيح البخاري كتاب الجهاد والسير

Khalid ibn Ma'dan related that 'Umair ibn Al-Aswad Al-'Ansi told him that he went to 'Ubada ibn Al-Samit while he was staying on the coast of Hims in a house of his, and Umm Haram was with him. 'Umair said: Umm Haram told us that she heard the Prophet (SAW) say: The first army of my *ummah* that goes on an attack at sea will certainly enter *Jannah*. Umm Haram asked: Oh Messenger of Allah, am I among them? He said: You are among them. Then the Prophet (SAW) said: The first army of my *ummah* that attacks the city of Caesar will be forgiven. I asked: Am I among them, oh Messenger of Allah? He said: No.

Sahih Al-Bukhari, The book of jihad and campaigns

عن سلمة رضي الله عنه قال بايعتُ النبي ﷺ ثم عدلت إلى ظل الشجرة فلما خفَّ الناس قال يا إبن الأكوع ألا تبايع قال قلت بايعت يا رسول الله قال وأيضاً فبايعتُه الثانية فقلت لا يا أبا مسلم على أي شيء كنتم تبايعون يومئذ قال على الموت

صحيح البخاري كتاب الجهاد والسير

From Salama (may Allah be pleased with him), who said: I made my pledge to the Prophet (SAW), then moved over to the shade of a tree. And when there were less people around, He said: Oh Ibn Al-Akwa', will you not make your pledge? I said: I have made my pledge already, oh Messenger of Allah. He said: Again. So I made my pledge a second time. And I asked: Oh Abu Muslim, what did you all make your pledge for that day? He said: For death.

Sahih Al-Bukhari, The book of jihad and campaigns

عن ابي هريرة رضي الله عنه عن النبي ﷺ قال غزا نبيٌ من الأنبياء فقال لقومه لا يتبعني رجل ملك بُضع إمرأة وهو يريد أن يبني بها ولم يبنِ بها

صحيح البخاري كتاب النكاح

Abu Huraira (may Allah be pleased with him) related from the Prophet (SAW), who said: One of the prophets went out on a raid, and said to his people: Any man who has come into possession of a woman's vagina [*malaka bud'a imra'a*; i.e. contracted marriage], and wants to have sex with her but has not yet had sex, should not come with me.

Sahih Al-Bukhari, The book of marital relations

إبن عوف قال كتبت إلى نافع فكتب إلي أن النبي ﷺ أغار على بني المصطلق وهم غارُّون وأنعامهم تُسقى على الماء فقتل مقاتلتهم وسبى ذراريَّهم وأصاب يومئذ جُوَيرية

صحيح البخاري كتاب العتق

Ibn 'Awf said: I wrote to Nafi' and he wrote back to me that the Prophet (SAW) raided the Banu Mustaliq when they had no idea and their flocks were being given water to drink. He killed their fighting men and took their women and children captive. And He got Juwairiyah on that day.

Sahih Al-Bukhari, The book of freeing slaves

عن أنس بن مالك رضي الله عنه قال صبّحنا خيبر بكرة فخرج أهلها بالمساحي فلما بصروا بالنبي ﷺ قالوا محمد والله محمد والخميس فقال النبي ﷺ الله أكبر خربت خيبر انا إذا نزلنا بساحة قوم فساء صباح المنذَرين فأصبنا من لحوم الحُمُر فنادى منادي النبي ﷺ إن الله ورسوله ينهَيانِكم عن لحوم الحُمر فإنها رجس

صحيح البخاري كتاب المغازي

From Anas ibn Malik (may Allah be pleased with him), who said: We got to Khaibar early in the morning, and the inhabitants were coming out with their shovels, and when they saw the Prophet (SAW) they said: Muhammad, by Allah! Muhammad and his army! And the Prophet (SAW) said: Allah is bigger [*Allahu akbar*]! Khaibar is ruined! Indeed when we descend onto a people, the morning gets bad for those who have been warned! Then we came upon some donkey meat, but the Prophet's (SAW) proclaimer announced: Indeed Allah and his Messenger prohibit you from eating donkey meat, for truly it is a filthy thing.

Sahih Al-Bukhari, The book of military raids

قوله خربت خيبر زاد في الجهاد فرفع يديه وقال الله أكبر خربت خيبر وزيادة التكبير في مُعظَم الطرق عن أنس وعن حميد قال السهيلي يؤخذ من هذا الحديث التفاؤل لأنه ﷺ لما رأى آلات الهَدم مع أنَّ لفظ المِسحاة من سَحَوتُ إذا قَشَرتَ أخذ منه أنَّ مدينتهم ستخرَب إنتهى ويُحتمل أن يكون قال خربت خيبر بطريق الوحي ويؤيِّده قوله بعد ذلك انا إذا نزلنا بساحة قوم فساء صباح المنذَرين

فتح الباري لإبن حجر العسقلاني كتاب المغازي

His words "Khaibar is ruined!" added as extra support in *jihad*: He raised his hands and said "*Allahu Akbar*! Khaibar is ruined!". The addition of *takbeer* ["*Allahu akbar*"] is in most of the narrations from Anas and Humaid. Al-Suhaili said: Saying this conveyed optimism, for when He (SAW) saw implements of destruction – even though saying "shovel" is like saying "I dug" or "I scraped" – He took it to mean that their city would be destroyed. (end quote). And so it is implied that He said "Khaibar is destroyed" by way of divine inspiration, and what He said after that supported this: "Indeed when we descend onto a people, the morning gets bad for those who have been warned".

Ibn Hajar Al-Asqalani, Fath Al-Bari, The book of military raids

عن عكرمة أن علياً قتل قوماً كفروا بعد إسلامهم وأحرقهم بالنار فبلغ ذلك إبن عباس فقال لو كنتُ لقتلتهم
ولم أحرّقهم لأن رسول الله ﷺ قال من بدّل أو قال من رجع عن دينه فأقتلوه ولا تعذّبوا بعذاب الله يعني
النار قال فبلغ قول إبن عباس علياً فقال وَيْحَ إبن عباس

المصنف لعبد الرزاق كتاب الجهاد

'Ikrama related that 'Ali killed some people who had renounced their Islam; he burned them with fire. News of this reached Ibn 'Abbas, and he said: If I were to have killed them I wouldn't have burned them, because the Messenger of Allah (SAW) said: Whoever changes ... or He said: Whoever turns away from his religion, kill him, but do not punish with Allah's punishment, that is, by fire. And news of what Ibn 'Abbas had said reached 'Ali, but he said: Screw Ibn 'Abbas!

'Abd Al-Razzaq, the Musannaf, The book of jihad

عن أبي هريرة رضي الله عنه أنه قال بعثنا رسول الله ﷺ في بعث فقال إن وجدتم فلاناً وفلاناً فأحرقوهما بالنار ثم قال رسول الله ﷺ حين أردنا الخروج إني أمرتكم أن تحرقوا فلاناً وفلاناً وإنّ النار لا يعذّب بها إلا الله فإن وجدتموهما فاقتلوهما

صحيح البخاري كتاب الجهاد والسير

From Abu Huraira (may Allah be pleased with him), who said: The Messenger of Allah (SAW) sent us out on a mission, and said: If you find So-and-so and So-and-so, burn them both with fire. Then the Messenger of Allah (SAW) said, when we were intending to leave: I indeed told you to burn So-and-so and So-and-so, but truly only Allah punishes with fire, so if you find the two of them, just kill them.

Sahih Al-Bukhari, The book of jihad and campaigns

عن أبي هريرة رضي الله عنه عن النبي ﷺ قال لا تمنّوا لقاء العدو فإذا لقيتموهم فاصبروا

صحيح البخاري كتاب الجهاد والسير

Abu Huraira (may Allah be pleased with him) related from the Prophet (SAW), who said: Do not desire to face the enemy, but whenever you face them, be steadfast.

Sahih Al-Bukhari, The book of jihad and campaigns

عن أبي سعيد عن النبي ﷺ قال لكل غادر لواءٌ عند استه يوم القيامة

صحيح مسلم كتاب الجهاد والسير

Abu Sa'id related from the Prophet (SAW), who said: Every traitor will have a flag on his ass at resurrection day.

Sahih Muslim, The book of jihad and campaigns

عن أنس بن مالك رضي الله عنه أن رسول الله ﷺ دخل عام الفتح وعلى رأسه المِغفر فلما نزعه جاء رجل فقال إن إبن خطل متعلّقٌ بأستار الكعبة فقال اقتلوه

صحيح البخاري كتاب الجهاد والسير

Anas ibn Malik (may Allah be pleased with him) related that the Messenger of Allah (SAW) came in once during the year of the conquest [of Mecca] with a helmet on his head, and when he took it off, a man came and said: Indeed Ibn Khatal is clinging onto the curtains of the Ka'ba. And He said: Kill him.

Sahih Al-Bukhari, The book of jihad and campaigns

عن ابي طلحة رضي الله عنه عن النبي ﷺ أنه كان إذا ظهر على قومٍ أقام بالعرصة ثلاث ليال

صحيح البخاري كتاب الجهاد والسير

Abu Talha (may Allah be pleased with him) related from the Prophet (SAW) that whenever He prevailed over a people, He stayed in the town square for three days.

Sahih Al-Bukhari, The book of jihad and campaigns

عن عبدالله رضي الله عنه أن النبي ﷺ كان إذا قفل كبّر ثلاثاً قال آيبون إن شاء الله تائبون عابدون حامدون لربنا ساجدون صدق الله وعده ونصر عبده وهزم الاحزاب وحده

صحيح البخاري كتاب الجهاد والسير

Abdullah (may Allah be pleased with him) related that the Prophet (SAW), whenever He returned, would say three *takbeer* [*"Allahu akbar"*] and say: We are returning, if Allah wills, repenting, worshipping, and praising, bowing before our Lord; Allah has fulfilled His promise, has made His servant victorious, and He alone has defeated the parties.

Sahih Al-Bukhari, The book of jihad and campaigns

عن عبدالله بن واقد السعدي قال وفدتُ إلى رسول الله ﷺ في وفد كلنا يطلب حاجة وكنتُ آخرهم دخولاً على رسول الله ﷺ فقلتُ يا رسول الله إني تركت من خلفي وهم يزعُمون أن الهجرة قد انقطعت قال لا تنقطع الهجرة ما قوتل الكفار

سنن النسائي كتاب البيعة

From Abdullah ibn Waqid Al-Sa'di, who said: I paid a visit to the Messenger of Allah (SAW) as part of a delegation, each of us asking something, and I was the last of them to enter in to see the Messenger of Allah (SAW); I said: Oh Messenger of Allah, indeed

I have abandoned those who were behind me – they allege that emigration has ceased. He said: Emigration will not cease as long as the disbelievers [*kuffar*] are being fought.

Sunan Al-Nasa'i, The book of the pledge of allegiance

عن سبرة بن ابي فاكه قال سمعت رسول الله ﷺ يقول إن الشيطان قعد لابن آدم بأطرُقه فقعد له بطريق الاسلام فقال تُسلم وتذَر دينك ودين آبائك وآباء ابيك فعصاه فأسلم ثم قعد له بطريق الهجرة فقال تهاجر وتدع أرضك وسماءك وإنما مَثَل المهاجر كمثل الفرس في الطِوَل فعصاه فهاجر ثم قعد له بطريق الجهاد فقال تجاهد فهو جَهْد النفس والمال فتقاتل فتُقتل فتُنكح المرأة ويُقسَم المال فعصاه فجاهد فقال رسول الله ﷺ فمن فعل ذلك كان حقاً على الله عز وجل أن يدخله الجنة ومن قُتل كان حقاً على الله عز وجل أن يدخله الجنة وإن غرِق كان حقاً على الله أن يدخله الجنة أو وقصته دابّته كان حقاً على الله أن يدخله الجنة

سنن النسائي كتاب لجهاد

From Sabra ibn Abi Fakih, who said: I heard the Messenger of Allah (SAW) say: Surely Satan sits in wait for a man along the paths he takes; he sits in wait for him on the path to Islam, saying: Will you yield into Islam, and forsake your religion and the religion of your fathers and the fathers of your father? But he pays no attention, and enters into Islam. Then Satan sits in wait for him on the path to emigration [*hijra*], saying: Will you emigrate, and leave your land and your sky – truly one who emigrates is like a horse on a rope. But he pays no attention, and emigrates. Then Satan sits in wait for him on the path to *jihad*, saying: Will you wage *jihad*, when this means waging yourself and your wealth? You will fight and be killed, and your woman will be given for marital relations with another, and your wealth will be divided up. But he pays no attention, and wages *jihad*. And the Messenger of Allah (SAW) said: Whoever does this, Allah Mighty and Sublime must admit him into *Jannah*, and whoever gets killed, Allah Mighty and Sublime must admit him into *Jannah*, even if he is drowned, Allah must admit him into *Jannah*, or if his animal throws him off and this breaks his neck, Allah must admit him into *Jannah*.

Sunan Al-Nasa'i, The book of jihad

عن ابي قتادة قال ... وجلس النبي ﷺ فقال من قتل قتيلاً له عليه بيّنة فله سَلَبه

صحيح البخاري كتاب المغازي

From Abu Qadata, who said ... and the Prophet (SAW) sat down and said: Whoever kills a man with proof of it, gets his belongings.

Sahih Al-Bukhari, The book of military raids

وثبت من فعله ﷺ أنه كان يبيّت العدو ويغير عليهم مع الغدوات فمن الناس وهم الجمهور من ذهب إلى أن فعله ناسخ لقوله وأن ذلك إنما كان في أول الاسلام قبل أن تنتشر الدعوة بدليل دعوتهم فيه إلى الهجرة ومن الناس من رجح القول على الفعل وذلك بأن حمل الفعل على الخصوص

بداية المجتهد ونهاية المقتصد لإبن رشد كتاب الجهاد الجملة الأول في معرفة أركان الحرب ألفصل الرابع في شرط الحرب

It is well-established from what He (SAW) did, that He would scheme against the enemy and change on them when setting out in the morning. Some people, and they are the majority, hold that what He did abrogates what He said, and that this indeed was in the beginning of Islam, before the call to Islam [*da'wah*] spread, on the basis that their *da'wah* in Islam was to emigrate. But some people give more weight to words than actions, and this is because actions apply to specific situations.

Ibn Rushd, Bidaya Al-mujtahid wa Nihaya Al-Muqtasid, The book of jihad, Part one: knowing the elements of war, Section four: on the stipulations for war

عن الحسن أن رسول الله ﷺ نهى عن قتل النساء

كتاب السير الصغير للشيباني ١٩

Al-Hasan related that the Messenger of Allah (SAW) prohibited the killing of women.

Al-Shaybani, Kitab Al-siyar Al-saghir, item 19

عن سعيد بن المسيب قال أمّن رسول الله ﷺ من الأسارى يوم بدر أبا عزة عبدالله بن عمرو بن عبد الجمحي وكان شاعراً وكان قال للنبي ﷺ يا محمد إن لي خمس بنات ليس لهن شيء فتصدق بي عليهن ففعل وقال أبو عزة أعطيك موثقاً أن لا أقاتلك ولا أكثر عليك أبداً فأرسله رسول الله ﷺ

السنن الكبرى للبيهقي كتاب السير

From Sa'id ibn Al-Musayyib, who said: The Messenger of Allah (SAW) secured Abu 'Azza Abdullah ibn 'Amr ibn 'Abd Al-Jumahi from among the prisoners on the day of Badr; he was a poet. He said to the Prophet (SAW): Oh Muhammad! Indeed I have five daughters who have nothing; be charitable to them for me. So He did. And Abu 'Azza said: I give you my word that I will not fight you and I will not ever be superior over you. So the Messenger of Allah (SAW) sent him off.

Al-Bayhaqi, Al-sunan Al-kubra, The book of campaigns

عن عبدالله بن يزيد عن النبي ﷺ أنه نهى عن النُّهبة والمُثلة رواه البخاري
النُّهبة - الغارة . المُثلة - تشويه الخلق بقطع الأنف والأذن وفقء العين
مشكاة المصابيح للتبريزي كتاب البيوع

Abdullah ibn Yazid related from the Prophet (SAW) that He prohibited excessive booty [*nuhbah*] and mutilation [*muthlah*]. Related by Al-Bukhari.

Nuhbah is an overzealous attempt to take a large portion [*ghara*]; *Muthlah* is disfigurement of someone's innate constitution by cutting off the nose, the ears, or gouging out the eyes.

Al-Tabrizi, Mishkat Al-masabih, The book of transactions

عن الضحاك أن رسول الله ﷺ خرج يوم أحد فإذا كتيبة حسناء فقال ما هؤلاء قالوا يهود كذا وكذا فقال
لا نستعين بالكفار
كتاب السير الصغير للشيباني ٢٥

Al-Dahhak related that the Messenger of Allah (SAW) went out on the day of Uhud and saw a fine-looking contingent; He asked: Who are those? They said: Such-and-such Jews. And He said: We do not seek aid from disbelievers [*kuffar*].

Al-Shaybani, Kitab Al-siyar Al-saghir, item 25

عن عبدالله بن بريدة عن أبيه قال كان رسول الله ﷺ إذا بعث جيشاً أو سريّة أوصى صاحبهم في خاصّة نفسه بتقوى الله وأوصاه بمن معه من المسلمين خيراً ثم قال اغزوا بسم الله وفي سبيل الله قاتلوا من كفر بالله ولا تغلّوا ولا تغدروا ولا تمثّلوا ولا تقتلوا وليداً وإذا لقيتم عدوّكم من المشركين فادعوهم إلى الاسلام فإن أسلموا فاقبلوا منهم وكفّوا عنهم
كتاب السير الصغير للشيباني ١

Abdullah ibn Buraida related from his father, who said: The Messenger of Allah (SAW), whenever he sent forth an army or a brigade, He would order the person in charge of them, in his personal character, to fear Allah, and He would order him to do good towards the Muslims who were with him, then He would say: Attack in the name of Allah and in the cause of Allah, fight those who have disbelieved in Allah, do not steal from the spoils, do not betray, do not mutilate, and do not kill children; and whenever you face your enemy the idolaters, call them to Islam, and if they yield into Islam, accept it from them and cease from them.

Al-Shaybani, Kitab Al-siyar Al-saghir, item 1

وذا إرتد المسلم عن الاسلام عرض عليه الاسلام فإن أسلم وإلا قتل مكانه إلا أن يطلب أن يؤجله فإن طلب ذلك أُجّل ثلاثة أيام بلغنا نحو ذلك عن النبي ﷺ في قتل المرتد

كتاب السير الصغير للشيباني ١٠٠-١٠١

If a Muslim apostatizes from Islam, Islam is to be presented to him. If he yields back into Islam, fine; otherwise, he is killed then and there, unless he asks to be deferred. If he asks for this, he is deferred for three days. We have been made aware of similar reports from the Prophet (SAW) regarding the killing of apostates [murtadd].

Al-Shaybani, Kitab Al-siyar Al-saghir, items 100 and 101

ولا تقتل المرتدة ولكنها تحبس أبداً حتى تسلم بلغنا عن إبن عباس رضي الله عنهما أنه قال إذا إرتدت المرأة عن الاسلام حبست ولم تقتل وبلغنا عن رسول الله ﷺ أنه نهى عن قتل نساء المشركين في الحرب

كتاب السير الصغير للشيباني ١١٢

Woman who apostatize are not to be killed, but they are to be permanently locked up until they yield into Islam. We have been made aware that Ibn 'Abbas (may Allah be pleased with them both) said: If a woman apostatizes from Islam, she is to be locked up but not killed. And we have been made aware that the Messenger of Allah (SAW) prohibited killing the women of the idolaters in wartime.

Al-Shaybani, Kitab Al-siyar Al-saghir, items 112

ذكر عبدالله بن ابي أوفى رضي الله عنه أن النبي ﷺ كان إذا لقي العدو وقبل أن يواقعهم قال اللهم إنا عبادك وهم عبادك نواصينا ونواصيهم بيدك اللهم اهزمهم وانصرنا عليهم وفيه دليل على أنه ينبغي لكل غاز أن يقتدي برسول الله ﷺ في الدعاء عند القتال قال وإذا لقي المسلمون المشركين فإن كانوا قوماً لم يبلغهم الاسلام فليس ينبغي لهم أن يقاتلهم حتى يدعوهم فإن كان قد بلغهم الاسلام ولكن لا يدرون أنا نقبل منهم الجزية فينبغي أن لا نقاتلهم حتى ندعوهم إلى إعطاء الجزية به أمر رسول الله ﷺ أمراء لجيوش وهو آخر ما ينتهي به القتال

كتاب السير الكبير للشيباني باب الدعاء عند القتال

Abdullah ibn Abi Awfa (may Allah be pleased with him) mentioned that the Prophet (SAW), whenever He faced the enemy, before combating them, would say: Oh Allah! Indeed we are your servants and they are your servants; our forelocks and their forelocks [i.e. control over us and them] are in your hand; oh Allah! Subdue them and grant us victory over them. From this it is evident that every warrior ought to emulate the Messenger of Allah (SAW) in issuing the call to people [du'a] at the time of fighting. And whenever the Muslims faced the Idolaters, if it was a group which had not been made aware of Islam, they were not to fight them until giving the du'a to them. If they had already been made aware of Islam, but did not know that we take *jizya* from them, then we were not to fight them until giving the *du'a* to them regarding giving *jizya*; this is what the Messenger of Allah (SAW) ordered the commanders of the army, and was the last thing by which fighting could be halted.

Al-Shaybani, Kitab Al-siyar Al-kabir, Section: calling people at the time of fighting

عن عمير بن مالك رضي الله عنه قال قال رجل يا رسول الله إني لقيت أبي في العدو فسمعت منه مقالة لك سيئة فقتلته فسكت رسول الله ﷺ

كتاب السير الكبير للشيباني باب قتل ذي الرحم المحرم

From 'Umair ibn Malik (may Allah be pleased with him), who said: A certain man said: Oh Messenger of Allah, indeed I faced my father among the enemy, and I heard him say some bad things of you, so I killed him. But the Messenger of Allah (SAW) said nothing.

Al-Shaybani, Kitab Al-siyar Al-kabir, Section: killing relatives

وإذا بعث ملك العدو إلى أمير الجند بهدية فلا بأس بأن يقبلها ويصير فيئاً للمسلمين وإذا طمع في إسلامهم فهو مندوب إلى أن يؤلفهم فيقبل الهدية ويهدي إليهم عملاً بقوله عليه السلام تهادوا تحابوا وإذا لم يطمع في إسلامهم فله أن يظهر معنى الغلظة والشدة عليهم برد الهدية

كتاب السير الكبير للشيباني باب هدية أهل الحرب

If a messenger from the enemy sends a gift to the commander of the army, there is no problem for him to accept it, and it becomes booty for the Muslims. If he is intent on them becoming Muslims, then he is allowed to be on good terms with them, and accept the gift, as well as give to them, acting in accordance with what He (peace upon him) said: Give gifts to each other to love each other. However if he is not intent on them becoming Muslims, he may show them the sense of harshness and severity by returning the gift.

Al-Shaybani, Kitab Al-siyar Al-kabir, Section: gifts from a warring party

قال إبن شهاب ولم أسمع يرخّص في شيء مما يقول الناس كذب إلا في ثلاث - الحرب والاصلاح بين الناس وحديث الرجل امرأته وحديث المرأة زوجها

صحيح مسلم كتاب البر والصلة والآداب

Ibn Shihab said: I never heard that He (SAW) gave license for anything in which people would tell lies except for three things – war, reconciliation between people, and a man's conversation with his woman and a woman's conversation with her husband.

Sahih Muslim, The book of devotion, family ties, and proprieties

عن ابن عمر قال قال رسول الله ﷺ بُعثتُ بالسيف حتى يُعبد الله لا شريك له وجُعل رزقي تحت ظل رُمحي وجُعل الذِلّة والصَغار على من خالف أمري ومن تشبّه بقوم فهو منهم

مسند أحمد مسند عبدالله بن عمر بن الخطاب رضي الله عنه

From Ibn 'Umar, who said: The Messenger of Allah (SAW) said: I have been sent forth with the sword until Allah is worshipped and no other alongside Him; and I have been made to prosper under the shadow of my spear; and disgrace and cringing for whoever goes against my orders; and whoever imitates a group of people, he is one of them.

Musnad Ahmad, The narrations of Abdullah ibn 'Umar ibn Al-Khattab (may Allah be pleased with him)

وسئل رحمه الله هل يجوز للجندي أن يلبس شيئاً من الحرير والذهب والفضة في القتال أو وقت يصل رسل العدو إلى المسلمين فأجاب الحمد لله أما لباس الحرير عند القتال للضرورة فيجوز باتفاق المسلمين وذلك بألا يقوم غيره مقامه في دفع السلاح والوقاية وأما لباسه لإرهاب العدو ففيه قولان للعلماء أظهرهما أن ذلك جائز فإن جند الشام كتبوا إلى عمر بن الخطاب إنا إذا لقينا العدو ورأيناهم قد كفروا أي غطوا اسلحتهم بالحرير وجدنا لذلك رعباً في قلوبنا فكتب اليهم عمر وأنتم فكفّروا أسلحتكم كما يكفرون اسلحتهم ولأن لبس الحرير فيه خيلاء والله يحب الخيلاء حال القتال كما في السنن عن النبي ﷺ أنه قال إن من الخيلاء ما يحبه الله ومن الخيلاء ما يبغضه الله فأما الخيلاء التي يحبها الله فإختيال الرجل عند الحرب وعند الصدقة وأما الخيلاء التي يبغضها الله فالخيلاء في البغي والفخر ولما كان يوم أحد إختال أبو دجانة الأنصاري بين الصفين فقال النبي ﷺ إنها لمشية يبغضها الله إلا في هذا الموطن وأما يسير الحرير مثل العلم الذي عرضه أربعة أصابع ونحو ذلك فيجوز مطلقاً وفي العلم الذهب نزاع بين العلماء والأظهر جوازه أيضاً فإن في السنن عن النبي ﷺ أنه نهى عن الذهب إلا مقطّعاً

مجموع الفتاوى لإبن تيمية كتاب الفقه الجزء الثامن الجهاد

He (may Allah have mercy on him) was asked: Is it permissible for a soldier to wear some silk, gold, or silver to fight, or at the time the enemy's messengers reach the Muslims? He answered: Praise be to Allah. Muslims agree that wearing silk when fighting, if necessary, is permitted; this is so nothing else substitutes for it in fending off weapons and assuring protection. As far as wearing it to terrorize the enemy, the scholars have two points of view; the most substantiated of which is that this is permissible. Indeed the army in Sham wrote to 'Umar ibn Al-Khattab: Whenever we have faced the enemy, and have seen that they cover – that is, wrap their weapons with silk – we met with terror in our hearts. 'Umar wrote back to them: So you all cover your weapons like they cover theirs. Even more so since wearing silk is flaunting, and Allah likes flaunting during fighting, as it is in the *sunnah* that the Prophet (SAW) said: Indeed there is flaunting that Allah likes, and there is flaunting that Allah hates; the flaunting that Allah likes is when a man shows off for war and in giving alms, and the kind of flaunting that Allah hates is flaunting to oppress or out of pride. On the day of Uhud, Abu Dujana Al-Ansari was going around arrogantly among the ranks, and the Prophet (SAW) said: Indeed Allah hates walking like this except in this situation. However a small amount of silk, like what is shown by four fingers or approximately that, is generally permitted; but there is disagreement among scholars regarding the gold that can be shown, although the most substantiated view is that it is permitted as well, since it is in the *sunnah* that the Prophet (SAW) prohibited gold except in small pieces.

Ibn Taymiyya, *Majmu' Al-fatawa*, The book of jurisprudence [*fiqh*], Section eight: jihad

عن إبن عمر قال سمعت رسول الله ﷺ يقول إذا تبايعتم بالعينة وأخذتم أذناب البقر ورضيتم بالزرع وتركتم الجهاد سلّط الله عليكم ذُلاً لا ينزِعه حتى ترجعوا إلى دينكم

سنن ابي داود كتاب الإجارة

From Ibn 'Umar who said: I heard the Messenger of Allah (SAW) say: If you all engage in *'inah* transactions [selling and buying back for profit], or grab the tails of cattle, or take pleasure in agriculture, or neglect *jihad*, Allah will inflict disgrace on you, and will not remove it until you come back to your religion.

Sunan Abu Dawud, The book of wages

عن ابي أمامة عن النبي ﷺ قال من لم يغزُ أو يجهّز غازياً أو يخلُف غازياً في أهله بخير أصابه الله بقارعة

سنن ابي داود كتاب الجهاد

Abu Umama related from the Prophet (SAW), who said: Whoever does not go out to fight, nor equips a fighter, nor stays behind to gainfully look after a fighter's household – Allah will bring swift affliction on him.

Sunan Abu Dawud, The book of jihad

عن زيد بن خالد الجهني قال قال رسول الله ﷺ من جهّز غازياً فقد غزا ومن خلف غازياً في أهله فقد غزا

صحيح مسلم كتاب الامارة

From Zaid ibn Khalid Al-Juhani, who said: The Messenger of Allah (SAW) said: Whoever equips a fighter – he has fought; and whoever stays behind to look after a fighter's household – he has fought.

Sahih Muslim, The book of governance

عن سليمان بن بريدة عن أبيه قال قال رسول الله ﷺ حُرمة نساء المجاهدين على القاعدين كحُرمة أمهاتهم وما من رجل من القاعدين يخلُف رجلاً من المجاهدين في أهله فيخونه فيهم إلا وُقف له يوم القيامة فيأخذ من عمله ما شاء فما ظَنُّكم

صحيح مسلم كتاب الامارة

Sulaiman ibn Buraida related from his father, who said: The Messenger of Allah (SAW) said: The inviolability of the women of the *Mujahideen* for those who sit it out is like the inviolability of their own mothers; and any man among those who sit it out who substitutes for one of the *Mujahideen* in looking after his household, and then betrays him in it – he will be made to stand up on resurrection day, and he [the *Mujahid*] will take whatever of his deeds he wishes; so what do you all think?

Sahih Muslim, The book of governance

عباية بن رفاعة قال أدركني أبو عبس وأنا اذهب إلى الجمعة فقال سمعت النبي ﷺ يقول من اغبرّت قدماه في سبيل الله حرَّمه الله على النار

صحيح البخاري كتاب الجمعة

'Abaya ibn Rifa'a said: Abu 'Abs caught up with me when I was going to the Friday prayer, and he said: I heard the Prophet (SAW) say: Anyone whose feet get covered with dust in the cause of Allah – Allah will keep him from Hellfire.

Sahih Al-Bukhari, The book of the Friday assembly

أخبرني عمر بن الخطاب أنه سمع رسول الله ﷺ يقول لأُخرجن اليهود والنصارى من جزيرة العرب حتى لا أدع إلا مسلماً

صحيح مسلم كتاب الجهاد والسير

'Umar ibn Al-Khattab heard the Messenger of Allah (SAW) say: Surely I will drive the Jews and Christians out of the Arabian Peninsula until I do not leave any but Muslims.

Sahih Muslim, The book of jihad and campaigns

عن إبن شهاب أن رسول الله ﷺ قال لا يجتمع دينان في جزيرة العرب قال مالك قال إبن شهاب ففحص عن ذلك عمر بن الخطاب حتى أتاه الثَلج واليقين أن رسول الله ﷺ قال لا يجتمع دينان في جزيرة العرب فأجلى يهود خيبر قال مالك وقد أجلى عمر بن الخطاب يهود نجران وفدك

موطأ مالك كتاب المدينة

Ibn Shihab related that the Messenger of Allah (SAW) said: Two religions can not coexist in the Arabian peninsula. Ibn Shihab said: 'Umar ibn Al-Khattab scrutinized this until he was satisfied and certain that the Messenger of Allah (SAW) had said: Two religions can not coexist in the Arabian peninsula. And so he expelled the Jews of Khaybar. Malik added: And 'Umar ibn Al-Khattab also expelled the Jews of Najran and Fadak.

Muwatta Malik, The book of Medina

أن أبا أيوب الأنصاري حدثه أن رسول الله ﷺ قال من جاء يعبد الله لا يشرك به شيئاً ويقيم الصلاة ويؤتي الزكاة ويجتنب الكبائر كان له الجنة فسألوه عن الكبائر فقال الاشراك بالله وقتل النفس المسلمة والفرار يوم الزحف
السنن الكبرى للنسائي كتاب المحاربة

Abu Ayub Al-Ansari related that the Messenger of Allah (SAW) said: Whoever comes along worshipping Allah, not associating anything with Him, observing prayer, giving *zakat*, and avoiding the major sins, *Jannah* is his. And they asked him about the major sins; He said: Associating others in worship with Allah, killing a Muslim individual, and running away on the day the army advances.

Al-Nasa'i, Al-sunan Al-kubra, The book of warfare

أبو عمر بن مرة قال سمعت بلال بن يسار بن زيد مولى النبي ﷺ قال سمعت أبي يحدّثنيه عن جدي أنه سمع رسول الله ﷺ يقول من قال استغفر الله الذي لا إله إلا هو الحي القيّوم وأتوب إليه غُفر له وإن كان فرّ من الزحف
سنن أبي داود كتاب الوتر

Abu 'Umr ibn Murra said: I heard Bilal ibn Yasar ibn Zaid, the freed slave of the Prophet (SAW), say: I heard my father relating from my grandfather, that he heard the Messenger of Allah (SAW) say: Whoever says "I seek forgiveness from Allah, He who there is no god but Him, the Living, the Everlasting, and I repent unto Him" – he will be forgiven, even if he ran away from advancing with the army.

Sunan Abu Dawud, The book of witr prayer

عن عائشة رضي الله عنها قالت أغار قوم على لِقاح رسول الله ﷺ فأخذهم فقطّع أيديهم وأرجلهم وسمَل أعينهم
سنن النسائي كتاب تحريم الدم

From 'Aishah (may Allah be pleased with her), who said: A group of people raided the Messenger of Allah's (SAW) milking camels, so He caught them, cut off their hands and feet, and gouged out their eyes.

Sunan Al-Nasa'i, The book of the prohibition of bloodshed

عن عائشة أم المؤمنين عن رسول الله ﷺ أنه قال لا يحل قتل مسلم إلا في إحدى ثلاث خصال زان محصَن فيُرجم ورجل يقتل مسلماً متعمّداً ورجل يخرج من الاسلام فيحارب الله عز وجل ورسوله فيُقتل أو يصلَّب أو يُنفى من الأرض

سنن النسائي كتاب القسامة

'Aishah, the Mother of the Believers, related that the Messenger of Allah (SAW) said: It is not permissible to kill a Muslim except in one of three instances: A married adulterer – who is to be stoned; a man who intentionally kills a Muslim; and a man who leaves Islam, waging war against Allah Mighty and Sublime and His Messenger – he is to be killed, crucified, or banished from the land.

Sunan Al-Nasa'i, The book of taking qasamah oaths

كان جرير يحدث عن النبي ﷺ إذا أبق العبد لم تُقبل له صلاة وإن مات مات كافراً وأبق غلام لجرير فأخذه فضرب عنقه

سنن النسائي كتاب تحريم الدم

Jarir used to relate from the Prophet (SAW): "If a slave runs away, no prayer of his will be accepted, and if he dies, he dies a disbeliever [*kafir*]." Then a slave of Jarir's ran away, and he caught him and decapitated him.

Sunan Al-Nasa'i, The book of the prohibition of bloodshed

البراء بن عازب رضي الله عنهما يحدث قال جعل النبي ﷺ على الرَّجالة يوم أحد وكانوا خمسين رجلاً عبدالله بن جبير فقال إن رأيتونا تخطفنا الطير فلا تبرحوا مكانكم هذا حتى أرسل إليكم وإن رأيتونا هزمنا القوم وأوطأناهم فلا تبرحوا حتى أرسل إليكم فهزموهم قال فأنا والله رأيت النساء يشتددن قد بدت خلاخلهن وأسوقهن رافعات ثيابَهن فقال أصحاب عبدالله بن جبير الغنيمة اي قوم الغنيمة ظهر أصحابكم فما تنتظرون

صحيح البخاري كتاب الجهاد والسِيَر

Baraa ibn 'Azib (may Allah be pleased with them both) related, saying: The Prophet (SAW), on the day of Uhud, put Abdullah ibn Jubair in charge of the troops – there were fifty men. He said: If you see us get snatched away by birds, do not leave your post until I send for you; and if you see that we have defeated the people and made them stomp away, do not leave until I send for you. They defeated them; and I swear by Allah I saw the women lifting up their clothes and hurrying away, with their anklets and their legs showing. And Abdullah ibn Jubair's companions said: The booty! Anybody, the booty! Your companions have prevailed, so what are you waiting for?

Sahih Al-Bukhari, The book of jihad and campaigns

عن سلمة بن نفيل الكندي قال كنت جالساً عند رسول الله ﷺ فقال رجل يا رسول الله أذال الناس الخيل ووضعوا السلاح وقالوا لا جهاد قد وضعت الحرب أوزارها فأقبل رسول الله ﷺ بوجهه وقال كذبوا الآن الآن جاء القتال ولا يزال من أمتي أمة يقاتلون على الحق ويُزيغ الله لهم قلوب أقوام ويرزقهم منهم حتى تقوم الساعة وحتى يأتي وعد الله والخيل معقود في نواصيها الخير إلى يوم القيامة وهو يوحى إليّ أني مقبوض غير مُلبَّث وأنتم تتّبعوني أفناداً يضرب بعضكم رقاب بعضٍ وعُقر دار المؤمنين الشام

سنن النسائي كتاب الخيل

From Salama ibn Nufail Al-Kindi, who said: I was sitting with the Messenger of Allah (SAW), and a man said: Oh Messenger of Allah, people have left the steeds behind, they have laid down their weapons, and they say there is no more *jihad*, since the war has put down its burdens. And the Messenger of Allah (SAW) turned his face towards him and said: They lie; now, now the fighting has come, and there will not cease to be in my *ummah* an *ummah* who fights for the truth, of which Allah will cause the hearts of some to deviate, and grant them bounty from them, until the hour comes, until the promise of Allah is fulfilled. The finest things are tied to the forelocks of steeds until resurrection day. And it is revealed to me that I am about to be taken and have not been given much more time; and you all will follow after me in falsehood, striking each other's necks. And the place of shelter in the land of the Believers is Sham.

Sunan Al-Nasa'i, The book of steeds

عن ابي أمامة عن النبي ﷺ قال ليس شيء أحب إلى الله من قطرتين وأثرين قطرة من دموع في خشية الله وقطرة دم تُهَراق في سبيل الله وأما الأثران فأثر في سبيل الله وأثر في فريضة من فرائض الله

جامع الترمذي كتاب فضائل الجهاد

Abu Umama related from the Prophet (SAW), who said: There is nothing more pleasing to Allah than two kinds of drops and two kinds of legacies – a drop of tears shed in fear of Allah, and a drop of blood shed in the cause of Allah; as for the two kinds of legacies – a legacy from being in the cause of Allah, and a legacy from carrying out one of Allah's prescribed obligations.

Sunan Al-Tirmidhi, The virtues of jihad

عن أنس بن مالك رضي الله عنه قال قدم النبي ﷺ خيبر فلما فتح الله عليه الحصن ذُكر له جمال صفية بنت حُيي بن أخطب وقد قُتل زوجها وكانت عروساً فاصطفاها رسول الله ﷺ لنفسه فخرج بها حتى بلغنا سد الروحاء حلّت فبنى بها ثم صنع حيساً في نطع صغير ثم قال رسول الله ﷺ آذن من حولك فكانت تلك وليمة رسول الله ﷺ على صفية ثم خرجنا إلى المدينة قال فرأيت رسول الله ﷺ يحوّي لها وراءه بعباءة ثم يجلس عند بعيره فيضع ركبته فتضع صفية رجلها على ركبته حتى تركب

صحيح البخاري كتاب البيوع

From Anas ibn Malik (may Allah be pleased with him) who said: The Prophet (SAW) came to Khaybar, and when Allah broke the strongholds for him in victory, the beauty of Safiyah bint Huyay ibn Akhtab was mentioned to Him; her husband had been killed while she was still a new bride. And the Messenger of Allah (SAW) chose her for himself, and set out with her until we reached the bulwark of Al-ruhaa, where she became purified from her menstruation and He had sex with her, and then made *hais* [date meal with cheese/butter] on a small leather mat. Then the Messenger of Allah (SAW) said: Notify those around you. And this was the banquet that the Messenger of Allah (SAW) had for Safiyah. Then we set out for Medina; I saw the Messenger of Allah (SAW) drape a cloak over her behind him and then sit by his camel. And He situated his knee and Safiyah put her foot on his knee so she could ride.

Sahih Al-Bukhari, The book of transactions

عن شرحبيل بن السمط عن عمرو بن عبسة قال قلت يا عمرو بن عبسة حدّثنا حديثاً سمعته من رسول الله ﷺ ليس فيه نسيان ولا تنقّص قال سمعت رسول الله ﷺ يقول من رمى بسهم في سبيل الله فبلغ العدو أخطأ أو أصاب كان له كعدل رقبة ومن أعتق رقبةً مسلمةً كان فداء كل عضو منه عضواً منه من نار جهنم ومن شاب شيبة في سبيل الله كانت له نوراً يوم القيامة

سنن النسائي كتاب الجهاد

Shurahbil ibn Al-Simt related from 'Amr ibn 'Abasa; he said: Oh 'Amr ibn 'Abasa, tell us a *hadith* that you heard from the Messenger of Allah (SAW), of which no part has been forgotten or left out. He said: I heard the Messenger of Allah (SAW) say: Whoever shoots an arrow in the cause of Allah and it reaches the enemy, whether he misses or hits the mark, it will be like a freed slave to him; whoever frees a Muslim slave, it will be a ransom for every limb of his, limb by limb, out of the fire of Hell; and whoever gets a gray hair in the cause of Allah, is will be light for him on resurrection day.

Sunan Al-Nasa'i, The book of jihad

عن جابر إبن عبدالله أن رسول الله ﷺ كان يجمع بين الرجلين والثلاثة من قتلى أحد في ثوب واحد ثم يقول أيهم أكثر أخذاً للقرآن فإذا أُشيرَ له إلى احدهم قدَّمه في اللحْد وقال أنا شهيد على هؤلاء وأمر بدفنهم في دمائهم ولم يصلِّ عليهم ولم يغسَّلوا

سنن إبن ماجه كتاب الجنائز

Jabir ibn Abdullah related that the Messenger of Allah (SAW) would put two or three of the dead at Uhud into one garment, and then He would ask: Which of them had more of the Qur'an? And if one of them was pointed out to him, He would put him first into the niche of the grave, and would say: I bear witness to these men. Then He ordered them to be buried in their blood, and not to be prayed over or washed.

Sunan Ibn Majah, The book of funerals

عن أنس بن مالك قال كان رسول الله ﷺ إذا غزا قال اللهم أنت عَضُدي ونصيري بك أحُول وبك أصُول وبك أقاتل

سنن ابي داود كتاب الجهاد

From Anas ibn Malik, who said: Whenever the Messenger of Allah (SAW) went out on an attack, He said: Oh Allah! You are my aid and my supporter, by you I move around, by you I attack, and by you I fight.

Sunan Abu Dawud, The book of jihad

وكان يلبس الدِرع والخوذة ويتقلد السيف ويحمل الرمح والقوس العربية وكان يتترس بالترس وكان يحب الخيُلاء في الحرب وقال إن منها ما يحبه الله ومنها ما يُبغضه الله فأما الخيلاء التي يحبها الله فإختيال الرجل بنفسه عند اللقاء وإختياله عند الصدقة وأما التي يبغض الله عز وجل فإختياله في البغي والفخر

زاد المعاد لإبن قيم الجهاد والغزوات

He would wear armor, a headpiece, put on a sword, carry a spear and a bow, and He would shield himself with a shield. And He loved being conceited in war; He said: Indeed in it there are things that Allah loves and things that Allah abhors. The conceit that Allah loves is for a man to flaunt himself in confrontations and to show off in giving charity, but the conceit that Allah Mighty and Sublime abhors is for a man to show off in trespasses and in boasting.

Ibn Qayyim, Zad Al-Ma'ad, Jihad and Raids

وكان يأمر أمير سريّته أن يدعو عدوه قبل القتال إما إلى الاسلام والهجرة أو إلى الاسلام دون الهجرة ويكونون كأعراب المسلمين ليس لهم في الفيء نصيب أو بذل الجزية فإن هم أجابوا إليه قبل منهم وإلا إستعان بالله وقاتلهم

زاد المعاد لإبن قيم الجهاد والغزوات

He would command the leader of his troops to give a call to his enemy before fighting: either a call to Islam and emigration, or to Islam with no emigration, in which case they would be like the Muslim Bedouins – they would have no part of the loot and would not have to give *jizya*. If they answered him, he was to accept, otherwise, seek the aid of Allah and fight them.

Ibn Qayyim, Zad Al-Ma'ad, Jihad and Raids

نافع قال حدثني إبن عمر رضي الله عنهما أن رسول الله ﷺ عرضه يوم أحد وهو إبن أربع عشرة سنة فلم يُجزني ثم عرضني يوم الخندق وأنا إبن خمس عشرة فأجازني قال نافع فقدمتُ على عمر بن عبد العزيز وهو خليفة لحدثته هذا الحديث فقال إن هذا لَحدٌ بين الصغير والكبير وكتب إلى عماله أن يَفرضوا لمن بلغ خمس عشرة

صحيح البخاري كتاب الشهادات

Nafi' said: Ibn 'Umar (may Allah be pleased with them both) related to me that the Messenger of Allah (SAW) brought him out on the day of Uhud, when he was fourteen years old, "but He did not allow me to go; He brought me out on the day of Khandaq [the Trench], when I was fifteen, and then He allowed me." Nafi' said: I went to see 'Umar ibn 'Abd Al-'Aziz, who was caliph at the time, and I told him this hadith, and he said: Indeed this is the threshold between children and grown men. And he wrote to his officers that they should allocate to anyone who had reached fifteen years of age.

Sahih Al-Bukhari, The book of testimonies

لما كان الجهاد ذِروة سنام الاسلام وقبّته ومنازل أهله أعلى المنازل في الجنة كما لهم الرِفعة في الدنيا فهم الأعلون في الدنيا والآخرة كان رسول الله ﷺ في الذروة العليا منه وإستولى على أنواعه كلها لِجاهد في الله حق جهاده بالقلب والجنان والدعوة والبيان والسيف والسنان وكانت ساعاته موقوفة على الجهاد بقلبه ولسانه ويده ولهذا كان أرفع العالمين ذكراً وأعظمهم عند الله قدراً

زاد المعاد لإبن قيم الجهاد والغزوات في هديه ﷺ في الجهاد والمغازي والسرايا والبعوث

As *jihad* reached the pinnacle of Islam's highest point, and its ceiling, and the dwellings of those who engage in it are the highest dwellings in *Jannah*, as they have special honor in this world, being the uppermost in this world and the next, the Messenger of Allah (SAW) attained its highest pinnacle and mastered all its diverse forms. He waged *jihad* for Allah as is due His *jihad*, with heart and soul, by calling people and by argument, by sword and by spear. His hours were dedicated to *jihad* with his heart, his tongue, and his hands, and for this reason He was the most highly celebrated of the worlds and the most highly esteemed of them in the sight of Allah.

Ibn Qayyim, Zad Al-Ma'ad, Jihad and Raids, Section: regarding his (SAW) guidance in jihad and making incursions [maghazi], troops, and sending out detachments

وكان يستحب القتال أول النهار كما يستحب الخروج للسفر أوله فإن لم يقاتل أول النهار أخّر القتال حتى تزول الشمس وتهب الرياح وينزل النصر

زاد المعاد لإبن قيم الجهاد والغزوات

He preferred to fight first thing in the morning, just as He preferred to set out on a journey early. If He did not fight first thing in the morning, He would postpone fighting until the sun went down, and the winds blew, and victory came down.

Ibn Qayyim, Zad Al-Ma'ad, Jihad and Raids

عن أنس بن مالك رضي الله عنه عن النبي ﷺ قال لَغدوة في سبيل الله أو روحة من خير من الدنيا وما فيها

صحيح البخاري كتاب الجهاد والسير

Anas ibn Malik (may Allah be pleased with him) related from the Prophet (SAW), who said: An early morning in the cause of Allah, or an afternoon, is better than this world and all that is in it.

Sahih Al-Bukhari, The book of jihad and campaigns

عن إبن عباس أن النبي ﷺ كتب إلى هِرَقل من محمد رسول الله إلى هرقل عظيم الروم سلام على من إتبع الهدى قال إبن يحيى عن إبن عباس أن أبا سفيان أخبره قال فدخلنا على هرقل فأجلسنا بين يديه ثم دعا بكتاب رسول الله ﷺ فإذا فيه بسم الله الرحمن الرحيم من محمد رسول الله إلى هرقل عظيم الروم سلام على من إتبع الهدى أما بعد

سنن ابي داود كتاب الأدب باب كيف يكتب إلى الذمي

Ibn 'Abbas related that the Prophet (SAW) wrote to Hiraql [Heraclius]: From Muhammad the messenger of Allah to Hiraql chief of Rome; peace to those who follow guidance. Ibn Yahya said, relating from Ibn 'Abbas, that Abu Sufyan told him: So we went in to see Hiraql, and he sat us down before him, then called for the Messenger of Allah's (SAW) letter, in which was written: In the name of Allah compassionate and merciful, from Muhammad the messenger of Allah to Hiraql chief of Rome; peace to those who follow guidance; now then ...

Sunan Abu Dawud, The book of manners, Section: how to write to dhimmis

وكتب إلى كسرى بسم الله الرحمن الرحيم من محمد رسول الله إلى كسرى عظيم فارس سلام على من إتّبع الهدى وآمن بالله ورسوله وشهد أن لا إله إلا الله وحده لا شريك له وأن محمداً عبده ورسوله أدعوك بدعاية الله فإني أنا رسول الله إلى الناس كافة ليُنذر من كان حياً ويحقّ القول على الكافرين أسلم تسلم فإن أبيت فعليك إثم المجوس فلما قُرِئ عليه الكتاب مزّقه فبلغ ذلك رسول الله ﷺ فقال مزّق الله مُلكه

زاد المعاد لإبن قيم الجهاد والغزوات فصل ذكر هديه ﷺ في مكاتباته إلى الملوك وغيرهم

And He wrote to Kisra [Khosrow]: In the name of Allah the Merciful the Compassionate, from Muhammad the Messenger of Allah to Kisra the Great One of Persia: Peace to those who follow guidance and believe in Allah and His Messenger, and bear witness that there is no god but Allah alone, none associated with Him, and that Muhammad is His Servant. I announce to you the announcement of Allah, for indeed I am the Messenger of Allah unto all people, to warn those who are alive and so that what is said against the disbelievers may be fulfilled [c.f. *Ya-sin 70*]: Yield into Islam and be safe! If you refuse, the sin of the Magians is upon you. And when the letter was read to him, he tore it to pieces. When news of this reached the Messenger of Allah (SAW), He said: May Allah tear up his kingdom.

Ibn Qayyim, Zad Al-Ma'ad, Jihad and Raids, Section: mention of his (SAW) guidance in his correspondence with kings and others

وكتب إلى النجاشي بسم الله الرحمن الرحيم من محمد رسول الله إلى النجاشي ملك الحبشة أسلم أنت فإني أحمد إليك الله الذي لا إله إلا هو الملك القدوس السلام المؤمن المهيمن وأشهد أن عيسى إبن مريم روح الله وكلمته ألقاها إلى مريم البتول الطيبة الحصينة فحملت بعيسى فخلقه من روحه ونفخه كما خلق آدم بيده واني أدعوك إلى الله وحده لا شريك له والموالاة على طاعته وأن تتبّعني وتؤمن بالذي جاءني فاني رسول الله واني أدعوك وجنودك إلى الله عز وجل وقد نلغتُ ونصحت فاقبلوا نصيحتي والسلام على من إتبع الهدى

زاد المعاد لإبن قيم الجهاد والغزوات فصل ذكر هديه ﷺ في مكاتباته إلى الملوك وغيرهم

And He wrote to Najashi: In the name of Allah the Merciful the Compassionate, from Muhammad the Messenger of Allah to Najashi king of Abyssinia: Yield into Islam you! Indeed I praise Allah for you, He besides who there is no god, the Holy King, Giver of Peace, Granter of Security, the Protector, and I bear witness that 'Isa son of Maryam is the spirit of Allah and His word that He cast onto Maryam the pleasant and well-protected virgin, who carried 'Isa; He created him from His spirit and His breath, just as He created Adam by His hand. Indeed I call you to Allah alone, none associated with Him, to be constant in obedience to Him, and to follow me and to believe in what has come to me, for indeed I am the Messenger of Allah, and indeed I call you and your armies to Allah Mighty and Sublime; I have given you the news and have advised you, so take my advice. Peace to those who follow guidance.

Ibn Qayyim, Zad Al-Ma'ad, Jihad and Raids, Section: mention of his (SAW) guidance in his correspondence with kings and others

وكتب إلى المقوقس ملك مصر والاسكندرية بسم الله الرحمن الرحيم من محمد عبدالله ورسوله إلى المُقَوقِس عظيم القبط سلام على من إتبع الهدى أما بعد فإني أدعوك بدعاية الاسلام أسلم تَسلم وأسلم يؤتِك الله أجرك مرتين فإن توليّتَ فإن عليك إثم القبط ﴿ يا أهل الكِتاب تعالوا إلى كلمة سواء بيننا وبينكم أن لا نعبد إلا الله ولا نشرك به شيئاً ولا يتَّخذ بعضنا بعضاً أرباباً من دون الله فإن تولوا اشهدوا بأنا مسلمون ﴾
زاد المعاد لإبن قيم الجهاد والغزوات فصل ذكر هديه ﷺ في مكاتباته إلى الملوك وغيرهم

And He wrote to Maqawqis king of Egypt and Alexandria: In the name of Allah the Merciful the Compassionate, from Muhammad the Servant of Allah to Maqawqis the Great One of the Copts: Peace to those who follow guidance. Now then, indeed I proclaim to you the proclamation of Islam: Yield into Islam and be safe! Yield into Islam, that Allah may come to you with your reward twice over. But if you turn away, indeed the sin of the Copts is upon you; { Say: "Oh People of the Book! Come to a word of equal terms between you and us, that we worship Allah alone, nothing do we associate with Him, and we do not take some of us as lords besides Him". But if they turn away, [then say]: "Bear witness that we are Muslims" } [Al 'Imran 64].

Ibn Qayyim, Zad Al-Ma'ad, Jihad and Raids, Section: mention of his (SAW) guidance in his correspondence with kings and others

وكتب إلى ملك عمان كتاباً وبعثه مع عمرو بن العاص بسم الله الرحمان الرحيم من محمد بن عبدالله إلى جَيفر و عبد ابني الجُلندى سلام على من إتبع الهدى أما بعد فإني ادعوكما بدعاية الاسلام أسلما تَسلما فاني رسول الله إلى الناس كافة لأنذر من كان حياً ويحق القول على الكافرين فإنكما إن أقررتما بالاسلام ولّيتُكما وإن أبيتما أن تُقرّا بالاسلام فإن مُلككما زائل عنكما وخيلي تَحُلّ بساحتكما وتظهر نبوتي على ملككما وكتب أبي بن كعب وختم الكِتاب
زاد المعاد لإبن قيم الجهاد والغزوات فصل ذكر هديه ﷺ في مكاتباته إلى الملوك وغيرهم

And He wrote a letter to the king of Oman, and dispatched it with 'Amr ibn Al-As: In the name of Allah the Merciful the Compassionate, from Muhammad ibn Abdullah to Jaifar and 'Abd, sons of Al-Julanda: Peace to those who follow guidance. Now then, indeed I proclaim to both of you the proclamation of Islam: Yield into Islam and be safe! For indeed I am the Messenger of Allah unto all people, to warn those who are alive and so that what is said against the Disbelievers may be fulfilled. Indeed both of you, if you attest to Islam, I will commission you, but if you refuse to acknowledge Islam, then indeed your reign will pass from you, my horsemen will come upon your dominion, and my prophethood will be manifest over your kingdom. Ubay ibn Ka'b wrote and sealed the letter.

Ibn Qayyim, Zad Al-Ma'ad, Jihad and Raids, Section: mention of his (SAW) guidance in his correspondence with kings and others

وكتب النبي ﷺ إلى صاحب اليمامة هوذة بن علي وأرسل به مع سليط بن عمرو العامري بسم الله الرحمن الرحيم من محمد رسول الله إلى هوذة بن علي سلام على من اتبع الهدى واعلم أن ديني سيظهر إلى منتهى الخفّ والحافر فأسلم تسلم وأجعل لك ما تحت يديك

زاد المعاد لإبن قيم الجهاد والغزوات فصل ذكر هديه ﷺ في مكاتباته إلى الملوك وغيرهم

And the Prophet (SAW) wrote to the ruler of Al-Yamama, Hawdha ibn 'Ali, and sent it with Salit ibn 'Amr Al-'Amiri: In the name of Allah the Merciful the Compassionate, from Muhammad the Messenger of Allah to Hawdha ibn 'Ali: Peace to those who follow guidance; know that my religion will spread to the ends of dominion, so yield into Islam and be safe! And I will let you have what is in your power.

Ibn Qayyim, Zad Al-Ma'ad, Jihad and Raids, Section: mention of his (SAW) guidance in his correspondence with kings and others

وكان يشاور أصحابه في أمر الجهاد وأمر العدو وتخيّر المنازل وفي المستدرك عن ابي هريرة ما رأيت احداً أكثر مشورة أصحابه من رسول الله ﷺ

زاد المعاد لإبن قيم الجهاد والغزوات

He would seek advice from his Companions on the issue of *jihad*, the issue of the enemy, and chosing places to camp. In the *Mustadrak*, related from Abu Huraira: I never saw anyone who asked his companions for advice more than the Messenger of Allah (SAW).

Ibn Qayyim, Zad Al-Ma'ad, Jihad and Raids

قال إبن إسحاق فحدثني يحيى بن عروة بن الزبير عن أبيه عروة بن الزبير عن عبدالله بن عمرو بن العاص قال قلت له ما أكثر ما رأيتَ قريشاً أصابوا من رسول الله ﷺ فيما كانوا يُظهرون من عداوته قال خضرتهم وقد إجتمع أشرافهم يوماً في الحجر فذكروا رسول الله ﷺ فقالوا ما رأينا مثل ما صبرنا عليه من أمر هذا الرجل قط سفّه أحلامنا وشتم آباءنا وعاب ديننا وفرّق جماعتنا وسبّ آلهتنا لقد صبرنا منه على أمر عظيم أو كما قالوا فبينما هم في ذلك إذ طلع رسول الله ﷺ فأقبل يمشي حتى إستلم الرُكن ثم مر بهم طائفاً بالبيت فلما مر بهم غمزوه ببعض القول قال فعرفتُ ذلك في وجه رسول الله ﷺ قال ثم مضى فلما مر بهم الثانية غمزوه بمثلها فعرفت ذلك في وجه رسول الله ﷺ ثم مر بهم الثالثة فغمزوه بمثلها فوقف ثم قال أتسمعون يا معشر قريش أما والذي نفسي بيده لقد جئتُكم بالذبح قال فأخذت القوم كلمتُه حتى ما منهم رجلٌ إلا كأنما على رأسه طائر

واقع حتى إن أشدَّهم فيه وصاة قبل ذلك ليرفؤُه بأحسن ما يجد من القول حتى إنه ليقول إنصرف يا أبا القاسم فوالله ما كنت جهولاً قال فإنصرف رسول الله ﷺ

السيرة النبوية لإبن هشام ذِكر بعض ما لَقي رسول الله ﷺ من قومه

Ibn Ishaq said: Yahya ibn 'Urwa ibn Al-Zubair related to me from his father 'Urwa ibn Al-Zubair, who related from Abdullah ibn 'Amr Al-'As, who said: I asked him: What was the most that you saw come upon the Quraish from the Messenger of Allah (SAW) when they made known their enmity towards him? He replied: I was with them when their nobles had gathered together one day at the *hijr* [by the Ka'ba], and they mentioned the Messenger of Allah (SAW), saying: We have never ever seen anything like what we have endured in dealing with this man – He calls our insight foolish, he insults our fathers, degrades our religion, disperses our gatherings, and slanders our gods; we have put up with a great deal from him (or whatever they said). And while they were talking like this, suddenly the Messenger of Allah (SAW) showed up, turned, and walked over to touch the corner, then He passed by the group while walking around the House [Ka'ba]. And when He passed by them, they said some things to him. He [the narrator] said: And I could see this on the Messenger of Allah's (SAW) face. Then He proceeded on, and when He passed by them the second time, they said the same kind of things; and I saw it on the Messenger of Allah's (SAW) face. Then He passed by them a third time, and they said the same kind of things. And He stopped, and said: Will you hear, oh people of Quraysh? But indeed I swear by Him who holds my soul, I have come to slaughter you all! His words gripped the people to the point that there was not a man who did not stand still as though a bird had landed on his head. Even those who had been most severe in talking about him before this made amends to him with the best possible words, finally saying: Turn away now, oh Abu Qasim, by Allah you are not foolish. And the Messenger of Allah (SAW) departed.

Ibn Hisham, Al-sirah Al-nabawiya, Topic section: mention of some of what the Messenger of Allah (SAW) faced from his people

عن ابي موسى رضي الله عنه أن رسول الله ﷺ كان إذا خاف قوماً قال اللهم إني اجعلك في نحورهم وأعوذ بك من شرورهم

السنن الكبرى للبيهقي كتاب السير باب كراهية تمني لقاء العدو وما يفعل وما يقول عند اللقاء

Abu Musa (may Allah be pleased with him) related that the Messenger of Allah (SAW), whenever He feared a certain people, said: Oh Allah! Truly I put you at their throats, and I seek refuge in you from their evils.

Al-Bayhaqi, Al-sunan Al-kubra, The book of campaigns, Section: aversion towards wishing for confrontation with the enemy, and what He did and said in confrontation

عن عتبة بن عبد السلمي وكان من أصحاب النبي ﷺ قال قال رسول الله ﷺ القتل ثلاثة رجل مؤمن قاتل بنفسه وماله في سبيل الله حتى إذا لقي العدو وقاتلهم حتى يقتل فذلك الشهيد المفتخر في خيمة الله تحت عرشه لا يفضله النبيون إلا بدرجة النبوة ورجل مؤمن فرق على نفسه من الذنوب والخطايا جاهد بنفسه وماله في سبيل الله حتى إذا لقي العدو قاتل حتى يقتل محيت ذنوبه وخطاياه إن السيف محاء الخطايا وأدخل من أي أبواب الجنة شاء فإن لها ثمانية أبواب ولجهنم سبعة أبواب بعضها أفضل من بعض ورجل منافق جاهد بنفسه وماله في سبيل الله حتى إذا لقي العدو قاتل في سبيل الله حتى يقتل فإن ذلك في النار السيف لا يمحو النفاق

مسند أحمد حديث عتبة بن عبد السلمي أبي الوليد رضي الله تعالى عنه

From 'Utba ibn 'Abd Al-Sulami, one of the Prophet's (SAW) Companions, who said: The Messenger of Allah (SAW) said: There are three kinds of killings: a believing man who fights in the cause of Allah with himself and his wealth until he faces the enemy and fights them until he is killed; he is the proud martyr in the tent of Allah beneath His throne, exceeded by the prophets only by their status of prophethood. Then a believing man who fears sins and wrongdoings for himself, and wages *jihad* with himself and his wealth in the cause of Allah until he faces the enemy, and fights until he is killed, his sins and wrongdoings wiped away; indeed the sword wipes away sins. And He will be admitted by any of the gates of *Jannah* that he wishes; indeed it has eight gates – and Hell has seven gates – some of which are better than others. Then finally a hypocrite who wages *jihad* with himself and his wealth in the cause of Allah until he faces the enemy and fights in the cause of Allah until he is killed; indeed he is in Hellfire – the sword does not wipe away hypocrisy.

Musnad Ahmad, The narrations of 'Utba ibn 'Abd Al-Sulami Abi Al-Walid (may Allah Most High be pleased with him)

عن عتبة بن عبد السلمي رضي الله عنه وكانت له صحبة أن رسول الله ﷺ قال القتل ثلاثة رجل مؤمن خرج بنفسه وماله فلقي العدو فقاتل حتى يقتل فذلك الممتحن في خيمة الله تحت عرشه لا يفضله النبيون إلا بدرجة النبوة ورجل مؤمن فرق على نفسه من الذنوب والخطايا لقي العدو فقاتل حتى يقتل فتلك مصمصة تحت ذنوبه وخطاياه إن السيف محاء للخطايا وقيل له ادخل من أي أبواب الجنة الثمانية شئت فإنها ثمانية أبواب ولجهنم سبعة أبواب بعضها أفضل من بعض يعني أبواب الجنة ورجل منافق خرج بنفسه وماله فقاتل حتى يقتل فذاك في النار إن السيف لا يمحو النفاق

السنن الكبرى للبيهقي كتاب السير باب فضل الشهادة في سبيل الله عز وجل

'Utba ibn 'Abd Al-Sulami (may Allah be pleased with him) – he was of the Companions – related that the Messenger of Allah (SAW) said: There are three kinds of casualties: a believing man who sets out with his life and his wealth, faces the enemy, and fights him until he is killed; he is the examined one, in the tent of Allah beneath His throne, exceeded by the prophets only by their status of prophethood. Then a believing man who fears sins and wrongdoings for himself, faces the enemy, and fights until he is killed; and that is like a rinse flowing under his sins and wrongdoings; indeed the sword wipes away sins. And it will be said to him: Enter from whichever of the eight gates of *Jannah* that you wish. For indeed there are eight gates; Hell has seven gates; some of them are better than others (that is, the gates of *Jannah*). Then a hypocrite who sets out with his life and his wealth, and fights until he is killed; he is in Hellfire; indeed the sword does not wipe away hypocrisy.

Al-Bayhaqi, Al-sunan Al-kubra, The book of campaigns, Section: the distinction of martyrdom in the cause of Allah Mighty and Sublime

وروينا عن سعد بن أبي وقاص وأنس بن مالك عن النبي ﷺ أنه كان يتعوذ من الجبن
السنن الكبرى للبيهقي كتاب السير باب الشجاعة والجبن

We have related from Sa'd ibn Abi Waqqas and Anas ibn Malik, from the Prophet (SAW), that He would seek refuge against cowardice.

Al-Bayhaqi, Al-sunan Al-kubra, The book of campaigns, Section: bravery and cowardice

عن ثوبان رضي الله عنه مولى رسول الله ﷺ قال قال رسول الله ﷺ عصابتان من أمتي أحرزهما الله من النار عصابة تغزو الهند وعصابة تكون مع عيسى إبن مريم عليهما السلام
السنن الكبرى للبيهقي كتاب السير باب ما جاء في قتال الهند

From Thawban (may Allah be pleased with him), the freed slave of the Messenger of Allah (SAW), who said: The Messenger of Allah (SAW) said: Two groups of my *ummah* – Allah will preserve them both from Hellfire: One group who attacks India, and another group who is with 'Isa ibn Maryam (peace be upon them both).

Al-Bayhaqi, Al-sunan Al-kubra, The book of campaigns, Section: what is mentioned concerning fighting India

عن إبن عباس قال قال رسول الله ﷺ ما من أيام العمل الصالح فيها أحب إلى الله من هذه الأيام يعني أيام العَشر قالوا يا رسول الله ولا الجهاد في سبيل الله قال ولا الجهاد في سبيل الله إلا رجل خرج بنفسه وماله فلم يرجع من ذلك بشيء
سنن أبي داود كتاب الصوم

From Ibn 'Abbas, who said: The Messenger of Allah (SAW) said: There are no days in which good deeds are done that are more pleasing to Allah than these days – meaning the days of *'Ashr* [the first ten days of the month of *Dhul-Hijjah*]. The people said: Oh Messenger of Allah, not even *jihad* in the cause of Allah? He said: Not even *jihad* in the cause of Allah, except for someone who sets out with his life and his wealth, and does not return with any of it.

Sunan Abu Dawud, The book of fasting

كعب بن مالك قال قلّما كان رسول الله ﷺ يخرج في سفرٍ إلا يوم الخميس

سنن أبي داود كتاب الجهاد

Ka'b ibn Malik said: The Messenger of Allah (SAW) seldom went out on a journey except on Thursdays.

Sunan Abu Dawud, The book of jihad

عن سليم بن عامر قال سمعت أبا أمامة يقول سمعت رسول الله ﷺ يقول شهيد البحر مثل شهيدَي البرّ والمائد في البحر كالمتشحّط في دمه في البر وما بين الموجتين كقاطع الدنيا في طاعة الله وإن الله عز وجل وكل مَلك الموت بقبض الأرواح إلا شهيد البحر فإنه يتولى قبض أرواحهم ويغفر لشهيد البر الذنوب كلها إلا الدَين ولشهيد البحر الذنوب والدين

سنن إبن ماجه كتاب الجهاد

From Sulaim ibn 'Amir, who said: I heard Abu Umama say: I heard the Messenger of Allah (SAW) say: A martyr at sea is like two martyrs on dry land, and someone who gets sick at sea is like someone soaked in his own blood on dry land, and what is between two waves is like traversing this world in obedience to Allah. And indeed Allah Mighty and Sublime has appointed the Angel of Death to take hold of spirits, except a martyr at sea, for indeed He himself handles their spirits. And He forgives all the sins of a martyr on dry land except debt, but of a martyr at sea, sins and debt.

Sunan Ibn Majah, The book of jihad

أبا هريرة حدثه قال جاء رجل إلى رسول الله ﷺ فقال دُلّني على عمل يعدِل الجهاد قال لا أجده هل تستطيع إذا خرج المجاهد تدخل مسجداً فتقوم لا تفتُر وتصوم لا تفطر قال من يستطيع ذلك

سنن النسائي كتاب الجهاد

Abu Huraira said: A certain man came to the Messenger of Allah (SAW) and said: Tell me about a deed equal to *jihad*. He replied: I find none; can you – if a *Mujahid* sets out – go into a mosque, stand, and not rest, or fast and not break the fast? He said: Who can do that?

Sunan Al-Nasa'i, The book of jihad

وكان جميع ما غزا رسول الله ﷺ بنفسه سبعاً وعشرين غزوة ... قاتل منها في تسع غزوات

السيرة النبوية لإبن هشام ذكر جملة الغزوات

The Messenger of Allah himself (SAW) went on twenty-seven attacks in all. ... Of these He fought in nine attacks.

Ibn Hisham, Al-sirah Al-nabawiya, Topic section: mention of the total number of attacks

أبو هريرة قال سمعت رسول الله ﷺ يقول مثل المجاهد في سبيل الله والله أعلم بمن يجاهد في سبيله كمثل الصائم القائم وتوكّلَ الله للمجاهد في سبيله بأن يتوفاه أن يُدخله الجنة أو يَرجعه سالماً مع أجرٍ أو غنيمة

صحيح البخاري كتاب الجهاد والسير

Abu Huraira said: I heard the Messenger of Allah (SAW) say: A *Mujahid* in the cause of Allah – and Allah knows best who wages *jihad* in His cause – is like someone who fasts and observes prayer. And to the *Mujahid* in His cause to whom He brings death, Allah has guaranteed that He will admit him into *Jannah*; otherwise He will send him back safely with a reward or with booty.

Sahih Al-Bukhari, The book of jihad and campaigns

عن عبدالله بن نوفل قال قال لي رسول الله ﷺ الميت في سبيل الله شهيد

المصنف لعبد الرزاق كتاب الجهاد

From Abdullah ibn Nawfal, who said: The Messenger of Allah (SAW) said to me: Anyone who is dead for the cause of Allah is a martyr [*shaheed*].

‘*Abd Al-Razzaq, the Musannaf, The book of jihad*

عن سمرة قال قال النبي ﷺ رأيت الليلة رجلين أتياني فصعدا بي الشجرة فأدخلاني داراً هي أحسن وافضل لم أر قط أحسن منها قالا أما هذه الدار فدار الشهداء

صحيح البخاري كتاب الجهاد والسير

Samura related that the Prophet (SAW) said: Last night I had a vision that two men came to me and brought me up the tree and had me enter a house, most beautiful and superior; I have never seen more beautiful than this. The two of them said: But indeed this house is the house of the martyrs.

Sahih Al-Bukhari, The book of jihad and campaigns

أنس بن مالك رضي الله عنه عن النبي ﷺ قال ما من عبد يموت له عند الله خير يسرّه أن يرجع إلى الدنيا وأنّ له الدنيا وما فيها إلا الشهيد لما يرى من فضل الشهادة فإنه يسره أن يرجع إلى الدنيا فيُقتل مرة أخرى

صحيح البخاري كتاب الجهاد والسير

Anas ibn Malik (may Allah be pleased with him) related from the Prophet (SAW), who said: There is no servant who dies, to gain good fortune with Allah, who would desire to return to this world, even if he had this world and all that is in it, except the martyr, when he sees how excellent martyrdom is; indeed he would desire to return to this world and get killed once again.

Sahih Al-Bukhari, The book of jihad and campaigns

أبو هريرة رضي الله عنه قال سمعت النبي ﷺ يقول والذي نفسي بيده لولا أن رجالاً من المؤمنين لا تطيب
أنفسُهم أن يتخلفوا عني ولا أحد ما احملهم عليه ما تخلفتُ عن سريّة تغزو في سبيل الله والذي نفسي بيده
لَوَدِدتُ أني أُقتَل في سبيل الله ثم أحيا ثم اقتل ثم أحيا ثم اقتل ثم أحيا ثم اقتل

صحيح البخاري كتاب الجهاد والسير

Abu Huraira (may Allah be pleased with him) said: I heard the Prophet (SAW) say: I swear by Him who holds my soul, were it not for some of the men among the Believers who are displeased to stay behind me, and no means by which to carry them, I would not stay behind any brigade going on a raid in the cause of Allah. And I swear by Him who holds my soul, I would love to be killed in the cause of Allah, then come back to life, then be killed again, then come back to life again, then be killed again, then come back to life again, then be killed again!

Sahih Al-Bukhari, The book of jihad and campaigns

عن إبن عباس رضي الله عنه قال جاءت إمرأة إلى النبي ﷺ فقالت يا رسول الله أنا وافدة النساء إليك ما
من إمرأة تسمع مقالتي إلى يوم القيامة إلا سرها ذلك الله رب الرجال والنساء وآدم أبو الرجال والنساء
وحواء أم الرجال والنساء وأنت رسول الله إلى الرجال والنساء كتب الله الجهاد على الرجال فإن استشهدوا
كانوا أحياء عند ربهم يرزقون وإن ماتوا وقع أجرهم على الله وإن رجعوا أجرهم الله ونحن النساء نقوم على
المرضى ونداوي الجرحى فما لنا من الآخرة قال رسول الله ﷺ يا وافدة النساء أبلغي من لقيت من النساء أن
طاعة الزوج واعترافها بحقه يعدل ذلك كله

أحكام النساء لإبن الجوزي الباب الخامس والستون في ثواب طاعة الزوج

From Ibn 'Abbas (may Allah be pleased with him) who said: A woman came to the Prophet (SAW) and said: Oh Messenger of Allah, I am the delegate of the women to you; there is no woman up until the day of resurrection who will hear my account and not be pleased by it. Allah is the Lord of men and women, Adam is the father of men and women, Eve is the mother of men and women, and you are the Messenger of Allah to men and women. Allah has ordained *jihad* for men; if they are martyred, they are alive with their Lord, favored and blessed; if they die, Allah owes them their reward, and if they return, Allah rewards them also. Us women take care of the sick and nurse the wounded – so what do we have in the hereafter? The Messenger of Allah (SAW) said: Oh delegate of the women, tell any women you meet that obeying the husband and recognizing his rights is equal to all of that.

Ibn Al-Jawzi, Ahkam Al-nisaa, Chapter sixty-five: regarding the reward in obeying the husband

عن ابي هريرة قال قال رسول الله ﷺ تضمّن الله لمن خرج في سبيله لا يُخرجه إلا جهاداً في سبيلي وإيماناً بي وتصديقاً برسلي فهو عليّ ضامن أن أدخله الجنة أو أرجعه إلى مسكنه الذي خرج منه نائلاً ما نال من أجر أو غنيمة والذي نفس محمد بيده ما من كَلْمٍ يُكلَم في سبيل الله إلا جاء يوم القيامة كهَيئته حين كُلم لونه لون دم وريحه مسك والذي نفس محمد بيده لولا أن يشُقّ على المسلمين ما قعدتُ خلاف سريّة تغزو في سبيل الله أبداً ولكن لا أجد سعةً فأحملهم ولا يجدون سعة ويشق عليهم أن يتخلّفون عني والذي نفس محمد بيده لوددتُ أني أغزو في سبيل الله فأُقتَل ثم أغزو فاقتل ثم أغزو فاقتل

صحيح مسلم كتاب الامارة

From Abu Huraira, who said: The Messenger of Allah (SAW) said: Allah guarantees whoever sets out in His cause that He will only have him set out on *jihad* "in My cause, believing in Me, attesting to My messengers – I must guarantee to admit him into *Jannah* or return him to the home he set out from having received his due reward or part in the spoils". And I swear by Him who holds Muhammad's soul, anyone who is wounded in the cause of Allah will appear on resurrection day in the same condition he was when he was wounded, its color the color of blood but its scent that of musk. And I swear by Him who holds Muhammad's soul, if it were not hard on the Muslims, I would never sit out behind any brigade that went out to attack in the cause of Allah; but I do not find ample supply of transport for them, and neither do they have ample supply; and it is hard on them to stay behind me. And I swear by Him who holds Muhammad's soul, I would love to set out and attack in the cause of Allah, and be killed, then attack and be killed again, then attack and be killed again!

Sahih Muslim, The book of governance

عن أنس بن مالك رضي الله عنه قال خطب النبي ﷺ فقال أخذ الراية زيد فأُصيبَ ثم أخذها جعفر فأصيب ثم أخذها عبدالله بن رواحة فأصيب ثم أخذها خالد بن الوليد عن غير إمرةٍ ففُتح له وقال ما يسرنا أنهم عندنا قال أيوب أو قال ما يسرهم أنهم عندنا وعيناه تذرفان

صحيح البخاري كتاب الجهاد والسير

From Anas ibn Malik (may Allah be pleased with him), who said: The Prophet (SAW) gave an address and said: Zaid took the banner and was overcome, then Ja'far took it and was overcome, then Abdullah ibn Rawaha took it and was overcome, then Khalid ibn Al-Walid took it, without authority to do so, and he was given victory. And He said: It would not please us for them to be among us. (Ayub said: Or He said, his eyes weeping: It would not please them to be among us).

Sahih Al-Bukhari, The book of jihad and campaigns

عن ابي هريرة رضي الله عنه أن رسول الله ﷺ قال والذي نفسي بيده لا يُكْلَمُ أحد في سبيل الله والله أعلم بمن يكلم في سبيله إلا جاء يوم القيامة واللون لون الدم والريح ريح المسك

صحيح البخاري كتاب الجهاد والسير

Abu Huraira (may Allah be pleased with him) related that the Messenger of Allah (SAW) said: I swear by Him who holds my soul, no one is wounded in the cause of Allah – and Allah knows best who is wounded in His cause – but that he will come to resurrection day with its color the color of blood but its scent the scent of musk.

Sahih Al-Bukhari, The book of jihad and campaigns

البراء رضي الله عنه يقول أتى النبي ﷺ رجلٌ مقنّعٌ بالحديد فقال يا رسول الله أقاتل وأُسلم قال أسلم ثم قاتل فأسلَم ثم قاتل فقُتل فقال رسول الله ﷺ عمل قليلاً وأُجِرَ كثيراً

صحيح البخاري كتاب الجهاد والسير

Al-Baraa (may Allah be pleased with him) said: A man came to the Prophet (SAW) with an iron visor on, and said: Oh Messenger of Allah, should I fight or yield into Islam? He said: Yield into Islam, then fight. So the man yielded into Islam, and then fought, and was killed. And the Messenger of Allah (SAW) said: He labored little and was rewarded much.

Sahih Al-Bukhari, The book of jihad and campaigns

مقنع وهو كناية عن تغطية وجهه بآلة الحرب و أُجِرَ كثيراً أي أُجِرَ أجراً كثيراً وفي هذا الحديث أنّ الأجر الكثير قد يحصل بالعمل اليسير فضلاً من الله واحساناً

فتح الباري لإبن حجر العسقلاني كتاب الجهاد

"With an iron visor on" : this is an allusion to covering his face with a war implement. And "he was rewarded much" : that is, he was rewarded with a great reward; and this hadith shows that great reward comes with modest work done to the good favor of Allah and excellence in deed.

Ibn Hajar Al-Asqalani, Fath Al-Bari, The book of jihad

عن ابي بكر بن عبدالله بن قيس عن أبيه قال سمعت ابي وهو بحضرة العدو يقول قال رسول الله ﷺ إن أبواب الجنة تحت ظلال السيوف فقام رجل رثّ الهيئة فقال يا أبا موسى أنت سمعت رسول الله ﷺ يقول هذا قال نعم قال فرجع إلى أصحابه فقال أقرأ عليكم السلام ثم كسر جفن سيفه فألقاه ثم مشى بسيفه إلى العدو فضرب به حتى قُتل

صحيح مسلم كتاب الإمارة

Abu Bakr ibn Abdullah ibn Qais related from his father; he said: I heard my father, while he was up against the enemy, say: The Messenger of Allah (SAW) said: Indeed the gates of *Jannah* are under the shades of swords. And a man with a tattered look got up and said: Oh Abu Musa, you heard the Messenger of Allah (SAW) say that? He said: Yes! So the man went back to his companions and said: I bid you all *salaam*. Then he broke off the sheath of his sword and tossed it away, and marched with his sword towards the enemy, and struck at them with it until he was killed.

Sahih Muslim, The book of governance

عن ابي بكر بن ابي موسى الأشعري قال سمعت ابي تجاه العدو يقول سمعت رسول الله ﷺ إن السيوف مفاتيح الجنة فقال له رجل رث الهيئة أنت سمعت هذا من رسول الله ﷺ قال نعم فسل سيفه وكسر غمده والتفت إلى أصحابه وقال اقرأ عليكم السلام ثم تقدم إلى العدو فقاتل حتى قتل

المصنف لإبن ابي شيبة كتاب الجهاد ما ذكر في فضل الجهاد والحث عليه

From Abu Bakr ibn Abi Musa Al-Ash'ari, who said: I heard my father, while he was up against the enemy, say: I heard the Messenger of Allah (SAW): "Indeed swords are the keys to *Jannah*". And a certain man with a tattered look said to him: You heard this from the Messenger of Allah (SAW)? He said: Yes! So the man drew his sword, broke off its sheath, turned to face his companions, and said: I bid you all *salam*. Then he went off towards the enemy and fought until he was killed.

Ibn Abi Shayba, Al-musannaf, The book of jihad, Section: what is mentioned of the merit of jihad and urging it

اسامة بن زيد قال قال رسول الله ﷺ ذات يوم لأصحابه ألا مشمّر للجنة فإن الجنة لا خطر لها هي ورب الكعبة نور يتلألأ وريحانة تهتزّ وقصر مشيد ونهر مطرّد وفاكهة كثيرة نضيجة وزوجة حسناء جميلة وحلل كثيرة في مقام أبداً في حبرة ونضرة في دار عالية سليمة بهية قالوا نحن المشمرون لها يا رسول الله قال قولوا إن شاء الله ثم ذكر الجهاد وحضّ عليه

سنن إبن ماجه كتاب الزهد

Usama ibn Zayd said: One day the Messenger of Allah (SAW) said to His Companions: Is there anyone that sincerely strives for *Jannah*? Truly there is nothing more honorable and glorious than *Jannah*; I swear by the Lord of the Ka'ba it is a gleaming light, swaying basil, a mansion raised up, a never-ending river, abundant and fully ripened fruit, a fine and beautiful wife, abundant garments in an eternal abode, ease and riches in a radiant high and secure dwelling. They said: We strive for it, oh Messenger of Allah. He said: Say "If Allah wills" ["*In shaa Allah*"]. Then He mentioned *jihad* and urged it.

Sunan Ibn Majah, The book of abstinence

عن أبي هريرة قال قال رسول الله ﷺ ما يجد الشهيد مسَّ القتل إلا كما يجد أحدكم مس القَرصة

سنن ابن ماجه كتاب الجهاد

From Abu Huraira, who said: The Messenger of Allah (SAW) said: A martyr feels getting killed only as any of you might feel getting pinched.

Sunan Ibn Majah, The book of jihad

عن أنس بن مالك قال قال رسول الله ﷺ تُفتح عليكم الآفاق وستفتح عليكم مدينة يقال لها قزوين من رابط فيها أربعين يوماً أو أربعين ليلة كان له في الجنة عمود من ذهب عليه زبرجدة خضراء عليها قبة من ياقوتة حمراء لها سبعون ألف مصراع من ذهب على كل مصراع زوجةٌ من الحور العين

سنن ابن ماجه كتاب الجهاد

From Anas ibn Malik who said: The Messenger of Allah (SAW) said: The horizons have opened over you, and a city called Qazwin will be opened to you in victory; whoever remains in it for forty days or forty nights, he will have in *Jannah* a pillar of gold, upon which is a stone of green peridot, upon which is a dome of red rubies having seventy thousand golden shutters; at every shutter there is a wife from among the wide-eyed maidens.

Sunan Ibn Majah, The book of jihad

عن أبي هريرة رضي الله عنه أن رسول الله ﷺ قال يضحك الله إلى رجلين يقتل أحدهما الآخر يدخلان الجنة يقاتل هذا في سبيل الله فيُقتل ثم يتوب الله على القاتل فيُستشهد

صحيح البخاري كتاب الجهاد والسير

Abu Huraira (may Allah be pleased with him) related that the Messenger of Allah (SAW) said: Allah greets two men with a chuckle, one of which kills the other but both enter *Jannah*. The one fights in the cause of Allah and is killed, and then Allah turns in forgiveness toward the killer as he seeks to be martyred.

Sahih Al-Bukhari, The book of jihad and campaigns

عن أبي سعيد الخدري أن رسول الله ﷺ قال يا أبا سعيد من رضي بالله رباً وبالإسلام ديناً وبمحمد نبياً وجبتْ له الجنة فعجب لها أبو سعيد قال اعدها عليّ يا رسول الله ففعل ثم قال رسول الله ﷺ وأخرى يُرفع بها العبد مائة درجة في الجنة ما بين كل درجتين كما بين السماء والأرض قال وما هي يا رسول الله قال الجهاد في سبيل الله الجهاد في سبيل الله

سنن النسائي كتاب الجهاد

Abu Sa'id Al-Khudri related that the Messenger of Allah (SAW) said: Oh Abu Sa'id, whoever is pleased with Allah as Lord, with Islam as religion, and with Muhammad as Prophet, *Jannah* is certainly his. And Abu Sa'id was amazed at this and said: Say it to me again, oh Messenger of Allah. And so He did. Then the Messenger of Allah (SAW) said: And there is something else, by which a servant is raised up in *Jannah* one hundred levels, between every two levels like that which is between heaven and earth. He said: And what is it, oh Messenger of Allah?! He said: *Jihad* in the cause of Allah! *Jihad* in the cause of Allah!

Sunan Al-Nasa'i, The book of jihad

عن ابي هريرة رضي الله عنه قال قال رسول الله ﷺ من آمن بالله وبرسوله وأقام الصلاة وصام رمضان كان حقاً على الله أن يُدخله الجنة جاهد في سبيل الله أو جلس في أرضه التي وُلد فيها فقالوا يا رسول الله أفلا نبشّر الناس قال إنّ في الجنة مائة درجة أعدّها الله للمجاهدين في سبيل الله ما بين الدرجتين كما بين السماء والأرض فإذا سألتم الله فاسألوه الفردوس فإنه أوسط الجنة وأعلى الجنة

صحيح البخاري كتاب الجهاد والسير

From Abu Huraira (may Allah be pleased with him), who said: The Messenger of Allah (SAW) said: Whoever believes in Allah and in His Messenger, observes prayer and fasts Ramadan, Allah owes him to be admitted into *Jannah*, whether he wages *jihad* in the cause of Allah or stays in the land he was born in. The people said: Oh Messenger of Allah, shall we not declare the good news to people? He said: Indeed in *Jannah* there are one hundred levels which Allah has prepared for those who wage *jihad* in His cause; the distance between two levels is like what is between heaven and earth; so whenever you ask something of Allah, ask Him for *Firdaus*, for indeed this is the best and highest part of *Jannah*.

Sahih Al-Bukhari, The book of jihad and campaigns

عن إبن كعب بن مالك عن أبيه أن رسول الله ﷺ قال إن أرواح الشهداء في طير خُضر تعلُق من ثمرة الجنة أو شجر الجنة

جامع الترمذي كتاب فضائل الجهاد

From Ibn Ka'b ibn Malik, who related from his father, that the Messenger of Allah (SAW) said: Indeed the spirits of the martyrs are in green birds, hanging from the fruit of *Jannah* or the trees of *Jannah*.

Sunan Al-Tirmidhi, The book of virtues of jihad

عن معاذ بن جبل عن النبي ﷺ قال من قاتل في سبيل الله من رجل مسلم فُواق ناقة وجبت له الجنة ومن جُرح جرحاً في سبيل الله أو نُكب نكبة فإنها تجيئ يوم القيامة كأغزر ما كانت لونها الزعفران وريحها كالمسك

جامع الترمذي كتاب فضائل الجهاد

Mu'adh ibn Jabal related from the Prophet (SAW), who said: Any Muslim man who fights in the cause of Allah for the time that lapses between two milkings of a camel, *Jannah* is indispensably his. And whoever is wounded in the cause of Allah or is made to suffer affliction, indeed it will appear on the day of resurrection more profusely than it was, with the color of saffron and the aroma of musk.

Sunan Al-Tirmidhi, The book of virtues of jihad

عن المقدام بن معديكرب قال قال رسول الله ﷺ للشهداء عند الله ست خصال يُغفر له في أول دفعة ويرى مقعده من الجنة ويُجار من عذاب القبر ويأمَن من الفزع الأكبر ويوضع على رأسه تاج الوقار الياقوتة منها خير من الدنيا وما فيها ويُزوَّج اثنتين وسبعين زوجة من الحور العين ويُشفَّع في سبعين من أقاربه

جامع الترمذي كتاب فضائل الجهاد

From Miqdam ibn Ma'dikarib, who said: The Messenger of Allah (SAW) said: A martyr has six virtues with Allah: he is forgiven at the first flow [i.e. of blood]; he sees where he will take his seat in *Jannah*; he is saved from the punishment of the grave; he is safe from the greatest dread; the crown of dignity is placed on his head, the rubies of which are better than the world and all that is in it; he is given in marriage to seventy-two of the wide-eyed maidens [*hur 'ain*]; and he is allowed to intercede for seventy of his relatives.

Sunan Al-Tirmidhi, The book of virtues of jihad

عن يحيى بن ابي كثير قال قال رسول الله ﷺ أفضل الشهداء الذين يُلقَون في الصف فلا يلفتون وجوههم حتى يقتلوا أولئك يتلبَّطون في الغرف العلى من الجنة يضحك إليهم ربك إن ربك إذا ضحك إلى قوم فلا حساب عليهم

المصنف لإبن ابي شيبة كتاب الجهاد ما ذكر في فضل الجهاد والحث عليه

From Yahya ibn Abi Kathir, who said: The Messenger of Allah (SAW) said: The best martyrs are those who are thrown into the ranks, and do not turn their faces away until they are killed. These are the ones who are cast into the highest chambers of *Jannah*, and your Lord chuckles at them; indeed your Lord, whenever He chuckles at people, they are no longer held to account.

Ibn Abi Shayba, Al-musannaf, The book of jihad, Section: what is mentioned of the merit of jihad and urging it

عن ابي هريرة رضي الله عنه أن رسول الله ﷺ قال الشهداء خمسة المطعون والمبطون والغَرِق وصاحب الهَدم والشهيد في سبيل الله

صحيح البخاري كتاب الجهاد والسِّيَر

Abu Huraira (may Allah be pleased with him) related that the Messenger of Allah (SAW) said: Five are martyrs – someone stricken by plague, someone stricken by abdominal sickness, someone who drowns, someone crushed under a building, and the martyr in the cause of Allah.

Sahih Al-Bukhari, The book of jihad and campaigns

عن إبن عمر أن رسول الله ﷺ أمر بقتل الكلاب

صحيح مسلم كتاب المساقاة

Ibn 'Umar related that the Messenger of Allah (SAW) ordered dogs to be killed.

Sahih Muslim, The book of sharecropping

قال إبن عمر بعث رسول الله ﷺ في قتل الكلاب فكنت فيمن بعث فقتلنا الكلاب حتى وجدنا إمرأة قدمت من البادية فقتلنا كلباً لها

مسند أحمد مسند عبدالله بن عمر بن الخطاب

Ibn 'Umar said: The Messenger of Allah (SAW) sent out a contingent to kill dogs; I was one of those He sent out, and we killed the dogs, and even when we came across a woman coming from the desert, we killed a dog she had with her.

Musnad Ahmad, Narrations from Abdullah ibn 'Umar ibn Al-Khattab

عن أم شريك أن النبي ﷺ أمرها بقتل الأوزاغ

صحيح مسلم كتاب السلام

Umm Sharik related that the Prophet (SAW) ordered her to kill lizards.

Sahih Muslim, The book of greeting [salaam]

عن سائبة مولاة الفاكه بن المغيرة أنها دخلت على عائشة فرأت في بيتها رمحاً موضوعاً فقالت يا أم المؤمنين ما تصنعين بهذا قالت نقتل به هذه الأوذاغ فإن نبي الله ﷺ أخبرنا أن ابراهيم لما ألقي في النار لم تكن في الأرض دابة إلا أطفأت النار غير الوزغ فإنها كانت تنفخ عليه فأمر رسول الله ﷺ بقتله

سنن إبن ماجه كتاب الصيد

Sa'ibah, the freed slave of Fakih ibn Al-Mughira, related that she went in to see 'Aishah, and she saw a spear placed there in her house. She said: Oh Mother of the Believers, what do you do with that? She said: We kill lizards with it, for indeed the Prophet of Allah (SAW) told us that Ibrahim, when he was thrown into the fire, there was no animal on earth that did not go to extinguish it, except the lizard, who was blowing on it; and so the Messenger of Allah (SAW) ordered that they be killed.

Sunan Ibn Majah, The book of hunting

قال علي رضي الله عنه سمعتُ النبي ﷺ يقول يأتي في آخر الزمان قوم حُدثاء الأسنان سفهاء الأحلام يقولون من خير قول البريَّة يمرُقون من الاسلام كما يمرق السهم من الرمية لا يجاوز ايمانهم حناجرهم فأينما لقيتموهم فاقتلوهم فإن قتْلهم أجرٌ لمن قتلهم يوم القيامة

صحيح البخاري كتاب فضائل القران

'Ali (may Allah be pleased with him) said: I heard the Prophet (SAW) say: In the end times people of young age will come around, foolish dreamers, speaking the best words on earth, who will pierce through and out of Islam like an arrow pierces through and out of its target; their belief will not go past their throats. So wherever you come across them, kill them, for indeed killing them will be a reward, on resurrection day, for those who kill them.

Sahih Al-Bukhari, The book of virtues of the Qur'an

عن ابي هريرة أن رسول الله ﷺ قال لا تقوم الساعة حتى يقاتل المسلمون اليهود فيقتلهم المسلمون حتى يختبئ اليهودي من وراء الحجر والشجر فيقول الحجر أو الشجر يا مسلم يا عبد الله هذا يهودي خلفي فتعال فأقتله إلا الغرقد فإنه من شجر اليهود

صحيح مسلم كتاب الفتن وأشراط الساعة

Abu Huraira related that the Messenger of Allah (SAW) said: The hour will not come until the Muslims fight the Jews and the Muslims kill them, to the point that a Jew will hide behind a stone or a tree, and the stone or tree will say: Oh Muslim! Oh servant of Allah! It's a Jew behind me, so come and kill him! – except the *gharqad* tree, since this is a tree of the Jews.

Sahih Muslim, The book of trials and signs of the hour

The way of Allah

والجهاد بكسر الجيم أصله لغةً المشقّة يقال جهدتُ جهاداً بلغتُ المشقة وشرعاً بذْل الجهْد في قتال الكفار ويُطلَق أيضاً على مجاهدة النفس والشيطان والفُسّاق فأما مجاهدة النفس فعلى تعلُّم أمور الدين ثم على العمل بها ثم على تعليمها وأما مجاهدة الشيطان فعلى دفع ما يأتي به من الشُبُهات وما يزيِّنه من الشهوات وأما مجاهدة الكفار فتقع باليد والمال واللسان والقلب وأما مجاهدة الفساق فباليد ثم اللسان ثم القلب

فتح الباري لإبن حجر العسقلاني كتاب الجهاد

The linguistic basis of *jihad* is *mashaqqa* [hardship, striving, laborious effort]. One may say: I have labored [*jahadtu*] heavily – I have hit hardship. With respect to the decrees of Islam, this means expending effort in fighting the disbelievers [*kuffar*], but also refers to fighting one's self, Satan, and the immoral. For indeed fighting one's self is in learning the matters of religion, then doing them, then teaching them. Fighting Satan is in averting the suspicions he brings and how he adorns them with desires. Fighting the disbelievers takes place by one's hand, wealth, tongue, and heart. And fighting the immoral is by one's hand, then tongue, then heart.

Ibn Hajar Al-Asqalani, *Fath Al-Bari*, The book of jihad

جهاد الهوى إن لم يكن أعظم من جهاد الكفار فليس جهاد رجل دونه قال للحسن البصري رحمه الله تعالى يا أبا سعيد أي الجهاد أفضل قال جهادك هواك وسمعت شيخنا يقول جهاد النفس والهوى أصل جهاد الكفار والمنافقين فإنه لا يقدر على جهادهم حتى يجاهد نفسه وهواه أولاً حتى يخرج اليهم

روضة المحبين ونزهة المشتاقين لإبن قيم الجوزية الباب التاسع والعشرون في ذم الهوى وما في مخالفته من نيل المنى

Jihad against passion, if not greater than *jihad* against the Disbelievers, is certainly not less than it. A certain man said to Hasan Al-Basri (may Allah Most High have mercy on him): Oh Abu Sa'id, What *jihad* is the best? He said: Your *jihad* against your passion. And I heard our *sheikh* say: *Jihad* of the self and against passion is the foundation for *jihad* against the disbelievers and hypocrites, for indeed one is not capable in *jihad* against them until one first engages in *jihad* against himself and his passion, so that he may then set out to them.

Ibn Qayyim, *Rawda Al-muhibeen wa Nuzha Al-mushtaqeen*, The twenty-ninth section: regarding disapproval of passion and how it can be opposed in the attainment of destiny

فقام ثابت فقال الحمد لله الذي السموات والأرض خلقه قضى فيهن أمره ووسع كرسيَّه عليه ولم يكُ شيءٌ قط إلا من فضله ثم كان من قدرته أن جعلنا ملوكاً وإصطفى من خير خَلقه رسولاً أكرمه نسباً وأصدقه حديثاً وأفضله حسباً فأنزل عليه كتابه وائتمنه على خلقه فكان خيرة الله من العالمين ثم دعا الناس إلى الإيمان به فآمن برسول الله ﷺ المهاجرون من قومه وذوي رحمه اكرم الناس حَسَباً وأحسن الناس وجوهاً وخير الناس

فعالاً ثم كان أول الخلق إجابةً واستجاب لله حين دعاه رسول الله ﷺ نحن فنحن أنصار الله ووزراء رسوله نقاتل الناس حتى يؤمنوا بالله فمن آمن بالله ورسوله منع ماله ودمه ومن كفر جاهدناه في الله أبداً وكان قتلُه علينا يسيراً أقول قولي هذا واستغفر الله لي وللمؤمنين والمؤمنات والسلام عليكم

السيرة النبوية لإبن هشام، قدوم وفد بني تميم ونزول سورة الحجرات، خطبة ثابت بن قيس

And so Thabit got up and said: Praise be to Allah who created the heavens and the earth, decreed His command in them, and whose knowledge surrounds His throne; nothing exists at all except by His bounty. Then it was in His power to make us rulers, and He chose a messenger from among the best of His creation, honored him in lineage, made him truthful in speech, favored him in esteem, sent down His book to him, and entrusted him with it above all His creation; He was the blessing of Allah to the worlds. Then He called people to believe in him; and the emigrants [*muhajirun*] from among his people and his kinsfolk believed in the Messenger of Allah (SAW), the most esteemed of people, the best of people in conduct, and the best of people in deeds. Then the first of mankind to answer and respond to Allah, when the Messenger of Allah (SAW) called them, were us. We are Allah's helpers and the ministers of His Messenger. We fight people until they believe in Allah; whoever believes in Allah and His Messenger, He forbids their property and their blood, but whoever disbelieves, we wage *jihad* on them for Allah again and again. Killing them is trivial for us. These are my words I speak, and I seek forgiveness from Allah for myself, the Believers, and the believing women. And peace be upon you.

Ibn Hisham, Al-sirah Al-nabawiya, Topic section: the arrival of the delegation of the Banu Tamim and the sending down of Sura Al-Hujurat, Subsection: Thabit ibn Qais's address

والملة الاسلامية لما كان الجهاد فيها مشروعاً لعموم الدعوة وحمل الكافة على دين الاسلام طوعاً أو كرهاً اتّحدت فيها الخلافة والمُلك لتوجّه الشوكة من القائمين بها اليهما معاً وأما ما سوى الملة الاسلامية فلم تكن دعوتهم عامةً ولا الجهاد عندهم مشروعاً إلا في المدافعة فقط

مقدمة ابن خلدون ٣ الدول الفصل الثالث والثلاثون في شرح إسم البابا والبطرك في الملة النصرانية والكوهن عند اليهود

In the Islamic religion, when *jihad* was prescribed to make a broad call [*da'wah*] and bring all people into the religion of Islam voluntarily or forcibly, the caliphate and the right of dominion were consolidated so that the power of those in power might be focused together towards both. Religions other than the Islamic religion do not make a call to all men, and *jihad* is not legislated for them except for defense alone.

Ibn Khaldun, Al-muqaddimah, Section 3: States, Chapter 33: Explanation of the name Baba (Pope) and Batrak (Patriarch) in the Christian religion and Kohen among the Jews

إذا عُرف هذا فالجهاد أربع مراتب جهاد النفس وجهاد الشيطان وجهاد الكفار وجهاد المنافقين
فجهاد النفس أربع مراتب أيضاً احداها أن يجاهدها على تعلّم الهدى ودين الحق الذي لا فلاح لها ولا سعادة
في معاشها ومعادها إلا به ومتى فاتها علمهُ شقيت في الدارين الثانية أن يجاهدها على العمل به بعد علمه وإلا
فمجرد العلم بلا عمل إن لم ينفعها لم يضُرّها الثالثة أن يجاهدها على الدعوة إليه وتعليمه من لا يعلمه وإلا كان
من الذين يكتمون ما أنزل الله من الهدى والبينات ولا ينفعه علمه ولا ينجيه من عذاب الله الرابعة أن يجاهدها
على الصبر على مشاقّ الدعوة إلى الله وأذى الخلق ويتحمّل ذلك كله لله فإذا استكمل هذه المراتب الأربع صار
من الربّانيين فإن السلف مُجمعون على أن العالم لا يستحق أن يسمى ربانياً حتى يعرف الحق ويعمل به ويعلّمه
فمن علم وعمل وعلّم فذاك يدعى عظيماً في ملكوت السماوات
وأما جهاد الشيطان فمرتبتان احداها جهاده على دفع ما يلقي إلى العبد من الشبهات والشكوك القادحة في الايمان
الثانية جهاده على دفع ما يلقي إليه من الارادات الفاسدة والشهوات فالجهاد الأول يكون بعده اليقين والثاني
يكون بعده الصبر قال تعالى ﴿ وجعلنا منهم أئمة يهدون بأمرنا لما صبروا وكانوا بآياتنا يوقنون ﴾ فأخبر أن إمامة
الدين انما تُنال بالصبر واليقين فالصبر يدفع الشهوات والارادات الفاسدة واليقين يدفع الشكوك والشبهات
وأما جهاد الكفار والمنافقين فأربع مراتب بالقلب واللسان والمال والنفس وجهاد الكفار أخصّ باليد وجهاد
المنافقين أخص باللسان وأما جهاد أرباب الظلم والبدع والمنكرات فثلاث مراتب الأول باليد إذا قدر فإن
عجز إنتقل إلى اللسان فإن عجز جاهد بقلبه
فهذه ثلاثة عشر مرتبة من الجهاد و "من مات ولم يغزُ ولم يحدث نفسه بالغزو مات على شُعبة من النفاق "

زاد المعاد لإبن قيم الجهاد والغزوات

This being known then, there are four degrees of *jihad*: *jihad* against one's self, *jihad* against Satan, *jihad* against the disbelievers [*kuffar*], and *jihad* against the hypocrites.

Jihad against one's self is of four degrees as well; one of them is to wage *jihad* against the self in learning guidance and the religion of truth, that without which there is no success for one's self, nor happiness in its life or afterlife; when this knowledge leaves one's self, it is wretched in both worlds. The second degree is to wage *jihad* against the self in deed after having learned, otherwise it is mere knowledge without works; if this does not oblige one's self, it is of no use to it. The third is for one to wage *jihad* against the self in calling people to it and teaching it to those who do not know it, otherwise he is one of those who conceal the guidance and signs that Allah has sent down, and his knowledge is of no use to him, nor does it save him from Allah's punishment. The fourth is for one to wage *jihad* against the self in being steadfast in the hardships of calling people to Allah and the offense of people, and to bear all of this for Allah. If one accomplishes these four degrees, he will become one of those who are perfect in knowledge and deed [*rabani*]; indeed the forefathers agreed that a man of knowledge is not worthy of being called *rabani* until he knows the truth, acts on it, and teaches it; whoever knows, does, and teaches – he will be called great in the kingdom of heaven.

And *Jihad* against Satan has two degrees; one of them is to wage *jihad* on him by pushing back against the suspicions and doubts that he casts on servants, which detract from belief. The second is to wage *jihad* on him by pushing back against the depraved desires and the lusts that he casts on servants. Conviction follows the first *jihad*; steadfastness follows the second; the Most High said: { And We made leaders [*imams*] from among them to guide by our commandments, when they were steadfast and had conviction in our signs } [*Al-sajda* 24]. He has made known that leadership in religion is attained by steadfastness and conviction; steadfastness averts lusts and depraved desires, while conviction averts doubts and suspicions.

Jihad against the disbelievers and the hypocrites has four degrees: by one's heart, tongue, wealth, and life. *Jihad* against the disbelievers is specifically more by one's hand, while *jihad* against the hypocrites is specifically more by the tongue. *Jihad* against the leaders of oppression, innovation [*bid'*], and abominable deeds is of three degrees: the first is by the hand, if possible; if one is unable, he proceeds to it by the tongue, and if he is still unable, then he wages *jihad* in his heart.

These, therefore, are thirteen degrees of *jihad*, and "Whoever dies without having gone out on an attack or having talked to himself about attacking, has died on a limb of hypocrisy."

Ibn Qayyim, Zad Al-Ma'ad, Jihad and Raids

قال ابن إسحاق وحدثني يحيى بن عباد بن عبدالله بن الزبير عن أبيه عباد قال كانت صفية بنت عبد المطلب في فارع حصن حسان بن ثابت قالت وكان حسان بن ثابت معنا فيه مع النساء والصبيان قالت صفية رضي الله عنها فمرّ بنا رجل من يهود فجعل يطيف بالحصن وقد حاربت بنو قريظة وقطعت ما بينها وبين رسول الله ﷺ وليس بيننا وبينهم أحد يدفع عنا ورسول الله ﷺ والمسلمون في نحور عدوهم لا يستطيعون أن ينصرفوا عنهم إلينا إن أتانا آتٍ قالت فقلت يا حسان إن هذا اليهودي كما ترى يطيف بالحصن وإني والله ما آمَنُه أن يدلّ على عورتنا مَن وراءنا من يهود وقد شُغِل عنا رسول الله ﷺ وأصحابه فانزل إليه فاقتله قال يغفر الله لك يا إبنة عبد المطلب والله لقد عرفتِ ما أنا بصاحب هذا قالت فلما قال لي ذلك ولم أر عنده شيئاً احتجزتُ ثم أخذت عموداً ثم نزلت من الحصن إليه فضربته بالعمود حتى قتلته فلما فرغت منه رجعت إلى الحصن فقلت يا حسان إنزل إليه فاسلبُه فإنه لم يمنعني من سَلَبه إلا أنه رجل قال مالي بسلبه من حاجة يا إبنة عبد المطلب

السيرة النبوية لإبن هشام غزوة الخندق في سنة خمس شأن صفية بنت عبد المطلب واليهودي الذي يطيف بالحصن

Ibn Ishaq said: Yahya ibn 'Abbad ibn Abdullah ibn Al-Zubair related from his father 'Abbad, who said: Safiyah bint 'Abd Al-Muttalib was up in the fortification of Hassan ibn Thabit. She said: Hassan ibn Thabit was with us there, along with the women and children. Safiyah (may Allah be pleased with her) said: And a man from the Jews passed by us and began to walk around the fortification. The Banu Quraiza had gone off to war and cut off contact between themselves and the Messenger of Allah (SAW), so between us and them there was no one to protect us while the Messenger of Allah (SAW) and the Muslims were out slaughtering their enemy; they were unable to break away from them and come to us if someone were to come upon us. Safiyah said: So I said: Oh Hassan, there is this Jewish man, as you see, going around the fortification, and truly I swear by Allah I don't trust him not to disclose our nakedness [exposure] from the Jews that are behind us, but the Messenger of Allah (SAW) and his Companions have become occupied away from us; so go down to him and kill him. Hassan said: May Allah forgive you, oh daughter of 'Abd Al-Muttalib, you know that I am not the man for that. She said: When he said that to me, and I didn't see any way with him, I tightened my robe, grabbed a pole, and then went down from the fortification to him. And I struck him with the pole until I killed him, and when I was finished with him I went back to the fortification and said: Oh Hassan, go down to him and pilfer him, for indeed I wouldn't be prohibited from pilfering him except that he is a man. He said: I have no need to pilfer him, oh daughter of 'Abd Al-Muttalib.

Ibn Hisham, Al-sirah Al-nabawiya, Topic section: the raid of Al-khandaq [the Trench] in year five, Subsection: the account of Safiyah bint 'Abd Al-Muttalib and the Jew who was walking around the fortification

عن معمر قال أخبرنا ثمامة بن عبدالله بن أنس بن عبدالله إبن مالك أن حرام بن ملحان وهو خال أنس بن مالك لما طُعن يوم بئر معونة أخذ بيده من دمه فنضحه على وجهه ورأسه قال فُزت ورب الكعبة فُزت ورب الكعبة

المصنف لعبد الرزاق كتاب الجهاد

From Ma'mar who said: Thumama ibn Abdullah ibn Anas ibn Abdullah Ibn Malik told us that Haram ibn Milhan, the uncle of Anas ibn Malik, when he was stabbed on the day of Bi'r Ma'una, took some of his blood with his hand and sprinkled his face and his head and said: By the Lord of the Ka'ba I am victorious! By the Lord of the Ka'ba I am victorious!

'Abd Al-Razzaq, the Musannaf, The book of jihad

قال إبن اسحاق ثم استنزلوا فحبسهم رسول الله ﷺ في دار ابنة الحارث إمرأة من بني النجار ثم خرج رسول الله ﷺ إلى التي هي سوقها اليوم فخندق بها خنادق ثم بعث إليهم فضرب أعناقهم في تلك الخنادق يُخرَج بهم إليه أرسالاً وفيهم عدو الله حيي بن أخطب وكعب بن أسد رأس القوم وهم ستّمائة أو سبعمائة المكثّر لهم يقول كانوا من الثمانمائة إلى التسعمائة وقد قالوا لكعب بن أسد وهم يُذهَب بهم إلى رسول الله ﷺ أرسالاً

يا كعب ما ترى ما يصنع بنا فقال كعب في كل موطن لا تعقلون ألا ترون الداعي لا ينزع وأنه من ذُهب به منكم لا يرجع هو والله القتل فلم يزل ذلك الدأب حتى فرغ منهم رسول الله ﷺ

تاريخ الطبري سنة ٥ غزوة بني قريظة

Ibn Ishaq said: Then they [the Banu Quraiza] were called down and the Messenger of Allah (SAW) held them in the house of Al-Harith's daughter, a woman of the Banu Al-Najjar. Then the Messenger of Allah (SAW) went out to the market in Medina, the one which is still its market today, and dug trenches in it. Then He sent for them, and struck their necks [beheaded them] in these trenches, they being brought out to him in groups. Among them was the enemy of Allah Huyayy ibn Akhtab and Ka'b ibn Asad, the leader of the tribe. There were six or seven hundred of them; the one with the most ominous report of them said that there were eight to nine hundred. And while they were being taken in groups to the Messenger of Allah (SAW), they said to Ka'b ibn Asad: Oh Ka'b, what do you think He's going to do to us?! And Ka'b said: You all don't ever get it! Don't you see that the one who is summoning us does not dismiss anyone, and that everyone of you who is taken away does not come back? By God this means killing! And the affair went on until the Messenger of Allah (SAW) had finished with them.

Tarikh Al-Tabari [Al-Tabari's History], Year five, Section: The attack on the Banu Quraiza

ثم قال لهم [أهل الحيرة] خالد إني أدعوكم إلى الله وإلى عبادته وإلى الاسلام فإن قبلتم فلكم ما لنا وعليكم ما علينا وإن أبيتم فالجزية وإن أبيتم فقد جئناكم بقوم يحبون الموت كما تحبون أنتم شرب الخمر ... عن الشعبي قال كتب خالد إلى هرمز قبل خروجه مع آزاذبة أبي الزياذبة الذين باليمامة وهرمز صاحب الثغر يومئذ أما بعد فأسلم تسلم أو اعتقد لنفسك وقومك الذمة وأقرر بالجزية وإلا فلا يلومنّ إلا نفسك فقد جئتك بقوم يحبون الموت كما تحبون الحياة

تاريخ الطبري ثم كانت سنة اثنتي عشرة من الهجرة

Then Khalid told them [the people of Al-Hira]: Indeed I call you to Allah and to worship Him, and to Islam; if you accept, what is ours is yours and our obligations are your obligations; but if you refuse, then pay *jizya*; and if you still refuse, then we will bring people to you who love death as much as you all love to drink wine. ... From Al-Sha'bi who said: Khalid wrote to Hurmuz before he set out with Azadhiba – the father of the Ziyadhiba who were in Al-Yamamah; at the time Hurmuz held a vacancy. He wrote: Now then, yield into Islam and be safe, or concede to being under safeguard [*dhimma*] for yourself and your people, and accede to the *jizya*; otherwise, there is no one to blame but yourself; I will bring to you a people who love death as much as you love life.

Tarikh Al-Tabari, Section: year twelve after the hijra

ويقاتِل اليهود والنصارى والمجوس إلا أن يسلموا أو يبذُلوا الجزية ويقاتل من سواهم إلا أن يسلموا

عمدة السالك وعدة الناسك لإبن النقيب المصري كتاب الجنايات

And he [the leader, i.e. caliph] fights the Jews, Christians, and Magians unless they become Muslims [*yuslimu*; yield] or give *jizya*; but anyone other than these he fights just unless they become Muslims.

Ibn Al-Naqib Al-Misri, 'Umda Al-salik wa 'Udda Al-nasik [ ], The book of serious crimes

عن عبدالله بن مسعود قال إن الله نظر في قلوب العِباد فوجد قلب محمد ﷺ خير قلوب العباد فاصطفاه لنفسه فابتعثه برسالته ثم نظر في قلوب العباد بعد قلب محمد فوجد قلوب أصحابه خير قلوب العباد فجعلهم وزراء نبيه يقاتلون على دينه

مسند أحمد مسند عبدالله بن مسعود رضي الله تعالى عنه.

Frm Abdullah ibn Mas'ud, who said: Indeed Allah looked upon the hearts of men, and He found the heart of Muhammad (SAW) to be the best of the hearts of men, so He chose him for Himself, and sent him out with His message; then He looked upon the hearts of men after the heart of Muhammad, and found the hearts of his Companions to be the best of the hearts of men, and so He made them ministers of His Prophet, to fight for His religion [*deen*].

Musnad Ahmad, The narrations of Abdullah ibn Mas'ud (may Allah Most High be pleased with him)

قال إبن مسعود رضي الله عنه السعيد من وعظ بغيره فقال أبو الدرداء رضي الله عنه إذا ذكر الموتى فعد نفسك كأحدهم

مختصر منهاج القاصدين لإبن قدامة باب ما جاء في فضل ذكر الموت

Ibn Mas'ud (may Allah be pleased with him) said: Happy is he who admonishes otherwise. And Abu Al-Dardaa (may Allah be pleased with him) said: Whenever the dead are mentioned, count yourself as one of them.

Ibn Qudama, Mukhtasar, Section: Regarding the merit in remembrance of death

وقال إبن دقيق العيد القياس يقتضي أن يكون الجهاد أفضل الأعمال التي هي وسائل لأن الجهاد وسيلة إلى إعلان الدين ونشره وإخماد الكفر ودحضه ففضيلته بحسب فضيلة ذلك والله أعلم

فتح الباري لإبن حجر العسقلاني كتاب الجهاد

Ibn Daqiq Al-'Eid said: Reasonable analogy [*qiyas*] calls for *jihad* to be the best of deeds that are means toward something, for *jihad* is a means toward proclaiming and spreading news of the religion [*deen*] and quashing and refuting disbelief, and its virtue is commensurate with the virtue of these things. But Allah knows best.

Ibn Hajar Al-Asqalani, Fath Al-Bari, The book of jihad

عن أنس رضي الله عنه أن عمّه غاب عن بدر فقال غبتُ عن أول قتال النبي ﷺ لئن أشهدني الله مع النبي ﷺ ليرينّ الله ما أُجِدّ فلقي يوم أُحُد فهُزم الناس فقال اللهم إني اعتذر إليك مما صنع هؤلاء يعني المسلمين وأبرأ إليك مما جاء به المشركون فتقدّم بسيفه فلقي سعد بن معاذ فقال أين يا سعد إني أجد ريح الجنة دون أحد فمضى فقُتل فما عُرف حتى عرفته أخته بشامة أو ببنانه وبه بضع وثمانون من طعنة وضربة ورمية بسهم

صحيح البخاري كتاب المغازي

Anas (may Allah be pleased with him) related that his uncle was absent from the battle of Badr; he said: I was absent from the first fighting the Prophet (SAW) did; if Allah would have me be present with the Prophet (SAW), truly Allah would see how I would strive. So he showed up for the day of Uhud. The people were defeated, and he said: Oh Allah! I apologize to you for what these people have done – meaning the Muslims – and I am absolved to you for what the Idolaters have brought. And he went forward with his sword, and encountered Sa'd ibn Mu'adh, and said: Where are you going, oh Sa'd? Indeed I can smell the aroma of *Jannah* in front of Uhud! Then he proceeded ahead and was killed. And no one recognized him until his sister recognized him by a birthmark or by his fingertips. There were eighty-something stabs, strikes, and arrow pierces on him.

Sahih Al-Bukhari, The book of military raids

قال إبن بطال وغيره يحتمل أن يكون على الحقيقة وأنه وجد ريح الجنة حقيقة أو وجد ريحاً طيبة ذكّره طيبها بطيب ريح الجنة ويجوز أن يكون أراد أنه إستحضر الجنة التي أُعدّت للشهيد فتصوّر أنها في ذلك الموضع الذي يقاتل فيه فيكون المعنى إني لأعلم أنّ الجنة تُكتسب في هذا الموضع فأشتاق لها

فتح الباري لإبن حجر العسقلاني كتاب الجهاد

Ibn Battal and others said: This implies that it is correct and that he indeed perceived the aroma of *Jannah* or perceived a pleasant aroma, the scent of which reminded him of the scent of *Jannah*. It is probable that he wanted to call to mind the *Jannah* that has been prepared for martyrs, and he pictured it in the place where he was fighting. And so the meaning is: "Indeed I know that *Jannah* is attained in this place, and I long for it."

Ibn Hajar Al-Asqalani, Fath Al-Bari, The book of jihad

وفي قصة أنس بن النضر من الفوائد جواز بذل النفس في الجهاد وفضل الوفاء بالعهد ولو شقّ على النفس حتى يصل إلى إهلاكها وأنّ طلب الشهادة في الجهاد لا يتناوله النهي عن الإلقاء إلى التهلكة وفيه فضيلة ظاهرة لأنس بن النضر وما كان عليه من صحة الإيمان وكثرة التوقّي والتورُّع وقوة اليقين

فتح الباري لإبن حجر العسقلاني كتاب الجهاد

In the story of Anas ibn Al-Nadr [the uncle of Anas] there are several things worth pointing out: the permissibility of someone sacrificing himself in *jihad*, the virtue of loyalty to commitment, even if it overwhelms one's self to the point of bringing it to destruction, and that the prohibition against throwing oneself into ruin does not apply to seeking martyrdom in *jihad*. And here there is clear excellence in Anas ibn Al-Nadr, and the genuine belief, great yearning, self-restraint, and strength of assurance that drove him on.

Ibn Hajar Al-Asqalani, Fath Al-Bari, The book of jihad

قال إبن إسحاق وحدثني الحصين بن عبدالرحمن بن عمرو بن سعد بن معاذ عن ابي سفيان مولى إبن ابي أحمد عن ابي هريرة رضي الله عنه قال كان يقول حدثوني عن رجل دخل الجنة لم يصلّ قط فإذا لم يعرفه الناس سألوه من هو فيقول أصيرم بني عبد الأشهل عمرو بن ثابت بن وقش قال الحصين فقلت لمحمود بن أسد كيف كان شأن أصيرم قال كان يأبى الاسلام على قومه فلما كان يوم خرج رسول الله ﷺ إلى أحد بدا له في الاسلام فأسلم ثم أخذ سيفه فعدا حتى دخل في عُرض الناس فقاتل حتى أثبتته الجراحة قال فبينا رجال من بني عبد الأشهل يلتمسون قتلاهم في المعركة إذا هم به فقالوا والله إن هذا للأصيرم ما جاء به لقد تركناه وإنه لمُنكر لهذا الحديث فسألوه ما جاء به فقالوا ما جاء بك يا عمرو أحدبٌ على قومك أم رغبة في الاسلام قال بل رغبة في الاسلام آمنتُ بالله وبرسوله وأسلمت ثم أخذت سيفي فغدوتُ مع رسول الله ﷺ ثم قاتلتُ حتى أصابني ما أصابني ثم لم يلبَث أن مات في أيديهم فذكروه لرسول الله ﷺ فقال إنه لمَن أهل الجنة

السيرة النبوية لإبن هشام غزوة أحد شأن أصيرم أحد بني عبد الأشهل

Ibn Ishaq said: Al-Husain ibn 'Abd Al-Rahman ibn 'Amr ibn Sa'd ibn Mu'adh related to me from Abu Sufyan, the freed slave of Ibn Abi Ahmad, who related that Abu Huraira (may Allah be pleased with him) used to say: Tell me about a man who entered *Jannah* without ever having prayed. And when people did not know who he was, they asked him: Who was he? And Abu Huraira would say: Usayrim Bani 'Abd Al-Ashhal 'Amr ibn Thabit ibn Waqsh. Husain said: So I asked Mahmud ibn Asad: What was the story of Usayrim? He said: He had refused Islam from his people, but on the day when the Messenger of Allah (SAW) set out to Uhud, Islam became clear to him, and he yielded into Islam. Then he took his sword and rushed out until he reached the thick of people, and he fought until the wounds put him out of action. And while the men of Banu 'Abd Al-Ashhal were searching around for their dead on the battlefield, behold they came upon him, and said: By Allah this is Usayrim! What brought him out? – we had left him while he had indeed refused what was being said [i.e. Islam]. And they asked him what had brought him out, saying: What brings you, oh 'Amr – fondness for your people or a desire for Islam? He said: Well, a desire for Islam – I have believed in Allah and in His Messenger, and have yielded into Islam, then I took my sword and went out with the Messenger of Allah (SAW), then I fought until what happened to me happened to me. Then not long afterwards he died among them. And they mentioned him to the Messenger of Allah (SAW), and He said: Indeed he is surely among the people of *Jannah*.

Ibn Hisham, Al-sirah Al-nabawiya, Topic section: the raid on Uhud, Subsection: the subject of Usayrim, one of the Banu 'Abd Al-Ashhal

قال جمهور العلماء يحرُم الجهاد إذا منع الأبوان أو احدهما بشرط أن يكونا مسلمَين لأن برّهما فرض عينٍ عليه والجهاد فرض كفاية فإذا تعيّن الجهاد فلا إذن ويشهد له ما أخرجه إبن حبان من طريق أخرى عن عبدالله بن عمرو جاء رجل إلى رسول الله ﷺ فسأله عن أفضل الأعمال قال الصلاة قال ثم مهْ قال الجهاد قال فإن لي والدين فقال آمرك بوالديك خيراً فقال والذي بعثك بالحق نبياً لأجاهدنّ ولأتركنّهما قال فأنت أعلم وهو محمول على جهاد فرض العين توفيقاً بين الحديثين

فتح الباري لإبن حجر العسقلاني كَاب الجهاد

The body of scholars have said that *jihad* is forbidden if the parents, or one of them, prohibit it, provided they are both Muslims, since devotion to them is one's individual obligation [*fard 'ain*], while *jihad* is a collective obligation [*fard kifaya*]. But whenever *jihad* is determined as one's duty, permission need not be considered. The separate narration recorded by Ibn Hibban as related by Abdullah ibn 'Amr testifies to this: A certain man came to the Messenger of Allah (SAW) and asked him about the best of deeds. He said: Prayer. The man said: And then what? He said: *Jihad*. The man said: But indeed I have parents. He said: I command you to be good to your parents. And the man said: I swear by Him who sent you forth with the truth as a prophet, surely I will wage *jihad*, and surely I will leave them. He said: You know best. And so this implies a *jihad* of personal duty, reconciling both hadiths.

Ibn Hajar Al-Asqalani, Fath Al-Bari, The book of jihad

عن عمرو قال سمعت جابراً يقول قال رجل يوم أحد أرأيت إن قُتلتُ في سبيل الله فأين أنا قال في الجنة فألقى تمرات في يده ثم قاتل حتى قُتل

سنن النسائي كَاب لجهاد

From 'Amr who said: I heard Jabir say: On the day of Uhud a certain man said: If I am killed in the cause of Allah, where do you reckon that I will be? He said: In *Jannah*. So the man tossed away some dates that were in his hand, then fought until he was killed.

Sunan Al-Nasa'i, The book of jihad

عن البراء بن عازب رضي الله عنهما قال بعث رسول الله ﷺ رهطاً من الأنصار إلى ابي رافع فدخل عليه عبدالله بن عتيك بيته ليلاً فقتله وهو نائم

صحيح البخاري كتاب الجهاد والسير

From Al-Baraa ibn 'Azib (may Allah be pleased with them both), who said: The Messenger of Allah (SAW) sent out a group of people from the *Ansar* to Abu Rafi', and Abdullah ibn 'Atik went in to him in his house at night and killed him while he was sleeping.

Sahih Al-Bukhari, The book of jihad and campaigns

وفيه جواز التجسيس على المشركين وطلب غِرَّتهم وجواز إغتيال ذَوي الأذيَّة البالغة منهم وكان أبو رافع ينادي رسول الله ﷺ ويؤلِّب عليه الناس ويؤخذ منه جواز قتل المشرك بغير دعوة إن كان قد بلغته الدعوة قبل ذلك وأما قتله إذا كان نائماً فمحلَّه أن يُعلم أنه مستمرّ على كفره وأنه قد يُئِسَ من فلاحه وطريق العلم بذلك إما بالوحي وإما بالقرائن الدالَّة على ذلك

فتح الباري لابن حجر العسقلاني كتاب الجهاد

In this is the permissibility of spying on idolaters [*mushrikeen*] and finding out when they are not watching, and the permissibility of assassinating (by surprise) those of them who are causing excessive harm; Abu Rafi' used to shout at the Messenger of Allah (SAW) and rally people against him. From this it can be taken that it is permissible to kill an Idolater without calling him to Islam [*da'wah*] if he had been given *da'wah* before this, and moreover, to kill him if he is asleep and his state is such that it is known that he persists in his disbelief, and that there is no hope for his deliverance; the way to know this is either by divine inspiration or by evidence that indicates it.

Ibn Hajar Al-Asqalani, Fath Al-Bari, The book of jihad

وما عدا جهاد المشركين من قتال ينقسم إلى ثلاثة أقسام قتال أهل الردة وقتال البغي وقتال المحاربين فأما القسم الأول من قتال أهل الردة فهو أن يرتد قوم حكم بإسلامهم سواء على فطرة الاسلام أو أسلموا عن كفر فكلا الفريقين في حكم الردة سواء فإن ارتدوا عن الاسلام إلى أي دين انتقلوا إليه مما يجوز أن يُقَرَّ أهله عليه كاليهودية والنصرانية أو لا يجوز أن يقر أهله عليه كالزندقة والوثنية لم يزج من ارتد إليه لأن الإقرار بالحق يوجب إلتزام احكامه قال رسول الله ﷺ من بدّل دينه فأقتلوه فإذا كانوا ممن وجب قتلهم بما ارتدوا عنه من دين الحق إلى غيره من الأديان لم يخل حالهم من أحد أمرين إما أن يكونوا في دار الاسلام شذاذاً وأفراداً لم يتميزوا بدار يتميزون بها عن المسلمين فلا حاجة بنا إلى قتالهم لدخولهم تحت القدرة ويكشف عن سبب ردتهم

... ومن أقام على ردته ولم يتب وجب قتله رجلاً كان أو إمرأة وقال أبو حنيفة لا أقتل المرأة بالردة وقد قتل رسول الله ﷺ بالردة إمرأة كانت تُكنى أم رومان ... وإختلف الفقهاء في قتلهم هل يُعجل في الحال أو يؤجلون فيه ثلاثة أيام على قولين احدهما تعجيل قتلهم في الحال لئلا يؤخر لله عز وجل حق والثاني ينظرون ثلاثة أيام لعلهم يستدركونه بالتوبة وقد أنذر عليّ عليه السلام المستورد العجلي بالتوبة ثلاثة ثم قتله بعدها ويُقتل صبراً بالسيف وقال إبن سريج من أصحاب الشافعي يُضرب بالخشب حتى يموت لأنه أبطأ قتلاً من السيف الموحي وربما إستدرك به التوبة ... والحالة الثانية أن يحتازوا إلى دار ينفردون بها عن المسلمين حتى يصيروا فيها ممتنعين فيجب قتالهم على الردة بعد مناظرتهم على الاسلام وإيضاح دلائله ويجري على قتالهم بعد الإنذار والاعذار حكمُ قتال أهل الحرب في قتالهم غِرّة وبياتاً ومصافتهم في الحرب جهاراً وقتالهم مقبلين ومدبرين

الأحكام السلطانية والولايات الدينية للماوردي الباب الخامس في الولاية على حروب المصالح ألفصل الأول في قتال أهل الردة

Other than *jihad* against the idolaters, fighting is divided into three categories: fighting apostates, fighting wrongdoers, and fighting those who make war. The first category is fighting apostates, namely, when people whose Islam has been ordained for them apostate – either those who have been born into the innate disposition [*fitra*] of Islam, or those who have yielded into Islam out of prior disbelief; both groups fall equally under judgment of apostasy. If they have apostatized from Islam and converted to any religion whose adherents are permitted to remain in it, like Judaism and Christianity, or whose adherents are not permitted to remain in it, like atheism [*zandaqa*] or idol worship [*wathaniya*, paganism], it is not permitted for someone who has apostatized to remain there, given that remaining in the truth necessitates abiding by its precepts; the Messenger of Allah (SAW) said: Whoever changes his religion, kill him. Whenever they are of those whose killing is necessitated because they have apostatized from the religion of truth into any other religion, they unavoidably fall into one of two situations:

1) When they are out of the way and isolated in Islamic territory [*Dar Al-Islam*], and have not withdrawn into a place which would single themselves out from the Muslims, we have no need to fight them in order for them to be subdued and to reveal the reason for their apostasy. … But whoever remains firm in his apostasy and does not repent must be killed, men and women. Abu Hanifa said: I would not kill a woman for apostasy. However the Messenger of Allah (SAW) killed a woman known as Umm Ruman for apostasy. … The legal scholars have differed regarding killing them – must it be carried out immediately or may it be delayed for three days? – into two points of view. One calls for it to be carried out immediately, lest any obligation to Allah Mighty and Sublime be delayed. The second is to watchfully wait for three days, that perchance they may correct him through repentance. 'Ali (peace be upon him) admonished Al-Mustawrid Al-'Ijli to repentance for three days, then killed him afterwards. And as a captive one is to be killed by the sword, although Ibn Suraij, one of the companions of Al-Shafi'i, said: They are to be beaten with a wooden stick until

they die, since this is a slower killing than by a hasty sword, and they may thereby be corrected unto repentance.

2) The second situation is that they withdraw to a certain place in order to isolate themselves from the Muslims to the point of becoming unattainable there; they must be fought for their apostasy, after speaking to them about Islam and making its evidence clear. Fighting is engaged with them, after warning and formal notice, in the same way as for fighting people in war territory [*ahl al-harb*], who are fought by trickery, by night, or openly lined up for battle; they can be fought from the front or from behind.

Al-Mawardi, Ahkam Al-sultaniya, Chapter 5: On the administration of authority in wars of general interest, Section one: On fighting apostates

وإذا بغت طائفة من المسلمين وخالفوا رأي الجماعة وانفردوا بمذهب ابتدعوه فإن لم يخرجوا عن المظاهرة بطاعة الإمام ولا تحيّزوا بدار اعتزلوا فيها وكانوا أفراداً متفرقين تنالهم القدرة وتمتد اليهم اليد تُركوا ولم يحاربوا وأُجريت عليهم أحكام العدل فيها يجب لهم وعليهم من الحقوق والحدود ... فإن تظاهروا باعتقادهم وهم على إختلاطهم بأهل العدل أوضح لهم الإمام فساد ما اعتقدوا وبطلان ابتدعوا ليرجعوا عنه إلى إعتقاد ألحق وموافقة الجماعة وجاز للإمام أن يعزّر منهم من تظاهر بالفساد أدناً وزجراً ولم يتجاوزه إلى قتل ولا حدّ روي عن النبي ﷺ لا يحلّ دم امرئ مسلم إلا بإحدى ثلاث كفر بعد إيمان أو زنى بعد إحصان أو قتل نفس بغير نفس
الأحكام السلطانية والولايات الدينية للماوردي الباب الخامس في الولاية على حروب المصالح الفصل الثاني في قتال أهل البغي

If a party of Muslims acts unjustly, clashes with the opinion of the community, and sets itself apart with a doctrine that they have devised, if by this they have not deviated from supporting obedience to the *imam*, and have not withdrawn somewhere to isolate themselves there, but are only separate and spread out, such that authority can reach them and they may be apprehended, then they can be left alone and not combatted, although all just rulings are applied to them, including the rights and legal punishments they are entitled to as well as what they are obliged to. ... If they make pretense of their creed, being at odds with those who rightly engage in justice, the *imam* is to make clear to them the corruption of what they have embraced and the vanity of what they have devised, so that they might turn from it back to the doctrine of truth and conformity to the community. The *imam* is permitted to rebuke by condemning and scolding those among them who are pretentious in corruption, and not go to the extreme of killing or imposing a legal punishment. It is narrated from the Prophet (SAW): The blood of no Muslim man is permissible except in one of three instances: disbelief after having believed, adultery after having married, and killing a life for other than another life.

Al-Mawardi, Ahkam Al-sultaniya, Chapter 5: On the administration of authority in wars of general interest, Section two: On fighting wrongdoers

وإذا اجتمعت طائفة من أهل الفساد على شهر السلاح وقطع الطريق وأخذ الأموال وقتل النفوس ومنع السابلة فهم المحاربون الذين قال الله تعالى فيهم ﴿ إنما جزاء الذين يحاربون الله ورسوله ويسعون في الأرض فساداً أن يُقتّلوا أو يصلّبوا أو تُقطّع أيديهم وأرجلهم من خلاف أو يُنفوا من الأرض ﴾ فإختلف الفقهاء في حكم هذه الآية على ثلاثة مذاهب احدها أن الإمام ومن استنابه على قتالهم من الولاة بالخيار بين أن يقتل ولا يصلب وبين أن يقتل ويصلب وبين أن يقطع أيديهم وأرجلهم من خلاف وبين أن ينفيهم من الأرض وهذا قول سعيد بن المسيب ومجاهد وعطاء وبراهيم النخعي والمذهب الثاني أن من كان منهم ذا رأي وتدبير قتله ولم يعفَ عنه ومن كان ذا بطش وقوة قطع يده ورجله من خلاف ومن لم يكن منهم ذا رأي ولا بطش عزّره وحبسه وهذا قول مالك بن أنس وطائفة من فقهاء المدينة لجعلها مرتبة بإختلاف صفاتهم لا بإختلاف أفعالهم والمذهب الثالث أنها مرتبة بإختلاف أفعالهم لا بإختلاف صفاتهم فمن قتل وأخذ المال قتل وصلب ومن قتل ولم يأخذ المال قتل ولم يُصلب ومن أخذ المال ولم يقتل قُطعت يده ورجله من خلاف ومن كرّه وهيّب ولم يقتل ولم يأخذ المال عُزّر ولم يصلب وهو قول إبن عباس والحسن وقتادة والسدي وهو مذهب الشافعي رضي الله عنه وقال أبو حنيفة إن قتلوا وأخذوا المال فالإمام بالخيار بين قتلهم ثم صلبهم وبين قطع أيديهم وأرجلهم من خلاف ثم صلبهم وبين قطع أيديهم وأرجلهم من خلاف ثم قتلهم ومن كان معهم مهيباً مكثراً فحكمه كحكمهم

الأحكام السلطانية والولايات الدينية للماوردي الباب الخامس في الولاية على حروب المصالح الفصل الثالث في قتال من إمتنع من المحاربين وقطاع الطرق

If a group of those who foster corruption get together to declare arms, block roadways, steal, kill people, or impede travel, these are the ones that Allah refers to who war against Him: { Indeed the recompense of those who war against Allah and His Messenger, and who pursue corruption in the land, is that they be slaughtered, or crucified, or their hands and feet cut off on opposite sides, or they be banished from the land } [Al-ma'ida 33]. The legal scholars are split into three schools regarding the ruling of this verse. One is that the *imam,* and the officials he has delegated to fight them, have the choice of killing without crucifying, killing and crucifying, cutting off hands and feet from opposite sides, or banishing from the land. This is what Sa'id ibn Al-Musayyib, Mujahid, 'Ataa, and Ibrahim Al-Nakh'i said. The second school holds that those among them who are competent and capable are to be killed without excuse, those among them who are aggressive and forceful are to have their hands and feet cut off on opposite sides, and those of them who are neither competent nor strong are chastened and detained; this is what Malik ibn Anas and a group of legal scholars from Medina said; they made the distinction based on the difference in their characteristics, not based on the difference in what they had done. The third school makes the distinction based on the difference in what they do, not based on their characteristics: whoever kills and steals is to be killed and crucified, whoever kills but does not steal is to be killed but not crucified, whoever steals but does not kill is to have his hand and foot cut off on opposite sides, and whoever sows hatred and inspires terror, but does not kill or steal, is to be rebuked but not killed or crucified; this is what Ibn 'Abbas, Al-Hasan, Qatada, and Al-Suddi said, and this is the school of Al-Shafi'i (may Allah be pleased with him). Abu Hanifa said: If they kill and steal, then the *imam* has the choice of killing then crucifying them, cutting off their hands and feet on opposite sides then crucifying them, or cutting off their hands and feet on opposite sides then killing them; and whoever was terrorizing and rallying along with them receives the same ruling as they do.

Al-Mawardi, Ahkam Al-sultaniya, Chapter 5: On the administration of authority in wars of general interest, Section three: On fighting those who resist among combatants and those who block roadways

وهذا قول كثير من أهل العلم كالشافعي وأحمد وهو قريب من قول ابي حنيفة رحمه الله ومنهم من قال للإمام أن يجتهد فيهم فيقتل من رأى قتله مصلحة

السياسة الشرعية لإبن تيمية

This is what many scholars say, like Al-Shafi'i and Ahmad, and it is close to what Abu Hanifa (may Allah have mercy on him) says; among these are those who say that the leader may use his best judgment regarding them – he may kill those whose killing he deems advantageous.

Ibn Taymiyya, Al-siyasa Al-shar'iya

مسألة قال ويقاتَل أهل الكتاب والمجوس ولا يُدعون لأن الدعوة قد بلغتهم ويدعى عَبَدَة الأوثان قبل أن يحاربوا

المغني لإبن قدامة كتاب الجهاد

He [Al-Khiraqi] said: The People of the Book and the Magians are to be fought against without being called [to Islam], as the call [*da'wah*] has already come to them; but the idol worshippers are to be called to Islam before war is made against them.

Ibn Qudama, Al-mughni, The book of jihad

والمشركون في دار الحرب صنفان صنف من بلغتهم دعوة الاسلام فامتنعوا منها وقاتلوا عليها فأمير الجيش مخيّر في قتالهم بين أمرين يفعل منهما ماعَلِم أنه الأصلح للمسلمين وأنكأ للمشركين من بياتهم ليلاً ونهاراً بالقتال والتحريق وأن ينذرهم بالحرب ويصافهم بالقتال والصنف الثاني لم تبلغهم دعوة الاسلام وقلّ أن يكونوا اليوم لما قد أظهره الله من دعوة رسوله إلا أن يكون قوم من وراء من يقابلنا من الترك والروم في مبادئ المشرق وأقاصي المغرب لا نعرفهم فيُحرم علينا الإقدام على قتالهم غرة وبياتاً بالقتل والتحريق وأن نبدأهم بالقتل قبل إظهار دعوة الاسلام لهم واعلامهم من معجزات النبوة وإظهار المحجة بما يقودهم إلى الإجابة فإن قاموا على الكفر بعد ظهورها لهم حاربهم وصاروا فيه كمن بلغتهم الدعوة قال الله تعالى ﴿ أدعُ إلى سبيل ربك بالحكمة والموعظة الحسَنة وجادلهم بالتي هي أحسن ﴾ يعني أدعُ إلى دين ربك بالحكمة وفيها تأويلات

احدهما بالنبوة والثاني بالقرآن قال الكلبي وفي الموعظة الحسنة تأويلات احدهما القرآن في ليّن من القول والثاني ما فيه من الأمر والنهي ﴿ وجادلهم بالتي هي أحسن ﴾ أي يبين لهم ألحق ويوضح لهم الحجة

الأحكام السلطانية والولايات الدينية للماوردي الباب الرابع في تقليد الإمارة على الجهاد

Idolaters in war territory [*dar al-harb*, house of war, i.e. lands governed by non-Muslims] are of two classes: one class are those who have received the call to Islam, but have rejected it and fought against it. The commander of the army has the choice between two options regarding fighting them, carrying out whichever of the two he knows to be the best for the Muslims and the most detrimental to the idolaters: either to come at them by surprise night and day with fighting and burning, or to declare war to them and line up to fight against them. The second class of idolaters are those who have not received the call to Islam – and at present these are small in number considering what Allah has made manifest of His Messenger's call, unless there are people beyond the Turks and Romans that have faced us, people we do not know from the beginnings of the east or the farthest reaches of the west – it is prohibited for us to be intrepid in fighting them, by trickery or at night, killing and burning, to begin killing them without first presenting them with the call to Islam and informing them of the miracles of the prophethood and presenting the argument by which the commander may lead them into compliance. If they persist in disbelief after this being evident to them, he is to make war with them, and they become like those who have already received the call. Allah Most High said: { Call to the cause of your Lord with wisdom and fitting exhortation, and dispute with them in what is best } [*Al-nahl* 125]. That is, make the call to the religion [*deen*] of your Lord with wisdom; regarding this there are two interpretations: one is by the prophethood and the other is by the Qur'an. Al-Kalbi said: Regarding { fitting exhortation } there are two interpretations: one is the Qur'an, from its gentle and tempered speech, and the other are the orders and prohibitions contained in it. { Dispute with them in what is best } : that is, to make the truth evident to them and to make the argument clear.

Al-Mawardi, Ahkam Al-sultaniya, Chapter 4: On appointing authority (an emirate) over jihad

قال إبن إسحاق وقال رسول الله ﷺ من ظفرتم به من رجال يهود فاقتلوه فوثب محيصة بن مسعود قال إبن هشام ويقال محيصة بن مسعود بن كعب بن عامر بن عدي بن مجدعة بن حارثة بن الحارث بن الخزرج بن عمرو بن مالك بن الأوس على إبن سنينة قال إبن هشام ويقال إبن سنينة رجل من تجار يهود كان يلابسهم ويبايعهم فقتله وكان حويصة بن مسعود إذ ذلك لم يسلم وكان أسنّ من محيصة فلما قتله جعل حويصة يضربه ويقول أي عدو الله أقتلته أما والله لربّ شحم في بطنك من ماله قال محيصة فقلت والله لقد أمرني بقتله من

لو أمرني بقتلك لضربتُ عنقك قال فوالله إن كان لأول إسلام حويصة قال أوالله لو أمرك محمد بقتلي لقتلتني قال نعم والله لو أمرني بضرب عنقك لضربتها قال والله إن ديناً بلغ بك هذا لعجبٌ فأسلم حويصة

السيرة النبوية لإبن هشام أمر محيصة وحويصة

Ibn Ishaq said: The Messenger of Allah (SAW) said: Any of the Jewish men you get the upper hand over – kill him. So Muhayyisa ibn Mas'ud (Ibn Hisham said: He was known as Muhayyisa ibn Mas'ud ibn Ka'b ibn 'Amir ibn 'Adiy ibn Majda'a ibn Haritha ibn Al-Harith ibn Al-Khazraj ibn 'Amr ibn Malik ibn Al-Aws) pounced on Ibn Sunaina (Ibn Hisham said: He was known as Ibn Sunaina, one of the Jewish merchants who was their close associate and did business with them), and killed him. Huwayyisa ibn Mas'ud had not yet yielded into Islam when this happened. He was older than Muhayyisa. And when Muhayyisa killed Ibn Sunaina, Huwayyisa began to beat him, saying: What enemy of Allah are you, have you killed him?! Indeed I swear by Allah the heavy fat on your belly comes from his wealth. Muhayyisa replied: I said, by Allah, I was ordered to kill him by him who, if he ordered me to kill you, I would decapitate you too. (He said: I swear by Allah this was part of the beginning of Huwayyisa's yielding into Islam.) Huwayyisa said: And by Allah, if Muhammad ordered you to kill me, you would kill me?! Muhayyisa replied: Yes, I swear by Allah if He ordered me to decapitate you, I would! Huwayyisa said: I swear by Allah, a religion that can bring you to this is indeed amazing! And Huwayyisa yielded into Islam.

Ibn Hisham, Al-sirah Al-nabawiya, Topic section: the issue of Muhayyisa and Huwayyisa

ويجوز للمسلم أن يقتل من ظفر به من مقاتلة المشركين محارباً وغير محارب وإختُلف في قتل شيوخهم ورهبانهم من سكان الصوامع والأديرة فأحد القولين فيهم أنهم لا يُقتلون حتى يقاتلوا لأنهم موادعون كالذراري والثاني يقتلون وإن لم يقاتلوا لأنهم ربما أشاروا برأي هو أنكى للمسلمين من القتال

الأحكام السلطانية والولايات الدينية للماوردي الباب الرابع في تقليد الإمارة على الجهاد

It is permissible for a Muslim to kill any of the fighters of the idolaters over whom he has prevailed, whether they have engaged in combat or not. There is disagreement regarding killing their elders and monks living in hermitages and monasteries. One viewpoint regarding them is that they are not to be killed until they themselves fight, since a truce has been made with them, like women and children. The second viewpoint is that they are to be killed even if they do not fight, since perhaps they may be sources of advice with ideas even more harmful to the Muslims than fighting.

Al-Mawardi, Ahkam Al-sultaniya, Chapter 4: On appointing authority (an emirate) over jihad

والقسم الثالث من أحكام هذه الإمارة من أمير الجيش في سياستهم والذي يلزمهم فيهم عشرة أشياء أحدها حراستهم من غرة يظفر بها العدو منهم وذلك بأن يتتبع المكامن فيحفظها عليهم ويحوط سوادهم بحرس يأمنون به على نفوسهم ورحالهم ليسكنوا في وقت الدعة ويأمنوا ما وراءهم في وقت المحاربة ... والرابع أن يعرف أخبار عدوه حتى يقف عليها ويتصفح أحواله حتى يخبرها من مكره ويلتمس الغرّة في الهجوم عليه ... والسادس أن يقوي نفوسهم بما يشعرهم من الظفر ويخيل إليهم من أسباب النصر ليقل العدو في أعينهم فيكون عليه أجرأ وبالجراءة يتسهل الظفر قال الله تعالى ﴿ إِذْ يُرِيكَهُمُ اللَّهُ فِي مَنَامِكَ قَلِيلًا وَلَوْ أَرَاكَهُمْ كَثِيرًا لَفَشِلْتُمْ وَلَتَنَازَعْتُمْ فِي الْأَمْرِ ﴾ والسابع أن يَعِد أهل الصبر والبلاء منهم بثواب الله لو كانوا من أهل الآخرة وبالجزاء والنفل من الغنيمة إن كانوا من أهل الدنيا قال الله تعالى ﴿ وَمَنْ يُرِدْ ثَوَابَ الدُّنْيَا نُؤْتِهِ مِنْهَا وَمَنْ يُرِدْ ثَوَابَ الْآخِرَةِ نُؤْتِهِ مِنْهَا ﴾ وثواب الدنيا الغنيمة وثواب الآخرة الجنن لجمع الله تعالى في ترغيبه بين أمرين ليكون أرغب للفريقين

الأحكام السلطانية والولايات الدينية للماوردي الباب الرابع في تقليد الإمارة على الجهاد

The third section of rulings for this position of authority concern the army commander regarding managing them. concern their course of action; he is to attend to them in ten things. One of them is to guard them from negligence by which the enemy might prevail over them, this by paying close attention to ambushes and preserving them from such, surrounding their compound with a guard by which their souls and their gear may rest secure, so that they may be at ease in time of mildness and be secure of their rear in time of combat. ... The fourth is that he should be aware of news of his enemy, so that he may take up position against them and survey their situation until he is fully aware of them, so he can be safe from their schemes and seek stealthily to attack them. ... The sixth is that he strengthen their spirits by informing them of the victory and evoking to them the reasons for the divine aid, so that the enemy may be reduced in their sight, and so they may be bolder, for by boldness victory is facilitated. Allah Most High said: { Indeed Allah showed them to you in your dreams as small in number, for if He had showed them to you as numerous, you would have lost courage and disputed about the issue } [Al-anfal 43]. The seventh is that he promise Allah's reward to those of them that are steadfast and brave if they are of those that will belong to the hereafter, and of the reward and the taking of spoils if they are of those that will still be of this world. Allah Most High said: { Whoever desires the reward of this world, We will bring of it to him; and whoever desires the reward of the hereafter, we will bring of it to him } [Al 'Imran 145]. The reward of this world is the booty, and the reward of the hereafter is *Jannah*; Allah Most High brought both issues together when He roused desire, so that it might be more desirous to both groups.

Al-Mawardi, Ahkam Al-sultaniya, Chapter 4: On appointing position of authority (an emirate) over jihad

عن إبن عباس قال الفيء الجماع
المصنف لعبد الرزاق كتاب الطلاق باب الفيء، الجماع

From Ibn 'Abbas who said: The loot is sex. [Al-fai' al-jima']

'Abd Al-Razzaq, the Musannaf, The book of divorce, Section: loot is sex

أن يقصد بقتاله نصرة دين الله تعالى وإبطال ما خالفه من الأديان ﴿ ليُظهره على الدين كله ولو كره المشركون ﴾ فيكون بهذا الإعتقاد حائزاً لثواب الله تعالى ومطيعاً له في أوامره ونصرة دينه ومستنصراً به على عدوه ليستسهل ما لاقى فيكون أكثر ثباتاً وأبلغ نكاية ولا يقصد بجهاده إستفادة المغنم فيصير من المكتسبين لا من المجاهدين

الأحكام السلطانية والولايات الدينية للماوردي الباب الرابع في تقليد الإمارة على الجهاد

One must strive, in his fighting, to uphold the religion of Allah Most High, and to abolish other religions that oppose it, { to make it prevail over all religion, even if the idolaters dislike this } [Al-saff 9]; that by this conviction he may take hold of the reward of Allah Most High, be obedient to Him in His orders and in upholding His religion, and by this seek aid over his enemy, thereby making easy whatever he comes across; that he may be greater in endurance and more rigorous in causing harm; and let him not aim, in his *jihad*, to gain the spoils, thereby becoming just someone looking to acquire things, and not a *mujahid*.

Al-Mawardi, Ahkam Al-sultaniya, Chapter 4: On appointing position of authority (an emirate) over jihad

ويُشترط لوجوب الجهاد سبعة شروط الاسلام والبلوغ والعقل والحرية والذكورية والسلامة من الضرر ووجود النفقة

المغني لإبن قدامة كتاب الجهاد

There are seven conditions stipulated in the duty of *jihad*: being a Muslim, having attained puberty, being of sound mind, being a free person, being male, being free from injuries, and being able to spend.

Ibn Qudama, Al-mughni, The book of jihad

وإذا كانت مصابرة القتال من حقوق الجهاد فهي لازمة حتى يظفر بخصلة من أربع خصال احداهن أن يسلموا فيصير لهم بالاسلام ما لنا وعليهم ما علينا ويُقرّوا على ما ملكوا من بلاد وأموال قال رسول الله ﷺ أمرت أن أقاتل الناس حتى يقولوا لا إله إلا الله فإذا قالوها عصموا مني دماءهم وأموالهم إلا بحقها ... والخصلة الثانية أن يظفره الله تعالى بهم مع مقامته على شركهم فتُسبى ذراريهم وتغنم أموالهم ويُقتل من لم

يحصل في الأسر منهم ويكون في الأسرى مخيّراً في إستعمال الأصلح من أربعة أمور احدها أن يقتلهم صبراً بضرب العنق والثاني أن يسترقهم ويجري عليهم أحكام الرق من بيع أو عتق والثالث أن يفادي بهم على مال أو أسرى والرابع أن يمنّ عليهم ويعفو عنهم قال الله تعالى ﴿ فإذا لقيتم الذين كفروا فضرب الرقاب ﴾ وفيه وجهان احدهما أنه ضرب رقابهم صبراً بعد القدرة عليهم والثاني أنه قتالهم بالسلاح والتدبير حتى يفضي الى ضرب رقابهم في المعركة ثم قال ﴿ حتى إذا أثخنتموهم فشدّوا الوثاق ﴾ يعني بالاثخان الطعن وبشد الوثاق الأسر ... والخصلة الثالثة أن يبذلوا مالاً على المسالمة والموادعة فيجوز أن يقبله منهم ويوادعهم على ضربين احدهما أن يبذلوه لوقتهم ولا يجعلوه خراجاً مستمراً ... والضرب الثاني أن يبذلوه في كل عام فيكون هذا خارجاً مستمراً ويكون الأمان به مستقراً ... والخصلة الرابعة أن يسألوا الأمان والمهادنة فيجوز إذا تعذر الظفر بهم وأخذ المال منهم أن يهادنهم على المسالمة في مدة مقدرة يعقد الهدنة عليهم إذا كان الإمام قد أذن له في الهدنة أو فوّض الأمر إليه قد هادن رسول الله ﷺ قريشاً عام الحديبية عشر سنين وتقتصر في مدة الهدنة على أقل ما يمكن ولا يجاوز أكثرها عشر سنين

_{الأحكام السلطانية والولايات الدينية للماوردي الباب الرابع في تقليد الإمارة على الجهاد}

In that perseverance in fighting is one of the obligations of *jihad*, it is obligatory until one of four dispositions is attained. The **first** of these is that they yield into Islam, in which case what is ours becomes theirs because of Islam, our obligations become theirs, and they are granted to hold onto the lands and wealth they possess. The Messenger of Allah (SAW) said: I have been ordered to fight people until they say "There is no god but Allah" [*"La ilaha illa Allah"*]; and if they say this, their blood and their property are safe from me, except when these are due. ... The **second** disposition is that Allah Most High grants him [the *emir*, military commander] victory over them, but they remain in their idolatry [*shirk*]; their women and children are taken captive, their wealth is plundered, and those of them who are not taken into captivity are killed. With regard to the captives, he has the choice to carry out the most advantageous of four options: one is to kill them as captives by decapitation [*darb al-'unuq*, striking the neck], the second is to enslave them and to apply the rulings for slaves to them as regards buying and selling, the third is to ransom them for money or other prisoners, and the fourth is to show kindness to them and pardon them. Allah Most High has said: { Whenever you face those who have disbelieved, strike the necks } [*Muhammad* 4]. There are two points of view regarding this: one of these is to strike their necks as captives after gaining power over them, and the other is to fight them in organized armed combat until being able to strike their necks in battle. Then He said: { Until you have thoroughly brought them down; and tighten the shackles } , "brought down" meaning piercing, and "tightening the shackles" means taking captive. ... The **third** disposition is for them to pay money for conciliation and to make peace. This may be levied from them, and peace made, in two ways: one of these is for them to pay at that time, and not make it a perpetual revenue ... the second is for them to pay every year, and for this to be a perpetual tax, and thereby security is permanent.

... The **fourth** disposition is that they ask for security and a truce. It is permissible, if victory over them or taking a payment is difficult, to establish a truce with them for conciliation, for an appointed duration by which he establishes a truce with them, if the leader [*imam*] has given him [the *emir*] permission for the truce or authorized him to do so. The Messenger of Allah (SAW) established, with the Quraish in the year of Hudaibiyya, a ten-year truce. The duration of the truce must be as short as is possible, and must not exceed ten years.

Al-Mawardi, Ahkam Al-sultaniya, Chapter 4: On appointing a position of authority (an emirate) over jihad

فأما الذين يحاربون فاتفقوا على أنهم جميع المشركين لقوله تعالى ﴿ وقاتلوهم حتى لا تكون فتنة ويكون الدين كله لله ﴾ إلا ما روي عن مالك أنه قال لا يجوز إبتداء الحبشة بالحرب ولا الترك لما روي أنه ﷺ قال ذروا الحبشة ما وذرتكم

بداية المجتهد ونهاية المقتصد لإبن رشد كتاب الجهاد الجملة الأولى في معرفة أركان الحرب الفصل الثاني في معرفة الذين يحاربون

Concerning those who are to be fought, they have agreed that they are all the Idolaters [*Mushrikun*], from the word of the Most High: { So fight them until there is no more sedition and religion is all for Allah } [*Al-anfal* 39]. The exception is what is related from Malik, who said: It is not permissible to initiate war with the Ethiopians [*Habasha*], nor with the Turks, based on what is related that He (SAW) said: Leave the Ethiopians alone as long as they leave you alone.

Ibn Rushd, Bidaya Al-mujtahid wa Nihaya Al-Muqtasid, The book of jihad, Part one: knowing the elements of war, Section two: knowing those who are to be fought

ومن قتل من شهداء المسلمين زُمِّل في ثيابه التل قُتل فيها ودُفن بها ولم يُغسل ولم يصلَ عليه قال رسول الله ﷺ في شهداء أحد زمّلوهم بكلومهم فإنهم يُبعثون يوم القيامة وأوداجهم تشخب دماء اللون لون الدم والريح ريح المسك وانما فعل بهم تكريماً لهم إجراء لحكم الحياة في ذلك قال الله تعالى ﴿ ولا تحسبنّ الذين قُتلوا في سبيل الله أمواتاً بل أحياء عند ربهم يُرزقون ﴾

الأحكام السلطانية والولايات الدينية للماوردي الباب الرابع في تقليد الإمارة على الجهاد

Those of the Muslim martyrs who are killed are wrapped in the garments that they were killed in, buried in them, and are neither washed nor prayed over. The Messenger of Allah (SAW) said regarding the martyrs at Uhud: Wrap them with their wounds, for surely they will be brought forth on resurrection day with their jugular veins flowing blood, its color the color of blood but its scent the scent of musk. Indeed thus

He did with them to honor them, and to fulfill the decree of life in this; Allah Most High said: { Do not at all deem those who have been killed in the cause of Allah to be dead, but rather alive with their Lord, bestowed with favor } [Al 'Imran 169].

Al-Mawardi, Ahkam Al-sultaniya, Chapter 4: On appointing position of authority (an emirate) over jihad

فأما حكم هذه الوظيفة فأجمع العلماء على أنها فرض على الكفاية لا فرض عين إلا عبدالله بن الحسن فإنه قال إنها تطوّع وإنما صار الجمهور فرضاً لكونه ﴿ كتب عليكم القتال وهو كرهٌ لكم ﴾ الآية ... وأما على من يجب فهم الرجال الأحرار البالغون الذين يجدون بما يغزون الأصحاء إلا المرضى وإلا الزمنى

بداية المجتهد ونهاية المقتصد لإبن رشد كتاب الجهاد الجملة الأولى في معرفة أركان الحرب الفصل الأول في معرفة حكم هذه الوظيفة

Concerning the ruling in this duty [jihad], the scholars have come together unanimously that it is a collective obligation, not an individual obligation, except Abdullah ibn Al-Hasan, who said that indeed it is voluntary. Indeed the community took it as an obligation from what the Most High said: { Fighting is ordained for you, being something you dislike ... } to the end of the verse [Al-baqara 216]. ... Those who are obliged to it are men, free, who have come of age, those who have the means to go out on attacks, and healthy, excepting the sick and chronically ill.

Ibn Rushd, Bidaya Al-mujtahid wa Nihaya Al-Muqtasid, The book of jihad, Part one: knowing the elements of war, Section one: knowing the ruling concerning this duty

والتحقيق أن جنس الجهاد فرضُ عين إما بالقلب وإما باللسان وإما بالمال وإما باليد فعلم كل مسلم أن يجاهد بنوع من هذه الأنواع

زاد المعاد لإبن قيم الجهاد والغزوات

It is affirmed that the nature of jihad is the personal obligation, whether by the heart, by the tongue, by one's wealth, or by the hand; it is every Muslim's duty to wage jihad in one of these ways.

Ibn Qayyim, Zad Al-Ma'ad, Jihad and Raids

مسألة قال والجهاد فرض على الكفاية إذا قام به قوم سقط عن الباقين
معنى فرض الكفاية الذي إن لم يقم به من يكفي أثِمَ الناس كلهم وإن قام به من يكفي سقط عن سائر الناس
فالخطاب في ابتدائه يتناول الجميع كفرض الأعيان ثم يختلفان أن فرض الكفاية يسقط بفعل بعض الناس له
وفرض الأعيان لا يسقط عن أحدٍ بفعل غيره والجهاد من فروض الكفايات في قول عامة أهل العلم

المغني لإبن قدامة كتاب الجهاد

His [Al-Khiraqi] statement: *Jihad* is a collective duty; if some people carry it out, the obligation is lifted from the rest.

The meaning of collective duty is that if those who are sufficient to carry it out do not carry it out, all the people are guilty of sin, but if sufficient people carry it out, the obligation is lifted from the rest of the people. This communication initially addresses everyone, as an obligation to individuals, then makes the distinction that a collective duty is lifted if some people perform it, while individual obligation is not lifted from anyone if someone else performs it. *Jihad* is one of the collective obligations according to what scholars in general say.

Ibn Qudama, Al-mughni, The book of jihad

ويتعيَّن الجهاد في ثلاثة مواضع احدها إذا إلتقى الزحفان وتقابل الصفّان حرُم على من حضر الإنصراف وتعين عليه المُقام ... الثاني إذا نزل الكفار ببلد تعين على أهله قتالهم ودفعهم الثالث إذا استنفر الإمام قوماً لزمَهم النفير معه

المغني لإبن قدامة كتاب الجهاد

Jihad becomes an individual duty in three instances; one of them is if two armies meet and two ranks face each other, it is forbidden for anyone present to depart, and it is their individual duty to stand their ground. ... The second is whenever the Disbelievers descend upon a region, its people are given the individual duty to fight them and push them back. The third is if the leader asks people to mobilize, they must mobilize with him.

Ibn Qudama, Al-mughni, The book of jihad

وأما ما يجوز من النكاية في العدو فإن النكاية لا تخلو أن تكون في الأموال أو في النفوس أو في الرقاب أعني الإستعباد والتملك فأما النكاية التي هي الإستعباد فهي جائزة بطريق الاجماع في جميع أنواع المشركين أعني ذكرانهم وإناثهم وشيوخهم وصبيانهم صغارهم وكبارهم إلا الرهبان ... وأكثر العلماء على أن الإمام مخير في الأسارى في خصال منها أن يمن عليهم ومنها أن يستعبدهم ومنها أن يقتلهم ومنها أن يأخذ منهم الفداء ومنها أن يضرب عليهم الجزية ... وأما النكاية التي تكون في النفوس فهي القتل ولا خلاف بين المسلمين أنه يجوز في الحرب قتل المشركين الذكران البالغين المقاتلين وأما القتل بعد الأسر ففيه الخلاف الذي ذكرنا وكذلك لا خلاف بينهم في أنه لا يجوز قتل صبيانهم ولا قتل نسائهم ما لم تقاتل المرأة والصبي فإذا قاتلت المرأة استبيح دمها ... واختلفوا في أهل الصوامع المنتزعين عن الناس والعميان والزمنى والشيوخ الذين لا يقاتلون والمعتوه والحراث والعسيف فقال مالك لا يقتل الأعمى ولا المعتوه ولا أصحاب الصوامع ويترك لهم من أموالهم بقدر ما يعيشون به وكذلك لا يقتل الشيخ الفاني عنده وبه قال أبو حنيفة وأصحابه وقال الثوري والأوزاعي لا تقتل الشيوخ فقط وقال الأوزاعي لا تقتل الحراث وقال الشافعي في الأصح عنه تقتل جميع هذه الاصناف والسبب في اختلافهم معارضة بعض الآثار بخصوصها لعموم الكتاب ولعموم قوله ﷺ الثابت أمرت أن أقاتل الناس حتى يقولوا لا إله إلا الله الحديث وذلك في قوله تعالى ﴿ فإذا انسلخ الأشهر الحرم فاقتلوا المشركين حيث وجدتموهم ﴾ يقتضي قتل كل مشرك راهباً كان أو غيره وكذلك قوله ﷺ أمرت أن أقاتل الناس حتى يقولوا لا إله إلا الله

<small>بداية المجتهد ونهاية المقتصد لإبن رشد كتاب الجهاد الجملة الأولى في معرفة أركان الحرب الفصل الثالث في معرفة ما يجوز من النكاية في العدو</small>

Concerning the harm permissible towards the enemy: clearly harm can be towards property, or life, or to liberty [*riqab*, necks], by this I mean enslavement or taking possession. Harm as enslavement is permissible by way of universal consensus for all types of idolaters [*mushrikun*], by this I mean their males, their females, their elderly, their youth, insignificant or distinguished, except for monks. ... Most of the scholars agree that the leader [*imam*] has the choice of several dispositions regarding captives, among them to show favor to them, to take them as slaves, to kill them, to take a ransom from them, or to levy tax [*jizya*] from them. ... Harm towards life is to kill, and there is no disagreement among the Muslims that it is permissible in war to kill the idolaters, males who have come of age and who fight. Regarding killing after taking captive, however, there is the disagreement we have mentioned. Similarly, there is no disagreement among them that it is not permissible to kill their youth or kill their women, as long as the women and youth are not fighting; if a woman fights, her blood becomes permissible. ... They disagree regarding those who live in hermitages isolated from people, the blind, the chronically ill, the elderly who do not fight, the insane, peasants, and laborers. Malik said: Neither the blind nor the insane nor the hermits are to be killed, and they are left with whatever of their possessions suffice for them to live by. Similarly, the most advanced in years are not to be killed in his view, and this is what Abu Hanifa and his companions said. Al-Thawri and Al-Awza'i said that only the elderly are not to be killed. Al-

Awza'i said that peasants are not to be killed. But Al-Shafi'i said, according to what is most correctly related from him, that all of these classes of people are to be killed. The reason for their disagreement is the disparity of certain reports in their matters of concern against the generality of the Book and the generality of what He (SAW) indisputably said: I have been ordered to fight people until they say "There is no god but Allah" ["La ilaha illa Allah"] and the rest of the hadith. This is also seen in the word of the Most High: { But when the sacred months have passed, kill the idolaters wherever you find them } [Al-tawba 5], which implies the killing of all Idolaters, monks or otherwise, as does His (SAW) word: I have been ordered to fight people until they say "La ilaha illa Allah".

Ibn Rushd, Bidaya Al-mujtahid wa Nihaya Al-Muqtasid, The book of jihad, Part one: knowing the elements of war, Section three: knowing what harm is permissible to inflict on the enemy

وصح النهي عن المُثلة واتفق المسلمون على جواز قتلهم بالسلاح واختلفوا في تحريقهم بالنار

بداية المجتهد ونهاية المقتصد لإبن رشد كتاب الجهاد الجملة الأولى في معرفة أركان الحرب ألفصل الثالث في معرفة ما يجوز من النكاية في العدو

The prohibition on mutilating is resolute; Muslims agree on the permissibility of killing them with weapons, but differ regarding burning them with fire.

Ibn Rushd, Bidaya Al-mujtahid wa Nihaya Al-Muqtasid, The book of jihad, Part one: knowing the elements of war, Section three: knowing what harm is permissible to inflict on the enemy

فأما شرط الحرب فهو بلوغ الدعوة بإتفاق أعني أنه لا يجوز حرابتهم حتى يكونوا قد بلغتهم الدعوة وذلك شيء مجتمع عليه من المسلمين لقوله تعالى ﴿ وما كنّا معذّبين حتى نبعث رسولاً ﴾ وأما هل يجب تكرار الدعوة عند تكرار الحرب فإنهم اختلفوا في ذلك فمنهم من أوجبها ومنهم من استحبها ومنهم من لم يوجبها ولا استحبها

بداية المجتهد ونهاية المقتصد لإبن رشد كتاب الجهاد الجملة الأولى في معرفة أركان الحرب ألفصل الرابع في شرط الحرب

Concerning the stipulations for war: it is agreed that this is making known the call to Islam [da'wah]; by this I mean that it is not permissible to wage war on them until the da'wah has reached them. This is something that Muslims agree on universally, based on the word of the Most High: { We do not punish until we send forth a messenger } [Al-israa 15]. However, is it necessary to repeat the da'wah when war is repeated? They differed with respect to this; some of them made it obligatory, some of them encouraged it, and some of them neither obliged nor encouraged it.

Ibn Rushd, Bidaya Al-mujtahid wa Nihaya Al-Muqtasid, The book of jihad, Part one: knowing the elements of war, Section four: on the stipulations for war

فأما هل تجوز المهادنة فإن قوماً اجازوها إبتداء من غير سبب إذا رأى الإمام مصلحة المسلمين وقوم لم يجيزوها إلا لمكان الضرورة الداعية لأهل الاسلام من فتنة أو غير ذلك إما بشيء يأخذونه منهم

بداية المجتهد ونهاية المقتصد لإبن رشد كتاب الجهاد الجملة الأولى في معرفة أركان الحرب الفصل السادس في جواز المهادنة

Now then, is truce permissible? Indeed one group made it permissible initially, with no reason given, whenever the leader [*imam*] saw an advantage for the Muslims. Another group did not make it permissible except in the case of an imperative need for the people of Islam to prevent any sedition [*fitnah*] or anything else, or for something that they could take from them.

Ibn Rushd, Bidaya Al-mujtahid wa Nihaya Al-Muqtasid, The book of jihad, Part one: knowing the elements of war, Section six: on the permissibility of truce

ومما يتعلق بهذه الجملة من المسائل المشهورة النهي عن السفر بالقرآن إلى أرض العدو وعامة الفقهاء على أن ذلك غير جائز لثبوت ذلك عن رسول الله ﷺ وقال أبو حنيفة يجوز ذلك إذا كان في العساكر المأمونة

بداية المجتهد ونهاية المقتصد لإبن رشد كتاب الجهاد الجملة الأولى في معرفة أركان الحرب الفصل السابع لماذا يحاربون

Among the well-known matters associated with this Part One is the prohibition of travelling with a Qur'an into enemy territory. The majority of legal scholars hold that this is not permissible, based on this being affirmed from the Messenger of Allah (SAW). Abu Hanifa said that this is permitted, if it is in the secured military encampments.

Ibn Rushd, Bidaya Al-mujtahid wa Nihaya Al-Muqtasid, The book of jihad, Part one: knowing the elements of war, Section seven: why is war waged on them?

وأما المسألة الرابعة وهي هل يجب سَلَب المقتول للقاتل أو ليس يجب له إلا إن نفله له الإمام فإنهم اختلفوا في ذلك فقال مالك لا يستحق القاتل سلب المقتول إلا أن ينفله له الامام على جهة الإجتهاد وذلك بعد الحرب وبه قال أبو حنيفة والثوري وقال الشافعي وأحمد وأبو ثور وإسحاق وجماعة السلف واجب للقاتل ذلك قال ذلك الامام أو لم يقله ومن هؤلاء من جعل السلب له على كل حال ولم يشترط في ذلك شرطاً ومنهم من قال لا يكون له السلب إلا إذا قتله مقبلاً غير مدبر وبه قال الشافعي ومنهم من قال انما يكون السلب للقاتل إذا كان القتل قبل معمعة الحرب أو بعدها وأما إن قتله في حين المعمعة فليس له سلب وبه قال الأوزاعي وقال قوم إن استكثر الإمام السلب جاز أن يخمسه

بداية المجتهد ونهاية المقتصد لإبن رشد كتاب الجهاد الجملة الثانية الفصل الثالث في حكم الانفال

The fourth issue is: Shall the killer have the spoils of someone who is killed, or is he not to have them except if the leader [*imam*] grants them to him? They disagreed regarding this; Malik said a killer does not have the right to the spoils of the one killed unless the *imam* grants them to him on the basis of his own judgment, and this after the battle. This is what Abu Hanifa and Al-Thawri said. Al-Shafi'i, Ahmad, Abu Thawr, Ishaq, and a group of those who preceded said that the killer is to have them, whether or not the *imam* says so. Of these there are those who would grant him the spoils in any circumstance, and they did not impose any conditions regarding this. Some of them said that the spoils are not his except if he has killed him facing him, not from behind; Al-Shafi'i said this. Some of them said that indeed the killer is to have the spoils if the killing was before the battle rages or after it, but if he kills him at the time the battle rages, there are no spoils for him. Al-Awza'i said this. And a group of people said that if the *imam* deems the spoils excessive, he is permitted to take one-fifth of it.

Ibn Rushd, Bidaya Al-mujtahid wa Nihaya Al-Muqtasid, The book of jihad, Part two, Section three: on the ruling of the spoils

وإذا غزا الجيش أرضاً قد بلغتهم الدعوة فإن دعوهم أيضاً فحسن وإن تركوا ذلك فحسن ولا بأس بأن يغيروا عليهم ليلاً أو نهاراً بغير دعوة ويحرقوا حصونهم ويغرقونها

كتاب السير الصغير للشيباني ٣٢

Whenever the army attacks a land which has been made aware of the call to people [to Islam; *da'wah*], if they make a *da'wah* again, fine, and if they omit this, fine. And there is no objection for them to raid them at night or by day, without a *da'wah*, and for them to burn their strongholds or flood them.

Al-Shaybani, Kitab Al-siyar Al-saghir, item 32

ولا شيء على من قتل المرتدين قبل أن يدعوهم إلى الاسلام

كتاب السير الصغير للشيباني ١٢٩

No one is held accountable for killing apostates before calling them back to Islam.

Al-Shaybani, Kitab Al-siyar Al-saghir, item 129

ولا يقسم السبي منهم وإن إحتاج الناس إليه ما لم يخرجوهم إلى دار الاسلام ولا يبيعهم ويمشيهم حتى يخرجوهم إلى دار الاسلام إن أطاقوا المثى وإن لم يطيقوه ولم يكن معه فضل حمولة ولم تطب أنفس من معه فضل حمولة من أهل العسكر بحملهم عليه قتل الرجال وترك النساء والصبيان

كتاب السير الصغير للشيباني ٣٥

Those of them taken as prisoners are not apportioned, even if people need them, as long as they have not yet been brought into Islamic territory [Dar Al-Islam]. He must not sell them, but make them march until they have brought them into Dar Al-Islam, provided they can make the trek. If they can not make it, and he does not have extra transport, and none of those with him who have extra transport is of a mind to take them, then the men are killed and the women and children are left.

Al-Shaybani, Kitab Al-siyar Al-saghir, item 35

وإن أعتق رجل من الجند جارية من الغنيمة لم يجز عتقه إستحساناً وإن استولدها لم يجز ولم يثبت النسب وأخذ منه العقر وكانت هي وولدها في الغنيمة

كتاب السير الصغير للشيباني ٤٤

If one of the soldiers frees a slave girl from among the spoils, his freeing her will not pass juristic discretion [istihsan]. If he seeks to have a child by her, this will not pass, the offspring will not be affirmed, and payment will be taken from him ['uqr, for unlawful relations with a slave girl]. She and her child will remain part of the spoils.

Al-Shaybani, Kitab Al-siyar Al-saghir, item 44

ولا يقتل الأعمى والمقعد والمعتوه من الأسرى

كتاب السير الصغير للشيباني ٥٥

Blind, disabled, or insane prisoners are not to be killed.

Al-Shaybani, Kitab Al-siyar Al-saghir, item 55

وإن خرج الرجل أو الرجلان من مثل هذه المدائن بغير إذن الإمام فأصاب غنيمة لم يكن فيها خمس وكانت كلها له وإن كانت جارية لم يطأها حتى يخرجها

كتاب السير الصغير للشيباني ٦٤

If one or two men come out from cities like these without permission from the leader [imam], and come upon some spoils, a fifth portion [khums] is not taken, and he may have all of it. If there is a slave girl, he is not to have sex with her until he brings her out.

Al-Shaybani, Kitab Al-siyar Al-saghir, item 64

وإن استأمن اليهم مسلم فإشترى جارية كتابية واستبرأها كان له أن يطأها هناك وأكره لكل مسلم أن يطأ امرأته أو أمته في دار الحرب مخافة أن يكون له هناك نسل

كتاب السير الصغير للشيباني ٦٥

If a Muslim seeks protection from them, and buys a Christian or Jewish slave girl, and observes the required period of abstinence for her [*istibra'*], he may have sex with her there; however I find it aversive for any Muslim to have sex with his woman or his servant girl in war territory [*dar al-harb*; non-Muslim lands], out of fear that he might have offspring there.

Al-Shaybani, Kitab Al-siyar Al-saghir, item 65

وإذا طعن المسلم بالرمح في جوفه لم أكره له أن يمشي إلى صاحبه والرمح في جوفه حتى يضربه بالسيف ولم اجعله بذلك معيناً على نفسه

كتاب السير الصغير للشيباني ٦٩

If a Muslim is stabbed in the stomach with a spear, I am not averse to him going over to whoever did it, with the spear still in his stomach, to strike him with his sword; in doing this I do not regard him as assisting in taking his own life.

Al-Shaybani, Kitab Al-siyar Al-saghir, item 69

حربي دخل دار الاسلام بغير أمان فمن أخذه فهو عبده

كتاب السير الصغير للشيباني ٩١

Any warrior who enters Islamic territory [*Dar Al-Islam*] without a warrant of security [*aman*], he is the slave of whoever takes him.

Al-Shaybani, Kitab Al-siyar Al-saghir, item 91

وسألت أبا حنيفة عن قتل لنساء والصبيان والشيوخ الذين لا يقدرون على القتال والذين بهم زمانة لا يطيقون قتالاً فنهى عن ذلك وكرهه وسألت عن قتل المترهبين وأصحاب الصوامع والزنار فرأى قتلهم حسناً وكره استبقائهم وسألت عن الرجل يأسر الرجل من العدو هل يقتله أو يأتي به الإمام قال أي ذلك فعل فهو حسن وقال أبو يوسف ومحمد أي ذلك كان أفضل للمسلمين فليفعله ... وسألت عن المسلمين يستعينون بأهل الشرك على أهل الحرب قال لا بأس بذلك إذا كان حكم الاسلام هو القاهر الغالب

كتاب السير الصغير للشيباني ١٦٢

I asked Abu Hanifa about killing women, children, and elderly who are not able to fight, as well as those with chronic illness who are unable to withstand fighting. He prohibited and was averse to it. I asked about killing monks, those who live in hermitages, and those who wear sashes around the waist. He felt that killing them was fine, and was adverse to sparing them. And I asked about someone who takes a man prisoner from the enemy – should he kill him or bring him to the leader [*imam*]? He said: Either of those is fine for him to do. But Abu Yusuf and Muhammad said: He should do whichever is better for the Muslims. ... And I asked about Muslims seeking aid from non-Muslims [*ahl al-shirk*, Idolaters] against the people they are at war with [*ahl al-harb*]; he said: There is no problem with that, as long as the decrees of Islam are forceful and victorious.

Al-Shaybani, Kitab Al-siyar Al-saghir, item 162

قال رسول الله ﷺ الحرب خدعة وفيه دليل على أنه لا بأس للمجاهد أن يخادع قرنه في حالة القتال وأن ذلك لا يكون غدراً منه وأخذ بعض العلماء بالظاهر فقالوا يرخص في الكذب في هذه الحالة واستدلوا بحديث ابي هريرة رضي الله عنه أن النبي ﷺ قال لا يصلح الكذب إلا في ثلاث في الصلح بين إثنين وفي القتال وفي إرضاء الرجل أهله والمذهب عندنا أنه ليس المراد الكذب المحض فإن ذلك لا رخصة فيه وإنما المراد إستعمال المعاريض

شرح كتاب السير الكبير للسرخسي باب الحرب خدعة

The Messenger of Allah (SAW) said: War is deceit. From this it is evident that there is no problem for a *Mujahid* to deceive his opponent in times of fighting, and that this does not constitute treason on his part. Some of the scholars took this literally and said: This gives license to tell lies during these times. They drew this conclusion from the hadith of Abu Huraira (may Allah be pleased with him), that the Prophet (SAW) said: Telling lies is not appropriate except in three instances – in reconciliation between two people, in fighting, and in a man pleasing the women of his household. Our school of thought is that this does not mean telling pure lies, since license is not given for this, but rather the meaning is to use misleading speech.

Al-Sarakhsi, Sharh Kitab Al-siyar Al-kabir, Section: war is deceit

> فإن التقية أن يقول العبد خلاف ما يعتقده لإتقاء مكروه يقع به لو لم يتكلم بالتقية
>
> أحكام أهل الذمة لإبن قيم فصل ١٨٧

Taqiyya is when one says something different from what he believes, as a precaution against something aversive that could befall him if he were not to speak with *taqiyya*.

Ibn Qayyim, *Ahkam Ahl Al-Dhimma*, Section 187

> قال لا يعجبنا أن يقاتل النساء مع الرجال في الحرب لأنه ليس للمرأة بنية صالحة للقتال كما أشار إليه رسول الله ﷺ في قوله هاه ما كانت هذه تقاتل وربما يكون في قتالها كشف عورة المسلمين فيفرح به المشركون وربما يكون ذلك سبباً لجرأة المشركين على المسلمين ويستدلون به على ضعف المسلمين فيقولون احتاجوا إلى الإستعانة بالنساء على قتالنا فليتحرز عن هذا ولهذا المعنى لا يستحب لهن مباشرة القتال إلا أن يضطر المسلمون إلى ذلك فإن دفع فتنة المشركين عند تحقق الضرورة بما يقدر عليه المسلمون جائز بل واجب
>
> شرح كتاب السير الكبير للسرخسي باب قتال النساء مع الرجال وشهودهن الحرب

He [Al-Shaybani] said: We are averse to women fighting with men in combat. This is because women have no sincere firm will for fighting, as the Messenger of Allah (SAW) pointed out when He said [after passing by a slain woman]: "Huh, this one should not have been fighting." And perhaps, by having women fight, the weaknesses of the Muslims might be revealed, and the idolaters might rejoice at that; and perhaps this might be reason for the idolaters' determination against the Muslims, drawing the conclusion that the Muslims are weak, and they might say: They had to seek help from the women to fight us. So let them avoid this. For this reason it is not desirable that women go directly into fighting, except if the Muslims are compelled to this, since it is permissible, indeed obligatory, to drive away the adversity of the Idolaters when the need is clear, by whatever means the Muslims are able.

Al-Sarakhsi, *Sharh Kitab Al-siyar Al-kabir*, Section: women fighting with men, and being present for combat

---

> (و) يمنع (نساء) للافتتان بهن مع أنهن لسن من أهل القتال لاستيلاء الفتور والجبن عليهن ولأنه لا يؤمن ظفر العدو بهن فيستحلون منهن ما حرم الله تعالى قال بعضهم (إلا إمرأة الأمير لحاجته) لفعله ﷺ (و) إلا إمرأة (طاعنة في السن لمصلحة فقط كسقي الماء ومعالجة الجرحى) لقول الربيع بنت معوذ كنا نغزو مع النبي ﷺ نسقي الماء ونخدمهم ونردّ الجرحى والقتلى إلى المدينة رواه البخاري وعن أنس معناه رواه مسلم ولأن الرجال يشتغلون بالحرب عن ذلك فيكون معونة للمسلمين
>
> كشاف القناع عن متن الإقناع للبهوتي كتاب الجهاد باب ما يلزم الإمام والجيش

And women are prohibited, due to the temptation they cause, and because they are not meant to fight, as they are overcome by frailty and cowardice, and because there is no guarantee that the enemy will not take hold of them and find it permissible to do to them what Allah Most High has forbidden. Some say: except the emir's woman, to fulfill his need – based on what He (SAW) would do. And except women advanced in age, only to be of use, such as in supplying water and taking care of the injured, based on what Rubayyi' bint Mu'awwidh said: We used to go on attacks with the Prophet (SAW) to supply water and serve them, and we would bring the injured and the dead back to Medina. Al-Bukhari related this, and Muslim related similarly from Anas. Moreover men are distracted from battle by these things, so this would provide support for the Muslims.

Al-Buhuti, Kashaf Al-qina' 'an Matn Al-Iqnaa', The book of jihad, Section: the duties of the leader [imam] and the army

وإذا تزوج الحربي في دار الحرب إمرأة وابنتها في عقدة واحدة أو عقدتين ثم أسلموا قبل أن يمس واحدة منهما فعند ابي حنيفة رضي الله تعالى عنه إن كان تزوجهما في عقدة واحدة فنكاحهما فاسد وإن كان تزوجهما في عقدتين فنكاح الثانية فاسد وبمجرد العقد الصحيح على الإبنة تحرم الأم وبمجرد العقد على الأم لا تحرم الإبنة فلهذا صح نكاح البنت في الوجهين وبطل نكاح الأم وإن كان دخل بهما فنكاحهما باطل على كل حال بالاتفاق وإن كان دخل بإحداهما دون الأخرى فعلا قول محمد رحمه الله تعالى إن كان دخل بالأم بعدما تزوج الإبنة فنكاحهما باطل وإن كان دخل بالأم قبل أن يتزوج الابنة فنكاح الأم صحيح وإن كان دخل بالإبنة فنكاحها صحيح وإن كان تزوجهما في عقدتين فإن كان تزوج الإبنة أولاً ودخل بها فنكاحها صحيح ونكاح الأم باطل لأجل المصاهرة وإن كان دخل بالأم فنكاحهما باطل لأن العقد على الإبنة كان صحيحاً وذلك يوجب حرمة الأم وقد دخل بالأم وذلك يوجب حرمة الإبنة وإن كان تزوج الأم أولاً فإن دخل بها فنكاحها صحيح وإن دخل بالابنة بطل نكاحهما جميعاً لأن العقد على الإبنة لم يكن صحيحاً لمعنى الجمع والدخول بالابنة مبطل نكاح الأم ثم له أن يتزوج الإبنة دون الأم قال ولو تزوج الحربي أمة وحرة ثم أسلموا جاز نكاحهما في قول محمد رحمه الله قال وإذا تزوج الحربي أربع نسوة في عقدة أو عقدتين ثم سبي وسبين معه فعلى قول محمد رحمه الله تعالى يختار إثنتين منهن ولو تزوج حربي رضيعتين ثم أرضعتهما إمرأة ثم أسلموا فهذا وما لو كانتا أختين حين تزوجهما سواء على الخلاف الذي بينا وإن كانت امما أرضعتهما بعدما أسلموا فقد فسد نكاحهما جميعاً وكذلك لو أسلم الزوج وهم من أهل الكتاب ثم أرضعتهما إمرأة ولو كان تزوج الحربي كبيرة ورضيعة وللكبيرة لبن فأرضعت الصغيرة ثم أسلموا ففي قول ابي حنيفة رضي الله تعالى عنه نكاحهما فاسد ولو كان الارضاع بعد الاسلام بطل نكاحهما بالاتفاق بمنزلة ما لو تزوجهما بعد الاسلام وكذلك لو أسلم الزوج ثم أرضعت الكبيرة الصغيرة فقد فسد نكاحهما ولو كانت الكبيرة أسلمت وحدها ثم أرضعت الصغيرة فعند محمد رحمه الله يفسد نكاحها ويجوز نكاح البنت ولو كان الذي أسلم أبو الصغيرة ثم أرضعت الكبيرة الصغيرة فقد فسد نكاحهما جميعاً

كتاب السير الكبير للشيباني باب من نكاح أهل الحرب مما لا يجوز في دار الاسلام

If a fighter marries a woman and her daughter in enemy territory [dar al-harb] with a single marriage contract or with two contracts, and they yield into Islam before he has touched either of them, then according to Abu Hanifa (may Allah Most High be pleased with him): if he has married both of them in a single contract, marital relations [nikah] with them are invalid, but if he has married them in two contracts, marital relations with the second one are void, simply because a valid contract with the daughter makes the mother unlawful, but a contract with the mother does not make the daughter unlawful. For this reason marital relations with the daughter are upheld in both instances, while marital relations with the mother become invalid. If he has sex with both of them, then it is agreed that marital relations with both become invalid in all instances, but if he has sex with one of them and not the other, then according to what Muhammad (may Allah Most High have mercy on him) said, if he has sex with the mother after marrying with the daughter, then marital relations with both of them become invalid, but if he has sex with the mother before marrying with the daughter, then marital relations with the mother are sound; if he has sex with the daughter, then marital relations with her are sound. If he marries both of them with two separate contracts, and if he marries the daughter first, and has sex with her, then marital relations with her are sound and marital relations with the mother become invalid, due to the relationship established by marriage. But if he has sex with the mother, then marital relations with both of them become invalid, since the contract with the daughter was sound, and this necessarily prohibits the mother; however, he had sex with the mother, and this necessarily prohibits the daughter. If he marries the mother first, then if he has sex with her, marital relations with her are sound, but if he has sex with the daughter, marital relations with both of them become invalid, since the contract with the daughter was not sound, and by virtue of him getting together with and having sex with the daughter, this annuls marital relations with the mother. He may then marry the daughter without the mother. If an enemy fighter marries a servant girl and a free woman, and then they all yield into Islam, marital relations with both of them are permitted based on what Muhammad (may Allah have mercy on him) said. If a fighter marries four women in one contract or two, and is then taken prisoner, and the women are taken prisoner with him, then according to what Muhammad (may Allah Most High have mercy on him) said, he is to chose two of them. If a fighter marries two infant girls [radi'atain], and then another woman suckles them, and then they all yield into Islam, there is no difference between this and if the two of them were sisters when he married them, in contrast to what we explained earlier. If indeed she suckles both of them after they have yielded into Islam, then marital relations with both of them become invalid; similarly if the husband yields into Islam and they are People of the Book, and then another woman suckles them. If a fighter marries a grown girl and an infant girl, and the grown one has milk and suckles the little one, and then they yield into Islam, then according to what Abu Hanifa (may Allah Most High be pleased with him) said, marital relations with both of them become invalid. Even if the suckling occurred after the Islam [after becoming Muslims], it is agreed that marital relations with both of them become invalid, by the same consideration as if he had married them after the Islam; similarly if the husband yields into Islam and then the grown one suckles the little one – marital relations with both of them become invalid. If only the grown one yields into Islam, and then suckles the little one, then according to Muhammad (may Allah have mercy on him), marital relations with her become invalid, but marital relations with the girl are permitted. If the one who yields into Islam is the father of the little one, and then the grown one suckles the little one, marital relations with both of them become invalid.

Al-Shaybani, Kitab Al-siyar Al-kabir, Section: marital relations of the warring party [ahl al-harb] that are not permitted in Islamic territory [dar al-Islam]

قال ولو أن أهل بلدة ارتدوا حتى صارت دراهم دار الحرب ثم وقع الظهور عليهم فإنه يقتل رجالهم ويسبى نساءهم وذراريهم كما فعله الصديق رضي الله تعالى عنه ببني حنيفة حين ارتدوا فإن قالت النساء حين ظفر المسلمون بهن ما إرتددنا قط وانا لمسلمات على ديننا فالقول قولهن لتمسكهن بما هو الأصل وهو الاسلام ولا يسبين وأولادهن الصغار بمنزلتهن إلا أن تقوم البينة من المسلمين عليهن بالردة

كتاب السير الكبير للشيباني باب من ارتد من المسلمين أو نقض العهد من المعاهدين

If the inhabitants of a certain territory apostatize, such that their land now becomes enemy land [dar al-harb], and the upper hand is gained over them, then their men are to be killed and their women and children taken captive, just as Al-Siddiq (may Allah Most High be pleased with him) did with the Banu Hanifa when they apostatized. If the women, when the Muslims defeat them, say: "We have not apostatized at all – truly we are Muslimas in our religion", then they should say what they need to say for them to adhere to what is established, that is, Islam; and they are not taken captive, and likewise their young children, except if evidence arises among the Muslims of their apostasy.

Al-Shaybani, Kitab Al-siyar Al-kabir, Section: Muslims who apostatize or those who make covenants and violate them

عن الحسن قال لا تقتل النساء إذا هن إرتددن عن الاسلام ولكن يدعين إلى الاسلام فإن هن أبين سبين وجعلن إماء للمسلمين ولا يقتلن

المصنف لإبن ابي شيبة كتاب السير ما قالوا في المرتدة عن الاسلام

From Al-Hasan, who said: If women apostatize from Islam they are not to be killed, but they are to be called back to Islam; if they refuse, they are taken captive and made the Muslims' slave girls, but they are not killed.

Ibn Abi Shayba, The Musannaf, The book of campaigns, Section: what is said regarding women who apostatize from Islam

قد بينا في المبسوط أن سبي أحد الزوجين موجب للفرقة لا لعينه بل لتباين الدارين حقيقةً أو حكماً بين الزوجين ولهذا لم تقع الفرقة إذا سبيا معاً فنقول إذا سبيت المرأة وأخرجت إلى دار الإسلام فلمن وقعت في سهمه أن يطأها بعدما يستبرئها بحيضة إن لم تكن حاملاً وبوضع الحمل إن كانت حاملاً

كتاب السير الكبير للشيباني باب الاستبراء

We have made clear in *Al-mabsut* that taking one of two spouses captive necessarily means their separation, not because of each other but because of the difference in the two territories, either in actual reality or in legal consequence. Because of this there is no separation if they are taken captive together. We say that whenever a woman is taken captive and brought into Islamic territory, the person into whose portion she falls may have sex with her after he observes the period of abstinence of one menstrual cycle if she is not pregnant, or by giving birth if she is pregnant.

Al-Shaybani, Kitab Al-siyar Al-kabir, Section: required periods of abstinence [istibra']

الكبيرة التسعون والحادية والثانية والتسعون بعد الثلثمائة ترك الجهاد عند تعينه بأن داخل الحربيون دار الإسلام أو اخذوا مسلماً وأمكن تخليصه منهم وترك الناس الجهاد من أصله وترك أهل الاقليم تحصين ثغورهم بحيث يخاف عليها من إستيلاء الكفار بسبب ترك ذلك التحصين

الزواجر عن إقتراف الكبائر لإبن حجر الهيتمي كتاب الجهاد

The three hundred nintieth, ninety-first, and ninety-second major sins are: neglecting *jihad* when it is called for due to enemy fighters entering Islamic territory or seizing a Muslim, with the possibility of rescuing him from them; fundamental neglect of *jihad*; and the neglect of the inhabitants of a region to fortify the passages that they fear the disbelievers might capture if such fortification is neglected.

Ibn Hajar Al-Haytami, Al-zawajir 'an Iqtiraf Al-kaba'ir, The book of jihad

الصديق وسائر الصحابة بدؤوا بجهاد المرتدين قبل جهاد الكفار من أهل الكتاب فإن جهاد هؤلاء حفظ لما فتح من بلاد المسلمين وأن يدخل فيه من أراد الخروج عنه وجهاد من لم يقاتلنا من المشركين وأهل الكتاب من زيادة إظهار الدين وحفظ رأس المال مقدم على الربح

مجموع الفتاوى لإبن تيمية كتاب الحدود باب حكم المرتد

Al-Siddiq and the rest of the Companions began with *jihad* against the apostates before *jihad* against the Disbelievers from among the People of the Book. Indeed *jihad* against these people safeguards Muslim lands that have been granted victory, and that those who desire to depart will remain there. *Jihad* against the idolaters and People of the Book who do not fight us is further manifestation of the religion. Safeguarding the capital takes precedence over profits.

Ibn Taymiyya, Majmu' Al-fatawa, The book of legal punishments [hudud], Section: the rulings for apostates

عن جبير بن حية قال بعث عمر الناس في أفناء الأمصار يقاتلون المشركين فأسلم الهرمزان فقال إني مستشيرُك في مغازيَّ هذه قال نعم مثلها ومثل من فيها من الناس من عدو المسلمين مثل طائر له رأس وله جناحان وله رجلان فإن كُسر أحد الجناحين نهضت الرجلان بجناح والرأس فإن كسر الجناح الآخر نهضت الرجلان والرأس وإن شُدخ الرأس ذهبت الرجلان والجناحان والرأس فالرأس كسرى والجناح قيصر والجناح الاخر فارس فُرَّ المسلمين فلينفروا إلى كسرى وقال بكر وزياد جميعاً عن جبير بن حية قال فندبنا عمر واستعمل علينا النعمان بن مقرن حتى إذا كنّا بأرض العدو وخرج علينا عامل كسرى في أربعين ألفاً فقام تُرجُمان فقال ليكلِّمني رجل منكم فقال المغيرة سَل عما شئتَ قال ما أنتم قال نحن أناس من العرب كنّا في شقاءٍ شديد وبَلاءٍ شديد نَمَصّ الجلد والنوى من الجوع ونلبس الوَبَر والشعر ونعبد الشجر والحجر فبينا نحن كذلك إذ بعث رب السموات ورب الأرضين تعالى ذكره وجَلّت عظمته إلينا نبياً من أنفسنا نعرف أباه وأمه فأمرنا نبينا رسول ربنا ﷺ أن نقاتلكم حتى تعبدوا الله وحده أو تؤَدّوا الجزية وأخبرنا نبينا ﷺ عن رسالة ربنا أنه من قُتل منا صار إلى الجنة في نعيم لم ير مثلها قط ومن بقي منا ملك ملك رقابكم

صحيح البخاري كتاب الجزية والموادعة

From Jubair ibn Hayya, who said: 'Umar would send people out to regions of large cities to fight the idolaters [*Mushrikeen*]. And Al-Hurmuzan yielded into Islam; 'Umar said: Indeed I want to ask your advice about these attacks of mine. He said: Sure; the people there who are enemies of the Muslims are like a bird who has a head, two wings, and two legs; if one if the wings is broken, its legs will rise with one wing and the head, if the other wing is broken, its legs will rise with the head, but if its head gets smashed in, then the two legs, the two wings, and the head will come to nothing. The head is Kisra [Khosrow], one wing is Caesar, and the other wing is Faris; so command the Muslims to mobilize towards Khosrow. Bakr and Ziyad both related from Jubair ibn Hayya, who said: So 'Umar charged us and put Al-Nu'man ibn Muqarrin as our leader, until we reached the land of the enemy. A representative of Khosrow came out to us with forty thousand men, and an interpreter got up and said: Let one of your men talk to me. Al-Mughira said: Ask whatever you wish. He said: Who are you all? He said: We are people of the Arabs; we were under great misery and affliction, sucking on skins and seed pits out of hunger, dressed in camel and rabbit hair and pelts, worshipping trees and stones; and while we were in this state, indeed the Lord of the heavens and Lord of the earths – may His remembrance be exalted and his greatness revered – sent forth to us a prophet from among us, whose father and mother we knew; our Prophet, the Messenger of our Lord (SAW), ordered us to fight you until you worship Allah alone or fulfill the *jizya*; and our Prophet (SAW) made the message of our Lord known to us that whoever of us gets killed goes to *Jannah* in bliss like he has never seen, and whoever of us remains will be master of your necks.

Sahih Al-Bukhari, The book of jizya and peacemaking

ويجب على كل مسلم أن يقوم في ذلك بحسب ما يقدر عليه من الواجب فلا يحل لأحد أن يكتم ما يعرفه من أخبارهم بل يفشيها ويظهرها ليعرف المسلمين حقيقة حالهم ولا يحل لأحد أن يعاونهم على بقائهم في الجند والمستخدمين ولا يحل لأحد السكوت عن القيام عليهم بما أمر الله به ورسوله ولا يحل لأحد أن ينهى عن القيام بما أمر الله به ورسوله فإن هذا من أعظم أبواب الأمر بالمعروف والنهي عن المنكر والجهاد في سبيل الله تعالى وقد قال الله تعالى لنبيه ﷺ ﴿ يا أيها النبي جاهد الكفار والمنافقين وأغلظ عليهم ﴾ وهؤلاء لا يخرجون عن الكفار والمنافقين

والمعاون على كف شرهم وهدايتهم بحسب الإمكان له من الأجر والثواب ما لا يعلمه إلا الله تعالى فإن المقصود بالقصد الأول هو هدايتهم كما قال الله تعالى ﴿ كنتم خير أمة أخرجت للناس ﴾ قال أبو هريرة كنتم خير الناس للناس تأتون بهم في القيود والسلاسل حتى تدخلوهم الاسلام فالمقصود بالجهاد والأمر بالمعروف والنهي عن المنكر هداية العباد لمصالح المعاش والمعاد بحسب الامكان فمن هداه الله سعد في الدنيا والآخرة ومن لم يهتد كف الله ضرره عن غيره

مجموع الفتاوى لإبن تيمية كتاب الحدود باب حكم المرتد

Every Muslim is obliged to undertake whatever duty he can regarding this. No one is permitted to conceal any information about them that he is aware of, but rather he is to disclose and announce it so that the Muslims can accurately know their situation. No one is permitted to aid them in staying among the soldiers or hired men. No one is permitted to remain silent in carrying out against them what Allah and His Messenger have ordered. No one is permitted to disallow carrying out what Allah and His Messenger have ordered. For indeed this is one of the greatest ways to prescribe what is right and prohibit what is wrong, and *jihad* in the cause of Allah Most High; Allah Most High said to His Prophet (SAW): { Oh Prophet! Wage *jihad* on the Disbelievers and the hypocrites, and be harsh to them } [Al-tahrim 9]. Such people do not in fact oppose the Disbelievers and hypocrites.

Anyone who aids in the cessation of their evil, and in guiding them to the extent possible, his is the reward and the recompense that only Allah knows. Indeed the purpose of the first aim is to guide them, as Allah Most High has said: { You all are the best nation that has been sent out to people } [Al 'Imran 110]. Abu Huraira said: You are the best people for people, you who bring them in shackles and chains until you make them enter Islam. The purpose of *jihad*, and prescribing what is right and prohibiting what is wrong, is to guide humanity to what is beneficial in living and in the hereafter, to the extent possible; for whoever Allah guides is happy in this world and in the next, although whoever is not guided – Allah will hold back his detriment from others.

Ibn Taymiyya, Majmu' Al-fatawa, The book of legal punishments [hudud], Section: the rulings for apostates

عن أنس بن مالك قال لما توفي رسول الله ﷺ ارتدّت العرب قال عمر يا أبا بكر كيف تقاتل العرب فقال أبو بكر إنما قال رسول الله ﷺ أمرت أن أقاتل الناس حتى يقولوا لا إله إلا الله وأني رسول الله ويقيموا الصلاة ويؤتوا الزكاة والله لو منعوني عناقاً مما كانوا يعطون رسول الله ﷺ لقاتلتهم عليه قال عمر فلما رأيت رأي أبي بكر قد شرح عرفت أنه الحق

السنن الكبرى للنسائي كتاب المحاربة

From Anas ibn Malik, who said: When the Messenger of Allah (SAW) passed away, the Arabs apostatized. 'Umr said: Oh Abu Bakr, how are you going to fight the Arabs?! Abu Bakr said: Indeed the Messenger of Allah (SAW) said "I have been ordered to fight people until they say 'There is no god but Allah' ['*La ilaha illa Allah*'] and that I am the Messenger of Allah, and observe prayer, and give *zakat*"; and I swear by Allah that even if they withheld from me a young she-goat that they had given to the Messenger of Allah (SAW), I would fight them for it. 'Umar said: When I saw Abu Bakr's attitude and how he had been laid bare, I knew that it was true.

Al-Nasa'i, Al-sunan Al-kubra, The book of warfare

عن أبي هريرة قال لما توفي رسول الله ﷺ واستخلف أبو بكر بعده وكفر من كفر من العرب قال عمر لأبي بكر كيف تقاتل الناس وقد قال رسول الله ﷺ أمرت أن أقاتل الناس حتى يقولوا لا إله إلا الله فمن قال لا إله إلا الله عصم مني ماله ونفسه إلا بحقه وحسابه على الله فقال والله لأقاتلنّ من فرّق بين الصلاة والزكاة فإن الزكاة حق المال والله لو منعوني عقالاً كانوا يؤدّونه إلى رسول الله ﷺ لقاتلتهم على منعه فقال عمر فوالله ما هو إلا أن رأيت الله قد شرح صدر أبي بكر للقتال فعرفت أنه الحق

صحيح البخاري كتاب الاعتصام بالكتاب والسنة

From Abu Huraira, who said: When the Messenger of Allah (SAW) passed away, and Abu Bakr was made caliph after him, and whoever of the Arabs who apostatized had apostatized, 'Umar said to Abu Bakr: How are you going to fight people, seeing that the Messenger of Allah (SAW) said "I have been commanded to fight people until they say 'There is no god but Allah', and whoever says 'There is no god but Allah' has kept their property and themself safe from me, except when these are due, and his reckoning is with Allah"? Abu Bakr replied: I swear by Allah truly I will fight anyone who makes a distinction between prayer and *zakat*; indeed *zakat* is a monetary duty; and I swear by Allah even if they withheld from me a hobbling cord that they had provided to the Messenger of Allah (SAW), I would fight them for keeping it! And 'Umar said: Indeed I swear by Allah, when I had only seen Allah lay open Abu Bakr's chest for fighting, I knew that it was true.

Sahih Al-Bukhari, The book of adherence to the Book and the Sunnah

عن إبن جريج قال أخبرني حيان عن أبن شهاب أنه قال إذا أشرك المسلم دُعِيَ إلى الاسلام ثلاث مرات فإن أبى ضُربت عنقه
المصنف لعبد الرزاق كتاب العقول باب الكفر بعد الإيمان

From Ibn Juraij, who said: Hayyan related to me from Ibn Shihab that he said: If a Muslim commits *shirk* [ascribing others in worship to Allah], he is to be called back to Islam three times; but if he refuses, he is decapitated.

'Abd Al-Razzaq, the Musannaf, The book of blood monies, Section: disbelief after having believed

عن ابي عمرو الشيباني أن المستورد العجلي تنصّر بعد اسلامه فبعث به عتبة بن فرقد إلى علي فاستتابة فلم يتُب فقتله فطلبت النصارى جيفته بثلاثين ألفاً فأبى وأحرقه
المصنف لعبد الرزاق كتاب العقول باب الكفر بعد الإيمان

'Amr Al-Shaybani related that Al-Mustawrid Al-'Ijli became a Christian after having been in Islam. So 'Utba ibn Farqad sent word of this to 'Ali; he called him to repent, but he did not repent, so he killed him. And the Christians asked for his carcass [*jifa*] for thirty thousand, but he refused, then burned him.

'Abd Al-Razzaq, the Musannaf, The book of blood monies, Section: disbelief after having believed

عبد الملك بن عمير قال شهدت علياً رضي الله عنه وأتي بأخي بني عجل المستورد بن قبيصة تنصر بعد اسلامه فقال له علي رضي الله عنه ما حُدِّثتُ عنك قال ما حدثت عني قال أنك تنصرت قال أنا على دين المسيح فقال له علي وأنا على دين المسيح فقال له علي ما تقول فيه فتكلم بكلام خفيَ علي فقال علي طؤوه فوطئ حتى مات فقلت للذي يليني ما قال قال المسيح ربه
السنن الكبرى للبيهقي كتاب المرتد باب من قال في المرتد يستتاب مكانه فإن تاب وإلا قتل

'Abd Al-Malik ibn 'Umair said: I was with 'Ali (may Allah be pleased with him), and he had brought a brother of mine from the Banu 'Ijl, Al-Mustawrid ibn Qabisa, who had become a Christian after having been in Islam. 'Ali (may Allah be pleased with him) said to him: What have I been told about you? He replied: What have you been told about me? 'Ali said: I have been told that you have become a Christian. He said: I am in the religion of the Messiah. 'Ali said to him: And I am in the religion of the Messiah. Then 'Ali asked him: What do you say about him? And he said something that made 'Ali change his look. Then 'Ali said: Trample him! So he was trampled until he died. Then I asked the person close to me: What did he say? He replied: He said that the Messiah is his lord.

Al-Bayhaqi, Al-sunan Al-kubra, The book of apostates, Section: those who say regarding apostates that they are to be called to repentance on the spot, and if they repent, fine, otherwise they are killed

عن ابي عمرو الشيباني أن رجلاً تنصر بعد إسلامه فأتي به علي لجعل يعرض عليه فقال ما أدري ما يقول غير أنه شهد أن المسيح إبن الله فوثب إليه علي فوطئه وأمر الناس أن يطؤوه ثم قال كُفوا فكفوا عنه وقد مات

معرفة السنن والآثار للبيهقي كتاب المرتد المكره على الردة

Abu 'Amr Al-Shaybani related that a certain man became a Christian after having been in Islam, and he was brought to 'Ali, who asked to be told about him. And the person said: The only thing I know he said was that he bears witness that the Messiah is the son of Allah. Then 'Ali rushed on him and trampled him, and ordered the people to trample him. Then he said: That's enough! So they stopped, since he had already died.

Al-Bayhaqi, Ma'rifa Al-sunan wa Al-athar, The book of apostates, Section: those forced to apostatize

عن إبن عباس قال لا يساكنكم اليهود والنصارى في أمصاركم فمن أسلم منهم ثم إرتد فلا تضربوا إلا عنقه

المصنف لإبن ابي شيبة كتاب السير ما قالوا في الرجل يسلم ثم يرتد ما يصنع به

From Ibn 'Abbas, who said: Let not the Jews and Christians live with you all in your cities; whoever of them yields into Islam but then apostatizes – strike his head off straightaway.

Ibn Abi Shayba, The Musannaf, The book of campaigns, Section: what is said regarding a man who yields into Islam and then apostatizes; what should be done with him?

عن علي بن ابي طالب أنه أتي برجل كان نصرانياً فأسلم ثم تنصر فسأله عمر عن كلمة فقال له فقام إليه علي فرفسه برجله فقام الناس إليه فضربوه حتى قتلوه

المصنف لإبن ابي شيبة كتاب السير ما قالوا في الرجل يسلم ثم يرتد ما يصنع به

A certain man was brought to 'Ali ibn Abi Talib who had been a Christian, and yielded into Islam, then became a Christian again. 'Umar asked him for a word, and he said something. Then 'Ali got up towards him and kicked him with his foot; and the people got up and beat him until they killed him.

Ibn Abi Shayba, The Musannaf, The book of campaigns, Section: what is said regarding a man who yields into Islam and then apostatizes; what should be done with him?

ولما كان من أفضل الجهاد قول ألحق مع شدة المعارض مثل أن يتكلم به عند من تُخاف سطوته وأذاه كان للرسول صلوات الله عليه وسلامه من ذلك الحظّ الأوفر وكان لنبينا صلوات الله عليه وسلامه من ذلك أكمل الجهاد وأتمّه ولما كان جهاد أعداء الله في الخارج فرعاً على جهاد العبد نفسه في ذات الله كما قال النبي ﷺ المجاهد من جاهد نفسه في طاعة الله والمجاهد من هجر ما نهى الله عنه كان جهاد النفس مقدماً على جهاد العدو في الخارج وأصلاً له فإنه ما لم يجاهد نفسه أولاً لتفعل ما أُمرت به وتترك ما نُهيت عنه ويحاربها في الله لم يمكنه جهاد عدوه في الخارج فكيف يمكنه جهاد عدوه والانتصاف منه وعدوه الذي بين جنبيه قاهرٌ له متسلّطٌ عليه لم يجاهده ولم يحاربه في الله بل لا يمكنه الخروج إلى عدوه حتى يجاهد نفسه على الخروج فهذان عدوان قد إمتحن العبد بجهادهما وبينهما عدو ثالث لا يمكنه جهادهما إلا بجهاده وهو واقف بينهما يثبّط العبد عن جهادهما ويخذّله ويُرجف به ولا يزال يخيّل له ما في جهادهما من المشاق وترك الحظوظ وفوت اللذات والمشتهيات ولا يمكنه أن يجاهد ذينك العدوين إلا بجهاده فكان جهاده هو الأصل لجهادهما وهو الشيطان قال تعالى ﴿ إِنَّ الشَّيْطَانَ لَكُمْ عَدُوٌّ فَاتَّخِذُوهُ عَدُوّاً ﴾ والأمر باتخاذه عدواً تنبيه على استفراغ الوُسع في محاربته ومجاهدته كأنه عدو لا يفتُر ولا يقصّر عن محاربة العبد على عدد الأنفاس فهذه ثلاثة أعداء أمر العبد بمحاربتها وجهادها وقد بُلي بمحاربتها في هذه الدار وسُلّطت عليه إمتحاناً من الله له وإبتلاء فأعطى الله العبد مدداً وعُدَّةً وأعواناً وسلاحاً لهذا الجهاد وأعطى أعداءه مدداً وعدةً وأعواناً وسلاحاً وبلا أحد الفريقين بالآخر وجعل بعضهم لبعض فتنة ليبلو أخبارهم ويمتحن ممن يتولّاه ويتولى رسله ممن يتولى الشيطان وحزبه كما قال تعالى ﴿ وَجَعَلْنَا بَعْضَكُمْ لِبَعْضٍ فِتْنَةً أَتَصْبِرُونَ وَكَانَ رَبُّكَ بَصِيراً ﴾ وقال تعالى ﴿ ذَلِكَ وَلَوْ يَشَاءُ اللَّهُ لَانْتَصَرَ مِنْهُمْ وَلَكِن لِّيَبْلُوَ بَعْضَكُم بِبَعْضٍ ﴾ وقال تعالى ﴿ وَلَنَبْلُوَنَّكُمْ حَتَّى نَعْلَمَ الْمُجَاهِدِينَ مِنكُمْ وَالصَّابِرِينَ وَنَبْلُوَ أَخْبَارَكُمْ ﴾

زاد المعاد لإبن قيم الجهاد والغزوات في هديه ﷺ في الجهاد والمغازي والسرايا والبعوث

Since part of the best *jihad* is to speak the truth, in spite of the severity of those who oppose, just like you tell it in the face of someone from whom you fear attack or harm, the Messenger (the prayers of Allah and His peace be upon him) had the most good fortune in this, and our Prophet (the prayers of Allah and His peace be upon him) had the most perfect and most complete *jihad* in this respect.

And since *jihad* against the enemies of Allah on the outside is part of one's *jihad* against himself for the sake of Allah, as the Prophet (SAW) said: A *Mujahid* is one who wages *jihad* on himself in obedience to Allah, and a *Mujahid* is one who abstains from what Allah has forbidden, therefore *jihad* against the self precedes *jihad* against the enemy on the outside, and is the basis for it. Indeed as long as one does not first wage *jihad* against his self, so that it does what it has been commanded to do, and abandons what it has been forbidden to do, and if one does not combat it for Allah, he will not be able to wage *jihad* against the enemy on the outside. And how can he wage *jihad* on his enemy and take revenge on him while his enemy – the one between his own flanks – has conquered him and prevailed over him? He can not wage *jihad* on him nor combat him for Allah, but instead will be unable to set out towards his enemy until he wages *jihad* on himself in priority to setting out.

These are two enemies by which a man is put to the test in *jihad* against them. But between them there is yet a third enemy, by which one is not able to wage *jihad* against the other two except by *jihad* against this one. He stands between the two, frustrating a man from *jihad* against the other two; he will betray him, spread lies about him, and will not cease to give him the impression of hardship in *jihad* against the other two, neglect of his good fortune, and the loss of delights and desires. One can not wage *jihad* against those two enemies except by *jihad* against this one, and *jihad* against this one is the basis for *jihad* against the other two. This is Satan. Allah Most high said: { Truly Satan is an enemy to you, so take him as an enemy } [*Al-fatir* 6]. The command to take him as an enemy is a warning to expend one's full capacity in combatting him and striving in *jihad* against him, as he is an enemy who does not grow weary and does not fail to war against a man in a number of ways.

A man is commanded to combat and wage *jihad* on these three enemies; he is put to the test in combatting them in this world, and they have been given power over him as a test to him from Allah and as a tribulation. To His servants Allah has given reinforcements, gear, assistance, and weapons for this *jihad*. And He has also given their enemies reinforcements, gear, assistance, and weapons. Each of the two groups is put to the test by the other, and He has made each a trial for the other, so that He might know what they do, and to discern those who turn away from Him and His Messengers from those who turn away from Satan and his party. As the Most High said: { We have made some of you a trial for others; will you be steadfast? And your Lord is aware } [*Al-furqan* 20]; and the Most High said: { Such it is; and if Allah had willed, He would have avenged Himself of them, but rather that some of you might put others of you to the test } [*Muhammad* 4]; and the Most High said: { Surely We will put you all to the test so We can know those among you who wage jihad, and those who are steadfast; and We will test your reports } [*Muhammad* 31].

Ibn Qayyim, Zad Al-Ma'ad, Jihad and Raids, Section: regarding his (SAW) guidance in jihad and making incursions [*maghazi*], troops, and sending out detachments

وأكمل الخلَق عند الله من كلّ مراتب الجهاد كلها والخلق متفاوتون في منازلهم عند الله تفاوتهم في مراتب الجهاد ولهذا كان أكمل الخلق وأكرمهم على الله خاتم أنبيائه ورسله فإنه كمل كل مراتب الجهاد وجاهد في الله حق جهاده وشرع في الجهاد من حين بُعث الى أن توفاه الله عز وجل فإنه لما نزل عليه ﴿ يا أيها المدَّثِّر قم فأنذر وربك فكبِّر وثيابك فطهِّر ﴾ شمَّر عن ساق الدعوة وقام في ذات الله أتمَّ قيام ودعا إلى الله ليلاً ونهاراً وسرّاً وجهاراً ولما نزل عليه ﴿ فاصدع بما تؤمر ﴾ فصدع بأمر الله لا تأخذه فيه لومة لائم فدعا إلى الله الصغير والكبير والحر والعبد والذكَّر والانثى والأحمر والأسود والجن والانس

زاد المعاد لإبن قيم الجهاد والغزوات

The most perfect of people in the sight of Allah are those who accomplish all of the degrees of *jihad*. People diverge in their standing with Allah; their divergence concerns the degrees of *jihad*. This is why the most perfect of people and the most noble of them unto Allah is the Seal of His prophets and messengers; indeed He completed the degrees of *jihad*. He waged *jihad* for Allah as is due His *jihad*, and set out to wage *jihad* from the time he was sent forth until Allah Mighty and Sublime took him. Indeed, when this came down to him: { Oh enshrouded one! Arise and warn, and make your Lord great, and purify your garments } [Al-muddathir 1-4], He rolled up his sleeves and got to work in making the call to people, and undertook the most complete undertaking for the sake of Allah; He called people to Allah day and night, in private and openly. When this came down to him: { So come out openly with what you have been commanded } [Al-hijr 94], He came out openly with the commands of Allah, with no regard for the rebukes of the rebukers, and He called people to Allah, young and old, free and slaves, male and female, red and black [i.e. all mankind], genies [*jinn*] and men.

Ibn Qayyim, Zad Al-Ma'ad, Jihad and Raids

ولما مصّ مالك أبو ابي سعيد الخدري جرح رسول الله ﷺ حتى أنقاه قال له مجّه قال والله لا أمجه أبداً ثم أدبر فقال النبي ﷺ من أراد أن ينظر إلى رجلٍ من أهل الجنة فلينظر إلى هذا

زاد المعاد لابن قيم الجهاد والغزوات في غزوة أحد

When Malik Abu Abi Sa'id Al-Khudri sucked on the Messenger of Allah's (SAW) wounds until he had cleansed them, He said to him: Spit it out. He replied: I swear by Allah I will never spit it out. Then he turned and left. And the Prophet (SAW) said: Whoever wants to see a man from among the inhabitants of *Jannah*, let him look at this man.

Ibn Qayyim, Zad Al-Ma'ad, Jihad and Raids, Section: regarding the attack at Uhud

فنها محاربة الكفار ومقاتلتهم في الأشهر الحرم فإن رسول الله ﷺ رجع من الحديبية في ذي الحجة فمكث بها أياماً ثم سار إلى خيبر في المحرم كذلك قال الزهري عن عروة عن مروان والمسور بن مخرمة وكذلك قال الواقدي خرج في أول سنة سبع من الهجرة ولكن في الاستدلال بذلك نظر فإن خروجه كان في اواخر المحرم لا في أوله وفتحها كان في صفر وأقوى من هذا الاستدلال بيعة النبي ﷺ أصحابه عند الشجرة بيعة الرضوان على القتال وألا يفرّوا وكانت في ذي القعدة ولكن لا دليل في ذلك لأنه إنما بايعهم على ذلك لما بلغه أنهم قد قتلوا عثمان وهم يريدون قتاله فحينئذ بايع الصحابة ولا خلاف في جواز القتال في الشهر الحرم إذا بدأ العدو وإنما الخلاف أن يقاتل فيه إبتداء فالجمهور جوّزوه وقالوا تحريم القتال فيه منسوخ وهو مذهب الأئمة الأربعة رحمهم الله

زاد المعاد لابن قيم الجهاد والغزوات فصل فيما كان في غزوة خيبر من الأحكام الفقهية

Included [in the legal rulings from Khaibar] is the waging of war on the disbelievers [*kuffar*] and fighting them during the sacred months. Indeed the Messenger of Allah (SAW) returned from Hudaibiyya in the month of *Dhu Al-hijja*, and remained for a few days, then He set out towards Khaibar in the month of *Muharram*. For this reason Al-Zuhri related from 'Urwa, from Marwan and Miswar ibn Makhrama, and Al-Waqidi said as well: He set out at the beginning of year seven following the *hijra*, although regarding the reasoning from this there is one judgment: Indeed He set out at the end of the month of *Muharram*, not in the beginning of it, and the victory there was in the month of *Safar*. Even more convincing than this reasoning is the Prophet's (SAW) pledge He took from his Companions at the tree, the pledge of agreement to fight, and that they would not run away. This was in the month of *Dhu Al-Qa'da*. However there is no evidence in this, because He took the pledge from them when He became aware that they had killed 'Uthman while wanting to fight him, and so He then took the pledge from the Companions. There is no disagreement regarding the permissibility of fighting during a sacred month, whenever the enemy initiates it; the disagreement is if fighting can be initiated then. The majority made it permissible, saying that the prohibition of fighting at those times was abrogated; and this is the position taken by the Four Imams (may Allah have mercy on them).

Ibn Qayyim, Zad Al-Ma'ad, Jihad and Raids, Section: regarding the legal rulings from the attack at Khaybar

فالشوق يحمل المشتاق على الجد في السير إلى محبوبه ويقرّب عليه الطريق ويطوي له البعيد ويهوّن عليه الآلام والمشاقّ وهو من أعظم نعمةٍ أنعم الله بها على عبده

زاد المعاد لإبن قيم الجهاد والغزوات

The yearning is what makes someone who yearns strive forward towards the beloved, brings the path near to him, hastens what is far away, and makes afflictions and hardship easy for him; it is of the greatest grace by which Allah graces His servants.

Ibn Qayyim, Zad Al-Ma'ad, Jihad and Raids

وقد قدمنا أن أبا رافع كان ممن ألّب الاحزاب على رسول الله ﷺ ولم يُقتل مع بني قريظة كما قتل صاحبه حيي بن أخطب ورغبت الخزرج في قتله مساواةً للأوس في قتل كعب بن الأشرف وكان الله سبحانه وتعالى قد جعل هذين الحيّين يتصاولان بين يدي رسول الله ﷺ في الخيرات فإستأذنوه في قتله فأذن لهم فإنتدب له رجال كلهم من بني سلمة وهم عبدالله بن عتيك وهو أمير القوم وعبدالله بن أنيس وابو قتادة الحارث بن

ربعي ومسعود بن سنان وخزاعي بن أسود فساروا حتى أتوه في خيبر في دار له فنزلوا عليه ليلاً فقتلوه ورجعوا إلى رسول الله ﷺ وكلهم ادّعى قتله فقال أروني أسيافكم فلما أروه اياها قال لسيف عبدالله بن أنيس هذا الذي قتله أرى فيه أثر الطعام

زاد المعاد لإبن قيم الجهاد والغزوات

We have already related how Abu Rafi' was among those who incited the Confederates against the Messenger of Allah (SAW), and how he was not killed with the Banu Quraiza like his companion Huyay ibn Akhtab was. And the Khazraj [a tribe among the *Ansar*] wanted to kill him to have the same standing as the Aws people, who had killed Ka'b ibn Al-Ashraf. (Allah – most High and Exalted – had made these two tribes go after each other in front of the Messenger of Allah (SAW) in regards to the blessings.) So the people sought permission from him to kill him, and He gave them permission, so they assigned some men, all of them from the Banu Salama; these were Abdullah ibn 'Atik, the people's leader, Abdullah ibn Unais, Abu Qatada Al-Harith ibn Rib'i, Mas'ud ibn Sanan, and Khuza'i ibn Aswad. They set out until they reached him at Khaybar in a dwelling of his, and they descended upon him at night and killed him. Then they returned to the Messenger of Allah (SAW), and all of them claimed to have killed him. So He said: Show me your swords. And when they showed them to him, He said to the sword of Abdullah ibn Unais: This is the one who killed him – I can see traces of food on it.

Ibn Qayyim, Zad Al-Ma'ad, Jihad and Raids

وانتهى أنس بن النضر إلى عمر بن الخطاب وطلحة بن عبيدالله في رجال من المهاجرين والأنصار وقد ألقوا بأيديهم فقال ما يُجلسكم فقالوا قُتل رسول الله ﷺ فقال فما تصنعون بالحياة بعده فقوموا فموتوا على ما مات عليه رسول الله ﷺ ثم إستقبل القوم فقاتل حتى قُتل

زاد المعاد لإبن قيم الجهاد والغزوات في غزوة أحد

Anas ibn Al-Nadr ran into 'Umar ibn Al-Khattab and Talha ibn 'Ubaid Allah by some men of the Emigrants [*Muhajireen*] and the Helpers [*Ansar*] who had given themselves up, and he said: What has made you all sit down? They said: the Messenger of Allah (SAW) has been killed. And he said: So what are you all going to do with your life after him? Get up and die as the Messenger of Allah (SAW) died! Then He went to face the people, and fought until he was killed.

Ibn Qayyim, Zad Al-Ma'ad, Jihad and Raids, Section: regarding the attack at Uhud

ومنها جواز الغزو بالنساء والاستعانة بهن في الجهاد

زاد المعاد لإبن قيم الجهاد والغزوات فيما اشتملت عليه هذه الغزاة من الأحكام والفقه

Among them [the rulings] is the permissibility of setting out on attacks with women, and seeking help from them in *jihad*.

Ibn Qayyim, Zad Al-Ma'ad, Jihad and Raids, Section: regarding the rulings and laws comprised in this attack

ومنها جواز دعاء الرجل أن يُقتل في سبيل الله وتمنيه ذلك وليس هذا من تمني الموت المنهي عنه كما قال عبدالله بن جحش اللهم لقِّني من المشركين رجلاً عظيماً كفره شديداً حرده فأقاتله فيقتلني فيك ويسلبني ثم يجدع أنفي وأذني فإذا لقيتَك فقلتَ يا عبدالله بن جحش فيم جُدعْت قلت فيك يا رب

زاد المعاد لإبن قيم الجهاد والغزوات فيما اشتملت عليه هذه الغزاة من الأحكام والفقه

Among the rulings is the permissibility for a man to make supplication to be killed in the cause of Allah and for him to desire this. This is not merely a desire for death, which is prohibited. As Abdullah ibn Jahsh said: Oh Allah! Let me face someone from among the Idolaters, whose disbelief is great and whose fury is strong, and I will fight him, and he will kill me for you, and plunder me, then cut off my nose and ears; then when I meet you, you say: Oh Abdullah ibn Jahsh, for what were you mutilated? And I will say: For you, oh Lord!

Ibn Qayyim, Zad Al-Ma'ad, Jihad and Raids, Section: regarding the rulings and laws comprised in this attack

ومنها أن المسلم إذا قتل نفسه فهو من أهل النار لقوله ﷺ في قزمان الذي أبلى يوم أحد بلاءً شديداً فلما اشتدت به الجراح نحر نفسه فقال ﷺ هو من أهل النار

زاد المعاد لإبن قيم الجهاد والغزوات فيما اشتملت عليه هذه الغزاة من الأحكام والفقه

Among the rulings is that if a Muslim kills himself, he will be among those in Hellfire, from what He (SAW) said regarding Qurman, who was put to the test severely on the day of Uhud, and when his wounds became intense, he slayed himself; He (SAW) said: He will be among those in Hellfire.

Ibn Qayyim, Zad Al-Ma'ad, Jihad and Raids, Section: regarding the rulings and laws comprised in this attack

ومنها جواز بناء الرجل بامرأته في السفر وركوبها معه على دابة بين الجيش

زاد المعاد لإبن قيم الجهاد والغزوات فصل فيما كان في غزوة خيبر من الأحكام الفقهية

Among the rulings is the permissibility for a man to have sex with his woman while journeying, and for her to ride with him on an animal among the army.

Ibn Qayyim, Zad Al-Ma'ad, Jihad and Raids, Section: regarding the legal rulings from the attack at Khaybar

وفيها جواز تبييت الكفار ومغافصتهم في ديارهم إذا كانت قد بلغتهم الدعوة وقد كانت سرايا رسول الله ﷺ يبيّتون الكفار ويُغيرون عليهم بإذنه بعد أن بلغتهم دعوته

زاد المعاد لإبن قيم الجهاد والغزوات فصل في الإشارة إلى ما في الغزوة من الفقه واللطائف

In these is the permissibility to plot by night against the disbelievers and to take them unexpectedly in their homes, provided the call [da'wah] has been made to them; the Messenger of Allah's (SAW) troops would plot by night against the Disbelievers and make raids on them with his permission after his call had been made to them.

Ibn Qayyim, Zad Al-Ma'ad, Jihad and Raids, Section: in regards to indicating the laws and clever remarks in making incursions

ومنها أن التبسم قد يكون عن الغضب كما يكون عن التعجب والسرور فإن كلاً منهما يوجب إنبساط دم القلب وثورانه

زاد المعاد لإبن قيم الجهاد والغزوات فصل في الإشارة إلى بعض ما تضمنته هذه الغزوة من الفقه والفوائد

Among them is that smiling may reflect anger, just as it reflects amazement or pleasure; indeed both of these involve the heart filling with and pumping out blood.

Ibn Qayyim, Zad Al-Ma'ad, Jihad and Raids, Section: in regards to indicating some of the laws and benefits included in this raid

عن عروة بن الزبير قال بعث رسول الله ﷺ بعثه إلى مؤتة في جمادى الأولى من سنة ثمان ...ثم مضوا حتى نزلوا معان من أرض الشام فبلغ الناس أن هرقل قد نزل مآب من أرض البلقاء في مائة ألف من الروم وإنضمّ اليهم من لخم وجذام والقين وبهراء وبليّ مائة ألف منهم رجل عليهم رجل من بلي ثم أحد إراشة يقال له مالك بن زافلة فلما بلغ ذلك المسلمين أقاموا على معان ليلتين يفكّرون في أمرهم وقالوا نكتب إلى رسول الله ﷺ فنخبره بعدد عدونا فإما أن يُمدّنا بالرجال وإما أن يأمرنا بأمره فنمضي له قال فشجّع الناس عبدالله بن رواحة وقال يا قوم والله إن التي تكرهون للّتي خرجتم تطلبون الشهادة وما نقاتل الناس بعددٍ ولا قوة ولا كثرة ولا نقاتلهم إلا بهذا الدين الذي أكرمنا الله به فانطلقوا فإنما هي إحدى الحُسنيَين إما ظهور وإما شهادة قال فقال الناس قد والله صدق إبن رواحة فمضى الناس

السيرة النبوية لإبن هشام ذكر غزوة مؤتة في جمادى الأولى سنة ثمان ومقتل جعفر وزيد وعبدالله بن رواحة

From 'Urwa ibn Al-Zubair, who said: The Messenger of Allah (SAW) sent out his mission to Mu'ta in the month of Jumada Al-ula in the eighth year ... Then they set out until reaching Mu'an in the land of Sham, and the people found out that Hiraql had reached Mu'ab in the land of Balqaa with one hundred thousand Romans, and another hundred thousand from Lakhm, Judham, Al-qayn, Bahraa, and Baliy had joined up with them, led by a man from Baliy, then one of the Irasha clan called Malk ibn Zafila. When the Muslims found out about this, they stayed in Mu'an for two nights thinking about their predicament. They said: We should write to the Messenger of Allah (SAW) and let him know the large number of our enemy; either He sends men to us as reinforcements, or He will tell us what his orders are and we will proceed. But Abdullah ibn Rawaha emboldened the people, saying: Oh people! By Allah truly that which you dislike is indeed that which you have set out in search of – martyrdom. We do not fight people by large numbers, nor by strength, nor by abundance; we only fight them for this religion that Allah has honored us with. So hurry on! Indeed this means one of two good things – either victory or martyrdom. And the people said: By Allah Ibn Rawaha is right! And so the people proceeded on.

Ibn Hisham, Al-sirah Al-nabawiya, Topic section: mention of the raid in Mu'ta in the month of Jumada Al-ula in the eighth year, and the killing of Ja'far, Zaid, and Abdullah ibn Rawaha

عن إبن عباس رضي الله عنهما قال قوله ﴿ وأعرض عن المشركين ﴾ و ﴿ لست عليهم بمصيطر ﴾ يقول لست عليهم بجبار ﴿ فاعفُ عنهم واصفَح ﴾ ﴿ وإن تعفوا وتصفحوا ﴾ ﴿ فاعفوا واصفحوا حتى يأتي الله بأمره ﴾ ﴿ قل للذين آمنوا يغفروا للذين لا يرجون أيام الله ﴾ ونحو هذا في القرآن أمر الله بالعفو عن المشركين وأنه نسخ ذلك كله قوله ﴿ اقتلوا المشركين حيث وجدتموهم ﴾ وقوله ﴿ قاتلوا الذين لا يؤمنون بالله ولا باليوم الآخر ﴾ إلى قوله ﴿ وهم صاغرون ﴾ فنسخ هذا العفو عن المشركين

السنن الكبرى للبيهقي كتاب السير باب ما جاء في نسخ العفو عن المشركين ونسخ النهي عن القتال حتى يقاتلوا والنهي عن القتال في الشهر الحرام

From Ibn 'Abbas (may Allah be pleased with them both), who said: His word { Turn away from the idolaters } [Al-hijr 94] and { You are not master over them } [Al-ghashiya 22], that is, you are not all-powerful over them; { But pardon them and be forbearing } [Al-ma'ida 13], { But if you all pardon and are forbearing } [Al-taghabun 14], { So pardon and be forbearing, until Allah brings his command } [Al-baqara 109], { Say to those who have believed that they should forgive those who do not hope in the days of Allah } [Al-jathiya 14], and other verses like this in the Qur'an where Allah has ordered for the idolaters to be pardoned – all of this was abrogated by His word: { Kill the Idolaters wherever you find them } [Al-tawba 5] and His word: { Fight those who do not believe in Allah nor in the last day } up until His word { and they are abased } [Al-tawba 29]; this abrogated any pardon for the idolaters.

Al-Bayhaqi, Al-sunan Al-kubra, The book of campaigns, Section: what came regarding abrogation of pardoning the idolaters, and abrogation of the prohibition to fight until being fought and the prohibition of fighting in a sacred month

عن ابي بردة قال قدم على أبي موسى الأشعري معاذ بن جبل من اليمن وإذا برجل عنده فقال ما هذا فقال رجل كان يهودياً فأسلم ثم تهود ونحن نريده على الإسلام منذ أحسبه قال شهرين قال معاذ والله لا أقعُدُ حتى تضربوا عنقه فضُربت عنقه ثم قال معاذ قضاء الله ورسوله

المحلى لإبن حزم كتاب الحدود

From Abu Burda who said: Mu'adh ibn Jabal came to Abu Musa Al-Ash'ari from Yemen, and there was a man with him. He said: What is this? Abu Musa replied: A man who was Jewish and yielded into Islam, then became Jewish again, and we want him back in Islam as of – I reckon – two months. Mu'adh said: I swear by Allah I will not sit down until you decapitate him! So he was decapitated. Then Mu'adh said: The sentence of Allah and His Messenger.

Ibn Hazm, Al-muhalla, The book of legal punishments [hudud]

والجهاد فرض على المسلمين فإذا قام به من يدفع العدو ويغزوهم في عقر دارهم ويحمي ثغور المسلمين سقط فرضه عن الباقين وإلا فلا قال الله تعالى ﴿ انفروا خفافاً وثقالاً وجاهدوا بأموالكم وأنفسكم ﴾

المحلى لإبن حزم كتاب الجهاد

Jihad is an obligation for Muslims, but whenever there are those who can carry it out, push back and attack the enemy within their own land, and protect the frontlines of the Muslims, the obligation is lifted from the rest; otherwise, it is not. Allah Most High said: { Mobilize, light or heavy, and wage *jihad* with your wealth and with yourselves } [Al-tawba 41].

Ibn Hazm, Al-muhalla, The book of jihad

٩٢٨ مسألة وجائز قتل كل من عدا من ذكرنا من المشركين من مقاتل أو غير مقاتل أو تاجر أو أجير وهو العسيف أو شيخ كبير كان ذا رأي أو لم يكن أو فلاح أو أسقف أو قسيس أو راهب أو أعمى أو مقعد لا تحاش أحداً وجائز استبقاؤهم أيضاً قال الله تعالى ﴿ فاقتلوا المشركين حيث وجدتموهم وخذوهم واحصروهم واقعدوا لهم كن مرصد فإن تابوا وأقاموا الصلاة وآتوا الزكاة فخلوا سبيلهم ﴾ فعمّ عز وجل كل مشرك بالقتل إلا أن يسلم

المحلى لإبن حزم كتاب الجهاد

It is permissible to kill among the idolaters – with the exception of those we have mentioned – all fighters, non-fighters, merchants, workmen – that is, laborers – the elderly, of sound mind or not, peasants, bishops, priests, monks, the blind, and the crippled who do not hinder anyone. It is also permissible to spare them; Allah Most High said: { Kill the idolaters wherever you find them, and take hold of them, and bring them under siege, and sit in wait for them at every place of ambush; but if they turn in repentance, and observe prayer, and bring *zakat*, then let them go on their way } [*Al-tawba* 5]. And the Mighty and Sublime made killing general for all idolaters unless they yield into Islam.

Ibn Hazm, Al-muhalla, The book of jihad (issue 928)

٩٢٩ مسألة ويغزى أهل الكفر مع كل فاسق من الامراء وغير فاسق ومع المتغلب والمحارب كما يغزى مع الإمام ويغزوهم المرء وحده إن قدر أيضاً قال الله تعالى ﴿ وتعاونوا على البرّ والتقوى ولا تعاونوا على الإثم والعدوان ﴾
المحلى لإبن حزم كتاب الجهاد

People of disbelief can be attacked with any commander who has defected, or not defected, and with those who dominate and those who are warriors, just as they can be attacked with the leader; a man may attack them by himself if he is able; the Most High said: { Aid each other towards righteousness and piety, but do not aid each other in sins and hostility } [*Al-ma'ida* 2].

Ibn Hazm, Al-muhalla, The book of jihad (issue 929)

٩٣٠ مسألة فمن غزا مع فاسق فليقتل الكفار وليفسد زروعهم ودورهم وثمارهم وليجلب النساء والصبيان ولا بد فإن إخراجهم من ظلمات الكفر إلى نور الاسلام فرض يعصي الله من ترك من قادراً عليه وإثمهم على من غلهم وكل معصية فهي أقل من تركهم في الكفر وعونهم على البقاء فيه
المحلى لإبن حزم كتاب الجهاد

Whoever goes on a raid with a defector, let him kill the disbelievers and destroy their cultivated fields, their homes, and their crops, and bring the women and children; this is indispensable. Indeed bringing them out of the darknesses of disbelief into the light of Islam is an obligation; whoever neglects this, being capable of it, disobeys Allah, and their sins are on anyone who puts them in shackles. Any act of wrongdoing is less serious than leaving them in disbelief and enabling them to remain in it.

Ibn Hazm, Al-muhalla, The book of jihad (issue 930)

٩٣٧ مسألة وإذا أسلم الكافر الحربي فسواء أسلم في دار الحرب ثم خرج إلى دار الاسلام أو لم يخرج أو خرج إلى دار الاسلام ثم أسلم كل ذلك سواء
المحلى لإبن حزم كتاب الجهاد

If a disbeliever being warred against yields into Islam, then it is the same whether He yields into Islam in war territory, and then sets out to Islamic territory, or if he does not set out, or if he sets out into Islamic territory and then yields into Islam; all that is the same.

Ibn Hazm, Al-muhalla, The book of jihad (issue 937)

٩٣٩ مسألة وأيما إمرأة أسلمت ولها زوج كافر ذمي أو حربي فحين إسلامها إنفسخ نكاحها منه سواء أسلم بعدها بطرفة عين أو أكثر أو لم يسلم لا سبيل له عليها إلا بإبتداء نكاح برضاها وإلا فلا فلو أسلما معاً بقيا على نكاحهما فإن أسلم هو قبلها فإن كانت كتابية بقيا على نكاحهما أسلمت هي أم لم تسلم وإن كانت غير كتابية فساعة إسلامه قد إنفسخ نكاحها منه أسلمت بعده بطرفة عين فأكثر لا سبيل له عليها إلا بإبتداء نكاح برضاها إن أسلمت وإلا فلا سواء حربيين أو ذميين كانا

المحلى لإبن حزم كتاب الجهاد

Any woman who yields into Islam and has a disbeliever husband, either a *dhimmi* or part of a warring party, then when she yields into Islam, marital relations with her are invalidated for him, whether he yields into Islam in the twinkling of an eye after her, or later on, or does not yield into Islam at all – there is no recourse for him to have her except by initiating marital relations with her approval; otherwise, no. If both of them yield into Islam together, they both remain in their marital relations. If he yields into Islam before she does, and she is of the People of the Book, then they both remain in their marital relations – whether or not she yields into Islam. If she is not of the People of the Book, then at the moment he yields into Islam, marital relations with her are invalidated for him; whether she yields into Islam in the twinkling of an eye or later on, there is no recourse for him to have her, except by initiating marital relations with her approval if she yields into Islam; otherwise, no, regardless of whether the two of them are of a warring party or are *dhimmis*.

Ibn Hazm, Al-muhalla, The book of jihad (issue 939)

٩٤٠ مسألة ومن قال من أهل الكفر مما سوى اليهود والنصارى أو المجوس لا إله إلا الله أو قال محمد رسول الله كان بذلك مسلماً تلزمه شرائع الاسلام فإن أبى الاسلام قتل وأما من اليهود والنصارى والمجوس فلا يكون مسلماً بقول لا إله إلا الله محمد رسول الله إلا حتى يقول وأنا مسلم أو قد أسلمت أو أنا بريء من كل دين حاشا الاسلام

المحلى لإبن حزم كتاب الجهاد

Whoever of the Disbelievers – besides Jews, Christians, and Magians – say "There is no god but Allah" or say "Muhammad is the Messenger of Allah", this makes them a Muslim, subject to the laws of Islam; but if they refuse Islam, they are killed. However

Jews, Christians, and Magians do not become Muslim by saying "There is no god but Allah, Muhammad is the Messenger of Allah", not until they also say "And I am a Muslim" or "I have yielded into Islam" or "I am absolved of all religion but Islam".

Ibn Hazm, Al-muhalla, The book of jihad (issue 940)

٩٤١ مسألة ولا يقبل من يهودي ولا نصراني ولا مجوسي جزية إلا بأن يقروا بأن محمداً رسول الله إلينا وأن لا يطعنوا فيه ولا في شيء من دين الاسلام لحديث ثوبان الذي ذكرنا آنفاً ولقول الله تعالى ﴿ وطعنوا في دينكم فقاتلوا أئمة الكفر إنهم لا إيمان لهم ﴾ وهو قول مالك قال في المستخرجة من قال من أهل الذمة انما أُرسِل محمد اليكم لا إلينا فلا شيء عليه قال فإن قال لم يكن نبياً قتل

المحلى لإبن حزم كَتاب الجهاد

Jizya is not accepted from a Jew, Christian, or Magian, except by them agreeing that Muhammad is the Messenger of Allah to us, and that they not defame him or anything in the religion of Islam, based on the hadith of Thawban that we mentioned earlier, and the word of the Most High: { ... and defame your religion, then fight the leaders of disbelief – for indeed they have no oaths ... } [*Al-tawba* 12]. And this is what Malik said, in *Al-mustakhrija* [by Al-'Utbi]; he said: Any *dhimmi* who says "Indeed Muhammad has been sent to you all, not to us" – there is no issue with him. But if he says "He was not a prophet", he is killed.

Ibn Hazm, Al-muhalla, The book of jihad (issue 941)

٩٥٨ مسألة ولا يقبل من كافر إلا الاسلام أو السيف الرجال والنساء في ذلك سواء حاشا أهل الكتاب خاصة وهم اليهود والنصارى والمجوس فقط فإنهم إن اعطوا الجزية اقروا على ذلك مع الصغار وقال أبو حنيفة ومالك أما من لم يكن كتابياً من العرب خاصة فالاسلام أو السيف

المحلى لإبن حزم كَتاب الجهاد

Nothing is accepted from a disbeliever except Islam, or the sword – men and women alike – except the People of the Book in particular, these being Jews, Christians, and Magians only. Indeed if these people give *jizya*, they can stay that way as long as they are abased. Abu Hanifa and Malik said: However, those Arabs who are not specifically People of the Book – either Islam or the sword.

Ibn Hazm, Al-muhalla, The book of jihad (issue 958)

والقتل المشروع هو ضرب الرقبة بالسيف ونحوه لأن ذلك أروح أنواع القتل وكذلك شرع الله قتل ما يباح قتله من الآدميين والبهائم إذا قدر عليه على هذا الوجه قال النبي ﷺ إن الله كتب الإحسان على كل شيء فإذا قتلتم فأحسنوا القتلة وإذا ذبحتم فأحسنوا الذبحة وليحد أحدكم شفرته وليرح ذبيحته رواه مسلم وقال إن أعف الناس قتلة أهل الإيمان

السياسة الشرعية لإبن تيمية

The type of killing prescribed by law is a blow to the neck with a sword or similar, since this is the most amenable way to kill. Similarly, Allah prescribed that humans and animals made permissible to kill, be killed, if possible in this manner. The Prophet (SAW) said: Indeed Allah has ordained for things to be done well, so whenever you kill, make it a good killing, and whenever you sacrifice, make it a good sacrifice; and let each of you sharpen his blades, to make it amenable for what is being sacrificed. (Related by Muslim). And He said: Indeed the people who kill most decently are those who believe [ahl al-iman].

Ibn Taymiyya, Al-siyasa Al-shar'iya

فالصواب الذي عليه جماهير المسلمين أن من قاتل على أخذ المال بأي نوع كان من أنواع القتال فهو محارب قاطع كما أن من قاتل المسلمين من الكفار بأي نوع كان من أنواع القتال فهو حربي ومن قاتل الكفار من المسلمين بسيف أو رمح أو سهم أو حجارة أو عصي فهو مجاهد في سبيل الله

السياسة الشرعية لإبن تيمية

The correct view, which the majority of Muslims hold, is that whoever fights to take hold of possessions, by whatever means of fighting, he is unmistakeably a warrior, just as whoever of the disbelievers fights the Muslims, by whatever means of fighting, he is part of the warring party. And whoever of the Muslims fights the disbelievers with a sword, a spear, arrows, stones, or a truncheon, he is a *Mujahid* in the cause of Allah.

Ibn Taymiyya, Al-siyasa Al-shar'iya

مسألة قال ويقاتَل أهل الكتاب والمجوس حتى يسلموا أو يعطوا الجزية عن يد وهم صاغرون ويقاتل من سواهم من الكفار حتى يسلموا

المغني لإبن قدامة كتاب الجهاد

He [Al-Khiraqi] said: The People of the Book and the Magians are to be fought against until they yield into Islam or give *jizya* from their hands and are abased; disbelievers other than them are to be fought until they yield into Islam.

Ibn Qudama, Al-mughni, The book of jihad

وأقل ما يُفعل مرة في كل عام لأن الجزية تجب على أهل الذمة كل عام وهي بدلٌ عن النصرة فكذلك مُبدَلها وهو الجهاد فيجب في كل عام مرة إلا من عذرٍ مثل أن يكون بالمسلمين ضعف في عدد أو عُدة أو يكون منتظراً لمدد يستعين به أو يكون الطريق إليهم فيها مانع أو ليس فيها علف أو ماء أو يعلم من عدوه حُسن الرأي في الاسلام فيطمع في إسلامهم إن أخّر قتالهم ونحو ذلك مما يرى المصلحة معه ترك القتال

المغني لإبن قدامة كتاب الجهاد

And it must be done at least once a year – since *jizya* is obligatory from those held under safeguard [*dhimma*] every year, this being compensation for protection and likewise in exchange for it – and this is *jihad*. It is obligatory once a year, except with an excuse such as if the Muslims are weak in number or equipment, or waiting for reinforcements from which they seek assistance, or something is in the way of them reaching them, or there is no feed for animals or water there, or they are aware of a favorable opinion on the part of their enemy towards Islam, and they eagerly desire for them to yield into Islam if they postpone fighting against them, and other such things for which abandoning fighting is advantageous.

Ibn Qudama, Al-mughni, The book of jihad

ومن طلب الأمان ليسمع كلام الله ويعرف شرائع الاسلام وجب أن يُعطاه ثم يُرَدّ إلى مأمنه لا نعلم في هذا خلافاً

المغني لإبن قدامة كتاب الجهاد

Whoever seeks protection [*aman*] in order to hear the word of Allah and find out about the laws of Islam – it is obligatory for this to be granted to him, and then he is to be returned to his place of safeguarding. We know of no disagreement regarding this.

Ibn Qudama, Al-mughni, The book of jihad

أما العدو إذا قُدر عليه فلا يجوز تحريقه بالنار بغير خلاف نعلمه وقد كان أبو بكر الصديق رضي الله عنه يأمر بتحريق أهل الردة بالنار وفعل ذلك خالد بن الوليد بأمره فأما اليوم فلا أعلم فيه بين الناس خلافاً

المغني لإبن قدامة كتاب الجهاد

Now then, the enemy, if they are conquered, it is not permissible to burn them by fire; there is no disagreement that we know of. Abu Bakr Al-Siddiq (may Allah be pleased with him) ordered the apostates to be burned by fire, as did Khalid ibn Al-Walid by his orders, but today I know of no disagreement among people regarding this.

Ibn Qudama, Al-mughni, The book of jihad

ولو وقفت إمرأةٌ في صف الكفار أو على حصنهم فشتمت المسلمين أو تكشّفت لهم جاز رميُها قصداً لما روى سعيد حدثنا حماد بن زيد عن أيوب عن عكرمة قال لما حاصر رسول الله ﷺ أهل الطائف أشرفت إمرأة فكشفت عن قُبُلها فقالت هادونكم فارموا فرماها رجل من المسلمين فما أخطأ ذلك منها ويجوز النظر إلى فرجها للحاجة إلى رميها لأن ذلك من ضرورة رميها وكذلك يجوز رميها إذا كانت تلتقط لهم السهام أو تَسقيهم الماء أو تحرّضهم على القتال لأنها في حكم المقاتل وهكذا الحكم في الصبي والشيخ وسائر من مُنع من قتله منهم

المغني لإبن قدامة كتاب الجهاد

If a woman gets up amidst the ranks of the disbelievers, or on top of their bulwark, and insults the Muslims or exposes herself to them, it is permissible to intentionally shoot at her, based on what Sa'id narrated: Hammad ibn Zayd related to us from Ayub, from 'Ikrama, who said: When the Messenger of Allah (SAW) besieged the people of Ta'if, a woman got close, exposed her front parts, and said: Here you go, so shoot! And a man from among the Muslims shot at her, and did not miss that part of her. It is permissible, then, to look at a woman's vagina if needed to shoot at her, since this is out of necessity for shooting at her. Similarly, it is permissible to shoot at a woman if she collects arrows for them, gives them drinking water, or urges them on to fight, since she falls under the ruling for fighters. The ruling similarly applies to children, the elderly, and any others of them who are normally prohibited to be killed.

Ibn Qudama, Al-mughni, The book of jihad

وله قتل مرتد وأكله وقتل حربي ولو صغيراً أو إمرأة وأكله لأنهما غير معصومين وإنما حرم قتل الصبي الحربي والمرأة الحربية في غير الضرورة لا لحرمتهما بل لحق الغانمين وله قتل الزاني المحصن والمحارب وتارك الصلاة ومن له عليه قصاص وإن لم يأذن الإمام في القتل لأن قتلهم مستحق

بجيرمي على الخطيب كتاب الصيد والذبائح فصل في الأطعمة

And one may kill an apostate and eat him, or kill a combatant, even a child or a woman, and eat them, since children and women are not infallible; indeed the prohibition on killing a boy combatant or a woman combatant, when there is no necessity, is not because of their sanctity, but rather for the claims of those who go after the spoils. And one may kill a married adulterer, a fighter, someone who abandons prayer, or anyone for whom retaliation is due, even if the imam has not given permission to kill, because such as these deserve to be killed.

Al-Bujairmi, Hashiya Al-Bujairmi, The book of hunting and sacrifices, Chapter: foods

وله قتل مرتد وأكله وقتل حربي ولو صغيراً أو إمرأة وأكلها لأنهما غير معصومين وإنما حرم قتل الصبي الحربي والمرأة الحربية في غير الضرورة لا لحرمتهما بل لحق الغانمين وله قتل الزاني المحصن والمحارب وتارك الصلاة ومن له عليه قصاص وإن لم يأذن الإمام في القتل لأن قتلهم مستحق وإنما اعتبروا إذنه في غير حال الضرورة تأدباً معه وحال الضرورة ليس فيها رعاية أدب وحكم مجانين أهل الحرب وأرقائهم وخناثهم كصبيانهم قال إبن عبدالسلام ولو وجد مضطر صبياً مع بالغ حربيين أكل البالغ وكف عن الصبي لما في أكله من ضياع المال ولأن الكفر الحقيقي أبلغ من الكفر الحكمي

الإقناع في حل ألفاظ أبي شجاع للخطيب الشربيني كتاب الصيد والذبائح

And one [i.e. who feels compelled] may kill and apostate and eat him, or kill a combatant, even a child or a woman, and eat them, since women and children are not infallible; indeed the prohibition on killing a boy combatant or a woman combatant, when there is no necessity, is not because of their sanctity, but rather for the claims of those who go after the spoils. And one may kill a married adulterer, a fighter, someone who abandons prayer, or anyone for whom retaliation is due, even if the Imam has not given permission to kill, because such as these deserve to be killed. Although people consider the Imam's permission out of corteous discipline when there is not a state of necessity, there is no concern for respectability in a state of necessity. And the ruling for those of the warring party who are insane, or slaves, or hermaphrodites [i.e. sexually undeveloped], as are children: Ibn 'Abd Al-Salaam said that if someone under pressure finds a child as well as someone mature, both of them combatants, then he may eat the mature one but is to refrain from the child, since eating him would be a waste of assets, and because true disbelief is more severe than determined unbelief.

Al-Khatib Al-Sharbini, Al-iqna' fi Hal Alfadh Abi Shuja' [Persuasion in the Requirements of the Pronouncements of Abu Shuja' ; a commentary on Al-ghaya wa Al-taqrib or Matan Abi Shuja', a legal manual by Abu Shuja'], The book of hunting and sacrifices

وإن خاف نقض العهد منهم جاز أن ينبذ اليهم عهدهم لقول الله تعالى ﴿ وإما تخافنّ من قومٍ خيانة فانبذ اليهم على سواء ﴾ يعني أعلِمْهم بنقض عهدهم حتى تصير أنت وهم سواء في العلم ولا يكفي وقوع ذلك في قلبه حتى يكون عن أمارة تدل على ما خافه

المغني لإبن قدامة كتاب الجهاد

If one fears that they will break their treaty, it is permissible for him to default on the treaty with them, based on the word of Allah Most High: { And if indeed you fear betrayal from people, default on them likewise } [Al-anfal 58]. That is, let them know that their treaty is being broken, so that you and them are both equally aware – it is not sufficient for this to occur in one's heart – so that they might have a clear sign that gives evidence of what is feared.

Ibn Qudama, Al-mughni, The book of jihad

مسألة قال ولم يغرّقوا النحل

وجملته أن تغريق النحل وتحريقه لا يجوز في قول عامة أهل العلم

المغني لإبن قدامة كتاب الجهاد

He [Al-Khiraqi] said: And they did not drown the bees.

His statement is that drowning bees or burning them is not permitted, according to what the majority of scholars say.

Ibn Qudama, Al-mughni, The book of jihad

وقد أشار الله سبحانه وتعالى إلى أمهاتها وأصولها في سورة آل عمران حيث إفتتح القصة بقوله ﴿ وإذ غدوت من أهلك تُبوِّئ المؤمنين مقاعد للقتال ﴾... ومنها أن الشهادة عنده من أعلى مراتب أوليائه والشهداء هم خواصه والمقرَّبون من عباده وليس بعد درجة الصِّدِّيقية إلا الشهادة وهو سبحانه يحب أن يتخذ من عباده شهداء تُراق دماؤهم في محبته ومرضاته ويؤثرون رضاه ومحابَّه على نفوسهم ولا سبيل إلى نيل هذه الدرجة إلا بتقدير الأسباب المفضية إليها من تسليط العدو

زاد المعاد لإبن قيم الجهاد والغزوات فصل في ذكر بعض الحكم والغايات المحمودة التي كانت في وقعة أحد

Allah Most High and Exalted indicated the essence and fundamentals of these [the commendable aims at Uhud] in *surah Al 'Imran* when He introduced the story by His words: { And when you set out in early morning, leaving those of your household to set up the believers in their stations to fight } [verse 121]. ... One of these is that martyrdom, in His sight, is one of the highest ranks of His associates, and martyrs are distinctively His, those of His servants who have been brought nearest. There is nothing beyond the status of righteous devotion except martyrdom. And He (may He be exalted) loves to take martyrs from among His servants, whose blood is shed out of love for Him and His gratification, preferring His pleasure and fondness over their own selves. And there is no way to attain this status except by the decreeing of causes that lead to it arising from the onslaught of the enemy.

Ibn Qayyim, Zad Al-Ma'ad, Jihad and Raids, Section: mention of certain commendable wise sayings and goals in the engagement at Uhud

مسألة قال قال أبو عبدالله لا أعلم شيئاً من العمل بعد الفرائض أفضل من الجهاد روى هذه المسألة عن أحمد جماعةٌ من أصحابه قال الأثرم قال أحمد لا نعلم شيئاً من أبواب البر أفضل من السبيل وقال الفضل بن زياد سمعت أبا عبدالله وذُكر له أمر الغزو فجعل يبكي ويقول ما من أعمال البر أفضل منه وقال عنه غيره ليس يعدل لقاء العدو شيءٌ

المغني لإبن قدامة كتاب الجهاد

His statement: Abu Abdullah said: I don't know of any thing besides the obligatory duties that is better than *jihad*.

This issue has been related by Ahmad from a group of his companions; Al-Athram said that Ahmad said: We don't know of any of the doors of devotion better than the path itself. Al-Fadl ibn Ziyad said: I heard Abu Abdullah, when the issue of going on raids was mentioned to him – it made him weep and say: There is no act of devotion better than this. Others have related from him: Nothing is equal to facing the enemy.

Ibn Qudama, Al-mughni, The book of jihad

ثم ذكر حكمة أخرى وهي اتخاذه سبحانه منهم شهداء فإنه يحب الشهداء من عباده وقد أعدّ لهم أعلى المنازل وأفضلها وقد اتخذهم لنفسه فلا بد أن يُنيلهم درجة الشهداء

زاد المعاد لإبن قيم الجهاد والغزوات فصل في ذكر بعض الحِكم والغايات المحمودة التي كانت في وقعة أحد

Then He mentions another piece of wisdom, and that is the Exalted taking martyrs from among them, for indeed He loves his servants who are martyrs, and has prepared the highest and best echelon for them, and has taken them unto Himself; He must therefore grant them the level of the martyrs.

Ibn Qayyim, Zad Al-Ma'ad, Jihad and Raids, Section: mention of certain commendable wise sayings and goals in the engagement at Uhud

عن أنس قال قال رسول الله ﷺ يؤتى بالرجل من أهل الجنة فيقول الله عز وجل يا إبن آدم كيف وجدت منزلك فيقول أي رب خير منزل فيقول سَلْ وتمنّ فيقول أسألك أن تردّني إلى الدنيا فأُقتل في سبيلك عشر مرات لما يرى من فضل الشهادة

سنن النسائي كتاب الجهاد

From Anas who said: The Messenger of Allah (SAW) said: A man from the people of *Jannah* was brought, and Allah Mighty and Sublime said: Oh son of Adam, what do you think of your dwelling? And he said: Oh Lord, the best dwelling. He said: Ask for and desire anything. And the man said: "I ask that you send me back into the world that I might be killed for your cause ten times" – because of the excellence he sees in martyrdom.

Sunan Al-Nasa'i, The book of jihad

إذا تعارض الشرع والعقل وجب تقديم الشرع

درء تعارض العقل والنقل لإبن تيمية الجزء الأول الوجه السادس

Whenever *sharia* and sound reasoning contradict each other, *sharia* must be given precedence.

Ibn Taymiyya, Dar' Ta'arud Al-'aql wa Al-naql, Part 1, the sixth aspect

أن صبيغ بن عِسل قدم المدينة فجعل يسأل عن متشابه القران وعن أشياء فبلغ ذلك عمر رضي الله عنه فبعث إليه عمر فأحضره وقد أعدّ له عراجين من عراجين النخل فلما حضر قال له عمر من أنت قال أنا عبد الله صبيغ فقال عمر رضي الله عنه وأنا عبد الله عمر ثم قام إليه فضرب رأسه بعرجون فشجّه ثم تابع ضربه حتى سال دمه على وجهه فقال حسبك يا أمير المؤمنين فقد والله ذهب ما كنت أجد في رأسي

تفسير القرطبي آل عمران ٧

Sabigh ibn 'Isl arrived in Medina and began to ask questions about the ambiguous verses in the Qur'an and about some other things. News of this reached 'Umar (may Allah be pleased with him), and 'Umar sent for the man and had him brought to him, having had some palm branch sticks prepared for him. When the man arrived, 'Umar said to him: Who are you? The man said: "I am Sabigh the servant of Allah". And 'Umar (may Allah be pleased with him) said: "And I am 'Umar the servant of Allah". Then he got up towards him and beat his head with a palm branch stick, cutting his head open, and continued to beat him until blood ran down his face. And the man said: Enough oh Leader of the Believers! I swear by Allah all the questions I had in my head are gone.

Tafsir Al-Qurtubi, Al 'Imran 7

Scholars and sources

'Abd Al-Razzaq

أبو بكر عبد الرزاق بن همام الصنعاني, *Abu Bakr 'Abd Al-Razzaq ibn Hammam Al-San'ani*. Hadith scholar from Yemen. He wrote the extensive *Musannaf* [Categorized Collection], one of the earliest compilations of hadith and therefore rich in narrations directly from the Prophet (SAW) and Companions. Died 211 A.H./826 A.D.

Abu Dawud

أبو داود سليمان بن الاشعث بن إسحاق بن بشير الازدي السجستاني, *Abu Dawud Sulaiman ibn Al-Ash'ath ibn Ishaq ibn Bashir Al-Azdi Al-Sajistani*. From Sajistan (Sistan; Persia/Afghanistan) and later Basra (Iraq). Compiled *Sunan Abi Dawud*, one of the six leading Sunni hadith collections. Died 275 A.H./888 A.D.

Abu Hayyan

أبو حيان الغرناطي, *Abu Hayyan Al-Gharnati*, known as أثير الدين, Beloved of the *Deen*. From Andalusia. His greatest and most famous work is the tafsir and reference *Al-bahr Al-muheet* [The All-embracing Sea]. Died 745 A.H./1344 A.D.

Ahmad

أبو عبدالله أحمد بن محمد بن حنبل الشيباني, *Abu Abdillah Ahmad ibn Muhammad ibn Hanbal Al-Shaybani* or simply *Ahmad ibn Hanbal*. From Baghdad. Revered figure in Islamic history and founder of the Hanbali school of law, most known for his extensive hadith collection the *Musnad*. Died 241 A.H./855 A.D.

Al-Baghawi

أبو محمد الحسين بن مسعود بن محمد الفراء البغوي, *Abu Muhammad Al-Husain ibn Mas'ud ibn Muhammad Al-Farra' Al-Baghawi*. Hadith scholar from Central Asia and Shafi'i jurist most known for his well-respected commentary on the Qur'an *Ma'alim Al-tanzil* [Guideposts to the Revelation] or *Tafsir Al-Baghawi*. Died 516 A.H./1122 A.D.

Al-Baydawi

ناصر الدين أبو الخير عبدالله بن ابي القاسم عمر بن محمد بن ابي الحسن علي البيضاوي, *Nasr Al-din Abu Al-Khair Abdullah bn Abi Al-Qasim 'Umar ibn Muhammad ibn Abi Al-Hasan 'Ali Al-Baydawi*. Persian theologian and judge. His major work is the commentary on the

Qur'an *Anwar Al-tanzil wa Asrar Al-ta'wil* [Lights of Revelation and Secrets of Interpretation], a standard tafsir and one of the most important and popular. Died 685 A.H./1286 A.D.

Al-Bayhaqi

أبو بكر أحمد بن الحسين بن علي بن موسى الخسروجردي الخراساني البيهقي, *Abu Bakr Ahmad ibn Al-Husain ibn 'Ali ibn Musa Al-Khusrawjirdi Al-Khurasani Al-Bayhaqi*. Persian and of the Shafi'i school; well-known scholar of hadith and prolific writer, among whose works are *Ma'rifa Al-sunan wa Al-athar* [Knowledge of the Sunnah and the Hadith] and *Al-sunan Al-kubra* [The Larger Compilation of Sunnah] also known as *Sunan Al-Bayhaqi*. Died 458 A.H./1066 A.D.

Al-Buhuti

أبو السعادات منصور بن يونس البهوتي, *Abu Al-Sa'adat Mansur ibn Yunus Al-Buhuti*. Hanbali theologian and jurist from Egypt. Among his works is the well-known exposition *Kashaf Al-qina' 'an Matn Al-iqnaa'* [Lifting the Veil on Firmness of Conviction]. Died 1051 A.H./1641 A.D.

Al-Bujairmi

سليمان بن محمد بن عمر الشافعي البجيرمي, *Sulaiman ibn Muhammad ibn 'Umar Al-Shafi'i Al-Bujairmi*. Jurist and hadith collector from Egypt. Wrote *Hashiya Al-Bujairmi 'ala Al-Khatib* [Al-Bujairmi's Commentary on Al-Khatib], an explanatory treatise on *Al-iqna' fi Hall Alfadh Abi Shuja'* [Conviction in Reconciling the Words of Abu Shuja'] by Al-Khatib Al-Sharbini, one of the most important and well-known books of Shafi'i jurisprudence. Died 1221 A.H./1806 A.D.

Al-Bukhari

أبو عبدالله محمد بن إسماعيل بن ابراهيم بن المغيرة بن بردزبة الجعفي البخاري, *Abu Abdillah Muhammad ibn Isma'il ibn Ibrahim ibn Al-Mughira ibn Bardizba Al-Ju'fi Al-Bukhari*. From Bukhara (now Uzbekistan). Compiled *Sahih Al-Bukhari*, one of the six leading Sunni hadith collections and one of the two most highly regarded compilations (along with *Sahih Muslim*); also compiled *Al-adab Al-mufrad* [Exemplary Manners], a collection of hadith concerning the behavior and morals of the Prophet (SAW). Died 256 A.H./870 A.D.

Al-Maturidi

أبو منصور محمد بن محمود الماتُريدي السمرقندي الأنصاري, *Abu Mansur Muhammad ibn Muhammad ibn Mahmud Al-Maturidi Al-Samarqandi Al-Ansari* or simply Abu Mansur

Al-Maturidi. From Samarqand (present-day Uzbekistan). Prominent scholar, jurist, and exegete of the Hanafi school. His tafsir is the *Ta'wilat Ahl Al-Sunna* [Interpretations for the Followers of the Sunnah]. Died 333 A.H./944 A.D.

Al-Mawardi

أبو الحسن علي بن محمد بن حبيب البصري الماوردي, *Abu Al-Hasan 'Ali ibn Muhammad ibn Habib Al-Basri Al-Mawardi.* Shafi'i jurist from Iraq. Compiled a tafsir – *Al-nukat wa Al'uyun* [Anecdotes and Springs] – as well as *Ahkam Al-sultaniya wa Al-wilayat Al-diniyya* [Sovereign Rulings and Religious Jurisdictions]. Died 450 A.H./1058 A.D.

Al-Nasa'i

أبو عبد الرحمن أحمد بن شعيب بن علي بن سنان بن بحر بن دينار النسائي, *Abu 'Abd Al-Rahman Ahmad ibn Shu'aib ibn 'Ali ibn Sinan ibn Bahr ibn Dinar Al-Nasa'i.* From Nisa (now Turkmenistan), later Palestine. Judge and compiler of several collections of hadith, including *Al-sunan Al-sughra* [The Lesser Sunan] also called *Sunan Al-Nasa'i*, one of the leading Sunni hadith collections, and *Al-sunan al-kubra* [The Greater Sunan]. Died 303 A.H./915 A.D.

Al-Nasafi

أبو البركات النسفي, *Abu 'Al-Barakat Al-Nasafi.* From Nisa (now Turkmenistan), given the title حافظ الدين, Guardian of the Deen. A prominent Hanafi jurist whose works include the commentary *Madarik Al-Tanzil wa Haqa'iq Al-ta'wil* [Perceptions of the Revelation and True Meanings of Interpretation]. Died 710 A.H./1310 A.D.

Al-Nawawi

أبو زكريا يحيى بن شرف الحزامي النووي, *Abu Zakariya Yahya ibn Sharaf Al-Hizami Al-Nawawi.* Scholar of hadith, theology, law, and lexicology, and one of the foremost in the Shafi'i school. From Nawa (now Syria). Author of many works, including *Al-minhaj fi Sharh Sahih Muslim* [Open Path to Exposition of Sahih Muslim], also called *Sahih Muslim bi Sharh Al-Nawawi* [Al-Nawawi's Commentary on Sahih Muslim], one of the most regarded commentaries on Sahih Muslim. Died 676 A.H./1277 A.D.

Al-Nisaburi

نظام الدين حسن النيسابوري, *Nidham Al-deen Hasan Al-Nisaburi.* Commentator, mathematician, astronomer, legal scholar, and poet From Nishapur (Persia). Wrote *Ghara'ib Al-Qur'an wa Ragha'ib Al-Furqan* [Wonders of the Qur'an and Aspirations of the Criterion] – or *Tafsir Al-Nisaburi.* Died 728 A.H./1328 A.D.

Al-Qurtubi

محمد بن أحمد بن ابي بكر بن فرح الأنصاري القرطبي, *Muhammad ibn Ahmad ibn Abi Bakr ibn Farh Al-Ansari Al-Qurtubi*; شمس الدين, Sun of the *Deen*. From Cordoba (Andalusia) and later lived in Egypt. Scholar of hadith, law, and commentary, of the Maliki school, most known for his important commentary on the Qur'an *Al-jami' Li-Ahkam Al-Qur'an* [Collection of Rulings of the Qur'an] or *Tafsir Al-Qurtubi*. Died 671 A.H./1273 A.D.

Al-Razi

أبو عبدالله محمد بن عمر بن الحسن بن الحسين بن علي الرازي, *Abu Abdillah Muhammad ibn 'Umar ibn Al-Hasan ibn Al-Husain ibn 'Ali Al-Razi*, given the title فخر الدين, Pride of the *Deen*. From Persia, later lived in Afghanistan. Wrote on ethics, medicine, history, law, and other subjects, and authored the extensive Qur'anic commentary *Mafatih Al-ghaib* [Keys to the Unseen] also called *Al-tafsir Al-kabir* [The Great Exegesis] or simply *Tafsir Al-Razi*. Died 604 A.H./1210 A.D.

Al-Samarqandi

أبو الليث نصر بن محمد بن إبراهيم بن الخطاب السمرقندي, *Abu Al-Laith Nasr ibn Muhammad ibn Ibrahim ibn Al-Khattab Al-Samarqandi*. Hanafi Jurist from Samarqand (present-day Uzbekistan). His most well-known work is the commentary *Bahr Al-'ulum* [Vast Sea of Knowledge], or *Tafsir Al-Samarqandi*. Also wrote *Tanbih Al-ghafileen* [Warning to the Unwary]. Died 373 A.H./983 A.D.

Al-Sarakhsi

محمد بن أحمد بن ابي سهل السرخسي, *Muhammad ibn Ahmad Abi Sahl Al-Sarakhsi*, known as شمس الأئمة, Sun of the Imams. Influential Hanafi scholar and jurist from Sarakhs (Persia/Turkmenistan). His writings include *Sharh Kitab Al-Siyar Al-Kabir* [Commentary on the *Kitab Al-siyar Al-kabir* of Al-Shaybani]. Died 483 A.H./1090 A.D.

Al-Shaybani

محمد بن الحسن بن فرقد الشيباني الكوفي, *Muhammad ibn Al-Hasan ibn Farqad Al-Shaybani Al-Kufi*. Jurist from Iraq. Studied under Abu Hanifa and wrote several legal expositions, among them *Kitab Al-siyar Al-saghir* [The Lesser Book on Campaigns] and *Kitab Al-siyar Al-kabir* [Greater Book on Campaigns]. Died 189 A.H./805 A.D.

Al-Suyuti

عبد الرحمن بن كمال الدين ابي بكر بن محمد سابق الدين خضر الخضيري الأسيوطي, *'Abd Al-rahman ibn Kamal Al-din Abi Bakr ibn Muhammad Sabiq Al-din Khadar Al-Khadiri Al-Asyuti*; known by the honorary title جلال الدين, Majesty of the *Deen*. Prolific comentator, historian, and scholar of hadith from Egypt. Compiled the popular exegesis of the Qur'an *Tafsir Al-Jalalain* with his mentor *Jalal Al-Din Al-Mahalli*. Among his other works are the authoritative Qur'anic exegesis based on direct narrations *Al-durr Al-manthur fi Al-tafsir Al-ma'thur* [Scattered Pearls on the Transmitted Commentary]. Died 911 A.H./1505 A.D.

Al-Tabarani

أبو القاسم سليمان بن أحمد بن أيوب بن مطير اللخمي الشامي الطبراني, *Abu Al-Qasim Sulaiman ibn Ahmad ibn Ayyub ibn Mutayyir Al-Lakhmi Al-Shami Al-Tabarani*. A well-known scholar and narrator of hadith from Palestine and later Persia; compiled *Al-tafsir Al-kabir* [The Great Exegesis]. Died 360 A.H./971 A.D.

Al-Tabari

أبو جعفر محمد بن جرير بن يزيد بن كثير بن غالب الطبري, *Abu Ja'far Muhammad ibn Jarir ibn Yazid ibn Kathir ibn Ghalib Al-Tabari*. Early commentator, historian, and jurist from Tabaristan (Persia), later Baghdad; given the title إمام المفسرين, Leader of the Commentators. His main and most influential work is his commentary on the Qur'an *Jami' Al-bayyan fi Ta'wil Al-Qur'an* [Collection of Explanations on Interpretation of the Qur'an] also called *Tafsir Al-Tabari*, the earliest extant work among the well-known commentaries and often considered the most important; he also wrote the historical account *Tarikh Al-rusul wa Al-Muluk* [History of Messengers and Kings], or simply *Tarikh Al-Tabari*. Died 310 A.H./923 A.D.

Al-Tha'alibi

عبد الرحمان الثعالبي, *'Abd Al-Rahman Al-Tha'alibi*. Comentator, jurist, and linguist of the Sufi Maliki school from Algeria. Wrote *Al-jawahir Al-hisan fi Tafsir Al-Qur'an* [Splendid Jewels in Exegesis of the Qur'an]. Died 875 A.H./1479 A.D.

Al-Tha'labi

أبو اسحاق أحمد بن محمد بن ابراهيم الثعلبي, *Abu Ishaq Ahmad ibn Muhammad ibn Ibrahim Al-Tha'labi*. Shafi'i scholar from Persia. His tafsir is *Al-Kashf wa Al-bayan fi Tafsir Al-Qur'an* [Discovery and Declaration on Exegesis of the Qur'an]. Died 427 A.H./1035 A.D.

Al-Tabrizi

محمد الخطيب التبريزي, *Muhammad Al-Khatib Al-Tabrizi*. Scholar of hadith who wrote the well-read collection *Mishkat Al-Masabih* [Niche of the Lamps], which builds on a collection of Al-Baghawi. Died 741 A.H./1340 A.D.

Al-Tirmidhi

أبو عيسى محمد بن عيسى بن سورة بن موسى بن الضحاك السلمي الترمذي, *Abu 'Isa Muhammad ibn 'Isa ibn Sawra ibn Musa ibn Al-Dahhak Al-Sulami Al-Tirmidhi*. From Termez (now Uzbekistan). His collection *Jami' Al-Tirmidhi* or *Sunan Al-Tirmidhi* is one of the leading collections of Sunni hadith. Died 279 A.H./892 A.D.

Al-Wahidi

أبو الحسن علي بن أحمد بن محمد إبن علي الواحدي النيسابوري, *Abu Al-Hasan 'Ali ibn Ahmad ibn Muhammad ibn 'Ali Al-Wahidi Al-Nisaburi*. From Nishapur (Persia). The earliest of the scholars concerned with the context of revelation of the Qur'an. His most renowned work is *Asbab Al-nuzul* [Reasons for the Revelations], which presents known occasions and incidents related to the revelation of specific verses in the Qur'an. Died 468 A.H./1076 A.D.

Al-Zamakhshari

أبو القاسم محمود بن عمر بن محمد بن عمر الخوارزمي الزمخشري, *Abu Al-Qasim Mahmud ibn 'Umar ibn Muhammad ibn 'Umar Al-Khawarzami Al-Zamakhshari*; given the title جار الله, Companion of Allah. From Turkmenistan. His most well-known work is the *tafsir Al-Kashaf 'an Haqa'iq Al-tanzil* [The Revealer of the True Meanings of the Revelation]. Died 538 A.H./1143 A.D.

Fairuz Abadi

أبو طاهر محمد بن يعقوب بن محمد بن إبراهيم الشيرازي الفيروزآبادي, *Abu Tahir Muhammad ibn Ya'qub ibn Muhammad ibn Ibrahim Al-Shirazi Al-Fairuzabadi*; given the title مجد الدين, Glory of the *Deen*. Judge and lexicographer from Persia, later Mecca and other places. Died 817 A.H./1414 A.D.

Ibn Abi Shaybah

أبو بكر عبد الله بن محمد بن أبي شيبة إبراهيم بن عثمان بن خواستي العبسي مولاهم الكوفي, *Abu Bakr Abdullah ibn Muhammad ibn Abi Shaybah Ibrahim ibn 'Uthman ibn Khuwasti Al-'Abasi Mawlahim Al-Kufi*. Scholar of hadith from Kufa (Iraq) and among the most significant of early authors; his *Musannaf* [Categorized Collection] is one of the largest existing compilations of hadith. Died 235 A.H./849 A.D.

Ibn 'Adil

أبو حفص عمر بن علي بن عادل الدمشقي, *Abu Hafs 'Umar ibn 'Ali ibn 'Adil Al-Dimashqi*, given the title سراج الدين, Lamp of the *Deen*. Hanbali jurist and commentator from Damascus.

Best known for *Al-lubab fi 'Ulum Al-kitab* [Kernels of Knowledge of the Book], also called *Tafsir Ibn 'Adil*. Died 880 A.H./1475 A.D.

Ibn Al-Jawzi

أبو الفرج عبد الرحمن بن أبي الحسن علي بن محمد التيمي البكري, *Abu Al-Faraj 'Abd Al-Rahman ibn Abi Al-Hasan 'Ali ibn Muhammad Al-Taimi Al-Bakri*, known as إبن الجوزي, Ibn Al-Jawzi. Hanbali jurist, collector of hadith and historian; influential in his native Baghdad. One of the most copious writers in the history of Islam, he wrote extensively on many areas of study, including *Zad Al-masir fi 'Ilm Al-tafsir* [Expanding the Course in Exegetical Knowledge], or simply *Tafsir Ibn Al-Jawzi*. Died 597 A.H./1201 A.D.

Ibn Al-Naqib Al-Misri

أبو العباس أحمد بن لؤلؤ بن عبد الله الرومي, *Abu Al-'Abbas Ahmad ibn Lu'lu' ibn Abdillah Al-Rumi*, known as شهاب الدين ابن النقيب المصري, Shining Star of the *Deen* Ibn Al-Naqib Al-Misri. From Cairo. Wrote the leading manual of Shafi'i law *'Umda Al-salik wa 'Udda Al-nasik* [Reliance of the Traveler and Instruments of the Devout]. Died 769 A.H./1368 A.D.

Ibn 'Atiyya

أبو محمد عبد الحق بن غالب بن عطية الأندلسي, *Abu Muhammad 'Abd Al-Haqq ibn Ghalib ibn 'Atiyya Al-Andalusi*. Jurist and scholar of tafsir, legal decrees, and hadith, from Analusia. His large commentary on the Qur'an is *Al-muharrar Al-wajeez fi Tafsir Al-kitab Al-'aziz* [Concise Compilation in Exegesis of the Great Book]. Died 541 A.H./1148 A.D.

Ibn Hajar Al-'Asqalani

أبو الفضل أحمد بن علي بن محمد بن محمد بن علي بن محمود بن أحمد بن أحمد الكناني العسقلاني, *Abu Al-fadl Ahmad ibn 'Ali ibn Muhammad ibn Muhammad ibn 'Ali ibn Mahmud ibn Ahmad ibn Ahmad Al-Kanani Al-'Asqalani*; given the title شهاب الدين, Flaming star of the *Deen*. Of the Shafi'i school, from Egypt. Compiled many volumes of hadith. His most well-known work is *Fath Al-bari* [Victory of the Creator], a highly acclaimed commentary on *Sahih Al-Bukhari*. Also among his works is *Bulugh Al-maram min Adilla Al-Ahkam* [Attainment of the Goal in Affirmations of the Rulings]. Died 852 A.H./1449 A.D.

Ibn Hajar Al-Haytami

أحمد بن محمد بن محمد بن علي بن حجر الهيتمي, *Ahmad ibn Muhammad ibn Muhammad ibn 'Ali ibn Hajar Al-Haytami*. Shafi'i jurist, historian, and scholar of hadith from Egypt, later

Mecca. His works include *Al-zawajir 'an Iqtiraf Al-kaba'ir* [Injunctions against Perpetrating the Major Sins]. Died 974 A.H./1566 A.D.

Ibn Hazm Al-Andalusi

أبو محمد علي بن أحمد بن سعيد بن حزم بن غالب بن صالح بن خلف بن معدان بن سفيان بن يزيد الأندلسي القرطبي, *Abu Muhammad 'Ali ibn Ahmad ibn Sa'id ibn Hazm ibn Ghalib ibn Salih ibn Khalaf ibn Ma'dan ibn Sufyan ibn Yazid Al-Andalusi Al-Qurtubi*. From Andalusia; he is the greatest scholar (along with Al-Tabari and Al-Suyuti) in terms of authorship and compilation, writing much on law, theology, science, and other subjects. Wrote *Al-muhalla bi Al-athar* [Sweetened by the outcomes], highly esteemed as a legal encyclopedia. Died 456 A.H./1064 A.D.

Ibn Hisham

أبو محمد عبد الملك بن هشام بن أيوب الحميري البصري, *Abu Muhammad 'Abd Al-Malik ibn Hisham ibn Ayyub Al-Himyari Al-Basri*. Biographer and historian from Basra (Iraq), later lived in Egypt, scholar of genealogies, language, and chronicles of the Arabs. *Al-sira Al-nabawiya* [The Biography of the Prophet] is a revision of Ibn Ishaq's work, and is the standard and earliest extant biography of the Prophet (SAW). Died 218 A.H./833 A.D.

Ibn Kathir

أبو الفداء إسماعيل بن عمر بن كثير القريشي الحصلي البصروي الدمشقي, *Abu Al-fidaa Isma'il ibn 'Umar ibn Kathir ibn Al-Quraishi Al-Hasli Al-Busrawi Al-Dimashqi*; honorary title عماد الدين, Pillar of the *Deen*. Salient scholar from Syria in exegesis and law. Wrote *Tafsir Al-Qur'an Al-'adhim* [Exegesis of the Great Qur'an], one of the most esteemed *tafsir*. Died 774 A.H./1373 A.D.

Ibn Khaldun

أبو زيد عبد الرحمن بن محمد بن خلدون الحضرمي, *Abu Zaid' Abd Al-Rahman ibn Muhammad ibn Khaldun Al-Hadrami*, given the title ولي الدين, Master of the *Deen*. Scholar of religion, philospher, and historian from Tunisia. His best-known work is *Al-muqaddimah* [The Introduction], the first part of a universal history. Died 808 A.H./1406 A.D.

Ibn Majah

أبو عبد الله محمد بن يزيد بن ماجه الربعي القزويني, *Abu Abdillah Muhammad ibn Yazid ibn Majah Al-Rab'i Al-Qazwini*. From Qazvin (Persia). Noted early scholar and prominent among the collectors of hadith; his collection (*Sunan*) is generally regarded as one of the leading works of Sunni hadith. Died 273 A.H./886 A.D.

Ibn Qayyim

أبو عبدالله محمد بن ابي بكر بن أيوب بن سعد بن حرير الزرعي, Abu Abdillah Muhammad ibn Abi Bakr ibn Ayyub ibn Sa'd bn Harir Al-Zur'i, given the title شمس الدين, Sun of the Deen and primarily known as ابن قيّم الجوزية, Ibn Qayyim Al-Jawziyya [son of the principal of the Jawziya school]. From Damascus. Jurist, compiler of hadith, commentator, and important member of the Hanbali school. His works include *Rawda Al-muhibeen wa Nuzha Al-mushtaqeen* [Meadow of Those who Love and Stroll of Those who Yearn], *Ahkam Ahl Al-dhimma* [Rulings for Those Being Safeguarded], and *Zad Al-Ma'ad fi Hadi Khair Al-'ibad* [Provisions for the Hereafter in the Guidance of the Best of Mankind], a book on the life and times of the Prophet (SAW). Died 751 A.H./1350 A.D.

Ibn Qudama

أبو محمد عبد الله بن أحمد بن قدامة بن مقدام المقدسي الجمّاعيلي, Abu Muhammad Abdullah ibn Ahmad ibn Qudama ibn Miqdam Al-Maqdisi Al-Jama'ili, given the title موفق الدين, Prosperous in the Deen. From Palestine, later Damascus. One of the most prominent figures of the Hanbali school; authored the highly regarded *Al-mughni* [The Enricher], one of the largest works of Islamic law, itself a commentary on *Al-Mukhtasar* by Al-Khiraqi; he also wrote *Mukhtasar Minhaj Al-Qasideen* [Compendium on Course of Study for the Motivated]. Died 620 A.H./1223 A.D.

Ibn Rushd

أبو الوليد محمد بن أحمد بن محمد بن أحمد بن أحمد بن رشد الأندلسي, Abu Al-Walid Muhammad ibn Ahmad ibn Muhammad ibn Ahmad ibn Ahmad ibn Rushd Al-Andalusi, known in Europe as Averroes. Judge, philosopher, physician, jurist, astronomer from Cordoba. Wrote a large number of works on many subjects, among these *Bidaya Al-mujtahid wa Nihaya Al-Muqtasid* [Primer for the Deducers and Resolution for the Moderate]. Died 595 A.H./1198 A.D.

Ibn Taymiyyah

أبو العباس أحمد بن عبد الحليم بن عبد السلام بن عبدالله بن الخضر بن محمد بن الخضر بن علي بن عبدالله إبن تيمية الحراني, Abu Al-'Abbas Ahmad ibn 'Abd Al-Halim ibn 'Abd Al-Salam ibn Abdillah ibn Al-Khidr ibn Muhammad ibn Al-Khidr ibn 'Ali ibn Abdillah Ibn Taymiyyah Al-Harrani, given the title تقي الدين, Pious in the Deen. Theologian, jurist, commentator, and compiler of hadith; of the Hanbali school. From Harran (now Turkey) and later Damascus. Among his works are the *Majmu' Al-fatawa* [Collection of Fatwas], *Al-siyasa Al-shar'iya* [Lawful Political Authority], and the celebrated *Dar' Ta'arud Al-'aql wa Al-naql* [Averting the Conflict of Reason and Revelation]. Died 728 A.H./1328 A.D.

Malik

أبو عبدالله مالك بن أنس بن مالك بن ابي عامر الأصبحي الحميري المدني, *Abu Abdillah Malik ibn Anas ibn Malik ibn Abi 'Amir Al-Asbahi Al-Hamiri Al-Madini*. Jurist, theologian, and compiler of hadith from Medina, most known for the *Muwatta* [The Well-trodden Path], one of the earliest collections of Sunni hadith and therefore considered one of the most authentic. Founder of the Maliki school of law. Died 179 A.H./795 A.D.

Muqatil ibn Sulaiman

أبو الحسن مقاتل بن سليمان بن بشير الأزدي البلخي, *Abu Al-Hasan Muqatil ibn Sulaiman ibn Bashir Al-Azdi Al-Balkhi*. His tafsir is considered one of the first, if not the first, complete *tafsir* of the Qur'an. From Khorasan (Persia/Afghanistan). Died 150 A.H./767 A.D.

Muslim

مسلم بن الحجاج بن مسلم بن ورد بن كوشاذ القشيري النيسابوري, *Muslim ibn Al-Hajaj ibn Muslim ibn Ward ibn Kawshadh Al-Qushairi Al-Nisaburi*. From Nishapur (Persia). Compiled *Sahih Muslim*, one of the leading Sunni hadith collections and one of the two most highly regarded (along with *Sahih Al-Bukhari*). Died 261 A.H./875 A.D.

www.ingramcontent.com/pod-product-compliance
Lightning Source LLC
Chambersburg PA
CBHW021954160426
43197CB00007B/128